the bondservant's life

Foundation for Understanding Prophecy, and
a Call to Maturity, Love, and Unity
in the Knowledge of God

JOHN BRENNER CHANDLER

DOULOS BOOKS
Rapid City, South Dakota

The Bondservant's Life

Copyright © 2012 by John Brenner Chandler
Published by Doulos Books, Rapid City, South Dakota

Scripture quotations were taken from multiple English versions and are marked as follows:

AMP: Scripture quotations marked **AMP** taken from the Amplified® Bible, Copyright © 1954, 1958, 1962, 1964, 1965, 1987 by The Lockman Foundation. Used by permission. (www.Lockman.org)

CJB: Scripture quotations marked **CJB** are taken from the Complete Jewish Bible, copyright 1998 by David H. Stern. Published by Jewish New Testament Publications, Inc. www.messianicjewish.net/jntp. Distributed by Messianic Jewish Resources Int'l. www.messianicjewish.net. All rights reserved. Used by permission.

DARBY: Scripture quotations marked **DARBY** are from the John N. Darby translation, 1890. Public Domain.

ESV: Scripture quotations marked **ESV** are from The Holy Bible, English Standard Version® (ESV®), copyright © 2001 by Crossway, a publishing ministry of Good News Publishers. Used by permission. All rights reserved.

GW: Scripture quotations marked **GW** are taken from GOD'S WORD®, © 1995 God's Word to the Nations. Used by permission of Baker Publishing Group.

HCSB: Scripture quotations marked **HCSB** are taken from the Holman Christian Standard Bible®, Copyright © 1999, 2000, 2002, 2003, 2009 by Holman Bible Publishers. Used by permission. Holman Christian Standard Bible®, Holman CSB®, and HCSB® are federally registered trademarks of Holman Bible Publishers.

ISV: Scripture quotations marked **ISV** are taken from the Holy Bible: International Standard Version®. Copyright © 1996-2008 by The ISV Foundation. ALL RIGHTS RESERVED INTERNATIONALLY. Used by permission.

KJV: Scripture quotations marked **KJV** are from the Holy Bible, King James Version. 1987 printing. Public Domain.

NASB: Scripture quotations marked **NASB** taken from the New American Standard Bible®, Copyright © 1960, 1962, 1963, 1968, 1971, 1972, 1973, 1975, 1977, 1995 by The Lockman Foundation. Used by permission. (www.Lockman.org)

NIV: Scripture quotations marked **NIV** are from THE HOLY BIBLE, NEW INTERNATIONAL VERSION®, NIV® Copyright © 1973, 1978, 1984, 2011 by Biblica, Inc.™ Used by permission. All rights reserved worldwide.

NKJV: Scripture quotations marked **NKJV**™ are taken from the New King James Version®. Copyright © 1982 by Thomas Nelson, Inc. Used by permission. All rights reserved.

NLT: Scripture quotations marked **NLT** are taken from the *Holy Bible*, New Living Translation, copyright © 1996, 2004, 2007 by Tyndale House Foundation. Used by permission of Tyndale House Publishers, Inc., Carol Stream, Illinois 60188. All rights reserved.

THE MESSAGE: Scripture quotations marked **THE MESSAGE** are taken from *THE MESSAGE*. Copyright © by Eugene H. Peterson 1993, 1994, 1995, 1996, 2000, 2001, 2002. Used by permission of NavPress Publishing Group.

YLT: Scripture quotations marked **YLT** are taken from Young's Literal Translation, by Robert Young, 1898. Public Domain.

Boldface words in passages were added for emphasis by author throughout the book.

ISBN 978-0-9838102-0-9

All rights reserved. Permission is granted to copy portions of this book for non-profit non-commercial use with the exception of posting more than brief quotations for reviews on a website. Other electronic use or storage in any retrieval system is prohibited without prior written permission of the publisher. Any commercial use is limited to brief quotations or reviews with proper bibliographical citation.

Library of Congress Control Number: 2011934015

    Subject Headings: 1.Religion 2.Christian Life 3.Spiritual Growth 4.Biblical Studies

Cover design by C.G. Taylor.
Cover photo: royalty free image purchased at istockphoto.com

To all who search for

Truth;

to Lee Loker,

whose faithful witness

pointed me in the right direction—

the Word;

and to the Lord

and His purposes for

the words on these pages.

May they bear much fruit for His Kingdom.

I have used a pen name to honor my fathers.

Centuries of pastors who labored in both the field and the Word of God, some who were also professors and theologians, are the heritage of the Brenner side of my family. My grandfather, Rev. Rudy Brenner, lived as he taught. Brenner means 'one who burns.'

In 1610, John Chandler came to America at the age of ten. The pioneering spirit of the Chandler side of my family is the legacy I inherited from my father, Joseph Chandler. John means 'God is gracious.' Chandler means 'candle maker' or 'lamp bearer.'

The name I have chosen came to me as I sat before the Lord one morning. It is not meant to cause offense or to deceive, but only to honor where I have been and where I am going. My fathers have all gone on to be with the Lord and left me an inheritance of love for God and His Word. This is worth taking note of and honoring, for I never got a chance to say this before they were gone. In some small way, this name embodies everything they are and passed on to me.

Chandler Family Crest
Motto: *Quae arguuntur a lumine manifestantur*
'Things which are in dispute are made clear by the light'

John was a burning and shining lamp.
-John 5:35

Table of Contents

Preface 7
Acknowledgments 11

SECTION 1: INTRODUCTION TO THE BONDSERVANT'S LIFE

Chapter 1   Foundation 15
Chapter 2   What Is a Bondservant? 25
Chapter 3   Who Are the Bondservants? 39
Chapter 4   How Does a Bondservant's Life Differ? 49

SECTION 2: PASSIONATE PURSUIT OF GOD

Chapter 5   Cultivating Intimacy 69
Chapter 6   Learning God's Language 80
Chapter 7   Correctly Dividing the Word 93

SECTION 3: HARMONIZED VIEW OF LAW AND FREEDOM

Chapter 8   The Role of the Law 117
Chapter 9   The Covenants 159
Chapter 10   Freedom in Christ 185
Chapter 11   The Goal: One New Man 214

SECTION 4: WHOLEHEARTED LIFESTYLE OF OBEDIENCE

Chapter 12   Qualities of a Believer's Life 249
Chapter 13   When You Give 262
Chapter 14   When You Pray 307
Chapter 15   When You Fast 334

SECTION 5: TACTICAL KNOWLEDGE OF THE ADVERSARY

Chapter 16   Role as Adversary 351
Chapter 17   The Process of Corruption 384
Chapter 18   The Goal: Defiling Our Actions 395

SECTION 6: RESPONSIVE DEPENDENCE ON THE HOLY SPIRIT

Chapter 19   Ministry and Work of the Holy Spirit 419
Chapter 20   Discernment 451

SECTION 7: DESTINATION OF BONDSERVANTS

Chapter 21   Eternal Salvation 467
Chapter 22   Adoption as Sons 483

Epilogue 508
End Notes 513

PREFACE

> *The Revelation of Jesus Christ, which God gave Him* **to show to His bond-servants***, the things which must soon take place.* -Rev. 1:1a, NASB

A phrase in this verse captured my attention a few years ago: 'to show His bondservants.' The book you have in front of you is based on this portion of the opening verse. It suddenly dawned on me that the book of Revelation was not meant for everyone to understand. It was written for the *bondservants* of Christ, just as the parables were meant for the disciples to understand (Luke 8:10). This begged the question, 'Who are the bondservants of Jesus?' Through this study, I have learned the foundation of our walk as believers is initiated by God and established with our heart's commitment to serve Christ despite the cost to us personally. Without this foundation, the prophetic passages are closed to us no matter what our education or title may be.

Comprehending the written word is difficult for those whose aptitudes run along very different lines, namely the math kind. Math has precision; words with their subjective meanings do not. Left-brained people have to put forth more effort to understand literary works and their deeper meanings, as I do. For example, after going through two sets of teaching tapes on the Song of Songs (I wore out the first set) and five years of constant exposure to this teaching, I finally understood the allegorical meaning. Only then did I come to the realization that the preacher was right—believers are lovers of God who struggle with sin, not sinners who struggle to love God.[1]

This book is a compilation of insights I have gathered in my search to understand the concept of a bondservant. The topics included in this study will help the believer follow Christ as defined in the Word and relate to others in a way that demonstrates the love of God. Embracing the lifestyle of a bondservant will provide the reader with what I believe to be the *foundation* for receiving understanding of the events prior to Jesus' return as well as help him/her prepare for those events. This foundation is built as we invest our lives in the study of the Word by the illumination of the Holy Spirit. The book to follow will discuss the actual *framework* for understanding those events (*The Bridegroom's Warning: Framework for Understanding Prophecy*; projected publication date, Lord willing, Fall 2014).

Attempting to study prophecy without the proper foundation can be frustrating. I had been discouraged by study of biblical prophecy before. Though I had read the book of Revelation dozens of times, understanding eluded me. Everything after chapter 3 seemed like the scene in *The Wizard of Oz* where all the farm hands, animals, neighbors, and trees swirled around in the cyclone, devoid of any setting that would give them real meaning—just all floating in a nebulous cloud. The only difference in the Revelation 'cyclone' is that it had beasts, horns, vials, trumpets, burned trees, and 666 instead.

Lack of personal aptitude contributed to the difficulty I experienced in understanding much of what is written in the Bible. Many of us are far more comfortable with directions, formulas, programs, and bulleted ideas than with interpreting the rich meanings cached in the living Word of God. Discovering what has been deftly and masterfully placed just below the surface in the guardian literary style of God is a lifetime pursuit that cannot be achieved in sporadic, cursory devotional readings. Yet unearthing the treasure secreted in the Word takes both kinds of thinkers—the literary *and* the logical-analytical types.

Many of the logical-analytical types enjoy doing logic puzzles for fun. Those who do quickly come to realize how important it is not to jump to conclusions by making assumptions of facts not in evidence, especially at the beginning, lest a cascade of erroneous deductions follow. When this happens, the entire solution derived ends up far from the correct answer. The following is a typical logic problem, beginner's level:

At the Farmers Market[2]

At the Meyersdale Farmers Market yesterday, Sally Salada bought five different farm-fresh fruits and vegetables for her family's enjoyment, purchasing a different amount— 1, 2, 3, 4, and 5 lbs.—of each from a different local vendor's stand. Given the facts that follow about her purchases, can you decide how much of each fruit or vegetable Sally bought and from which grower she selected it?

1. After buying some crisp red lettuce from one vendor, Sally Salada made a purchase at the Raindrop Acres stand; after her buy at the Raindrop Acres stand, she bought 1 lb. of produce at a third farmer's booth.
2. Sally tasted the large, sweet blueberries and the juicy Maryland Red peaches before buying them at two different stands; neither is the item she chose at the Tiller Gardens stand.
3. Sally Salada got 2 lbs. of the item she purchased at Grow Bros. Produce.
4. The weight of the produce Sally bought at the Freshly Fruits & Vegetables stand was less than that of the white potatoes she purchased at another stand.
5. Sally bought 5 lbs. of Granny Smith apples to make pies.
6. The item Sally got at the Sunset Farm stand wasn't the peaches.
7. Raindrop Acres didn't have white potatoes for sale.
8. The produce Sally purchased at the Freshly Fruits & Vegetables stand wasn't the red lettuce and wasn't 1 lb. in weight.

(The solution is in the endnotes for those who actually attempt to solve this.[3])

Especially in the more challenging puzzles, there is a temptation to believe there are not enough clues to solve the problem. But with careful observation and organizing the clues in a meaningful way so holes and relationships between clues can be easily determined, chains of deductions where accurate conclusions can be drawn become easier. This is also true of understanding biblical prophecy under the supervision of the Holy Spirit and in concert with the community of believers, for each 'only sees in part.'

There are those who memorize easily and those better at grasping concepts. Typically we lean one way or the other. Concept people are usually poor memorizers. Henri Nouwen, a dedicated Catholic priest who reached out to the oppressed throughout the world through his many acts of kindness, has written several thought-provoking works. My favorite is the *Way of the Heart*. Nouwen quotes a Taoist monk who expresses the philosophy of a concept person: "Words exist because of meaning; once you've gotten the meaning, you can forget the words. Where can I find a man who has forgotten words? He is the one I would like to talk to." This is the essence of a concept person.

Bible study requires understanding the concepts the Lord has established in the Word. But if we limit ourselves to only understanding the concepts, we will miss the subtle hints and connections God placed in the Word because of the specific language or phrases He uses. Having in our memories the specific language God uses allows the Holy Spirit to draw on that input to link relevant passages together. This is the memorizer's forte. Therefore, the Bible was written for the concept person *and* the memorizer, but understanding won't come easily to either. It takes time spent in the Lord's presence in prayer and meditation in the Word, because few of us are both strong concept people and competent memorizers.

Though philosophy and other wordy subjects may not come easily to some, we come to appreciate words through our study of *God's* Word. I thought it odd that the Lord would instill in us a passion for knowing His Word, but give some of us natural ability in seemingly unrelated areas. Through the study of prophecy, however, I have realized it is precisely this background in math, science, and logic submitted to the guidance of the Holy Spirit that enables us to see presuppositions and assumptions present in many theological arguments not expressly stated in the Word.

This typically leads to more questions than it does answers. Allowing the Lord to reveal truths in His timing requires a great deal of patience and diligence—qualities we are not born with but which the Holy Spirit cultivates in our lives as He conforms us to the character of Jesus. The entire process of getting to know God and understanding His Word is necessarily one of advancing in a posture of prayer out of a sheer lack of natural ability to achieve this on our own, and birthed in zeal to accomplish something outside the realm of inherent skill. Calculus and statistical analysis seem like mere child's play in comparison.

The bondservant identity and understanding prophecy are inseparable. Jesus, who loves us with intense passion, is committed to letting His followers know what is going to happen *before* it happens so we have every chance of passing the tests given. 'To be forewarned is to be forearmed.' God spoke through the Old Testament prophets and stated plainly that He does nothing without first showing His servants what will take place (Amos 3:7). Jesus not only told His disciples ahead of time what would take place (Matt. 24:25; Mark 13:23), but He also quoted Psalm 78:2 in proclaiming He would declare things kept secret from the foundation of the world (Matt. 13:34-35). The entire book of Revelation was written in order to show the *bondservants* what will take place (Rev. 1:1). Jesus promised the Holy Spirit would guide us into all truth *and reveal the things to come:*

> *I still have many things to say to you, but you cannot bear them now. However, when He, the Spirit of truth, has come, He will guide you into all truth... He will tell you things to come.* -John 16:12-13, NKJV

We must frequently keep these words in our prayers: that the Holy Spirit would guide us into all truth and reveal the things to come. The phrase, 'you cannot bear them now' refers to the disciples' inability to comprehend what Jesus had yet to say. In other words, they had not yet arrived at a place in their walk as disciples where they had a 'grid' to fathom what Jesus wanted to impart. Jesus had much to say, but some of it had to wait until the disciples were ready to receive it.

When it comes to prophecy, the average believer throws his hands in the air in frustration and determines to leave understanding to the scholars and seminary students. If our focus is the prophetic word void of heart engagement in a dynamic relationship with God, we will either continue to be frustrated or settle for convoluted and incomplete understanding of the prophetic events revealed in the Bible.

Many centuries ago, the Lord declared His zeal for His house, and many burn with the desire to see the Word of God portrayed accurately and truthfully. This book was written for those who share this passion. Volumes have been written on subjects for which I can donate only a few pages. For the ideas that pique interest, it is my hope you will explore those matters more fully in your own study. Keep in mind that what is written here is the result of personal study. What I have shared is obviously not infallible or exhaustive. I expect my own understanding to be 'tweaked' by further study and dialogue with other believers.

Concepts and ideas are introduced utilizing bulleted lists on occasion to help organize the information. I have included a good deal of Scripture, often inserting the text but mostly leaving only a reference. There is something about reading the Word itself that evokes a response at the heart level that cannot be captured any other way. For literary types, these interruptions may prove distracting. But for the left-brained, this makes the information stand out rather than being lost in a sea of words.

While I appreciate economy of words, I also understand that in some instances more words are needed to ensure a point is adequately explained. It is my hope you will bear with the length of this book (and dare I say, some tedious moments...) in order to have the basic foundation needed for your own study of the Word and your walk as a bondservant of Christ. It might prove helpful to view this book as a compilation of several books gathered in one volume. Each section is written with this goal in mind. Please also bear in mind this is not Shakespeare. The LBLS (left-brained literary style) is not for everyone.

My prayer is that these pages will not be lifeless academic rhetoric, but that the reader will be edified and incited to know our Beloved Redeemer better, as well as walk in harmony with fellow believers. Even if we do not agree on the conclusions drawn, perhaps we can agree that the greater purpose in any study of the Word is to incite love and draw us ever closer to the Eternal Flame; a Flame that makes our heart, mind, and vision burn ever brighter with the expectation we will one day be like Him.

Until our beloved King returns,

J.B. Chandler
February 14, 2012

ACKNOWLEDGMENTS

There are many people to thank, but the bulk of my gratitude goes to the Lord. How He can make something out of nothing never ceases to amaze me. This book started out with four words and a question mark: 'What is a bondservant?' He really does fill the hungry with good things.

My parents, Joe and Lois Chandler, raised us in the church and I loved going. In second grade, I wanted to copy the entire Bible so I could have my own. I only got partway into Genesis, but I already knew I liked what God had to say, even though I didn't understand the words. Mom used her incredible music gift to serve the Lord and taught us to do likewise (though our music gifting wasn't quite so incredible). Daddy was meticulous and creative—he could fix anything with duct tape, old coffee cans, and wire coat hangers. He was an amazingly talented man and thought all of us should be as persistent as Thomas Edison, my first lesson in perseverance. Their faithfulness gave me a great foundation. Thanks, Mom and Dad—I love you both.

My own family deserves a huge 'thank you.' They took care of nearly everything while I was engrossed in this work. They kept the house in order and gave much needed humor to my days. The older children actually read an early draft to give feedback and helped with the 'techy' parts of the manuscript. My wonderful spouse was a gem—never complained about the lack of attention and even painstakingly reviewed the first and last drafts with very helpful suggestions and contributions, a reflection of the time spent in prayer and the Word. I love you all.

My brother Steve also made his way through a very rough draft and offered much needed insight and suggestions on each chapter. His well-rounded knowledge and understanding of the Word was invaluable. I owe you one.

Editor Jeff Criswell gave excellent suggestions during the editing process, which made for a much more readable end-product. His meticulous copyediting is outstanding. If there are any mistakes in the manuscript, it's because I fiddled around with it after he was finished. His intervention and counsel were an answer to prayer.

Dear friends prayed for and encouraged me during this project: Virgil and Agatha Dawson, Nancy Berg, and Pastors Gaylord and Sharon Lemke. It was an incredible blessing to know others took the time to intercede on my behalf. I am so blessed by your friendship and love for the purposes of God. You are each so precious and dearly loved.

Mrs. Farnham and Mr. Jones, two of my grade school teachers, let me learn at my own pace. They gave me unlimited access to library and math books outside of what we used in class. This fueled my passion for learning and discovering knowledge on my own. Mr. Drinkall, my high school math teacher and Mathletes coach, helped me learn to think 'outside the box.' Matrix Algebra became a breeze. Mr. Potts was my high school chemistry-physics teacher, and his love for science was contagious. Both of these men took time to work with me and help me reach for understanding of concepts beyond the textbook. I will never forget them or their efforts to open doors of understanding and stretch my mind to *really think* and not merely regurgitate facts.

There is not room to mention all the preachers of the thousands of sermons I've heard or the authors of the hundreds of books I've read that shaped my understanding of the Word. Listening to and reading the teaching of others made the work you see here possible. Anyone who has written a work of this nature realizes we stand on the labors of those who have gone before us. Many of their thoughts have become my thoughts, though our views may not be exactly the same. These thoughts have formed the composite of understanding for my spiritual foundation.

So little space to give honor to the deserving. I've debated whether to include at least some of their names. Some readers will embrace the work because of certain names, and others will shun the work for the same reason. Hopefully no one will throw the baby out with the bathwater. Honor is due where honor is due:

Abraham Lincoln	Spiro Zodhiates	J.I. Packer	A.W. Tozer
William Wilberforce	Martin Luther	David Stern	Asher Intrater
Richard Wurmbrand	Henry Blackaby	John Stott	John Bevere
Charles Spurgeon	James Strong	C.S. Lewis	C.R. Oliver
Dietrich Bonhoeffer	Wesley Deuwel	Mike Bickle	Henri Nouwen
William Tyndale	Charles Stanley	R.C. Sproul	David Pawson
John Wycliffe	John MacArthur	Rick Joyner	George E. Ladd

This list could easily quadruple in size if I checked my library shelves. I've left out so many who deserve to be mentioned. Like the many meals we eat, forgetting who made what and when it was served, we don't always remember who gave us the insight that becomes part of our spiritual foundation. I have tried to footnote everything I have used, but some thoughts I have shared on certain topics undoubtedly originated in others' teaching. These are not footnoted because I simply can't remember who served that meal. I hope no one will be offended if I have failed to give credit; such an omission is totally unintended. Perhaps, in the grace of God, those who did not receive credit would choose to be encouraged that someone heard and took to heart what they shared with the body of Christ.

I learned true fellowship by investing time in intercession with Agatha Dawson, Cathy Herman, Steve Jarasek, and Dan O'Brien. These people walk in the heart of God. We met weekly to pray that the purposes of God be done on earth as in heaven. The unity we experienced in prayer was unlike any other ministry experience. I love you guys.

I am deeply grateful for the work of those who have fed the community of believers with their rich insight and revelation in the Word, and all of the pastors who put up with my spiritual 'growing pains.' I would not have been able to complete this book without their contributions, the guidance of the Holy Spirit, and the prayers of family and friends. I am truly blessed.

SECTION 1

INTRODUCTION TO THE BONDSERVANT'S LIFE

Chapter 1

Foundation

> *The Revelation of Jesus Christ, which God gave Him to **show to His bond-servants**, the things which must soon take place... And he said to me, "These words are faithful and true"; and the Lord, the God of the spirits of the prophets, sent His angel **to show to His bond-servants** the things which must soon take place.* -Rev. 1:1; 22:6, NASB

The Book of Revelation begins and ends with God's purpose in announcing these prophetic events: to show His bondservants what must soon take place. Our focus can become so engrossed in the events themselves that we fail to notice to whom this is addressed—*the bondservants of Jesus*. But who, exactly, are the bondservants? Isn't 'bondservant' just another name for a Christian? That would depend on our definition of 'Christian.' The Word of God has definite things to teach us about the life of an authentic follower of Christ, quite different from the popular definition today.

Correctly interpreting prophecy is bound together with the concept of bondservanthood. Living life as a bondservant of Christ *in sincerity* builds on the foundation of our relationship with God and the body of Christ. Without this foundation, our interpretation of prophecy is an academic exercise resulting only in educated guesses of what makes sense to our finite minds. Understanding does not come from years in seminary school learning scriptural facts, history, and legitimate methods of interpretation, though this certainly can help. Any subject outside the Bible is mastered in this fashion, resulting in diverse interpretations of the material presented. While approaching the Bible in this manner has some efficacy, we must acknowledge the Bible is no ordinary book. The Word of God is living and breathing, filled with the power and wisdom of God not only to change lives, but also to enable us to know and be known by the God of the universe.

Through our relationship with God in Christ—our foundation—we begin to understand His heart and plans for the hour in which we live as well as foster love and unity in the community of believers. In this section, we will look at the biblical definition of the bondservant, laying a grid through which we can understand the commands of Christ, the instructions of the apostles, and the prophetic revelation given in the Word.

Bondservanthood: The Foundation for Understanding Prophecy

Understanding Scripture, particularly prophecy, evokes different responses in different people. The scope of responses ranges from passionate and fascinated to bewildered or even indifferent. For some, the responses are a mixture of these with a bit of frustration thrown in if attempts have been made to accomplish this without help. Be encouraged. The very fact that you care and want to understand puts you in a great place to receive understanding if you persevere in your quest. This book was written for all but the indifferent.

The book of Revelation in particular has engendered more thought-provoking and controversial debate than any other book in the Bible. Mysterious and cryptic, the imagery has inspired widely varied interpretations from the deeply philosophical and scholarly to the sophomoric and fantastically convoluted. Yet for all our interpreting and defining, it is still apparent we have not yet fully grasped the content of its message with any sort of consistency across the body of believers. After two thousand years, we must pause to ask ourselves, 'Why?' Through reflection on available Scripture, the answer seems to be two-fold. It involves both the *right timing* for the message to unfold, and the *readiness* of the believer (bondservant) to receive the message.

Timing

Timing is designated by God, an example of which can be seen in the life of Daniel. Though Jeremiah had written much earlier regarding the length of the Babylonian captivity, Daniel grasped the meaning of Jeremiah's message when the time was nearly upon them for the return to the land. This realization drove Daniel to prayer and fasting so the Word of God would be fulfilled (see Dan. 9).

Jeremiah wrote something else of use to us for our current study. He stated the prophetic events of the Bible would be understood 'perfectly' in the latter days. Taking our cue from Daniel, those alive at the close of the age should also respond to Jeremiah's words with prayer and fasting to see God's Word fulfilled.

> *The anger of the LORD will not turn back until He has executed... the thoughts of His heart.* ***In the latter days you will understand it perfectly.*** -Jer. 23:20, NKJV

In Habakkuk, we note that the revelation the prophet received was for an 'appointed time' (Hab. 2:2-3). The Lord chooses the appointed time for every event (Ecc. 3:1; Ps. 75:2). Even Jesus had an appointed time to be revealed.

> *And [now] in His own appointed time He has made manifest (made known) His Word and revealed it.* -Titus 1:3a, AMP

Before Jesus arrived, the Scriptures were carefully studied so the Messiah would be recognized. But what does the Word record of the actual response of the majority in Israel? Most had not interpreted the prophecies accurately in the timing of God and ultimately rejected their Savior. As a result, they missed the day of their visitation because their expectation of the Messiah's ministry and purpose had been clouded by their own rigid interpretation. Even the disciples, who spent much time with Jesus personally, did not fully understand His ministry and message until after Jesus ascended and the Holy Spirit was given.

> *Jesus answered him, "What I am doing you do not understand now, but afterward you will understand."* -John 13:7, ESV

From these passages, it becomes apparent that God chooses the specific timing to bring forth understanding as well as the specific individuals to whom understanding is given. Regarding the matters concerning the end of the age, He has promised in His Word that we will understand perfectly 'in the latter days.'

Daniel assumed a posture of prayer, fasting, and mourning before God when he discovered the captivity of Judah was nearly completed. He understood the appointed time was at hand. Daniel's heart was so closely knit with God's that the matters and purposes of God meant more to Daniel than anything else. Likewise, we must have God's will and purposes rooted in our hearts so we can show the wisdom Daniel demonstrated by interceding in a timely fashion. Intercession rooted in understanding of God's Word and timing will bear fruit for God's kingdom.

While John the Baptist's message of repentance and returning to God is appropriate for all time, the greatest impact and understanding of that message could only take place in the context of the Messiah's first advent and in anticipation of the new covenant's establishment.[1] Just as John burned with the message entrusted to him to prepare the way for Jesus, there is a time appointed for those entrusted with the messages that will prepare the hearts of the people before Jesus' return. These messages will necessarily include clarity on the prophesied events prior to His second coming, and the Word itself verifies they will understand this *perfectly*.

Peter also spoke of the timing of prophetic revelation, disclosing that even the prophets themselves did not comprehend all they wrote because it was intended for those in this age to understand. Even though they earnestly sought understanding, God had determined their prophecies would not be made plain until the days of Jesus' ministry (1 Pet. 1:12). Obedience to God's will does not always come with complete understanding.

Further proof that the prophets of old did not always understand the prophecies given to them can be found in Daniel. Though God highly esteemed and loved Daniel, the timing for granting understanding of the vision had been determined for the future. Even though Daniel asked for the explanation, God told him understanding would not be revealed until the 'time of the end.'

> *I heard, but I did not understand... "O my lord, what shall be the outcome of these things?" He said, "Go your way, Daniel, for* **the words are shut up and sealed until the time of the end.** *Many shall purify themselves and make themselves white and be refined... And none of the wicked shall understand,* **but those who are wise shall understand."** -Dan. 12:8-10, ESV

Even the disciples did not have full revelation. In response to the disciples' questions about the restoration of the kingdom, Jesus replied it was not given *to them* to understand God's appointed timing regarding those events. Their allotted portion—their *charge*—was to spread the message of the kingdom as far and wide and as quickly as possible by the power of the Holy Spirit (Acts 1:6-8).

The appointed time for everything has been determined by God on His own authority. Jesus came at His appointed time, heralded by John the Baptist. The disciples were appointed to spread the gospel until it filled the earth ('like yeast working its way through a batch of dough,' Matt. 13:33). According to Jeremiah and Daniel, those at the end of the age are appointed to understand 'perfectly' the events and timing of God before the second coming of Jesus.

The Pioneers

Desiring to grasp the contents of the book of Revelation, those who have gone before us have put forth much effort in laying the groundwork for what we understand today. Born out of season, they are like the proverbial salmon swimming upstream to the spawning ground, planting seed for future generations. Their passion, zeal, and tenacity in searching out the contents of Revelation are evidence of the kingly spirit spoken of in Proverbs:

> *It is the glory of God to conceal a matter, but the glory of kings is to search out a matter.* -Pr. 25:2, NKJV

Despite the grand efforts of these dedicated believers, we still need clarity and the 'aha' feeling that comes when Holy Spirit inspired exposition takes place in conjunction with the timing of God. Despite being out of season for understanding perfectly, those who have 'seized the day' and brought their understanding forward have given us much to consider. On the other hand, some of their more speculative conclusions have contributed a degree of confusion! These individuals have been described in the book of Daniel:

> *[M]any shall run to and fro and search anxiously [through the Book], and knowledge [of God's purposes as revealed by His prophets] shall be increased and become great.* -Dan. 12:4, AMP

The first key to acquire understanding of biblical prophecy is to hold opinions as loosely as possible until the appointed time. If we cling to any model, no matter how closely it might resemble the truth, we may get hung up on a detail that is out of place. This could cause us to miss the day of our visitation, just as the Pharisees did.

Maturity and Heart Posture

The proper timing of a message is understandable, but what does being a bondservant have to do with understanding prophecy? The answer involves the readiness and maturity of believers to grasp or carry the message:

I have still many things to say to you, but you are not able to bear them or to take them upon you or to grasp them now. But when He, the Spirit of Truth (the Truth-giving Spirit) comes, He will guide you into all the Truth (the whole, full Truth)... and He will announce and declare to you the things that are to come [that will happen in the future]. -John 16:12-13, AMP

Jesus explained this to His disciples, who later described themselves as Jesus' bondservants. In the prologue to Revelation, Jesus proclaimed that His message is intended for His bondservants. It is important to note at the time the book of Revelation was written (c. A.D. 95-96, though a minority of scholars disagree, contending for A.D. 68-69), most of the original disciples/apostles were no longer living. Therefore we cannot conclude this book was written for the original bondservants, the disciples.

[Note: Irenaeus, one of the early church fathers (c. A.D. 150-202), gives the earliest external testimony in existence, verifying that the book of Revelation was written during the reign of Domitian (A.D. 81-96).[2]]

The word *bondservant* provides the second key to understanding biblical prophecy concerning the end of the age. Contrary to popular belief, the book of Revelation was not written for anyone and everyone to understand, just as understanding of the parables hadn't been given to everyone who heard them (see also Luke 8:10).

> *And the disciples... said to Him, "Why do You speak to them in parables?" Jesus answered them,* **"To you it has been granted to know the mysteries** *of the kingdom of heaven, but to them it has not been granted."* -Matt. 13:10-11, NASB

The introductory passage to Revelation makes clear the *bondservants* of Jesus Christ are the targeted audience. Only after reading many different English versions of the book of Revelation dozens of times did this stand out to me. The word rendered in the opening passage as 'bond-servants' in the NASB is the more precise translation of the Greek word *doulos*. This leads to the obvious questions:

- What is a bondservant?
- Who are the bondservants?
- How are bondservants different?

This book will explore the answers to these questions and more, starting in Chapter 2 with a broad discussion of the biblical definition of a bondservant and its complementary application to the New Testament believer. In the context of biblical prophecy, particularly as it pertains to understanding the book of Revelation, it is important we first grasp the concept of the bondservant, to whom the book of Revelation is addressed.

Progressing from there, we will take a more detailed look at who the bondservants are and the general qualities of a bondservant's life. The process of voluntarily becoming a bondservant is initiated in love and results in bearing much fruit, including the maturity needed to stand firm in the day of calamity. It is nothing less than the total transformation of the soul and spirit to be conformed to Christ. When Jesus returns, this will include the total transformation of our physical bodies as well—the adoption as sons—enabling us to fulfill His call to rule and reign with Him in the age to come. There isn't a better offer in the whole universe.

It is my hope that through this study you will find awakened in your spirit a renewed passion to know God. When we truly follow Christ, we experience the power of His resurrection as He takes us from a dead existence to one of a transformed mind and heart. This includes participating in the fellowship of His suffering by hearing and obeying as Jesus did—without reservation. This means dying to our own desires, will, and lives to embrace God's purposes instead. Then the apostle's words will be true in our lives as well: 'I am crucified with Christ.' By embracing the lifestyle of the bondservant, we will be in a position to hear from God with clarity and know perfectly what will soon take place.

The goal? To possess the mind of Christ, walk in the discernment of the Spirit, and know the timing and movement of the Father's heart. Add to this the hope that in the day we meet Jesus, we will hear Him say, 'Well done, thou good and faithful bondservant!'

First Things First

How is it that you don't know how to interpret this present time? -Luke 12:56b, NIV

Before we can understand the last days, or more precisely the close of this age, it cannot be emphasized enough that we must pay attention to and struggle with all our strength to enter into the salvation we have been freely offered. This involves:

- knowing our God,
- understanding and carrying out what is expected of us as bondservants,
- recognizing the tactics of our enemy,
- cooperating as the Holy Spirit transforms our character, and
- receiving with submission the discernment and illumination of the Holy Spirit.

These are foundational criteria for understanding the prophetic word. The beauty of the way God transforms us allows for increasing our understanding *along the way* while the foundation is being laid. In other words, He doesn't wait until we've arrived at our destination of maturity before He begins to share with us the secrets of His kingdom. What a privilege to be called into God's family and to have God as our Father.

Laying a foundation can be swift if all we are building is a chicken coop. But if a large, multistory building is being constructed, the foundation and footings must go down deeply to support the structure. Foundational work is below ground and not impressive to the uninstructed eye. In fact, very few even notice the work taking place below the surface, let alone are impressed by it. But it is this very foundation that allows the building to stand and not collapse when storms, wind, and quakes come against it. Does this sound familiar? The Word admonishes us to be wise builders with solid foundations (Matt. 7:24-25). The edifice seen above ground will be built in its time.

Painting a room illustrates the same principle. If done properly, preparing the walls and taping the woodwork can easily consume seventy percent of the time for the project. The actual act of painting is the least frustrating yet most praised part of the job, despite taking the least amount of time and effort. Laying a proper and sound foundation is critical in the believer's walk so we do not falter when it counts the most.

Cultivating Good Fruit

A proper foundation provides fertile ground for bearing good fruit. The principle given in Levitical law regarding fruit trees furnishes an object lesson for believers to follow. After planting a fruit tree, the Israelites were to regard its fruit as forbidden the first three years. In the fourth year, the fruit was considered holy and given only to the Lord. The fruit could not be eaten until the fifth year. The reason for these instructions? 'So that your harvest would be increased' (Lev. 19:23-25).

Fruit production in the early stages of a tree's life can stunt its growth. This is due to an immature root system in combination with the inability of the soil to provide nutrients for both producing fruit and bringing the needed growth for the tree itself. Until the tree is of mature size to bear fruit, the flowers that appear on the tree should be pinched off as they emerge. This will encourage the development of a healthy root system and above ground growth that can support a much larger yield of fruit. The tree should not be allowed to produce fruit until then, typically requiring three or four years' growth to reach this desirable point of maturity, the same principle stated in the Levitical passage. The tree continues to grow after it begins to bear fruit, requiring pruning to maintain its health and optimum fruit-bearing capability.

The parallel, of course, is that many Christians are so anxious to produce fruit for the kingdom (or at least want to appear this way) that they have gotten very busy in their effort to accomplish this. The desire to do so is admirable in some cases, but this kind of 'zeal without knowledge' (Rom. 10:2) will lead to the ruination of their soul through pride, ambition to be approved by man, envy when they are not the one out in front, rejection when their efforts are not noticed, promulgation of error through misinterpretation or improper handling of the Word, or worse.

The sad part for many is that excessive busyness for the kingdom has stunted personal spiritual growth. These have very little real depth in intimacy with and understanding of the Word by the standard of God. To their peril, they have only a shallow root system that is in very real danger of causing them to wither in a time of persecution. Consequently, they bear sparse fruit of very little value, far less than expected for the effort put forth. Many feel as though they are 'spinning their wheels' and not getting enough attention or making enough progress in ministry.

While the waiting can be frustrating, allowing the Lord to bring forth beneficial and lasting fruit requires the input of time and effort into the believer's spiritual growth and maturity. The dangers of not following this principle are not fabricated but found in the Word. Paul advised Timothy to select elders who were not new believers because young believers are more prone to pride. A posture of pride will cause us to fall (1 Tim. 3:6). Until a firm root system is established, no stability will be found:

> *The one on whom seed was sown on the rocky places, this is the man who hears the word and **immediately receives it with joy; yet he has no firm root** in himself, but is only temporary, and when affliction or persecution arises because of the word, immediately he falls away.* -Matt. 13:20-21, NASB

For this reason, we must encourage and exhort each other to persevere in establishing our own foundation and history in God. This process takes time—years—depending on what has been ordained for us to accomplish and how much time and energy we devote to its pursuit. Paul may seem like an exception because the Word tells us he began preaching immediately. But by his own admission, Paul was a learned Pharisee when he met Jesus on the road to Damascus. He already had extensive knowledge of the Scriptures. However, only after this experience did he have the proper perspective to interpret accurately the Scriptures he previously learned so well. Even the disciples needed more than three years at Jesus' side, night and day, to prepare them for their callings.

Does this mean we do nothing but sit around and read the Word? Hardly. We put faith and compassion to work immediately, helping those in need as God places them in our path. We show hospitality. We learn to serve in our families and the church (in that order) in the most mundane or menial tasks. We train our children to live by God's standards. We resolve to hold our resources with an open hand for those truly in need. We determine to govern our time in prayer and Bible study. We discipline ourselves to control our appetites through grace for fasting and to shun those practices which will shipwreck our faith. Preparing ourselves God's way and in His timing will bring thirty-, sixty-, and hundred-fold increases (Matt. 13:23).

We gain wisdom and insight as we endure trials and testing. The Holy Spirit uses these to bring maturity if we will only focus on the lesson rather than: 1.) our feelings toward the trial, or 2.) self-condemnation if we miss the mark. We experience the patience and love of God during these tests because He never gives up on us—even when we give up on ourselves. If we turn to Him, He is faithful to pick us up and set us back on the right path.

Sharing Our Part in the Timing of God

Many have been given something to share with the body of Christ but disdain their part as somehow insignificant because they haven't grasped the entirety of the message or feel inadequate because they don't have credentials. If this is the case, consider that the disciples didn't have credentials either. Jesus, the Word, was their teacher. All who come to Christ, turning from sin and the ways of the world, receive the *same* Holy Spirit who instructed the disciples. We come to know God by the work of the Holy Spirit and by washing our minds with the Word. Nowhere do we read that the knowledge of God has been reserved only for those who have been to seminary or Bible College.

Now is the time for God's people to establish themselves in the Word so they can stand in the days to come. The foundation must be laid *now* so we can have discernment when it matters most, speaking truth and wisdom when the Lord prompts. Focusing our lives *now* on what matters most will put us in good position when dire circumstances come our way.

Questions will remain throughout our lives that require further study and prayer. Keep in mind that each of us sees only in part (1 Cor. 13:12). Knowing this limitation, please prayerfully continue this book, always seeking the witness of the Holy Spirit and the proof in the Word. We grow in knowledge as each member does his part and shares with the others, continually gaining understanding as we spend our energies plumbing the depths and riches of the Word. By this continued effort, the body of Christ will mature in the unity of faith and knowledge in God as each faithfully executes his charge (Eph. 4:13).

Closing Thoughts

If we endeavor to understand prophecy, our life must reflect a bondservant's heart to serve in spirit and in truth. Whether we see perfectly, as Jeremiah prophesied, or not is dependent on our own readiness as well as the timing and purpose of God. Ambition, presumption, and arrogance would claim to have the whole matter sorted out ahead of time. This fosters a contentious or adversarial spirit among those who seek to put their views in the forefront as the only tenable position. We must move in grace, preferring others to ourselves, testing every spirit and searching the Scriptures daily if we are to understand what the Lord desires to impart in this hour. Having tested the words of others, we hold onto the good (1 Thes. 5:21).

Paul taught the Ephesians that the church is built up as everyone does their part. The goal of what we have been given in the grace of God is to equip believers for ministry, promoting unity in faith and knowledge so we are no longer spiritual babes. Only by striving for the maturity available in Christ will the church stand firm against deception. The gifts of the Spirit are effective in edifying the body only if they are performed in love with the goal of unity (Eph. 4:7,12-16). To ignore doing our part because it seems worthless in our eyes equals negligence and will receive rebuke from God.

We've all experienced tremendous growth and have been edified countless times by the works of others. We consider pastors, authors, and teachers our spiritual fathers and mentors, some having gone on to be with the Lord before we were born. It is my prayer this book will help equip the body of Christ to lay the foundation needed for walking in

SECTION 1 INTRODUCTION TO THE BONDSERVANT'S LIFE

unity as well as for understanding the last hour before Jesus returns. I also hope those who take the time to complete this book will be provoked to go deeper in their relationship with God, searching the Word and drinking deeply on their own. Our hearts will one day kneel in agreement with the Holy Spirit and say, 'Amen. Come Lord Jesus.'

> *Who then is that **faithful steward**, the wise man whom his master will set over those in his household service **to supply them their allowance of food at the appointed time**? Blessed (happy and to be envied) is that servant whom his master finds so doing when he arrives.* -Luke 12:42-43, AMP

Note: The reader will get the most out of this book by thinking of it as a text book. Tackling each section as a separate book will be more profitable for remembering what has been studied. In this way, the topics covered will lend themselves to greater congruency and prevent the study fatigue that will surely overcome anyone trying to read this entire volume in one sitting.

Chapter 2

What Is a Bondservant?

> **bond·ser·vant**: n. a person bound to service without wages; devoted to another to the disregard of one's own interests[1]

While researching biblical understanding of the bondservant, the transcript of one sermon in particular helped bring together my fragmented knowledge on the subject. I have woven my own ideas together with those of Mike Fischer, whose excellent sermon is posted at cke1st.com ('seek ye first').

In order to grasp the relevance of bondservanthood in the believer's life, we will first look at the 'type and shadow' given in Exodus. Paul explained that the things written in the Old Testament were given to the followers of Christ for instruction so that through their encouragement, we will persevere and have hope (Rom. 15:4; 1 Cor. 10:11). While the events recorded in the Word are historical in nature, not every historical event was included. The events that have been recorded in the Word are there to teach us spiritual truths. Paul used the following example to validate this precept:

> *For it is written in the Law of Moses, "YOU SHALL NOT MUZZLE THE OX WHILE HE IS THRESHING." God is not concerned about oxen, is He? Or is He speaking altogether for our sake? Yes,* ***for our sake it was written.*** -1 Cor. 9:9-10a, NASB

The Setting

The setting for the teaching on the bondservant takes place when Israel received the law at Mt. Sinai. Having been redeemed from Egypt, the Israelites were now at the place where their redeemer God revealed the regulations by which they were to govern themselves. The Ten Commandments had been received amidst the frightening spectacle of thunder, lightning, smoke, and the tremor of the mountain. After the Ten Commandments were given, the people begged Moses to hear from God for them because they were seized with the fear they would die (Deut. 5:23-27).

Their fear appears to be the result of a heart posture not grounded in love and desire but in performance and fear of consequences. Now that the expectations of God had been made known, fear of the legal ramifications for disobedience surfaced. When our hearts are not resolved to obey out of love and relationship, the *empowerment* to obey is not given. Rigid obedience will not make the heart tender toward the Lord. More likely, a heart with this disposition will become resentful and critical of the leadership and laws, particularly over time.

As slaves in Egypt, the hearts of the Israelites were not committed to what they were forced to do. Their actions were simply rooted in self-preservation. When witnessing the awesome power of the God to whom they were now beholden, fear gripped their hearts because obedience born out of love had not. At this point, the courage to remain in God's presence evaporated. They stood 'afar off' and asked Moses to hear from the Lord for them (Ex. 20:18-21).

> *You go near and hear all that the LORD our God may say, and tell us all that the LORD our God says to you, and we will hear and do it.* -Deut. 5:27, NKJV

Their final statement shows they were performance-based in their hearts: 'we will hear (*sh'ma*) and do (*asah*).' It is no coincidence that the word *sh'ma* not only means to hear, but also to obey. God told Moses the people were right in what they had spoken, for their hearts were not motivated to obey out of love, but to *asah* (to do, labor, accomplish, earn) out of fear of the consequences rather than the true fear of God (see Deut. 5:28-30). In his book to the Roman believers, Paul reminded them they did not receive the spirit of bondage again *to fear*. As bondservants of God, we receive the spirit of adoption that enables us to relate to God as Father by not fearing judgment, while at the same time retaining the proper sense of the fear of the Lord (Rom. 8:14-15).

The Israelites' decision to obey was, for most, an emotional one based on fear. Any decision made during a time of heightened emotion without a commitment of the will probably won't be carried out—at least not without regret. As in Egypt, fear and self-preservation were their motives to obey God's commands, not love. What happened to them after the memory of the frightful events began to fade? What happens to anyone who makes an impulsive decision based on heightened emotion? Many later regret their decision because they did not consider or 'count the cost.' Likewise, the Israelites who turned from God in fear later complained about the very freedom God had given them, grumbled at every challenging circumstance, and doubted God's faithfulness.

Instruction About Slaves Came First

Teaching about slaves first would capture the Israelites' attention because they had just been freed from bondage. The imagery would speak of their recent redemption by God's hand. God intended to solicit the following response from them: 'I love you, Lord. You rescued me from bondage. My heart is so captured by Your love and the awesome power You displayed on my behalf that it is unthinkable to go my own way. I cannot leave You, not ever. You rescued me out of a hopeless situation, and You didn't have to. My life is free because of You. Let me stay with You and serve in Your house to be a part of Your work. This is what I want for my whole life.' This is the response God wanted but did not get from most of the Israelites. A nearly identical situation occurred when Jesus healed the ten lepers. Only the Samaritan returned to thank Him (Luke 17:11-19).

When it became apparent the Israelites' hearts were far from Him (Deut. 5:23-27), God's lament could be heard in His response (Deut. 5:29): 'Oh, that they had such a heart in them, that they would fear Me and always keep My commandments, that it may be well with them and with their children forever!' Jesus' lamentation over Jerusalem carried the same heart-rending emotion, demonstrating God's longing for reconciliation with man:

> *O Jerusalem... How often I wanted to gather your children together, as a hen gathers her chicks under her wings, but you were not willing!* -Matt. 23:37, NKJV

God's next statement to Israel through Moses is disheartening: 'Return to your tents.' The scepter had been extended to them by the Almighty King of the universe, and they declined to approach. At the beginning of this encounter, the Israelites came out of their tents eager to meet God. Now they were admonished to turn back to the place where they started. But Moses, the bondservant of God, was told to stand before God in order to hear the rest of what God would say (Deut. 5:31). The people, however, stood 'afar off.' *Selah* (Hebrew for 'think about that').

A Perfect Heart Towards God

From our study of the bondservant, we learn that the obedience God looks for is rooted in the heart and affects the actions. While the *actions* may not always be perfect, the *heart* can be perfect toward the Lord. Moses applied this to the law as well:

> *The LORD your God commands you... to follow these decrees and laws;* **carefully observe them with all your heart and with all your soul.** -Deut. 26:16, NIV

Notice the Lord called them to *carefully* observe the law with all their *heart and soul*. Our actions involving legs, arms, or even our tongues for speech are the fruit of what is in our hearts. It is the posture of our will, affections, and motives that defines us before God. No one who desires to be obedient out of love can willfully sin and enjoy it. With our heart and soul in agreement, we can experience the sanctification of our behavior. This can only be accomplished by the power of the Holy Spirit. God first loved us, and we reciprocate love back through obedience as He empowers us to do so.

> *In fact, this is love for God: to keep his commands. And his commands are not burdensome.* -1 John 5:3, NIV

The Making of a Bondservant

In discussing the concept of a bondservant, we will first look at the relevant phrases in the following passage and then apply the teaching to believers under the new covenant.

> *Now these are the rules that you shall set before them. When you buy a* **Hebrew slave**, *he shall serve six years, and* **in the seventh he shall go out free**, *for nothing... But if the slave plainly says,* '**I love my master**, *my wife, and my children; I*

will not go out free,' *then his master shall* ***bring him to God****, and he shall* ***bring him to the door*** *or the doorpost. And his master shall* ***bore his ear through with an awl****, and* ***he shall be his slave forever****.* -Ex. 21:1-2,5-6, ESV

We may find it odd that the first ordinance mentioned after the Ten Commandments dealt with treatment of Hebrew slaves, but its spiritual significance sets the tone for the whole law. Once we grasp this, we are better able to understand the heart of the law. As with most corporate documents today that begin with a stated mission, objective, and purpose, the first ordinance God gave Moses to 'set before the people' established the whole purpose of the law. The teaching of the bondservant first presents *prima facie* evidence that the heart must be involved for God to judge our obedience as acceptable.

The heart posture of the bondservant as the basis for the law establishes the primary objective: heartfelt commitment to obey out of love. Only secondarily are outward actions considered. When love and loyalty for God have gripped the heart, the Lord knows He has us. If only our minds and actions are involved, we will eventually burn out in our striving. Even the *Sh'ma* reinforces this:

> *Hear, O Israel: The LORD our God, the LORD is one! You shall love the LORD your God with all your heart, with all your soul, and with all your strength. And* ***these words which I command you today shall be in your heart****.* -Deut. 6:4-6, NKJV

It is important to note that the bondservant teaching applied only to Hebrew slaves. Other slaves were not subject to being released in the seventh year, according to Levitical law. This made the enslavement of Hebrews resemble that of indentured servants rather than slaves with little hope of freedom. So why would a Hebrew person enslave one of his brothers in the first place? Typically, a Hebrew was only enslaved in the event he could not pay his debt, whether because of poverty (Lev. 25:39-41) or the fine imposed from a charge of theft (Ex. 22:2-3). Both instances required labor in lieu of payment on the debt.

This inability to repay a debt owed has an obvious spiritual equivalence in the debt we owe because of sin, causing us to be in bondage to death. Paul stated all were slaves of sin before coming to Christ. Because Jesus paid our debt for us, we are now freed from the bondage of sin and death and become the bondslaves of Christ. All who repent and turn from the ways of the world, whether Jew or Greek, male or female, slave or free, become the spiritual seed of Abraham (Gal. 3:6-9,29). The analogy of the Hebrew slave is appropriate for all who by faith believe in Jesus and the salvation He offers (see also Acts 11:17-18). This establishes the preeminence of the Savior and our position as His bondslaves, here at the beginning of the law as given to Moses.

'In the Seventh Year He Is to Be Freed'

At the end of every seven years, the law required all Hebrew slaves be set free. No matter what time during the seven year period an Israelite became a slave, he was to be set free with all the rest in the Sabbatical year. The Sabbatical year was a year of rest for everyone. For the slave who had grown to love his master and his ways, however, no freedom was sought because the slave desired to be with his master more than he desired his freedom.

Jesus taught about the freedom given in the seventh year by the miracles He performed on Sabbath days during His ministry. On a Sabbath day, Jesus set free the woman who had been 'bound for eighteen years' (Luke 13:16). He also healed on the Sabbath the man with the withered hand (Luke 6:5-10), the lame man who picked up his mat (John 5:5-10), and the blind man (John 9:1-14).

The author of Hebrews also spoke of a Sabbath rest yet to come for God's people, alluding to the return of Christ and His Sabbath reign (Heb. 4:9-11). This is better understood in light of comments made by Moses, Peter, and Jesus Himself.

- **Moses**: A thousand years are like one day in the sight of God (Ps. 90:4).
- **Peter**: One day is as a thousand years, and a thousand years as one day from God's perspective (2 Pet. 3:8).
- **Jesus**: Jesus stated He is the Lord of the Sabbath (Matt. 12:8) and testified He will reign for a thousand years after the great tribulation (Rev. 20:4-6).

By professing He is Lord of the Sabbath, Jesus prophetically spoke of His millennial reign. As the author of Hebrews testified, this Sabbath is yet to come. Jesus explained that both He and His Father were working at the present time (John 5:17), revealing that the spiritual season in which Jesus walked the earth was *not* the Sabbath rest. He also told His disciples that the *works* He did, they would do also. Likewise, James explained any believer who had real faith would do *works* as the result of their faith (James 2:24-26). We are in the age of labor, not rest; the Sabbath is a picture of things to come.

In other words, all those who are bondslaves of Jesus will do works, just as He did. In each of these passages about works, the same basic Greek word is used, *ergon*. Jesus expected those who laid hold of His righteousness and experienced the release of all their debt because of His sacrifice and victory would become His bondservants. Out of love, the bondslave would obey His voice and accomplish all that the Lord set before him to do. This is how we keep the charge given to us as Abraham did (Gen. 26:5). Our labor in this age will cease when Jesus returns and the Sabbath rest begins.

'I Love My Master… I Will Not Go out Free'

In the Old Testament, we find the bondservant (Hebrew *ebed*) described as one who chooses voluntary servitude because of his love and gratitude for the one he serves. It is unthinkable to the bondservant to be separated from the master he has grown to love. With his whole heart he desires to remain in his master's presence for the rest of his life. In like manner, David professed his yearning for the house of the Lord where His glory dwelled (Ps. 26:8). The following verses likewise describe the heart of the bondservant:

SECTION 1 *INTRODUCTION TO THE BONDSERVANT'S LIFE*

> ***My soul yearns, even faints, for the courts of the LORD; my heart and my flesh cry out for the living God...*** *Better is one day in your courts than a thousand elsewhere; I would rather be a doorkeeper in the house of my God than dwell in the tents of the wicked.* -Ps. 84:2,10, NIV

The Israelites had been redeemed from slavery in Egypt. The Lord then invited them to become His bondslaves out of love. Many only felt fear. This is the fear that comes from a heart that will not relinquish control but rather clings to self-centered desires. Though God had shown Himself to be totally trustworthy in rescuing them from Egypt, fear and conflict reigned in their hearts. Having been slaves in Egypt, were they now to be slaves of God? How is that freedom? This same conflict is seen in believers who enter into the new covenant of freedom expecting to do as they please, not realizing freedom in Christ requires obedience to God.

David, on the other hand, showed the heart posture of a bondservant:

> ***One thing I ask from the LORD,*** *this only do I seek:* ***that I may dwell in the house of the LORD all the days of my life,*** *to gaze on the beauty of the LORD and to seek him in his temple.* -Ps. 27:4, NIV

When the bondservant said, 'I love my master,' the word 'master' was translated from the Hebrew word, *Adonai*. Throughout the Old Testament, we see this word primarily rendered 'lord' or 'Lord,' depending on who is referenced. The New Testament writers continually referred to Jesus as Lord, and without this designation accompanying His title of Savior, we are prone to adopt an erroneous idea that it's all about us and our privilege as children of God.

The use of 'I am' in both of the following verses comes from the Greek word *eimi* and is the designation for God (Ex. 3:14). Jesus used this to describe Himself, revealing He is God in the flesh.

> *Ye call me, The Teacher and The Lord, and ye say well, for I am.* -John 13:13, YLT

> *Truly, truly, I say to you, before Abraham was born, I am.* -John 8:58, NASB

If Jesus is not Lord, then we will not have the works that accompany faith and are pleasing in His sight. We will only have self-will, and no matter how 'good' the works we accomplish may seem, they will all burn up because He is not the author of them (1 Cor. 3:12-15). A dying ember He will not snuff out (Isa. 42:3). However, to be the agency of our demise because all we accomplished originated in our own mind and was done for reputation, honor, or out of humanistic compassion, will prove to be a cause for tears and shame at His coming. In order for Jesus to be Lord in truth, we must voluntarily take the form of a bondservant. The wonderful picture of the bondslave as depicted in the book of Exodus shows we have time to grow and mature in our love and gratitude toward the Lord until we reach the point where we say, 'I love my Lord, I will not go out.'

To walk as Jesus walked and love as He loved requires we walk in His Spirit and place priority on loving the Lord with all our heart, soul, mind, and strength. Only then will we make the transition from focusing on *our* will to focusing on *His*. Our lives will only have worth as they are a legacy of obedience to the will of God at the expense of our own. This is how we demonstrate our love for God (John 14:15,21; 2 John 1:6).

> *But my life is worth nothing to me unless I use it for finishing the work assigned me by the Lord Jesus.* -Acts 20:24, NLT

'Bring Him to Elohim'

When offered his freedom, the bondservant declares he will not go out free because he loves his master and wants to voluntarily stay with him in servitude. In order to 'seal the deal,' the servant is taken to *elohim*, which is translated 'God' in the ESV (Ex. 21:6). This is appropriate, though other versions are equally correct in using 'judges' as the translation. When *elohim* is used in this context, it most likely refers to human agents rendering judicial decisions by reason of their delegated authority, thereby acting as agents of God (cf. Rom. 13:1; see also Ps. 58; 82).

In the Old Testament context, the servant is brought before the delegated authorities. As new covenant believers, however, we come before the Lord with our hearts bared and a Holy Spirit driven desire to be obedient as an expression of our love for God. Both Old and New Testament writers frequently remind us that obedience to God is a heart issue rooted in love. Jesus declared the *Sh'ma* to be the most important commandment and quoted Deuteronomy 6:4-5:

> *The most important one... is this: 'Hear, O Israel: The Lord our God, the Lord is one. Love the Lord your God with all your heart and with all your soul and with all your mind and with all your strength.' The second is this: 'Love your neighbor as yourself.' There is no commandment greater than these.* -Mark 12:29-31, NIV

Jesus goes on to say that having this heart posture as the foundation for our obedience is more important than all the outward activities and sacrifices we may make (Mark 12:33). Once He has captured our hearts, God knows He will have all of us—our soul, mind, and strength. This takes place by the power of His love working through us via the ministry and work of the Holy Spirit. By this we will be equipped to follow His commands in all we do, giving our lives eternal worth.

Notice the emphasis on the heart rather than the actions themselves in this passage:

> *My son, do not forget my law, but* **let your heart keep my commands**... *Let not mercy and truth forsake you; bind them around your neck, write them on the tablet of your heart.* -Pr. 3:1,3, NKJV

'Bring Him to the Door'

At this point, the bondservant is brought to the door of his master's house. Not only is the door part of the permanent structure of the house, it is the entrance by which the servant must enter. Jesus described Himself as the door, and no one can enter except through Him (John 14:6). Present in the teaching of the *Torah*, then, is the concept of being fixed to the door, which is Jesus, the only way we gain entrance to the Master's house.

> *I am the door. If anyone enters by Me, he will be saved, and will go in and out and find pasture.* -John 10:9, NKJV

The next act of fixing the servant to the door by driving an awl through his ear lobe symbolizes the permanence of his decision. The slave is forever bonded to his master, becoming 'part of the house' through this act. By renouncing his right to his own will, he has received in exchange the right to enter his master's house and be involved in his master's concerns. In many instances, though still remaining a lowly servant, the bondservant was treated more like family, privy to much of the master's business and private concerns.

Jesus admonished us to make *every effort* to enter through Him, the door (Luke 13:24). Entrance is not gained through self-will but through love. This love is resolute in its commitment to obey the Master, even if this obedience is not performed perfectly. The door will never be closed for true bondservants as long as they never cease striving to enter. Striving is directly related to a heart laboring to obey. For those bondservants alive at the end of the age, an open door will be presented to them—for revelation.

> **I have put before you an open door which no one can shut**, because you have... kept My word, and have not denied My name... After these things I looked, and behold, **a door standing open in heaven**... Come up here, and I will show you things which must take place after this. -Rev. 3:8; 4:1, NASB

'Bore His Ear Through with an Awl'

In Hebrew, the ear symbolized hearing. As previously mentioned, the Hebrew equivalent for the word 'hear' is the same as for the word 'obey': *sh'ma*. This is probably the most critical concept to understand. If we remember nothing else from this entire study but *sh'ma*, we will have gained ground. Jesus said His sheep *hear* His voice (John 10:27), and it is vitally important we understand the spiritual concept that true hearing always involves obedience to what has been heard.

Piercing the ear with an awl into the doorframe of the house signified the bondslave's voluntary obligation to hear and obey his master. His heart is bent on obedience because of love. Desire to obey births in us a spirit that is waiting, watchful, and expectant to hear the voice of the master in order to demonstrate love through obedience.

Hearing is equated with obedience in the New Testament as well ('be doers of the word, and not hearers only,' James 1:22). Though remaining a slave, the bondservant became much more than a slave because he was now bonded to his master for life. Such a bondservant was typically entrusted with more of the master's affairs than the other slaves were. But the fact remained that he was still a slave and obligated to obey. The bondservant's position was not exalted, but rather pointed to the special bond of love that existed between the master and bondslave.[2] Being a slave is still a lowly position, even if the position is voluntarily chosen. In exchange, the bondslave does not have to worry about his next meal or clothing because his Master provides these for him (Matt. 6:32-34).

Bondservants in the New Testament

The New Testament equivalent of the bondservant can be found in the Greek word *doulos*, defined as someone who gives up his own will for that of another out of utter devotion. It is a decision based not on fear or reasoning but on love. Disregarding his own interests and desires, the bondservant actually seeks to serve with no aspiration or ambition for the exaltation of self. Indeed, the concepts of slavery and personal ambition are at odds. The opposite of being a bondservant is not being a master, as some would think. Jesus is both our Master and the one who came *to serve*. The opposite of serving is the very thing which hinders us from giving all to Christ: self-centeredness and self-will. A servant asks what he can do for others. A self-centered person gratifies only his own desires, including using others to further his own agenda.[3]

Being a bondservant of Jesus means complete and utter devotion to God, His Word, and His will. It is disregarding our own will, desires, and interests in order to lay down our lives at the cross to follow Christ. It is not about walking in sinless perfection, yet it is a dedication to following God in all things no matter the cost.

When we come across passages in Scripture where we read God did not give them ears to hear (e.g., Isa. 6:10; Rom. 11:8), we may become confused as to why these people are still held at fault if they are unable to understand the point God is trying to make. The answer may simply be connected to heart posture. Consider the following:

> To whom shall I [Jeremiah] speak and give warning, that they may hear? Behold, **their ears are uncircumcised** [never brought into covenant with God or consecrated to His service], and they cannot hear or obey. Behold, the word of the Lord has become to them a reproach and the object of their scorn; **they have no delight in it**. -Jer. 6:10, AMP

They don't hear because they don't wish to hear and have no delight in hearing what God has to say. If we are not seeking to hear, God will not provide us with understanding. Only God can give us spiritual eyes to see or ears to hear for understanding spiritual truth (Pr. 20:12; 1 Cor. 2:11-16). This understanding is only available to those who seek it.

If we are not rooted in love for God, our obedience will not be obedience at all by God's standard but only an outward show. This type of heart disconnect with the actions carried out in the name of the law excludes us from the empowerment to *sh'ma*, which would otherwise be ours if our actions were initiated from a heart of love.

This is not new teaching. We find the same thoughts written by David in Psalm 40. When our heart moves toward God out of love and desire to obey, God empowers us to do what our heart desires to do. The phrase, 'my ears You have opened' in the following verse is translated in the Amplified as, "You have given me the capacity to hear and obey Your law." This reminds us we are not to be hearers only who later forget the message, but *doers* who put what they have heard into action.

> *Sacrifice... You have not desired; My ears You have opened.* -Ps. 40:6, NASB

Jesus often spoke in parables to hide the message from those who were wise and learned in their own eyes. He often concluded the parables with, 'He who has ears to hear, let him hear' (e.g., Matt. 11:15; Mark 7:16; Luke 14:35). In the book of Revelation, the letters to each of the churches have counsel followed by the words, 'He who has an ear, let him hear what the Spirit says to the churches.' Only true bondservants can hear the message because their ears have been opened for the purpose of obeying.

> *Blessed are your eyes because they see, and your ears because they hear. For... many prophets and righteous people longed to see what you see but did not see it, and to hear what you hear but did not hear it.* -Matt. 13:16-17, NIV

In this passage, we note again that what we hear and understand is not only dependent on whether or not we are bondservants but also on the timing and purpose of God.

A Slave Forever

Though still a servant, the newly dedicated bondservant was often given more privilege and responsibility, demonstrating his unique standing in the master's house. This also included greater knowledge of the master's business pursuits and concerns. Yet he receives only as much privilege as his master decides to give him. It is not a way for the servant to maneuver into a position of privilege. In the life of the believer, it is the way to fulfill the Master's plan and purpose for his life.

Of his own free will, the servant has now become a bondslave for the rest of his life. The paradox of being both free in the liberty of Christ and the bondslave of Christ becomes difficult in our thinking only when we view these two states as mutually exclusive. Yet Jesus has forever linked our freedom from the bondage of sin with our unrestrained willingness to be His servants as slaves of righteousness (Rom. 6:18).

> *[S]ince you have been set free from sin and have become the slaves of God, you have your present reward in holiness and its end is eternal life.* -Rom. 6:22, AMP

Our 'present reward in holiness' is the empowerment to do what is acceptable in God's sight. The Holy Spirit works in our hearts and minds to conform us to the character of Christ (Gal. 4:19). Jesus is our example of the perfect bondservant who came to do God's will and finish the work (John 4:34). As bondservants who have been given ears to hear and a heart that understands, we have a foretaste of eternity in this age:

> *This is eternal life, that they may know You, the only true God, and Jesus Christ whom You have sent.* -John 17:3, NASB

Use Your Freedom to Serve

The New Testament writers remind us that without love we are nothing, we gain nothing (1 Cor. 13). Freedom from sin as well as freedom from being bound to the works of the law is a gift that allows us to love God and our fellowman. Our freedom is not an occasion to harm another person's faith so we can have our own desires fulfilled. Quite the opposite, our freedom must be walked out in faith that comes with wisdom to understand freedom through the lens of love and servanthood.

Paul modeled this in his life and teaching. Though he was free and belonged to no one, he made himself a slave to everyone in order to win as many as possible to faith in Jesus (1 Cor. 9:19). Those who have made themselves bondservants would not think of using their freedom in Christ as a covering for sin. Their freedom is seen as power to choose the will of God (1 Pet. 2:16-17).

> *"I have the right to do anything," you say—but not everything is beneficial... not everything is constructive. No one should seek their own good, but the good of others.* -1 Cor. 10:23,24, NIV

Learning to deny ourselves and esteem others' needs first is a recurring theme in the Bible. Only the power and grace of God can accomplish this, for we came out of the womb screaming to have our way. This only increases in intensity as we grow up, though we may find more civilized ways of expressing it. There are many Scriptures that show us the way of love and its requirement in fulfilling the law. Each points to the heart of the servant as the key. In our minds, it is easy to serve Jesus, God's perfect Son, but serving others is another story! The following list of related Bible passages shows the emphasis the apostles placed on looking out for the interests of others. We are to:

- use our freedom to serve others humbly out of love, for the entire law is fulfilled in loving others as ourselves (Gal. 5:13-14);
- do good and share with others as a 'sacrifice' pleasing to God (Heb. 13:16);
- be concerned first about others' welfare rather than our own (1 Cor. 10:24);
- do nothing out of selfish ambition or vain conceit, but in humility value others above ourselves, which includes looking out for the interests of others and not just our own (Php. 2:3-4);

- meet the urgent needs of others (Titus 3:14);
- walk in the wisdom from above, which is willing to yield to others, full of mercy and good deeds, showing no favoritism (James 3:17); and
- offer hospitality to one another without grumbling, faithfully using whatever gift we have been given to serve others (1 Pet. 4:9-10).

Not only is the bar very high, it is a stumbling block to most of us who are obsessed with getting our own way, manipulating, intimidating, and taking advantage of others until we succeed. But there is hope for everyone who is in Christ! If we will cooperate with the Holy Spirit as He does His work of sanctification, we can be empowered to love others. Then we will be free to love as God intended. The directives to love one another are many, but Jesus' command is direct and to the point:

My command is this: Love each other as I have loved you. -John 15:12, NIV

Wow—love others as Jesus loves us. Bing Crosby defined 'wow' as 'somewhere between *ouch* and *boing*.' Wow. The apostles also frequently remind us to love each other because this fulfills the law. This cannot be accomplished on our own. We have no comprehension of how much God loves us, and without a broader perspective and bigger heart, we will fail miserably at this command. The author of Hebrews went further, stating we need to love others *so we can make certain* we attain what we hope for: salvation and the transformation of our bodies from mortal to immortal (Heb. 6:11). John also stated that if we do not love fellow believers, we are still in darkness (1 John 2:5-10).

Only those who walk in love live in the light of God's presence with nothing to make them stumble. This love is not based merely on affection, but on mental ascent that seeks the highest good for others—even those who are difficult to get along with and sorely try our patience. This *agape* love originates with God and is available to all who walk by the Holy Spirit. If it were up to love based on feelings, everyone would fail.

The apostle John gives us a wonderfully circular command. 'Anyone who loves God must also love his brother and sister' (1 John 4:21), and 'this is how we know that we love the children of God: by loving God and carrying out his commands' (1 John 5:2). I am convinced this apostle walked in the love of God and theologically understood and experienced God's love in the deepest way.

A Hireling Is Not a Bondservant

The hireling is paid for his work. His relationship is a business transaction with the owner of the house. Wages are the primary reason for the relationship, not love. He has received his reward in full. Owing nothing to his boss, his only requirement is to put in an honest day's work. Because he is not involved at the heart level, he will typically be more concerned about saving his own skin in a day of trouble rather than staying to help the vulnerable ones under the protection of the owner (John 10:13).

Because the primary concern of the hireling is the wage he collects, his master is not God but mammon. Without the ear opened, as in the case of the bondservant, he is unable to comprehend the ways and knowledge of God.

> *Such are the shepherds who cannot understand; they have all turned to their own way, each one to his own gain.* -Isa. 56:11, AMP

Enough said.

Closing Thoughts

The bondservant's whole motivation is his relationship with the One he loves. It is not about an ulterior motive to get an exalted position. A bondservant is still a slave in a lowly position and expected to do his Master's bidding. Becoming a bondservant grates against our natural inclination toward selfishness, self-centeredness, self-actualization, and self-fulfillment. As infants, we cannot help but be selfish, seeking always to have our needs met for survival. Because we are born this way, we scarcely recognize that we are selfish because selfishness is birthed in subtlety and promoted in all the world regards as normal and healthy. The realization we are selfish typically does not surface until we get married or have children. Then we find out just how self-centered we really are!

Though we are expected as believers to grow out of this mindset, it does not come naturally. Many are able to help others, perform selfless acts, and share what they have, but even these acts are an assertion of will if they are not performed in submission to the will of God. Because these activities are by definition selfless, we assume they are not selfishly motivated. But so far as we are still on the throne of our will, even these acts are tainted with selfishness and humanistic compassion that is perverted by its short-sightedness. Only by the Holy Spirit's grace can we hope to be transformed into the bondservant who, like Jesus, can from the heart utter the words, 'Not my will, but Yours be done.'

There are times when we will wander from this calling, but the Lord is persistent and will bring us back because we are His and under His protection. Even in ministry it is easy to wander, especially if our heart posture changes and we only perform ministry tasks for our own pleasure, for recognition, or out of a sense of duty. Many have constructed a religious covering for all their self-willed deeds, which receive praise from men but are not honored by God. It is the difference between choosing what *we* want to do for God, rather than doing what *He* determined for us to accomplish.

Being a bondservant does not mean sinless perfection but dedication and commitment to do God's will. The examples we have of bondservants in the Bible record their obedient acts alongside their sins, fears, doubts, and lack of faith. This helps remind us they are just regular people like us. All who are in Christ grow in the grace to live as Jesus did—in complete obedience to the Father.

SECTION 1 *INTRODUCTION TO THE BONDSERVANT'S LIFE*

It is utterly unnatural to choose to be a bondservant because the position is both lowly and permanent. It says, 'I give up my right to be on the throne of my life.' The bondservant has abrogated self and the trappings of this world. To be a bondservant is to utterly trust and love the One to whom we are bonded and have given our rights. God is deserving of all our trust because He never gives us more than we can bear. "Faith knows not where it goes but it loves the one it follows."[4]

Bondservants are the only people who are truly free from the grip of this world. If we serve God alone and have eyes only for Him, we will not be tricked into bondage to the world's ways or the god of this age. A true servant of God will walk in peace, for it is only in Him that we have peace. He protects us, reminding us to turn the other cheek and agree with our adversary because vengeance belongs to God and He will repay in due season. Being a bondservant of Christ entails devotion to the Word, which is a description of Jesus (the 'Word made flesh'). For the bondservant, spending time with God through obedient service and study of the Word is the preoccupation of his heart, soul, and spirit.

> *Come to Me, all you who labor and are heavy laden, and I will give you rest. Take My yoke upon you and learn from Me, for I am gentle and lowly in heart, and you will find rest for your souls. For My yoke is easy and My burden is light.* -Matt. 11:28-30, NKJV

Chapter 3

Who Are the Bondservants?

> *[A]m I now seeking the favor of men, or of God? Or am I striving to please men? If I were still trying to please men, I would not be a bond-servant of Christ.* -Gal. 1:10, NASB

No one would be surprised to learn that the prophets and apostles were depicted as bondservants of God. Enoch walked with God and was no more. Abraham was called God's friend. God talked with Moses face to face. David was a man after God's own heart. Daniel was a man highly esteemed by God. Jesus said John the Baptist was the greatest man ever born of a woman and friend of the Bridegroom. All the Old Testament prophets were called bondservants.

What do believers today have in common with these heroes of the faith? The answer is both extremes: much and little. 'Much' because we share the same scarlet thread that delivers us from bondage to sin and reconciles us with God. 'Little' in that most Christians today are far more concerned with their own affairs and taking every shrewd advantage to get ahead than they are with their Father's business. Both ministers and 'laymen' alike can be deceived into giving greater priority to self than to God. This must change if we are to finish the race marked out for us and bring the Lord something other than a cloud of smoke when we meet Him face to face (1 Cor. 3:15).

How we see ourselves from a spiritual standpoint says a great deal about where we are in our walk as servants. If we see ourselves as people loaded with talent waiting to be discovered, we are over the top with ambition and pride. If we see ourselves as rejected orphans continually hoping and searching for affirmation, we are still in a place of self-centeredness. Even if our minds are focused on demonstrating our servanthood nature by taking every opportunity to serve because we enjoy doing so or want to prove we are so inclined, our motives are askew. While bondservants may start out this way due to immaturity, a mind focused on God and His kingdom provides evidence that we have crossed over into the realm of mature bondservanthood.

Love and Loyalty

If the characteristics of a bondservant could be boiled down to just two, the most likely attributes would have to be love and loyalty. Loyalty flows out of love and a shared vision. If we love someone but don't share his or her passion or vision, our relationship can only go so far. We will be more focused on our own vision, and the end result will be that we drift apart from the one we professed to love. David admonished his son

Solomon to serve the Lord with a loyal heart and willing mind because the Lord searches the heart and discerns our motives (1 Chron. 28:9).

When our actions are dictated by our own narrow-minded idea of how our lives should be lived with no greater context than our culture, self, and immediate family, we may love God but no loyalty will be found there. Our loyalty will be to our own personal objective or vision with no room for a broader vision that may be in conflict with our own. Eventually we will discover that our objectives and what we value are at odds with God's purposes. How we handle this conflict will determine who is lord of our life. We will follow whomever or whatever has captivated our affections and therefore our loyalty.

The Lord is seeking those who will worship in spirit and truth (John 4:23). Worship includes the sacrifices of praise, thanksgiving, and prayer, but this is only a part. Biblical worship of God requires submission to Him in service. Paul urged the believers to present their bodies as 'living and holy' sacrifices acceptable to God. This expresses worship through obedient service (Rom. 12:1). By presenting our bodies to God, we are making a statement that our lives are not our own. Serving God by making *His* will *our* will is the most authentic expression of worship. Only when our actions validate our confession of Christ as Savior and our profession that we are His followers can we make certain our worship is genuine—in spirit and in truth.

In the next passage, the Greek word *latreuo* is translated 'serve,' but it can also be translated 'worship' (e.g., Acts 7:42; 24:14; Php. 3:3; Heb. 10:2). Serving is integral to worship just as obedience is inseparable from truly hearing.

> *I thank God, whom I serve* (**latreuo**)... *with a clear conscience, as night and day I constantly remember you in my prayers.* -2 Tim. 1:3, NIV (parenthetical added)

Worshipping God and serving Him in obedience go hand in hand. Peter stated that all those who treat God with worshipful obedience and live uprightly are acceptable to God (Acts 10:34-35). Paul also wrote that good deeds are to accompany those who profess to worship God (1 Tim. 2:10).

> *We know that God does not listen to sinners, but if anyone is a* **worshiper of God and does his will,** *God listens to him.* -John 9:31, ESV

From this we have clarity as to what John meant when he wrote God is looking for those who worship in spirit and in truth. While there are more applications than this, for our study we will focus on 'in spirit' as designating those whose will and desire are in keeping with the Spirit of God. Likewise, 'in truth' characterizes those who are connected at the heart level in their submission to God, seen in their voluntary obedience to His Word and will in acts of service. The loyal of the earth are the ones God is searching for:

> *[T]he eyes of the LORD run to and fro throughout the whole earth,* **to show Himself strong on behalf of those whose heart is loyal to Him**. -2 Chron. 16:9a, NKJV

In David's song of deliverance (2 Sam. 22), he stated God shows Himself loving and loyal to those who love Him and are loyal to His will (see v. 26, AMP). In contrast, Adam's loyalty was found wanting. He had received one command from God: 'Don't eat from the tree of knowledge in the center of the garden.' His loyalty was to be centered on God. When Eve entered the picture, Adam's heart wavered. Eve ate the fruit after being deceived, but Adam ate the fruit in disobedience because his heart was now divided. This is made more apparent from the following passage:

> For **I delight in loyalty rather than sacrifice**, And in the knowledge of God rather than burnt offerings. But **like Adam** they have **transgressed the covenant**; there they have **dealt treacherously against Me**. -Hos. 6:6-7, NASB

Our loyalty will be either to God and His purposes, or to self, personal preferences and desires, and/or the world. For some, loyalty leans toward the needs of others or doing what is agreeable in our circle of friends because of peer pressure. But even this loyalty is rooted in self because those who do so crave the acceptance and approval of others. The allurement of the world and its ways will win over our affections without the aid of God's grace and the discernment available to us by the Holy Spirit.

Jesus: The Perfect Example of a Bondservant

The life of a bondservant is first and foremost the life of someone who does the will of God at the expense of his own. There is no greater example of this than in the life of Jesus. During His time as a man on the earth, Jesus walked in complete surrender to the will of the Father (John 6:38). Paul described Jesus as humbling Himself by becoming a bondservant, obedient even to death on the cross because it suited the plan and purpose of God (Php. 2:5-8).

Throughout Jesus' life, we witness the heart of a man loyal to the Father He loves, perfect in His submission to the Father's will. By becoming a man, Jesus is able to identify with us in our humanity on the matter of obedience and the struggle this engenders in our flesh. While in Gethsemane, Jesus pleaded three times for God to remove the trial of suffering set before Him, each time deferring in His request to the will of God (Matt. 26:39,42,44). We know His request was not answered in the way that He prayed. Does this actually mean Jesus did not have enough faith to get what He asked for, as some would suggest? I speak as a fool... No, this was written for our benefit, and it actually helps us understand the following passage. Notice the writer stated Jesus' loud cries were heard because He submitted His request with reverence. If His cries were heard, how was this prayer answered if it didn't cause the Father to grant Jesus' request? The answer came in the form of angelic aid sent to strengthen Him for the task (Luke 22:43).

> *In the days of his flesh, Jesus offered up prayers and supplications, with loud cries and tears, to him who was able to save him from death, and he was heard*

> because of his reverence. **Although he was a son, he learned obedience through what he suffered.** And **being made perfect,** he became the source of eternal salvation to all who obey him. -Heb. 5:7-9, ESV

At first glance, this Scripture boggles the mind with the words, 'He learned obedience,' and 'made perfect.' Why would Jesus have to learn anything, especially obedience? How could Jesus be 'made perfect' if He was already the perfect Son of God?

On the first question, the key lies in the word 'learned.' This particular word in the Greek (*manthano*) means to understand in an *experiential* way. In other words, through this experience of crying out for a way different than the one set before Him, yet understanding from the Father that His will on the matter had not changed despite Jesus' cries for an altered course, Jesus acquired firsthand *experiential* knowledge of what it means to submit to God in the face of tremendous struggle and conflict of desire. He is now able to intercede for us as our high priest because of His ability to empathize with our struggles against the flesh in our efforts to comply with God's will.

> *We do not have a high priest who cannot sympathize with our weaknesses, but One who has been tempted in all things as we are, yet without sin.* -Heb. 4:15, NASB

By submitting to God's will in all God ordained for Him to do, Jesus was made *perfect*— He obeyed God's will (even when He sought a different way in Gethsemane) and completed His course. All through His ministry on earth, we find evidence of Jesus' obedience to the Father, whether in the things He said or things He did. Jesus stated the Father shows Him all that He is doing because of love (John 5:20). Jesus did nothing of His own accord but only what He saw the Father doing. Neither did Jesus speak on His own initiative; He spoke only as the Father commanded Him (John 12:49). Notice in the following verse that speaking as the Father commands is equated with 'works':

> *Do you not believe that I am in the Father, and the Father is in Me? The words that I say to you **I do not speak on My own** initiative, but the Father abiding in Me **does His works**.* -John 14:10, NASB

This helps us understand the second question. Jesus' heart was *perfect* (obedient) before God, as prophesied by David. While most of us recoil at the thought of doing someone else's will, Jesus stated that God's will is a delight. Notice that God gave Him an open ear, just as described in the case of an actual bondslave's ear pierced with an awl:

> *In sacrifice and offering you have not delighted, **but you have given me an open ear**... Then I said, "Behold, I have come; in the scroll of the book it is written of me: **I delight to do your will**, O my God; your law is within my heart."* -Ps. 40:6a,7-8, ESV (see also Heb. 10:7)

As Jesus taught, so He lived. When the 'sons of thunder' sought to secure themselves a favorable position in the Court of Heaven, the other disciples were incensed (probably because they hadn't asked first). Jesus taught them about servanthood using Himself as the example to follow. Only the worldly lord authority over one another. Among Jesus' followers, however, those who wished to be great would have to become servants. Even Jesus, the King of kings, did not come to be served but to serve others (Mark 10:42-45; Luke 22:27). We, also, are *made perfect* through obedience to serve.

Servanthood inhabits the core of Jesus' teaching, whether by His example or His words. The Word teaches that the fulfillment of the law exists in love—love for God and love for man. Serving others is the natural result of serving God. It requires faith that what God determines is best and humility to accept we are shortsighted in our thinking and plans. If we truly have these qualities as our foundation, we will not transgress against God or man. Jesus fulfilled this perfectly. The final outcome of Jesus' obedience is this:

> ***Therefore God also has highly exalted Him and given Him the name which is above every name***, *that at the name of Jesus every knee should bow, of those in heaven, and of those on earth, and of those under the earth, and that every tongue should confess that Jesus Christ is Lord, to the glory of God the Father.*
> -Php. 2:9-11, NKJV

Other Examples of Bondservants in the Bible

Kings, priests, shepherds, farmers, mothers, intercessors, apostles, prophets—examples of each are depicted as bondservants in the Word. We might be intimidated by apostles and prophets, but probably not by moms, farmers, and shepherds! The apostles, who described themselves as bondservants of God and Jesus Christ, were not perfect. They were ordinary people like us (Acts 14:15) who had an extraordinary encounter and calling. Even Elijah is described as a man 'just like us' (James 5:17). They did not know everything. They prophesied in part and understood only in part. Yet the entire Bible was written by the bondservants whom God had entrusted with writing His Word.

There are examples of bondservants in both Old and New Testaments. Some identified themselves as bondservants of God while others were defined by God in that way. Here is an incomplete list of the 'Bondservant Hall of Fame.' A short description of the particular quality the individual exemplified in his life as a bondservant introduces each one.

Enoch: walked with God in habitual fellowship (Gen. 5:24); did not experience death and was commended as one who pleased God (Heb. 11:5).

Job: was blameless before God and upright in conduct and heart; feared God and shunned evil (Job 1:8).

Abraham: believed God's promises, which was credited to him as righteousness; was called 'God's friend' (James 2:23).

Moses: heard from God as a friend (Ex. 33:11); walked in humility and was faithful to obey (Num. 12:7).

SECTION 1 *INTRODUCTION TO THE BONDSERVANT'S LIFE*

Joshua: delighted in the Lord's presence (Ex. 33:11); was known as God's servant (Jdg. 2:8); courageously led the charge to take the Promised Land (book of Joshua).

Caleb: followed the Lord wholeheartedly despite the odds or opposition (Num. 13:30; 14:6-10,24).

Phinehas: had as much zeal for God's name as God Himself and was given a covenant of a lasting priesthood as a result (Num. 25:11-13); his loyalty was credited to him as righteousness for endless generations (Ps. 106:30-31).

Hannah: called herself the Lord's servant; took her 'bitterness of soul' to the Lord and her request was honored (1 Sam. 1:11).

Samuel: postured his heart to hear from the Lord during a time of apostasy, and became God's voice at a time when the word of the Lord was rare (1 Sam. 3:1,10).

David: called a man after God's own heart and credited with doing all of God's will (Acts 13:22); served God with an upright heart whether watching sheep or guiding the nation with discernment and skill (1 Kings 3:6; Ps. 78:72).

Elijah: followed the Lord despite incredible opposition and intimidation; asked God to make it known he was the Lord's obedient servant (1 Kings 18:36).

Jonah: humbled himself before God to accomplish a mission he neither liked nor believed in (salvation of the Assyrians in Nineveh; see the book of Jonah) but was still called God's servant (2 Kings 14:25).

Isaiah: was obedient in politically incorrect prophetic acts (Isa. 20:3) and unpopular messages (e.g., Isa:1).

Hezekiah: loved the Lord and followed His commands in faithfulness with all his heart (2 Chron. 31:20-21).

Josiah: lived the *sh'ma*; loved the Lord with all his heart, soul, and strength, in word and deed (2 Kings 23:25).

Daniel: sought the Lord for wisdom and understanding, humbling himself before the Lord in prayer three times each day; highly esteemed by God (Dan. 9:17,23; 10:11,19).

Nehemiah: loved God's people and His Word; used his position to see God's Word fulfilled through intercession and faithful, steadfast action at the appointed time (see the book of Nehemiah).

Ezra: loved the Word of God; devoted himself to study and observance of the law, and sought to restore this love to the people (Ezr. 7:10).

Zerrubabel: was given great authority in Israel to rebuild the temple; called God's servant and was granted God's authority to rule Israel (Hag. 2:23).

The prophets: loved the Lord and heard His voice to speak His messages to the people in God's timing no matter the consequences (Amos 3:7; Luke 11:48).

Mary: walked humbly before the Lord and was favored by God; called herself the bondslave of the Lord (Luke 1:38).

Simeon: deemed righteous and devout; stayed in step with and heard from the Holy Spirit; was promised he would see the Messiah before he died (Luke 2:25-29).

Anna: served the Lord night and day with prayer and fasting (Luke 2:36-38).

John the Baptist: called the greatest man ever born of a woman (Matt. 11:11) though he never performed a single miracle (John 10:41); humbly but fearlessly and incessantly proclaimed the way of salvation (Matt. 21:32; Luke 1:15-17; 76-80).

Paul: overtaken with love for his Savior; often risked his life to fulfill God's will (2 Cor. 11:23-29); wrote much of the New Testament; called himself a bondservant of Christ (Rom. 1:1).

Peter: gave his life out of love for God; transformed from an emotion-based follower of Christ to conviction-based; called himself a bondservant of Christ (2 Pet. 1:1).

John: loved and served God in true understanding of the identity we have in Christ (identified himself as the 'one Jesus loved'; see John 13:23; 19:26; 20:2; 21:7,20); called himself a bondservant of Christ (Rev. 1:1).

Timothy (Php. 1:1), Epaphras (Col. 1:7), Tychicus (Col. 4:7), James (James 1:1), Jude (Jude 1:1), and even angels (Rev. 22:9, *sundoulos*: fellow bondservants) are referred to as bondservants of Christ. A look at Hebrews 11 gives us a picture of the quality of faith these bondservants demonstrated. What each has in common is their love for God, faith in His promises, active loyalty to His work, and their submission (albeit imperfect) to His will, even if their submission cost them their lives. Each one has character qualities and behaviors that define who a bondservant is and what he looks like. Aspiring to be included in this group starts with love for God and loyalty to His purposes.

It may surprise some to know that God also described Nebuchadnezzar as His servant (Hebrew *ebed*; see Jer. 25:9; 27:6; 43:10). He was God's instrument to discipline the nation of Judah. In other words, Nebuchadnezzar carried out God's will in fulfilling prophetic judgment, warranting his inclusion as a bondservant. While Nebuchadnezzar was not necessarily known as a man of faith, his confession after a brief (seven year) period of pride-induced insanity was a good start:

> *Now I, Nebuchadnezzar, praise, exalt and honor the King of heaven, for all His works are true and His ways just, and He is able to humble those who walk in pride.* -Dan. 4:37, NASB

Cyrus, on the other hand, was not described as God's servant but as His anointed shepherd (Isa. 44:28; 45:1). Twice Isaiah recorded that Cyrus did not know God (Isa. 45:4,5). Yet he was given the mandate to cause the exiles to return to Israel and rebuild the temple in Jerusalem, which he began in the first year of his reign (Ezr. 1:1-2). The Lord stirred Cyrus' heart to righteousness and equipped him to accomplish His purposes for

Israel. This example alone should be inspiration enough to pray that God would move on the hearts of ungodly governmental leaders to accomplish His will.

> *I will raise up Cyrus in my righteousness: I will make all his ways straight. He will rebuild my city and set my exiles free, but not for a price or reward, says the LORD Almighty.* -Isa. 45:13, NIV

Bondservants Run to God

With Nebuchadnezzar being the one possible exception, those described as bondservants walked in love for God and trust in His will and ways. Moses is a man who understood and walked out the lifestyle of a bondservant. Though the people were afraid to draw near to God, Moses walked in the reverential fear of the Lord and approached God to know Him and understand His ways.

The proper fear of the Lord makes us run *to* Him in order to be reconciled. Fear that makes believers run *from* Him results from a superficial relationship with God and is rooted in fear of judgment because of sin. Paul admonished believers to do what is right for then there is no fear from those in authority (Rom. 13:3-4). Only those who habitually walk in sin, stubbornly defiant to God's standards, are in danger of experiencing the severity and judgment of God. Those who love God but are struggling with sin will find grace to overcome that sin, and lovingkindness and mercy when they fail.

Unwarranted fear also plagues believers who haven't discerned the unfailing mercy available to those who love God and are committed to Him, His Word, and His ways. Moses, David, Daniel, and the other Old Testament prophets understood this. This inspired them to be wholehearted in their pursuit of God. With this piece of revelation, they were free to love God and do the best they could without letting their hearts grow cold and die through self-condemnation. The Psalmist wrote that God *always* shows mercy to those who love His name (Ps. 119:132). Jeremiah stated the faithfulness of God is so great that His steadfast love and mercy *never cease*, His compassions *never fail*, and they are new *every* morning (Lam. 3:22-23). If you struggle with self-condemnation, let the message of the following passage settle into your soul:

> *And therefore **the Lord [earnestly] waits [expecting, looking, and longing] to be gracious to you**; and therefore He lifts Himself up, **that He may have mercy on you** and **show loving-kindness to you**.* -Isa. 30:18, AMP

Our hearts can be unlocked by understanding His love as conveyed by His mercy toward those who love Him in spirit and in truth. Anyone who has been born again and desires to live for God can be a bondservant. While the examples in the Bible may seem heroic compared to us, it is our heart posture and the fact we are running to Him that define us. We may stumble and fall while we are running, momentarily taking our eyes off our goal, but we get up, reaffix our gaze on Him, and continue running, knowing His compassion *never* fails and His mercy is new *every* morning.

The Determining Factor: Heart Response

Peter wrote that God does not show partiality to anyone, but embraces all who fear Him and do His will, regardless of age, gender, social status, or race (Acts 10:34-35). The last word on bondservants is found in the book of Revelation. Included in this company are not only apostles and prophets, but also 'the saints and all those who fear His name, small and great' (Rev. 19:5-6; see also 11:18).

It is not how we or others perceive the worth of the charge given to us in this age that matters. What does matter is our heart posture toward the One assigning us our portion, and our faithfulness to His will. This is evidenced by obedient actions flowing out of a conquered heart. The parable of the talents warns those given a smaller portion not to esteem their one talent as unworthy of their attention, devaluing it as insignificant. Rather, we are to put everything we have into being faithful with our one talent. In so doing, we multiply the Lord's investment in our own hearts by passing it along to others through our obedient actions. Whether the small portion we've been given concerns our role in the community of believers or the amount of time we have left, we must put all our strength into running hard the race set for us.

> *Only, let each one [seek to conduct himself and regulate his affairs so as to] lead the life which the Lord has allotted and imparted to him and to which God has invited and summoned him. This is my order in all the churches.* -1 Cor. 7:17, AMP

Bearing Fruit

When Zechariah, the father of John the Baptist, received his voice back, he prophesied by the Holy Spirit. He testified that the Messiah would come to rescue us from our enemies and enable us to serve Him without fear, in holiness and righteousness all of our days (Luke 1:74-75). This is a promise we can count on. The fruit we bear is in direct proportion to our heart response to His will and purpose in our lives.

Dying to our own will and religious self-righteousness is required for fruitfulness (John 12:24; Rom. 7:4). If we are receptive to the Bible's teaching and listen with the intent to be obedient, the Word planted in our hearts will bear much fruit (Matt. 13:23). The fruit we bear for God's kingdom comes primarily from the Word sown in our hearts rather than following religious ceremonial observances.

Scripture gives the requisite for bearing fruit: abiding in Christ, who is the Word. The fruit of our relationship with Christ is obedience to God's will, just as Jesus demonstrated, no matter the cost. Apart from Christ we can do *nothing* that matters (John 15:4-5).

SECTION 1 *INTRODUCTION TO THE BONDSERVANT'S LIFE*

Believers in Christ are appointed to bear fruit that lasts, and they have been given the privilege of prayer to ask God for whatever they need to accomplish His will (John 15:16). Only by dying to self and abiding in Christ (the Word) will we bear fruit recognized by God. This is the fruit He is looking for—the fruit that proves we are His.

> *By this my Father is glorified, that you bear much fruit and so prove to be my disciples.* -John 15:8, ESV

Closing Thoughts

The love and loyalty of bondservants are anchored to their Lord, Jesus Christ. They do not consider their lives their own, evidenced by their willing obedience to follow Him no matter where He takes them. They are free from allegiance to what the world has to offer. Because of this, they are free to worship in spirit and in truth. Every believer can be a bondservant if his heart is postured before God in faith, if he yearns for God's presence out of love, and if he desires to know God and His ways, pledging his heart to obey. Their lives will not be a testimony of sinless perfection, but of unrestrained love and the desire to be pleasing to God in all things, struggling with all their might to overcome whatever hinders that love.

> *With great delight I sat in his shadow… I will seek him whom my soul loves.* -Songs 2:3b; 3:2b, ESV

Chapter 4

How Does a Bondservant's Life Differ?

> *If anyone desires to be My disciple, **let him deny himself** [disregard, lose sight of, and forget himself and his own interests] and **take up his cross and follow Me** [cleave steadfastly to Me, conform wholly to My example in living and, if need be, in dying, also].* -Matt. 16:24, AMP

Though Jesus is addressing the disciples, His directive applies to all who would follow Him. In this passage, we see the definition of a bondservant outlined by the Master Himself. The two pillars that authenticate a bondservant's life are a *change of heart* ('let him deny himself') and a *change of behavior* ('let him take up his cross and follow Me'). Following Christ is not mere belief in Jesus as Savior and a weekly commitment to attend church. Following Jesus as a bondservant requires radical commitment and most often a radical change in focus and lifestyle.

We see two responses in the Bible from those invited to follow Jesus. They either dropped what they were doing and came after Him immediately (Matt. 4:19-22; 9:9; Mark 2:14; Luke 18:28), or they made excuses for why they couldn't follow Him 'just yet' (Matt. 8:21-22; Luke 9:57-62; 14:18-20). Some in the former group came to the realization that following Christ cost much more than they ever dreamed, but their captured heart persevered through the hardships. Those in the latter group discovered their zeal to live righteously by following the commandments and attending to religious duties was present, but their willingness to forego comfort, their own plans and goals, and the lifestyle they had chosen and cherished was not (Matt. 8:19-20; 19:16-23).

> *No one who puts his hand to the plow and looks back is fit for the kingdom of God.* -Luke 9:62, ESV

All who would follow Jesus must count the cost. Jesus taught that anyone who does not give up everything he has cannot be His disciple (Luke 14:33). This means giving up emotional attachment to our possessions, lifestyle, and dreams, leaving them at the Lord's disposal. It may mean giving up physical comfort and embracing a simpler lifestyle. Following Jesus may mean giving up a job as the disciples did (Matt. 19:27; Luke 5:28). It may mean giving away property, houses, and earthly possessions (Acts 4:32-34). It may mean dissolving investments or giving up retirement accounts. It may mean hardship, moving to a foreign country, controversy, or persecution. Following Jesus requires a radical departure from the ideal life sought by those in Western culture (Luke 14:25-33).

> *Whoever does not take his cross and follow me is not worthy of me.* -Matt. 10:38, ESV

SECTION 1 *INTRODUCTION TO THE BONDSERVANT'S LIFE*

Change of Heart

Repent (think differently; change your mind, regretting your sins and changing your conduct), for the kingdom of heaven is at hand. -Matt. 3:2, AMP

The first step in becoming a bondservant is repentance born of godly sorrow. We gently instruct those who oppose the truth in the hope God may grant them repentance, the means by which we come to the right knowledge of truth (2 Tim. 2:25). Being granted repentance from wrong thinking is an act of God, yet we are also told if we draw near to God, He will draw near to us (James 4:8). There is tension in this because of the paradox it creates in our minds: only God can draw us, but it is also implied we can draw near to Him, especially through godly sorrow. We are reminded that whoever would draw near to God must believe He exists and that He rewards those who seek Him (Heb. 11:6). This requires faith, and even our measure of faith has been given to us by God (Rom. 12:3).

Repentance literally means 'to change one's mind,' particularly as it pertains to moral judgment. Acquiring godly wisdom is not automatic, but God promised that those who seek Him *will* find Him. Paul told Timothy to *gently* instruct those who oppose the knowledge of truth, not debate with them in frustration. Debate often leads to anger. Some of the angriest people we know are that way because subconsciously their inner man is seeking truth while their conscious mind is holding onto the teachings of the god of this age. The resulting internal conflict keeps them in a smoldering temper until this issue is resolved through 'repentance.'

Jesus stated no one can come to Him for salvation unless he is first drawn by the Father (John 6:44). Perhaps this is the origin of the tension in the first place. God is drawing us subconsciously, in our inner man, and we are initially at odds with this drawing because the paradigm or worldview we have fashioned for ourselves is contrary to truth. In many cases, we have shaped God in the image we prefer Him to be, one that suits our refined, politically correct 21st century sagacity.

In the book of Ephesians, Paul began his description of worldly thinkers by stating they are hopelessly confused and in darkness (see Eph. 4:17-24). They have wandered from God because their minds are closed and hardened against truth. This takes place when we live to fulfill our own sinful desires and pleasures yet yearn to be free from condemnation and guilt. The only way we can accomplish this is to deny God's standards, deceiving ourselves into thinking our actions are justifiable under our new moral relativism. Only by rejecting this broad path of corruption will we come to repentance and adopt the new nature of righteousness in God.

Once our intellect and inner man are in agreement with God, we experience what may be called an epiphany, similar to what we experience when the left and right lenses of a pair of binoculars are adjusted and finally line up to form one field of view. When we line up *our intellect* with *God's eternal perspective and truth*, we have experienced repentance (the turning of our mind to truth) and can say as Jesus did to Zacchaeus, 'Today, *salvation* has come to this house' (Luke 19:9). The veil has been removed. This constitutes the first step in cleansing the mind of wrong ideology and of what is falsely called wisdom and knowledge. The washing continues as we go deeper in the Word and mature.

Change of Behavior

Bear fruits that are deserving and consistent with [your] repentance [that is, conduct worthy of a heart changed, a heart abhorring sin]. -Luke 3:8a, AMP

Take a look at what immediately accompanied Zacchaeus' change of heart and mind in Luke 19:1-10. His outward behavior changed to conform to his newly found understanding of truth. He gave half his possessions to the poor and pledged to pay back anyone he had defrauded four times as much as he took from them—twice as much as required by law (Ex. 22:4,7). The reader can almost feel the joy and exuberance Zacchaeus was experiencing when he made this declaration.

His sudden change of paradigm resulted in an immediate change of behavior. This is the second marker distinguishing the life of a bondservant—an obedient heart *compelled* to act in accordance with God's will. From this example, then, we can draft a crude definition of salvation as being repentance leading to a change of paradigm that demands a change of behavior, all founded on the finished work of the cross and grace.

Zacchaeus no longer worshipped mammon. He was now gripped by love for God. True religion, by God's standard, takes care of the poor. God also loves justice, especially when we voluntarily right the wrongs we have committed. Zacchaeus acted upon both of these right away. Jesus desired this for the rich young ruler as well, for He loved him, but the young man couldn't let go of his vast accumulation just then. The young man left 'sad and grieving' because he owned much property (Mark 10:21-23).

The heart of the rich young ruler can be likened to the thorny ground described in the parable of the sower. Even though the Word had been sown in the heart (he kept all the commandments), the cares, anxieties, and distractions of this age prevented its growth. Pleasure, false glamour, the deceitfulness of riches, and craving for other things suffocate the Word and make it fruitless (Mark 4:18-19).

Either the young ruler still clung to his paradigm that worldly wealth defines the degree of God's favor, or his god truly was mammon. If it was merely the former, the war described earlier had now been deposited into his heart. Sometimes it just takes a while for new teaching to settle in. But if we reject Jesus' teaching outright as most of the Pharisees did, clinging brazenly to our own ideas, we share their fate. Rejecting the Word of God is the same as rejecting the Son, for Jesus is the Word.

*Whoever believes in the Son has eternal life, but **whoever rejects the Son will not see life, for God's wrath remains on them**.* -John 3:36, NIV

SECTION 1 *INTRODUCTION TO THE BONDSERVANT'S LIFE*

Without a change in our outlook and behavior, we must ask ourselves if repentance has truly taken place. This is not to say that at the moment of repentance we begin walking perfectly before the Lord. It is merely the first step, and many of us discover that when we experience true repentance, a good measure of our anger evaporates as well as other unwholesome behaviors. The bottom line is that a changed heart will lead to changed behavior—immediately *and* over time. 'Prove by the way you live that you have repented and turned to God' (Matt. 3:8).

> *Walk as children of light (for the fruit of light is found in all that is good and right and true), and try to discern what is pleasing to the Lord.* -Eph. 5:8b-10, ESV

The Aroma of Myrrh

Jesus, John the Baptist, and the apostles all taught that the evidence of a redeemed life is seen in a change in behavior, just as the evidence a seed has been planted in the soil is seen when a seedling emerges. A seed cannot bring forth a plant unless the right conditions for germination and growth are present. These are the presence of water, the sun, and good soil. In fact, when the seed germinates, it 'dies' as a seed (John 12:24).

> *Those who love their life in this world will lose it. Those who care nothing for their life in this world will keep it for eternity.* -John 12:25, NLT

This is what the Lord is looking for in each one of us—death to wrong ideas and to self-will so fruit may be brought forth. When the casing around a seed becomes soft enough for a sprout to spring forth, germination takes place. This process is governed by both internal and external conditions. The adequate hydration required for the seed to germinate can be compared to soaking our minds in God's Word. Once truth softens the hard seed coat, the seed 'dies' and a new plant is birthed. This 'death' brings forth the aroma of myrrh, a resin used for millennia in preparing the dead for burial and for wound treatment. Like the Levitical sacrifices, a life yielded to God is a 'pleasing aroma.'

> *Live a life filled with love, following the example of Christ. He loved us and offered himself as a sacrifice for us, a pleasing aroma to God.* -Eph. 5:2, NLT

Repentance comes first so the resulting change in behavior is sincere and genuine before God. The Spirit of God is intimately involved in this process. We may cooperate as we are changed, but the strength, desire, and understanding to do so come from Him.

In other words, this change does not come by our own effort but by the enabling power of the Holy Spirit. Paul explained it was the grace of God that enabled him to work harder than the others. It did not come by his own effort but by the Spirit of God who gave him the strength and endurance to complete his assignment (1 Cor. 15:10). As we cooperate with the Spirit's leading, we find ourselves desiring less and less of the world and more and more of God's presence. This includes an eagerness to know Him and walk in perfect step with God as Jesus did. This will bear lasting fruit.

Examine Yourselves

Paul exhorted us to examine ourselves to confirm transformation is taking place. This is not meant to measure how perfectly we behave but to observe how far we have progressed from our old nature to being conformed to the character of Christ. Many of us are eternally grateful for how far He has already taken us from former days of futility.

> *Examine and test and evaluate your own selves to see whether you are holding to your faith and showing the proper fruits of it.* -2 Cor. 13:5a, AMP

Jesus admonished His disciples to observe the fruit in a person's life to test the validity of their claims (Matt. 7:15-20). Actions speak louder than words. Only those who actually do God's will are allowed entrance to heaven (Matt. 7:21; Heb. 3:18). Those undergoing true sanctification will not necessarily walk in perfection, but over the length of their lives, the progress becomes apparent and the obedient nature of Christ is seen.

We have an active role in the sanctification process. As we will find out later, we must make it our business to cooperate with the Holy Spirit and continually cleanse our minds from the wrong paradigms we have accumulated. As long as we persevere in our endeavor, we will make the Word of the Lord our habitation and receive from the Holy Spirit the grace to walk faithfully to God's Word (Col. 2:6).

The Objective: To Glorify God

> *May you abound in and be filled with the fruits of righteousness (of right standing with God and right doing) which come through Jesus Christ (the Anointed One), to the honor and praise of God [that His glory may be both manifested and recognized].* -Php. 1:11, AMP

By Jesus' example, we learn that a life dedicated in bond service to God brings glory to the One who gave us life. We are repeatedly exhorted to live in accordance with the Spirit and not according to our sinful nature. The standard today has been lowered to such a degree that some actually have a false confidence before the Lord if they dedicate Sunday morning to church. The rest of the week they think only of themselves and their own goals, cheating on taxes, running over others to gain an advantage, taking legal but unethical entitlements, boldly airing opinions at every turn, or similar pursuits. Every waking moment is consumed with getting ahead, satisfying every unwholesome urge, and working ambitiously to make a name for themselves (cf. Gen. 11:4).

These are not the traits of someone who has experienced repentance in spirit and in truth. The unsaved who see no difference between Christians and themselves think our faith futile and filled with hypocrisy. Or worse, they see unbelievers who have more of the qualities of Christ than we do! Our lives must bear fruit in order to confirm repentance has taken place and to bring honor to God.

SECTION 1 INTRODUCTION TO THE BONDSERVANT'S LIFE

> *Be careful to live properly among your unbelieving neighbors. Then even if they accuse you of doing wrong, they will see your honorable behavior, and they will give honor to God when he judges the world.* -1 Pet. 2:12, NLT

We are brought to repentance for the specific purpose of learning to conduct ourselves in a manner worthy of the name of the Lord (Col. 1:10). This includes having the desire to please Him in all things. The fruit of this will be apparent in good works and steady growth in and by the knowledge of God. Spiritual growth through the knowledge of God results in the transformation of our minds. Transformation of the mind will always be followed by transformation of behavior. This is fruit that brings God glory.

> *Let your light so shine before men that they may see your moral excellence and your praiseworthy, noble, and good deeds and recognize and honor and praise and glorify your Father Who is in heaven.* -Matt. 5:16, AMP

This verse is not talking about parading good deeds so much as just operating in the realm of service and purity as a way of life. However, this is only honored if done from the heart and not begrudgingly or under compulsion. No one likes to be served by a grump who hates their work and is only trying to score 'servanthood' points. No one will be impressed or glorify God by angry holiness which bites at those who don't likewise behave. These types of feigned behavior cause red flags to rise up within the hearts of those who witness them because of the incongruency between the profession and the attitude or tone with which the actual behavior is executed. These people will most likely corner their target with a memorized message on the 'Roman's road' to salvation. I believe the apostolic directive would be, 'From such, run!'

The life that truly glorifies God will be obedient even if following God's will is injurious financially, physically, in reputation, or in any other way. Jesus showed Peter that although he used to do as he pleased, as a bondservant of Christ he would make the ultimate sacrifice—'the last full measure of devotion,' just as Jesus did when He turned His will over to the Father on the matter of the cross (John 21:18-19).

Suffering by obeying God instead of doing what we want is evidence we have been 'perfected' as Jesus was when He walked the earth. It is the requirement for everyone who desires to spend eternity with God. Walking in obedience and completing all God has set before us brings God glory, as Jesus did:

> *I brought glory to you here on earth by completing the work you gave me to do.*
> -John 17:4, NLT

This glory is rooted in honoring God through obedience to His Word and His will as ordained for us. Righteous acts that flow out of a redeemed heart in the will of God are the steps marked out for us in the race we have been given, which includes letting go of sin. Jesus is our example, and His surrendered life is still bearing fruit. True disciples surrender their lives to the Lord and will produce much fruit (John 15:8). The very act of declaring Jesus Lord over our lives brings glory to God in itself because it is acknowledgment of God's will for Jesus to be so (Php. 2:11).

Outwardly Obedient but Inwardly Disloyal

The transformation of our heart and mind must come first in order for the resultant change in our behavior to be in spirit and in truth. Compliant outward behavior born from a striving heart and a strong will to succeed or earn favor will burn up under the lens of God's scrutiny. Some behave properly only because they know it is expected of them, not because they are captured with desire at the heart level.

The first example recorded in the Word of mere outward obedience is in the life of Cain. Abel's sacrifice was accepted because his heart posture was right before the Lord. In humility, Abel acknowledged his need for a Redeemer, typified by the firstborn lamb he sacrificed. Cain's heart posture, most likely filled with pride for his accomplishment, was not pleasing to the Lord. Both offered sacrifices, but Cain's offering was determined as evil by God's standard—evil in a moral or spiritual sense by use of the Greek word *poneros* (1 John 3:12). The action itself was not evil, but the heart posture in which he executed the sacrifice was.

We have already noted God is looking for those whose right actions flow out of a heart of love and loyalty to God. Any other heart posture as the basis for our obedience is evil in His sight, whether compulsion, ambition, pride, self-righteousness, or guilt. 'Whatever is not of faith is sin' (Rom. 14:23). Faith, from the Greek word *pistis*, means 'to be persuaded in our intellect and convictions, especially as it pertains to confidence in divine truth which produces good works.'[1] Acts that originate from any other motive are defiled no matter how good the actions may look on the outside. Those who are 'willfully contrary' in the following passage are those who insist on their own will rather than God's. They are still in control of their lives.

> *They who are willfully contrary in heart are extremely disgusting and shamefully vile in the eyes of the Lord, but such as are blameless and wholehearted in their ways are His delight!* -Pr. 11:20, AMP

The old covenant was written on tablets of stone, sadly representative of the hearts of the majority present at Mt. Sinai. The new covenant is living, intended for the tender heart of flesh God will give to any who accept His invitation. This invitation includes empowerment to follow God wholeheartedly. Following Jesus is the same as following the Word, for Jesus is the 'Word made flesh.' The *Torah* of stone becomes the *Torah* of the tender heart. Only the way of the bondservant allows us to enter into the wholeheartedness required for following the new covenant.

King Amaziah was typical of the majority of Israelites under the old covenant. The Word tells us that he did what was right in God's sight, but he did not do it with a loyal heart

(2 Chron. 25:1-2). There are numerous passages that speak to this issue, mostly describing how the Israelites would go astray, God would send some sort of chastisement, and then they would turn back to God so the consequences of their sin would be removed. However, as soon as they felt relieved, they would begin the process all over again, slowly drifting away until another judgment was sent. The book of Judges illustrates this cycle. This happened in similar fashion at Kadesh Barnea when the newly redeemed Israelites refused to enter Canaan because they gave greater weight to their own wisdom than God's (Num. 13-14). The consequences for their disobedience brought great sorrow.

In the following Psalm, we have proof the hearts of the Israelites were only briefly turned back to God because they were not truly loyal to Him. While they were sincerely grateful for the relief, they were not truly dedicated in turning back to God. Their gaze was fixed on their *circumstances* rather than their relationship with God. In fact, after momentarily turning to God in their distress, their gaze drifted back to where it had been all along—on self.

> *In spite of all this, they kept on sinning; in spite of his wonders, they did not believe. So he ended their days in futility and their years in terror. Whenever God slew them, they would seek him;* **they eagerly turned to him again.** *They remembered that God was their Rock, that God Most High was their Redeemer. But* **then they would flatter him with their mouths, lying to him with their tongues; their hearts were not loyal to him, they were not faithful to his covenant. Yet he was merciful.** -Ps. 78:32-38a, NIV

When our heart is focused primarily on self, any negative change in circumstances, no matter how slight, may cause us to doubt God's love or precipitate anger, despair, self-pity, self-condemnation, blame-casting, depression, or fear. For some, the first authentic prayer offered in months is spoken in panic, grasping at any straw to remedy the painful circumstances. After 9.11.2001, there were record numbers of Americans in churches across the nation. Some well-known religious leaders hailed the phenomenon as the beginning of revival. However, many slowly drifted back to their self-focused lives after the pain had dulled and returned to the lifestyle they had chosen for themselves. A decade later, we find, as the Israelites before us, that we have gone back to our own lives. We have not learned from history as Paul had hoped (1 Cor. 10:11).

On a similar theme, much of the 'good' behavior we witness in ourselves and others is born of a man-pleasing spirit. As long as we are fixated on reputation and appearances, we will not be bondservants of God but of the expectations of others. All our activity and goals will be directed toward fueling this objective. This produces actions not born of loyalty but of this man-pleasing preoccupation. Only that which is born of faith in love and loyalty to God will produce obedience pleasing to God.

> *For if I still pleased men, I would not be a bondservant of Christ.* -Gal. 1:10, NKJV

Psalm 131

The Lord could rarely mention David's name without the accompanying phrase, 'My servant.' In fact, David rarely left out this description of himself as the 'servant of the Lord.' Despite his many faults, David is a prime example of someone who loved God with all his heart, ran to God when he stumbled, and walked in the spirit of the law. The Lord was his strength and the object of his affection (Ps. 18:1).

Psalm 131 gives us needed insight into what it means to have a heart in pursuit of God as David had. It is short (three verses) but packed with rich layers of meaning. We will look at the meaning most pertinent to our topic of bondservanthood.

> *My heart is not proud, LORD, my eyes are not haughty; I do not concern myself with great matters or things too wonderful for me. But I have calmed and quieted myself, I am like a weaned child with its mother; like a weaned child I am content. Israel, put your hope in the LORD both now and forevermore.* -Ps. 131:1-3, NIV

David did not lift up his heart to grasp at matters or realms not meant for him. His focus on beholding the beauty of the Lord (which comes through revelation and understanding God's Word) preempted any desire to be opinionated or self-conceited in striving after things beyond his station. He did not run after the way of Korah to usurp the authority of another (see Num. 16), but remained content and diligent in what had been assigned to him by the Lord. This was true whether he was shepherding his father's flock, fighting Israel's battles, or ruling as monarch.

Those who are not content with the portion appointed to them by God find themselves involved in vain ambitions in their pursuit of honor and power. Consider this quote from the *Treasury of David*: "High things may suit others who are of greater stature, and yet they may be quite unfit for us. A man does well to know his own size. Ascertaining his own capacity, he will be foolish if he aims at that which is beyond his reach, straining himself, and thus injuring himself. Such is the vanity of many men that if a work be within their range they despise it, and think it beneath them: the only service which they are willing to undertake is that to which they have never been called, and for which they are by no means qualified.

"What a haughty heart must he have who will not serve God at all unless he may be trusted with five talents at the least! His looks are indeed lofty who disdains to be a light among his poor friends and neighbours here below, but demands to be created a star of the first magnitude to shine among the upper ranks, and to be admired by gazing crowds. It is just on God's part that those who wish to be everything should end in being nothing. It is a righteous retribution from God when every matter turns out to be too great for the man who would only handle great matters, and everything proves to be too high for the man who exercised himself in things too high for him. Lord, make us lowly, keep us lowly, fix us forever in lowliness. Help us to be in such a case that the confession of this verse may come from our lips as a truthful utterance which we dare make before the Judge of all the earth."[2]

These thoughts are further examined in the next excerpt. From the *Keil and Delitzsch Commentary on the Old Testament,* we gain the keen insights of these two commentators, giving us an expanded view of what it means to be a man after God's heart. "I esteem myself still less than I now show it, and I appear base in mine own eyes. In general David is the model of the state of mind which the poet expresses here. He did not push himself forward, but suffered himself to be drawn forth out of seclusion. He did not take possession of the throne violently, but after Samuel has anointed him he willingly and patiently traverses the long, thorny, circuitous way of deep abasement, until he receives from God's hand that which God's promise had assured to him. The persecution by Saul lasted about ten years, and his kingship in Hebron, at first only incipient, seven years and a half. He left it entirely to God to remove Saul and Ishbosheth. He let Shimei curse. He left Jerusalem before Absalom. **Submission to God's guidance, resignation to His dispensations, contentment with that which was allotted to him, are the distinguishing traits of his noble character...** (emphasis added).

"Pride has its seat in the heart, in the eyes especially it finds its expression, and great things are its sphere in which it diligently exercises itself... He has leveled or made smooth his soul, so that humility is its entire and uniform state; he has calmed it so that it is silent and at rest, and lets God speak and work in it and for it... As a weaned child... lies upon its mother without crying impatiently and craving for its mother's breast, but contented with the fact that it has its mother—like such a weaned child is his soul upon him... his soul, which is by nature restless and craving, is stilled; it does not long after earthly enjoyment and earthly good that God should give these to it, but it is satisfied in the fellowship of God...

"By the closing strain... the individual language of the Psalm comes to have a reference to the congregation at large. Israel is to renounce all self-boasting... and to wait in lowliness and quietness upon its God from now and for evermore. For He resisteth the proud, but giveth grace unto the humble."[3]

Ambitious for God

Toward the end of his life, a lofty idea came to David. He wanted to build a temple for God. At first the prophet Nathan was in agreement with this ambitious idea. But after a visit from the Lord, he told David the Lord had reserved this task for another—his son Solomon (1 Kings 8:17-19). All of our ambitious plans to accomplish important and effective work for God must be submitted to Him first. This can be difficult because many of us put a good deal of heart involvement into those plans and would rather not have them cancelled or even delayed. In this example, David gives us a look at the correct response when our plans are not in line with God's.

The tender exchange between the Lord and David is absolutely beautiful. King David looks at the wonderful house of cedar he has been living in. How can he enjoy this house when the ark of the Lord's presence has only a tent? The Lord answers with such tenderness. 'David, I have never complained about the tent. And I have dwelt with you from the days I took you from the pasture and made you ruler over My people. You have fought many wars and shed much blood in My sight, so your son will build My house instead. I will build an everlasting house for you, David, from your family line.'

Rather than being disappointed at the news he will not be appointed to build the temple, David is overwhelmed by God's promise to give him an everlasting kingdom. His prayer shows the heart posture of a man who not only understands his lowly stature before the Lord but is also taken with gratitude for the promises given (see 2 Sam. 7:18-29).

Claiming to Know God Without a Changed Life

Nothing in Scripture supports the idea of claiming to know God without a resultant change in behavior. If our hearts are still focused on sin, we deceive ourselves and the truth is not in us. To walk in sincerity, we must be brutally honest when we answer the following question: What *preoccupies* our thoughts throughout the day? If we have answered truthfully, we know where our heart's desire is focused. [Note: There will be seasons of life where we must be focused on the tasks at hand, such as a new job, moving, childbirth, war, life-threatening illness, etc. Our thoughts are understandably engrossed with these all-consuming circumstances. We are, after all, only human! But even during these times, the bondservant keeps a posture of open communication with the Lord and looks forward to the day when more time can be set aside for greater focus on the Lord.]

We cannot expect to have genuinely transformed behavior until our heart is gripped by the bondservant reality. Our actions betray what is in our heart. To the pure, all things are pure. But to the corrupt and unbelieving, nothing is pure. Paul stated their mind and their conscience are corrupted. Though they claim to know God, their actions speak otherwise. These are judged as detestable and unfit for doing anything good (Titus 1:15-16).

Paul's letter to Titus also reminds us of our tendency to judge others by our standards and practice. Those who make a habit of lying also suspect others of lying or having ulterior motives. A spouse who frequently allows his mind to wander into adulterous imaginings will be quick to assume his partner is unfaithful as well. Those who are upfront and honest think others are the same way, which at times leads to being deceived. Those who desire to know truth no matter how it may impact their cherished beliefs are surprised by those who want truth only if it fits their traditions, religious paradigms, and goals.

A bondservant may not be perfect in his actions, but he is being transformed. His loyalty is to God, and he will not stop in his pursuit to dethrone himself in the area of his will. He has a teachable spirit and thirsts to know truth. This is a lifelong struggle, but the Lord gives each believer grace and the power needed to persevere.

SECTION 1 *INTRODUCTION TO THE BONDSERVANT'S LIFE*

Parable of the Ten Minas

Right after meeting Zacchaeus, Jesus seizes the teachable moment to clarify the kingdom principle exhibited in Zacchaeus' newfound salvation. This takes place in conjunction with His approach to Jerusalem. Jesus introduced the parable of the ten minas (Luke 19:11-27), contrasting three responses to Him: outright rejection, acceptance leading to multiplication, and acceptance that falls short of fruitfulness.

In this parable, Jesus is the nobleman departing to receive His kingdom. His disciples are His servants (*doulos*), and the Pharisees and all Jews who rejected Him are the subjects/citizens. [Note: This parable is not to be confused with the parable of the talents. The parable of the minas was taught before Jesus reached Jerusalem, each servant receiving the same amount of money. The parable of the talents was taught after Jesus arrived in Jerusalem, and involved different amounts of money given to the servants.]

Each of the *bondservants* was given a mina 'to do business with.' *Diapragmateuomai*, the Greek word translated 'to do business,' literally means 'to thoroughly occupy oneself with.' As an allegory, Jesus taught of His desire that we preoccupy ourselves with searching out knowledge and understanding of Him and His kingdom, even if we have other jobs by which we make our living. No matter what our line of work is, as bondservants our hearts will be 'thoroughly occupied' with God and His kingdom.

The *subjects* in this story reject the nobleman as their king and show only contempt for him and his message. The only other mention of them is found when the nobleman returns as king at the end of the parable, and they are executed for their disloyalty. The *servants*, on the other hand, are left to 'do business' while he is away. When the nobleman returns, he will judge how well each governed the deposit given.

> Now **it is God who makes both us and you stand firm** in Christ. He anointed us, set his seal of ownership on us, and **put his Spirit in our hearts as a deposit**, *guaranteeing what is to come.* -2 Cor. 1:21-22, NIV

All who have been granted repentance receive the same 'deposit'—the Holy Spirit. From this point, it is the individual believer's responsibility to follow the leading of the Spirit to gain ground in their understanding. Most of us have experienced the need to strike while the iron is hot lest the iron cool and with it the desire to reach the objective. Advancing our walk by enlarging our hearts through greater understanding of the Word and acts of service provides the only way to maintain the zeal we experienced at the beginning. This, in effect, multiplies the initial deposit we received at repentance.

By constantly renewing our minds through study of the Word, God reproduces the character of Christ in us (Gal. 4:19; Eph. 4:21-24). New believers must not endanger the deposit entrusted to them by responding with indolence. They must guard and nurture their deposit from the start. Tireless and conscientious scrutiny of the Word maintains our zeal for the kingdom of God. This sets a pace in our spirit with the goal being to attain the highest height possible in the wisdom and revelation of God in this life. Our relationship with God must be dynamic if it is to be productive and ultimately withstand the fire of testing. This will lead to transformed and fruitful behavior.

The first two servants responded to the deposit given them with an immediate change of behavior. They began occupying themselves with multiplying their deposit, just as Zacchaeus immediately demonstrated. The third servant, however, did not put forth any effort or risk.

At the king's return, the first two servants brought ten- and five-fold increases on their deposits. These two were the opposite of indolent. They were industrious, laboring productively, thoroughly occupying themselves with the king's business. They are examples for us to follow, exhorting us to move in passionate zeal toward the things of God. We accomplish this by searching the Scriptures as often as we can to learn the way of the kingdom. This includes the change of behavior that follows as we discover what is pleasing to God. Our spirits must be alert and attentive, thoughtfully and painstakingly searching the Word as well as diligently applying the knowledge we've gained. Those with open hearts toward God are always ready for that teachable moment.

The way we cherish the Word in our lives can be determined by the percentage of our *free* time it occupies. Some of us have precious little free time, and the fact that we would even think of using it to read the Word instead of watching the news, surfing the web in honorable ways, or having a relaxing meal at our favorite restaurant is pleasing to God. [Note: None of these things are wrong for us to do. The point here is the willingness to forego legitimate pleasures to pursue God.]

Demonstrating perseverance in our walk defines the bondservant on his way to 'perfection.' This is evidenced by intentional discipline in study of the Word as well as concern and respect for the things of God. Perfection can be defined as keeping the charge we have been assigned and pursuing the transformation of our character to match Christ's.

Definition of Poor Stewardship

The third servant, however, received the same deposit but did not move on from there. He stewarded his portion poorly. There was no change in his behavior. Whether indolence, indifference, negligence, carelessness, ignorance, love for other things, fear, or simply dereliction of the duty required of a bondservant, this one did not occupy himself with God's kingdom. He knew of the severity of God, but did not expand his understanding to comprehend the kindness of God. He was slothful, excusing his laziness by rationalizing that he didn't want to take a risk with the mina he had. Rather than the deposit effecting any change in his life, he kept it covered. Out of sight, out of mind. Erroneously thinking he could justify his lack of effort, this servant would soon realize God had a very different view of his rationalized behavior.

The third servant handled the deposit given to him irresponsibly. Among believers, this is the equivalent of experiencing true repentance without taking the time to fuel a relationship with God. Perhaps those who procrastinate or who have filled their lives with the time-consuming obsessions and activities of our technology- and sports-centered society can be placed in this group as well. Being devoured by activity might make us feel as though we have purpose and are accomplishing something, but in the end we will only know leanness of soul. Content with a once-a-week message from someone else, these avoid the exertion needed to learn personally from God's Word. They are careless and disrespectful toward the One who extended great grace to them, disregarding their deposit as insignificant. For some, inclusion in the body of Christ is primarily for the hope of avoiding hell, not as a means to grow in love for God.

Because he viewed the nobleman as harsh, the third servant had the same fear that gripped the Israelites at Mt. Sinai when they returned to their tents, and at Kadesh Barnea when they refused to go in and claim the land. Joshua recorded that the spies who went with him to explore the land made the hearts of the people 'melt in fear' (Josh. 14:7-8). Even though all ate the same *spiritual* food and drank the same *spiritual* drink from the rock (Christ), God was not pleased with most of them and they died in the wilderness (1 Cor. 10:4-5). The same fate awaits the slovenly servant in this parable. His heart was not captured to obey out of love, but to feign fear of God through the same fear of judgment that grips the heart of the disobedient (Rom. 13:3).

Since he had not taken the time to expand the deposit given to him, the third servant made up an easy excuse (taken in part from God's Word) to justify his slothfulness and neglect. The nobleman's reply, however, shows that this man's excuse contradicts his actions and is therefore a covert lie. 'If this is what you thought of me, then common sense would have told you to at least put the mina in the bank to earn a bit of interest. Your actions do not match your excuse. I gave the mina to you instead of putting it in the bank because I was looking for a multiplied return by your faithful action. But you neither knew me nor took the time to expend the effort to do so. The deposit and trust given to you did not bear fruit as was intended. Only fear could be found in your heart— fear of punishment birthed by your neglect and disobedience. Now what you have received will be taken from you and given to the one who loves me and serves me wholeheartedly as evidenced by the return his mina earned. Whoever produces fruit from what I have deposited in him will be given more, and those who produce no fruit are worthless. As for those who hate me and don't want to accept my authority and rule (the subjects), they will lose their lives.'

The way in which some have taught this parable, equating it only with stewardship of money, would have our Master shake His head and say, 'How is it that you did not know I was not talking about money?' (cf. Matt. 16:5-12). We do desire to be good stewards of material wealth, but the way in which we handle true riches, the heavenly deposit given to us, will either make or break us at His return.

Who is wise and understanding among you? By his good conduct let him show his works in the meekness of wisdom. -James 3:13, ESV

Application for Our Time: The Sons of Zadok and King Jotham

All Scripture is written so we can learn and apply the lessons to our own lives (Rom. 15:4). The sons of Zadok, Levites from the line of Phinehas, were honored by God because they did not stray into idolatry as the other Levites had during a time of generalized apostasy in Israel (Ezk. 48:11). God determined they were the only ones who could approach to minister before Him from that point forward (Ezk. 40:46). This family line is noted to be particularly faithful to God throughout the Old Testament. The Hebrew word used for the Zadok priests' ministry, *sharath*, carries the meaning of service delegated to a servant of higher rank to perform. It is also used of the worship ministry performed by the priests and constituted Israel's access to God.[4] Truly, these are special bondservants in the sight of God.

Likewise, King Jotham maintained a steadfast heart when all Israel went astray:

> *Jotham was twenty-five years old when he became king, and he reigned in Jerusalem sixteen years. His mother's name was Jerusha **daughter of Zadok. He did what was right in the eyes of the LORD**... The people, however, continued their corrupt practices... Jotham grew powerful because **he walked steadfastly before the LORD his God**.* -2 Chron. 27:1-2,6, NIV

It should not surprise us that Jotham was also of the line of Zadok on his mother's side. The Zadok priests were from the line of Phinehas, the grandson of Aaron. In the previous chapter, we learned that God had blessed Phinehas because he demonstrated his zeal for the honor of God's name during a time of tremendous apostasy. God promised Phinehas' family the covenant of an everlasting priesthood. His actions were credited to him as righteousness throughout all his generations. It is interesting to note Jotham is listed in the genealogy of Jesus (Matt. 1:9), and therefore Jesus, though legally of the tribe of Judah, is remotely of the line of Phinehas and the Zadok priests as well—those who alone minister to the Lord.

How does this apply to us? Look around you and see the generation as in the days of Noah. Corruption has made its way through all levels of our society and the church. The first two traits of perilous times, as defined by the Lord, are that people will be self-centered and motivated primarily by the attainment of wealth. When these conditions exist, all other ungodly practices follow. As in Israel during the time of the Judges, everyone exists to do what is right in their own eyes, willfully contrary in heart to the will of God. Paul revealed that in the last days there will be times of great stress because people will be lovers of self and utterly self-centered, lovers of money with an inordinate desire for wealth, and lovers of sensual pleasures and vain amusements rather than lovers of God. Paul's closing statement implied these would be the traits of many professing believers in the church. He described them as looking religious but that their conduct and lack of transformation witness against them (2 Tim. 3:1-5).

God always reserves a remnant who will not bow to the god of the culture and times. The Word of God is our plumb line, not the shifting sands of cultural knowledge and wisdom, or scientific theories continually replaced by new and improved or adjusted versions of 'fact.' Paul encourages us to persevere in working out our salvation in the midst of a crooked and perverse generation so we will prove ourselves innocent, blameless, and above reproach as the children of God. The Holy Spirit supplies us with the power to do this. As we hold fast to the Word, we will be light to a dark world and unashamed at Jesus' return (Php. 2:12-16).

Closing Thoughts

Bondservants march to the beat of a different drummer. They long to hear the voice of their Master. They make mistakes, sin, and lose their way at times, but they run back to God because He truly is their anchor. They long for His appearing and strive to complete all God has ordained for them to accomplish in this age. Bit by bit, they divorce themselves from the things of the world until nothing captivates their attention more than He does.

If we can walk away with one idea from this chapter, let it be that we can love God freely, and He will supply the power for us to become obedient, even unto death, as evidenced by the lives of the bondservants in the Bible. Our part is to cooperate and work diligently in the realm God has appointed to us. The teaching of salvation by grace as evidenced by works, which is difficult for some, is the same as the teaching of freedom and love as evidenced by obedience. In each reality, the concepts are not at odds with each other. Obedient works are the natural outcome of salvation, grace, freedom, and love.

The remainder of this book will take a more in-depth look at the specific traits that define a bondservant's life:

The bondservant sets his affections on God

- ♦ preoccupies his heart and mind with the knowledge of God
- ♦ seeks to hear the Master's heart and share in His work
- ♦ longs for an ever-deepening relationship with God

The bondservant voluntarily relinquishes lordship over his life

- ♦ maintains a teachable spirit
- ♦ denies himself in order to be obedient
- ♦ follows through even when it is not in the best interest of self

The bondservant guards his position by discerning his Master's voice

- won't follow another
- is alert to the tactics of the enemy
- relies on his Master's strength
- is not naive but shrewd in dealing with the crafty

The bondservant remains connected through the Word and the Spirit

- cooperates in the process of sanctification
- makes study of the Word a priority in his life
- keeps eternity in view and longs for his full adoption as a son

The bondservant is given ears to hear

- allows the Spirit to guide him into truth
- applies what he learns to his conduct in everyday life
- listens as the Spirit reveals the things to come

SECTION 2

PASSIONATE PURSUIT OF GOD

Chapter 5

Cultivating Intimacy

> *O God, you are my God; earnestly I seek you; my soul thirsts for you; my flesh faints for you, as in a dry and weary land where there is no water.* -Ps. 63:1, ESV

[Note: I would not have the understanding I have today of intimacy with God without the help of a powerful teaching series on the book of Song of Songs by Mike Bickle. This teaching redirected my walk with the Lord and opened up a whole new realm of understanding, and for that I am indebted to him. What I have written here is a blend of his work and my grasp of his teaching.[1]]

Bondservants are driven to know God. They are unable to escape the desire for ever deeper and broader understanding of God and His ways, longing to hear what He would say. They are consumed with acquiring friendship with God. At the commencement of our pursuit to know God, understanding that Jesus is the Word sets the cornerstone for our journey:

> *In the beginning was the Word, and the Word was with God, and the Word was God... In him was life, and the life was the light of men. The light shines in the darkness, and the darkness has not overcome it... And the Word became flesh and dwelt among us.* -John 1:1,4-5,14a, ESV

Grasping the truth that *Jesus is the Word* revolutionizes our understanding of the way we get to know God and multiply the deposit given to us. Oftentimes we can substitute the name of Jesus in Scripture wherever the Word is spoken of, or substitute 'Word' for Jesus. This can bring greater clarity or an added dimension to a passage. For example, this substitution principle, a fundamental principle from mathematics, can be used in verses 4-5 above: 'In the Word is life, and that life in the Word is the light of men. The Word shines in the darkness, and the darkness has not overcome it.' Moving forward in the newness of life given to us means multiplying the deposit we have been granted and increasing our understanding of God. These have one common denominator—the Word. Allocating time to study the Word and listen to sound biblical teaching is critical for our growth and relationship with God.

Many have presumed the Old Testament is for those under the old covenant, and the New Testament for those who believe in Jesus as Messiah. This contradicts New Testament teaching, which informs us that *all* Scripture has been given to teach us spiritual truths. The *entire* Word of God is living and breathing. It is spirit and life. None of the Word was done away with at the cross because God's Word is eternal.

Knowing God

> *With my whole heart I seek you; let me not wander from your commandments. I have stored up your word in my heart, that I might not sin against you... I will meditate on your precepts and fix my eyes on your ways... I will not forget your word.* -Ps. 119:10-11,15,16b, ESV

Relationships with a spouse and with friends are built and cultivated over years of spending time with them. It is no different with the Lord. Time spent in His presence hearing and reading the Word, and pondering, brooding over, and praying through His Word provide the way in which we get to know Him. The Word and the Holy Spirit accomplish the transformation of our mind and heart so we can receive God's truth and walk with Him in meaningful relationship. This is why groups such as Wycliffe are so vitally important. Having the Bible in one's own language is an invaluable gift.

Cultivating intimacy can be a major challenge for broken people who have set up barriers around their wounded hearts. Others have constructed elaborate spiritual or religious paradigms of what makes sense to them or what they like, preventing them from recognizing truth. Still others have set multiple obstacles in place through sin they won't relinquish. For many, the lure and trappings of the world, including the deceptive intellectualism of our day, erect a bulwark that shrouds the heart and mind in darkness.

The only real remedy for these is to continually wash the mind with the Word. It may seem like nothing is happening at first, just as a watched pot never boils, but the promised transformation and freedom will take place if we persevere.

Investing Time

Athletes and musicians discipline themselves by investing time and effort in practice and training, persevering through frustration and pain to reach a goal. Others have spent time training and preparing for a profession or work of some sort and made countless sacrifices to accomplish this. Why is it, then, when it comes to spiritual matters, we quit before we reach the goal? We put forth only minimal effort and time, yet expect the results to be dramatic or obtained by automatic download. Peter taught we should be like newborns, *craving* milk (1 Pet. 2:2-4). When we first experience repentance, this craving for the Word and the truth it imparts is insatiable. Whether we satisfy this craving or let it die of neglect is the choice each makes.

We must continue to wrestle with the truth in the Word until it becomes part of who we are. This pursuit is worth all the wealth we have and deserves every bit of our time and attention. If we really desire this relationship, the sacrifices we have to make to nurture it will not seem like sacrifices at all. The Lord takes us through this process incrementally, helping us let go of anger and the pain of old wounds, holding one hand as we let go of things we have held so tightly in the other. Throughout this process, the

Holy Spirit transforms our mind to understand truth and converts our heart and desire to focus on God and His kingdom instead of ourselves.

Proper Paradigm

The study of the Song of Songs gives the proper framework for comprehending the love God has for us. Proper understanding destroys the misconception that God dwells in anger and disappointment with man, condemning all to a life of shame and guilt by disapproving our every word and action. Thinking this way is a prison constructed in our minds. It is a cage where Satan wants us to remain to keep our hearts and minds closed to the truth of who God is and His passionate love for those who fear His name.

Once the truth sets us free from that prison, we can begin to comprehend the depth and height and breadth of His love for us. With hearts no longer locked in shame and guilt, we are set free to wholeheartedly pursue the relationship that is above all we could ask or think—knowing the God of the universe and the creator of our being.

There are different ways of interpreting the Song of Songs: *literally*, as natural human love between a man and a woman, and *allegorically*, as the love between Israel and God, Jesus and the community of believers, or Jesus and the individual believer. Our focus will be on the last interpretation for this brief and limited discussion.

God Draws Us

> *Let him kiss me with the kisses of his mouth! For your love is better than wine; your anointing oils are fragrant; your name is oil poured out; therefore virgins love you. Draw me after you; let us run. The king has brought me into his chambers.* -Songs 1:2-4a, ESV

Song of Songs begins with the desire of the Shulamite to know her Beloved. Kisses symbolize intimacy, and His mouth represents the Word. She is asking the Lord to impart His Word to her and draw her to Him. Being drawn to God is a supernatural work. Jesus stated no one can come to Him unless the Father draws him and gives him the desire to do so (John 6:44). God richly rewards those who 'turn aside' in response to this drawing, as Moses discovered when God spoke to him from the burning bush (Ex. 3:1-4).

The king's chambers are the place of intimacy where secrets and affection are shared. The secrets are the treasures in His Word, and the affection comes with understanding the truth of His passion for us. His 'anointing oils are fragrant' and His 'name is oil poured out' are associated with and identified by the meaning of His name and character. 'Jesus' is the Greek translation of the Hebrew name *Yeshua* ('Yahweh is salvation'). Jesus is identified as the Christ, 'the anointed One,' and John designated Jesus as the Word made flesh (John 1:1,14). These descriptions of Jesus help us understand the use of the word 'anointing' in the following passage:

> *As for you, **the anointing which you received from Him abides in you**, and you have no need for anyone to teach you; but as **His anointing teaches you about all things**, and is true and is not a lie, and just as it has taught you, you abide in Him.* -1 John 2:27, NASB

Jesus, both our salvation and the Word by which we are saved and sanctified, sent forth or poured out His Spirit—His *anointing*—to guide us into all truth. This *anointing*, resident in us when we come to repentance, teaches us about all things as we abide in Christ, the Word. His *anointing* draws forth the love of the virgins (Songs 1:3). The virgins are those who believe and cling to His salvation, and revel in the understanding that His love for them is all-consuming. They are virgins because they will not accept other lovers, which are the temptations of this world in whatever form. Jesus' oil poured forth is manifested in the free gift of righteousness.

While We Were Yet Sinners

> *I am dark, but lovely...* -Songs 1:5a, NKJV

Through this intimacy, we come to realize that despite being dark in our understanding and dark due to our fallen nature and sin, we are lovely to Him and loved by Him. God demonstrated His love for us because *'while we were yet sinners*, Christ died for us' (Rom. 5:8). Intimacy flourishes when we pore over the Word with desire for His presence, not from a legalistic mindset hoping to earn the relationship by sinless perfection.

The struggle we have with sin and the remorse we have over it are contrasted with giving ourselves *over* to sin in rebellion. Knowing the difference enables us to properly answer the question I heard many years ago that changed my life: 'Do you see yourself as a sinner who struggles to love God, or a lover of God who still struggles with sin?'

The latter is the correct answer for the believer in Christ. The fact that we struggle with sin rather than embrace it furnishes evidence we are on the right track. But in order for our hearts to be unlocked to the truth of His love, we must view His love as our primary focus, not our battle with sin issues and error. God does not view things as we do. His generous evaluation of David's life helps us realize this truth:

- He walked uprightly and faithfully before Me with integrity of heart (1 Kings 9:4).
- He kept My commands and followed Me with all his heart, doing only what was right in My eyes (1 Kings 14:8b).
- He shepherded Israel with integrity of heart and skillful hands (Ps. 78:72).
- David is a man after My own heart and fulfilled all My will (Acts 13:22).

This is high praise from God, who covered David's repented sins of adultery, murder, and pride in taking a census without God's consent. This is *amazing* redemptive editing. God said David *only* did what was right in God's eyes. Truly, we are blessed because the

Lord does not hold the sins of the repentant against them (Ps. 32:2; Rom. 4:8). Not only this, but God declares He will *not even remember* our sins (Jer. 31:34). It should make us hopeful that we have the same quality of praise awaiting us if we posture our hearts before the Lord as David did, and pursue God with all of our heart, mind, and strength as he modeled throughout his life. God's forgiveness erases our sins completely:

> *As far as the east is from the west, so far has He removed our transgressions from us.* -Ps. 103:12, HCSB

The Dove and the Rock

With her profession of love and desire, the Bridegroom responds with His affirmation of the Shulamite's beauty in His eyes:

> *Behold, you are beautiful, my love! Behold, you are beautiful! You have doves' eyes.* -Songs 1:15, AMP

Here and in Songs 4:1, her eyes are described as 'doves' eyes.' The singleness of vision represented by doves' eyes describes the wholehearted commitment of one whose soul is not divided in its loyalty. This defines true beauty by God's standard.

The double-minded, in contrast, are exhorted to purify their hearts to have one love (James 4:8). James' exhortation to those divided in their loyalty entails cleansing our thoughts from the duplicity that results when we want to experience all the world has to offer in this life, while at the same time feeling the tug on our spirit to come up higher to know God. We cannot have both.

Doves' eyes express the qualities of modesty, faithfulness, and humility. As a believer matures in faith, longing for the Beloved intensifies. It is common knowledge that eyes reflect the desire of the heart. For example, think of cartoon characters drawn with dollar signs in the eyes to indicate the greed in the heart. In our lives as believers, the singleness of vision describes the intense longing and love for the Beloved as reflected in the 'eyes,' which becomes more fervent as we grow in knowledge and understanding. This takes place through a relationship nurtured by the Word and prayer. Upon seeing this fervent desire and longing for His presence, the Bridegroom responds:

> *Turn your eyes away from me, for they have overcome me.* -Songs 6:5, NKJV

Expositor John Gill stated, "[H]er eyes… had made a conquest of his heart; which does not imply weakness in Christ but condescending grace, that he should suffer himself, as it were, to be overpowered by the faith and love of his people."[2] Such is the passion of our Lord for His people. Laying hold of this truth will set the heart of the believer free to run without reservation or fear into the arms of her Beloved.

The dove imagery applied to the believer is both lovely and rich in meaning. Doves are monogamous, having only one mate. Paul regards the believer similarly, speaking of believers as virgins before the Lord:

> *I am jealous for you with a godly jealousy. I promised you to one husband, to Christ, so that I might present you as a pure virgin to him.* -2 Cor. 11:2, NIV

While we see many doves in our cities, the biblical writers describe doves as taking up residence in rocky hillsides and caves (cf. Jer 48:28b).

> **O my dove, in the clefts of the rock, in the secret places of the cliff,** *let me see your face, let me hear your voice; for your voice is sweet, and your face is lovely.*
> -Songs 2:14, NKJV

This also gives us a spiritual picture of the refuge the dove seeks in the Rock. 'There is no rock like our Rock' (1 Sam. 2:2). This is an allusion to the nature of God as our refuge, derived from the Hebrew word *tsuwr*, which literally means 'rock' but figuratively speaks of refuge. Paul spoke of Christ as the spiritual Rock that followed Israel and provided them with water in the desert (1 Cor. 10:4; cf. Ps. 78:16).

Moses also called God 'the Rock whose work is just and perfect, faithful and upright in all His ways' (Deut. 32:4). The person who used this metaphor the most was David, who understood that his salvation (refuge) was found in the Lord, and he called God his 'mighty Rock' (Ps. 62:7; see also Ps. 61:2; 71:3).

> *The LORD is my rock, my fortress, and my savior; my God is my rock, in whom I find protection. He is my shield, the power that saves me, and my place of safety. He is my refuge, my savior, the one who saves me from violence.* -2 Sam. 22:2-3, NLT

The fountain of living water, which God used to describe Himself (Jer. 2:13; 17:13), is coupled with the imagery of the Rock to teach us that living water flows from Christ, the Rock, the Word of God on which the wise build their homes (Matt. 7:24). Jesus (the Rock) gives us living water—His words are spirit and life. Anyone who believes in Jesus will have rivers of living water flowing out of his heart (John 7:37-38), a spring of water welling up to eternal life (John 4:14). Eternal life is knowing God (John 17:3).

> *Trust in the LORD forever, for the LORD GOD is an everlasting rock.* -Isa. 26:4, ESV

A further application of the water that flows from the rock can be seen in the case of the rocky ground. These are the ones who receive the word 'immediately with joy,' but in a time of testing fall away because the Word has no root in them (Matt. 13:20-21). But by the grace of God, those who were once rocky ground can be transformed through repentance and the power of the Holy Spirit.

> *Bear fruits in keeping with repentance... God is able from these stones to raise up children for Abraham.* -Luke 3:8, ESV

In this passage, Jesus reminds the Jews that God has the power to raise up children for Abraham *from stones*. God is able to turn 'the rock into a pool of water, the flint into a spring of water' (Ps. 114:8). Rocky ground can be made to bring forth water through the Word (see Jer. 23:29), faith, and the power of God's Spirit. Many of us are living proof this is indeed true by the testimony of our own lives.

The Quiet Place

Seeking the quietness of the rocky places, the dove gives us a parallel in nature that is true in the believer's life. The secret places are where we get away from the noise and distractions of life. The dove leaves the place of bustling activity and settles in the distant sanctuary of the rocky crags. This place of intimacy is where we, as doves, find solitude, rest, and growth by spending time with the Lover of our souls away from the commotion, diversions, and amusements of life. Even Jesus retreated to solitary places to fellowship with His Father (Matt. 14:13; Mark 1:35; Luke 4:42).

David used this same imagery:

> *Oh, that I had the wings of a dove! I would fly away and be at rest. I would flee far away and stay in the desert; Selah. I would hurry to my place of shelter, far from the tempest and storm.* -Ps. 55:6-8, NIV

God desires intimacy from each of us: quiet fellowship on a regular basis. Corporate gatherings have their purpose as well, but the intimate fellowship between God and the individual believer is necessary to develop our relationship with God. If we depend only on corporate gatherings to fuel our hearts, we miss out on the intimacy and sharing that occurs when we set our hearts before the Lord in private contemplation of the Word.

By the repeated washing of our heart and mind with the Word of God, we are transformed and renewed. A general principle of both chemistry and microbiology, especially as applied to the environmental and biological arenas, states that 'dilution is the solution for pollution.' Applying this to our lives, the pollution with which our carnal nature and living in the world have defiled our mind and heart is washed away by the Word of God. Washing with the water of the Word incrementally dilutes the 'pollution' (wrong thinking, pain, guilt, anger, etc.) clinging to us.

As the story progresses and the Shulamite matures, she is transformed from being darkened because of her fallen nature to being undefiled and pure in His sight. Here the Lord references the perfect posture of her heart towards Him as evidenced by her desire to obey—even if it turns out to be an *imperfect* obedience.

> *But my **dove, my undefiled and perfect one**, stands alone...* -Songs 6:9a, AMP

Both David (Ps. 68:13) and Asaph (Ps. 74:18-19) use the imagery of a dove to refer to the beloved people of the Lord. Gentleness and guilelessness are the strengths of doves as described in the Word. Juxtaposed to these strengths are their shortcomings, namely being unwary and easily deceived. This describes Eve in the garden as she unwittingly capitulated in the first step of Satan's scheme to divest man of his kingdom authority over the earth. Hosea wrote that Ephraim was unaware of what was taking place around him, causing him to be baited and trapped, 'a silly dove without heart or understanding' (Hos. 7:11). Jesus exhorted His disciples to be alert and shrewd to prevent exploitation via this Achilles' heel, and at the same time remain in their strength as guileless and innocent of evil before God (Matt. 10:16).

As an interesting side note, both male and female doves (a.k.a. 'pigeons') produce crop milk to feed their young, a highly digestible mixture of fat and protein for the newly hatched chicks. Seeds are added into their diet only incrementally by first being mixed with the crop milk. This crop milk is so peculiar to doves/pigeons (only flamingoes produce something similar) that it is also known as 'pigeon milk.'

As spiritual fathers and mothers, we need to feed new believers with the pure milk of the Word, introducing first the love of our Father, the Bridegroom Redeemer nature of Jesus, and the comforting friendship of the Holy Spirit. Too often we have fed new converts 'rules of religion' first, before their hearts are captured by God's love. This can lead to austere and cranky holiness or frustration with religion that promised much but delivered so little. There have been many believers locked into this wrong paradigm for decades, ending their walk in disappointment, confusion, or apathy. The truth of who God really is and how He feels toward us will set us free, even from legalistic religious practices that are devoid of meaningful relationship with God.

The Bondservant Is the Bridal Identity

When we are in a loving relationship with God, we gradual cross over into the role of the bondservant without realizing it. The bondservant becomes more loyal to his Master than to his own interests, just as a bride lays down her name and her right to make her own decisions for the one she marries. A bride in love will not quit when the going gets tough. Workers for hire, on the other hand, will either wear down or burn out in their zeal to be obedient because their hearts have not been engaged in the process. If the heart is captured, the zeal and perseverance to continue will follow.

Both the bondservant illustration and the bridal identity are rooted in love. This love is first received from the Master/Bridegroom, enabling the bondservant/bride to reciprocate love back. The following gives us proper perspective regarding the degree to which God loves us:

> *May... the world... know that you sent me and that* ***you love them as much as you love me****.* -John 17:23b, NLT

This passage sums up perfectly what so many of us find difficult to believe: God the Father loves *us* as much as He loves *His Son Jesus*. Because of the volume of judgment writing in the Old Testament, many have drawn the erroneous conclusion that God is angry all of the time. While there are passages of just judgment executed on the hostile and rebellious, these incidents are few in number relative to the amount of time covered, which is approximately four thousand years. The bulk of judgment prophecies were made over the span of only a few hundred years, many of which deal with a future day when everything will be made right. In the mind of the bondservant, these writings are not examples of God's disdain for mankind but words of warning for those He loves and disciplines as sons as well as righteous judgment executed on the persecutors of His people or the apostate among them. We must keep perspective on this issue lest we make false assumptions about the character and nature of God's heart toward His children.

Paul called this the kindness and severity of God (Rom. 11:22). The lovingkindness that the Lord showed David is the same lovingkindness He shows to each one of us whose heart is captured by and occupied with His love. Those who are like King Saul, mere man-pleasers who operate out of selfish desire for the promotion of self, give God either no thought or only secondary consideration. These will experience the severity of God and find He does not spare the branches that persist in unbelief and willful sin.

Knowing that those who are in Christ are desired, loved, and cherished by the father heart of God brings tremendous freedom, unlocking our hearts in the process. With this freedom, we come *to* God instead of hide *from* Him when we sin, as David did. Instead of a dutiful worker trying to accomplish as much as possible for the boss, Jesus will return for a loving and spotless Bride, fit to partner with Him in His reign over the earth. A worn out and harried worker fears the expected harsh and exacting evaluation of his work and does not look forward to the return of his Master. But a Bride, with longing in her heart, will say, 'Come quickly; I can't stand the separation any longer!'

Proper Garments

We must divest ourselves of the worker mentality and embrace the Bridal paradigm of God's kingdom. A worker keeps track of all his accomplishments, hoping to score some points with his overseer. He keeps an updated resume with him at all times and wears his self-initiated achievements as a garment. But the King has provided wedding garments for us through the righteousness of Christ. We cannot show up to the wedding feast in work clothes, parading our own accomplishments. To do so shows disrespect to the King who has already provided the wedding garment. Furthermore, doing so endangers our place at the wedding feast. Rather than God's lovingkindness, we provoke His rejection of our lives because we rejected His gift (Matt. 22:11-14).

All who are in Christ will be arrayed as He is. Even at the cross we find something unusual noted about Jesus' garments. His coat was noted to be without seam, just as Josephus described the garments of the high priest (see Ex. 39:22-23).[3] Jesus' designation as our high priest and our role as priests in His kingdom make the comparison significant. No priest under the old covenant could show up for temple duty in common, sweaty work clothes.

> *Be silent before the Lord GOD! For the day of the LORD is near; the LORD has prepared a sacrifice and consecrated his guests. And on the day of the LORD's sacrifice—**I will punish** the officials and the king's sons and **all who array themselves in foreign attire**.* -Zeph. 1:7-8, ESV

Only laziness, pride in our accomplishments, or false humility that says 'I'm not worthy' would cause us to wear our own garments when His have been provided for us. It is a 'given' that we are not worthy, which is why our worthiness must be found in Christ alone. Either we believe the Word on this point or we are lacking faith that His Word is true. *Our* garments are viewed by God as filthy rags (Isa. 64:6), but *His* are righteousness and salvation:

> *I delight greatly in the LORD; my soul rejoices in my God... he has clothed me with **garments of salvation** and arrayed me in a **robe of his righteousness**.*
> -Isa. 61:10a, NIV

The righteousness of Christ provides the wedding garment for each believer. When we experience repentance and accept His free gift of righteousness and reconciliation with God, our filthy, sin-stained (including the stain of pride in accomplishment) clothes are removed and we are given fine, clean garments to replace them. This occurred in Zechariah's vision at the time the exiles returned, an example of the mercy and lovingkindness of God (Zech. 3:4). This is also an example that God's forgiveness and loving concern have always existed, even under the old covenant.

We must take care to understand this principle, foregoing laziness by instead striving to work out our salvation. At the same time, we take neither pride nor false humility in our accomplishments. 'All that we have accomplished He has done for us' (Isa. 26:12), and 'all we have given we first took from His hand' (1 Chron. 29:14). A bondservant understands this at the heart level and is only grateful to be involved in the process of what is accomplished in whatever measure he is given. He wears the garments provided for him with joy and gratitude. These are the garments of the Bride of Christ.

Closing Thoughts

The following thoughts from C.S. Lewis' book, *Mere Christianity*, accurately reflect how many of us feel about the subject of loving God: "Some writers use the word charity to describe not only Christian love between human beings, but also God's love for man and man's love for God. About the second of these two, people are often worried. They are told they ought to love God. They cannot find any such feeling in themselves. What are they to do? The answer is the same as before. Act as if you did. Do not sit trying to manufacture feelings. Ask yourself, 'If I were sure that I loved God, what would I do?' When you have found the answer, go and do it.

"On the whole, God's love for us is a much safer subject to think about than our love for Him. Nobody can always have devout feelings: and even if we could, feelings are not what God principally cares about. *Christian Love, either towards God or towards man, is an affair of the will.* If we are trying to do His will we are obeying the commandment, 'Thou shalt love the Lord thy God.' He will give us feelings of love if He pleases. We cannot create them for ourselves, and we must not demand them as a right. But the great thing to remember is that, though our feelings come and go, His love for us does not. It is not wearied by our sins, or our indifference; and, therefore, it is quite relentless in its determination that we shall be cured of those sins, at whatever cost to us, at whatever cost to Him."[4] (emphasis added)

In hindsight, many of us can look back on the striving and busy lifestyles that took priority over our relationship with God and agree with Paul that it was all for loss. Swapping reputation, a full resume, and self-satisfaction in a long list of accomplishments for time that could have been spent with God begins to look like a bowl of Esau's red stew. But take heart—the scepter is extended to all who are in Christ. 'Today, if you hear His voice, do not harden your heart.'

> *Therefore the LORD longs to be gracious to you, and therefore He waits on high to have compassion on you.* -Isa. 30:18a, NASB

Chapter 6

Learning God's Language

> *I have also spoken by the prophets, and have multiplied visions; I have given symbols through the witness of the prophets.* -Hos. 12:10, NKJV

The events of the Bible, both historic and prophetic, are couched in symbolic language and imagery in a literary style difficult for anyone to grasp on first exposure, or even second or third for that matter. The more obvious truths spelled out in the Word are the milk we thrive on in the early days of our walk, building the foundation for the meat we will consume later.

Many of us are under the assumption we lack the time, tools, or energy to tackle the Word of God in all its complexity on our own. We leave it to the 'big boys'—the scholars and clergy. But the Lord made the Word both simple and complex for a reason. Beyond the simple, He wanted us to wrestle with the Word to gain deeper understanding; to persevere and not give up. Understanding what He desires to communicate is not available to mere curious observers, but to His bondservants who struggle with all their might to understand and know the One who has brought them freedom and life. He will be found by those who seek Him, which includes deepening comprehension of His Word.

First Contact

At first reading, however, all of us struggle with understanding the Word, especially the Old Testament. While it is easier to understand those truths spelled out more clearly in the New Testament or to dive into some of the Psalms which beautifully express the emotions we feel, much of what we read bypasses our intellect and therefore our ability to understand in a meaningful way. Because of the degree of mental exertion required, most believers who start out tackling the Word end up settling for devotionals (though some can be challenging) or sticking to passages that are easier to understand. But God never intended for us to settle for a continual diet of mashed bananas and gruel. There is a banquet prepared for us in the Word, and we need to use our teeth to lay hold of it.

The two greatest obstacles preventing us from understanding God's Word are His manner of communication and our dull minds. We all struggle in communication, at least since the tower of Babel. The following conversation shows how we misunderstand each other due to misplaced modifiers:

> A wife asks her husband, an engineer, "Could you please go shopping for me and buy one carton of milk, and if they have eggs, get a dozen."

A short time later the husband comes back home with a dozen cartons of milk. The wife asks him, "Why in the world did you buy a dozen cartons of milk?"
He replied, "They had eggs."

At other times, true communication escapes because one person may be trying to communicate a thought without giving sufficient background for the listener to follow precisely what he is saying. The following conversation illustrates this point. It took place between a staff member and pastor in a church where we formerly served. The pastor had received some criticism from local 'religious' people for an outreach he had undertaken to engage the youth in the area. The conversation went something like this (the name of the staff person's brother is Dave, who also worked at the church):

Pastor: Now I know how David felt when Shimei threw stones at him.
Staff member: Someone was throwing stones at Dave?
Pastor: Yes, and he just stood by and took his insults, without taking action but just relying on the Lord to vindicate him (see 2 Sam. 16:5-14).
Staff member: That doesn't sound like Dave. I'm surprised he didn't go around the block and get some of his buddies to go after this guy...

These humorous misunderstandings help us to see, in hindsight, how we could have more effectively communicated the intended meaning. Sometimes being misunderstood is funny, but often it can be frustrating, or worse.

Most of us will be able to relate to the following movie illustrations, the first from *Star Trek: The Next Generation*, which illustrates a communication barrier. The second is from *Monty Python and the Holy Grail*, which parallels our general lack of inherent ability in understanding God's Word.

Communication Barrier

In this particular *Star Trek: The Next Generation* episode, the *Enterprise* is hailed from Tama, aliens whose language is not yet understood despite the use of the universal translator. Hoping to establish friendship, Captain Picard of the *Enterprise* and Captain Dathon of Tama attempt to communicate but without success. Though a people with no history of aggressive violence, Dathon turns to Picard with two daggers in hand and they are immediately beamed to the surface of an uninhabited planet below.

On the planet, Dathon offers Picard a dagger, saying, "Darmok and Jalad at Tanagra." Piccard mistakes this as a challenge to duel or as an act of war, and refuses the dagger. Dathon shakes his head, disappointed, and says, "Shaka, when the walls fell," which we later understand to mean, 'failure to understand' in this usage. After building a fire because of the approaching night, Picard sleeps. Waking a while later, he hears Dathan cry out, and at the same time hears the roar of a beast. Once again, Dathan offers Picard the dagger and, under the circumstances, Picard accepts it. During the fight with the beast, the two continue to struggle to communicate, though Picard is starting to understand that the Tamarians communicate by analogous comparisons to historical events. Once Picard has this 'epiphany,' Dathon responds enthusiastically to Picard's newfound understanding.

Due to the rescue efforts of the crew on the *Enterprise*, Picard dematerializes briefly. While Picard is on the *Enterprise*, the beast strikes Dathan. Picard returns to the planet and finds Dathon dying from the wound. He continues to struggle to understand the events and realizes the Tamarian was reenacting the event of Darmok and Jalad, two friends on an island called Tanagra, fighting together to slay a beast.

He further realizes Dathan brought Picard there specifically with the hope that this concrete example would dissolve the communication barrier so the two societies could communicate and begin relations—become friends, like Darmok and Jalad. When all is said and done, Picard wonders whether he would have sacrificed his life as Dathon had, simply in the hope communication would be established.[1]

The frustration Picard felt in trying to understand Dathon is the type of frustration we experience when first trying to understand some of the more cryptic literary expressions used in the Word. This includes understanding the point of some stories included for our instruction. Our basic assumption about these stories must line up with God's Word, which states they have something to teach us. They are not there so we can merely acquire knowledge, but so we can be equipped for good works (2 Tim. 3:16-17).

The first time I read Judges 19-20 and much of the prophetic writings, including Revelation, I thought, 'Shaka, when the walls fell.' Other treasures completely escaped my grasp: some of the Levitical laws regarding clean and unclean states, lying on one side for three hundred ninety days, foreskins as a marriage price, a wheel within a wheel, cooking food over dung, snapping a bird's neck under running water to cleanse a moldy house, the epithet 'the house of him whose sandal was removed'... well, it's unusual. I struggled to understand what the Lord wanted to communicate in these passages. But over time, my understanding of many biblical expressions has increased, though there is still much to learn. Step-by-step, the truth begins to sink in if we will only persevere. Love and understanding are then able to take root and flourish.

Intellectual Insufficiency

The second movie example, *Monty Python and the Holy Grail*, illustrates our dullness of mind in comparison with the genius of God. (Using this movie may seem sacrilegious to some—no offense is intended. The goal is to illustrate the futility of human 'logic.') In our human wisdom and reasoning, we can only come up with the simple-minded logic epitomized in this scene. This portrays our inability to understand by our own effort what God is saying in the Word. Anyone who is familiar with the scene will recall the ludicrous exchange of 'reasoning' that takes place to determine if the woman is a witch.

Bedemir: *Quiet, quiet. Quiet! There are ways of telling whether she is a witch.*
Crowd: Are there? What are they?
Bedemir: *Tell me, what do you do with witches?*
Villager #2: Burn!
Crowd: Burn, burn them up!
Bedemir: *And what do you burn apart from witches?*
Villager #1: More witches!
Villager #2: Wood!
Bedemir: *So, why do witches burn?*
   [pause]
Villager #3: [haltingly] Be-... 'cause they're made of wood...?
Bedemir: *Good!*
Crowd: Oh yeah, yeah...
Bedemir: *So, how do we tell whether she is made of wood?*
Villager #1: Build a bridge out of her.
Bedemir: *Aah, but can you not also build bridges out of stone?*
Villager #2: Oh, yeah.
Bedemir: *Does wood sink in water?*
Villager #1: No, no.
Villager #2: It floats! It floats!
Villager #1: Throw her into the pond!
Crowd: The pond!
Bedemir: *What also floats in water?*
Villager #1: Bread!
Villager #2: Apples!
Villager #3: Very small rocks!
Villager #1: Cider!
Villager #2: Great gravy!
Villager #1: Cherries!
Villager #2: Mud!
Villager #3: Churches—churches!
Villager #2: Lead—lead!
King Arthur: A duck.
Crowd: Oooh.
Bedemir: *Exactly! So, logically...,*
Villager #1: If... she... weighs the same as a duck, she's made of wood.
Bedemir: *And therefore...?*
Villager #1: A witch![2]

We either laugh at this type of obtuse reasoning or roll our eyes because it is absolutely ridiculous. But this is how many of us feel when we first start out in our journey to understand God's Word. And some of what has been labeled intelligent scholarship might just look this way to God! Most of our minds are concrete and literal, and it really takes exercise and the Spirit of God for us to 'understand that He was not speaking about bread' (see Matt. 16:11).

For example, look at the following passage. This is part of Hezekiah's lament when he was told his days were numbered and he would soon die:

> *I waited patiently till dawn, but like a lion he broke all my bones; day and night you made an end of me.* -Isa. 38:13, NIV

God broke all his bones? He killed him day and night? Obviously this isn't to be taken literally. When I first saw the next two passages, I thought, who wrote this? These passages are only three chapters apart—did they think we would forget what the first one said or that we wouldn't notice? Are we supposed to *remember* the former things or *forget* them?

> **Forget the former things;** *do not dwell on the past.* -Isa. 43:18, NIV

> **Remember the former things long past**, *for I am God, and there is no other; I am God, and there is no one like Me.* -Isa. 46:9, NASB

For those of us with more of the $ax^2 + bx + c = 0$ mentality, this is difficult water to tread; a real communication barrier.

The Postulates

There are two postulates we must accept in order to proceed with any cohesiveness in our hope to know God and understand His Word. A postulate is defined as "a proposition that requires no proof, being self-evident, or that is for a specific purpose assumed true, and that is used in the proof of other propositions; something taken as self-evident or assumed without proof as a basis for reasoning; a fundamental principle; a necessary condition; prerequisite."[3] For our study of God's Word, the following postulates must be firmly fixed in our minds:

- We must have conviction that God's Word is inerrant in the original languages and inspired by the Holy Spirit.
- We must believe God is smarter and wiser than we are; hence, if we don't understand something, it is not because His Word is contradictory but because we aren't smart enough to understand how it fits together (or as a third possibility, the translators' bias may have corrupted or obscured the original meaning).

Once we have these two issues settled, we can proceed by placing our teachable hearts before the Word, trusting that God's Spirit will guide us into all truth, teaching us whatever we are ready to hear, each truth building on the former truths we have learned. This is how a spiritual house is built.

There are 31,175 verses in the Bible. There are layers of meaning, dual fulfillments of prophecies, literal events alongside symbolic ones, near events described with far fulfillments—clues everywhere. Think of it this way: mix several puzzles together made by the same company (many pieces with identical shapes), each with a thousand reversible pieces, and then sort them out into their respective pictures. This was my view of the difficulty and perplexity of putting the prophetic passages in the Word into any semblance of order. But do not despair—the Lord has sent His Holy Spirit to help us.

The Poetry of God

Our God is a poet, whether we understand His language or not. When I first started seriously reading the Word of God, it could be described as Joe Friday ('Just the facts, ma'am') of *Dragnet* meets the poetic, romantic bridegroom God, author of the languages, and also warrior King and righteous Judge. Concrete sequential thinking confined in the fallen, finite mind of man striving to understand the infinite, unfathomable genius of the God of the universe (who takes literal events and infuses them with poetic language: hyperbole, parables, allegory, symbols, personification, metaphors, metonymy, synecdoche, and word plays) is a lesson in futility if it is attempted without the Holy Spirit. The only literary devices I haven't found in God's literary style are onomatopoeia and alliteration, probably only because I don't possess the skill to read the original manuscripts.

Limericks are the poetry I have the ability to compose. Here is a sample of my work:

> There once was a chemist from Maine,
> Whose poems were all inane.
> Much as he tried,
> He just couldn't hide,
> There was no talent to feign.

> Though his teachers sought to train,
> That poetry he should gain,
> Instead you must know,
> His poems plainly show,
> To read them caused people much pain.

Note the appalling lack of poetic skill. Realizing the Lord wants to be known by each of us affirms that He loves a challenge and no challenge is too big for Him. We can't begin to comprehend God and His ways without His active involvement in the endeavor. Human nature defaults to fitting everything into a box of what makes sense to our limited perspective, finite base of knowledge, and unbalanced sense of justice.

> *No one can know God's thoughts except God's own Spirit. And we have received God's Spirit (not the world's spirit), so we can know the wonderful things God has freely given us.* -1 Cor. 2:11b-12, NLT

SECTION 2 PASSIONATE PURSUIT OF GOD

Some Challenges

Other misunderstandings or difficulties arise when attempting to interpret biblical illustrations detail by detail in a manner God never intended. When the Lord conveys a principle through an analogy, it is important to remember He may be driving home only one major point. This is important because not all facets of an illustration will have a parallel counterpart in the principle God desires to impart. The Word gives examples that pedantic treatment of the parables or dreams was never intended. For example, to illustrate the sudden and unexpected nature of His return to those who are not ready, Jesus used the idea of a thief breaking into a house (Matt. 24:42-44). His purpose is to incite believers to be prepared at all times. There is no further parallel between the Lord and the thief.

Example: Luke 16

At other times, seemingly isolated, unrelated ideas are introduced into a train of thought. Using the parable of the unjust steward and the story of the rich man and Lazarus will more effectively highlight this point (see Luke 16).

In the first parable, Jesus described a dishonest manager confronted by his rich boss for wasting his possessions. The manager, a very worldly and self-serving man, searches for a solution to his dilemma because he doesn't want to beg or dig ditches to make a living after he loses his position. His solution is both resourceful and shrewd, ensuring once he is dismissed, his goal of being provided for is met. Jesus' praise is for the clever and astute remedy he devised for his objective and obviously not for his dishonesty. Jesus advised His followers to likewise resourcefully and ably use the means at their disposal while they have them in this age for the furtherance of God's kingdom in order to secure reward from God. His rebuke is that His followers do not use the same creative thought processes in attaining *righteous* objectives.

Jesus then explained true riches (spiritual) will not be entrusted to those who are dishonest with unrighteous wealth. In other words, a covetous person cannot have both his covetous desires in this world and the riches of God, for we are the slave of the one that occupies our affections, thoughts, and desires. Only the slaves of God will receive the riches of God imparted through the Spirit of wisdom and revelation (see Luke 16:10-13).

After saying this, the Pharisees ridiculed Jesus because, according to their interpretation of the law, the wealthy are so because the favor of God rests on them. Jesus proceeded to show that what they have interpreted from the law as God's favor is not what God referred to when He spoke of bestowing blessing. What is sought after as a blessing from man's perspective is detestable from God's point of view (Luke 16:14-15).

Jesus next briefly explained that just as the law and the prophets were subjected to man's interpretation, now likewise the good news of the kingdom is being subjected to a violent wresting of its intended meaning. The Pharisees' 'violence' to God's Word affects those they teach and sets them against the truth because those being taught accept the Pharisees' interpretation as authoritative. The Amplified captures this meaning:

> *Until John came, there were the Law and the Prophets; since then the good news (the Gospel) of the kingdom of God is being preached, and **everyone strives violently to go in [would force his own way rather than God's way into it]**. Yet it is easier for heaven and earth to pass away than for one dot of the Law to fail and become void.* -Luke 16:16-17, AMP

Jesus is emphasizing that the law in its original meaning cannot be made void because of their carnal interpretation. He used this same illustration in the Sermon on the Mount (Matt. 5:17-20). At this point, we note a seemingly unrelated idea interjected into the conversation recorded in Luke where they had been discussing wealth:

> *For example, a man who divorces his wife and marries someone else commits adultery.* -Luke 16:18a, NLT

The NLT inserts the words 'for example' as a way to clarify the intended meaning, indicating that the law cannot be altered merely because the social norms have changed. The law stands 'as is' and cannot be made void by the 'reasonable' alterations of man.

After this one verse interjection, Jesus continued with the theme of wealth in a story further emphasizing that man's idea of riches—money—is not a sign of God's favor or even right standing with God. The rich man goes to hell and the poor man to the place of the departed righteous, which can safely be said to have vexed the paradigm of the Pharisees. Once again, Jesus concluded with reference to the law (Moses) and the prophets as being that which witness to us in this life if we are open to hearing and understanding the *God*-given meaning and intent.

> *If they do not listen to Moses and the Prophets, they will not be convinced even if someone rises from the dead.* -Luke 16:31, NIV

What we can conclude about the interjected thought on divorce must be related to the general theme Jesus is discussing. It is apparent from the context that Jesus is citing another example of the Pharisees' interpretation of the law corrupted by man's desires and carnal thinking, rather than what is intended and important to God. In other words, Jesus is saying, 'You are wrong in your interpretation of the Scriptures in thinking that those rich in mammon have the favor of God, just as you are wrong in your liberal interpretation and application of God's law regarding divorce. Your interpretation has been brought about through your corrupt mind that seeks to justify its desires through willful misapplication of God's Word. It is willful because you were not truly seeking to know My will, but to justify the lusts of your hardened heart.' The outcome? The portion they had been entrusted with will be taken from them and given to those who will teach the kingdom principles the way God intended (Matt. 21:43).

The point we need to grasp is that the Word of God must be interpreted in context in order to walk away with the intended meaning. Does this mean we cannot use the words of Scripture for other purposes? Absolutely not, as long as it doesn't do violence to the Word of God. For example, in order to comfort someone who has experienced the loss of a loved one, can we use a verse lifted out of its original context to breathe love and encouragement into that person's situation? It is right and in keeping with the heart of God to do so (2 Cor. 1:3-4; 7:6). Such uses of Scripture are harmonious with God's desire that we bear each other's burdens.

Get to Know the Author

Understanding the Bible is impossible without also getting to know the Author and the manner of speech He uses to express His thoughts, ideas, warnings, and visions. Knowing God comes through understanding the Word by the Spirit of God. This is a painstaking loop, but by studying the Word, we gradually begin to grasp the way He communicates. Before we know it, we begin to think like Him. Our ability to understand the Word opens up—'Darmok and Jalad at Tanagra.'

This is seen in immersion-type language courses. In foreign language immersion, the language itself becomes the teaching tool. All subjects are taken in the foreign language, whether language-oriented or not, for instance math. Though difficult initially, over time the language gradually becomes more familiar, and understanding and fluency begin to flourish. Similarly, immersing ourselves in the Word exposes us to God's language until understanding begins to take root in our mind and heart by the power of God's Spirit.

Just as each friend or family member communicates in ways peculiar to them and through which we understand what they are saying to us, the Lord has a unique way of communicating as well. Yogi Berra, celebrated baseball player, had a very unique mode of communication. He is famous for combining mutually exclusive phrases and other incongruent, redundant, or otherwise hilarious statements. For example:

- It ain't the heat; it's the humility.
- Even Napoleon had his Watergate.
- He hits from both sides of the plate. He's amphibious.
- I wish I had an answer to that 'cause I'm tired of answering that question.
- You can observe a lot just by watching.
- If you come to a fork in the road, take it.
- You better cut the pizza in 4 pieces—I'm not hungry enough to eat 6.
- Nobody goes there anymore; it's too crowded.
- Baseball is 90% mental—the other half is physical.
- I didn't really say everything I said.
- The future ain't what it used to be.[4]

Even his son, Dale, picked up his style: "You can't compare me to my father. Our similarities are different."[5] If he had written the Bible, we would be in serious confusion without knowing Berra's way of communicating and what he *meant* to say.

Drawing careful conclusions from guarded deductions based on what we have grasped by the illumination of the Holy Spirit and the washing of the Word regarding God's nature, character, and the language with which He communicates is challenging. Accomplishing this is questionable in this life, for who can know everything about God?

Some doctrinal teaching we hold firmly because it is plainly delivered for all to see (unless one has a hidden agenda). Other teaching is meant to be held loosely until further light is brought forth to confirm or refute those beliefs, especially in the realm of prophecy. We are only given a foretaste in this age (we 'know in part and see in part'). Even this comes only with much effort and attention.

Isaiah wrote 'God's understanding is unsearchable' (Isa. 40:28). Similarly, Paul wrote of the unfathomable nature of the wisdom and knowledge of God (Rom. 11:33). Yet God desires to be known by us, His children, for He is a good Father. When we call out to Him, He will answer and tell us great, unsearchable, and remarkable things that we did not know (Jer. 33:2-3). When we cry out to Him, He will say, 'Here I am' (Isa. 58:9a). If we return to Him, He will return to us (Zech. 1:3).

> ***Here I am!*** *I stand at the door and knock. If anyone hears my voice and opens the door,* ***I will come in and eat with him****.* -Rev. 3:20, NIV

The fellowship meal promised to those who answer the door is a banquet of understanding and intimacy like no other. We must continue to stay in this teachable mode and in constant exposure to His Word if we are to understand fully. One of the Lord's most precious promises reveals that in the latter days we will understand perfectly (Jer. 23:20). Until we understand perfectly, we must hold our current understanding of prophetic passages as an open document, allowing the Lord to cut, paste, revise, and delete as He chooses.

Methods of Interpretation

There are available some helpful methods of studying the Word I have found particularly insightful. The rabbis made use of four different methods of interpretation, as explained by Dr. David H. Stern in his *Jewish New Testament Commentary*[6]:

- ♦ *P'shat* ("simple"): the plain, literal sense of the text, more or less what modern scholars mean by "grammatical-historical exegesis," which looks to the grammar of the language and the historical setting as a background for deciding what a passage means. Modern scholars often consider grammatical-historical exegesis the only valid way to deal with a text; pastors who use other approaches in their sermons usually feel defensive about it before academics. But the rabbis had three other modes of interpreting Scripture, and their validity should not be excluded in advance but related to the validity of their implied presuppositions.

- **Remez** ("hint"): wherein a word, phrase or other element in the text hints at a truth not conveyed by the p'shat. The implied presupposition is that God can hint at things of which the Bible writers themselves were unaware.
- **Drash or Midrash** ("search"): an allegorical or homiletical application of a text. This is a species of Eisegesis—reading one's own thoughts into the text—as opposed to exegesis, which is extracting from the text what it actually says. The implied presupposition is that the words of Scripture can legitimately become grist for the mill of human intellect, which God can guide to truths not directly related to the text at all.
- **Sod** ("secret"): a mystical or hidden meaning arrived at by operating on the numerical values of the Hebrew letters, noting unusual spellings, transposing letters, and the like... The implied presupposition is that God invests meaning in the minutest details of Scripture, even the individual letters.

Dr. Stern goes on to say, "The presuppositions underlying *remez, drash* and *sod* obviously express God's omnipotence, but they also express his love for humanity, in the sense that he chooses out of love to use extraordinary means for reaching people's hearts and minds. At the same time, it is easy to see how *remez, drash* and *sod* can be abused, since they all, indeed require, subjective interpretation; and this explains why scholars, who deal with the objective world, hesitate to use them."[7]

There are many examples throughout Stern's commentary indicating the authors of the New Testament used the *remez* method of interpretation by using Old Testament passages to justify the points they were making. This validates the *remez* method of interpretation if it is accomplished through prayerful consideration and the witness of the Holy Spirit. For example, Matthew quotes Hosea 11:1, 'When Israel was a child, I loved him, and out of Egypt I called my son,' to lend support that Jesus is the Son of God and intimately identified with God's son, Israel, as Israel's Messiah (see also Ex. 4:22). Hosea is plainly talking about Israel, not Jesus. But Matthew uses this *remez* as part of his 'proof' that Jesus is the Messiah who has fulfilled this prophecy (Matt. 2:13-15).

Another example is obvious from the Amplified text but not from the other English versions unless one has extensive knowledge of Greek vocabulary. Without the explanation that the Greek word translated Nazarene (*Nazoraios*) is a wordplay on the city of Nazareth and the Hebrew word *netzer* (or *netser*, which means a 'shoot,' or figuratively 'a descendant,' typically translated 'branch'), the Bible student would search in vain to find an Old Testament prophecy indicating the Messiah would be a Nazarene.

> He went and dwelt in a town called Nazareth, so that **what was spoken through the prophets might be fulfilled: He shall be called a Nazarene [Branch, Separated One].** -Matt. 2:23, AMP

Notice Matthew does not give a prophet's name, but merely states that the 'prophets,' plural, spoke of this. Jesus, the prophesied Messiah, the shoot of David, is the "Branch" prophesied by Isaiah (11:1), Jeremiah (23:5; 33:15), and Zechariah (3:8; 6:12).[8]

The Promise of Understanding

It is easy to feel dwarfed in our current understanding of the Lord, His Word, His ways, and the language He uses to express Himself. Add to this the sheer magnitude of moving forward in the task of grasping those things which we haven't yet understood, and feelings of being overwhelmed set in quickly. I am convinced a complete study of the richness and depth of the Word, with its layers of meanings and nuances, could not be completed in even a thousand lifetimes.

Yet the Lord has given very precious promises to those who persevere in their pursuit of God. Mark records that the hidden things are so only temporarily in order to be revealed at the proper time (Mark 4:22). Highlighting this same principle, Luke exhorts us to *be careful* how we listen. Remember, those who are truly listening will also be obedient to what they have heard and, as a result, receive more.

> *For there is nothing hidden that shall not be disclosed, nor anything secret that shall not be known and come out into the open.* ***Be careful therefore how you listen****. For to him who has [spiritual knowledge] will more be given; and from him who does not have [spiritual knowledge], even what he thinks and guesses and supposes that he has will be taken away.* -Luke 8:17-18, AMP

The following passage is as much about understanding revealed truth as it is about money. If we are not faithful in our use of money, we will not be entrusted with the true wealth found in God's Word. Likewise, if we are dishonest with a little of His Word, we will be dishonest with more. Despising the small portion we have been given also prevents us from receiving more. Everyone has to start somewhere.

> *He who is **faithful in a very little thing** is **faithful also in much**; and he who is unrighteous in a very little thing is unrighteous also in much. Therefore if you have **not been faithful in the use of unrighteous wealth**, **who will entrust the true riches to you**? And if you have not been faithful in the use of that which is another's, who will give you that which is your own?* -Luke 16:10-12, NASB

A parallel can be drawn here that explains some of the instances where we get stuck in our understanding of God and His Word, resulting in a stagnant and frustrated walk. Whether we have laid hold of error and refused to let go because we like the illusion (e.g., you can serve God *and* pursue money idolatrously as a primary pursuit), or we have laid hold of error and have been either too stubborn to admit we have camped out on the wrong side of the tracks, or too slothful in our search of Scripture to discern the error, the result is the same: we will not be given more. Reading the Word repeatedly with an open, teachable spirit alongside the discernment of the Holy Spirit is the best defense against this and the best offense against our flesh and the wiles of the enemy.

Notice also the Lord requires us to be faithful with that which is someone else's. This includes the teaching we have received from others that builds our spiritual foundation. All true illumination ultimately comes from the Lord, but we do well to remember and honor those who have gone before us to bring understanding for which we did not have to labor and who mentored us in our walk as believers.

Closing Thoughts

For those who are frustrated in their Bible study, let me encourage you to persevere. If God succeeded in helping someone with no natural literary talent, He can certainly help others of like ineptitude who endeavor to understand His Word and ways. All that is required are perseverance and a teachable heart, traits available to every believer abiding in the Spirit of grace. God's treasure is totally worth the time and effort we need to invest. You will be eternally blessed with both a deepening relationship with and knowledge of the God you serve.

Your word has given me life. -Ps. 119:50b, NKJV

Chapter 7

Correctly Dividing the Word

> *Be diligent to present yourself approved to God, a worker who doesn't need to be ashamed, correctly teaching ('accurately handling,' NASB) the word of truth.*
> -2 Tim. 2:15, HCSB (parenthetical added)

Every topic in the Bible requires a thorough search of the Word in order to understand with any sense of fullness the harmony of God's thought on a given subject. For example, are we the sons of God or the bride of Christ? Are we bondservants or friends? Are we free from being under the law or do we uphold the law? If all of these seem at odds with each other, might we consider that our presuppositions are at fault? The prophets were considered God's friends as well as His servants. In the infinite wisdom of God, might we not be at the same time the sons of God *and* the bride of Christ? Voluntary bondservants *and* friends? Free from being under the law *and* upholding the law in righteousness?

If we dogmatically hold one view at odds with the others, we have become like the blind sages who only understand the elephant by the part immediately within their grasp. The one grasping the tail thinks an elephant is like a rope. The one who feels the leg determines the elephant is like a tree trunk. Both are right, and yet if their idea of the elephant as a whole can only fit into their narrow, limited view, they would be dead wrong. Harmony comes when we look at the multifaceted explanation as an integrated whole, even when some descriptions initially *seem* to be diametrically opposed.

Avenues of Error

Whether we realize this or not, all of us come with assumptions and biases when we read the Word, including theologians. Wisdom dictates that in order to grasp the intended meaning of a passage, we must first understand the context in which it was given. This includes the intent of the author, the historical circumstances, the grammatical construct, and the audience to which the message is directed.

One essential consideration is to remember the Word was written primarily by people of Hebrew descent (with the possible exception of Luke) to a primarily Hebrew audience (with notable exceptions in the epistles). By virtue of this simple fact, Gentile believers are typically at a disadvantage from the start and in need of a proper lens through which to accurately interpret what is being said. Confusion and misinterpretation are understandable without attention to this preliminary consideration.

Add to this the matter of determining the type of literature used in any passage, and the permutations of possible error increase. If historical events are expressed in poetic language, we would be in error to assume that each expression used as a descriptive literary device literally happened, though this may be the case. As with most poetic literature, literary devices are used to give an emotional feel to the actual events that took place. In the case of visions and dreams, typically rife with poetic language and symbols, the actual meaning of the imagery becomes apparent only when an angel shows up to give the interpretation.

If we are to interpret correctly, we must heed Jesus' words to stop judging by appearances but rather with right judgment (John 7:24; cf. Isa. 11:3-5). Jesus chided the Pharisees and teachers of the law for improperly teaching the people, thereby leading them astray. By Jesus' teaching as well as the example of the Bereans, we are warned it is unwise to accept the teachings of others, no matter how learned, without comparing those teachings with the Word of God on our own. There is personal responsibility and accountability before God regarding those things that we believe and the convictions we hold as part of our faith.

Having said this, we do give honor to whom honor is due, but not by giving teachers carte blanche authority over our own spiritual progress and understanding of the Word. Honor is displayed by giving them our attention and respect when they have conclusions to present based on their hard work, scholarship, and perseverance. We grow in our faith as we read the Word ourselves, dialogue with others who also spend time in the Word, and read the works of those who have researched and written about topics in the Word, whether lettered by academia or not. I have yet to read a biblical study where I couldn't find some useful and edifying nugget of information, even if significant portions were contrary to the plain truth in the Word of God.

Ultimately, however, we cannot excuse ourselves before God for having turned our individual responsibility for searching and understanding the Word over to the scholars or the 'denominational position' when God has given us the Word and Holy Spirit to guide us personally into all truth. This is especially true of the English speaking peoples who have more translations of the Bible than any other language group. Leaving our understanding in the hands of the clergy causes us to miss all God desires to impart to us personally through time spent in prayer and meditation on His Word. Whether this is the result of slothfulness or of misunderstanding the gift given to us in the Holy Spirit, the result is the same. For those who have done so, there will be much regret at His coming.

Cross Pollination

Searching for truth is both a destination (Jesus, who is the Truth) and a journey that never ends (the unsearchable wisdom of God). Studying to show ourselves approved is not living in isolation with the Word, but living in the community of faith, exchanging views and thoughts, examining everything, and holding onto what is good. At times this includes contending for truth in the face of obvious error. Often our assumptions will be challenged by another's understanding, testing our allegiance as well as our discernment. Will we listen to the Word or our indoctrination? Will we follow the Holy Spirit's leading, or cling to a faulty paradigm handed down to us through the generations?

Mutual dialogue with others shouldn't bring division but grounded faith even if we don't agree on every point. Cross pollination is good for the body of Christ. Without cross pollination, most fruit trees will not bear fruit—an object lesson from nature we should heed. "Symptoms of inadequate pollination are small and misshapen apples, and slowness to ripen. The seeds can be counted to evaluate pollination. Well-pollinated apples are the best quality, and will have seven to ten seeds. Apples with fewer than three seeds will usually not mature and will drop from the trees in the early summer."[1]

> *The ax is already at the root of the trees, and every tree that does not produce good fruit will be cut down and thrown into the fire.* -Matt. 3:10, NIV

Without cross pollination, we produce little, if any fruit, and are found to possess 'leaves only,' just as the fig tree Jesus cursed to be withered (Matt. 21:19). From science, we know leaves have the function of feeding the tree, and fruit has the function of reproducing the tree as well as providing food for passersby. We learn from the fig tree that a tree with only leaves to feed itself, with no evidence of accepting cross pollination in order to bear fruit, is doomed to be judged for providing only for itself. When Jesus returns to evaluate what we have done with the good deposit He has given us, He will be looking for fruit (Matt. 16:27; Rom. 2:6-9; Rev. 2:23b).

Wolf Trees

Another object lesson comes from what are known as 'wolf trees.' A wolf tree is an unusually large tree that dominates the surrounding environment due to its size, monopolizing both the nutrients in the soil and the sunlight needed for growth. It has been suggested the term was derived from the historical view of wolves as thieves, a fitting description of a tree that robs resources from the other trees in its proximity.[2] These are older trees that "take up large amounts of space and are too twisted and gnarled to have value as lumber. Due to advanced age they grow very slowly, robbing smaller trees of sunlight and nutrients, and underutilizing the sunlight that they do absorb."[3]

Not only does the wolf tree produce nothing of value, it prevents the plants around it from being fruitful as well. The parallel seems fairly obvious. Older, unpruned trees that have ceased to bear fruit but cling to what God did last season, intimidating or manipulating others into this same mode, rob those in its shadow of today's life-giving nutrients and sunlight. This stunts the growth of every plant around it. The parable of the barren fig tree illustrates what happens to the fruitless (Luke 13:6-9). When the owner who planted the tree came to look for fruit and saw none, he ordered it to be cut down:

> *Cut it down! Why should it continue also to use up the ground [to deplete the soil, intercept the sun, and take up room]?* -Luke 13:7b, AMP

The vinedresser pleads on behalf of the useless tree, asking for time to 'cultivate' the ground around the tree to give the tree every opportunity to bear fruit (vv. 8-9). But if cultivating and fertilizing still do not produce fruit, the tree will be cut down. Whatever the case in a believer's life—lack of pollination or the existence of a wolf tree robbing those around it of light and nutrients—growth becomes stunted and fruit production is halted. Those who bear no fruit are in danger of being cut down and thrown in the fire.

Faulty Presuppositions and Disputable Matters

Another trap we can fall into unawares occurs when we take what we consider a 'given' and read into the Word something God never intended. For example, when God gave the Ten Commandments, He began by reminding the Israelites, 'I am the LORD your God (*elohim*), who brought you out of the land of Egypt' (Ex. 20:2). After this, Moses went into the thick darkness on the mountain to receive the rest of the law while the people remained in the camp below. While he was on the mountain, Aaron fashioned a calf and stated, "This is thy god (*elohim*), Israel, who has brought thee up out of the land of Egypt...Tomorrow shall be a feast to the LORD" (Ex. 32:4-5, DARBY).

In most translations, the word *elohim* is translated 'God' in the first passage, but 'gods' in the second. The two statements closely resemble each other, but the second was defiled by the Israelites' concept of who or what *elohim* represented. In other words, the people fashioned God in the image they understood, letting their own ideas or cultural familiarity from their time in Egypt influence their understanding. They were under the mistaken belief they were having a celebration to their *elohim* through their idolatrous act. In their minds, they were picturing the male calf as the unseen *elohim* who rescued them from Egypt. This had disastrous results. Their theology had corrupted their actions and turned them aside from the one true God. We must examine our own religious practices and mindsets to make certain they line up with God's Word, lest we succumb to this same error in our doctrine and religious ceremonial customs.

In the case of what Paul called disputable matters, those who are the most offended by the views and practice of others often have not searched out the matters for themselves or have only searched out one side of a matter. Patience and perseverance are the keys—patience with people, perseverance in the Word. These are the hallmarks of a bondservant. A bondservant will not castigate or ridicule those with different views as the Pharisees treated Jesus and Paul treated the believers prior to his Damascus road experience. Gentle instruction from the Word and patience are called for in most cases.

There are many scholarly works and commentaries that can help us grasp the truths in the Word. Those who have discovered and use these books love them and are deeply grateful to the authors who poured out their lives so we could have better understanding. Truly, we stand on the shoulders of giants. These are invaluable tools as long as we remember they are *tools* and do not have the same weight and reliability as Scripture.

Come up Higher

One drawback of these tools is that scholars often use theological terms and jargon with which the average Christian is not familiar. Jesus spoke in simple terms to portray deep truths—truths with more than one layer of meaning. At times we can be so caught up with the scholarly approach it can become a hindrance to hearing what the Spirit is saying to the servants of God to prepare them for what lies ahead. We are reminded to 'let the Word interpret the Word.' Our reliance on these wonderful tools of biblical scholarship cannot take the place of relationship and personal meditation on the Word.

There comes a time in our walk when the Lord desires to build on the foundation laid by sound biblical teaching received from mentors, teachers, and books. At these times, He calls us to 'come up higher' to a place of trusting the Word and the Spirit to guide us into all truth. It is God Himself who reveals understanding of His Word (Matt. 11:25-26), and He often chooses those who are nothing in the sight of men (1 Cor. 1:26-27).

The Holy Spirit really is a good teacher. While I am a firm believer in the corporate gathering, sound biblical teaching, and fellowship of the community of believers, I also know we are personally accountable for searching the Scriptures on our own to verify what we have been taught. Human sagacity will not give us the proper meaning of God's Word (1 Cor. 2:13). We must be like the Bereans:

> *Now the Berean Jews were of **more noble character** than the Thessalonians, for they received the message **with great eagerness** and **examined the Scriptures every day** to see if what Paul said was true.* -Acts 17:11, NIV

The Bereans were noted to be of a more noble character than the Thessalonians because they were eager to receive the message of the new covenant *and* searched the Scriptures daily to verify that Paul's teaching was accurate. Note the Bereans were *Jews* (see also v. 10) who received the message eagerly, and the Scriptures they searched could only have been the *Old Testament*. When verifying biblical teaching, the Word reminds us to validate by two or three witnesses (2 Cor. 13:1). Applying this to spiritual truth, we look for two or three 'witnesses' (passages) to verify our interpretation, though this is not always easily accomplished. Often we will find other passages that seem to teach something in opposition to the principle we want to verify. This is how we wrestle with the Word to understand with any sense of fullness the intent of God's thoughts on a particular subject.

The Lord gets hold of each one of us in our private study to show us the hidden treasure in His Word if we will only take the time to drink deeply. The first century church had none of the commentaries on which we have grown to rely so heavily—they didn't even have a New Testament (in its present form). Yet they grew in their knowledge and understanding of the Word by searching the (Old Testament) Scriptures daily.

Their task was a little different than ours because their Latin and Greek texts were translated from the original Hebrew and Aramaic. Our texts are translations, paraphrases, and transliterations of their primarily Latin and Greek texts, accomplished by scholars who gave valiant but admittedly imperfect efforts to preserve the original words and meanings for people of different languages, idioms, and structures of speech. Remember, it is the original Word given in the original languages that is accepted as infallible and inerrant, not our interpretations or translations. Because of this, making use of study aids (a concordance with Hebrew and Greek word studies, a Bible dictionary or encyclopedia, Hebrew and Greek interlinear Bibles, etc., most of which are available free online) is of great benefit.

By constant exposure to and study of the Word, we wash our minds of wrong assumptions and presuppositions that hinder us from understanding and entering into the mind of Christ, the heart of the Father, and the fellowship of the Holy Spirit. This can seem overwhelming for many of us. Our minds have been polluted by our culture, education, and fallen condition. As a result, we can become easily and quickly frustrated when trying to understand the Word at first glance. Add to this mix generations of religious tradition and dogma which shaped our minds as children, and we have a barrier sufficient to prevent us from grasping truth. Unless we become as teachable children before the Lord, willing to forego our positions in order to deepen our relationship with God in spirit and in truth, we will miss what He desires to impart.

Spiritual Growth

The example I have given my children to help them persevere in Bible Study is that of a six month old child learning to eat solid food. The baby has no idea what he is eating, and doesn't even eat very well—half of it is never even swallowed in the initial stages. But the infant continues to grow physically even though he hasn't got a clue as to what is being eaten, much less the physical process taking place that causes growth.

It is the same with our spiritual nature. When we first undertake to read the Word, we understand very little of it and most often only the obvious surface concepts. Some of it is just plain hard to swallow and falls to the wayside. But regardless of whether or not we are aware, our spiritual nature is being fed and grows in the knowledge of God, and our mind is renewed by encountering the truth. Jesus gave Himself for us and washes us by the 'cleansing of His Word' (Eph. 5:25-27). This is the way in which His Bride is made spotless and holy.

The sudden realization that wrestling with the Word of God is like learning Karate helped me to understand the process more clearly. When I first began to learn Karate, we focused on the basics for weeks. In some of the classes, we were required to create 'one-steps' to demonstrate a defensive skill using a combination of techniques. I found this very difficult and frustrating initially because of my limited knowledge of even the basic techniques. As I acquired new skills, however, it became easier to devise a sequence of techniques that went beyond the basic block, kick, and punch.

Understanding the Word of God is like this. The Lord has promised He will be found by those who *diligently* seek Him (Pr. 8:17). Time spent in the Word may initially seem like a loss of productivity, but if we stick with it, we will reap a bountiful harvest in righteousness, spiritual knowledge, and an ever-deepening, intimate relationship with our Lord. These are rare and priceless commodities today, the means by which we stand in future adversity, and the determining factors of our position in the age to come.

> [W]ithout faith it is impossible to please and be satisfactory to Him. For whoever would come near to God must [necessarily] believe that God exists and that **He is the rewarder of those who earnestly and diligently seek Him** [out]. -Heb. 11:6, AMP

The Wise Man Built His House upon the Rock

Knowing nuggets of God's truth, plucked out of the Word without seeing the Word as an integrated whole, can be compared to taking the solid foundation of God's Word (the Rock) and breaking it into *bits* of truth. These little pieces become sand if we do not consider all God has to say on a particular topic, or if we only pick the pieces we like. For example, if we take Jesus' words about prayer that we can ask for anything we want and, as long as we believe, we will have what we ask for (Matt. 21:22), we ignore the rest of Scripture which moderates unsanctified use of this verse.

Under the inspiration of the Holy Spirit, James expounded on Jesus' statement, explaining we cannot ask with wrong motives and expect to receive (James 4:3). John wrote that our confidence in prayer before the Lord comes from asking for what is in agreement with God's will (1 John 5:14). If we do not consider the whole counsel of God on any particular subject, we may find ourselves standing on an unstable foundation that consists of only partial truth. It is the *sum* of God's Word (Ps. 119:160) that gives us truth and a solid foundation.

Jesus made it clear we are to build our spiritual house upon the Rock—the entirety of God's Word. Without examining the context in which a verse is situated, the intended meaning can be greatly altered. Standing on a piece of rock broken off and isolated from the whole may, at the very least, cause us to lose our balance. We must guard ourselves against this tendency. As a crude example, consider the following verse read out of context. Using this as a basis for doctrinal belief would be devastating to a good percentage of the body of Christ:

> *Behold, I, Paul, say to you, that if ye are circumcised, Christ shall profit you nothing.* -Gal. 5:2, DARBY

If taken literally as a standalone truth, anyone who has been circumcised is out of luck—it's right there in black and white. Using this verse as an isolated principle, one could argue any male who has been circumcised has no hope of being saved because Christ will be of no benefit to him. But we know this is not true. It would be considered a preposterous conclusion and an abuse of the text based on our knowledge of the point Paul is making in the entire passage. Paul was speaking of reliance on circumcision, here equated with the law, to save. We need to examine ourselves on the more subtle points in the Word to see if we have done this with other verses, especially if those verses are difficult to reconcile with other seemingly 'contradictory' passages and examples in the Bible.

Chapter and Verse

Before we begin, remember the original Scriptures as written by the authors contained no chapter or verse markings. When quoting the Old Testament, New Testament writers only referred to the prophet's name and in some cases not even that. This is very encouraging for a concept person who is not a memorizer by nature. This is my favorite: the author of Hebrews quotes Psalm 8:4-6, starting with '...it is testified somewhere...' (Heb. 2:6). He also quotes Genesis 2:2, and says similarly, 'He has said somewhere...' (Heb. 4:4). This should be of *great* encouragement to anyone like me who cannot always remember the exact location of a particular passage, or even the exact words.

The Hebrew Tanakh (Old Testament) incorporated a multilevel system for dividing the text into sections, paragraphs, and phrases through special 'cantillation' markings. Their usefulness is immediately apparent. These divisions remain essentially unchanged today in the English translations through the labor of Rabbi Isaac Nathan (c. A.D. 1440), with the exception of a few isolated divergences.

The New Testament divisions, however, came in stages and were not completed until later. Stephen Langton, Archbishop of Canterbury (A.D. 1228), is the individual most often credited with the chapter divisions. Dividing those chapters into verses required extensive knowledge of the Greek dialect (*Koine*) used during the Roman Empire. The structure of *Koine* Greek causes the intent, relation, emphasis, and the forcefulness of the words to be easily corrupted by imprecise divisions. Because of this, most theologians were strongly opposed to further division of the New Testament into verses.

Robert Estienne (also referred to as Robert Stephens by eighteenth and nineteenth century English writers) was undaunted by these objections, and the numbering of New Testament verses he developed in 1551 is still used today. He is credited with having an exceptional grasp of the finer points of the ancient Greek language as well as knowledge of the Scriptures. After the Geneva Bible was printed in 1560 with both chapter and verse numberings in both Old and New Testaments, the system became accepted as the standard way to notate passage references.

Despite his skill in *Koine* Greek, Estienne's divisions have met with no small criticism because they often break the text into fragments and divisions seen even in the middle of a sentence. This division of the Scriptures was motivated by and implemented primarily for practical purposes with regard to reference and efficacy, and as such there are notable instances in which the train of thought caused by a division into verses and chapters is obscured, or worse. When we conduct our Bible study by reading a chapter a day, the continuity of what is being taught can be lost in some cases. This is why reading a verse in context is especially important. Once again, the Lord anticipates this potential source for introducing error and/or confusion. He reminds us we will find truth as we study the entirety of His Word:

The sum of Your word is truth. -Ps. 119:160a, NASB

Handling the Word of God properly is our priority, and the Lord's admonishment to search the whole of Scripture accompanied by the wisdom to take each 'verse' in context (checking the flow of thought before and after the verse being studied) will enable us to more fully understand the truth intended. Despite their disadvantages, the advantages of these verse notations outweigh their deficiencies.[4]

The Translators

The translators who have devoted their lives to getting the Word into the hands of the people are among my favorite heroes. Wycliffe Bible Translators have a very worthy goal, *Vision 2025*. "In 1999, translation projects started at a pace of about one every 18 days. At that rate it would have taken until 2150 before the last translation project was even begun. Wycliffe leaders challenged the Body of Christ to accelerate the pace. *Vision 2025* was born. The goal? To see a Bible translation program in progress in every language still needing one by the year 2025. The ultimate goal—God's Word accessible to all people, so that everyone has an opportunity to have an intimate and life changing relationship with Jesus Christ."[5]

These translators and those who went before them worked diligently to give us the Bible in words the common people could understand. But with few exceptions, languages are not simply a matter of *vocabulary*, i.e., word-for-word substitutions. The structure of a language and the way in which thoughts are conveyed are uniquely different and often incongruent from one language to another (sentence structure, verb tenses, use of masculine or feminine designations, etc.). Anyone who has studied another language has experienced this. The only presupposition one can make is that each language is uniquely idiomatic. Add to this the fact that the idioms of the culture at the time the work was written may be different than they are today, and we quickly realize we have a multifaceted and challenging project on our hands. Math is easier; remember I told you ahead of time.

A translation is a herculean effort by gifted and highly trained people doing their level best to stay true to the Word of God. The limitations, however, should be fairly obvious. Though checks and balances are put into rendering the translations by having several scholars work on them together, this safeguard does not preclude the occurrence of using one word or phrase where another may have been more suitable for the spiritual connotation intended. This is where study aids help us to capture the richness, depth, and congruency of Scripture.

The translators of the 1611 King James Bible understood this. In the preface to this translation, their heart for unity, understanding of the need for the Holy Spirit to interpret the Word, and lack of conceit regarding the work they offered to the English-speaking peoples in their translation of the Bible is remarkable. The spirit of humility and the fear of the Lord in which this version was written and offered, giving recognition to the limitations of the human translators, provides an example to us all. Those who have taken it upon themselves to personally wage war against all other versions, viewing the KJV as the only truly authorized version, would be at odds with those who brought it forth.

While later versions of the KJV dismissed the margin notes, the 1611 KJV translators were careful to include these alternate readings in case they had missed the mark in their choice of words. This portion of the translators' preface to the reader from the 1611 edition is worth reading (emphasis added):

> Some peradventure would have no varietie of sences to be set in the margine, lest the authoritie of the Scriptures for deciding of controversies by that shew of uncertaintie, should somewhat be shaken. But we hold their judgment not to be so sound in this point... **partly also to stirre up our devotion to crave the assistance of Gods spirit by prayer, and lastly, that we might be forward to seeke ayd of our brethren by conference**, and never scorne those that be not in all respects so complete as they should bee, being to seeke in many things our selves, it hath pleased God in his divine providence, heere and there to scatter wordes and sentences of that difficultie and doubtfulnesse, not in doctrinall points that concerne salvation, (for in such it hath beene vouched that the Scriptures are plaine) but in matters of lesse moment, that fearefulnesse would better beseeme us then confidence, and if we will resolve, to resolve upon modestie with *S. Augustine*... **it is better to make doubt of those things which are secret, then to strive about those things that are uncertaine**. There be many words in the Scriptures, which be never found there but once, (having neither brother nor neighbour, as the *Hebrewes* speake) so that we cannot be holpen by conference of places... **doth not a margine do well to admonish the Reader to seeke further, and not to conclude or dogmatize upon this or that peremptorily**? For as it is a fault of incredulitie, to doubt of those things that are evident: so to determine of such things as the Spirit of God hath left (even in the judgment of the judicious) questionable, can be no lesse then presumption. Therfore as *S. Augustine* saith, that **varietie of Translations is profitable for the finding out of**

the sense of the Scriptures: *so diversitie of signification and sense in the margine, where the text is not so cleare, must needes doe good, yea is necessary, as we are perswaded...* ***They that are wise, had rather have their judgements at libertie in differences of readings, then to be captivated to one, when it may be the other.***

In our effort to be accurate, our goal is to be approved by God and not men. In addition to the primary necessity of a relationship with God through Jesus, this requires diligence, perseverance, time, and prayer. Even the most diligent come to realize this goal cannot be accomplished in a few months—it takes years to make any significant headway. Like anyone who starts out in a technical profession, thinking pridefully they know a great deal about the work in which they are engaged, the realization of how little they actually know in comparison with what there is to know will not grip them until later. Staying teachable and moving in a spirit of humility will guard us from error or formulating doctrine on issues that are less defined than we suppose.

Correctly Dividing the Word

Knowing God as our Father, Savior, and Guide is the only prerequisite for proceeding into the life of the bondservant. This is absolutely the most important step since everything else flows out of this relationship. Once we receive the free gift of justification and the Holy Spirit, the way for getting to know God has been established. The journey of getting to know the Lord is accomplished through prayerful reading, study, and obedience to the Word, and accompanied by cooperation with the Holy Spirit's guidance.

Jesus prefaced Revelation by saying the contents are for the *bondservants* of Christ: those who willingly give up their personal desires and will for His, who follow His commands out of love and in the fear of the Lord, and who long for His appearing. It is not for the casual or social Christian, the merely curious person, or the solely scholarly individual to understand. It is for the *bondservants* of Jesus Christ without any further qualification as to intellectual endowment, scholastic achievement, natural aptitude, ambition, or any other manmade measurement of competence or qualification. The Lord will meet each one of us without regard to or in spite of ability.

Casual or even scholarly reading of this book will not lead the student to the correct conclusions (Matt. 22:28-29; John 3:10; 8:43; Acts 13:27; 1 Cor. 1:19). Our heart posture before the Lord as we delve into His book will determine what we receive from Him in true understanding. To use the Bible as a means to make a name for ourselves will have disastrous results for our spiritual well-being. Paul warned Timothy that some will come up with doctrine on their own in order to be seen as teachers, wanting to have a reputation as experts on religious issues, confidently speaking without actually having any real understanding of the Word (1 Tim. 1:5-8). These have swerved from 'love that is uncontaminated by self-interest and counterfeit faith, a life open to God' (1 Tim. 1:5, THE MESSAGE), bringing them to a place of error.

Paul labeled those who contradict the gospel of Jesus as 'arrogant and ignorant' (see 1 Tim. 6:3-5). These people thrive on debates, causing arguments that result in jealousy, division, slander, and 'evil suspicion.' They are not as interested in truth as they are in acquiring followers and profiting from the doctrine they peddle. Those who pass themselves off as teachers in this fashion will not receive true understanding of God's Word but only whatever principles they can conceive by the wisdom and reasoning of man.

The Lord does not divulge the hidden treasures in the Word to anyone who passes by (Matt. 13:13-14). Even those to whom He desires to impart these truths have difficulty grasping them, as evidenced by the many times the Word records that Jesus' disciples did not understand (Matt. 15:16; 16:11; Mark 4:13; 8:16-18; 9:32; Luke 2:49-50; 18:33-34; John 12:16; 20:8-9). But the Word also records that He does not give up on us, for He desires that those whose hearts are loyal to Him should understand these things in the timing and purposes of God (see also Amos 3:7). The secret of the Lord comes to those who fear Him; to these God reveals His covenant (Ps. 25:14).

> ***He reveals the deep and secret things***; *He knows what is in the darkness, and the light dwells with Him!* -Dan. 2:22, AMP

This explains why the Lord spoke so often in parables and with symbolic language. The underlying meaning will be made plain only to those who are truly His and who persevere in getting to know Him (see Mark 4:10-11). The gift of the Holy Spirit opens the door to understanding spiritual matters as we abide in Christ.

> *Jesus answered him, "What I am doing* ***you do not understand now, but afterward you will understand."*** -John 13:7, ESV

Even for Jesus' followers, understanding didn't (and still doesn't) come instantly. The disciples left their jobs and followed Jesus for an intense discipleship course. Paradigms had to be radically changed. The conventional understanding of God and practice of that knowledge had strayed from center. It took on the form of what men could understand (what *made sense* to them) and what fueled man's pride, namely legalistic practices and the recognition one gets from appearing spiritually dedicated.

Make Time to Understand

Jesus' followers must also take the time to 'turn aside' to understand, just as Moses turned from his daily routine to investigate the burning bush (Ex. 3:1-4). Having led the flock out to Mt. Horeb, Moses then turned to the burning bush:

> *Then Moses said, "****I will now turn aside*** *and see this great sight, why the bush does not burn."* ***So when the LORD saw that he turned aside to look****, God called to him from the midst of the bush.* -Ex. 3:3-4a, NKJV

In the midst of his daily routine, Moses allowed himself to be interrupted at the beckoning of God. Only after the Lord saw that Moses took interest did He call to him. When we continually give reading the Word and time set aside for God the least priority in our busy schedules, we miss the spiritual growth we desperately need as well as the revelation God desires to impart to us.

The *foremost* preoccupation of the heart must be the Lord and the establishment of His kingdom. This does not come easily in a society that praises constant activity and fills our minds with many distractions, hoping to steal our affection through as many different venues as are tempting to the human heart. In the *Sound of Music*, Captain Von Trapp stated with pain, "Activity suggests a life filled with purpose."

Many people keep busy to feel good about themselves and their lives. But when the activity has ceased and we are alone to face the void in our soul, an ache for *true* purpose and meaning emerges. For others, the true pain of a life without God is felt. When a person is antagonistic toward or bewildered by God due to their mistaken understanding of God, the pain will many times be disguised as seething anger, hatred, depression, self-condemnation, confusion, or apathy rooted in despair.

The bondservant lifestyle must be built on the foundation Jesus taught. Captured at the heart level, a bondservant's preoccupation is doing the will of God (Eph. 6:6; 1 Pet. 2:16). Not man-pleasers (Gal. 1:10) or quarrelsome, they are kind to all, able to teach, patient when wronged, and gentle when correcting those in error (2 Tim. 2:22-26). They continually labor in prayer for the edification and purification of the church (Col. 4:12). Does this sound impossible? To live it out with sinless perfection would be, but the Spirit gives us grace, empowering us to enter into this lifestyle. In addition, the mercy extended to us by the blood of Jesus keeps us in right standing with God. With all wrongs erased and self-accomplishment nullified in the sight of God, our lives become pretty condensed.

Jesus spoke during His earthly ministry in parables to those 'without,' thus veiling the true meaning so they would not understand. On the other hand, He explained in plain language the meaning of the parables to His own surrendered but imperfect followers (Matt. 13:13-17; Mark 4:10-12). Likewise, the book of Revelation and other prophetic passages in the Word are written so that those 'without' cannot understand them. Jesus will explain these things in plain language at the appointed time to His true followers who keep His Father's commandments and possess the Holy Spirit (John 16:13; Acts 5:32). It is not given to all to understand (Dan. 12:10).

> *The fear of the LORD is the beginning of wisdom;* **all who follow his precepts have good understanding.** *To him belongs eternal praise.* -Ps. 111:10, NIV
>
> *He changes the times and the seasons...* **He gives wisdom to the wise and knowledge to those who have understanding!** -Dan. 2:21, AMP

None of the Wicked Will Understand

With all the cataclysmic events and the insidious matters of intrigue shrouding the days before the second coming of Christ, it would behoove us to understand these matters and prepare our minds and hearts as much as possible beforehand. The Word clearly establishes that we will understand perfectly as the day approaches. It is equally clear that those who have not dedicated their hearts in love and loyalty to God will not understand. The hearts of those who are wicked in God's sight will melt with fear and their minds overcome by utter confusion when the judgments of God are seen in the earth.

> *None of the wicked will understand, but those who are wise will understand.*
> -Dan. 12:10, NIV

Without the fear of the Lord, we will never acquire wisdom. If our hearts are filled with pride in our intellect, extensive education, powers of reason, knowledge, accomplishment, or any other vain thing, we will walk in darkness. God views pride in these traits as wickedness. Be careful how you read this. It is the *pride* that is wicked, not the traits themselves. God desires to use the intellect and gifts of those so endowed for His glory and purposes, not their own.

Solomon wrote the Proverbs so people would know godly wisdom and instruction, gain discernment, and live righteously (Pr. 1:1-4). These traits can only be obtained by the Spirit of truth through the washing of the Word in the fear of the Lord. He further stated it is the wise who hear and gain understanding (Pr. 1:5-7). Those with understanding are the ones who acquire skill and sound counsel. The purpose for wisdom is so people can understand 'figures of speech, enigmas, riddles, and dark sayings.' But how do we become wise in the first place so we also receive understanding?

> *The fear of the LORD is the beginning of wisdom, and the knowledge of the Holy One is understanding.* -Pr. 9:10, HCSB

All wisdom and understanding are tied to the reverential fear and knowledge of God. James reminds the bondservant that good works are the goal of all the understanding the Lord deposits in our mind and heart. The traits of the wicked, conversely, lead not to wisdom but to 'disorder and every evil practice' (James 3:13-16). Without the proper fear of the Lord, we remain in the dark.

Understanding Comes Through Relationship

We must approach God based on relationship, advance through prayer, and come as teachable children. To approach Him casually or presumptuously with a once-a-week 'faith' will most likely end up in frustration, anger, confusion, indifference, or disappointment. Unless we become as little children, teachable and trusting, we will not enter the kingdom of heaven (Matt. 18:3). Those who, like the disciples, have been given spiritual knowledge of the secrets of the kingdom will be given more so that they will have abundance. Those who rely on their own wisdom and knowledge will find what little they thought they had will be taken from them (Matt. 13:10-12). Paul prayed for the believers to be filled with the knowledge of God so their walk would be worthy of the Lord (Col. 1:9-10).

While it would be easier and more convenient if the Lord would speak plainly, the wisdom behind the use of parables and layers of meaning in the Word is to restrain the acquisition of knowledge devoid of relationship. Understanding the Word is reserved for those who diligently seek to know God and lay all their natural abilities and pride at His feet so they can be taught by His Spirit. These show by their lifestyle, use of time, and heart posture that they are truly His.

This last requirement sounds simple enough, but for this to be accomplished *in truth* and not mere confession of a desire for this to be so takes years of sitting at the Lord's feet and cooperating with the Holy Spirit. This is how we are conformed to Christ, who is the Word. It is an impossible, not just improbable, task to understand the Word of God without having the mind of Christ. His Word is living because *He* is living. Gaining the mind of Christ comes through study of the Word with the Holy Spirit sanctifying us in the process. Our part is to study and cooperate. If we set aside time, He will help us let go of the world and its ways. If we focus on Him and His kingdom, He will help us let go of our focus on ourselves and building our kingdoms. If we earnestly desire His presence and wisdom, He will remove our fear of man and teach us the fear of the Lord. Even the desire to do this is birthed in believers by God. Our part is to cooperate with Him and determine to have this desire fulfilled. Paul told Timothy to fan his gifting into a flame. Each one of us must fan into flame this desire to know Him by pursuing the knowledge of the Holy One through stewardship of our time, affections, and resources.

Principles of Interpretation

There are some hermeneutical principles (guidelines of interpretation) theologians have devised to help us understand the Word properly. These have their place, as certain destructive heresies resulted from rampant allegorization of the Word early in church history. To hold heresy at bay, careful examination and interpretation of the Word was developed through a method called 'exegesis.' *Exegesis* is the process by which we *draw out* of the Word the plain meaning in the passage we are studying—explaining or commenting on what it says through critical interpretation. This critical interpretation involves taking into consideration primarily the literal historical context alongside the grammatical framework.[6]

Eisegesis, on the other hand, is the interpretation of a passage by *reading into* it our own ideas.[7] While exegesis is the only method acceptable in certain circles, eisegesis is utilized as a tool of application by many ministers to help believers see the utility of a passage for their own lives. While this involves a certain degree of subjectivity, insight can be gained that will be of benefit to those who hear. If we are perfectly honest about these two methods of interpretation, many scholars and theologians mix the two at times without realizing they are doing it, however subtly, because every single one of us have personal, covert, and subconscious grids through which we filter information.

Another principle some Bible teachers emphasize is 'when interpreting the Word, the text should be interpreted literally unless the text specifically *states* the imagery is symbolic or if it is *obviously* symbolic.' Problems can arise when what is obvious to one may not be obvious to another. For example, Revelation 6:13 prophesies the 'stars of heaven will fall to the earth.' Stars are large thermonuclear reactors. Even the smallest neutron stars, only ten miles in diameter, carry as much mass as the sun. Without this knowledge, some have actually interpreted this passage literally, envisioning stars impacting the earth in a horrendous cataclysmic event. After all, from our perspective stars are just little twinkling lights in the sky. But if just one star even came *close* to the earth, we would all perish and the earth with us.

An additional example can be seen in the passage where Jesus pronounced the woes on the hypocritical Pharisees, accusing them of straining out a gnat but swallowing a camel (Matt. 23:24). We've heard some interesting interpretations on this verse, but the bottom line reveals that Jesus was trying to urge the Pharisees to see how contradictory their teaching and ways really were. They strained itty bitty bugs like gnats out of their drinks so they would stay true to Levitical laws regarding clean and unclean food, yet they 'swallowed whole camels,' the largest unclean land animal in their region of the world. Were these Pharisees literally eating camel, as the Arabs did? This is doubtful. Jesus likely switched from discussing literal behaviors (straining the gnats) to go on to metaphorically describe the uncleanness that enters them because of their teaching, ways, and the preoccupation of their hearts—uncleanness of the magnitude of a camel.

Spiritual Discernment Is Required

When we purpose to keep our minds on literal fulfillment of the imagery in a vision (please note what is being referred to here are prophetic visions as well as parabolic messages with hidden meanings, *not* the historical events recorded in the Bible), we risk the rebuke the disciples received because they maintained a literal mode when Jesus was speaking figuratively:

> **"How is it you don't understand that I was not talking to you about bread?** But be on your guard against the yeast of the Pharisees and Sadducees." Then they understood that he was… telling them to guard against… the teaching of the Pharisees and Sadducees. -Matt. 16:11-12, NIV

Consider also there are numerous examples in prophetic or visionary passages where the Lord *combines* literal and symbolic imagery. One obvious example is the vision given to Nebuchadnezzar, warning him of the impending consequences for his pride (see Dan. 4:4-18 for the recounting of Nebuchadnezzar's dream). After hearing the dream, Daniel stated the following components of the dream (Dan. 4:23):

- cut down the tree and destroy it
- leave the stump bound with iron and bronze; its roots will remain in the ground
- the stump will be in the grass of the field
- he will be drenched with dew
- he will live like a wild animal for seven years

Daniel then interprets the dream (Dan. 4:24-26):

- Nebuchadnezzar will be driven from people and live like a wild animal
- the command to leave the stump with its roots meant his kingdom would be restored afterwards
- he will eat grass like cattle
- he will be drenched with dew
- this will last seven years until he acknowledges God's sovereignty

The vision starts out with symbolic language: the tree represents Nebuchadnezzar (see v. 22) and the stump bound with iron and bronze are representative of the symbolic shackles placed on him. Note that he was not literally destroyed, and a stump was not literally bound with shackles. Now the vision goes into literal mode. He literally ends up in a field of grass being drenched by dew for seven years, living with and acting like the animals. The interpretation returns to symbolic language, indicating that the stump with its roots represents the return of his kingdom after Nebuchadnezzar acknowledges God. This is the record of what actually happened to Nebuchadnezzar (i.e., an historical event):

> *He was driven away from people and ate grass like cattle. His body was drenched with the dew of heaven until his hair grew like the feathers of an eagle and his nails like the claws of a bird. At the end of that time... my sanity was restored.* -Dan. 4:33b-34a, NIV

Despite the use of metaphors to describe his appearance, the event was literal. Nebuchadnezzar turns from his pride and gives praise to God, similar to the turning of the King of Nineveh who heeded the warning through Jonah. These are wonderful examples of the grace of God, encouraging us to remember we cannot judge by outward appearances who will turn to God and who won't. Afterwards, Nebuchadnezzar offered a spontaneous profession of praise to God, demonstrating he not only understood Who was in charge, but also that God will humble all who walk in pride (Dan. 4:34-37).

Because we are dealing with the Word of God, which is living and flowing like a river, never stagnant but ever changing directions in expression, we must take our ignorance seriously enough to realize we are unable to judge whether prophetic passages are to be taken literally and/or symbolically without the aid of the Holy Spirit. Manmade principles of interpretation make it easier for us to understand and 'uniformly' decode the Word as well as erect a safety barrier we hope will keep us from error. But no matter how many hermeneutical principles we employ in our attempts to fit God's Word into a box, in the end we will miss the mark without the Holy Spirit.

Words with Contrasting Uses

Many of us have heard principles made from one verse that are clearly in contrast with other verses. For example, Paul talks about how the physical came first (Adam), and the spiritual last (Jesus) (see 1 Cor. 15:46). But we also know that the earthly tabernacle (physical) was a copy of the heavenly pattern (spiritual) (Heb. 8:5). In this example, the spiritual came first. Even Jesus taught us to pray that the will of God would be done on earth as it *already* has been done in heaven. The context of the passage should always be considered first—we should not be so quick to make spiritual principles out of one or two verses without consulting the whole of Scripture, no matter how correct it may seem to us when we first see and consider the proposed principle in the Word.

Another practice to avoid is labeling symbolic images as either bad or good. Jesus is described as the Lion of Judah, but Satan is described as a lion as well, seeking who he may devour. We build our house upon the rock, but those who have rock-like hearts will have no root for the Word they receive. Leaven is most often used to represent sin, but Jesus used this symbol to also represent how the kingdom of God quickly permeates whatever it touches. White hair is the glory of the aged, but it is also a sign of contagious skin disease. Wind is a description of the Holy Spirit, but it is also a description of people who are void of the true counsel of God and give birth only to wind. Who knows the mind of God except the Spirit of God?

Dream Interpretation

When interpreting visions or dreams, the use of scripturally-based dream handbooks with suggestions on how to interpret the imagery can be helpful, but they cannot be used mechanically to give an accurate interpretation. For example, take a look at the baker's dream as told to Joseph:

> *When the chief baker saw that the interpretation was good, he said to Joseph, "I also was in my dream, and there were three white baskets on my head. In the uppermost basket were all kinds of baked goods for Pharaoh, and the birds ate them out of the basket on my head."* -Gen. 40:16-17, NKJV

Using contemporary dream interpretation methods, the mechanical interpretation might draw on various prescribed definitions for the imagery. The baskets were on the bakers' *head*, meaning he was crowned or anointed for this task. The *white bread* (NASB) symbolizes the pure word of God, and the number *three* symbolizes obedience or divine perfection. *White baskets* symbolize purity or innocence of the vessel bearing the word. The uppermost basket had *goods for Pharaoh*, indicating the baker will have audience with the ruler to share this 'bread.' The *birds* signify the unsaved who will also feed on the manna he has been given. The summary would sound something like this: 'The Lord will anoint you and give grace to speak forth a pure Word from His heart. He will send you before Pharaoh to proclaim this word, and your innocence will be apparent. Your testimony will be given to the many unsaved who hear and partake of its goodness. Go forth, brother, in the power and anointing of the Lord!'

The real meaning, however, was far from this:

> *"This is what it means," Joseph said. "The three baskets are three days. Within three days Pharaoh will lift off your head and hang you on a tree. And the birds will eat away your flesh."* -Gen. 40:18-19, NIV

Notice each of the details given in the dream did not necessarily have a specific counterpart in the interpretation. To God belong the mysteries and to Him alone we must always look for the interpretation (Dan. 2:27-28). While hermeneutical principles keep us from obvious heresy on doctrinal issues and from allegorizing the historical events in the Word, they are no substitute for waiting on the Lord to reveal in His timing the prophetic meaning of the visions, mysteries, secrets, and sealed things in the Word.

Mixture of Truth and Error: We Know in Part

Hermeneutical principles allow us to interpret passages so we can gain some understanding *now*, but keep in mind that understanding obtained this way may not always be entirely accurate or free from mixture. Mixture is something with which we need to earnestly, soberly, and zealously concern ourselves, especially as it pertains to the Word. It is no coincidence Pentecost was chosen as the day of the birth of the new covenant as described by Jeremiah (Jer. 31:31-34) through the sending and receiving of the Holy Spirit. In Leviticus 23:15-21, we observe that Pentecost is the only feast where leaven is used. Other commands regarding sacrifices and feasts establish they are to be celebrated with *no* leaven whatsoever. This leads us to wonder, 'Why?'

Our understanding comes from parallels we can draw from the Word and is primarily two-fold. One interpretation comes from Jesus' teaching that the leaven is a 'type' or symbol of the quickly advancing kingdom of God. The two loaves in this scenario would represent Jewish and Gentile believers in Jesus. Hence, we have a picture of the rapidly advancing kingdom of God through both the Jews and Gentiles.

On the other hand, the more widely used application of leaven as symbolic of sin or the fallen nature lends itself to another interpretation. In this use, the main thrust would point out that throughout the age of Pentecost, known to most as the church age, the 'bread' of the church would be infused with mixture because *we* are still filled with mixture. Though we are in the process of being transformed, the process will not be complete until Jesus returns and we are all changed. In the meantime, our 'bread' (teaching) is not as pure as we would like to think.

This mixture is one where the actions, ideas, paradigms, and wisdom of man are mingled with the truths conveyed by the Holy Spirit through the Word and the gifts He imparts to believers. The prophetic voices among believers, whether they are an established voice or not, are to be compared with the Word and discerned by the witness of the Holy Spirit because there is always the possibility of mixture.

Several years ago, I began wondering why the Lord would even include us in His work because we have a way of making things more difficult, prolonging the process by our ineptitude, not to mention the havoc we sometimes leave in our wake. The example that immediately came to mind was a parent teaching a small child to bake cookies. Without the child, the cookies would be made more quickly, without the eggshells in the batter, and with virtually no mess to clean up afterward. But the whole point of having the child help is for fellowship and training. In the case of the kingdom of God, He fellowships with us as He trains us to partner with Him in the advancement of His kingdom in this age so we can become a partner suitable for Jesus in the age to come. The Holy Spirit has been given to us for this purpose.

There are two yeast-laden loaves required for celebrating Pentecost, speaking of the division not only in the nation of Israel (Judah and Ephraim; see Isa. 7:17; Ezk. 37:16), but also in the body of Christ (Jew and Gentile; Eph. 2:11-22). This is in spite of the fact the church began with the believers in one accord in Jerusalem. They were together praying on that day (Acts 2:1), but whether or not they were fasting is a matter of speculation. Pentecost, after all, was a feast. Most of these were Jewish believers, and as such they would have honored the command for all males to celebrate this feast each year in Jerusalem (see Deut. 16:16). No doubt this was the reason there were so many God-fearing Jews in Jerusalem from all of the surrounding nations at that time (Acts 2:5).

The Feast of Pentecost commemorates the giving of the law on Mt. Sinai. God chose this day to initiate the new covenant where the Spirit now writes the law on the heart of believers. The sheer number of devout Jews and proselytes who made their way to Jerusalem each year for this feast demonstrates the wisdom of God in selecting this day. This gave the broadest witness possible to the miracle of the impartation of the Holy Spirit to believers in this new covenant. The Holy Spirit gave the gift of tongues that day with a purpose: to garner the attention of those who came to celebrate the feast by speaking forth the message of the gospel in the language of their native countries.

Returning to the discussion of the loaves, both Old and New Testaments tell us these divisions will be reconciled. Paul told us the Jew and Gentile will become 'one new man' in Christ (Eph. 2:14-16). Similarly, Ezekiel speaks of the reconciliation of the Northern and Southern kingdoms in Israel, becoming as one 'stick' in the Lord's hand (Ezk. 37:19). We look forward to the unity God will create from the factions we now see.

Checks and Balances

As far as the mixture of Pentecost is concerned, the Lord provided ways to guard against the errors that occur when our minds form conclusions from the Word that are not what He intended. A system of checks and balances was given to the community of believers, building safeguards into interpreting the Word so that 'by the mouth of two or three witnesses every word may be established' (Matt. 18:16; John 8:17).

- He gave us **the Word** to verify or refute that which is taught (2 Tim. 3:16).
- He gave us **the Holy Spirit** to bear witness to what is true (John 16:13).
- He gave us **the corporate body of Christ** to allow those inspired to speak and the others to discern what was said (1 Cor. 14:29).

Much of the church's problem with divisiveness can be traced to the simple fact that we don't truly listen to the Word, the Spirit, or each other.

Closing Thoughts

The hermeneutical principles developed by devout church leaders were created as the answer to correct the problems of rampant mistreatment and exploitation of the Word, excessive and inappropriate allegorization, and other adulterated practices and license in interpreting the Word. But the bottom line must acknowledge that these principles are still guidelines formed by man and are not the ultimate authority for accurate interpretation, particularly of prophetic passages and visions. Wisdom invites us to listen to her counsel:

> *Wisdom cries aloud in the street, in the markets she raises her voice... **If you turn at my reproof**, behold, **I will pour out my spirit to you; I will make my words known to you**.* -Pr. 1:20,23, ESV

SECTION 3

HARMONIZED VIEW OF LAW AND FREEDOM

Chapter 8

The Role of the Law

> *For the law was given through Moses; grace and truth came through Jesus Christ.* -John 1:17, ESV

The path to life is narrow (Matt. 7:14). It is the path of righteousness found in Christ by faith alone and walked out in obedience to God's commands by the power of the Holy Spirit. There is a ditch on either side—legalistic self-righteousness on one side and lawlessness on the other. It is cold in either ditch, void of love, and filled with either vain ambition or unrestrained craving for the illusion of worldly success, happiness, and pleasure. The paradox of law and freedom creates tension in our minds until we understand one is necessary for the other to exist. For example, the American way of government founded on freedom is undergirded by laws that protect our freedoms.

This section may pose the greatest challenge for the reader because it does not reflect the view of mainstream Christianity. It definitely posed the greatest challenge for me. I lost much sleep while wrestling over the concepts of law and freedom. I struggled to find congruency where apostolic thought on the law seemed to be in conflict with teaching on freedom. How can our walk as believers be pleasing to the Lord if we don't fully understand the role of His law? If we have died to the law as the means for righteousness (Rom. 7:4; Gal. 2:19), why does Paul say we also uphold the law (Rom. 3:31)?

During this struggle, I often spontaneously woke between 1:30 and 3:30 in the morning, wide awake with the law immediately on my mind. This went on for many weeks, during which I devoted 16-20 hours each day to wrestle with all of the conflicting scholarship and debate on the subject. This included grappling with verses that seemed to pose irreconcilable, paradoxical concepts. I had to clear my mind with a periodic walk just to digest the material and try to somehow organize it in my mind to come to a cohesive conclusion.

I remember being severely frustrated during this time. I just couldn't make the passages fit together and desperately wanted to move onto something else. Only after reading dozens if not hundreds of articles, books, and essays by scholars in both Gentile and Jewish circles, as well as every Bible verse about the law or freedom in its context, did I finally have the 'aha' I was searching for. My response to the sudden realization of how everything fit together was, 'Could it be that simple?'

I urge you to study each chapter in this section and carefully weigh what is presented before making a decision on the interpretation offered. While it is difficult to refrain from basing our conclusions on a few well-known verses of Scripture without taking into consideration the hundreds of verses written on the subject of the law in both the Old and New Testaments, let me encourage you to consider the many seemingly contradictory passages on this subject as well. To build our theology regarding the law on only a small percentage of the verses available—ones that agree with our doctrinal views—is to build an inverted pyramid. Having said that, I will share that this section caused me the most mental, emotional, and physical pain because of its complexity and magnitude, exacting all the perseverance I had just to stay in the match. The conclusions of my study are presented here for your consideration.

Before we begin our discussion, please take the time to read Acts 15. This chapter was the key that unlocked the door for my understanding of the role of the law in the new covenant. When you have finished, keep in the back of your mind this question: If the Jewish apostles and elders in Jerusalem believed the law had been nullified by the new covenant, why did they need to convene to decide whether Gentiles should be required to follow the law as grafted-in believers? This section will explore the Scriptures to hopefully bring a cohesive answer to this question.

The Law and Freedom

The obvious questions that enter the mind with regard to the law, freedom, and bondservanthood are: How can the bondservant be under the new covenant of freedom through grace, and yet bound to obedience by virtue of being a slave of Christ? From what are we freed? To what commands are bondservants being obedient? If the new covenant is one of grace and faith, what role does the law have in our lives?

These questions need to be answered in our hearts and minds to give us the proper posture for doing everything from a position of faith; out of love (the spirit) rather than self-righteousness that seeks to *earn* favor or right standing with God (the letter). This was a very important issue among the early followers of Jesus, both Jews and Gentiles. Paul took great pains to address this concern in his letters.

There are many passages in the New Testament that refute any claims that the new covenant is without law (anarchy), for God is not the author of confusion (1 Cor. 14:33). Neither is the new covenant without a moral code (antinomian), as the apostles continually exhort the believers to keep from immorality. Rather, the new covenant sets us free specifically from *the curse* of the law by enabling us to be free from the power and consequences of sin. This is true whether referring to the general curse of death for sin, or the specific curses written in Deuteronomy 27-28 for breaking the Mosaic covenant. Freedom comes only by the power of the Spirit and the law now written on our hearts.

Without a suitable grid based on the Word, it is easy to get lost in the myriad of words on the subject of the law. For example, just what are the works of the law? How are they different from works of faith, which James declares are the fruit of a true believer's life? The works of faith not only include works of righteousness (walking morally upright in our thought, word, and action), but works of love and kindness to our fellow man. Jesus stated in Revelation that each man's works will be tested (Rev. 2-3), as did Paul when he stated the quality of each person's work will be tested by fire (1 Cor. 3:13b-14).

Confusion enters our mind because works are often equated with the law due to Paul's use of the expression 'works of the law.' Misunderstanding also surfaces when we fail to differentiate between righteousness received by grace and the righteousness pursued by following the law. The Word makes it crystal clear we do not gain righteousness before God by means of the law. Christ is the end of the law *for righteousness*. Our righteousness is a gift from God through the sacrifice of Christ and is accepted by faith. We are made righteous before God by grace alone, not by anything we've done. Thinking we can be made right with God through works precisely defines the error of Cain.

Works are to follow this free gift of righteousness, and on the point of works, not sin, believers will be evaluated at the judgment seat of Christ. For the truly repentant who abide in Christ, 'our sins He will remember no more.' Believers have been made righteous in Christ and stand before the Father as white as snow through no works of their own. At the judgment seat of Christ, we will be examined for our obedience to and heart involvement in the works God has ordained for us to do (Eph. 2:10).

[Note: The concept of salvation can be nearly as confusing as a discussion of the law, primarily because the term salvation is used in three distinct ways:

- to describe the restoration of an individual's relationship with God, accomplished by the free gift of *righteousness* through the blood of Christ, cleansing our conscience from the guilt and condemnation of sin. This happens at the time of rebirth through repentance.
- to describe the process of *sanctification* by which our character and desires are transformed by the power of the Spirit and the Word. The fruit of this transformation is the evidence God looks for to verify true repentance has taken place.
- to describe the *transformation* of our physical bodies at Jesus' return.

Each 'phase' of salvation depends on the previous. Notice *phase one* primarily involves the transformation of our spirit—our conscience is cleansed and we are made righteous before God; *phase two* involves the transformation of our soul—our desires, understanding, and will are brought in line with God's; and *phase three* involves the transformation of our physical bodies to be incorruptible—the salvation Jesus brings with Him at His return. We will discuss these distinct phases of salvation in more detail in Section 7.]

After looking at the establishment of law from the beginning, we will look at the fulfillment of the old covenant in Christ and the freedom we are granted under the new covenant ratified in Jesus' blood. The stated purpose of the new covenant is to be freed from condemnation and to have the law written on our hearts, 'in order that the righteous requirement of the law might be fulfilled in us' (Rom. 8:4).

SECTION 3 *HARMONIZED VIEW OF LAW AND FREEDOM*

Law Was Present from the Beginning

The first law was given in an idyllic setting to people who knew no sin and walked with God. It consisted of positive commands and one negative command, found in Genesis 1-2, basically as follows:

- be fruitful, with morality and monogamy assumed (cf. Gen. 2:24)
- multiply/increase in number
- fill the earth/spread out
- subdue/govern the earth
- have dominion over all animal life
- take all seed bearing plants for food
- do not eat of the tree of knowledge

The law was simple and the people sinless and walking with God, yet the fall occurred. None of us would have done better. This is our first lesson that no one can be made righteous by the law; we will fail no matter what. As a result of this failure, authority to rule the earth was given to another and darkness began to invade man's spirit. The image in which man was created became more and more veiled as the soul of self-will took over and obscured the most precious and unique gift given to man, the *neshamah*—the spirit or breath of God, which enables man to speak and relate to God.

As Paul explained in Romans, the downside of the law was used against Eve to awaken ambition for wisdom and acquisition of discernment outside the timing of God's plan. Jesus was also tempted in this way. Satan goaded Jesus to take what God had promised Him before the appointed time. The difference is that Jesus recognized this tactic of the enemy, while Eve, in her naiveté, did not.

From the Fall to the Flood, man walked in bondage to sin as the law written on the heart was eroded by self-will. The antediluvian 'lord of the flies' was the result, warranting destruction of all life save those in the ark. After the flood, God gave some basic laws to Noah with the promise He would never destroy the world by flood again. These laws were (see Gen. 9:1-7):

- be fruitful/multiply
- fill the earth
- everything that lives, plant and animal alike, will be allowed as food
- do not eat flesh while it is alive
- do not eat flesh with its blood still in it (e.g., animals found dead or strangled, in which case the congealed blood would still be in its body)
- do not murder; justice requires the murderer's life

Notice the mandate to have dominion (royal) authority over the earth is absent. While the provision for punishing murder is given as an inference to bring to justice those who transgress the command of God, there is no indication authority over the whole earth belongs to man. Man governs the behavior of his fellowman through just laws, but kingdom authority over the earth itself was lost to the adversary (Luke 4:5-7; John 14:30; 2 Cor. 4:4). God, however, remains in sovereign control (see Dan. 4:25; Rom. 13:1; cf. Hos. 8:4; Rev. 13:1-5) and delegates His governing authority to men as He sees fit (e.g., Isa. 45).

Though we no longer have access to the tree of life in Eden to provide physical immortality in our present state, God has made provision to gain life spiritually. Wisdom, understanding, and righteousness are a 'tree of life' to all who pursue them (Pr. 3:13-18; 11:30). All three of these are found in Christ through the work of the Holy Spirit.

Lawlessness Is the Work of Satan

For the secret power of lawlessness is already at work... The coming of the lawless one will be in accordance with the work of Satan displayed in all kinds of counterfeit miracles, signs and wonders. -2 Thes. 2:7,9, NIV

The Bible defines lawlessness as the work of Satan. Lawlessness (*anomia*) is used to describe the sin of anyone who moves in opposition to or in contempt for the will of God. Notice the miracles, signs, and wonders that follow the lawless one. Discerning the genuine activity of the Holy Spirit from Satan's in the realm of supernatural activity requires divine intervention. Signs and wonders are not the fruit we look for when discerning the legitimacy of teachers and prophetic people in the body of Christ. Righteous character and the absence of lawlessness (sin) are the hallmarks of true believers.

The person *struggling* with sin is not *anomia* ('lawless'), but rather incomplete in his sanctification by the Spirit of God. Still struggling in the area of self-control, sinning causes his conscience to suffer. The war to overcome sin is evidence of sanctification's process in the truly repentant. This defines every believer in this age. It is the *habitual* practice of sin without sorrow or regret that defines lawlessness (1 John 3:4).

Legalism Is Lawlessness

Legalistic adherence to the law cannot produce righteousness and is seen as lawlessness in God's eyes. In His comments to the Pharisees, contrary to their own estimation of themselves, Jesus rebuked them for practicing *lawlessness*, not righteousness. The reason the Pharisees were lawless was because their hearts were bent on an outward show to magnify themselves. They didn't care about what God wanted. If they had, they would have looked to the weightier matters of the law to dictate their practice. Lawlessness includes pride, selfish ambition, and self-righteousness. While outwardly appearing to be righteous to others, Jesus declared them full of hypocrisy and *lawlessness* (Matt. 23:28).

Those who focus on good works, yet continue willfully in sin, are deceived. Adhering to a rationalized theology that God wouldn't use them in ministry if He counted those willful sins against them will cause those so deceived to one day hear this:

> *Many will say to Me on that day, 'Lord, Lord, did we not prophesy in Your name, and in Your name cast out demons, and in Your name perform many miracles?' And then I will declare to them, 'I never knew you; DEPART FROM ME, YOU WHO PRACTICE LAWLESSNESS.'* -Matt. 7:22-23, NASB

The fruit of lawlessness is a cold heart: one who has love for neither God nor man. The heart of the lawless are bent on fulfilling their own desires and goals despite appearing righteous; they have little compassion or empathy for the plight of others, much like a sociopath. When things go well, they praise their discipline, ingenuity, and skill, counting it as God's favor. When things go poorly, they blame either God or other people. 'And because lawlessness will be increased, the love of many will grow cold' (Matt. 24:12, ESV).

Not only are we not to practice lawlessness, we are not to have close fellowship with those who do, lest we be carried away with their folly. This includes those who insist on legalistic adherence to the law for righteousness before God. Paul warns us not to be deceived—bad company corrupts good character (1 Cor. 15:33). He also instructs believers not to be bound to unbelievers, 'for what partnership can righteousness have with lawlessness' (2 Cor. 6:14).

To be without law was never the goal of the new covenant. This would be lawlessness—the activity of Satan. Rather, the new covenant gives us a clear conscience and right standing before God because of the blood of Jesus' sacrifice. By cooperating with the Holy Spirit, we can live uprightly before God in accordance with the law now written on the heart. This brings redemption and a place in the age to come.

Those who practice lawlessness will be gathered with those destined for fire. The *practice* of lawlessness implies habitual repetition of sinning with a 'high hand,' excluding those who do from inheriting the promised kingdom. Instead, they will find themselves in the place of weeping and gnashing of teeth (Matt. 13:40-42).

Ignorantia legis neminem excusat ("ignorance of the law excuses no one") is a legal principle specifying that a person who is unaware of a law may not escape liability for violating that law merely because he was ignorant of it. Now, by the grace of the new covenant, the law is being written on our hearts. In this way, we are no longer ignorant of the law, for the law written on our hearts will either testify for us or against us. We are no longer under the written law with its curse of death for violating those things of which we were not even aware. We are under the law of grace, which holds us accountable for those things the Spirit has written on our hearts. These laws on the heart come with the power to overcome temptation, and conviction when we fail.

Love Righteousness and Hate Lawlessness

Jesus not only loves righteousness—He also hates lawlessness (Heb. 1:8-9). Some have dubbed Paul the 'false apostle' due to the difficulty in understanding his writings about the law. This primarily occurs when we do not consider to whom or for what purpose the specific letters were written, and when bias is introduced into the text by translators. There is a distinction between Jew and Gentile in matters of the law, as we will soon discuss. Peter refuted rejection of Paul and honored Paul's teaching as part of Scripture. To reject Paul is to reject Peter, who had accepted Paul and his teaching (2 Pet. 3:16b).

Lawlessness is the work of Satan, whose version of 'freedom' results in the death penalty. A murderer from the beginning, his work of death continues insidiously in the hearts of men who believe his lie that God's law is bondage. Jesus came to redeem us from lawlessness and purify a possession for Himself who are zealous for good works (Titus 2:14). God's law enables us to be trained in righteousness toward God and our fellow man as long as we approach the law with faith that He will supply the grace we need to accomplish His will, and forgiveness when we fail.

> *Therefore, dear friends, since you have been forewarned, be on your guard so that you may not be carried away by the error of the lawless and **fall from your secure position**.* -2 Pet. 3:17, NIV

Law Is Not the Same as Covenant

The covenants with Israel are unconditional except for the Mosaic covenant, which can only be temporary because of the conflict it poses with the Abrahamic covenant. The unconditional covenant of faith made with Abraham, giving the land of Canaan to Israel forever, cannot be undone by a later, conditional covenant of stipulations that will thrust the Israelites out of the land for disobedience. This was our first clue this covenant could not last forever (Gal. 3:17-18).

The Mosaic *covenant*, however, must not be confused with the *stipulations* of the covenant, namely the Mosaic *law*. In this section, we will take a look at the eternal nature of the law as defined in the Word. To give a simple illustration of the difference between the *covenant* and its *stipulations*, we will use an imaginary business transaction involving land. Though this illustration is not without certain frailties, it will suffice for our discussion. Suppose Joe is considering the property Bob is selling. After looking around, Joe tells Bob he will buy the property if at least seven inches of rain fall over the next three months. At the end of the three months, only five inches of rain have fallen. The conditional contract between Joe and Bob is made void because the conditions have not been met. But does this mean that rain itself, as the stipulation of the contract, has been voided along with the contract? This would be an absurd conclusion.

We have to ask ourselves if this is precisely what the majority of the church has done with the Mosaic law because we understood neither the *Torah* nor the intention of the apostles in their discussions of 'the law.' Our primary concern when trying to discern what seem to be conflicting statements is to first determine the audience being addressed in the passage. Once this is established, the central point the writer is making must be excavated, keeping in mind the Greek term for law is a *general* term that does not always convey the specific aspect being discussed. We must also keep in mind that Paul uses idiomatic expressions, such as 'works of the law' and 'under the law,' as well as his proclamation that we do not discard the law but uphold it (Rom. 3:31).

Works of the Law

Since the discovery of the Dead Sea Scrolls, some have concluded that the expression 'works of the law' most likely refers to the rabbinic interpretations, amplifications, and extensions of the Mosaic law found in the Jewish oral traditions as later recorded in the Mishnah. The Dead Sea Scroll entitled *Miqsat Ma'ase Ha-Torah* (MMT) is translated 'Works of the Law.' In this scroll, the expression 'works of the law' was used to describe the *halakha* of the Essene teachers, which is the interpretation of the law with explanation as to how that law should be followed. While similar to the *halakha* of the Talmud, this sect of Jews had rejected the oral tradition of the Pharisees and came up with their own set of rules. Jesus had only negative comments for those who would add to God's law, not only because it became a heavy yoke for the people, but also because strict adherence to these manmade rules both nullified the Word of God and ignored the weightier matters of the law. In the *Biblical Archaeological Review*, Martin Abegg explains that 'works of the law' have everything to do with the way in which the Mosaic law is interpreted and practiced.[1]

The strict legalistic nature of the Essenes' teachings cannot be dismissed. "For the Essenes their halacha or *'works of the law'* was a binding legal requirement that demanded absolute compliance. In other words their religious tradition overruled basic *Torah* principles. Knowing how this phrase *'works of the law'* was used by the Essenes and their converts, we can now correctly apply this in Apostle Paul's letters."[2]

Both the Essenes and the Pharisees held to traditions outside the actual law, thinking they were doing everyone a favor by using these extra regulations to make it more difficult to break the actual written laws. This type of thinking began in the garden when Eve added the phrase, 'neither can we touch it,' which was not part of the original command. The Lord instructs us not to add or subtract from God's commands (see also Deut. 12:32):

> ***Do not add*** *to what I command you and* ***do not subtract*** *from it, but keep the commands of the LORD your God that I give you.* -Deut. 4:2, NIV

'Works of the law' could be interpreted to mean the various rabbinic interpretations of the Mosaic law prevalent in Jewish life during the first century. The different sects in Judaism each have their own interpretation of the law, just as the various church denominations have their own particular doctrinal statements. Those in the church should be wary of pointing the finger at the oral laws of the Jews as long as we have our own differences as to practice and interpretation to which we adhere outside the realm of biblical command. If we point the finger at the Jews for expanding or diminishing God's law because of their oral tradition, we need to take a look at the 'beam' in our own practice. Take a look at some of the laws the Gentiles added for Sunday observance here in the U.S.:

- All men must carry a rifle to church on Sunday. (MA)
- Dominoes may not be played on Sunday. (AL)
- It is illegal to wear a fake moustache that causes laughter in church. (AL)
- Pickles are not to be consumed on Sundays. (NJ)
- Musical instruments may not be sold on Sunday. (SC)
- You may not sell toothpaste and toothbrush to the same customer on Sunday. (RI)
- It is illegal to sell Limburger cheese on Sunday. (TX)
- No animal may be hunted on Sunday with the exception of raccoons, which may be hunted until 2:00 A.M. (VA)
- No Christian parent may require their children to pick up trash from the highway on Easter day. (TN)
- No person may walk around on Sun. with an ice cream cone in his pocket. (NY)
- You may not run machinery on Sundays. (NH)
- If a child burps during church, his parent may be arrested. (NE)
- It is illegal for a man to scowl at his wife on Sunday. (MI)
- One may not whisper in church. (DE)
- No one may practice the business of tattooing on Sunday. (GA)
- It is illegal to carry a chicken by its feet down Broadway on Sunday. (GA)
- It is unlawful to walk a cow down Main Street after 1:00 P.M. on Sunday. (AR)[3]

(To my knowledge, none of these are being enforced, but they are on the books.)

Returning to Paul's use of the 'works of the law,' we cannot be certain he used it as the equivalent of the oral *Torah*. The issue that could be brought up against such a view is Paul's own statement of the 'work of the law' the Gentiles follow instinctively:

> *For when Gentiles who do not have the Law do instinctively the things of the Law, these, not having the Law, are a law to themselves, in that they show **the work of the Law written in their hearts.*** -Rom. 2:14-15a, NASB

While the word 'work' in this case is singular, it is obvious Paul views the awareness of and adherence to the righteous moral code of God planted in each person's heart as 'the work of the law.' This evidence would attest in favor of viewing the 'works of the law' as being those things we do that are morally good and right before God, but which Paul stresses repeatedly are not the way to be made righteous before God. Everything we touch is mingled with tainted motives, imperfect heart posture, or vain ambition. This renders even a perfectly performed act profane in God's sight. 'Works of the law' as used by Paul seems to primarily point out a performance-based or self-made righteousness through perfection of outward behavior, in contrast with the righteousness freely given by grace through faith in Jesus.

Being declared righteous by faith will naturally lead to righteous behavior because of the gift of the Holy Spirit who governs our behavior. We may falter, but by faith we trust the power of God working in us to cleanse us from all sin. Daily we find His mercies are new every morning, and we live free from condemnation. The power of God is displayed in us as we are incrementally transformed to the character of Christ.

The Scope of the Law

At His first coming, Jesus provided the nation of Israel with the correct interpretation of the law of Moses both by His actions and by His teaching. At His second coming, the law will go forth from Zion (Isa. 2:3; Mic. 4:2). Jesus has and will fulfill the prophecy spoken about Him by Moses (see also Acts 3:22-23):

> *I will raise up for them **a Prophet like you** from among their brethren, and will put My words in His mouth, and He shall speak to them all that I command Him. And it shall be that whoever will not hear My words, which He speaks in My name, I will require it of him.* -Deut. 18:18-19, NKJV

If our view of what is meant by the law is too narrow, much of what Scripture has to say about the law will perplex us. Most of us have been taught to think of the law only as those ordinances and statutes Moses received while on Mt. Sinai. The Hebraic understanding of the word law, translated *torah,* means not only law but instruction, teaching, and guidance as well. It is derived from the word *yarah*, which means to 'shoot out the hand as pointing, or as an arrow; to show, indicate, teach, instruct, lay foundations; to sprinkle, to water.' This is in contrast with the word *lamadh*, 'to teach or instruct,' but with the implication of prodding as with an ox goad. This method of training is for "an animal or soldiers. How much better to be taught by pointing than by poking, by the demonstration of the hand rather than the discipline of the rod. *Torah* then derives from a root verb which has more to do with 'hand' led instruction than 'rod' following legalism."[4]

The first mention of *torah* occurs over four hundred years before the law was given at Mt. Sinai. Abraham obeyed every command God gave him: moving from his home, circumcising all the males in his house, obeying the command to sacrifice his son. Everything he did came from faith.

> *Abraham obeyed* (**sh'ma**) *My voice and kept... My laws* (**torah**). -Gen. 26:5, NKJV
> (parentheticals added)

The word translated 'laws' in this passage is the word *torah*. The only God-given laws known at the time were the commands given to Noah after the flood and those things the 'Gentiles know instinctively' (Rom. 2:14). Paul maintains that Abraham is the father of both the circumcised and the uncircumcised; those who follow *Torah* as written by Moses, and those who follow *torah* as practiced by Abraham. All must come by faith, for he is the father of all those who walk in obedience by faith.

Torah is used in various passages throughout the Old Testament to reveal the broad scope of its application. Whether in reference to all of God's instruction and guidance in the Bible, to the Pentateuch, or specifically to the laws given through Moses, *torah* is not to be understood as a rod of legalistic code. "Its basic idea, then, is 'instruction' or 'teaching' to a valued individual rather than to a beast of burden. Even when it is legitimately translated as 'law' the emphasis is still on instruction... In the modern Christian church 'law' has become a negative word and 'revelation' a positive one. But they are both the same. The famous verse in Proverbs 29:18 is usually quoted as half a verse only. Its second half, written in parallel terminology, says the same thing so that revelation and Torah instruction are virtually identical: 'Where there is no revelation, the people perish. But blessed is he who keeps the Torah/law' (Proverbs 29:18)."[5]

There is no problem with *Torah* as it was given. The problem arose when men took the *Torah* of Moses (the stipulations of the covenant), and made those stipulations an end in themselves. As Dr. Spiros Zodhiates explains, "...Torah was much more than a law or set of rules. It was not to be perceived as restrictions, but the very means by which one could reach a spiritual ideal. If Israel would keep Torah, then they would be safe. However, the people came to understand it as something which was imposed for its own sake rather than what God intended... instead of being seen as a guideline, it became a heavy external set of rules which were stifling."[6]

The Eternal Nature of the Law

The eternal nature of the *Torah* (the instruction God has given for our benefit to help us in our relationships with God and man) is noted in several passages of Scripture. None would deny the eternal nature of God's Word (Ps. 119:89), but we can misunderstand much of New Testament teaching on the law if we fail to recognize its purpose. Knowing the temporary nature of the Mosaic *covenant* in contrast with the eternal nature of the *instructions* or *stipulations* will help us understand the place of the *Torah* and more specifically the Mosaic law under the new covenant of grace.

The *Torah* of the Lord brings delight to the one seeking God. There are three general distinctions in the types of laws given in the *Torah*:

- ♦ ***Mishpatim***: the moral or ethical laws necessary for man to live in harmony; literally translated *'judgments'* or *'ordinances'*; the reasons for these laws are easily seen and understood, much like our own civil laws which protect the innocent and bring the guilty to justice for crimes committed.

- **Edot**: the rituals and festivals which reawaken us to important religious truths, such as Sabbath and holy days; also the *tefillin* placed on the head and hands, and the *mezuzah* placed on the doorposts to remind of God's presence; literally translated *'testimonies'* or *'witnesses'*; the reasons for these laws are given.
- **Chukim**: the laws that do not have any given or logical reason in our estimation, such as the kosher laws; literally translated as *'decrees'*; "Chukim test the purity of our commitment to Torah."[7]

The *chukim* are the laws that people performed without fully understanding why they were doing them. In the original movie *Karate Kid*, these would have been the 'wax on, wax off' commands. In the case of the *chukim*, however, we undoubtedly find object lessons that impart some truth about God, His plans, and His kingdom.

Notice in the following verses that the commands of the Lord are specifically singled out with different Hebrew words rather than using the general term, *'torah,'* which would have a much wider application. This broader application could be construed as opening the door for denying application of *olam* (everlasting) to the Mosaic law specifically, resulting in its application only to *Torah* instruction generally. Using the specific terms instead of *'torah'* gives very little latitude for dismissing the individual commands of the Mosaic law (see also Ps. 111:7-8, where *piqqud*, the collective and broad term for all God's commands, is described as firmly fixed and established forever).

> *Your statutes (**edhuth**) are my heritage forever; they are the joy of my heart.*
> -Ps. 119:111, NIV

> *I have inclined my heart to perform Your statutes (**choq**) forever, to the very end.*
> -Ps. 119:112, NKJV

> *Your righteous testimonies (**edhuth**) are everlasting and Your decrees are binding to eternity.* -Ps. 119:144a, AMP

> *Long ago I learned from your statutes (**edhah**) that you established them to last forever.* -Ps. 119:152, NIV

> *All your righteous laws (**mishpat**) are eternal.* -Ps. 119:160b, NIV

> *The statutes (**choq**) and the ordinances (**mishpat**) and the law (**torah**) and the commandment (**mitsvah**) which He wrote for you, you shall observe to do forever.* -2 Kings 17:37, NASB (parentheticals added)

We must cease looking at the instruction of God, the *Torah*, as stifling or as a curse. This is not what Paul or Peter were describing, but rather they were referring to one or more of the following as the bondage or yoke of the law: the prevailing legalistic attitude toward the law; the expansion of the law by the oral traditions heaped on top of God's original statutes; the burden of trying (and failing) to attain righteousness by following the law to the letter; and/or the physical curse for disobeying the commands and the self-condemnation failure imposed on the soul of man. The next passage clearly states that those who follow the law walk in *freedom*, not a stifling yoke or curse:

> *I will always obey your law (**torah**), forever and ever. I will walk about in freedom, for I have sought out your precepts (**piqqud**).* -Ps. 119:44-45, NIV (parenthetical added)

The Law as Israel's Possession

In the next passage, notice the reference to the law is singular. The Mosaic law is to be viewed as one law, not groups of laws from which we can pick and choose. The 613 mitzvot are one unified code of law for Israel.

> *Moses charged us with a law, a **possession** for the assembly of Jacob.* -Deut. 33:4, NASB

The Hebrew word translated 'possession' in this verse is *morashah*, and can be synonymously translated 'an inheritance.' *Morashah* is also the Hebrew word used to describe the land promised to Abraham in Exodus 6:8, the *possession* of his descendants forever. The law has been given to Israel *as a possession*, or *inheritance* (KJV), just as the land has been given to them as a possession. *Both* are their inheritance. God has not given this to any other nation (see also Deut. 29:29).

> *He has revealed his word to Jacob, his laws and decrees to Israel.* **He has done this for no other nation; he has not made his laws known to them.** -Ps. 147:19-20, NIV (the NIV footnoted ending from the Septuagint has been substituted)

'Obviously the law applies to those to whom it was given' (Rom. 3:19). Scripture tells us the Mosaic law was given *to Israel*. The stipulations of the law are types and shadows to teach us about the nature of God, our relationship with Him, and the way in which to honor, live with, and love those around us. Understanding the law fuels our desire to keep it, not in a legalistic way, but because we come closer to God through understanding His ways. For the Jew, this provokes desire to walk in the laws given to Israel with greater heart involvement. For the Gentile believer, this provokes deeper desire to know God through the spiritual understanding gained (see also Ps. 119:1).

> *Give me understanding, so that I may keep your law and obey it with all my heart... give me understanding that I may live.* -Ps. 119:34,144b, NIV

Psalm 119

The writer of Psalm 119 understood the purpose of the law and he delighted in it. The more we peer into the perfect law of freedom, the more we want to be drawn in. It is here we behold the face of God and are changed. Paul wrote that under the new covenant the veil has been removed. It is by the Word of God that we are transformed into His image (2 Cor. 3:18).

God's Word cannot go forth and return to Him void of accomplishing the purpose for which it was sent (Isa. 55:11): the transformation of our souls. This includes understanding with spiritual wisdom the value of the law and its application in the believer's life, particularly as it points to deeper revelation of Christ and His kingdom.

> *And do not be conformed to this world, but be transformed by the renewing of your mind, that you may prove what is that good and acceptable and perfect will of God.* -Rom. 12:2, NKJV

In *The Treasury of David*, Charles H. Spurgeon gave detailed insight of the worth of Psalm 119. Spurgeon compares this psalm to the New Jerusalem. "Many superficial readers have imagined that it harps upon one string, and abounds in pious repetitions and redundancies; but this arises from the shallowness of the reader's own mind: those who have studied this divine hymn, and carefully noted each line of it, are amazed at the variety and profundity of the thought. Using only a few words, the writer has produced permutations and combinations of meaning which display his holy familiarity with his subject, and the sanctified ingenuity of his mind. He never repeats himself; for if the same sentiment recurs it is placed in a fresh connection, and so exhibits another interesting shade of meaning. The more one studies it the fresher it becomes... It contains no idle word; **the grapes of this cluster are almost to bursting full with the new wine of the kingdom**... those who devoutly gaze into it shall not only see the brightness, but feel the glow of the sacred flame."[8] (emphasis added)

[Notice that Spurgeon describes this Psalm as 'bursting full with new wine,' just as Jesus described the new covenant.]

Inclining our ear to *sh'ma* out of love defines the primary characteristic of the bondservant. Without obedience to the law, we are lawless and have fallen into the trap of the evil one. Not even our prayers are heard when we are in a state of lawlessness.

> *He who turns away his ear from listening to the law, even his prayer is an abomination.* -Pr. 28:9, NASB

The Ten Commandments

The Ten Commandments are the bedrock on which the remainder of the Mosaic law is founded. Moses told the Israelites that God gave them specific statutes based upon the commandments written on the stone tablets. Those additional laws clarify and provide practical application for their national life and governance *in His land* (Deut. 4:13-14).

These statutes are distinctives ensuring enforcement of the moral code in the everyday life of Israel. The Ten Commandments begin with, 'I am the Lord your God, who brought you out of the land of Egypt' (Ex. 20:2; Deut. 5:6). God is speaking specifically to Israel. While a *midrash* could be applied for the use of the Ten Commandments under the new covenant, the historical context is indisputably Israel.

> *In it have I put the ark... in which is the covenant of the Lord [the Ten Commandments]* **which He made with the people of Israel.** -2 Chron. 6:11, AMP

Furthermore, the instruction about the Sabbath command, especially as described in Deuteronomy, specifically indicates its peculiarity to these chosen people who will inhabit His land. The Sabbath and holy days were given to be a sign between God and Israel so they would understand that He is the one who set them apart (Ezk. 20:12).

> *Say to the Israelites,* **Truly you shall keep My Sabbaths, for it is a sign between Me and you throughout your generations***, that you may know that I, the Lord, sanctify you [set you apart for Myself]... Wherefore* **the Israelites shall keep the Sabbath to observe it throughout their generations, a perpetual covenant. It is a sign between Me and the Israelites forever.** -Ex. 31:13,16-17a, AMP

In addition, we find laws that address the challenges of the culture at that time, particularly divorce and slavery. Laws regarding slavery and divorce were included not because God approved of these practices, but because these practices already existed. In a perfect world, these laws would be unnecessary. The practice of either militates against God's law to love your neighbor as yourself (although in the case of Hebrew slaves in Israel, it was a means by which the poor could pay off their debts, or thieves were brought to justice). For example, God made allowance for divorce due to the hardness of men's hearts, not because He approved of its practice (Matt. 19:8; Mal. 2:16). The laws were given so these practices could be governed justly as well as teach spiritual truths.

The Mosaic law is the specific and ongoing possession of Israel. We have to take issue with those who say the law itself has been rescinded. The Word testifies that God's law continues forever. Do we suppose ourselves to understand the purpose and duration of the law better than the Old Testament writers under the inspiration of the Holy Spirit, who stated God's law is everlasting? If we have done this, we have placed ourselves in the role of judge over the Word of God (cf. James 4:11-12).

In doing away with the law, how are we to understand the new covenant as presented by Isaiah and Jeremiah, where *the law* is written on our hearts, or the vision of Ezekiel, who describes in detail the millennial temple to be built, complete with daily sacrifice as described in the ceremonial law? Even Jesus, who emphasized that His words will never pass away (Matt. 24:35), spoke unequivocally when He told His primarily Jewish audience that He had not come to destroy the law:

> *Do not think that I came to destroy the Law or the Prophets.* **I did not come to destroy** *but to fulfill. For assuredly, I say to you,* **till heaven and earth pass away, one jot or one tittle will by no means pass from the law** *till all is fulfilled.*
> -Matt. 5:17-18, NKJV

> *But it is easier for heaven and earth to pass away than for one dot of the Law to become void.* -Luke 16:17, ESV

"The underlying idea of law, as it is used in the Bible, is that of teaching and instruction. Law is God instructing His people that they may know how to live in a moral and ethical way, pleasing unto Him, and at peace with our fellow man. Law is instruction that, if followed, will enrich one's life, if ignored will diminish it. Law was for the purpose of instructing man how he was to live here in this world."[9]

The Dynamic Nature of the Law

He has shown you, O man, what is good; and what does the LORD require of you but to do justly, to love mercy, and to walk humbly with your God? -Mic. 6:8, NKJV

The dynamic nature of the law is practically defined by the weightier matters of the law, which take priority over the laws themselves. The Ten Commandments as given by God were the only portion of the Mosaic law set in stone—literally and figuratively. After recounting the Ten Commandments in Deuteronomy (5:1-21), Moses testifies only these commands went on the tablets (v. 22). The remainder of the law was recorded as well, but not on the stone tablets.

By placing the cardinal moral code in stone, we are able to see more clearly the two divisions of commands that demonstrate love for God (Deut. 5:6-15) and love for man (Deut. 5:16-21). Without these foundational commandments, it is easy to get lost in the multitudinous collection of laws in the Levitical code. But observing the two distinctions enables us to remember the purpose of the law. Jesus reduced the law to love for God and love for neighbor. 'All the law and the prophets hang on these two commands' (Matt. 22:35-40).

Examples of Legitimate Deviations from the Law

There are examples in the Word which demonstrate the mutability of the specific stipulations of the law in the presence of extenuating circumstances, especially in matters of showing mercy. For example, when Aaron's sons died because they offered strange fire, the ordinance for eating the sin offering was set aside due to the circumstances (Lev. 10). Because of their great need, David's men ate the showbread reserved for the priests (1 Sam. 21:6). When the people returned to the land after the Babylonian exile to rebuild, Nehemiah reduced the half shekel temple tax to a third, presumably due to the widespread poverty of much of the nation (Neh. 5; 10:32-33). The Lord divorced Israel, but in great compassion and mercy will take her back again, contrary to the law (Deut. 24:1-4; Isa. 50:1; Jer. 3:8; Zech. 10:6). Because many of these laws are meant as object lessons to teach spiritual truths, setting them aside to take care of the needy or to show mercy in extenuating circumstances does not violate the law but demonstrates the foundational purpose of the law: to honor God and love others as ourselves.

One of the best examples of the dynamic nature of the law takes place during the reign of Hezekiah. In the first month of his reign, this good king reopened the temple and began the work of repairing and restoring what had fallen into neglect. After only sixteen days, the temple had been cleansed and consecrated, and the people rejoiced greatly. Because they missed the regular time for celebrating Passover in the first month, they decided to celebrate in the second month according to the provision in the law (Num. 9:9ff). The remnant in the northern kingdom was invited as well (Assyria had already invaded Israel and carried away the majority of the northern inhabitants).

When the people from the northern kingdom arrived, however, they were ceremonially unclean and therefore by law not allowed to partake in the Passover (2 Chron. 30:18). But because of the weightier matters that were taking place—the people returning to God, seeking the Lord whole heartedly, and moving in a spirit of unity—Hezekiah prayed that the Lord would pardon these sincere seekers who had violated the laws of ceremonial cleanness. The Lord heard Hezekiah and healed the people (2 Chron. 30:18-20).

Similarly, we find examples in the New Testament where the law is set aside to attend to weightier matters. If a male infant's day of circumcision falls on a Sabbath, the Sabbath ordinance is set aside (Matt. 12:5). If a person is in need of healing, the weightier matters of the law are satisfied by allowing this to take place on the Sabbath as well (Matt. 12:10-12; Luke 6:9-10). The woman with the issue of blood touched Jesus, which made Him ceremonially unclean (Lev. 15:19ff), yet He continued on His way to the house of one of the synagogue rulers where He grasped the hand of the dead girl and raised her back to life (Mark 5:21-43). Jesus, who has no legal lineage to Levi, becomes our high priest because it serves justice to have a high priest whose own innocent blood atones for the sins of all, and who can permanently mediate for man by virtue of His indestructible life (Heb. 7:15-19).

> *When the priesthood is changed, the law must be changed also.*   -Heb. 7:12, NIV

Weightier Matters

While on the earth, Jesus demonstrated a firm grasp of the weightier matters of the law. He allowed His Sabbath to be interrupted in order to show mercy to the infirm and the hungry. Being faithful in following the law requires attention to the needs of others. This is precisely so God's people would learn to heed His voice, which takes far more attention and discernment than following rules.

It also places our priority on relationships and love for others rather than tallying a perfect performance. If we reduce our relationships with God and man to a set of rules, we have become nothing more than automatons programmed to follow a code. Legalistic adherence to the law places the proud heart in a place of disobedience, for the truly righteous live by faithful hearing and obedience to the Master's voice (Hab. 2:4).

Prior to John the Baptist's ministry, the law and prophets were the focus of teaching (Luke 16:16). From John's time forward, however, the focus of teaching would change to proclamation of the gospel of the kingdom as fulfillment of everything taught in the law and prophets. After Jesus' resurrection, this would include teaching about the arrival of the new covenant in fulfillment of prophecy. The gospel of the kingdom and the new covenant help us to focus on the weightier matters of treating others as we want to be treated as our *first* consideration and not our *last*. With too much focus on law rather than love, mercy, and humility before God, the human mind becomes programmed to think of their performance scorecard before regarding the needs of others.

In the Sermon on the Mount, Jesus taught the laws are principles that could be adjusted or waived in the presence of circumstances requiring mercy or faithfulness to weightier matters. Mercy was shown the woman caught in adultery due at least in part to the partiality and hypocrisy of her accusers. Justice was not served in the manner prescribed by law because *both* parties were to be judged, not just the woman (Lev. 20:10; Jn. 8:3-10). It could also be argued her accusers were more sinful than she. On another occasion, a woman was freed from her eighteen-year physical bondage on a Sabbath, demonstrating the weightier matter of bringing freedom to a daughter of Israel (Luke 13:16).

The law has God-ordained flexibility only in the mind of one led by God's Spirit and governed by the weightier matters of love, mercy, justice, and faithfulness. To the performance-based follower of the law, everything must be done to the letter in order to have a perfect record before God so as to be rewarded and declared righteous due to the valiant effort given. Though righteous behavior is important, God is not looking for us to operate in this fashion. Indeed, He emphatically declares that we cannot keep His law righteously. He wants us to love what He loves and be led by His Spirit as we walk in a manner pleasing to Him. The law of God is beautiful to those whose hearts are captured by His love. To all others, it is a list of rules to be obeyed. Jesus reduced the law to two primary commands: loving God and loving our neighbor. If these are our foundation, we will walk out the minutiae of the law perfectly because love requires the weightier matters be given just that—greater weight than wooden obedience.

The Talmud, a written compilation of Jewish oral law, includes Jewish legal discussions and decisions on the law, known as *halakha*. The *halakha* discussions reveal differing views as well as flexibility in application of the law as each rabbi interprets in his own fashion. "Rarely are debates formally closed; in many instances, the final word determines the practical law, although there are many exceptions to this principle."[10]

Jesus taught that following the law was not merely a matter of knowledge and outward compliance, but an inward focus on loving God and on loving man, making the commands a joy. This allows us to move in flexibility, not in matters of morality (e.g., adultery, theft, fornication, false witness, covetousness, etc.), but in recognizing that the ceremonial stipulations of the law can be set aside for the good of another in need.

The parable of the good Samaritan illustrates this point (Luke 10:25-37). An expert in the law wanted to test Jesus on matters of the law. Jesus used the parable to show what true love for our fellowman entails. In the story, the priest and Levite did not want to become ceremonially unclean by coming in contact with a bloodied, half-dead man. They crossed on the other side, far enough away to prevent violation of this law. Only the Samaritan, who concerned himself with the man's safety ahead of all other concerns, demonstrated the weightier matters of the law. It is safe to say only his actions would be deemed lawful in the sight of God, not the two who legalistically adhered to the law at the expense of another's life.

When we are confronted with the needs of another, our immediate thoughts betray whether we are loving our neighbor as ourselves, or focusing on performance. The one who is concerned with his track record of performance of the stipulations of the law will think twice about helping someone if it will entail violating any laws (unrelated to actual moral or sin issues). This demonstrates why God defines legalism as lawlessness: it leads to a vanishing social conscience and lack of moral responsibility for our fellowman.

The law is good as long as it is followed with greater weight given to what really matters in the sight of God: humility, mercy, love, justice, and faithfulness to the voice of the Holy Spirit. This is how Jesus lived. He knew the law but viewed it as the way to express love for God and man. The law served as His framework, but Jesus listened to His Father for specific direction in each situation. He said and did only what He saw His Father saying and doing, which will always interpret compliance to the law through the lens of the weightier matters. This is fulfillment of the *Sh'ma*: <u>Hear</u>, O Israel.

The Purpose of the Law: A Guardian for Israel

In order to understand the role of the law in the new covenant, we must first understand the role of the law under the old covenant. The old covenant was to keep Israel as God's chosen people, a holy nation through whom the promised seed of Abraham would come to bless the whole earth (Ex. 19:5-6; Deut. 29:9-13).

We also must understand from start to finish, the Ten Commandments and the remaining 603 *mitzvot* were given specifically to Israel as one code of law. Although they can be categorized as civil, moral, and ceremonial, they cannot be viewed as three *separate* legal codes from which we can pick and choose. The Ten Commandments provide the outline, or framework, of the set of laws. The remaining statutes and ordinances dictate how those commands can be carried out on a day-to-day basis.

The point of much of the old covenant was to provide a standard of morality with the hope to prevent corruption of the 'seed.' In this way, God's promises to Abraham would be fulfilled. It not only provided for the moral, ceremonial, and civil governance of Israel, it was a shadow of the reality of Christ, though veiled to most. By first codifying His moral standard in the Ten Commandments and His standards of justice in the civil laws, God then provided ceremonial laws that would cover man's inability to keep either. These laws also furnished a means to celebrate the benevolence and mercy of God.

SECTION 3 HARMONIZED VIEW OF LAW AND FREEDOM

The veiling of Moses' face, just as the veil over the true purpose of the law as type and shadow of Christ, is contrasted with the new covenant where we behold the glory of Christ with an *unveiled* face. The primary purpose of the law—to point to Christ and draw forth loving obedience—remained veiled to most.

> *For since the law has but a shadow of the good things to come instead of the true form of these realities,* **it can never,** *by the same sacrifices that are continually offered every year,* **make perfect those who draw near.** -Heb. 10:1, ESV

The Mosaic laws were also meant to be object lessons for the people to learn something about their God; to better understand His heart and thereby better understand the One they were called to serve. The *tefillin* (Hebrew), or *phylacteries* (Greek), used by Jewish people are the literal execution of the command to bind the laws to their foreheads (thought) and to their arms (actions). Each time they thought about or carried out the requirements of the law, they would be reminded of an attribute of God, His kingdom, and the nature He implanted in man when he was created in God's image.

For example, one principle we learn from the allotment of the tribes into their land is the spiritual reality that each believer is given an allotted portion to tend—his charge. Just as the Israelites did not choose their specific lot in the land, we do not choose our calling. It is assigned to us by God. To neglect what we have been given by the Lord, longing for another's portion, is not only disrespectful to our Master, saying 'I will not do Your will, for I want to do something more significant...' but it also shipwrecks our relationship and faith. We end up treading on the allotment of another, causing division. The heart becomes cold because we have set our will above the Lord's. God calls this kind of substitution (of our will to do something 'grand' instead of the 'lowly' thing assigned to us) 'evil and lawlessness.' It is not wise or heroic to 'despise the day of small things' by coveting the calling of another. This is lawlessness.

Israel: Example to the Nations

Israel was to be an example to the nations of righteous living and right standing with God—a chosen nation for His special favor and promise through which the entire earth would be blessed. The law demonstrated the kind of behavior expected of a people who walk in love for God and love for neighbor. This law, as a temporary guardian or tutor (Gal. 3:23-25), would keep the Israelites in proper relationship with God so they could walk in the blessings of the covenant (which included staying in the land) until the promise of Messiah was fulfilled. The law was meant to keep them from the moral and religious depravity of the nations they replaced in the land God had given them.

The guardian imposes strict expectations on those under his care because they do not know how to conduct themselves wisely without that imposition. Tutors are necessary, considering young students do not immediately internalize, understand, or appreciate the instruction they receive. Only with maturity, revelation, and the development of wisdom do we realize the importance of what we have been taught. The 'tutor' functioned until the time of Christ, who embodied the types and shadows of the underlying meaning of the law. For those who were watching and to whom the Lord granted understanding, this became crystal clear—the veil was lifted.

Paul referred to the law as a witness against sin. Its purpose was to keep people from having excuses, showing that all have fallen short of God's righteous standard (Rom. 3:19-20). Our only recourse in light of this condemnation is to repent and ask for God's mercy through Jesus' righteousness. Paul also argued that the reason sin was introduced to the human race was to bring death, the legal penalty for disobeying the law (Rom. 7:13). The wages of sin is death. This has never changed. If all men die because of the death sentence imposed by the law, then there will be no one fit to take dominion over the earth, God's original and therefore primary mandate to mankind (Gen. 1:26). 'So we can see how terrible sin really is. It uses God's good commands for its own evil purposes' (Rom. 7:13b, NLT).

God made precious promises to Abraham by faith long before the Mosaic law was given. The law was introduced to make men more aware of their sin until the time when those promises were fulfilled in the person of Jesus Christ. The essence of the law was to be a guardian of the race through which the promise would be fulfilled. It pointed to the promised Heir who would fulfill the law and reconcile all the people of the earth to God through faith. Jesus fulfilled the promise made to Abraham, a promise made apart from the law. [Note: Though Moses said keeping the law was not out of their reach (Deut. 30:11), the sad and redundant fact of history testifies that man naturally defaults to doing his own will and what is perceived as beneficial or desirous for selfish reasons.]

Jewish Perspective on the Law

In his article, "Love and Brotherhood," Tracey Rich explains the purpose of the law from the perspective of a traditional observant Jew. "Many people think of Judaism as the religion of cold, harsh laws, to be contrasted with Christianity, the religion of love and brotherhood. This is an unfair characterization of both Judaism and Jewish law. Love and kindness has been a part of Judaism from the very beginning… The Talmud tells a story of Rabbi Hillel, who lived around the time of Jesus. A pagan came to him saying that he would convert to Judaism if Hillel could teach him the whole of the Torah in the time he could stand on one foot. Rabbi Hillel replied, "What is hateful to yourself, do not do to your fellow man. That is the whole Torah; the rest is just commentary. Go and study it." Sounds a lot like Jesus' "Golden Rule"? But this idea was a fundamental part of Judaism long before Hillel or Jesus. It is a common-sense application of the Torah commandment to love your neighbor as yourself (Lev. 19:18), which Rabbi Akiba described as the essence of the Torah.

"The true difference between Judaism and Christianity lies in Hillel's last comment: Go and study it. Judaism is not content to leave love and brotherhood as a general ideal, to be fulfilled as each individual sees fit. Judaism spells out, in intricate detail, how we are meant to show that love... [T]he Ten Commandments command us not to murder. The full scope of Jewish law goes much farther in requiring us to protect our fellow man. We are commanded not to leave a condition that may cause harm, to construct our homes in ways that will prevent people from being harmed, and to help a person whose life is in danger, so long as it does not put our own lives in danger. These commandments regarding the preservation of life are so important in Judaism that they override all of the ritual observances that people think are the most important part of Judaism."[11]

This is the heart of the law as Jesus described and lived out. While I appreciate and agree with the explanation of the function of the law shared by Mr. Rich, the fact remains that the law does not intrinsically include the ability to change the heart. The limitations of the law as surveyed by the apostles are that it does not:

- bring freedom from the power of sin (Rom. 8:1-3);
- justify (Gal. 2:16);
- impart the Spirit (Gal. 3:2);
- give life or righteousness (Gal. 3:21);
- fulfill, make perfect, or complete anything (Heb. 7:19); or
- change the heart (Rom. 2:29).

But what Paul declares as the weakness of the law—that it is not accompanied by the power to change the heart—is the strength of the new covenant as described by Jeremiah (see Jer. 31:33-34). Under the new covenant, the law would be inscribed on the believer's heart. Furthermore, each believer would know the Lord and be known by Him because their sins would be forgiven and erased completely. This is the free gift we are given through faith in Jesus: reconciliation by being justified before God in Christ, no longer bearing the shame for sins God no longer remembers.

The precursor for knowing God, then, is forgiveness, not a perfect track record in the law. New Testament teaching may not include specific and systematic *mitzvot* as laid out in the Mosaic law, as Tracey Rich's comments suggest, but there is much teaching on the behavior believers are to demonstrate in their relationships to God and fellow believers as well as direction for church governance. Loving God with all our heart, soul, mind, and strength will enable us to grow into the right posture for walking righteously with our fellowman. Love forms the foundation for our actions toward our brothers, soberly viewing ourselves in light of the standard set by Jesus and the apostles. This is walking in faith, and when faith has come we no longer need the old guardian:

> *The law was our guardian **until Christ came**; it protected us **until we could be made right with God through faith**. And now that the way of faith has come, we no longer need the law **as our guardian**. For you are all children of God through faith in Christ Jesus.* -Gal. 3:24-26, NLT

Notice this passage does not say the law is no longer needed, but it is no longer needed *as a guardian*. The purpose of the law is good. The fault lay squarely with the people's mistreatment of it through pride, ignorance, willful rebellion, and/or indifference.

> *Therefore I was provoked with that generation, and said, 'They always go astray in their heart; they have not known my ways.'* -Heb. 3:9b, ESV

The Fruit of the Law

The fruit of man's *legalistic* view and interaction with the law was all bad:

- hypocrisy (Matt. 23:28; Gal. 2:12-13);
- self-righteousness (Rom. 10:2-3);
- death (2 Cor. 3:6-7);
- curse (Gal. 3:10);
- condemnation (2 Cor. 3:9);
- increase in sin (Rom. 7:7-13); and
- bondage (Gal. 4:21-5:1).

The futility of the law *by itself* to change men's hearts continued until the new covenant was established in Jesus. Described as a parable, the outer court symbolizes the external observances of the law which are incapable of allowing the obedient practitioner entrance to the holy place (Heb. 9:9). These cannot absolve us from the sin that prohibits entrance. Thus we see God wanted us to learn that mere striving to enter in through obedience to the law cannot earn entrance into His presence. Only forgiveness of sin can accomplish this, exemplified by the blood required to enter the holiest place.

In the new covenant, the process is reversed. We are placed squarely at the mercy seat in the holy of holies for forgiveness of sin and are made right with God. We then proceed through the torn veil to bask in the light of His presence (the eternal light) through prayer (altar of incense) and partaking of the Word (showbread) in the holy place. As we behold Him and are washed clean of wrong thinking and practice, we find that we can fulfill the ordinances of the outer court: walking in moral uprightness and obedience with the proper posture of heart, out of love for both God and man. This is how we have a foretaste of things to come.

[Note: There is more than one way of looking at this. The author of Hebrews states the outer court is symbolic of the present age (9:9), which Paul calls 'this present evil age' (Gal. 1:4). This foreshadows two ages to come: the first spent in the holy place with Jesus during the millennial reign (Rev. 20:4,6), and the second in the holy of holies when the Lord God Almighty once more lives with men (Rev. 21:3).]

Lamentably, for most the law was merely a set of rules to be obeyed to avoid punishment. But for the relatively few who grasped the intent of the perfect law of God in even a small measure, the whole realm of God's nature and love for people opened up.

SECTION 3 HARMONIZED VIEW OF LAW AND FREEDOM

Helen Keller experienced this critical point of sudden understanding when she came to the realization the shapes formed in her hand were actually words describing the object for which they stood. Communication had now been established—a true epiphany.

Interestingly, transgressions of the Mosaic law that carried the death sentence required execution by stoning, the same material on which the law was written. How ironic that this parallels our expression of 'throwing the book at someone' who has broken multiple laws, since our laws are written in books. Object lessons are everywhere.

Jesus Fulfills the Law

Everything must be fulfilled that is written about me in the Law of Moses, the Prophets and the Psalms. -Luke 24:44, NIV

The tribe of Judah had to be preserved in order to bring forth the Messiah. Likewise, the tribe of Levi was required to serve in the temple at the time of the Messiah so Jesus could fulfill all the law. Without the temple and the Levitical priesthood in the land, this would not have been possible. One of the primary roles of priests included teaching the people. Jesus operated in this role while in Israel and now intercedes as our high priest today so that we grow in our knowledge of God.

Jesus was born under the law (Gal. 4:4), walked it out perfectly in His life on earth, and satisfied God's justice on the cross by becoming the sin offering for us. Jesus demonstrated the mercy of God as the sinless sacrifice for all who are under the curse of death. We are now reconciled to God and free to celebrate His benevolence and mercy every day of our lives.

*Christ is the end of the law **for righteousness**.* -Rom. 10:4, NKJV

This passage specifically points out that Jesus has fulfilled the law, making an end of the law *for righteousness.* The law can nevermore be considered the means for making one righteous before God. Jesus walked out the law perfectly, accomplishing all its requirements for Israel as well as for the Gentiles, thereby nullifying the curse of the law for disobedience. The curse of the law is never meant to refer to following the commands and living within the framework of *Torah*. Rather, the curse of the law is spelled out as such in the Mosaic covenant and was shouted from Mt. Ebal (Deut. 27:9-26; 28:15-68).

All have sinned and fallen short, whether by action or heart posture. By identifying Himself with the nation of Israel (Matt. 2:15; cf. Hos. 11:1), Jesus executed Israel's obligations to the Mosaic covenant as Israel's delegated proxy. By fulfilling the requirements of the old covenant for the nation of Israel, Jesus cancelled the curse forever. His blameless life and sacrifice made Him the legal heir of the covenant promise of the land of Israel. Those among Israel who have accepted *Yeshua* as the promised Messiah will rule and reign with Him in the land, as promised to Abraham.

But this was deemed too small a thing for so precious a sacrifice. Jesus also annulled the curse of death for Gentiles by His obedience to the universal laws known to all men. God therefore gave Jesus the nations as well: the people and the authority to govern all kingdoms. Those who are cleansed and follow the law written on their hearts will now partake of the original command in the Garden. What a marvelous thing Jesus has done for both Israel and those of us 'who were far off.' Through this new covenant, we are granted a cleansed conscience that includes engraving the law on our hearts. This part comes without cost. It is freely given; all who call upon the Lord will be saved.

Jesus came to fulfill the law. He followed it perfectly, walking in the authority of one who fully understood its import and utility for men. He kept all of its statutes, fully compliant with its requirements and complexities involving heart, mind, and strength, while not ignoring the weightier matters. He not only walked out the law in perfect outward obedience, His heart, soul, mind, and strength were engaged as well. By so doing, Jesus became the only man who fulfilled the *Sh'ma*—to actively hear and obey God in fulfilling the spirit of the law—and thereby became qualified to initiate the new covenant by virtue of having met the requirements of the first. The law is ended *for righteousness.*

The new law of the Spirit of life is ours in Christ and has set us free from the law of sin and death (Rom. 8:2). This is the principle Paul repeatedly hammered home in his letters. The old covenant has been fulfilled in Christ, and there is a new and superior covenant that has taken its place. Only in the new covenant will we find life (2 Cor. 3:6).

The Law Written on the Heart

Paul finds no fault with the law itself, but with those who reduced it to something merely written. 'Gentiles do not have the written law, yet they will still be condemned as guilty because of their sin. The Jews will be judged by the law when they fail to obey it. Merely listening to the law does not make us right before God; obedience is the key. This is seen in the Gentiles who do not have the written moral law, yet instinctively obey it without ever having heard it. By this they demonstrate that God's law is written on their conscience, which either accuses or exonerates their behavior. The day is coming when God will judge everyone's secret life' (Rom. 2:12-16). In other words, we may lie to ourselves and rationalize our immoral behavior, but deep down we know when we are doing wrong. This will be exposed by God on the appointed day.

There is a difference between the use of the word law in reference to the old covenant given to Israel at Mt. Sinai, and the law as God's commands and will for righteous living etched on the heart of every man. While there is much in common between the two, there are particular aspects of the Mosaic covenant peculiar to Israel (e.g., circumcision) and meant to serve as types and shadows, not standards of living for all people. This is not always clearly spelled out in Scripture, particularly in our English translations. Regardless, mere outward obedience doesn't constitute a proper response from God's

SECTION 3 HARMONIZED VIEW OF LAW AND FREEDOM

point of view, whether we follow the requirements of the old covenant in hopes of justification, or follow the universal laws of righteous living in order to earn God's favor.

The Word gives ample evidence that the morality of God is written on the hearts of all men, otherwise the destruction of Sodom and Gomorrah, for example, would be unjustified. Nine of the Ten Commandments are attested to in Scripture prior to the giving of the law at Mt. Sinai. The commandment to honor the Sabbath day is the only one absent from the list. Though God Himself set the seventh day apart as holy, there is no record that men honored this day as a day of rest prior to the Mosaic law.

1. **Do not have other gods before Me** (Gen. 5:22; 6:9; 17:1; 22:12; 28:21; Job 1:8; 31:24-28; see also Ex. 15:2).
2. **Do not make for yourself any graven image** (Gen. 35:2).
3. **Do not take the name of the Lord in vain** (Gen. 14:22-23; 24:3).
4. **Honor your father and mother** (Gen. 9:22-27).
5. **Do not murder** (Gen. 4:8-16).
6. **Do not commit adultery** (Gen. 12:18-20; 20:1-9; 26:1-10; 39:9; Job 31:1,9-10).
7. **Do not steal** (Gen. 31:7; 44:8).
8. **Do not bear false witness** (Job 31:5).
9. **Do not covet** (Job 31:7).

Job goes through a litany of wrongs he has kept himself from committing, including thwarting justice (31:13-14), ignoring the plight of the poor and needy (31:16-23), and rejoicing in the demise of enemies (31:29-30). From these accounts we have evidence of the God-given conscience every man possesses, testifying for or against their deeds, before the Mosaic law. Because of this, God is justified in having destroyed Sodom. The laws they transgressed are those which are condemned in almost every society. And what were the sins of Sodom?

> *Now this was the sin of your sister Sodom: She and her daughters were **arrogant, overfed and unconcerned** ('prosperous ease,' ESV; 'idleness,' AMP); **they did not help the poor and needy. They were haughty and did detestable things before me.** Therefore I did away with them as you have seen.* -Ezk. 16:49-50, NIV

The new covenant brings life because it does not operate from the external and move inward, but rather starts in our spirit by cleansing our conscience from sin. This produces life *inwardly* in order to produce godly behavior *outwardly*. The believer is enabled to obey the law of God on their hearts, which is the spirit of the law. Paul describes this as the law even the Gentiles obey because our spirits, made in the image of God, have His standards etched in them. 'Circumcision is a matter of the heart, by the Spirit, not by the letter' (Rom. 2:29). Satisfied in Christ, the requirements of the old covenant have been met and the curse removed.

External observance of the written law did not accomplish regeneration of the heart but only made us more aware of sin's dominion. More importantly, if we are under *any* part of the law for the hope of being made right with God, we are still under the curse of the law (Gal. 3:10). The old covenant fulfilled its purpose until the time of Christ as a witness against sin and as the guardian of the promise made to Abraham.

When the promise arrived, the old covenant was fulfilled and the contract set aside for the new covenant in Christ. The existence of the moral code (nine of the Ten Commandments) prior to Mt. Sinai has been noted. Paul wrote about the moral code's universality because of what could be seen in the behavior of righteous Gentiles who did not have the law of Moses. The laws kept by Abraham predated the Mosaic law, yet God called these *His* laws. It can be reasoned that the moral code is written in the conscience of man as he bears the image of God, whether he attends to that conscience or not.

The Mosaic law codified the universal moral laws already in existence into an expression targeted specifically for Israel, namely by the addition of Sabbath and ceremonial observances. In addition, the Mosaic law provided types and shadows of the nature of God's wisdom, kingdom, and promised Redeemer, particularly through the ceremonial laws. The primary point of the replacement of the old covenant is removal of the curse that accompanied violation of the law. The bottom line for believers: we have Christ's righteousness and therefore the law can't condemn us (Rom. 4:4-8; 5:1; 7:1-6; 8:1-2).

God's Standard for Israel

> *See, I have taught you decrees and laws as the LORD my God commanded me...* ***Observe them carefully, for this will show your wisdom and understanding to the nations****, who will hear about all these decrees and say, "****Surely this great nation is a wise and understanding people****."* -Deut. 4:5-6, NIV

Israel's observance of the law witnessed to other nations the wisdom and presence of God through the righteousness of the law given. As it is today with no temple, even *Torah* observant Jews are able to follow only 271 of the 613 mitzvot—less than half of the law. This is because many of the laws apply to the priests and Levites, temple duties and worship, and theocratic governance. "The modern scholar Rabbi Israel Meir of Radin, commonly known as the Chafetz Chayim, has identified 77 positive mitzvot and 194 negative mitzvot which can be observed outside of Israel today."[12]

Paul makes the distinction that Israel failed to uphold the law because they pursued it as performance rather than on the basis of faith (Rom. 9:31-33). This caused them to stumble over Jesus, who showed them the futility of their brand of righteousness. Only in the righteousness of Christ can we be accepted before God.

With the Mosaic covenant fulfilled, the new covenant prophesied in Isaiah, Jeremiah, and Ezekiel could be enacted. This covenant is built on better promises and sealed with the innocent blood of the Lamb of God. Moreover, with a conscience cleansed from sin, we are now free to follow God's righteous decrees by the empowerment of the Spirit through faith. No further sacrifice would ever be required to atone for sins. The old covenant sacrifices never atoned for sin (Heb. 9:9), but rather pointed to the promised Messiah who would one day offer Himself in our place, just as the sacrificial animal took our place under the old covenant. All of this required faith in the promise to come.

One of the traps the people fell into regarding the sacrificial animals is they did not understand that the unblemished animals represented the spotless Son of God who would come at the appointed time to be a sacrifice for sin. If they had truly understood this, it would have been unthinkable to offer as a picture of the promised Messiah the lame and sick animals for which they were rebuked (Mal. 1:8). The imagery of the perfect sacrifice escaped their understanding, and many viewed the sacrificial animals merely as commodities of marketable value.

The Jewish Apostles Continued to Keep the Law

Most of us have been under the impression Paul gave up following the Mosaic law when he evangelized the Gentiles. Quite the opposite, Paul's own confession reveals he continued to follow the law, however no longer with religious zeal. Look closely at the following verses. They are in agreement that not only did Paul observe the Mosaic law, he maintained Jewish believers in *Yeshua* were also to continue in the law of Moses. Keep in mind these statements were made later in his life as an apostle.

> *I admit that I worship the God of our ancestors as a follower of the Way, which they call a sect.* ***I believe everything that is in accordance with the Law*** *and that is written in the Prophets... So* ***I strive always to keep my conscience clear*** *before God and man.* -Acts 24:14,16, NIV

> *Paul argued in his defense, "****Neither against the law of the Jews, nor against the temple****, nor against Caesar* ***have I committed any offense.****"* -Acts 25:8, ESV

> *Paul said to them: "My brothers, although I* ***have done nothing against our people or against the customs of our ancestors,*** *I was arrested in Jerusalem and handed over to the Romans."* -Acts 28:17b, NIV

James was also eager to dispel rumors that Paul was teaching the believing Jews to cast off the Mosaic law. Thousands of Jews came to believe in Jesus as their Messiah but were troubled when they heard rumors that Paul taught other Jews to 'abandon Moses' by telling them not to circumcise their children or follow the Jewish customs. With Paul's arrival in Jerusalem, James wanted to destroy this rumor by asking Paul to demonstrate his loyalty and adherence to the law:

> *They will certainly hear that you've come. Therefore do what we tell you: We have four men who have obligated themselves with a vow. Take these men, purify yourself along with them...* ***Then everyone will know that what they were***

> ***told about you amounts to nothing***, *but that **you yourself are also careful about observing the law**.* -Acts 21:22b-24, HCSB

This was not conspiracy to commit hypocrisy, as I once thought. After confronting Paul about the situation, Paul was anxious to prove his faithfulness to the law by agreeing to James' plan. In the rest of this passage, James makes the distinction that the believing Gentiles, in contrast, were only obligated to keep the four commands decided upon at the Jerusalem Council (Acts 21:25; see Acts 15:1-32).

The law of Moses remains the inheritance for Israel, not as the means to righteousness but to be obeyed in faith that God will bring redemption and fulfill His oath to Abraham as *promised*, not through performance. For the Jew who has recognized *Yeshua* as his Messiah, this law no longer carries the curse. The Jew is saved by faith, just as the Gentile, and the ministry of the Holy Spirit will make sure the law becomes part of his heart and not mere outward obedience. This is accomplished through the process of sanctification and is the glory of the new covenant.

> *The righteousness based on faith says... The word is near you, in your mouth and in your heart... For there is no distinction between Jew and Greek; the same Lord is Lord of all, bestowing his riches on all who call on him. For "everyone who calls on the name of the Lord will be saved."* -Rom. 10:6a,8b,12-13, ESV

There are other passages that on surface inspection appear to say Peter and Paul no longer followed Jewish law (e.g., Gal. 2:14; Rom. 14). On closer scrutiny, however, these merely point out they had fellowship with Gentiles, who were considered 'common' or 'profane' to a people devoted to separation. In addition, they may have eaten the 'common' meats offered in the marketplace as the Gentiles did. 'Common' meats are not to be confused with 'unclean' meats (pork, shellfish, etc.). The 'common' meats were differentiated by the method of butchering, labeled 'common' because they were not butchered in an approved kosher manner.

This becomes more apparent when the Greek words used are compared. *Koinos* means to be 'common or defiled,' used in Romans 14 in the sense of being a 'clean' meat that is not fit for Jewish standards. *Koinos* does not refer to an *unclean* meat, as it is often translated, but rather to a 'clean' meat that is not butchered properly with respect to Jewish tradition. In the case of 'unclean' meats, the word *akathartos* (legal or ceremonial uncleanness) is used, as differentiated in Peter's vision (Acts 10:9-16,28).

In Peter's vision, the translation is given by Peter himself. His interpretation indicated he did not take the vision literally as a command to eat 'unclean' meats, but rather as a command to ignore the oral tradition that forbade fraternity with 'unclean' Gentiles:

> *Peter said to them, "You know it's forbidden for a Jewish man to associate with or visit a foreigner. But God has shown me that I must not call **any person** common (**koinos**) or unclean (**akathartos**)."* -Acts 10:28, HCSB

In any case, the kosher dietary laws were now seen as secondary to the greater purpose God had in mind: the salvation of the Gentiles and the forming of 'one new man' from Jew and Gentile in Christ. This focus enabled the apostles to view and walk in these weightier matters in lieu of their former rigid adherence to the law. The law itself would continue, though now written on the heart with the weightier matters taking priority. The Mosaic law in particular, as the inheritance of Israel, continues under the new covenant for the Jewish believer, as Paul, James, and Peter attest. Unfortunately, the *Torah* (including the oral traditions) and the land of Israel have become idols in the hearts of some, elevated to a position of worship that is reserved for God alone. This is not the spirit of Abraham, who was willing to put his inheritance on the altar at the behest of God, in faith knowing God is able to raise the dead; in faith knowing God could keep His promise no matter what. The precise point at which the law becomes an idol occurs when it is elevated above the One to whom it pointed—Jesus the Messiah.

God's Standard for Gentiles

> *Even Gentiles, who do not have God's written law, show that they know his law when they instinctively obey it, even without having heard it. They demonstrate that God's law is written in their hearts.* -Rom. 2:14-15a, NLT

Generally speaking, Gentiles were outside the covenants and promises made to Israel. Provision made for their inclusion came from conversion (Num. 9:14; 15:14-15). According to tradition, proselytes to Judaism were circumcised and baptized, and then presented a sacrificial offering as part of their initiation into Judaism. They were expected to follow the Mosaic law, including dietary laws, Sabbath observance, and the other regulations in order to partake of the covenant promises of Israel. Proselytes were afforded privileges not granted to those who merely sojourned with Israel in the land. But God promised even the sojourner an inheritance in the land of Israel in the millennial kingdom (Ezk. 47:21-23).

Sojourners

God's love and concern for the Gentiles is attested throughout the Bible (e.g., 2 Kings 5:1-18; Matt. 8:5-13; Mark 7:24-30; Luke 4:24-27). The poor sojourners in Israel were to receive the third year tithe along with the Levites, widows, and orphans (Deut. 14:28-30), and they were not to do any work for the Israelites on the Sabbath in order to partake of the blessing of Sabbath rest (Ex. 20:10). To those who oppressed and 'thrust aside' the sojourners, God promised He would be a 'swift witness' against them for judgment. Those who act in this manner do so from lack of the fear of the Lord (Mal. 3:5).

The sojourner was not forgotten by God. In fact, God kept watch over them for their good. Israel was to remember they were once sojourners in Egypt. God expected Israel to treat the sojourners fairly and neither wrong nor oppress them (Ex. 22:21). God loves the sojourners and makes sure they have food and clothing (Deut. 10:18), watching over them to protect them from the wicked (Ps. 146:9).

With the exception of the circumcised proselytes, sojourners could not eat the Passover unless they, too, became circumcised (Ex. 12:45-48). While the law required the same *mishpat* for native born and sojourner, the sojourners do not seem to be held to the *chukim* or *edot* unless they stood before the Lord as part of the congregation of Israel (Num. 15:15-16). Only the laws of civil governance (*mishpat*) seem to be in common, as noted by the different standard in the second passage.

> *You shall have the same rule* (**mishpat**) *for the sojourner and for the native, for I am the LORD your God.* -Lev. 24:22, ESV

> *You shall not eat anything that has died naturally. You may give it to the sojourner who is within your towns, that he may eat it, or you may sell it to a foreigner.* -Deut. 14:21a, ESV

God-fearers

The God-fearers, in contrast with Gentile proselytes or the sojourners who lived in Israel, were Gentiles outside of Israel who did not subject themselves to circumcision but identified with Israel through affiliation with their worship and belief in Israel's God. They endeavored to honor God through prayer, alms-giving, and engaging in *Torah* study by attending synagogue meetings. Generally speaking, they were excluded only from Passover celebration (which required circumcision for participation) and were considered outside the covenant promises to Israel. Gentiles received salvation by their inclusion in the scope of God's redemptive grace. This is seen in the redemptive preaching of Jonah to the Ninevites. The Feast of Tabernacles presents a picture of God's redemptive grace to the nations, represented by the seventy bulls sacrificed as a foreshadowing of the seventy nations of the world (see Gen. 10).

Cornelius the centurion lived the life of a God-fearer. He walked righteously, gave generously to the poor, prayed continually, and his whole household feared God (Acts 10:1-4,22). His prayers were heard by God, and God acknowledged Cornelius' alms-giving as worthy of remembrance ('recorded in His book,' cf. Mal. 3:16).

> *We know that God doesn't listen to sinners, but if anyone is God-fearing and does His will, He listens to him.* -John 9:31, HCSB

The presence of God-fearing Gentiles whose prayers are heard by God negates the Talmudic tradition that all Gentiles are sinners outside of God's redemptive grace. If they were sinners, their prayers would not have been heard. For God-fearing Gentiles, the morality of the Jews was adopted without necessarily taking on the ceremonial observances of specific days, dietary restrictions, or sacrifices. The code of behavior for God-fearing Gentiles can be understood as including several components:

- the laws given to Noah
- the moral aspects of the Jewish law, instinctively written on the heart
- alms-giving
- prayer
- *Torah* study
- (arguably) fasting

This code of behavior would be stressed under the new covenant as well, with the cornerstone being belief in Christ and faith in the atoning work He accomplished at the cross. The new covenant meant Gentiles were no longer required to become circumcised Jewish proselytes who followed Jewish law in order to be grafted in. With the advent of the new covenant in Christ, Gentiles found themselves in the happy position to be included in the promises of God without the requirement of becoming a proselyte.

Remain as You Are

> *[R]emain as you were when God first called you. This is my rule for all the churches. For instance... the man who was uncircumcised when he became a believer should not be circumcised now. For it makes no difference whether or not a man has been circumcised. The **important thing is to keep God's commandments** (**entole**).* -1 Cor. 7:17b-19, NLT (parenthetical added)

Paul exhorted each believer to remain as he was before coming to faith in Christ, a theme he reiterates in verses 20 and 24. A Jew was to remain a Jew and a Gentile was to remain a Gentile. In Romans, Paul states that all receive the gift of righteousness and salvation by faith. 'We are all certain to receive it, guaranteed not only to those who live according to the law of Moses but also to those with faith like Abraham' (Rom. 4:16-17). Paul here reinforces apostolic teaching that in Christ, Jews still practice the law of Moses, in contrast with Gentiles who are neither required nor encouraged to do so.

Notice in the above passage that circumcision is not included as part of 'God's commands.' What are these commands, then, if not those involving circumcision (i.e., the Mosaic law)? Since we have established that the Jewish law was to remain the standard for the Jew to follow, what standards are the Gentiles to follow? What law would be written on their hearts?

A New Command

The command most frequently given to those under the new covenant is to love one another. Jesus' answer to the Pharisees' question regarding the commandments of God was stated in such a way as to be universally applicable: 'Love the Lord your God with all your heart, mind, and strength, and love your neighbor as yourself' (Matt. 22:34-40). During His final intimate gathering with the disciples, Jesus gave the disciples a 'new command.' They were to love each other as He had loved them so everyone would know they were His disciples (John 13:34-35). John the apostle taught that we have assurance we have passed from death to eternal life if we love each other (1 John 3:14). As recorded by John, God's commandment is that we believe in the name of Jesus and love one another as *proof* we are abiding in Him (1 John 3:21-24). Jesus' command to love our neighbor as ourselves not only encompasses behavior that keeps us from harming another (e.g., adultery, murder, theft, slander), but includes commands to honor parents and help others in need (Luke 18:18-25). The apostles were anxious for believers under the new covenant to learn to demonstrate their love for one another and not merely talk about it.

By not focusing on the details of rules, we would be freer to follow the Spirit in matters of love, mercy, and justice without thinking twice about whether or not our action might break the laws of types and shadows, which were primarily meant to illustrate spiritual principles. This is not referring to laws about moral sins, but rather to ceremonial laws for washing, diet, Sabbath, etc. which do not harm another if not performed. The new covenant commands emphasized by Jesus and the apostles were simple:

- Love for God
- Love for neighbor
- Faith in Jesus as Messiah

This is the law reduced to its basic form in order to have one law for both Jew and Gentile under the new covenant. The way in which this law is expressed may be different, but the framework of the law is the same.

> *So in everything, do to others what you would have them do to you, for this sums up the Law and the Prophets.* -Matt. 7:12, NIV

The command or charge of God (*entole*) is not the equivalent of the law (*nomos*), though they are not mutually exclusive. We have previously noted that circumcision is not included as a 'command' (*entole*) of God for the Gentiles (1 Cor. 7:19), even though it remains a specific command (*nomos*) for the Jew as a sign. *Entole* gives greater weight to the authority of the One giving the command than to the command itself. Herein lies the difference between following the law by rote, and following the law by staying in step with the Holy Spirit, always ready to have your Sabbath observance interrupted by the needs of a neighbor; ready to show mercy to those who have wronged us and deserve punishment by the law's standards; ready to demonstrate the weightier matters of the law as the higher expression of faithfulness to the law than following the letter.

Following the law in the manner Jesus prescribed and practiced allows for the demonstration of mercy, kindness, and true justice. He neither did nor said anything unless it originated with the Father (John 12:49). In one way, the law exists so God can demonstrate His mercy (Rom. 11:28-32), and by His example we learn to demonstrate mercy to others. We abide in God's love by abiding in His Word and keeping His command that

SECTION 3 HARMONIZED VIEW OF LAW AND FREEDOM

we love one another, praying for whatever is in keeping with His love and Word abiding in us. This will bear much fruit for God's kingdom and bring Him glory (John 15:4-17). Love fulfills the law (Rom. 13:10).

Living as Jesus Did

> *This is how we know we are in him: Whoever claims to live in him must live as Jesus did.* -1 John 2:5b-6, NIV

To live as Jesus did is to place priority on the weightier matters of the law. He focused on hearing the will of God in any given situation rather than forging ahead based on legalistic observance of the law or walking presumptuously in humanistic mercy. The law is good, provided it is used properly.

We know that Abraham followed God's *torah*, which was not the Mosaic law but the moral law on his God-given conscience and the specific commands given to him personally. The 'God-fearers' who followed the laws given to Noah, turned from sin, had faith God would provide them with a redeemer Messiah, and gave generously to those in need as an expression of righteousness, were esteemed by the Jewish community as those who would have a part in the *olam habah* (the world to come).

The Gentiles never agreed to the Mosaic covenant made at Mt. Sinai, where those in agreement were sealed to that covenant by the blood of sprinkling. There has never been a command for those outside the Mosaic covenant to observe washings, tithing, festivals, holy days, or even the Sabbath. The Mosaic covenant was specifically made with the people of Israel and their generations after them who would inhabit the land of Israel as stewards over God's property. It was not a condition of inheriting the promise made to Abraham. That promise came by faith. Abel, Enoch, Noah, Abraham, Isaac, and Jacob were never under the Mosaic covenant or subject to Mosaic law, yet each received the promise of redemption by faith, as do all Gentiles.

Gentiles may not have been included in the Mosaic covenant, but certainly other passages attest to the morality and ethics common to the human race as a whole. Paul wrote that the Gentiles do what is right by nature because their conscience testifies for or against them. This conscience is nothing less than the image of God given only to man, and hence the only reliable witness against sin other than God Himself. But the fact remains we can ignore or sear our conscience through rationalization and repeated sin. Because of this, the Ten Commandments serve as a righteous standard for humanity in general.

Acts 15

Because of the influx of Gentiles into the new covenant, the Jewish leaders had to determine how much of the law, if any, the Gentiles should be required to follow. This was not for making one righteous before God, but possibly for the sake of fellowship with Jewish believers, clearing confusion regarding the inclusion of non-proselytized Gentiles into the covenant promises of Israel, or arguably as a starting point for sanctification.

Salvation and the Holy Spirit had already been given to Gentile believers apart from the law. Many of the Jewish believers had the understanding that those who would take part in the promises made to Israel must be circumcised, as were Abraham and all the males in his house. These tried to impose circumcision and obedience to the law of Moses on the Gentiles as a requirement for salvation (Acts 15:1). They correctly understood upright behavior as the evidence of abiding in Messiah. The Mosaic law would provide for a homogenous code of behavior, which is especially desirable by those who prefer uniformity.

Peter responded that doing so puts God to the test because all are saved by the grace of Christ (Acts 15:10-11). Peter understood: 1.) righteousness is granted to us *by grace*, 2.) sanctification of our behavior comes *by grace* working through us, and 3.) the redemption of our bodies is fulfilled *by grace* at Jesus' return. The question before the apostles and elders was this: Can the Gentiles be grafted into the promises and covenant blessings of Israel (in this case, the prophesied new covenant) without obedience to the Mosaic law?

After their discussion, James addressed the assembly by recalling the prophet Amos' words that the Gentiles called by God's name would seek the Lord when the promised Heir from David's line arrived (Amos 9:11-12). He then stated:

> **Therefore my judgment is that we should not trouble those of the Gentiles who turn to God**, *but should write to them to abstain from the **things polluted by idols**, and from **sexual immorality**, and from **what has been strangled**, and from **blood**. For from ancient generations Moses has had in every city those who proclaim him, for he is read every Sabbath in the synagogues.* -Acts 15:19-21, ESV

The last sentence of this passage can be interpreted various ways, of which these are two:

- Since the teachings of Moses are preached in every city that has a synagogue, the Gentiles will eventually learn what is pleasing to God by hearing *Torah* instruction. For now, they must immediately give up these four things they are currently practicing, because these practices inhibit fellowship with their Jewish brothers. Obedience to the rest of Mosaic law will come in time.
- Because the teachings of Moses are preached every Sabbath where the Gentiles learn alongside the Jews, we have to make sure they know the Mosaic law was given specifically to Israel. After all, the Gentiles received the Holy Spirit and salvation without the law of Moses. To hear Moses preached may continue to confuse them as to what role the law has for the Gentile believer in *Yeshua*. These four commands are sufficient to keep them walking in the 'perfect law of Christ,' fostering good relations with their Jewish brothers. The rest of Mosaic teaching will help them grow in wisdom and understanding.

The decisions rendered by the early believers can be viewed as *halakhic* decisions based on their knowledge of Scripture and the objectives of the new covenant. These objectives are to walk morally upright by freedom from the power of sin, to love God with all the heart, mind, soul, and strength, and to love others as we do ourselves.

SECTION 3 HARMONIZED VIEW OF LAW AND FREEDOM

Perhaps it was on this last point that the leaders in Jerusalem decided to impose guidelines as to the use of certain points of the law to promote fellowship between Jews and Gentiles. Certain pagan religious behaviors of the now converted Gentiles (namely odious dietary habits and the common practice of sexual immorality) were offensive to the Jews and made fellowship problematic.

In light of the Word and especially Peter's comments in Acts 15:10, the second conclusion offered would be the more likely. Gentiles learn a great deal about Jesus and the kingdom of God as they hear and understand the types and shadows embedded in the *Torah*. Though the law of Moses is not binding on Gentiles, learning the underlying spiritual significance fosters growth in knowledge of our Savior and the work He has accomplished. As for adherence to the Mosaic law, the Gentiles have no obligation except where there is overlap with the common moral laws of conscience given generally to mankind.

We can base these conclusions on James' statement that 'no greater burden' will be placed on the Gentiles other than the four requirements mentioned (Acts 15:28). Hearing this caused rejoicing because it encouraged the Gentiles by eliminating the confusion that existed at the time (Acts 15:31). They now understood they were not required to become Jewish proselytes in order to enter into the promise of life through the new covenant. This also shows the confidence the apostles had in the power of the Holy Spirit to guide the conscience of the new believers into righteous behavior befitting a follower of Christ.

This conclusion would also be in keeping with Paul's admonition for each to 'stay as he is' at the time he turns to Christ: Jews as Jews, and Gentiles as Gentiles. This is not segregation, but a matter of honoring the differences God created as well as demonstrating God is no respecter of persons. Anyone who accepts the righteousness of Christ is saved, not only those who follow the Mosaic law. Do men try to make women become as they are, or women force men to become like them? That would be senseless, and perhaps we can agree that making a Jew behave as a Gentile or vice versa is equally unfounded. As recorded in Acts 21:20-26, James was zealous for the thousands of Jewish believers to know that Paul did not teach *Jews* to abrogate the law, and that Paul himself was *Torah* observant. In contradistinction, James made certain he also mentioned that Gentiles were not obligated to follow Jewish law, but rather only the requirements decided upon earlier, as recorded in Acts 15 (see previous discussion on Acts 21:25).

As additional weight for this view, recall all the verses which hammer home the apostles' ruling that circumcision is not a requirement for the Gentile under the new covenant (Rom. 2:27-29; 1 Cor. 7:19; Gal. 5:6; 6:15; Col. 2:11; cf. Titus 1:10-11). If the new covenant then requires the Gentiles to somehow eventually become followers of the Mosaic law as part of the process of sanctification, how could the uncircumcised Gentiles possibly partake of the foundational festival of *Pesach* (Passover)? This festival requires that *all* who partake of it according to the Mosaic law be circumcised in the flesh (Ex. 12:48).

CHAPTER 8 *THE ROLE OF THE LAW*

Gentiles Keep the Spirit of the Law

> *Open my eyes so that I can see the wonderful truths in your law.* -Psalm 119:18, NIRV

Paul, however, made celebrating the festival of Passover in the Lord's Supper a spiritual exercise rather than one of adhering to the old requirements. For Gentiles, the way in which we honor the Lord is to remember Jesus is our Passover Lamb, and that we are to put out the leaven of malice and sin because we now have a circumcised heart (1 Cor. 5:7-11). For the Gentile, Paul emphasized the spiritual lessons to be learned from the pattern handed to Moses and recorded in the *Torah*.

Speaking to the predominantly Gentile believers at Colossae, Paul addresses the criticism or faulty teaching they had received and redirects their attention to the preeminence of Christ.

> *[D]o not let anyone judge you by what you eat or drink, or with regard to a religious festival, a New Moon celebration or a Sabbath day. These are a shadow of the things that were to come;* **the reality, however, is found in Christ.** -Col. 2:16-17, NIV

Being without law was never a question for the apostles, for it was understood that lawlessness is of Satan. The real question was deciding which laws were to be followed by the converts who entered from outside Judaism. This question was answered in a way that brought the witness of the Holy Spirit, and the body of Christ will benefit by operating in agreement with that decision. Paul's advice to Titus certainly anticipated the strife engendered by quarrels regarding the law within both the Gentile churches and the Jewish congregations.

> *[A]void foolish controversies and genealogies and arguments and quarrels about the law, because these are unprofitable and useless.* -Titus 3:9, NIV

While much of what has been written regarding the role of the Mosaic law in the life of a new covenant believer could be construed as teaching, there is also the presence of divisive rancor toward those of opposing views. Some have been so bold as to state if one rejects the Mosaic law as the charter for behavior, it is because they think it is okay to murder, steal, and commit adultery. Are we to believe that the only thing holding us back from these sins is a written law? Or is it the law of God written on our hearts and the presence of the Holy Spirit that guides us in upright living?

> *[T]he law is good, if one uses it lawfully, understanding this, that the law is not laid down for the just but for the lawless and disobedient.* -1 Tim. 1:8-9a, ESV

Those who have been made righteous by the blood of the new covenant in Christ do not need the law to tell them what is right and wrong because they have received the Spirit of God. The law is no longer a guardian, but it is still the possession of Israel. Is it because Messianic Jews are lawbreakers that they still require the law, as the above passage might suggest? No, but for the simple fact the Word declares the law is their inheritance. The divisiveness caused by quarrels about the role of the law is lamentable and grieves the heart of God. We must learn to keep our exalted opinions of our own teaching in perspective, for the arguments they generate are 'unprofitable and useless.'

The Whole Law

While the 613 commands in the Mosaic law have been categorized various ways, the commands are seen as one integrated whole, much as we view our U.S. Constitution. Paul and James also make this point, emphasizing we cannot rely on obedience to part of the law for justification before God. If we have failed *any* part of it, we have broken *all* of it.

- Those who rely on the law for righteousness are under a curse if they do not perform **all** of the law (Gal. 3:10), an impossibility without the temple and priests.
- If someone chooses one of the laws to obey as a means for right standing before God, he is obligated to obey the **whole** law (Gal. 5:3).
- Whoever stumbles in obeying just one point of the law is guilty of breaking **all** of it (James 2:10).

Surely it is obvious the believing Gentiles were not obeying Mosaic law but God's law on the heart. Otherwise, we cannot explain their lack of attention to circumcision. The type and shadow which indicated an individual was part of God's people—circumcision of the flesh by the law given to Abraham—is shown now to be circumcision of the heart by the Spirit in the life of the new covenant believer. Likewise, every time we see Jews observe the Sabbath, we are reminded that the Sabbath rest promised for God's people will be inaugurated at Jesus' return.

The Sabbath is a sign, kept by Jews to demonstrate that the promised Sabbath rest will come when the prophesied blessing from their race—the Davidic ruler *Yeshua*—returns to reign in righteousness and true justice over the earth. A Gentile may keep the Sabbath to rest from work and pursue God, reminding him of the future reign of the Jewish King when all men will cease from their religious striving and toil against one another. This sign is not to be understood as a commandment for the Gentile, but rather as a principle to promote fellowship with God. The Sabbatical kingship does not come from the Gentiles, but from the nation of Israel. God gave the Sabbath command to Israel alone. The sign of the Sabbath reminds us of the spiritual truth that the only righteous man to ever live, a Jew from Nazareth, will return to restore man's dominion authority over the earth.

A Truly <u>New</u> Covenant

Paul argues that the new covenant of the spirit is *superior* to the old covenant of the letter. He does not make any argument that the new covenant enables us to fulfill the old covenant. Taking such a view treats with contempt the Scriptures that confirm the *fulfillment* of the Mosaic covenant by Jesus alone. It is finished! Once again, if we are trying to fulfill old covenant obligations with the empowerment provided in the new covenant, as some have reasoned, we have usurped the authority of Christ and taken an allotment (fulfilling the Mosaic covenant) that not only is not our own (it was Christ's), it is redundant: He has already fulfilled it. God *set aside* the first covenant to establish the second (Heb. 10:8-10).

Though the emphasis of Gentile practice regarding the Mosaic law is spiritual in nature, James warns we are not to judge those who follow the law (James 4:11-12). Likewise, Paul exhorted believers to walk out their faith fully convinced of their practice before the Lord without passing judgment on those who practice differently (Rom. 14). Whatever our views are on matters of religious practice (not moral issues), Paul recommended we keep these things between ourselves and God.

Asceticism

The apostles addressed ascetic practices to caution believers. In their zeal to please the Lord, some have adopted lifestyles of severe treatment of the body frowned upon by the apostles (1 Tim. 4:1-5). Very few have the maturity to live this kind of lifestyle *voluntarily* without being puffed up in their accomplishment, or without it affecting how they feel as they stand before God. They feel connected, confident, and worthy if they do well, and the opposite if they don't carry out their commitment perfectly (cf. Gal. 6:15).

Many ascetics are unable to feel worthy before the Lord unless they deny themselves all the blessings God gives us in this life. This questionable position foregoes plain scriptural teaching that our worth is found in Christ. He alone has made us worthy before God. Even under the old covenant, the Lord encouraged worshippers coming from great distances to exchange their tithe for money beforehand so when they arrived in Jerusalem they could buy *whatever they liked* for the tithe meal they would eat joyfully in His presence (Deut. 14:26). [Note: Seasons of protracted fasting, Nazarite vows, etc. are not the subject of apostolic caution, but rather ascetic practices to prove piety and worth.]

The Lord wants us to enjoy the blessings He delights to give us. Neither strict asceticism nor the life devoid of discipline is fitting for believers (1 Thes. 4:4-8). We must trust the Holy Spirit to lead us gradually into the lifestyle of prayer, giving, and fasting as our hearts are gradually conformed by washing with the Word. At the same time, we are free to enjoy those legitimate pleasures of life God has also given to us as blessings.

The Utility of the Law

The utility of the law for the Gentile believer is found in discovering how the law teaches us about Christ. Gentiles who desire to observe the festivals and other practices in the law are not restrained from doing so as long as the observance is out of desire rather than compunction or some vain imagining that it will make one in better standing with God. How can we possibly be in a better position than standing before God in the righteousness of Christ?

SECTION 3 HARMONIZED VIEW OF LAW AND FREEDOM

Thomas Edison said, "Just because something doesn't do what you planned it to do doesn't mean it's useless." While this isn't precisely what needs to be said about the usefulness of the law, it comes very close. Apostolic teaching indicates the necessity for believers to act becomingly to bring God honor and demonstrate love for man. Many scholars have pointed out the fact that nine of the Ten Commandments are referred to in the epistles as standards for Jesus' followers (the Sabbath command being the only exception). In fact, these standards form the bedrock of any society whose goal is to honor God through righteous living.

Martin Luther delivered a sermon in 1525 entitled, "How Christians should regard Moses." This message gives us the proper approach to studying the books of the law *for Gentiles*. "We will regard Moses as a teacher, but we will not regard him as our lawgiver—unless he agrees with both the New Testament and the natural law... What Moses commands is nothing new. For what God has given the Jews from heaven, he has also written in the hearts of all men. Thus I keep the commandments which Moses has given, not because Moses gave the commandment, but because they have been implanted in me by nature, and Moses agrees exactly with nature... But the other commandments of Moses, which are not [implanted in all men] by nature, the Gentiles do not hold. Nor do these pertain to the Gentiles, such as the tithe and others equally fine which I wish we had too...

"I find something in Moses that I do not have from nature: the promises and pledges of God about Christ. This is the best thing. It is something that is not written naturally into the heart, but comes from heaven... But let God's word be what it may, ***I must pay attention and know to whom God's word is addressed***... I have stated that all Christians, and especially those who handle the word of God and attempt to teach others, should take heed and learn Moses aright... We have our own Master, Christ, and he has set before us what we are to know, observe, do, and leave undone. However it is true that Moses sets down, in addition to the laws, fine examples of faith and unfaith—punishment of the godless, elevation of the righteous and believing—and also the dear and comforting promises concerning Christ which we should accept... Many learned men have not known how far Moses ought to be taught. Origen, Jerome, and others like them, have not shown clearly how far Moses can really serve us. This is what I have attempted, to say in an introduction to Moses how we should regard him, and how he should be understood and received and not simply be swept under the rug."[13] (emphasis added)

The purpose of the law to illuminate sin and instruct in good conduct is beneficial as long as its use is in conformity to the new covenant (1 Tim. 1:8). We are to stand firm in the freedom of Christ and not be burdened by the yoke of slavery that comes when trying to earn right standing before God through obedience to the law (Gal. 5:1). Using the law properly requires we remember all Scripture is God inspired and useful for teaching, rebuking, correcting, and training in good conduct so we are thoroughly equipped for every good work (2 Tim. 3:16-17).

The importance of making the distinction between the Ten Commandments as legally binding vs. a new covenant standard to live by is precisely the point of the curse incurred by the law (James 2:8-10). While the standard is good and profitable for instruction in righteous conduct, the consequence of 'putting yourself under the yoke of the law' is not life but death. The new covenant provides for writing the law on our hearts as we place ourselves before the Word to be washed clean. The curse of the law has been lifted and the contract fulfilled.

> *God did what the law could not do. He sent his own Son in a body like the bodies we sinners have. And in that body God declared an end to sin's control over us by giving his Son as a sacrifice for our sins. He did this so that the just requirement of the law would be fully satisfied for us, who no longer follow our sinful nature but instead follow the Spirit.* -Rom. 8:3b-4, NLT

One of the roles of the law for the new covenant believer is to expose sin for Jew and Gentile alike. While the Jew received the Mosaic law as his inheritance, if he is in Christ he no longer follows the law as the means to inherit blessing, nor is he under the curse of the law for not carrying it out perfectly. Furthermore, demonstration of the ceremonial aspects of the law teaches everyone about our Messiah: His sacrifice, His plan of redemption, and the prophetic fulfillment of His mission. As for the moral and civil matters of the Mosaic law, are not the laws in civilized countries followed by the Gentiles for similar reasons and in similar fashion?

The utility of the law for the Gentile, therefore, is not its use as a code of legal requirement that promotes works from self-effort, but as a guide in agreement with the universal nature of morality imprinted on our spirit by God. As such, it allows for living in the grace, power, and leading of the Holy Spirit. James (Acts 15:13-21) and Martin Luther alike addressed the inclination of those who hear Moses read aloud to adopt the commands as bearing on the life of the Gentile believer in Christ. This results from inattention regarding who is being addressed in those commands, and the purpose for which the commands were instituted—as a guardian for Israel and to point to Christ.

Closing Thoughts

> *The law of the LORD is perfect, converting the soul; the testimony of the LORD is sure, making wise the simple.* -Ps. 19:7, NKJV

Clearly, the law is good and holy, but as the basis for making man righteous it failed. Any attempt to follow the law in our own strength will produce failure (sin), which in turn produces death. Is the law abolished? No, for God's Word testifies that it is everlasting. But as the chief cornerstone of covenant meant to keep man in good standing with God, yes, it is abolished. The moral law will always be binding, whether Jew or Gentile, but it is not the means by which we are declared righteous in God's sight. The chief cornerstone, the basis of the new covenant, is Jesus who fulfilled... accomplished... completed the contractual obligations of the old covenant *based on the law*, and nailed the fulfilled contract along with its curses to the tree.

The new covenant ratified in Jesus' blood is justification *by faith* through the sacrifice and righteousness of Christ as the fulfillment of the law. Now the veil of darkness is removed from our spirit and we are thus enabled to follow His commands in *spirit* (not a legalistic outward show) and in *truth* (not deceiving ourselves), leading to the salvation of our souls and attainment of the resurrection of the dead.

In other words, following the law no longer formed the *basis* for covenant (due to our inability to keep it without God's help), but became the *fruit* of the new covenant of grace initiated by accepting the free gift of righteousness in Christ. In order for this to happen, repentance must take place so the one in darkness can see the light, turn to that light, and have the veil removed (2 Cor. 3:15-16). The repentant are now free of the veil that kept them in bondage to the darkness of the god of this age. If repentance has taken place, the only course of action is to work progressively toward removing the old nature from the soul by the power of the Holy Spirit. By this we strive for the promised reward—eternal life and the promise of incorruptible flesh at the resurrection of the dead.

When Paul said he and Peter 'lived as the Gentiles do' when they were with them, this was not to say they had abandoned the Mosaic law. Rather, they clung to what God had spoken, divesting themselves of the perhaps well-intentioned but harmful entrapment of the oral traditions of their culture. They could now move in freedom to fellowship with the uncircumcised, partake in fellowship meals with the newly saved Gentiles, and in good conscience permit the Gentiles to remain Gentiles apart from Jewish practices, such as Sabbath keeping or circumcision.

The basic universal moral laws were enforced along with those noted in Acts 15, but no other 'yoke' was placed upon the Gentile believers. All mankind has the covenant sign of the rainbow, but only the Jews have the covenant signs of circumcision, Sabbath, festivals, and the *Levitical* priesthood. Additionally, whatever we are when we are called, Jew or Gentile, we are not to seek to be something else.

In order to fully walk in obedience to God, the bondservant will want to have these issues of the law straightened out in his mind. Confusion clouds our ability to hear the witness of God's Holy Spirit, and having clarity on the use of the law will go far to reduce any hesitation we may have concerning the Spirit's leading to help our neighbors. In addition, such clarity will foster unity with the rest of the body of Christ.

> *Finally, all of you, be like-minded, be sympathetic, love one another, be compassionate and humble... turn from evil and do good... seek peace and pursue it.*
> -1 Pet. 3:8,11, NIV

Chapter 9

The Covenants

> *God is not a man who lies, or a son of man who changes His mind. Does He speak and not act, or promise and not fulfill?* -Num. 23:19, HCSB

Before we go further in our study of law and freedom, reviewing the various covenants God has made with men will give us better insight as to the plan of redemption God has prepared for all. Covenants can be perpetual or conditional; for all people, specific groups, or with particular individuals. By taking a brief look at these covenants, we can get a better feel for the overall scope of God's plan without micro analyzing the finer points of each. The opening verse reminds us that God does not lie. He will not go back on His Word—He remains faithful even when we are faithless.

> *If we are faithless... He remains true (faithful to His Word and His righteous character), for He cannot deny Himself.* -2 Tim. 2:13, AMP

Why is this important in our study of the bondservant? It establishes that the promises of God have not been nullified. This is especially important when we endeavor to understand God's plan for the community of believers as well as the destiny of the nation of Israel. As we will see, Gentile believers have not replaced Israel. They are grafted into the promises and covenants of Israel through faith in the Jewish Messiah.

The Covenant with Noah

God's covenant with Noah was established after the flood. The covenant included not only Noah but all flesh and for all time. In this covenant, God promises to never again destroy all living creatures by flood (Gen. 9:8-11). As a sign, the rainbow was placed in the sky as God's seal of this everlasting promise (Gen. 9:16-17).

Although God gave Noah laws at the same time He made this covenant, there does not seem to be any conditional requirement for the laws to be kept in order for the promise to stand. The laws themselves presume relationship with God. If not, there would be no incentive to follow them. Indifference to, flat out rejection of, or scorn for God's laws given here to all mankind is included in the biblical understanding of blasphemy.

According to the Word, all of us have descended from Noah and therefore these laws apply to everyone. To forget these laws and live according to our own desires and 'wisdom' is to reject the foundational laws given to Noah for all men. By extension, this is rejection of God and His will—lawlessness. Presumably, Sodom and Gomorrah violated

SECTION 3 HARMONIZED VIEW OF LAW AND FREEDOM

these laws as well as those inscribed on the conscience of every man, and were destroyed by fire as a result.

The Covenant with Abraham, and Renewed with Isaac and Jacob

> *He has remembered His covenant forever, the word which He commanded to a thousand generations, the covenant which He made with Abraham, and His oath to Isaac. Then He confirmed it to Jacob for a statute, to Israel as an everlasting covenant, saying, "To you I will give the land of Canaan as the portion of your inheritance."* -Ps. 105:8-11, NASB (see also 1 Chron. 16:15-18)

The covenant made with Abraham is an everlasting covenant, specifically through his son Isaac and grandson Jacob. This covenant possesses only one condition, and it only applies to individual participation in the covenant promises. Every male descendant, as well as the male slaves in his house, must be circumcised as a sign of the covenant. To disregard this condition is to be cut off from the people of Israel and therefore from the promises as well (Gen. 17:10-14). The promises to corporate Israel as stated in this covenant, however, are unconditional and eternal. God promised:

- I will make you a great nation (Gen. 12:2).
- You will be the father of a multitude of nations; kings will come from you (Gen. 17:4-6; 35:11; 48:19).
- I will give you and your offspring this land forever (Gen. 12:7; 13:14-17; 15:18; 17:8; 35:12).
- I will make your offspring numerous (Gen. 13:16; 15:5; 22:17; 26:4).
- Your offspring will triumph over his enemies (Gen. 22:17).
- In your offspring all nations of the earth will be blessed (Gen. 22:18; 26:4).

Paul makes clear that 'the offspring' (singular) who will bless the entire earth is Jesus (Gal. 3:16). Many Jewish people will also cite the scientific and humanitarian blessings the people of Israel have brought to the world as evidence of this prophecy to bless the world, and there are many such examples. While I appreciate those who take pride in the accomplishments of their nation, we should note that other nations have notable accomplishments that have blessed the world, and at the same basic rate of accomplishment as those of the nation of Israel. But only one nation has brought forth the Messiah, and by Him shall the entire world be *truly* and eternally blessed.

Both Abraham *and Jacob* were told a multitude of nations would come from 'their body.' Perhaps the lineage of the dispersed northern tribes has accomplished more than once thought. It was to Jacob the Lord addressed this promise:

> *Be fruitful and multiply;* **a nation** *(Israel)* **and a company of nations** *shall proceed from you, and kings shall come from your body.* -Gen. 35:11b, NKJV (parenthetical added)

Israel as a nation cannot lose the land of promise because it is an unconditional promise from the perspective of eternity. The stipulation of circumcision affects only whether individual men of Israelite descent will be included. This does not mean Jacob's descendants will always inhabit the land in this age. But when all things are restored, as mentioned repeatedly in the Word, Israel will be regathered to the land *forever*.

The Covenant with Israel at Mt. Sinai

The Mosaic covenant is a conditional covenant dependent on the faith and obedience of the people of Israel. Specifically, their cooperation and ability to adhere to the 613 commands given at Mt. Sinai determined whether they would be allowed to remain in the land (Deut. 28:63-66).

In Deuteronomy 28:1-14, we see all the promised blessings for the nation of Israel if they continued to walk in obedience to the covenant. In this passage and others, the blessings pronounced for Israel pertain to blessing them *in the land*. These include primacy among the nations, prosperity, fertility, defeat of enemies, adequate rain, being set apart for the Lord, and long life in the land.

As promised at the time of Adam and Eve's fall, salvation and eternal life could only come by faith in God's Word to bring forth the promised seed that would defeat Satan and redeem all of mankind who look for their salvation and eternal life in Him (Gen. 3:15; Heb. 11:1-12:2). The Word teaches us that eternal life cannot come by the law, but only by faith. This is seen in the lives of Abel, Enoch, Abraham, David, and all the others who believed by faith, whose sins were not counted against them, and who walked out their faith in obedience, albeit imperfectly.

The covenant at Mt. Sinai promised they could live in the land and be blessed if they followed God's law. The Israelites were to 'take to heart' all the words of the law God warned them to observe. Doing so would mean prolonged life in the land (Deut. 32:46-47). If they transgressed this covenant by serving other gods, the Lord reminded them they would 'perish quickly from off the good land' He had given them (Josh. 23:16; see also Deut. 30:15-20).

The promise to possess the land unconditionally had been made *to Abraham* and his descendants. Because Abraham never received this promise in his lifetime, the only conclusion we can make is that God views this promise from an entirely different perspective—one with the view of eternity.

> [C]hoose life in order that you may live... by loving the LORD your God, by obeying His voice, and by holding fast to Him; for this is your life and the length of your days, that you may **live in the land which the LORD swore to your fathers, to Abraham, Isaac, and Jacob, <u>to give them</u>**. -Deut. 30:19b-20, NASB

Abraham and his descendants, by the sign of circumcision, were promised the land forever unconditionally. So why are there conditions for staying in the land under the Mosaic covenant? The answer is determined primarily through realization that the covenant with Abraham has the viewpoint of eternity, as do the Davidic and priestly covenants (discussion to follow). All the everlasting promises of God are 'yes and amen,' not necessarily in our personal lifetimes but assuredly in the age to come. The Mosaic covenant deals with the conditions for inhabiting the land in this age. At the same time, this covenant teaches the people how to properly relate to God and each other. Doing so demonstrates God's nature in justice, righteousness, faithfulness, mercy, love, and truth. This defines the guardian nature of the law.

Not an Eternal Covenant

The very purpose and nature of this covenant mitigates the weight of any consideration it was intended to be eternal. Why? The promise given to Abraham that the land would be Israel's forever is unconditional, but the conditions of the Mosaic covenant provide for loss of the land for disobedience.

This is why the curse of the Mosaic covenant, as written in Deuteronomy 27:9-26 and 28:15-68, was nailed to the tree. For all who accept Jesus as the prophesied promised seed of Abraham, there is no more curse for violating the Mosaic law. Only in Jesus will the Jews enter into the promise of Abraham to inhabit the land forever.

When the Abrahamic covenant is fulfilled at Jesus' second coming, the land will be given unconditionally to those descendants of Abraham, Isaac, and Jacob circumcised in flesh and heart. The Mosaic covenant will have no purpose because there will be no conditions for staying in the land, and the law will now go forth from Zion through the promised Davidic ruler, Jesus.

Despite the lack of explicit language stating the Mosaic covenant is eternal, there are several ordinances of this covenant depicted as *olam*, everlasting. Though the word *olam* is typically translated 'everlasting,' 'perpetual,' 'eternal,' 'forever,' or other similar words (and 'world' in other instances), there are uses where this meaning is not meant literally, but the context often makes this clear (e.g., Isa. 42:14; Jon. 2:6). These perpetual ordinances include the Sabbath, new moon, and festival keeping (Ex. 12:14,17,24; Lev. 16:29,31,34; 23:14,21,31,41; 2 Chron. 2:4) as well as everlasting ordinances for the priests, the gifts they receive, and some of their duties in the temple (Ex. 27:21; 28:43; 29:9; 30:21; Lev. 10:9; 24:3,8-9; Num. 10:8; 18:8,11,19,23; 19:10,21). The dietary restriction for not eating fat or blood is also a 'perpetual statute' (Lev. 3:17). In fact, all the offerings brought before the Lord are of a permanent nature because they are offered with salt (Lev. 2:13).

[Note: Recall that the 'sacrifice of our lips' (our speech; Hos. 14:2; Heb. 13:15) is to be seasoned with salt (Col. 4:6). Remember also that we will give an account of every idle word we have spoken (Matt. 12:36). From the Levitical offering of sacrifices seasoned with salt, the Word teaches us the spiritual truth that our words are likewise to be seasoned with salt because we will be judged by all we have spoken. How do we season 'the sacrifice of our lips' with salt? If we remember the eternal nature of God's Word, and understand that salt is a picture of something everlasting, we can conclude that the idea here is to season our speech with the eternal Word of God.]

The law that goes forth in the land of Israel will be the same for all, Israelite and alien alike, as a perpetual statute. Most civilized nations have a similar ruling ensuring that treatment of foreigners is just and impartial. This can only be accomplished if the law is the same for all. It is against God's wisdom and view of impartiality for a nation to adopt two sets of laws, for example, the adoption of Islamic sharia law alongside the already established law of the land, or laws for the common people that differ from the laws for politicians. A 'double-minded' nation will not stand.

Notice in the following passage that the ceremonial decrees for those who assemble before God as one people were to be uniform, just as the civil ordinances for the nation. Not everyone would assemble as part of the congregation before God (e.g., nonbelieving sojourners, foreigners, etc.), but all would be governed by the uniform civil laws:

> **As for the assembly** (those who congregate together before the Lord), *there shall be one statute* (**chukkah**) *for you and for the alien who sojourns with you, a perpetual statute throughout your generations; as you are, so shall the alien be before the LORD. There is to be one law* (**torah**; moral code) *and one ordinance* (**mishpat**; pertains to civil laws for crimes committed) *for you and for the alien who sojourns with you.* -Num. 15:15-16, NASB (parentheticals added)

This principle also applies to the body of believers. While the specifics for the 'two loaves' (Jew and Gentile) may be different, they are derived from the same foundational directives: faith in Jesus, love for God, and love for neighbors. The United States, for example, has a broad set of federal laws that apply to each state as well as the specific laws of governance determined by each state individually.

The Fading Glory of a Temporary Covenant

Paul gives three *kal v'homer* arguments (Hebrew for 'light and heavy,' i.e., proceeding from a lightweight argument to a weightier one) in 2 Cor. 3:7-11, all dealing with the supremacy of the new covenant:

- If the covenant on *stone* tablets came with glory (though fading), the covenant of the *Spirit* more glorious;
- If the covenant of *condemnation* was glorious, how much more the covenant that brings *righteousness*;
- If what was *temporary* came with glory, how much greater the glory of that which is *eternal*.

SECTION 3 HARMONIZED VIEW OF LAW AND FREEDOM

An analogy is made between the old covenant of death and the fading glory of Moses' face. 'Moses' and 'the law' are often used as interchangeable terms to refer to the old covenant. If the glory on Moses' face was fading, we are made to understand that something fading shortly after being given was never meant to be permanent. Both Jesus and Moses are the mediators of their respective covenants. Because of Jesus' indestructible life, we have a picture of the new covenant as everlasting. On the other hand, Moses died before entering the Promised Land, a harbinger of this covenant's fate.

> Having **canceled out the certificate of debt** consisting of decrees against us, which was hostile to us; and He has taken it out of the way, having nailed it to the cross. When He had **disarmed the rulers and authorities**, He made a public display of them, having triumphed over them through Him. -Col. 2:14-15, NASB

This passage provides rich detail of the work Jesus accomplished at the cross. A brilliant work, in fact, that not only reconciled man to God, but also cancelled the power of death that came through sin as well as the old covenant's curses for disobedience. This includes voiding the legal charges with which Satan accuses us before God.

'Certificate of debt' is translated from *cheirographon*, typically used to refer to a handwritten, legally binding document. This precisely describes the old covenant agreement between God and the Israelites. It is the same concept as a modern day contract. The initial contract is written up and both parties agree to the terms—the services to be provided by one, and the compensation pledged in return for the services by the other. Both then sign on the dotted line. When the terms of the contract are met and payment is received, the contract is *fulfilled*. Though the parties may or may not continue to do business with one another, that particular contract is no longer in force.

Jeremiah also attests to the fact that God would replace the old covenant with a new one, *unlike the previous covenant* (see Jer. 31:31-34). The old covenant based on rules to be obeyed (outer court) would be replaced with a new covenant based on a reconciled relationship through mercy and forgiveness (holy of holies). Through a restored relationship with God, the people would learn to walk out the *Torah* in love.

> In that He says, "A new covenant," He has made the first obsolete. Now what is becoming obsolete and growing old is ready to vanish away. -Heb. 8:13, NKJV

The author of Hebrews describes the Mosaic covenant as obsolete because the new covenant has arrived. But he also states the old covenant is *becoming* obsolete: *ready* to vanish but not yet dissolved. First, we note he is talking about the covenant itself, not the laws *per se*. Second, because the majority of Israel rejected the new covenant in Jesus, they remain under the old covenant that is fading away—fading until Jesus returns, at which point it will disappear. When Jesus returns their eyes will be opened. They will mourn for Him as for an only Son (Zech. 12:10) and will be granted repentance as a nation (Rom. 11:25-27), thereby entering into the new covenant.

The Covenant with the Levites

For the LORD your God has chosen him out of all your tribes to stand to minister in the name of the LORD, him and his sons forever. -Deut. 18:5, NKJV

The Levites rallied to the Lord on a day of great apostasy, which singled them out because their loyalty to the Lord took precedence over their loyalty to their families (Ex. 32:26-29). As a reward, the Levites were given no inheritance in the land—the Lord Himself would be their portion (Deut. 10:8-9). Though David was from the tribe of Judah, he also claimed the Lord as his portion. This is the heart of the bondservant.

Levi has been chosen to serve the Lord forever, made unequivocally clear in Jeremiah 33 where the indisputable and permanent nature of the covenant is plainly stated.

*For thus says the LORD... **the Levitical priests shall never lack a man in my presence** to offer burnt offerings, to burn grain offerings, and to make sacrifices **forever**... If you can break my covenant with the day and my covenant with the night, so that day and night will not come at their appointed time, then also... my covenant with the Levitical priests my ministers.* -Jer. 33:17a,18,20-21, ESV

Because of the destruction of the temple, the priests have been unable to perform their duties. Note the clause 'in my presence.' Ezekiel recorded in his vision the gradual exit of the Lord's presence from the temple (Ezk. 10). While God remains omnipresent, His manifest presence was removed from the temple.

From the viewpoint of eternity, however, the priesthood is perpetual and will be reinstated during the millennial reign when God's manifest presence returns. At that time, the priesthood will be conducted righteously, thereby fulfilling God's covenant. The Lord will not forget His covenant with Levi because He also stated that even when we are unfaithful, He is still faithful (2 Tim. 2:13).

While the majority of Malachi is a rebuke of the practices of the defiled Levitical priesthood, this section describes the covenant God made with Levi. The Lord is recalling a former time when Levi walked uprightly with God and instructed the people in God's ways. This will be true again one day under the reign of *Yeshua*.

*So shall you know that I have sent this command to you, that **my covenant with Levi may stand**, says the LORD of hosts. My covenant with him was one of life and peace, and I gave them to him. It was a covenant of fear, and he feared me. He stood in awe of my name. True instruction was in his mouth, and no wrong was found on his lips. He walked with me in peace and uprightness, and he turned many from iniquity. For the lips of a priest should guard knowledge, and people should seek instruction from his mouth, for he is the messenger of the LORD of hosts.* -Mal. 2:4-7, ESV

The Covenant with Phinehas

The covenant God made with Phinehas resulted from the zeal he demonstrated for the honor of God's name during the Moab debacle instigated by Balaam (see Num. 25). The Lord credited Phinehas with turning back His wrath because he was as zealous for the honor of God's name as God Himself. As a result, God gave Phinehas and his descendants a covenant of an everlasting priesthood. The Psalmist declared that Phinehas' actions were credited to him as righteousness forever (Ps. 106:30-31). Likewise, Phinehas' descendants, the sons of Zadok, displayed zeal for the Lord and 'kept His charge' when all Israel and the other Levites went astray (Ezk. 48:11). The sons of Zadok alone are promised the privilege of ministering before the Lord (see also Ezk. 40:46). This is an everlasting covenant of priesthood.

> *However, the Levitical priests of the family of Zadok continued to minister faithfully in the Temple when Israel abandoned me for idols. These men will serve as my ministers...* **They alone will enter my sanctuary and approach my table to serve me.** -Ezk. 44:15a,16, NLT

It is more than merely interesting to see the sons of Zadok figured prominently in the description of the temple in Ezekiel's vision (Ezk. 40-47). If one accepts the interpretation that this is the millennial temple, the covenants with Levi and Phinehas of an everlasting priesthood make sense from the perspective of Jesus' future reign. This would also render the everlasting nature of the festival keeping, etc. plausible with an operational temple and Levitical priesthood. The temple duties and sacrificial system are not so odd if one views them in the same way as the Lord's Supper—to 'do in remembrance' of Jesus' flesh and blood sacrifice. As types and shadows, the sacrifices point to Christ and His work. Commemorating days on which God fulfilled His prophetic promises is similar to our celebrations of providential historic events, such as the 4th of July.

There is further evidence a temple will be present in the millennial reign because of the emphasis that there will be *no* need for a temple *afterward*. When the New Jerusalem comes down out of heaven afterward, God will once again live in the midst of His people, just as He did in the Garden of Eden. The book of Revelation does not negate the presence of a temple during the millennial reign, but rather supports it. The following passage describes the New Jerusalem, *after* the millennial reign of Christ.

> *And I saw no temple in the city, for its temple is the Lord God the Almighty and the Lamb. And the city has no need of sun or moon to shine on it, for the glory of God gives it light, and its lamp is the Lamb.* -Rev. 21:22-23, ESV

Ezekiel's temple vision is difficult to understand. There are some interesting works on the subject, though they are few. The following is an excerpt from Paul Jablonski, who actually made a model of the temple Ezekiel described (you'll find pictures of it on his website). He references the feasts which were spoken of as perpetual statutes. "These appointed Feasts are for the purpose of changing us more into God's image thus giving Him glory. Ezekiel 46:9 tells the worshippers at the appointed Feasts not to leave by the same gate that they entered. Likewise, every time we come in worship to offer our lives as a sacrifice to the Lord we will be changed from glory to glory and not leave the same way that we entered... (2 Cor. 3:18). Every time we come into the presence of the Lord we are changed more into His likeness, and we leave different than when we came."[1]

The Covenant with David

> *Your house and your kingdom shall be made sure forever before me. Your throne shall be established forever.* -2 Sam. 7:16, ESV

The permanent nature of this covenant cannot be overlooked. It was made as a covenant of salt. "The term 'covenant of salt' is indicative of the everlasting nature of the relationship between the children of salt, and their Elohim Yahweh. When we hear the term salt, the understanding is that the things Yahweh addresses are eternal, enduring, never changing, and abiding forever. All salt covenants then are eternal, and eternally binding on the sons and daughters of Yisrael, regardless where they are to be found, and regardless of whether a physical temple stands on Mt. Moriyah or not."[2]

> *Do you not know that the LORD God of Israel gave the rule over Israel forever to David and his sons by a covenant of salt?* -2 Chron. 13:5, NASB

David's response is a prayer of gratitude (2 Sam. 7:18-29), well worth reading, but we will only look at the final verses:

> *And now, O Lord GOD, you are God, and your words are true, and you have promised this good thing to your servant. Now therefore may it please you to bless the house of your servant, so that it may continue forever before you. For you, O Lord GOD, have spoken, and with your blessing shall the house of your servant be blessed forever.* -2 Sam. 7:28-29, ESV

In the days of Jeremiah, the Lord confirmed the covenant He made with David. This came at the time when Judah and her Davidic kings were on their way to exile, which would seem to support the belief that God annulled the covenant made with David. In this passage, however, not only is the covenant reaffirmed, but the promise of the righteous branch—the Messiah—from David's line is prophesied as well. All believers long to see this promise fulfilled.

> *I will cause a righteous Branch to spring up for David, and he shall execute justice and righteousness in the land... If you can break my covenant with the day and my covenant with the night, so that day and night will not come at their appointed time, then also my covenant with David my servant may be broken, so that he shall not have a son to reign on his throne.* -Jer. 33:15b,20-21a, ESV

SECTION 3 *HARMONIZED VIEW OF LAW AND FREEDOM*

The Lord further denounces the claims of those who believe God has rejected David's line or the Levitical priesthood by reiterating the permanent nature of His promise. This is a warning for us who are 'far off' that some have been a bit hasty in taking part of new covenant teaching out of context, particularly that the Gentile church has replaced Israel.

> *Have you not observed that these people are saying, 'The LORD has rejected the two clans that he chose'? Thus* **they have despised my people so that they are no longer a nation in their sight.** *Thus says the LORD: If I have not established my covenant with day and night and the fixed order of heaven and earth, then I will reject the offspring of Jacob and David my servant and will not choose one of his offspring to rule over the offspring of Abraham, Isaac, and Jacob. For I will restore their fortunes and will have mercy on them.* -Jer. 33:24-26, ESV

Despite the evil done by some of the Davidic kings, the Lord would not cancel His covenant with David because the eternal nature of the covenant was unconditional from the view of heaven (2 Chron. 21:7). The right of the people (including the kings) to stay in the land in this age, however, was conditional based on their adherence to the Mosaic covenant (see Ps. 89:30-32). The Lord has made it clear He will keep His covenant with David, and one of his descendants, *Yeshua*, will sit on his throne forever.

> *I have made a covenant with My chosen, I have sworn to My servant David: 'Your seed I will establish forever, and build up your throne to all generations.' Selah... His seed also I will make to endure forever, and* **his throne as the days of heaven... My lovingkindness I will not utterly take from him, nor allow My faithfulness to fail. My covenant I will not break, nor alter the word that has gone out of My lips. Once I have sworn by My holiness; I will not lie to David: His seed shall endure forever, and his throne** *as the sun before Me; It shall be* **established forever***... Selah.* -Ps. 89:3-4,29,33-37a, NKJV

Just because there is no heir from David's line currently on the throne in Israel does not mean the covenant God made to David is nullified. God has sworn by His holiness and will not break His covenant with David. How could God break His own commandment that prohibits taking His name in vain? The answer is He would never swear falsely, but will be utterly faithful to do all He has sworn He will do.

Likewise, just because there is no temple standing in Israel or continuing priesthood today does not mean the promises made to the Levites have been made void. The covenants made to the line of Phinehas, Zadok, and the Levitical priests will be honored in the millennial temple. The law that goes forth from Zion during that time will include the revisions seen in what is recorded in Ezekiel, in keeping with the dynamic nature of the law but never violating the moral code from which the law was derived. The law that goes forth from Zion will always uphold the eternal law and, at the same time, express the weightier matters of the law in true righteousness and justice.

Foreshadowing of the New Covenant

The entire exodus story is a foreshadowing of the new covenant prophesied through the prophets. The sequence of events the Israelites experienced parallel the milestones of the believer as he progresses in the new covenant. This also helps us better understand the process of salvation.

- **Bondage in Egypt**: The believer is in bondage to sin.
- **The ten plagues**: God rescues the believer miraculously by putting to shame the powers and principalities that can no longer hold him back from freedom.
- **The Passover Lamb**: The blood of Christ rescues us from certain death.
- **The Red Sea**: When baptized, we cross from sin's bondage (death) to grace (life).
- **The law given at Mt. Sinai**: After we have declared publicly we are Christ's through baptism, He takes us to the Word and gives us His Spirit so we can learn what is acceptable, writing the law on our hearts.
- **The wilderness journey**: Our life in this age teaches us to rely on God and His provision (manna, water from the rock, etc.) while we strive to follow His leading and timing (moving when the cloud lifts/staying when it settles).
- **Joshua circumcises the new generation**: Those who are in the new covenant become circumcised in heart.
- **Taking the Promised Land**: We put our lives on the line to take the kingdom He has promised for us by dying daily to self.

Also note the law giver and mediator of the old covenant, Moses, died outside the Promised Land. This also testifies that the old covenant is not the way into the promised Sabbath rest when Jesus returns. Jesus, on the other hand, died and was raised *in the land*. Those who cling to the old covenant as the vehicle for inheritance when Jesus returns will be buried apart from the promises of God. Taking the Promised Land is a shadow of the future millennial kingdom where the Bride of Christ shares the authority of the Lamb and reigns with Him, extending His reign throughout the earth (Dan. 2:34-45; cf. 1 Cor. 15:24-28; Rev. 20:4).

The New Eternal Covenant in Jesus' Blood

Jesus took bread and, praising God, gave thanks... and when He had broken it, He gave it to the disciples and said, Take, eat; this is My body. And He took a cup, and when He had given thanks, He gave it to them, saying, Drink of it, all of you; For **this is My blood of the new covenant, which [ratifies the agreement and]** *is being poured out for many for the forgiveness of sins.* -Matt. 26:26-28, AMP

This new covenant sealed in the blood of Jesus fulfills Old Testament prophecy. Unlike the Mosaic covenant, this would be an everlasting covenant whereby the conscience is wiped clean of the guilt of sin. With a cleansed conscience, it is now possible to write the laws of God on the mind and heart. Step-by-step, the wrong thinking, assumptions,

SECTION 3 *HARMONIZED VIEW OF LAW AND FREEDOM*

and paradigms held under the tyranny of a stained conscience are overwritten by the wisdom and counsel of God.

Promised to Israel

The new covenant was prophesied when the old one had been broken. Before the Mosaic covenant was renewed by the returning exiles under the leadership of Ezra and Nehemiah, God revealed to the prophets His wonderful plan to redeem Israel (Ephraim) and Judah through a *new* covenant, unlike the old.

- **According to Isaiah**: prophesied of a new everlasting covenant according to the faithful mercy shown to David. This new covenant is promised to Israel for all generations. God promised His steadfast love and covenant of peace will not depart from them (Isa. 55:3; 59:21; 61:8; 54:10).
- **According to Jeremiah**: prophesied of a new covenant radically different from the Mosaic covenant. God would write His law on their hearts by His Spirit. All who enter into this covenant will know the Lord, no matter what their status, because God will forgive their sin and remember it no more. Israel will never cease to be a nation before God. His everlasting covenant is with them, and He will put the fear of the Lord in their hearts so they will not turn away from God. They will return to Zion to be joined to the Lord in an everlasting covenant that will not be forgotten (Jer. 31:31-37; 32:40; 50:5). [Note: On this last point, the people will return to Israel not because their first love is the land promised them, but because they want to be joined to the Lord.]
- **According to Ezekiel**: prophesied of the everlasting covenant of peace God would make with Israel. He will multiply them and make the land safe and secure. The people of Israel will receive a new heart by the gift of the Holy Spirit. This would cause them to walk in obedience to God's law. He will set His sanctuary in their midst forever (Ezk. 16:60; 34:25; 36:26-27; 37:26).

This everlasting covenant of peace was promised to Israel, inaugurated at Jesus' first coming, and ratified in Jesus' blood. It is a covenant God made with Israel and sealed by the blood of a *Torah* observant Jew who walked out the law perfectly and gave Himself as the sin offering for the sins of all mankind. It is important that we realize this covenant is offered first to Israel if we are to understand the context in which it was given.

> *Men, brethren, sons of the race of Abraham, and those among you fearing God, to you was the word of this salvation sent.* -Acts 13:26, YLT

At His first advent, Jesus was sent to the lost of Israel (Matt. 15:24), not to the Gentiles, in order to proclaim and inaugurate the new covenant the prophets had foretold. While the God-fearing are included, both Jesus and Paul verify that salvation is first to the Jew because the promises were made to Israel. Regardless of race, we must be grateful to be part of the 'mixed multitude' (cf. Ex. 12:38) included in this great promise.

The book of Hebrews is addressed to Jewish believers. The author made note of the sins committed under the *first* covenant—a covenant not made with any other nation. He then stated 'for this reason' Jesus came to set them free from those sins that violated the old covenant so they can receive the promised eternal inheritance (Heb. 9:15). Clearly, the new covenant ratified in Jesus' blood was provided for the people of Israel.

Gentiles Included

Jesus announced He had sheep other than Israel to bring into the kingdom as well. These would listen to His voice and become one flock with Israel under one Shepherd (John 10:16). Though the new covenant was prophesied for Israel, God had already made provision for the new covenant to include the Gentiles (see also Rom. 11:11-24).

> *Ask me, and I will make the nations your inheritance, the ends of the earth your possession.* -Ps. 2:8, NIV

> *You will do more than restore the people of Israel to me. I will make you a light to the Gentiles, and you will bring my salvation to the ends of the earth.* -Isa. 49:6, NLT

The Gentiles were included because God loves them as well. This would also help Israel understand that it is through grace, not works or special status, that we are made righteous before God. Just as Jacob was chosen *before* birth—*before* any works that might be construed as the reason for his selection (Rom. 9:10-12)—so we are also made righteous apart from any works we may have accomplished. We are all on equal footing with respect to righteousness before God (see also Rom. 9:30-33).

> *For we hold that one is justified by faith apart from works of the law. Or is God the God of Jews only? Is he not the God of Gentiles also? Yes, of Gentiles also, since God is one—who will justify the circumcised by faith and the uncircumcised through faith.* -Rom. 3:28-30, ESV

After striving to gain righteousness through following the law for the entirety of its existence, Israel's ingrained paradigm made righteousness through grace a difficult concept to embrace. For many, the law had become not the means but the goal of their existence. There is a huge chasm between a lifestyle that is lived for God as David lived, and one that is lived for the law as the Pharisees lived.

The law-based life leads to zeal without knowledge, as Paul demonstrated before he met Jesus. This blinds those so inclined to the righteousness of Christ because they are too busy striving to establish their own. Christ, the fulfillment of the law *for righteousness*, now extends the invitation to all who thirst for *His* righteousness, found only in the new covenant (see Rom. 10:2-4,9-10). Paul exhorted the Philippians to be found in Jesus with the righteousness that depends upon and comes through faith in Christ, not self-righteousness that comes from the law (Php. 3:9). Those who would be justified by the law have fallen from grace and are 'severed from Christ' (Gal. 5:4).

SECTION 3 HARMONIZED VIEW OF LAW AND FREEDOM

Every law given to man proved righteousness could not come by following the law, whether there was only one (negative) command given to a sinless man walking with God in the uncorrupted garden of paradise, a handful of laws given to the only surviving family of the worldwide flood, or 613 given to those chosen to bring forth the Messiah. It only served to show us our consistent failure to keep God's standards and inability to be reconciled to God through our own effort.

Only God's mercy and grace can reconcile us to God and enable us to do what is right in His sight. When we try to follow the law in our own strength, our actions are stained by pride, self-righteousness, feelings of spiritual superiority, self-satisfaction, and a sense of worthiness because of our accomplishment. If we fail, we feel condemned and unworthy. The entire focus of our behavior is *self*, glorying in the good that we have wrought of our own volition, or wallowing in despair for failure. The poison of self ruins anything we may do, no matter how good it looks outwardly. But there is hope in Christ:

> *There is therefore now no condemnation for those who are in Christ Jesus. For the law of the Spirit of life has set you free in Christ Jesus from the law of sin and death.* -Rom. 8:1-2, ESV

We all like to earn favor. It makes us feel good, and upright behavior is important. But unless we have accepted the righteousness of Christ as the only means of our righteousness before God, we ruin everything we touch because of the inner workings of our fleshly pride. To approach God through accomplishment defines the way of Cain. Those who approach God in this way, finding they are not accepted no matter how much effort they put forth, become enraged at those who lay hold of God's reconciliation by grace through faith. Surely the spirit of murder lurks in all those who approach God through their accomplishments or 'righteous' behavior, fuming that it is not fair to have worked so hard only to receive rebuke from God because of pride and self-righteousness.

What they have perhaps not fully understood is that God does reward those who work hard for His kingdom as long as two requisites are met. First, we must accept the mercy of God through Jesus by faith alone, the only means by which we are judged righteous in His sight. Only this will allow us an audience in His presence, and only in this way are we granted access to His throne. The scepter will always be extended to those who are in Christ. Second, we must perform the works God has given us to do and not our own. This is true whether what we desire to accomplish is 'less' than what He asks or 'greater'—both are rebellion against His will and the opposite of abiding in His Spirit.

Under the new covenant, it is our duty to offer ourselves in God's service as the proper expression of worship. We accomplish this as we die to the desires and temptations of the world, renew our minds through study of His Word, and live morally upright to attest to God's grace and bring honor to His name. Only in this way will we be able to discern God's will for our lives (Rom. 12:1-2).

The Goal of the New Covenant

The blessings of the new covenant are given freely by grace because Jesus paid our penalty for us. So how should the new covenant of righteousness affect our lives? Our response, by the power of the Spirit who enables us to accomplish the works ordained for us, compels us to:

- set our minds to die to self (Luke 9:23), setting us free from sin (Rom. 6:7);
- wrestle with our old nature so we can live holy (Gal. 5:16-17,24; Php. 2:12; Col. 3:5-10; Titus 2:12);
- renew our minds through study of the Word (Rom. 12:2; Eph. 4:23; Col. 3:10);
- live in obedience to God's will (Rom. 6:16; 8:13; 2 Tim. 1:14; 2 John 1:6); and
- walk in wholehearted love toward God and our fellow man, deferring to others as needed (Matt. 22:37-40; Php. 2:3; James 3:17).

Paul gave Titus a succinct overview of the new covenant of grace (see Titus 2:11-15). The first part of the passage defines the *provisions* of the covenant: 'to save us from the curse of death and train us to live righteously in this present age.' The second part of the passage defines the *purpose* of the covenant: 'to redeem us from lawlessness and purify us to be His own possession,' the same words spoken to Israel under the old covenant (Deut. 4:20).

Being led by the Spirit demonstrates we are not under the law. When we are led by the Spirit, our first concern will always be the will of God with demonstration of love for man by paying attention to the weightier matters. Under the new covenant, we fulfill the law to love one another by bearing each other's burdens. This goal of serving one another in love, thereby fulfilling the requirement of the law, is both the glory and hallmark of the new covenant (Gal. 5:18; 6:2).

The Blood of Sprinkling to Seal the New Covenant

> *And to Jesus the mediator of the new covenant, and to the blood of sprinkling, that speaketh better things than that of Abel.* -Heb. 12:24, KJV

Abel brought a blood sacrifice, demonstrating his faith that God would keep His promise to one day send the promised Redeemer. Cain came by effort and hard work, supposing his accomplishment could win God's approval. Cain was rejected, as are all who refuse the Messiah's substitutionary sacrifice. Those who choose self-atonement (working to make their way right before God by accomplishments, religious rituals, and self-righteous performance of the law) will find themselves in the same place of rejection before God.

In the New Testament, the new covenant is referred to by two Greek words, both translated 'new.' The word predominantly used is *kainos*, meaning 'new with respect to the quality of something; unlike anything previous' (Luke 22:20; 1 Cor. 11:25; Heb. 8:8,13; 9:15). This supports the idea that the law of the new covenant is a new law of the Spirit whereby God's decrees are written on our hearts. It is the difference between staying in the outer court devoid of the presence of God, just going through the motions for 'fire insurance,' in contrast to being in the holy of holies with God where His Spirit writes the law on our cleansed conscience so we joyfully obey in His presence.

The other word used to refer to the new covenant is *neos*, meaning 'new with respect to the age of something, the most recent or last one numerically' (see Heb. 12:24, previous). In this passage, Jesus is described as the mediator of the *neos* covenant, and His blood is described as the 'blood of sprinkling' by which we are purified. Likewise, the old covenant was sealed with the blood of sprinkling from animal sacrifice as the type and shadow of the new covenant.

"Sprinkling was the form of transfer of sacrificial blood in order to secure its atoning efficacy, the form of purifying connected with expiation. Sprinkling of persons took place only upon the ratifying of the covenant (Ex. 24:8); upon the consecration of Aaron to the priesthood (Ex. 29:21); in cleansing from leprosy and pollution from a dead body (Lev. 14:7,16; Num. 19:11-19). The first two cases dealt with the establishment of a covenant between God and His people and... the application of the atoning blood by the mediator. In the last two we have the removal of fellowship with that which is of the nature of judgment against sin... (the sprinkling) took place... on man's side once only at the outset and never afterward except when leprosy and contact with death... **had actually annulled the covenant relation**."[3] (emphasis added)

[Note: Notice that leprosy, the symbolic picture of sin, actually *annuls* the covenant relationship. Knowing this helps us to understand why the apostles were so insistent and relentless in teaching that believers must keep themselves from sinning with a *'high hand'*: the practice of lawlessness (sin) with calloused indifference. In the new covenant, there is only one act of the blood of sprinkling by Jesus' blood. This happens when a person experiences repentance and receives the Holy Spirit as God's seal, thereby entering into the new covenant ratified in Jesus' blood. To enter into a spiritually leprous state—to give oneself over to sin—annuls the blood of sprinkling received with repentance. In order to be restored under the old covenant, another sacrifice had to be made to restore the leprous individual into covenant relationship again. Under the new covenant, there is no more sacrifice for the one who sins with a 'high hand' (Heb. 10:26; cf. Num. 15:30).]

Connected with this understanding of the *neos* covenant is the word *prosphatos*, the 'new and living way' Jesus made for us through the veil into the holy places by the sacrifice of His body.

> [S]ince we have confidence to enter the Most Holy Place by the blood of Jesus, by **a new and living way opened for us through the curtain, that is, his body** (Jesus, the Word), *and since we have a great priest over the house of God, let us draw near to God with a sincere heart and with the full assurance that faith*

> brings, **having our hearts sprinkled** to cleanse us from a guilty conscience and having our bodies washed with pure water. -Heb. 10:19b-22, NIV (parenthetical added)

Prosphatos is a combination of *pro*, meaning 'fore,' (superior, primary, or in front), and *sphazo*, 'to butcher or slaughter' (as in a sacrifice). By offering Himself as a 'new' or superior sacrifice by virtue of an indestructible life, no further sacrifice for sin is needed. What is an indestructible life? It is a sinless life that cannot incur the death penalty because no crime has been committed. Christ has rescued us from the curse of death by taking our curse upon Himself and allowing us to share in His righteousness so that we, too, have an indestructible life (Gal. 3:13).

> *For by one offering He has perfected forever those who are being sanctified.*
> -Heb. 10:14, NKJV

The Curse of the Law Removed

The curse of the law as shouted from Mt. Ebal has been removed. The obligations of the old covenant were accomplished during Jesus' life, and now all Israel who will appropriate the sacrificial blood of Jesus by faith are free from the curse of the law. The blessings of the Abrahamic covenant will be realized when Jesus returns and the remnant of Israel is regathered to the land. Read the following carefully:

> *But now we have been released from the* (bondage or curse of the) *Law, having died to that by which we were bound* (bound to sin and therefore the curse of the law), *so that we serve* (**douleuo**, from **doulos**: bond servitude) *in newness of the Spirit* (a qualitatively different/new spirit that comes from a cleansed conscience, forgiveness, and reconciliation with God) *and not in oldness of the letter* (without heart connection; merely doing what is expected to earn favor rather than out of desire or gratitude). -Rom. 7:6, NASB (parentheticals added)

The new covenant is about being released from our heart of stone, represented by the law written on stone, and being brought into a binding and everlasting covenant that gives us a heart of flesh, on which is written the law by the Spirit. The word 'law' in the next passage is the same Greek word *ergon*, whether it refers to the law written on stone, or the law now written on our hearts by the Spirit of God (see also Heb. 8:10-13).

> *This is the covenant I will make with them after that time... I will put my laws in their hearts, and I will write them on their minds.* -Heb. 10:16, NIV

> *Do we then by [this] faith make the Law of no effect, overthrow it or make it a dead letter? Certainly not! On the contrary, we confirm and establish and uphold the Law* (now written on our hearts instead of the stones). -Rom. 3:31, AMP (unitalicized parenthetical added)

The old covenant was the temporary covenant of stony hearts on which God had to forcibly chisel the law, teaching us that it is impossible for us to earn righteousness through our own effort. The new covenant is the everlasting covenant of hearts made tender by the Spirit of grace through the sprinkling of Jesus' blood so the law could be written there gently as we progressively die daily to sin. If we can distinguish between the messages of the two covenants, then we can understand the role of the law under the new covenant of freedom. Paul counseled Timothy that the law is *good* if used properly (1 Tim. 1:8).

Legalistic Religious Practice Brings Death

Legalistic religious practice has always been a snare to make men feel pious and worthy before God. Problems arise when the law is seen as a way to make oneself righteous before God, or when meticulous attention to traditions usurps the authority of Scripture. Much of Paul's writing regarding the law was addressed to Gentile believers who were never under the Mosaic law in the first place.

There was also concern for those who adopted the religious practices mandated by the religious authorities of the day, which both Jesus and Paul refuted. These traditions and rules of men were seen as the yoke of bondage, as was legalistic adherence to the law devoid of any heart involvement. The law itself was considered a yoke not because of what it required, but because we were incapable of not sinning, which brought the curse for everyone under the performance-based old covenant (Gal. 3:10).

At the risk of being too repetitive, the law has not been nullified or abolished. The only difference is its place in the new covenant. While under the law, sin was the master and brought death to all because the very mention of a prohibited act immediately grips the mind with temptation to do it (Rom. 7:10-11). Under grace, we have a new Master because we are freed from the power of sin and can righteously uphold the law. This can only happen when our hearts are engaged, we are in right standing with God through the righteousness of Jesus, and we rely on the power and grace of the Holy Spirit.

> *For just as you once presented your members as slaves to impurity and to lawlessness leading to more lawlessness, so now present your members as slaves to righteousness leading to sanctification.* -Rom. 6:19b, ESV

The Glory of the New Covenant

The glory of the old covenant could not change the people to whom it was given because they could not see (understand) its glory (as written in the law). Moses alone beheld God's glory when God spoke with him face to face. The concept of God's glory is linked to His presence and His Word. Like Moses' face, the glory of the old covenant was veiled and therefore powerless to change the heart. In other words, the people were oblivious to the message of God's redemptive plan as expressed in the law because they became primarily focused on the performance of its requirements. Even though God's truth was present in the law, without a dynamic Spirit-filled relationship with God the people could not comprehend it. This brought death (Rom. 7:9-10).

The glory of the new covenant, however, initiated with the rending of the veil in the temple, can be seen by all. This glory has the power to transform our inner man by: 1.) wiping our conscience clean and giving us power over sin, and 2.) opening our mind and heart to understand God's Word. This affords us the glory Jesus gave the disciples: unity with God in heart and purpose (John 17:22). Jeremiah alludes to this same glory of knowing and being known, as both Jesus and Moses are known. He stated that under the new covenant, we would all know God because of the forgiveness of sins (Jer. 31:34). This brings life.

The transformation of the heart is not automatic but rather comes incrementally as we place ourselves before the Word and allow the Holy Spirit to wash away our wrong mindsets and practices. This is how we are changed to become like Jesus (the Word). Without the work of the Holy Spirit, we would not be able to walk in the grace of the new covenant.

> *But it is the spirit in man, the breath of the Almighty, that makes him understand.* -Job 32:8, ESV

In both Hebrew (*ruach*) and Greek (*pneuma*), the Holy Spirit is defined as 'breath.' This depiction of the Spirit as 'breath' reminds us that not only are we unable to support life without the act of breathing, we cannot even live off the air we inhaled in the previous hour. We must continue to draw breath to live, and the quality of the air we breathe greatly affects our quality of life at the cellular level.

Because of the vital necessity of physical breathing, God did not leave it up to our conscious ability but made it an autonomic function of the physical body. The ability to breathe automatically is interrupted only when the autonomic impulses from the brain are disrupted. The implication is clear: we must remain connected to the Head, Jesus (Eph. 4:15; Col. 1:18; 2:18-19), *who is the Word*, in order to operate in the Spirit.

The apostles agreed that this new life of freedom is not freedom from the law. Abiding in Christ does not produce lawlessness in us but power to live righteously. If we have died with Christ, we have been set free from the power of sin (Rom. 6:6-7).

Paul counseled the Romans to use their bodies to do what is right for the Lord. Because we no longer live under the law, sin is not our master and we now live in the freedom of God's grace. That freedom is not for the continuance of sin but rather to obey God, which can only be accomplished when we are no longer slaves of sin. Paul further stated we are either the slave of sin (leading to death) or the slave of righteousness (leading to life) (see Rom. 6:13-16). Being made holy and inheriting eternal life is the glory of the new covenant.

> *Now you are free from your slavery to sin, and you have become slaves to righteous living... But now you are free from the power of sin and have become slaves of God. Now you do those things that lead to holiness and result in eternal life.*
> -Rom. 6:18,22, NLT

The Initial Step: Repentance

John the Baptist heralded this new covenant, exhorting those listening to bear fruit in keeping with repentance. Repentance carries with it the meaning of a change of heart and mind with regard to God and accompanied by remorse on issues of sin. This remorse comes not because of the consequences but because of the desire to be one with God. *Shuv*, Hebrew for 'repent,' means 'to turn oneself, to turn back or return,' especially in reference to returning to the Lord. "The basic meaning of *shuv* is movement back to the point of departure."[4] The Greek word for repent, *metanoia*, essentially means to "repent with regret accompanied by a true change of heart toward God."[5]

The very nature of the new covenant with its emphasis on repentance makes living righteously an essential component. The change takes place in the heart and mind and affects the outward behavior. This is why the formerly greedy and covetous Zacchaeus could change his ways and give away half of what he owned.

When John the Baptist was asked what he meant by the fruit of repentance, he told the people to share what they had (whether food or possessions), be content with pay, and deal ethically in matters of money (Luke 3:8-14). All of these actions show love for the needy and poor, and satisfy God's requirements in the law of love, faithfulness, justice, and mercy. This use of the law surpasses the righteousness of those whose obedience is tainted by legalism in action and hypocrisy with respect to the heart of the law.

> [U]nless your righteousness exceeds the righteousness of the scribes and Pharisees, you will by no means enter the kingdom of heaven. -Matt. 5:20, NKJV

Fruit of the New Covenant

Some of the most amazing provisions of the new covenant include being conformed to the character and mind of Christ (Rom. 8:29). This is such a precious goal that it is worth all the effort we put forth to cooperate with the Holy Spirit as this transformation takes place. Paul affirmed that this transformation materializes when spiritual wisdom is imparted through spiritual truths. Without the Holy Spirit's help, we are at the same disadvantage as the natural man without the Spirit of God, who is simply incapable of understanding God's truth (1 Cor. 2:10-14).

> For who has understood the mind of the Lord so as to instruct him? But we have the mind of Christ. -1 Cor. 2:16, ESV

While this transformation takes time, the immediate fruit is a cleansed conscience through repentance. This was the charge of the forerunner John the Baptist to his listeners. Repentance brings with it a change of behavior as proof repentance has taken place (Matt. 3:8), in contrast with regret that is only sorry for the results of misbehavior. Worldly sorrow expresses remorse because of the unpleasantness of the consequences: the restitution required as the penalty for stealing, the child born out of wedlock as the consequence of fornication, divorce as the result of adultery, disinheritance because of rebellion, disease from abusing the body (not all disease comes from abusing the body), etc. This type of sorrow does not typically change the long term practice of the one who was 'caught.' Only the Spirit of God can impart godly sorrow for sin (Acts 11:18; 2 Cor. 7:10).

Hindrances to Fruitfulness

The cares and lure of the world in this present age interfere with repentance and keep God's Word from bearing fruit in our lives. These thorns choke the Word and make it barren and withered (Mark 4:19). The appeal of the world is an illusion of this present age and will end up in chasing wind:

> *But as I looked at everything I had worked so hard to accomplish, it was all so meaningless—like chasing the wind… Then I observed that most people are motivated to success because they envy their neighbors. But this, too, is meaningless—like chasing the wind.* -Ecc. 2:11; 4:4, NLT

If our hearts are continually occupied by worldly success and gain, we have set God aside and set up worldly gain as god in our heart. John the apostle warned us against love for the world and its ways. It is evidence the love of God is not present. We cannot serve both (Matt. 6:24; Luke 16:13; James 4:4). He reminds us that the world and its desires will pass away, but whoever does God's will lives forever (1 John 2:15-17).

Transformation of Carnal Desires

Transformation of our desires is crucial for our sanctification. This comes only by the work of God, who works in us to both *desire* and *do* His will (Php. 2:13). Without heart change, it would be extremely difficult to continue in God's will without a subsequent downward spiral into either pride or self-condemnation.

Jesus advised His disciples that they would know a person by their fruit (Matt. 7:20). The New Testament writers talk of not only the typical sins of fornication, murder, and stealing as being the fruit of the flesh/darkness, but also sins motivated by greed, vain ambition, selfishness, envy, and covetousness. When these latter are present, there will be 'disorder and every evil practice' as those serving the flesh strive to place themselves in positions of power and status to satisfy these carnal cravings. James calls envy and selfish ambition a 'demonic practice' (James 3:14-16). No unity can come from such an environment. Only deeds birthed in wisdom and performed in humility demonstrate God's heart.

The only remedy for those governed by the flesh is to begin walking in the Spirit. Walking in the Spirit can only come as we stay connected to the Head (the Word). The desires of the flesh (e.g., immorality, impure thoughts, sensuality, greed, divisiveness, strife, envy, outbursts of anger, arguing, dissensions, drunkenness, etc.) set themselves in opposition to the desires of the Spirit. Only those who are led by the Spirit are free from the curse of the law and enabled to deny the desires of the flesh (Gal. 5:16-21).

Transformation of desires also involves letting go of our emotional attachment to the rituals of religion. Many of these rituals give us comfort and a sense of stability in our faith. But they are no substitute for our relationship with God. If our religious rituals have captured our hearts more than the simplicity of sincere devotion to Christ, we have placed ourselves on slippery footing. Peter described following the tradition the Jews inherited from their fathers as futile, and something from which we have been redeemed (1 Pet. 1:18). Through Christ we have died to the law *for righteousness* so we can live by the law of God written on our hearts. This bears fruit that brings honor to God because it involves heart change—a return to the image of God stamped on our spirit. This stamp, or seal, identifies us as His (2 Cor. 1:22; Eph. 1:13; 4:30).

> *[Y]ou also died to the law through the body of Christ, that you might belong to another, to him who was raised from the dead, in order that we might bear fruit for God.* -Rom. 7:4, NIV

Forbearance: The Evidence of Grace

The process of bringing forth fruit begins at the moment of rebirth, as in the example of Zacchaeus, and increases over time as we place ourselves before the Word with grace as our tutor. Those who receive the Word on good soil ('an honest, noble, and virtuous heart') guard the deposit received so that it steadily bears fruit (Luke 8:15).

Because bearing fruit requires time and attention, we must remember each believer is a 'work in progress,' including ourselves. Just as we appreciate the patience extended to us by others while we are going through 'spiritual growing pains,' we must reciprocate this same grace. Herein lies the need for *makrothumia*, translated 'forbearance.' Zodhiates clarifies and refines the specific meaning of this word as restraining oneself *mentally* before taking action or succumbing to passion. Associated with mercy toward people rather than circumstances or things, *makrothumia* has the added component of enduring the actions of others despite the annoyance, anger, or provocation their actions engender in us.[6]

> *Be patient, therefore, brothers... Do not grumble against one another, brothers, so that you may not be judged.* -James 5:7a,9a, ESV

We also call this 'showing grace' to someone who continues to struggle with unsanctified behavior. John instructs believers that the fruit of the new covenant is walking in truth, not sinless perfection. By walking in truth, our actions definitely change incrementally to become more righteous and in line with God's universal laws. But it also means we are truthful when we stumble in sin and run to God for forgiveness.

> ***If we claim to be without sin, we deceive ourselves and the truth is not in us.*** *If we confess our sins, he is faithful and just and will forgive us our sins and purify us from all unrighteousness.* -1 John 1:8-9, NIV

Fruit in the believer's life grows and matures over time. Typically, those who walk in the least degree of forbearance toward the shortcomings of others are those who have immature fruit in their own lives as well. The entire process entails graduating from one truth to the next (see Eph. 5:9-10, AMP).

Overcoming our sin nature and the captivation of the world becomes possible through attention to the leading of the Spirit, day by day, each day built on the lessons learned previously. Walking in obedience by the Spirit reforms our natural inclinations as He gives us the grace required each day for overcoming the particular challenges we will face. We overcome the obstacles in our lives one day at a time, persevering through the failures and disappointments through reliance on the Word and Spirit.

> *Everyone born of God overcomes the world. This is the victory that has overcome the world, even our faith. Who is it that overcomes the world? Only the one who believes that Jesus is the Son of God.* -1 John 5:4-5, NIV

If we try to run in our own strength, we will soon rediscover the condemnation we felt while under the law. Human weakness is legendary. Trusting the Holy Spirit to get us to the destination of sanctification must be cultivated to prevent running ahead of the Spirit presumptuously in our own strength.

Understanding the Spirit's forbearance and grace extended toward us should enable us to be more gracious toward one another. One person may struggle with lust, while another with gossip or addiction to alcohol, and yet another with avarice and greed. Harshly or condescendingly judging another because the vice they struggle with is not one with which we struggle personally, and at the same time expecting others to show us grace as we struggle with our particular issue, is hypocrisy. For example:

- the one addicted to pornography shaking his head in revulsion at the homeless alcoholic
- the fornicator who looks in condescending disgust at the overweight person struggling to control his appetite
- the gossip incensed by the one still battling with the use of profanity
- the successful but covetous business woman who looks in haughty superiority at the single mother on government assistance

The beam is in our own eyes. We must forbear; we can't hypocritically judge others by their actions while we judge ourselves by our struggle and intentions.[7]

The Fruit: Spiritual and Character Development

The fruit of righteousness can primarily be described in terms of spiritual and character development. While following God's moral laws are part of this fruit, upright behavior only 'counts' as fruit when it flows out of the nature of Christ developing in us. In turn, this type of genuine fruit can only be generated as we abide in Christ, the true vine (John 15:4; 1 John 2:24). Examples of the fruit produced from walking in the Spirit can be seen throughout the New Testament. The best known comes from the book of Galatians: love, joy, peace, patience (forbearance), kindness, goodness (benevolence), faithfulness, gentleness (meekness, humility), and self-control (Gal. 5:22-23).

Paul, Peter, and James each addressed the fruit of walking in the Spirit. Paul called this the 'fruit of righteousness' that comes through Jesus and brings honor to God. It entails desiring and learning to recognize the things of real value in order to become pure and sincere in heart. By this we look forward to the day of Jesus' return without stumbling or causing others to stumble (Php. 1:10-11; 1 John 2:10; Jude 1:24).

James described the fruit as being rooted in the wisdom from above, which is pure, peace-loving, considerate, impartial, sincere, open to reason, yielding to others, and full of mercy (James 3:17). Peter described the process of sanctification as the way we bear fruit in the knowledge of God. We have a dynamic role in this process, requiring that we diligently pursue righteousness, self-control, knowledge, and love through perseverance. Those who ignore this aspect of salvation are 'shortsighted and have forgotten *why* they were cleansed from their former sins' (2 Pet. 1:5-9).

One of the standards we see frequently in the early church is the generosity of the early believers. The first action taken by Zacchaeus when he repented and received salvation was to give generously to those in need. Cornelius' generous alms-giving caught God's attention, and as a result, Peter was sent directly to his house to preach the gospel message. Because of the great economic need during the early church, believers sold property in order to assist those who had nothing. Generosity is a benchmark of the new covenant paradigm because it is the practical outcome of loving our neighbor as ourselves. It also demonstrates that the god of this age has no hold on us.

Abiding in the Word (Jesus) is the only way true transformation and fruitfulness can take place. Apart from Him we can do nothing that will withstand the fire of testing. Only the fruit born of the Spirit brings God glory and proves we are His disciples. Love for God is made complete in those who obey His Word and conduct their lives the way Jesus did: in complete obedience to the Father's will. This is proof we are abiding in Him (1 John 2:5-6). Abiding in Christ means abiding in His Word. Notice the disciples were made clean because of the Word:

> *Already **you are clean because of the word** that I have spoken to you. Abide in me, and I in you. As the branch cannot bear fruit by itself, unless it abides in the vine, neither can you, unless you abide in me... Whoever abides in me and I in him, he it is that bears much fruit, for **apart from me you can do nothing**... By this my Father is glorified, that you **bear much fruit and so prove to be my disciples**.* -John 15:3-4,5b,8, ESV

Jesus Is the Only Head

Some adverse effects of the freedom found in the new covenant were evident in the division caused when adherents to one leader pitted themselves against those who had taken sides with another. Paul spoke strongly against this practice in the Corinthian church because it caused division, wrangling, and dissension. He desired the Corinthians to be united in their 'common understanding, opinions, and judgments.' He urged them to be in harmony and agreement, not foster factions based on human leaders:

> *What I mean is this, that each one of you [either] says, I belong to Paul, or I belong to Apollos, or I belong to Cephas (Peter), or I belong to Christ.* **Is Christ (the Messiah) divided into parts?** *Was Paul crucified on behalf of you? Or were you baptized into the name of Paul?* -1 Cor. 1:12-13, AMP

The problem was that each believer chose a 'leader' to follow, as we do today. The only difference between us and the Corinthian church is the number of choices we have: I follow_____ (*fill in the blank,* e.g., the Pope, Luther, Calvin, Wesley, Scofield, MacArthur, Bickle, Stanley, Chernoff, etc.). The problem is not usually with the leaders, burdened to share what they believe, but with the people who have quickly forgotten it is *Christ* who we follow by the power of the Spirit. People who create division in this way Paul called 'carnal and infantile,' unable to move onto stronger teaching beyond the basics.

Righteous leaders are ministering servants, as Paul called them, not icons to be elevated in the same manner seen among the worldly Gentiles. Their writings and teaching are intended to edify the body of Christ and hopefully not cause division. The writings of the church are prolific and have become the Talmud of Christendom—some good and some divisive (please do not understand this to be pointing to the men previously mentioned, but rather to the writings in the body of Christ in general, especially the profuse internet opinions expressed on every issue imaginable).

According to Paul, the divisiveness in the body of Christ is a sure sign we are still carnal, for 'as long as there are envying, wrangling, and factions,' we are convicted as unspiritual and acting like those who do not know Christ. Paul would address the church in the West today, saying, 'What then is Wesley? What is Luther? What is Calvin?' And he would likewise answer his own question, stating, 'they are only ministering servants with their appointed tasks. Only God can bring spiritual growth' (see 1 Cor. 3:3-8).

Each one of us has understanding available to us if we will only place ourselves before the Word on a regular basis to be fed by the Spirit. This is how we grow. Gaining wisdom from those who are more mature and have spent more time with the Lord is not wrong. As a matter of fact, it is in our best interest to learn from the sages, and I have spent decades doing just that. Learning this way gives us a leap in understanding here, or a bit of redirection there. It also sharpens our discernment as we weigh what is taught and learn to discard faulty conclusions. The problem arises when we let these leaders do our thinking for us, not honoring but rather ignoring what the Holy Spirit stands poised to impart to us if we will only value His presence.

> So **let no one exult proudly concerning men** [boasting of having this or that man as a leader], for all things are yours, whether Paul or Apollos or Cephas (Peter), or the universe or life or death, or the immediate and threatening present or the [subsequent and uncertain] future—all are yours, and you are Christ's, and Christ is God's. -1 Cor. 3:21-23, AMP

We are all followers of *Christ*, the Word, as are the teachers. Each of us is accountable to God for the way we treat the deposit given to us. We must not despise the day of small things—everyone has to start at square one. By staying in step with the Holy Spirit, we will bear fruit that lasts and not have the shame of rebuke when we meet the Lord.

> *Only let your manner of life be worthy of the gospel of Christ, so that... I may hear of you that you are standing firm in one spirit, with one mind striving side by side for the faith of the gospel.* -Php. 1:27, ESV

Closing Thoughts

The covenants God made with men are founded on the faithfulness of God who cannot go back on His Word. In the case of the Mosaic covenant, curses were prescribed for the nation of Israel if they did not adhere to their part of the covenant. Under the new covenant made with Israel, Gentiles have the privilege of being grafted in and enjoying the promises made specifically for Israel. This is an everlasting covenant of peace and freedom. For those in Christ, there is no longer any curse. Truly, Jesus' first miracle heralded the truth that He saved the best wine for last (see John 2:10)—a new and lasting covenant that includes all men for all time through His free gift of righteousness and the Holy Spirit. The second death has no power over those in Christ, granting us the privilege of living in the presence of God forever as heaven and earth are once again reunited.

> *But now that you have been set free from sin and have become slaves of God, the fruit you get leads to sanctification and its end, eternal life.* -Rom. 6:22, ESV

The covenant sealed in Jesus' blood reconciles us to God, erases our sin, and imparts the Holy Spirit in order to sanctify our desires and actions. The goal of our faith and the fruit of sanctification is eternal life. Bearing fruit for God's glory is a priority for true disciples of Christ. The bondservant looks forward to the day when his corrupted flesh will put on immortality, completing God's promise to become as He is.

> *Beloved, now we are children of God; and it has not yet been revealed what we shall be, but we know that when He is revealed, we shall be like Him, for we shall see Him as He is.* -1 John 3:2, NKJV

Chapter 10

Freedom in Christ

> *Jesus said, "If you hold to my teaching, you are really my disciples. Then you will know the truth, and the truth will set you free... So if the Son sets you free, you will be free indeed."* -John 8:31b-32,36, NIV

The world espouses many truths, but there is only one truth that will set us free. This truth is found only in Christ Jesus, who described Himself as the Way, the Truth, and the Life. To be set free from sin requires we recognize Jesus as the only *way* to be reconciled to God, the only *truth* that sets us free, and the only *life* that saves us completely: spirit, soul, and body.

Jesus inaugurated His ministry on earth by announcing He had come at the appointed time to proclaim freedom. This proclamation set the tone and objective for His first coming and made reference to the freedom all men need from the power of sin. Man became a slave to sin when the lure of sin mastered him in the garden.

From that day forward, we have all come under the weight of judgment and the painful knowledge of the curse for sin: death. Man also lost dominion authority over the earth through sin. Even so, at the time the curse was pronounced, God also prophesied the coming seed of the woman who would defeat the serpent (Gen. 3:15). Jesus came first to: 1.) proclaim freedom from sin, condemnation, and death, and 2.) become the means of reconciliation between man and God. He will return to take dominion over the earth with all who enter into the freedom found in the new covenant.

The Inaugural Address

Jesus' inaugural address took place after being tempted during His forty day wilderness fast. Satan tempted Jesus to use God's power for selfish reasons (Matt. 4:3-4), to claim His kingdom out of God's timing (Matt. 4:8-11), and to prove He was God's Son by the wrong means (Matt. 4:5-7). Having passed all three tests, Jesus began teaching in the power of the Spirit in the Galilean synagogues. On the Sabbath day, He stood up to read and was given the scroll of Isaiah. He undeniably presented Himself as the Messiah by pronouncing the fulfillment of Isaiah 61:1-2a:

> *The Spirit of the LORD is upon Me,*
> *Because He has anointed Me*
> *To preach the gospel to the poor* (**ptochos**);
> *He has sent Me to heal the brokenhearted* (**suntribo**),

> *To proclaim liberty (**aphesis**) to the captives (**aichmalotos**),*
> *And recovery of sight to the blind,*
> *To set at liberty (**aphesis**) those who are oppressed (**thrauo**);*
> *To proclaim the acceptable year of the LORD.*
>
> *Then He closed the book… "Today this Scripture is fulfilled in your hearing."* -Luke 4:18-21, NKJV (parentheticals added)

[Note: Comparing the passage Jesus read aloud as recorded in Luke with the original prophecy in Isaiah 61:2, we notice Jesus stopped reading in the middle of the sentence: *To proclaim the acceptable year of the LORD, and the day of vengeance of our God.* Observing Jesus' use of the Isaiah passage, we learn principles of interpretation and not only the primary intent of the passage to proclaim the appointed year of God's favor. First, we learn Jesus is making it clear He will not be fulfilling this entire prophecy in His first coming. Second, through Jesus' demonstration of interpretation, we learn that prophetic passages that sound as though they describe concurrent events may not be. As a matter of fact, events written in one description that appear to belong together may be separated by a good deal of time and widely divergent purpose. Inductive reasoning may have its place, but when we use it for the interpretation of prophecy, we surely risk losing our way as did the 'prophecy watchers' of Jesus' day when they rejected their Messiah on this very point of misinterpretation—expecting the restored Davidic kingdom at the same time as the arrival of the Messiah.]

Taking a closer look at the Greek terms used in the passage reveals a good deal about the freedom Jesus was sent to proclaim. The poor to which the good news is proclaimed are the *ptochos*, not the *penes*, poor. This implies one who was not only poor but helpless; one who had fallen from a better estate. Zodhiates describes the difference: "The *penes* may be poor but he earns his bread by daily labor. The *ptochos* is so poor that he can only obtain his living by begging. The *penes* has nothing superfluous, while the *ptochos* has nothing at all."[1] This describes our spiritual state because of the weight of sin and the despair of having no hope for recovery.

Use of the word *suntribo* to describe the brokenhearted illustrates a completely shattered or crushed heart. Here we face the truth that we are completely lonely and broken people until the presence of God enters our hearts. In proclaiming freedom (*aphesis*) for the prisoners (*aichmalotos*), the Greek words used describe forgiveness for 'prisoners of war' taken in the battle of sin and the sentence of death it brings. The word *aphesis* is used again in regard to the oppressed, once again speaking of the forgiveness proclaimed for the oppressed (*thrauo*) who are crushed under the weight of guilt from sin, and burdened by sorrow due to separation from the source of life.

Zodhiates explains the use of *aphesis*: "This required Christ's sacrifice as punishment of sin, hence the putting away of sin and the deliverance of the sinner from the power of sin although not from the presence of sin."[2] Each of these proclamations makes reference to our spiritual condition prior to meeting Jesus. Because of the spiritual implications of the other proclamations, it is safe to say recovery of sight for the blind would include not only physical sight, but the ability to understand spiritual matters, as in 'my eyes were opened to the truth.'

To Proclaim Freedom

Jesus' mission, therefore, was to proclaim freedom to those who were experiencing the crushing weight of guilt from sin that holds them captive and keeps them from seeing the truth of who they are before God. All of Jesus' miracles demonstrated spiritual corollaries and truths about the freedom and deliverance He inaugurated at His first coming. Many times Jesus healed all who were present; He always did what He saw His Father doing. The following are only examples of the truths His miracles taught:

- **the water to wine**: The wine of the new covenant is able to heal and gladden the heart (John 2:1-11).
- **deliverance from demons**: He sets the captives free from the power of darkness (Luke 9:38-43; 4:33-36; 8:27-36).
- **the sick brought to Him in the evening**: He always has time for us (Matt. 8:16-17; Mark 1:32-34).
- **healing the leprous**: He removes our sin and reconciles us to God (Luke 5:12-13; 17:11-19).
- **healing the paralyzed, lame, and malformed**: He provides us with what we lack; His strength is displayed in our weakness; crippled souls can be made whole (Luke 5:18-25; 6:6-10).
- **restoring those whose infirmity was the direct consequence of sin**: He grants mercy to the repentant (John 5:2-15).
- **restoring those whose malady had nothing to do with sin**: He gives grace to the suffering (John 9:1-41).
- **raising the dead**: He brings life to the dead in sin (Luke 7:11-15; John 11:1-44).
- **authority over nature**: He miraculously intervenes to overcome natural laws (Luke 8:22-25; John 6:19-21).
- **internal bleeding**: He delivers from the pain of emotional wounds that no other physician can heal (Luke 8:43-48).
- **healing the blind, the mute, the deaf**: He helps us understand, hear, confess, and obey (Matt. 9:27-31; Mark 7:31-37; 8:22-26; Luke 11:14; 18:35-43).
- **feeding multitudes**: He has ample and abundant spiritual food for all the hungry (Matt. 15:32-38; Mark 8:2-9; John 6:5-13).
- **healing those bound by Satan**: No one is out of His reach—His name is above all names (Luke 13:11-17).
- **provision of necessary finances**: He pays our debt for us; He provides what is needed at the right time (Matt. 17:24-27).

- **healing a slave's ear**: He repairs damage we receive from His misguided followers (Luke 22:50-51).
- **healing of Gentile seekers**: His freedom is not only for Israel, but the whole world (Matt. 15:21-28; Luke 7:1-10; cf. Isa. 49:6).
- **enormous catch of fish**: His message has power to draw even the unsuspecting to Him; He acts to catch our attention so we will follow Him (Luke 5:1-11).
- **healing on the Sabbath**: His new covenant is founded on the weightier matters of law (Matt. 12:9-14; Mark 1:21-28; 3:1-6; Luke 13:10-17; 14:1-6; John 5:1-16).

[Note: Notice in matters of providing food, Jesus performed miracles that were above what anyone could ask or think, for example, the feeding of the five thousand with twelve baskets left over. In the miracle of providing for His and Peter's tax payment in the mouth of the fish, there was precisely enough.]

Jesus only did what He saw the Father doing, and through spiritual perception of the works Jesus accomplished, we learn more of the nature of God and His kingdom. Jesus was sent to bring freedom to all who were bound spiritually, mentally, emotionally, and physically. On this last point, we note true and lasting freedom will come when our bodies are redeemed at Jesus' second coming. The only way in which He could bring true, lasting freedom was through fulfilling the contract of the old covenant by walking in the moral, civil, and sacrificial requirements so the contract could be paid in full and the new covenant of life and freedom ushered in.

Perfect Law of Liberty

> *But he who looks into the **perfect law of liberty** and continues in it, and is **not a forgetful hearer but a doer of the work**, this one will be blessed in what he does.* -James 1:25, NKJV

Freedom means action. Our freedom in Christ releases us from sin so we can perform God's will. One of the ways the new covenant is superior to the old is that the laws are written on the heart and can be carried with us wherever we go, unlike being written on stone or in a book. In the book of Judges, God refutes the reasoning that each can do what is right in his own eyes, verifying that our consciences are, in fact, stained and corrupted. The new covenant does not duplicate the lifeless legalism that has no power to transform the heart and mind. Nor is it a do-as-you-please licentious liberty with fragmented and misrepresented New Testament language thrown in to legitimize lawlessness.

The new covenant is different than both the law written on stone and the natural law by which unregenerate men should live by their conscience, but instead devolve to living in selfish rationalization, vain imaginings, and pursuit of whatever they desire. Living to please self requires we give only secondary consideration to those we trample or defile to further our own purposes or lusts. The new covenant does what neither of these modes of law could accomplish. Now God's law is written on the heart, and His Spirit cleanses us from our former ways of thinking (whether legalistic duty or rationalized, self-centered license). The new covenant gives us freedom from the power of sin as well as freedom to love God and man through faith in Christ and the grace provided.

The outcome of righteousness through faith does not produce lawlessness, but striving against our flesh with our eyes fixed on God so that if we fail, we don't succumb to condemnation. The believer's life becomes a cycle of running, stumbling, conviction, and forgiveness. Christian liberty is not the right to do as one pleases, but the power, desire, and will to do as one ought, through the grace of God and a regenerated life.

It is as if the apostles are saying, 'Our liberty is not freedom to do whatever we please, especially in the arena of sin; this should be understood because sin is the opposite of love. Sin is born in selfishness and lawlessness. How can there be evidence the law is now written on our hearts if we continue in sin? No, the law of liberty means we no longer sin because we are now *free* from sin, and our conscience *won't allow* us to sin. It is killing the desires of the flesh because sin no longer controls us. The perfect law of liberty is liberty from sin. This is why it is perfect. A perfect law keeps crime from taking place, which can only be accomplished as the Holy Spirit lives in us and we listen to His voice. Proclaim liberty throughout the land, for we are free from the power under which Adam and Eve fell.'

License to sin is not freedom but slavery. The new covenant was never about freedom to sin. The damnable nature of sin will be witnessed in those 'Christians' who continue in sin only to hear 'depart, I never knew you, you who *practice lawlessness*.' Grieving the Holy Spirit in this manner will lead to our rejection at Jesus' return. Those who view their faith as an 'insurance policy,' granting immunity from the consequences of their willful practice of sin, have stepped off the narrow path and placed themselves squarely on the broad road to destruction.

Disputable matters of the law never had to do with sin issues because there is no dispute about sin. It is wrong, and the conscience of unbeliever and believer alike identify what is wrong: murder, theft, false witness, immorality, and so on. While covetousness is not as obvious, it is usually at the root of most sin. Those believers who allow themselves to indulge in fornication or pornography, rationalizing its practice in their own minds, would typically prefer no other believers know they are involved in these activities. Wanting to hide what we are doing is a sure sign that we recognize we are sinning. Unfortunately, in our day there is no blushing over these matters but instead a calloused indifference, which is the fruit of a seared conscience. Some search for scriptural ways to validate sin or will even discredit the Word in order to legitimize sin.

The apostles are clear on this: matters of sin are not debatable. It is to be understood by everyone that moral laws are written even on the conscience of the ungodly. It is a foundational 'given' by virtue of being human. When the apostles discuss matters of the works of the law, bondage to the law, the yoke of the law, or being under the law, they are not negating the commands against sin. These specifically refer to adherence to the oral law or traditions (which no one is required to follow), following the Mosaic law if one is a Gentile (thinking it is required to please God), or following the Mosaic law or universal moral code in order to *earn righteousness* before God.

Paul wrote that sin is no longer our master because we live under the freedom of God's grace. Since we are now free from the law as the means to establish righteousness, are we to use that freedom to go on sinning? Paul emphatically answers his own question: 'Of course not!' (Rom. 6:14-15).

Apostolic Teaching on Freedom in Christ

For you were called to freedom, brethren; only do not turn your freedom into an opportunity for the flesh, but through love serve one another. -Gal. 5:13, NASB

The apostles emphasized the freedom available to believers under the new covenant. This freedom is not only removal of the *curse* for sin by lifting the sentence mandated by law, but it is also freedom from the *power* of sin to enslave us.

The apostles made a clear distinction between following the law as a requirement for reconciliation with God, and upholding the moral code to fulfill the law of Christ to honor and love God as well as love our neighbor as ourselves. The perfect law of liberty is summed up in three main points:

- **freedom from the yoke and curse of the law**: freedom from death through forgiveness of sins and imputed righteousness (rather than performance-based righteousness), resulting in freedom to be led by the Spirit
- **freedom from the power of sin**: freedom and grace to keep from sin to pursue righteousness wholeheartedly without fear of blame, accusation, condemnation, or death if we stumble
- **freedom from the veil**: freedom to understand divine truth by the gift of the Spirit

In our discussion of freedom, we again note the freedom obtained for us at the cross is a gift. It is not earned by keeping the law or performing good works. Our spirits are *justified* (made in right standing with God) through the righteousness of Christ, which we accept by faith (Rom. 3:28; Gal. 2:16). The Amplified version actually spells this out in the parenthetical explanation in Galatians 2:16b: "...*because by keeping legal rituals and by works no human being can ever be justified (declared righteous and put in right standing with God)*." We are justified, made righteous, and pronounced not guilty in the Court of God by the blood of Christ. The command to all who have been cleansed by Christ's sacrifice is to 'go and sin no more' by the power of the Spirit.

The process of *sanctification*, where our selfish sin nature is confronted by the Word and the Spirit of God and guided through the process of being conformed to the nature of Christ, requires work and struggle on our part. We have freedom to choose whether or not to cooperate with this process of transformation, but it is wholly in our interest to do so (we will revisit this topic in Sections 6 and 7).

Those who have the strongest souls, the most ambition, the most lust for power, or the most greed will be far more drawn to the world than to Christ. Their soul will not relinquish control to another until, like Paul, they encounter God, repent from the heart through godly sorrow, and turn from their own version of truth to embrace the only truth that will bring freedom. True freedom exists only in the spirit of one who has been reconciled to God and over whom death no longer has power.

Paul warned in his letter to the Romans that setting our minds on natural or worldly desires is hostile to God and brings death (Rom. 8:5-8). James agreed, stating those who adopt the world's ways make themselves enemies of God (James 4:4). Elsewhere, Paul stated those who live in hostility toward God by virtue of their worldly lifestyle will not inherit the kingdom (Gal. 5:20-21). When we are under the sentence of death, we frantically search for ways to make our mark on the world to be remembered after we are gone. In contrast, the Word teaches we will only have lasting impact if we embrace Christ.

'The mind set on the Spirit is life and peace' (Rom. 8:6b). Walking in the Spirit focuses our heart on God as Father. In contrast, walking in the flesh causes fear to rise up in us because we know the light of judgment will reveal our guilt (Rom. 8:15). By this we note 1.) the *kindness* and *grace* of God as Father toward those who repent and come by faith in Jesus, and 2.) the *severity* of God as Judge toward those who refuse His mercy. If we refuse His mercy, we are placed under the law, judged by it, and found unrighteous, for which the sentence is death. Therefore fear God, tremble at His Word, and accept His free gift. The alternative is certain death.

Faith-Based Response

The three primary responses to the law are:

- legalism born of a religious spirit, self-righteousness, and pride
- apathetic indifference
- faith-based hope in salvation through the promised Messiah (requires humility and honest assessment of our position before God)

The three primary responses to grace (freedom in Christ) are:

- lawlessness, evidence of the desire to remain in full control (a slave of sin and stiff-necked toward the Word and the Spirit); born of pride, self-centered desires, and ignorance
- apathetic indifference
- faith-based hope in righteousness through faith and in the resurrection to come (requires humility and the desire to be right with God, evidenced by relinquishing control of personal desires)

SECTION 3 *HARMONIZED VIEW OF LAW AND FREEDOM*

Obviously, God is looking for those with a faith-based response. Many under the old covenant responded in faith, looking to the promise of redemption and embracing God as Father. Under the new covenant, we have been given the Holy Spirit to keep us in right relationship with God. Through the work of His Spirit, we have everything we need to grow and mature in faith, but it won't take place without effort and cooperation on our part. Incrementally, we are brought to a place of effectual labor, bearing good fruit for the kingdom. He has given us all the power and help we need to live a godly life.

This power is supplied by the living Word and the Holy Spirit, through which we have received 'great and precious promises.' These promises include deliverance from the power of sin and the corruption that results. We are now invited to participate in the divine nature—the character and mind of Christ. After explaining these things (2 Pet. 1:3-4), Peter exhorted believers to make *every effort* to build on their faith with virtue (moral excellence), knowledge, self-control, perseverance in circumstances, godliness (devotion to God), mutual affection (*philadelphia*), and finally love (*agape*) (2 Pet. 1:5-7). Each builds on and flows out of the previous.

> For **if you possess these qualities in increasing measure, they will keep you from being <u>ineffective and unproductive in your knowledge</u>** *of our Lord Jesus Christ. But whoever does not have them is nearsighted and blind, forgetting that they have been cleansed from their past sins.* -2 Pet. 1:8-9, NIV

Freedom from the Yoke and Curse of the Law

Many in the church superficially believe freedom from the law means there is no law. They would be in agreement with Thomas Edison's remark about his work: "... there are no rules here—we're trying to accomplish something." While this statement is useful for thinking 'outside the box,' the place where many creative ideas originate, this cannot be applied to moral or ethical issues. But his statement is close to what the new covenant is all about because God's objective is to capture our hearts. This is what He desires to accomplish through the freedom of the new covenant. Once our heart is captured and fascinated by Him, all righteousness and transformation will follow.

Jesus came to reconcile us to God by giving Himself as a sacrifice to atone for our sins. His fulfillment of the law *for righteousness* paid humanity's debt for sin and nailed the curse of death to the cross. The curse nailed to the cross was the curse of death spoken over all mankind in the Garden, and the curses pronounced from Mt. Ebal for Israel. 'The wages of sin is death,' and because life is in the blood, only by the shedding of blood can man pay the debt his soul owes for sin (Lev. 17:11).

Thankfully, God in His mercy allows for the blood of the innocent to take the place of the blood of the guilty in order to fulfill the requirement of the original law in the Garden, 'in that day you will die.' As the perfect Judge, God delayed the sentence so we could produce godly offspring (though many have been far busier satisfying the longing to be productive in the sight of men than following God's command to raise godly children), ensuring the survival of the human race until the appointed time of perfect redemption. Through God's plan, dominion of the world will be reinstated to man. Those who follow Christ and embrace His counsel for godly living will be appointed to reign with Jesus.

Because life is in the blood, it was used as the means for making atonement for transgression, starting in the garden with the animal sacrificed to make atoning garments for Adam and Eve. The author of Hebrews, however, makes it clear that it is impossible for the blood of animals to take away sin (Heb. 10:4). Not only this, but the blood of animals cannot cleanse our conscience from sin; only the blood of Christ accomplished this (Heb. 9:9,14). The purpose of the animal sacrifices for sin, then, is as an object lesson to remind us of the Redeemer that God promised to send. Jesus' obedient life and perfect blood would cleanse our conscience and reconcile us to God. What God desires from the redeemed is obedience (1 Sam. 15:22; Heb. 10:5).

Faith in this promised Redeemer prompted men to offer sacrifices, both as an acknowledgment of sin and as a demonstration of faith in the promise to come. Abel sacrificed one from the flock because of his humility before God, acknowledging the sinful inclination he inherently possessed. This was a symbolic act, pointing to the Redeemer who would one day shed His blood for all.

The innocent blood of Jesus became the instrument of redemption because innocent blood is not under any curse. Jesus set His face toward Jerusalem because He came to die to save mankind from the curse of death and to restore what had been lost in Eden. He came the first time to testify to the truth, to show us the way (John 18:37), and to lay down His life to redeem us from death (John 12:27). Jesus had the choice to do this, and He did it because of love—love for His Father who gave Him the authority, and love for the lost He ransomed from death. Regarding His life, Jesus stated:

> *No one has taken it away from Me, but I lay it down on My own initiative. I have authority to lay it down, and I have authority to take it up again. This commandment (**entole**) I received from My Father.* -John 10:18, NASB

The law's curse is indisputable and came as the Israelites agreed to put themselves under the law: 'Cursed is anyone who does not obey everything contained in the law' (Deut. 27:26; see also Gal. 3:10). However, Jesus freed us from the curse by becoming the curse (Gal. 3:13). Since 'the curse' was hung on the cross and died, it has been abolished. This selfless act provided us with a better covenant based on *promises*, not performance. From the first days of man in the Garden to the covenant at Sinai, law failed as the contingency for righteousness (right standing before God) and for life because the mention of sin grips the mind with desire to sin. Love and faith are the foundation for life and righteousness under the new covenant, the result of which provides reconciliation with God, a sanctified existence in the present age, and eternal life in the presence of God in a glorified, imperishable, ageless body in the age to come.

SECTION 3 *HARMONIZED VIEW OF LAW AND FREEDOM*

Paul concluded the law was the wall of hostility between the Gentiles and the Jews before they were reconciled by Jesus' blood (Eph. 2:11-16). Gentiles could not hope to enter into God's covenant because by law they were not allowed admission to the temple proper unless they converted to Judaism. Even so, the outer court was as far as even most Jews could go, illustrating that observance of the law will never give us access to God because it is impossible for us to keep it. Jesus' sacrifice put an end to the law as the means to gain access to (or relationship with) God (Eph. 2:14-15).

No Distinction Between Jew and Gentile Concerning Salvation

Both Jew and Gentile alike have cause for rejoicing in the Jewish Messiah. There is no more curse and no more distinction between Jew and Gentile as pertains to salvation. While it was difficult for Jews accustomed to the old covenant to enter into this new freedom, the Spirit is patient with both those established in the letter of the law (Jews) as well as the typically licentious (Gentiles).

God declared Abraham righteous by faith before the law and before circumcision, foreshadowing the universality of the new covenant (Rom. 4:9-10). The promise cannot come by both faith and the law—it is clearly only by faith (Rom. 4:13-14). All men are prisoners of sin; only by believing in Jesus can we receive the promise (Gal. 3:21-22). Anyone can partake of the promised gift of freedom if received by faith because Abraham is the father of all who believe. Those who embrace the new covenant comprise the 'many nations' God promised to Abraham (Rom. 4:16-17).

Understanding this kept the early believers from making the law a requirement for Gentiles to enter into the promises of the Jewish new covenant, as some of the Jewish believers would have preferred (see Acts 15:1-2). Many of us have difficulty letting go of our cherished traditions, beliefs, and ways; this should come as no surprise. Not only this, but we can become narrow-minded in our thinking and require everyone to do things the same way that we do. Sometimes it takes a while for the lure of the old wine to lose its grip on our mind and affections.

> *You are **trying to earn favor with God** by observing certain days or months or seasons or years. I fear for you... I plead with you to live as I do in freedom from these things, for I have become like you Gentiles—**free from those laws*** (legalistically, as a means to please God or merit salvation). -Gal. 4:10-12a, NLT (parenthetical added)

The religious spirit prefers to have rules and participate in atonement through religious rituals and ascetic practices to somehow make him worthy before God. Following a checklist is in some ways much easier than following the Spirit. When we follow the Spirit, we often find that either He won't let us go as fast as we would like, or He is pressing us to 'get going' when we want to pull back. In other instances, He wants us to go in a completely different direction, even though our own momentum is propelling us toward what seems to be a very worthy goal.

Paul warned the Gentile believers at Colossae not to return to rudimentary physical regulations, defining these as rules on eating, keeping special days, and abstinence of various sorts. Believers have died with Christ and are free from earthly regulations. He encouraged them to keep their focus on heavenly matters.

> *These **rules may seem wise** because they require strong devotion, pious self-denial, and severe bodily discipline. **But they provide no help** in conquering a person's evil desires* (e.g., pride, religious self-righteousness, cold legalism). -Col. 2:23, NLT (parenthetical added)

Paul similarly counseled the Galatians, admonishing them to keep from being tied up again in a yoke of slavery to religious law since Christ has truly set them free (Gal. 5:1). We have a glimpse of the freedom in which the apostles began to walk. Peter and Paul both fellowshipped with Gentiles in ways contrary to the Jewish traditions (known as the oral law), paying attention to the weightier matters, especially of love for each other.

> *But when I saw that they were deviating from the truth of the gospel, I told Cephas in front of everyone, "If you, who are a Jew, live like a Gentile and not like a Jew, how can you compel Gentiles to live like Jews?"* -Gal. 2:14, HCSB

In light of Paul's other comments, particularly that he had transgressed no laws of the Jews or temple (see Acts 25:8; 28:17), we must read this at more than face value lest we neglect to take into account the whole counsel of God. Paul operated within the framework of the Mosaic law with such freedom as to no longer move in legalistic performance. Instead, he focused on weightier matters, especially love, in the hopes of winning some to salvation.

In this way, and remembering Jesus as our example of someone who was perfectly obedient to the law by giving greater priority to the weightier matters, the particulars of the ceremonial laws could be adjusted or waived in circumstances which warranted the accommodation. Paul reminded us that the salvation of someone's eternal soul is justification enough for setting aside the law (the *edot* and *chukim*).

> *I became to the Jews as a Jew, that Jews I might gain; to those under law as under law, that those under law I might gain; to those without law, as without law—(**not being without law to God, but within law to Christ**)—that I might gain those without law; I became to the infirm as infirm, that the infirm I might gain; to all men I have become all things, that by all means I may save some.*
> -1 Cor. 9:20-22, YLT

Freedom from the Power of Sin

Having been freed from the power of sin, we are now free to be bondservants of God. Peter exhorted believers to live in this freedom not as a cover for sin, but as God's slaves (1 Pet. 2:16). This freedom defines the life of the bondservant, enabling him to

SECTION 3 HARMONIZED VIEW OF LAW AND FREEDOM

serve God wholeheartedly without condemnation or compulsion. The heart is free to focus on commitment to God, rather than remain captive to guilt and shame.

> *When you were slaves to sin, you were free from the obligation to do right. And what was the result? You are now ashamed of the things you used to do, things that end in eternal doom.* **But now you are free from the power of sin and have become slaves of God.** *Now you do those things that lead to holiness and result in eternal life.* -Rom. 6:20-22, NLT

The heart of the bondservant has been gripped with the reality of this freedom and turns back to thank his benefactor by pledging his service, just as the one leper returned to thank Jesus after being healed (Luke 17:11-19). This is the heart response God is seeking: the one whose heart is 'perfect' (loyal) toward Him.

In the process of becoming a bondservant, the Holy Spirit illuminates behaviors that are unbecoming in our lives and unacceptable for one in God's service—in one who bears His name. The apostles repeatedly addressed the conduct in the early believers' fellowships. They emphasized following the Holy Spirit and walking in the power to be free from sin. When we are directed by the Spirit, we are not under obligation to the law for right standing before God (Gal. 5:16-18).

In Romans, Paul reminded believers that sin must not control the way in which they live. Succumbing to sinful desires makes our bodies instruments of evil that 'serve sin.' By giving ourselves completely to God, we can live as instruments of righteousness to bring honor to God's name. Since sin is no longer our master, we live under the freedom of God's grace. Paul also stated that if we use this freedom to sin, then *sin is still our master* because we are the slave to whatever we obey. If we choose to obey sin, the consequence is death because those who obey their sin nature are under the law, not grace. If we obey God, we become slaves to righteous living and have life.

> *Once you were slaves of sin, but now you wholeheartedly obey this teaching we have given you. Now you are free from your slavery to sin, and you have become slaves to righteous living.* -Rom. 6:17-18, NLT

It was especially important that the newly appointed elders be chosen only after the Holy Spirit's work in their lives became evident (1 Tim. 3:1-7). James, whose letter is one of the earliest written, was burdened with the issue of seeing believers in the new covenant become fruitful in their freedom. With great zeal, James counseled new believers not to deceive themselves into believing they could get by with only listening to the Word, reducing the new covenant to mere academic acquisition of knowledge—a philosophical discussion for the mind only. He was adamant they also put into practice what they learned (James 1:22-25).

It is easy to understand why Martin Luther had such a difficult time with James. It would seem as though James wanted new believers to return to performance, especially with his comment 'we are also justified by works' (James 2:24). But if we remember that we are saved by grace *for righteousness*, we will better understand that the law's inability to save does not negate the moral code of God. The freedom of the new covenant now enables us to walk uprightly by cancelling the power of sin. The apostles continually mentioned the grace (empowerment) believers have been afforded to overcome sin. 'When we died with Christ, we were set free from the power of sin' so we can live righteously (Rom. 6:7, NLT; see also Rom. 6:10-11,22). We are free from the curse of the law and free from the power of sin so we can be separated and made righteous. Jesus gave His life to free us from 'every kind' of sin and to cleanse us from all unrighteousness. The goal is to make us His own people, committed to doing good deeds (Titus 2:14).

James warned us to speak and act with the knowledge that we will be judged by the law that gives freedom. In other words, now that we are free from the power of sin, Jesus will judge us when He returns on how we lived out our freedom (James 2:12). Paul exhorted Timothy to keep himself free from sin, implying the need to exercise his will in executing this command (1 Tim. 5:22). Peter charged the believers to live as free people, not as an excuse for sin, but for choosing to live as God's bondservants (1 Pet. 2:16).

Grace: Our New Tutor

> *For the grace of God has appeared (**epiphaino**), bringing salvation to all men, instructing (**paideuo**) us to deny ungodliness and worldly desires and to live sensibly, righteously and godly in the present age, looking for the blessed hope and the appearing of the glory of our great God and Savior, Christ Jesus, who gave Himself for us to redeem us from every lawless deed, and **to purify for Himself a people for His own possession, zealous for good deeds.*** -Titus 2:11-14, NASB (parentheticals added)

The use of *paideuo* in this passage to explain the nature of the teaching 'grace' provides is derived from the word *pais*, 'a child.' The reference to a child is a clear implication of the need for grace to tutor us from immature babes in Christ to maturity. Much as the law was guardian under the old covenant, grace appeared in order to tutor us under the new. Grace 'appeared,' *epiphaino*, relating the sense of suddenness, like light bursting forth at dawn, or the unexpectedness of this new teacher shining light upon the way of the new covenant life in the Spirit. This is exactly what happened at Pentecost, as well as in the life of every believer who has experienced true repentance.[3]

The guardian role of grace instructs us in the way to go so we can fulfill our lives as bondservants. "The verb *teaching* encompasses the whole concept of growth—discipline, maturing, obedience, progress, and the like. This involves denial of improper things and direction into proper channels. These five terms—godliness, worldly lusts, soberly, righteously, godly—do not describe the content of grace teaching so much as they indicate the object and purposeful goal of that teaching. And this intent is, according to this passage, the ultimate purpose of the Incarnation of Christ. He came to display the grace of God in the changed lives of his people. ***The final cause of the revelation of the grace of God in Christ is not creed but character.***"[4] (emphasis added)

The type of teaching to which *paideuo* refers is not knowledge that puffs up, but the moral and spiritual development of children.[5] Guiding conscious behavior and will by instructing the conscience through training, drilling, reproof, admonition, and chastisement defines the process of *paideuo*, resulting in the hoped for result of conforming the student to divine truth and the nature of God. These methods of teaching often come through the trials and testing the New Testament writers forewarned would come to perfect our faith (bring to mature obedience). The goal of the tutor in this case is to help the student learn to deny what is improper as well as impart yearning to walk in moral uprightness. This tutor pursues our character and heart. The difference between this tutor and the old guardian is the difference between life and death.

"God's grace teaches us by putting us under obligation negatively—to quit sinning—and positively—to grow and produce fruit. The Moffatt translation clarifies this obligation by defining the terms in more modern language. "For the grace of God has appeared to save all men, and it schools us to renounce irreligion and worldly passions and to live a life of self-mastery, of integrity, and of piety in this present world." These are the areas toward which we must turn our attention to fulfill our duty to Christ. Moffatt retains the positive and negative aspects in his version: first, the negative renouncing of 'irreligion and worldly passions,' then the positive living of a life of 'self-mastery, integrity, and piety.'"[6]

Grace is indispensible now that the Mosaic law as the task master of behavior has been set aside. The source of our righteousness is not the law, but the righteousness of Christ imparted to us at rebirth, granting us power over sin, condemnation, and death. Understood this way, grace and the freedom of believers become not the right to do as one's selfish nature would dictate, but the power and desire to do what is right in the sight of God. The goal is to demonstrate by our behavior that sin no longer has dominion over us (Rom. 6:14).

Is this beginning to sound like the law again, all about good behavior in compliance with God's standards? In a way, it is. We have the perfect law of liberty (James 1:25), the law of Christ (Gal. 6:2), and the law of the Spirit of life (Rom. 8:2), but all under the tutor of grace, not the guardianship of law. Paul calls these principles 'the righteousness of the law' (Rom. 8:4) and, as we have seen here, they are the goal of life in the Spirit by grace.

This helps us understand James' statement, which is difficult to reconcile with other apostolic teaching on justification without knowing the goal of the grace we have been given. The goal is to walk in accordance with God's will as *evidence* sin no longer has a hold on us (James 2:24). Therefore, we conduct ourselves in compliance with the Spirit in the fear of the Lord, free from the 'aimless conduct received by tradition' (1 Pet. 1:17-18).

> *Those who belong to Christ Jesus have nailed the passions and desires of their sinful nature to his cross and crucified them there. Since we are living by the Spirit, let us follow the Spirit's leading in every part of our lives.* -Gal. 5:24-25, NLT

Sanctification Is Individually Tailored by the Spirit

We cannot do the work of the Holy Spirit for Him by imposing lists of rules on members in the body of Christ. Sanctification is the result of the Holy Spirit's work and individualized for each person. The Lord knows each of us intimately, giving us baby steps initially in the transformation of our mind, heart, and actions. This allows us to experience the freedom of relinquishing sinful behaviors as well as the victory of the overcomer. As sanctification progresses, we incrementally let go of the more difficult or ingrained behaviors. This step-by-step sanctification is tailored for each person and is therefore not in the same order for any two believers. Imposing 'standards' has the same effect as the overprescribed use of Ritalin in very active children: it makes interaction with the group more tolerable, but it dulls the spirit, among other side effects.

The church does need standards of behavior, but the manner in which we treat those members having difficulty reveals whether we are moving in a religious spirit and self-righteousness, or the zeal of Phinehas and love. If we are moving in the right way, we will pray and maybe even fast for the strength and grace needed by the wayward believer. Many in the church who struggle in certain areas stop attending because of the wrong spirit of condemnation present among the 'more righteous.'

The guidelines imposed on believers must be based on the moral code for the honor of God's name and the promotion of fellowship but not without concern for the struggles of others. Typically, those who are most vocal about the behavioral shortcomings of others have ingrained battles with gossip, ambition, and self-righteous pride, all of which are terribly odious in God's sight. Sanctification is progressive as is revelation (Eph. 3:9; Col. 1:26-27). We need patience to live in harmony with those who continue to struggle. We must remind ourselves that a self-righteous attitude of condemnation, often expressed through gossip and slander, demonstrates our own defiled heart.

The law of the Spirit is life because of the righteousness freely given to all who are in Christ. Because of Jesus, we are no longer under the guardianship of the law but under the tutelage of grace (Rom. 7:6). Only while under the law can sin reign and have dominion over us. The wages of sin has always been death—this has not changed (Rom. 6:23). Under grace we die to sin and therefore it no longer has dominion over us. Through grace we become 'slaves to righteousness,' which leads to our sanctification. The end result or goal of sanctification is eternal life (Rom. 6:19,22).

Because of Jesus, we no longer stand condemned before God because of sin. This is true freedom. The law was powerless to produce righteousness because of our sin nature. Through Jesus' atoning sacrifice, the sin nature in each one of us was condemned so righteousness could be brought forth by the Spirit. Having minds no longer set on the flesh, we can follow the Spirit, which brings life and peace.

If the Spirit of God lives in us, we belong to Christ and no longer seek to follow our own desires. This does not mean the old desires are immediately gone, although this is true in some cases of instant deliverance at repentance, for example, from the use of foul language. But it does mean those carnal desires are now accompanied by conviction and the increasing desire to overcome their hold on our lives. Eternal life is promised to all who abide in Christ and overcome the ways of the world. Jesus' own resurrection supplied evidence that God will raise His followers as promised (Rom. 8:1-11).

Our obligation, then, is to live not for ourselves but for Christ, as bondservants out of love and gratitude, not out of compunction or for gain. Because of our willingness to be bondslaves out of love and not fear, God will adopt us as sons, giving us the witness of the Spirit by which we relate to God as 'Father.' As sons, we are coheirs with Christ as long as we abide in Him (Rom. 8:12-17).

Freedom from the Veil

[W]henever a person turns to the Lord, the veil is taken away. -2 Cor. 3:16, NASB

Notice God removes the veil after we turn aside from the world to God, as Moses did. Jeremiah prophesied a distinction of the new covenant: each will know God (Jer. 31:34). The unveiling of Christ enables us to change to be like Him by the power of the Spirit as He illuminates the Word. This opens up a realm of understanding that can be discerned by grasping John's description of Jesus as the 'Word of God made flesh.' When Jesus told His disciples to eat His flesh and drink His blood, He pointed to the new covenant where His flesh, the bread of life, is the Word, and His blood, the wine of the Holy Spirit, is the seal of the new covenant of grace (Eph. 1:13; 4:30). The Holy Spirit searches the deep things of God and reveals understanding to those under the covenant of grace.

- ◆ God made His light shine in our hearts to give us knowledge of His glory, displayed in Jesus' face, the Word (2 Cor. 4:6).
- ◆ God reveals His secret thoughts to us by His Spirit (1 Cor. 2:10).
- ◆ We are enriched with knowledge and speech through Christ, the Word (1 Cor. 1:5).
- ◆ God has showered us with wisdom and understanding (Eph. 1:8).

When we walk in the Spirit, we find as we persevere in our quest to know God that we begin to have greater, deeper, and clearer understanding of the Word. Staying connected to the Head, which is Jesus the Word, enables us to stay in the Spirit. The Spirit is the 'breath' that imparts to us the grace we need not only to overcome sin, but also to know what pleases God through progressive understanding of His Word. The Lord reveals His secrets to those who love and fear Him and walk uprightly before Him (see also John 15:14-15; Pr. 3:32; Amos 3:7; Matt. 10:26; Luke 12:2).

The secret of the LORD is for those who fear Him, and He will make them know His covenant. -Ps. 25:14, NASB

Those who stay connected to the Head and learn from the Spirit will be given deeper understanding of the Word, and at the appointed time, revelation of the things to come. This fulfills the words of Jeremiah that in the season preceding the Day of the Lord, those who are God's bondservants will understand clearly what has been prophesied (Jer. 23:20).

Jesus also told the disciples there was much He still wanted to teach them, but they were not able to understand or even receive it at that time (John 16:12-15). A simplistic example would be the pointlessness of teaching physics to a five year old. They are neither ready to grasp nor even capable of learning this. Each level of understanding builds on mastery of the principles from the previous level. Skipping several levels all at once will only bring frustration to the student.

So it is with spiritual understanding. This explains why the promise of the Holy Spirit is particularly precious. He reveals to us whatever we need and are ready to receive at the time. Furthermore, whatever we are searching for He helps us find, even to the point of telling us (at the right time) what lies ahead.

Ask me and I will tell you remarkable secrets you do not know about things to come. -Jer. 33:3, NLT

The Purpose of Revelation

The purpose of revelation is not only to give us insight into what lies ahead, but also to show what is pleasing to the Lord and enable us to obey.

The Lord our God has secrets known to no one. We are not accountable for them, but we and our children are accountable forever for all that he has revealed to us, so that we may obey all the terms of these instructions. -Deut. 29:29, NLT

Jesus exhorted His disciples to *really listen* in order to understand what He was saying. The effort with which we struggle to hear and understand will determine how much the Lord imparts to us of the riches buried in His Word, including clarity on the things to come. As with any school system, successfully learning the precepts of a lower level allows us to progress on toward learning at a higher level.

After asking the disciples whether a lamp is hidden under a basket or put on a table to let the light show, Jesus explained to the disciples that nothing hidden or kept secret will remain that way, including the secret and sealed things in His Word (Mark 4:21-22). For this reason, we are to pay attention to what we hear because the one who has heard (listens with the intent to understand and obey) will be given more. The one merely listening to be polite or out of a sense of duty (indifferent toward really comprehending the meaning and even less interested in obeying) will find what little he had will be taken from him and given to the one who is thirsty for more (Mark 4:23-25). Luke recorded the same teaching:

> [A]ll that is secret will eventually be brought into the open, and everything that is concealed will be brought to light and made known to all. So **pay attention to how you hear**. To those who listen to my teaching, more understanding will be given. But for those who are not listening, even what they think they understand will be taken away from them. -Luke 8:17-18, NLT

In other words, those who are sincerely studying the Word because they love the Lord, consumed and captivated with knowing Him and the workings of His heart, will be given further revelation because of their hunger. He does not send the hungry away empty. However, to those without this hunger, even the little they were given will be taken away. People who are not hungry do not eat what is set before them, and the Lord does not send forth His Word to have it return to Him void of fruitfulness (Isa. 55:11).

For this reason the Lord rebuked the Pharisees. They nullified the Word of God because they mishandled Scripture and taught others to do likewise (Matt. 15:6; Luke 11:52). They placed greater importance on and were more loyal to their own teaching and opinions than to God's truth, heart, or purposes. The result is that the hungry were not fed.

> For fools speak folly, their hearts are bent on evil: They practice ungodliness and spread error concerning the LORD; the hungry they leave empty and from the thirsty they withhold water. -Isa. 32:6, NIV

All born again believers have this hunger. This hunger is dulled in two primary ways. Preoccupation with self and with the cares and lure of this world are one way to dull the hunger of our spirits to know God. The second way is to become involved in a congregation that neither honors the Word nor focuses on the things that matter to God. Jesus will not send the hungry away empty, but those satisfied with what the world and the rituals of religion have to offer are left barren.

> For he satisfies the longing soul, and the hungry soul he fills with good things... He has filled the hungry with good things, and the rich (satisfied) He has sent away empty. -Ps. 107:9; Luke 1:53, ESV (parenthetical added)

Requires Perseverance

To test our sincerity and perseverance on this issue of hearing, the treasures of God's Word are often couched in language or literary devices that purposefully obscure the meaning (Matt. 13:10-16). This guards against acquiring knowledge that puffs up, ensuring that the casual, immature, and unbelieving are not given treasure they cannot handle or steward properly. With increased revelation about the kingdom comes greater accountability, and this is only given to the bondservants of God. Recall that the disciples identified themselves as bondservants to whom the following was addressed:

> *The knowledge of the secrets of the kingdom of God has been given to you, but to others I speak in parables, so that, 'though seeing, they may not see; though hearing, they may not understand.'* -Luke 8:10, NIV

Comprehension can only come as we resolve to pursue understanding and allow the Holy Spirit to work through repeated exposure to the Word of God. While it is the glory of God to conceal His treasure, it is the kingly spirit in man that searches the Word to understand what has been hidden (Pr. 25:2). Through this process, we gain the mind of Christ as carnal thinking and man-made paradigms concede to truth.

Believers have not received the spirit of the world but the Spirit of God so we can understand what God has given us. The words used to teach spiritual realities are not words of human wisdom but of divine wisdom. The person without the Spirit cannot accept the spiritual truths spoken in God's manner of expression. Those principles are foolish or illogical from his carnal perspective (1 Cor. 2:14-16).

The apostles emphasized the necessity of growing in understanding by frequently requesting this in their prayers for the believers (e.g., Col. 1:9-10). One of the prerequisites for growing in knowledge is to be united in love, which enables us to know Christ, who is the Word. By being united in love, we have available to us complete understanding of the 'mystery of God,' defined by Paul as Jesus Himself. In Jesus (the Word) are hidden all the treasures of wisdom and knowledge. Paul explained this to the Colossians so that no one would deceive them by their 'fine sounding arguments' (Col. 2:2-4).

This is why staying connected to the Head (the Word) is so crucial in the believer's walk. Comprehending and obeying the Word are our primary duties and concerns. Jesus explained that those who would call themselves His disciples must abide in His Word (John 8:31). Through immersion in the Word, we behold the face of Christ and are changed to be like Him—perfect in heart toward God and increasing in our love for others. By this we are able to fulfill the law of walking in love for God and our fellow man. It is our love for one another that will prove to the world we are His disciples (John 13:35).

> *If I had the gift of prophecy, and if I understood all of God's secret plans and possessed all knowledge, and if I had such faith that I could move mountains, but didn't love others, I would be nothing.* -1 Cor. 13:2, NLT

Regrettably, many in the church avoid reading their Bibles citing it is too hard to understand and/or they don't have enough time. Time is made for everything else: working out, weekly card games with friends, ball games, sporting events, music lessons, horseback riding, Christian romance books (fiction), landscaping, concerts, shopping at the mall, manicures, texting, crafts, concerts, potlucks, reading groups, television, web surfing—you name it. [Note: None of these are wrong to do, especially when they promote fellowship among believers. But they are no substitute for time with God. These activities feed our souls. Only time with God feeds our spirit, which is why a steady diet of this 'soul-food' can leave us feeling weak spiritually.] For many, it is simply feeling a lack of priority for reading the Word, frustration with the supposed daunting nature of Bible study, negative anticipation of the effort required, or indifference to the commitment.

Deep inside some, however, is the underlying fear the Word may expose a part of their life they would rather keep secret, or an area they may have to surrender and would rather hold onto—even if it is legitimate activity and not an issue of sin. The issue may be based in fear of relinquishing control over the life they so cherish and the things they love to do which they erroneously think define them. Our identity is found in Christ alone. We must remember that anything we accomplish outside the realm of God's will is judged worthless (evil), even if it is not inherently sinful.

> *This is the verdict: Light has come into the world, but people loved darkness instead of light because their deeds were evil. Everyone who does evil hates the light, and will not come into the light for fear that their deeds will be exposed. But whoever lives by the truth comes into the light, so that it may be seen plainly that what they have done has been done in the sight of God.* -John 3:19-21, NIV

The Word and Spirit bring light and life. We must be grateful for the ministers who faithfully discharge their duties in bringing the gospel to others, especially for those to whom access to the written Word has not yet been provided. For this reason, many of them seek to meet daily—to hear the Word. But for those who have access to the Word, personal study must have priority for our spiritual health, especially if we meet with others only weekly or less frequently. We have been saved for a purpose, and we discover that purpose as we grow in our understanding of God's Word. Applying the principle of substitution to Jesus as the Word, we can exchange 'Word' for 'Jesus' in the following passage to bring greater practical understanding of what the Lord is saying.

> *When Jesus spoke again to the people, he said, "I am the light of the world. Whoever follows me* (the Word) *will never walk in darkness* (lack of understanding), *but will have the light of life."* -John 8:12, NIV (parentheticals added)

Another Comforter Sent to Teach Us

It is important we keep our minds and hearts in a teachable mode as we sit before the Word in order to grow in our understanding. The Holy Spirit was sent to us as our teacher. When Jesus stated He would send another (*allos*) Comforter (*parakletos*), He revealed the nature of His own ministry as Advocate for the disciples. By saying the Holy Spirit is *allos*, Jesus indicated the Spirit is another of the same quality as He is. "The Holy Spirit... undertakes Christ's office in the world while Christ is away." The word *parakletos* conveys the notion of one who comes alongside a defendant to provide legal counsel; "one who comes forward on behalf of and as the representative of another."[7] Because of the Holy Spirit's function to guide us into all truth in the same way Jesus instructed the disciples, it is vital we place ourselves under the Spirit's tutelage.

Always keep in mind Jesus is the Word. This helps us understand the role of the Word in our lives and the imperative nature of understanding His Word for our own salvation. God's Word, by giving us understanding of divine wisdom and plans, keeps us in peace even under the direst circumstances. Jesus gave the promise that He will reveal Himself (the Word) to those that are His.

In Jesus' final message to the disciples before the cross, He explained in one word what love for God entails: obedience. Those who love Him will receive His Spirit as their Advocate forever. The Spirit of Truth is given to help us and always be with us if we love Jesus and keep His commands. The Holy Spirit is not given to or even recognized by those who are worldly, but He will live in those who abide in Christ (John 14:15-17).

Those who keep Jesus' commands are the ones who really love Him. These are the ones to whom Jesus promised to reveal Himself (the Word) (John 14:21). To those who love Jesus and obey His teaching, He and the Father will 'make their home with them.' The Holy Spirit, the believer's Advocate, will teach us all things and remind us of what we have already learned. This will give us peace no matter what our circumstances may be (John 14:23-27). Jesus reveals events ahead of time through His Spirit so when they happen we will believe (John 14:29). We no longer have to walk in darkness. Even if we are not gifted in the realm of literary understanding, He is faithful to satisfy the hungry with good things.

Apostolic Teaching on Conduct and the Law

> *The aim of our charge is love that issues from a pure heart and a good conscience and a sincere faith. Certain persons, by swerving from these, have wandered away into vain discussion, desiring to be teachers of the law, without understanding either what they are saying or the things about which they make confident assertions.* -1 Tim. 1:5-7, ESV

Love from a pure heart, clear conscience, and sincere faith describes our goal. Some have veered away from this goal by focusing on discussions of the law without clearly understanding what they are teaching, no matter how confidently they assert their positions (and there are many). Our focus is not to become teachers of the law, but rather to edify the body of Christ through loving acts of service to those in need, including those who need a word of encouragement or answers to questions in matters of faith.

Paul made very clear that sanctification of our desires and behavior through the work of the Holy Spirit and grace would take place *in this present age*. The Lord's goal is to purify a people for Himself who are fit to rule and reign with Jesus. Ask yourself this question: If you had the choice to select people for rulership in your kingdom, would you choose self-disciplined, self-controlled, not-easily-offended people who are farsighted enough and sincerely considerate of others that they are willing to deny their own interests in order to effectively care for the needs of those under their authority as well as uphold the mandate of the One in charge? Or would you choose those who only have their own welfare in mind, grasp for authority beyond their station, rationalize every unethical practice and hoard for themselves all the good a people and land can produce, and are easily offended and harbor bitterness toward all those who oppose them? The answer is obvious. So we must ask ourselves, what kind of people will Jesus be looking for to rule and reign with Him when He returns? Are we that kind of people?

God's grace appeared specifically to raise up a people trained to renounce ungodly passions and worldly pursuits. This comes through living self-controlled and upright lives *in the present age*, and focusing on the promise of Jesus' return and the redemption of our own bodies from mortal to immortal. He came to save us from our sinful nature and the lure of the world in order to purify for Himself a people who have zeal for accomplishing God's purposes, dedicated to seeing His kingdom established on earth (Titus 2:11-15).

The apostles emphasized proper instruction and teaching about the grace available to believers so they would be devoted to doing good works. Paul underscored that we are to avoid controversial matters, genealogies (especially regarding Jewish lineage, which is surely his meaning), divisive arguments, and quarrels about the law. Moreover, Paul called these activities unprofitable for the *ekklesia* and worthless. Those who continue in these types of divisive quarrels are subversive, sinful, and miss the mark, condemning themselves by their own actions. We are to warn these people to cease from their error, breaking fellowship if they will not listen (Titus 3:7-11). So why do we get caught up in these types of debates? Let everything be done from a posture of faith with love.

Order in the Assemblies of Believers

Paul's guidelines for proper order in the assemblies of believers in the early church are on the order of *halakhic* decisions (cf. 1 Cor. 7:12,25), based on knowledge of the Word and its application in a practical sense under the inspiration of God's Spirit. The goal is to honor God and show deference to each other by our conduct. This involves the common courtesy of taking turns, not speaking when someone else is trying to make a point, yielding to others by not monopolizing the conversation, making sure everyone is fed and treated equitably, and disciplining members in gross sin (this is not making reference to eating pork, smoking, drinking wine, or stopping at the store on a 'Sabbath' day). We are not to put a stumbling block before others, for example, by what we eat or the way we dress. We are to be sensitive to the needs of others out of love and deference to the Lord's desire that we treat others the way we want to be treated. We learned most of these things in kindergarten before we became so rigid in our thinking that we bristle at any correction, even if the source of the rebuke is the Word and the Spirit of God.

Outside of maintaining order in our assemblies, there is very little instruction about specific religious practice other than meeting with other believers regularly, baptism, the Lord's Supper, alms-giving, and prayer. The vast majority of apostolic instruction regarding conduct dealt with sin issues, not special religious formalism. We are to mortify our inclinations toward sexual immorality, covetousness, anger, unwholesome talk, lying, divisiveness, and other sins (Col. 3:5-11). By patient perseverance in doing good and denying the flesh, those who lay hold of the grace offered to them will inherit eternal life (Rom. 2:7). Only those who prove by their actions what has taken place in their heart will have a place in the kingdom to come (Rom. 2:8-11; Gal. 5:19-21; Rev. 21:8).

Paul gave clear teaching on which qualities must be emphasized for those who would be Jesus' followers—His bondservants (taken from Col. 3:1-17; see also Rom. 12-13). The reason we teach and admonish is to accomplish the apostolic mission to make disciples, not numbers. Soren Kierkegaard observed, "Everything that needs numbers in order to become significant is by that very fact insignificant."[8] Our goal is not numbers of 'decisions for Christ' void of true repentance. The goal is to bring every follower of Christ to maturity, competent and equipped for every good work (Col. 1:28-29; 2 Tim. 3:16-17).

- Set your mind and heart on things above, not earthly things.
- Put to death sinful desires: sexual immorality, lust, greed, anger, rage, malice, slander, unwholesome talk, lying.
- Renew your mind by increasing knowledge of God through study of the Word.
- Clothe yourself with compassion, kindness, humility, gentleness, and patience.
- Bear with others and forgive as the Lord forgave you—*completely*.
- Put on *agape* love that binds all these other qualities together in completeness.
- Let the peace of God rule in your heart.
- Do everything, whether word or deed, in the authority and way of Christ to bring honor to His name.
- Be thankful.
- Let the *logos* word of Christ dwell in you abundantly as you teach and admonish with all wisdom ("comprehensive insight into the ways and purposes of God," Col. 1:28, AMP).

We will never be transformed by adopting the behavior and customs of the world no matter how they appeal to our carnal sense of what defines success. Only God can truly transform us by changing the way we think. Then we will learn what pleases God as well as determine His will for our lives (Rom. 12:2).

Stewardship of Freedom: All Things from Love and Faith

> *Love does no harm to a neighbor; therefore love is the fulfillment of the law.*
> -Rom. 13:10, NKJV

SECTION 3 HARMONIZED VIEW OF LAW AND FREEDOM

How we treat others is the distinction of the new covenant as taught by Jesus. The world will know we are His disciples if we walk in love for one another (John 13:34-35). In the absence of a written charter, we have the law of God written on our hearts by which our conscience convicts us as guilty if we wrongfully use or abuse our fellowman (Gal. 5:13-15).

The Lord put us together without specific written laws precisely so we could demonstrate we are walking in love. It is easier to live in harmony with those whose religious practice conforms to ours, especially if it includes agreement on the more debatable points in Scripture. While we must be in agreement on the major points (e.g., salvation through Christ alone), it is specifically on this point of differences that we are tested as to the quality of our professed love. The quality of our love can be seen to the degree we walk in patience and kindness toward others, especially if we don't agree on the finer points of new covenant practice and teaching. If we rejoice in truth, bear and endure all things, hope and believe in all of God's Word, we are grasping the concept of abiding love.

We are to love one another as brothers and sisters (Heb. 13:1). There is no evidence in the Word that the Lord is pleased with an angry, debating, mocking, vainglorious, unteachable, critical, ridiculing spirit who thinks they have everything figured out. God defines those who operate in this spirit as evil (James 3:13-18).

> *The wise fear the LORD and shun evil, but a fool is hotheaded and yet feels secure.* -Pr. 14:16, NIV

We are all still learning. Many of us have found that others will observe something in Scripture we never considered or didn't even notice was there. Once again, our ignorance instructs us that we have not plumbed the depths of God's Word in every way, nor will we ever. We must stay teachable and compare everything with the standard of Scripture and the witness of the Spirit.

The Word and the Glory of God

Our excitement at grasping truth, however, does please the Lord, even if the way we walk out our interpretation is somewhat different from someone else's grasp of the same truth. If we commit to searching out the Word and place ourselves under the guardian of grace, we will one day walk in unity in both truth and love. John described the glory of God (seen in Jesus, the Word) as the means for being united in love, just as the Son and the Father are united.

> *I have given them the glory that you gave me, that they may be one as we are one—I in them and you in me—**so that they may be brought to complete unity**. Then the world will know that you sent me and have loved them even as you have loved me.* -John 17:22-23, NIV

The glory given to us depends on the Word taking root in our hearts, bringing our thoughts, words, and actions in harmony with the nature and purpose of God. This should be obvious because throughout His ministry, Jesus imparted to His disciples understanding of the kingdom and His Word, speaking only what the Father had given Him to say. This sums up Jesus' statement, 'I have given them Your glory.'

As for matters of faith and conscience, we must take care to avoid offending another who continues to observe certain practices not required for everyone, such as dietary restrictions, Sabbath keeping, or tithing. This obviously does not refer to giving latitude concerning morally upright behavior, etched on our conscience by virtue of being created in God's image, but rather those practices associated with religion: incense burning, sacrifices, the temple tax, and so on. By Paul's example, we do not condone the *requirement* of such practice for salvation, but neither do we criticize those who practice these things for the sake of conscience.

> *But you must be careful so that your freedom does not cause others with a weaker conscience to stumble.* -1 Cor. 8:9, NLT

Their conscience is weaker only in the sense that their faith requires them to do these things, in contrast with those who feel no obligation to operate in similar fashion to experience the acceptance God has promised in Christ. There are as many ways to make the perfect salad as there are people who eat salad. God made each one of us different, with different tastes, favorite colors, types of music—you name it. It is the person who wants to force his favorites or preferences on others that is walking in selfishness and a domineering spirit. This is not love. Paul disparaged any such behavior, promoting deference as the way of love. Though Paul spoke specifically about those who follow Jewish dietary restrictions and holy days (Rom. 14:1-12), application can be made to other religious practices as well (see Rom. 14:13-23):

- Don't criticize one another on issues of religious practice (though we do warn people practicing idolatry; this can occur even with legitimate religious practices if the practice itself has seized our affections or gives us our worth before God rather than the righteousness of Christ).
- Pursue what promotes peace and edification.
- Decide not to cause someone else to stumble by exercising our freedom in a way that provokes offense.
- Prioritize righteousness, peace, and joy in the Spirit over religious practice issues.
- Don't tear down God's work based on issues of ceremonial religious customs.
- Keep your convictions about religious practice between yourself and God.
- Do everything from a stance of faith and in accordance with God's Word.
- We are accountable before God for our own religious practice, not that of others.

Following Paul's advice in this regard promotes walking in love, which serves the body of Christ and Jesus Himself in a manner acceptable to God and pleasing in His sight. Paul's instruction did not include indulging those who made old covenant practice mandatory for all believers, however (see Acts 15; Gal. 2:11-14). His primary concern was that we refrain from using our freedom to hurt those who keep standards for themselves we do not share, for example, those who approve a glass of wine vs. those who prohibit the use of any alcoholic beverage. Paul excelled not only in teaching the practical aspects of walking in love in the new found freedom of the new covenant—he was one of the finest examples of its practice. After explaining that he adapted his behavior depending on the group he was trying to reach (not ignoring the law, but within the parameters of the weightier matters of the law; 1 Cor. 9:19-22), Paul summarizes:

> *I try to find common ground with everyone, doing everything I can to save some. I do everything to spread the Good News.* -1 Cor. 9:22b-23, NLT

Paul demonstrated this type of love when he defended the rights of the Gentiles to remain free from the requirements of the law. He also circumcised Timothy, who being Jewish would necessarily need to be circumcised in order to be included in the promises made to Israel in the Abrahamic covenant. Circumcision also allowed Timothy entrance into the temple. Paul himself fulfilled a vow, following the Mosaic law for the benefit of the Jewish converts who feared Paul was promoting termination of the law for Jews.

Paul upheld the law but recognized its place in the new covenant as being peculiarly Jewish and subject to the weightier matters, especially love, mercy, and faithfulness. His practice demonstrated that religious customs, though not required, can be practiced without harm to the conscience or the relationship we have with Jesus if practiced from a place of faith or desire, or out of deference to another, rather than a religious spirit trying to earn its own salvation through works of the law (or out of fear of condemnation if not practiced).

Cease Quarreling over Disputable Matters

> *Accept the one whose faith is weak, without quarreling over disputable matters.*
> -Rom. 14:1, NIV

Nearly everyone who has ventured out of a denominational church or a synagogue will struggle with neglecting the religious practices to which he is accustomed. The rites of lent, advent, the festivals, Sabbath keeping, burning candles, and other like practices each have their lure in making us feel pious. But the new covenant is not founded on what makes us *feel* righteous before God. It is founded on truth. The atoning work of the cross, which fulfilled the obligations of the old covenant, makes us *truly* and *legally* righteous before God. Now we are free to enjoy God and be enjoyed by God as we allow His Holy Spirit to conform us to the image of His Son, who walked in perfect obedience as a bondservant. Our focus must be on character transformation and relationship, not external religious rites. Paul admonished us not to seek our own good and what is to our advantage or profit, but the welfare of others (1 Cor. 10:23-24,31-33).

The focus is not on observing days and feasts, circumcision and tithing, sacrifices and altars. These things are all types and shadows to teach us spiritual principles. The inward moral code of how we treat others and honor God remains unchanged, but these outward exercises were given to teach spiritual matters that have parallel meaning under the new covenant, all pointing to Christ. Our behavior must now be ruled by the law of God in our hearts, deferring to those who still cling to the rules they view as acts of faith and proper before God—those whose hearts are in the right place because they want to be pleasing in God's sight and are operating from a posture of faith.

Keeping the Sabbath holy is a disputed topic. It may have more to do with keeping Jesus' millennial reign set apart in our hearts than with the debate between Saturday and Sunday Sabbath keepers. The primary principle is to set aside time for God to provoke longing for His presence. Paul specifically stated we are not to let others judge us on matters of Sabbath days or festival observances. We should let it go at that, convinced in our own mind as to how we will practice rather than try to convince others our view is right.

When it comes to moral issues, the supremacy of Christ, and salvation by faith through Jesus' free gift, we do everything we can to persuade others. But on issues of religious practice, each is to be convinced in his own mind through holding up his practice to the light of Scripture, not viewing those who differ as lawbreakers, but being respectful of those whose conscience requires something different in order to honor God from a place of faith.

So then, each of us will give an account of himself to God. -Rom. 14:12, HCSB

Leadership to Set an Example

Paul viewed leadership as accountable for the honor of the gospel message and God's name by the response of the people to the way in which the leader practiced his freedom. He admonished leaders to do what would lead to the edification of the believers under their care and avoid doing those things which may bring the honor of the message or God's name into question. As an example of this, Paul used himself as an illustration of not exercising his freedom to receive pay from those he taught in order that the focus would remain on the message (1 Cor. 9:17-18; 2 Thes. 3:7-9). The emphasis is on love and walking in faith.

Philemon furnishes another example of giving up rights. The entire book of Philemon is an exhortation to a slave owner to take back his runaway slave in brotherly love. Paul appeals to the slave owner to consider not only his rights when making decisions about Onesimus' fate, but to temper his actions with love and grace because Onesimus is a fellow believer. The law of Christ and the treatment the owner received from Paul would remind him not to succumb to hypocrisy by the way in which he treats Onesimus on his return, even if he has the legal right to take corrective disciplinary action.

The apostles and elders involved in the Jerusalem council decision brought peace to both sides of the issue while not making the law a requirement for salvation (Acts 15:1).

SECTION 3 *HARMONIZED VIEW OF LAW AND FREEDOM*

The decision promoted love and fellowship in keeping with the standards of the new covenant. Evidence that Jesus honored their *halakhic* decision is seen in Revelation, where the issues of sexual immorality and eating meat sacrificed to idols surfaced in the rebukes to Pergamum and Thyatira (Rev. 2:14,20). Notice that the seven churches were rebuked not only for these issues, but for lacking love despite all their activity in ministry, for tolerating false teachers, for apathy, and for self-deception as well. There is no mention of or rebuke for their lack of circumcision, tithing, or Sabbath observance because it doesn't apply.

> *For when we place our faith in Christ Jesus, there is no benefit in being circumcised or being uncircumcised.* **What is important is faith expressing itself in love.** -Gal. 5:6, NLT

Paul wrote we are not to quarrel about opinions or pass judgment on others regarding dietary habits or special days. In other words, do not try to convince others of your conclusions in matters of law or religious practice. This will not bear righteous fruit for God, but only sow bitterness, confusion, and division on matters of conscience that are left to the individual believer by the instruction of God's Word. (Paul reminds us that he was sent to the Gentiles, and as such, was not instructing fellow Jews on matters of the law.)

The following commentaries on Romans 14:1 concur with this view. Albert Barnes wrote, "Young converts have often a special delicacy or sensitiveness about the lawfulness of many things in relation to which older Christians may be more fully established. To produce peace, there must be kindness, tenderness, and faithful teaching; not denunciation, or harshness, on one side or the other."[9]

Adam Clarke thought similarly: "Do not reject any from your Christian communion because of their particular sentiments on things which are in themselves indifferent. Do not curiously inquire into their religious scruples, nor condemn them on that account. Entertain a brother of this kind rather with what may profit his soul, than with curious disquisitions on speculative points of doctrine. A good lesson for modern Christians in general."[10] C.I. Scofield sums up by saying, "The church has no authority to decide questions of personal liberty in things not expressly forbidden in Scripture."[11]

Habakkuk wrote, 'the righteous shall live by his faith' (Hab. 2:4), a theme carried over into the New Testament (Rom. 1:17; Gal. 3:11; Heb. 10:38). Paul expounded on this by reminding us that whatever is not of faith is sin, and on this point we will each give account to God. We are not to pass judgment on or demean the religious convictions of others in disputable matters, but each one needs to be fully convinced in his own mind in order to operate from a stance of faith (Rom. 14:5-23).

Nowhere are we commanded to persuade others about these matters. Quite the opposite, we are warned not to get entangled in disputes about the law, not to pass judgment or despise others' religious practice, to bear with those who have convictions in areas we are convinced do not matter, and to be wary of those who cause divisions and create obstacles because of these issues (Rom. 16:17; Titus 3:10). On this last point, we must make the distinction between those who stand up for the gospel message or take a stance against sin and doctrinal error, and those who wrangle about special days, religious customs, dietary discriminations, and so forth. We are to pursue peace and what leads to mutual edification (Rom. 14:19). Paul prayed we would live in such harmony in accordance with the Word that we would glorify God with one voice (Rom. 15:5-6). The Lord's Supper, baptism, alms-giving, prayer, and meeting together to pray, encourage, fellowship, and instruct are the only fundamental practices of new covenant believers. These form the foundation of our unity in Christ.

Closing Thoughts

We are not married to the law or religious ceremonial practices but to Christ. Submission to Christ now takes the place of submission to what is inferior. This is the only way we have true freedom. We follow Christ wherever He goes, which will not lead to lawlessness but rather to walking uprightly according to the weightier matters of the law: love, mercy, justice, and faithfulness. Walking by these principles is the only way we will look out for the interests of others *first,* rather than giving our religious practice preeminence. By this we bear fruit that lasts for the kingdom of God and display His love and righteousness to the world.

How can we tell if we are walking out our freedom in faith? Hunger for truth and demonstrating kindness toward others are the indicators proving the hidden faith of the believer is alive. Not all seeds planted will germinate, just as not all faith germinates. How do we know faith has germinated in the one who received the Word? They will show hunger for God and a desire to help others. God has ordained works for each of us to accomplish, and lack of obedience in this area is sin, which is lawlessness (James 4:17). The perfect and royal law of liberty in Christ includes being His agent: His hand extended to those whom He constantly watches over—the poor, the widow, the orphan, and the sojourner.

> *You have died with Christ, and he has set you free from the spiritual powers of this world.* -Col. 2:20a, NLT

Chapter 11

The Goal: One New Man

> *Other sheep I have which are not of this fold; them also I must bring, and they will hear My voice; and there will be one flock and one shepherd.* -John 10:16, NKJV

There is one flock only because Christ made it possible for all, Jew and Gentile alike, to have access to the holiest place by rending the veil that kept everyone out. The veil represented His flesh, and once it was torn by His sacrifice, the way was opened for all. This is the only way to be reconciled with and made righteous before God.

Paul defines the antagonism between Jew and Gentile as the law, which prevented the Gentiles from having access to the covenant relationship Israel enjoyed with God. While there were always God-fearers among the Gentiles through history, for example, Cornelius, no Gentiles were allowed to partake of covenant worship of God unless they became Jewish converts through circumcision and other rituals.

Through the new covenant, Jesus made it possible for both Jew and Gentile to be in covenant relationship with God through grace by the finished work of the cross. Now both receive the Holy Spirit and have access to the Father. Just as there is only one Spirit by which we cry, 'Abba, Father,' those who come to the Father in the new covenant are one new man (Eph. 2:14-22; Rom. 8:15; Gal. 4:6).

Without common access, the holy of holies as the type of God's presence had been shrouded in mystery, much like a wrapped gift until the paper is removed. The law and the prophets gave many hints about the package (the promised gift), adding suspense, excitement, and hope until the appointed day when the package would be opened. But the hints about the gift became more important to many in Israel than the gift itself. Nevertheless, many did witness the unveiling of the gift (access to the holiest place by the sacrifice of Jesus) and experienced the promised reconciliation with God.

The blessing *and* the vexation of the new covenant is that Jew and Gentile alike are invited to share in this gift, making them one in Christ. It is a blessing because no one in Christ remains under the curse. The vexation results from the frustration that followed when some interpreted this oneness to mean a unity based on uniformity rather than to indicate a body with its diverse parts as an integrated whole. The harmony of this oneness is centered on working as one unit to complete the mandate by each doing the part he has been specifically given. Much time has been lost as we try to control the part given to someone else while faltering on our own, or worse, abandoning our post to usurp the post of another. Let's forget about all that. Consider the military as an example of unity.

Even though no two soldiers are alike, they submit themselves to their commanding officer, laying aside their differences because of the nature of their mission to move as one unit. Their lives and the outcome of their mission depend on this unity.

God gave the Jews a particular mandate, and we are not to use our freedom to despise their portion. Or vice versa, the Jews are not to see their portion as more authentic or worthy. If, in the mind of the Gentile, the law is no longer to be followed by *anyone*, why would the leaders of the early church require any council at all to determine if the Gentiles needed to follow the law (Acts 15)? Doesn't the fact that they had a meeting indicate they understood the law continued for the Jewish believers, though no longer of the mindset that it could earn favor or establish their righteousness before God?

It is readily apparent and well-documented that the Jewish believers in *Yeshua* continued to observe the Mosaic law, including the apostles. The question arose only as to whether or not the Gentiles should likewise follow the law, for redemption or otherwise. This was likely due to the Jewish custom of imposing the law on Gentiles who joined the Jewish faith as proselytes under the old covenant. The answer was flatly 'no,' except for the few stipulations determined, on the witness that God had already given Gentiles His acceptance by imparting His Spirit (see discussion on Acts 15 in Chapter 8).

The Body of Christ

> *Consequently, when Christ came into the world, he said, "Sacrifices and offerings you have not desired, **but a body have you prepared for me**... Then I said, 'Behold, I have come to do your will, O God...'"* -Heb. 10:5,7a, ESV

Quoting Psalm 40, the author of Hebrews states that 'a body' was prepared for Jesus to accomplish God's will. In Psalm 40, however, the phrase is actually 'you have given me an *ear*' (v. 6). The seeming discrepancy can be explained when we remember we are given ears to hear in order to obey—something to be carried out by the body. In fact, the psalmist states that the Messiah delights to do the will of God because of the 'ear' He has been given to perform God's will.

This passage can also be metaphorically understood as referring to the spiritual body of Christ—Jesus was given a *body* (of believers) to do God's will. As His body, it is our duty to sh'ma not only to obey in the performance of good deeds, but also to follow His instructions, turn from iniquity, and have faith and trust in Him. For the bondservant completely captured by the love of God, it is a delight to do His will. Obedience is the best form of worship we can offer the Lord and the mark of the soul's 'perfection.'

> *Has the LORD as great delight in burnt offerings and sacrifices, as in obeying the voice of the LORD? Behold, **to obey is better** than sacrifice, **and to listen** than the fat of rams.* -1 Sam. 15:22, ESV

SECTION 3 *HARMONIZED VIEW OF LAW AND FREEDOM*

Following God's instruction assumes recognition of His voice and knowledge of His ways, which in turn lead to discernment. Marvin Vincent stated, "Love displays itself in knowledge and discernment. In proportion as it abounds it sharpens the moral perceptions for the discernment of what is best."[1] Again, we return to the hallmark of the new covenant, which is love. There can be no unity in the body of Christ without love based on the true knowledge of God and the ability to discern truth from error and right from wrong (Php. 1:9-11; Heb. 5:14).

> *He **opens their ears to instruction** and commands that they return from iniquity.*
> -Job 36:10, ESV

Diversity in the Body

Using the physical body as an example, Paul emphasized the diversity of function of the individual parts. Each part has a specific function different from the rest, yet the body functions as a unit as long as it remains attached to the Head (Rom. 12:4; Eph. 1:22-23). Paul instructed the new believers to respect differences and not despise the place they were given. God places each one in the body as He chooses, not as our ambition covets.

Despite all the vainglory in setting up the church to recognize status according to worldly standards, God maintains that the one who loves has attained the greatest honor (Mark 12:31; 1 Cor. 12:31-13:13). God honors all those who keep the position He has given them and who fulfill their duties in love. Ambitious striving to vie for a better position to be recognized by others destroys unity. We have been given one Spirit, have one Lord, and are one body, despite the diversity of gifts (1 Cor. 12:4,12-14,20).

> *God has so composed the body, **giving more abundant honor to that member which lacked, so that there may be no division** in the body, but that the members may have the **same** care for one another.* -1 Cor. 12:24b-25, NASB

Staying Connected to the Head

In severe head trauma, the brain tissue swells and the blood supply to the brain can be blocked. When this happens, the body itself can be kept alive for a limited length of time through mechanical and chemical life support, but death is certain short of a miracle. The same is true of Christ's body. If we are not connected to the Head, we will die or at the very least need life support to stay alive. Many books have been written with strategies to prop up the lifeless or frustrated—novel approaches to stimulate 'church growth' that are the equivalent of life support for those disconnected from the Head. It takes great patience to wait for the Lord to bring forth fruit in its season. Many church leaders are either unwilling to wait or pressured to produce results, shipwrecking their churches in pursuit of quick 'fruit' that will not last or withstand the fire of testing.

> *He is also head of the body, the church... He Himself will come to have first place in everything.* -Col. 1:18, NASB

The Head is Jesus, the Word. Being in a group of professing believers who are not teaching and leaning on the Word is hazardous. Preeminence of Christ as the Head will necessitate heavy reliance on the whole counsel of God as well as the timing and leading of the Spirit. Without this, our congregations will need the life support readily available from experts in marketing and business. In fact, some churches select their elders or deacons not based on apostolic criteria, but on the business skills they feel are required to fulfill the particular vision they have developed for their church—skills possessed by real estate agents, mortgage brokers, insurance agents, corporate attorneys, and financial investment experts. This makes for a well-rounded boardroom in the eyes of men.

Community of Love

The *ekklesia* ('the New Testament community of the redeemed'[2]) of God was meant to stand firm in unity by loving and staying connected to the Head. This includes walking with each other in love. Staying connected involves holding fast to our righteousness in Christ as well as growing in our understanding through study of the Word. We are able to refute lies by the collective wisdom given to the body by Christ, growing and building the church up by truth spoken in love so we encourage unity. It was understood unity would not come automatically. But as the Holy Spirit leads the body into greater knowledge, understanding, and wisdom in God, believers will have unity in faith and in knowledge, though not necessarily uniformity of expression. This is the mark of maturity.

Paul frequently communicated the idea of oneness and admonished the new believers to make every effort to keep unity in the Spirit through the bond of peace. When addressing the Ephesians, Paul repeatedly spoke of the idea of oneness: one body, one Spirit, one hope, one Lord, one faith, one baptism, one God and Father of all (Eph. 4:3-6). The diversity is seen in the particular grace given to individual believers so each can accomplish what the Lord has ordained specifically for each to do. Diversity in the body provides for training, building, and equipping for works of service in love. No 'one man shows' allowed. Since no one person or congregation is holding all the cards, we are dependent on each other to grow into unity in the faith and unity in the knowledge of God. The goal is for each to become 'complete and mature' (Eph. 4:11-13).

The bond of peace can only come with the activity of the Holy Spirit. Albert Barnes explained in his commentary, "the meaning here is that they should be bound or united together in the sentiments and affections of peace. It is not mere "external" unity; it is not a mere unity of creed; it is not a mere unity in the forms of public worship; it is such as the Holy Spirit produces in the hearts of Christians, when it fills them all with the same love, and joy, and peace in believing."[3]

Peace among believers is spoken of frequently, emphasizing the need to *pursue* peace and those things which build up the members of the body (Mark 9:50; Rom. 12:18; Rom. 14:19; Col. 3:15; 1 Thes. 5:13). We need to pursue these things because they won't happen automatically.

> *Finally, brethren, rejoice, be made complete, be comforted, be like-minded, live in peace; and the God of love and peace will be with you.* -2 Cor. 13:11, NASB

This can only be achieved when we become a people who honor and respect one another. Love is the only way in which this can be accomplished with any sincerity. Envy, quarrels, and divisions are present in the church precisely because of love that has grown cold, which happens when people become lovers of self more than lovers of God (2 Tim. 3:2-5). It is impossible for the self-centered person to esteem others more highly than himself, to defer to others in decisions, or to restrain himself from expressing his opinions (Rom. 12:3; Php. 2:3; Pr. 18:2).

Nowhere is this seen more tragically than in the practice of killing others to preserve reputation, finances, career, comfort, external beauty, or lifestyle—desires all centered on self. God's Word defines life as beginning at conception: '*Before* I formed you in the womb, I knew you' (Jer. 1:5). Our own Declaration of Independence establishes the right of every person to *life*: "We hold these truths to be self-evident, that all men are created equal, that they are endowed by their Creator with certain unalienable Rights, that among these are Life, Liberty and the pursuit of Happiness." Our forefathers called these rights 'self-evident.'

Perhaps these truths are only self-evident to those who walk in the eternal wisdom and counsel of God rather than the wisdom *du jour*. But now we elevate a woman's right to pursue happiness over another's right to life. The right to pursue happiness cannot and does not take precedence over personal responsibility for the consequences of our actions. A thief gives up his right to pursue happiness because his actions dictate that he must make restitution. As the Pharisees before us, we have set aside God's command and our own laws to have the desires of our selfish, deceived, hardened hearts.

If we were to judge the church by its current condition, the situation would seem utterly hopeless. But take heart; with God *all things are possible*.

Be Like-Minded

> *Be of the same mind toward one another. Do not set your mind on high things, but associate with the humble.* **Do not be wise in your own opinion.** -Rom. 12:16, NKJV

Like-mindedness does not come without effort because we are all infused with opinions as we progress down the road to a mature knowledge of the truth. An opinion based on feelings, Scripture taken out of context, or religious ideas born of tradition without basis in the Word are to be handled by clear refutations from Scripture. When Satan tried to use the Word to tempt Jesus to sin, Jesus exposed his faulty premise by wielding the Word accurately, destroying any consideration of Satan's error.

> *We destroy arguments and every lofty opinion raised against the knowledge of God.* -2 Cor. 10:5a, ESV

Unity accompanied by peace, maturity, and knowledge are not achieved without effort and cooperation with the Holy Spirit. James declared the tongue that cannot be tamed causes all manner of problems (James 3). Perhaps as a preliminary measure, members of the body of Christ should heed the advice in Proverbs:

> *Even fools are thought wise if they keep silent, and discerning if they hold their tongues.* -Pr. 17:28, NIV

The road to unity is paved with practical expressions of love, not rabid arguments about opinions or disputable matters. Not thinking more highly of ourselves than we ought is also good advice (Rom. 12:3). It keeps us open to the wisdom of others, and as we grow in love, true dialogue that brings understanding and growth can take place. We must remain teachable as an expression of honoring others and showing patient love. Does this mean we accept everything in the name of love? Of course not. Everything must be held to the light of Scripture. But we cannot become so conceited in our doctrine or convinced of our position that we are unwilling to listen to others, including the Holy Spirit and the Word.

In Acts 18, we meet Apollos, a man who thoroughly understood the Word and was gifted in speaking (see vv. 24-28). He had been 'instructed in the way of the Lord,' was passionate about God, and taught boldly and accurately on those things he understood. When Priscilla and Aquila heard him, they realized that although he knew the baptism of John (repentnce), he hadn't yet heard the gospel message. They did not correct him in front of everyone, but took him aside privately to expound the Scriptures more accurately in light of the gospel. They taught the truth in love, and Apollos accepted because of his teachable spirit and love for truth. The characteristics of someone with a teachable spirit are based on humility and seen in the one who does not think more highly of himself or his opinions than he ought. The fruit of this meeting was that Apollos became a great help to new believers since he was enabled to vigorously refute from the Scriptures the Jews who opposed the message of Jesus as the promised Messiah. Being bold or vigorous in our testimony can help others be convinced of teaching and increase in their understanding. This story, however, shows that we can speak boldly and with conviction while at the same time come short in our theology.

Another example is seen in the life of David. After defeating the Philistines, he and all Israel were rejoicing before the Lord in a great celebration when they brought the ark of the covenant back from the house of Abinadab (2 Sam. 6:1-11). But the Lord was not pleased when they did not follow the way He had prescribed for carrying the ark. As a result, Uzzah died when he tried to steady the tottering ark on the cart. This demonstrates that our delight, enthusiasm, and unified participation in religious practices are not the criteria that determine whether those practices are pleasing in God's sight. After this tragedy, David searched the Scriptures for God's regulations for carrying the ark, and it was later brought back properly with much rejoicing (1 Chron. 15:1-16:7). It was because of David's fear of the Lord that he accepted correction from God's Word.

Before his Damascus road experience, Paul was *absolutely convinced* he should do everything possible to stop the spread of the gospel message (Acts 26:9) until Jesus knocked him off his horse and showed him the truth (Acts 9:1-19). What do we learn from Apollos, David, and Paul? We learn that speaking boldly, rejoicing before the Lord corporately with joy and unified spiritual zeal, or being entirely convinced of the error of others is not proof we are in the right. The acid test may come when someone shows us a more accurate interpretation of what we so confidently proclaim. If we bristle and dig our heels in, not really listening to what is being said, pride has overtaken us. If we weigh what is said, probing to find the truth through questions and sharing knowledge of the Word, we are operating in unity for the love of truth. Our minds may not be convinced by the other's position, but we will have operated in a spirit of love and humility, pleasing to God.

Paul exhorted us to walk in all humility and gentleness with patience and forbearance. Our demeanor should display eagerness for unity as we are equipped for works of service to build up Christ's body. In this way, we have hope to reach unity in faith and knowledge. *Then* we will no longer be infants who don't know the Word, but rather we will be enabled to speak the truth in love so the body is equipped to maturity. With Jesus as the Head, we will be built up in love as each person does what God has chosen for him to do (Eph. 4:2-16). The requirements for accomplishing this are: 1.) putting off the old self corrupted by its deceitful desires, and 2.) putting on the new self created to be like God in righteousness and holiness. This occurs as we renew our minds through hearing and studying the Word (Eph. 4:22-24).

Paul urged the Ephesians to live their lives in such a way as to be worthy of their calling (Eph. 4:25-32). This entailed:

- putting off falsehood and speaking truthfully instead;
- giving no foothold to the devil by clinging to anger;
- working—doing something useful 'with our hands' so believers are not dependent on others and will always have something to share with those in need;
- refraining from speaking in an unwholesome way;
- speaking only what edifies/benefits others according to their needs;
- heeding rather than grieving the Holy Spirit;
- renouncing all bitterness, anger, fighting, slander, and malice; and
- walking in kindness and compassion, forgiving each other.

Love and Truth

Love and truth spoken in humility are the keys for unity and peace in the body, and for this reason Jesus spent His final prayer meeting with the disciples emphasizing both. Knowledge of the truth comes from the Holy Spirit's activity as we read the Word, and love fills us more and more as we abide in truth. If we are devoid of love, then none of the following count for anything ('I am nothing… I gain nothing,' 1 Cor. 13):

- **speaking in tongues**: they will be stilled
- **having the gift of prophecy**: prophecies will cease
- **understanding all mysteries**: they will be known/fulfilled
- **having all (experiential, present, and fragmentary) knowledge**: it will pass away (replaced by clear and exact knowledge)
- **having faith that can move mountains**: dead without love
- **giving to the poor**: actions without love are perfunctory, and therefore the fire that tests each man's work will burn them away
- **giving the body over to hardship that we may boast**: burned away because it is rooted in pride

Agape Love

How do we know if we are moving in love? Paul described the characteristics of *agape* love in 1 Corinthians 13, an unselfish love based on commitment to the needs of others and not on ever-shifting feelings. This can only be acquired by the Spirit's work in our lives to make us mature and whole. *Agape* love can only come through relationship with God because it originates in God. 'Anyone who does not love does not know God, because God is love… and whoever abides in love abides in God, and God abides in him' (1 John 4:8,16, ESV). Each use of 'love' in these verses is *agape* love, rooted in commitment, not *phileo* love, rooted in affectionate feelings that can change like shifting sand.

Love centered on how we feel is rooted in self. It is not wrong to have affection for others. But as the basis for relationship, *phileo* love will not withstand testing because it can change with our ever-shifting emotions. Decisions become based on how we feel about the other person, or what another person can do for us to make us feel good about ourselves. While there is nothing wrong with feeling affection for another person, our decisions cannot be based on what *feels* right, but what *is* right. Defining love by our feelings explains many of the divorces in the church. The attributes of *agape* love, in contrast, are centered on the needs of others (taken from 1 Cor. 13 and Eph. 4):

- patient, kind
- not envious
- not boastful
- not proud—completely humble and gentle
- not easily angered or resentful
- does not dishonor others (not rude)
- does not seek its own advantage or insist on having its own way
- does not delight in evil (e.g., for gain, advantage, revenge, etc.)
- keeps no record of wrongs
- rejoices in the truth
- always protects (covers over the wrongs of others, not retaliating or retelling)

- always trusts
- always hopes
- always perseveres

Love never fails... Now I know in part; then I shall know fully, even as I am fully known. And now these three remain: faith, hope and love. But the greatest of these is love. -1 Cor. 13:8a,12b-13, NIV

Loving our neighbor means working for his good, the opposite of the selfish nature which seeks its own good. We are to work for the good of all in whatever timely, ordained opportunities come our way. Though we are not limited to demonstrating kindness to the needy in the church, care for other believers takes precedent (Gal. 6:10).

As each one has received a special gift, employ it in serving one another as good stewards of the manifold grace of God. -1 Pet. 4:10, NASB

Speech

So also the tongue is a small part of the body, and yet it boasts of great things. See how great a forest is set aflame by such a small fire! -James 3:5, NASB

Speech must be for edification, not promoting self. This is the final frontier for most believers. Once the tongue is tamed, perfection has been achieved. Exerting more effort in this area will foster unity more quickly than any potluck or Bible class. Our speech is to be full of grace and seasoned with salt (the Word) so we can respond to others for their edification (Col. 4:6). Unwholesome talk has no place in the believer's life. We are to edify and impart grace through our words according to the need of the moment (Eph. 4:29). Speaking the truth in love fosters growth toward maturity in Christ (Eph. 4:15).

Discerning the Lord's Body

I am the bread of life... the living bread that came down from heaven. If anyone eats of this bread, he will live forever. And the bread that I will give for the life of the world is my flesh... The words that I have spoken to you are spirit and life.
-John 6:35a,51,63b, ESV

Jesus described Himself as the 'bread of life.' He further explained that the bread He gives for the world is His body. When we partake of the Lord's Supper, we partake of the bread as a symbol of Jesus' body, the bread of heaven—a body that is not divided (1 Cor. 1:13). Partaking of this bread (Jesus) leads to eternal life. To partake of the body of Christ requires participation in the new covenant, the covenant of abiding in Christ.

In his first letter to the Corinthians, Paul addressed the divisions among them by using the example of the way in which they practiced the Lord's Supper (see 1 Cor. 11:17-34). It is because of these divisions that Paul rebuked them. Division meant they could not possibly be celebrating the *Lord's* Supper. Earlier in the letter, Paul laid the foundation that the bread of the Lord's Supper is one loaf, signifying the unity of the Lord's body.

> *For we, though many, are **one bread and one body**; for we all partake of that one bread.* -1 Cor. 10:17, NKJV

The fellowship meals of the Corinthians were characterized by self-centeredness, each looking to his own appetite rather than to the needs of others who may not have had the means to bring anything to the meal. This rendered their meal common, causing humiliation for the poor among them, making it no more a fellowship meal than a meal eaten at home. Eating in this manner is sin against the body of Christ (v. 27) because it divides the body into haves and have-nots, showing no concern for the poor who are part of the body. Paul summed it up this way:

> *[W]hen you gather to eat, you should all eat together. Anyone who is hungry* (**peinao:** 'famished') *should eat something at home, so that when you meet together it may not result in judgment.* -1 Cor. 11:33-34a, NIV

The setting for his comment is stated in the beginning of this letter. After the initial greeting, Paul jumped right into the problem they were having with divisions (1 Cor. 1:10-13), explaining the reasons for those divisions throughout the letter. In this particular section, Paul also exposed the division that manifested in the way they celebrated the Lord's Supper. Jesus is the bread from heaven, and Paul reminded the Corinthians that Christ is not divided. As the body of Christ, we eat of one loaf to symbolize our unity in His flesh.

Eating the Lord's Supper together when there are factions and division brings judgment on those who harbor: unforgiveness, rancor for not getting their way in church decisions, resentment for not being selected for a coveted position, vain ambition to grab authority, envy for the gifts of another, or other divisive internal conflicts. The greedy way in which some of the Corinthians ate, causing others to be utterly neglected and rejected, was the outward display of what was taking place internally.

This concept of unity is so important that Jesus admonished us not to offer any gift unless we have been reconciled with a fellow believer by whom we have been offended and with whom we have not sought reconciliation (Matt. 5:22-24). This is not to say we will be reconciled right away or that reconciliation will even take place, especially if the other individual is immature in their walk, has been deeply offended, or is only a professing Christian rather than a true believer. Even Jesus was not reconciled with most of the Pharisees, nor was Paul with Alexander the coppersmith as far as we know (1 Tim. 1:20; 2 Tim. 4:14). We are not accountable for their response, but only for our sincere attempt to be reconciled to our offended brother.

> *If it is possible, **as far as it depends on you**, live at peace with everyone.* -Rom. 12:18, NIV

Unity is the theme of much of new covenant teaching. The content of Jesus' prayer (John 17) before the cross is focused on:

- knowing God (who is both love and truth)
- believing in Jesus
- seeking unity
- growing in love and truth

Jesus prayed that His followers would be sanctified by the truth and come to unity so the world would know Jesus was sent from God. He also prayed God's *agape* love and the Word would reside in them so unity would result. Only those who are walking in humility with the heart of a bondservant are able to receive the necessary sanctification of the Holy Spirit for this to be realized.

Unity by partaking of the bread of the fellowship meal is illustrated in the ceremonial law. Under Mosaic law, a purchased slave may eat of the showbread reserved for the priest and his family (Lev. 22:10-11). Jesus, the high priest of the new covenant, purchased men for Himself who would become His bondslaves. These are the ones who are commanded to eat His flesh, the bread of His presence, which is the Word of God. No hired servant could eat this bread.

The following description of the table of showbread by Rusty Russell ties in the new covenant application. "The table of shewbread was referred to as the table of the Presence. God's light forever shines on His people. The 12 baked cakes of bread spoke of God's people who were one with Him as the priests joined together for the fellowship of eating the bread and becoming one. Jesus referred to Himself as the bread of life and said if we eat this bread we will live forever. The very nature of bread is to provide physical sustenance and as you eat the bread and digest it, it becomes part of you. The very nature of the Word of God is to provide spiritual sustenance and as it is received it becomes part of our very nature. Just as the table always speaks of fellowship and communion, so the table of the shewbread points to Jesus who has made a covenant built on better promises and provided a blood covenant meal for us to partake that we might all be one in the Spirit."[4] The Lord's Supper, then, is symbolic of the unity we have when we partake of the bread (Jesus, the Word), which becomes part of us and promotes unity in understanding through the knowledge of God and a shared vision of His purposes.

The Jewish priests stood together in unity to eat the showbread, unlike the Corinthians. There can be no unity when each grasps for a greater slice, ignores those who have gone without, and refuses to cooperate in a spirit of unity because of a mistaken notion that he has a higher calling or is spiritually superior to those he tramples. Where there is selfishness, vain ambition, rivalry, and envy there will also be every evil practice. This is how Christ is divided and we treat His body with contempt: we use the body for our own personal gain, caring little for the unity it is to represent. We make His body common ('profane') in our own eyes by seeing it as a means for satisfaction of our desires through vying for position and taking more for ourselves than we ought. This occurs when personal agendas and a domineering spirit take control of our fellowships.

Jesus' body is defined as the people who have come to faith in Him as Redeemer—people who are to be one loaf. John calls Jesus 'the Word made flesh.' If we would also learn from the picture of the Word (Jesus) as the bread of life, the Corinthians are an example to us of how ignorance of the Word ('not discerning the body') is another way of looking at the cause of division. Abiding in Christ, the Word, is the foundation of walking in unity and love as the body of Christ.

Reconciliation of Christianity with Its Hebraic Roots

With one possible exception (Luke), all the books of the Bible have Hebrew authorship. Our Savior is from the tribe of Judah, as prophesied, and the events of the Bible are primarily centered on the nation of Israel. Believing Gentiles have been grafted into Israel—the cultivated olive tree (Rom. 11:17-24). Gentiles have not replaced Israel but will provoke Israel to jealousy so that Israel turns to their Messiah. We must guard ourselves against the tendency to impose upon Jews who recognize their Messiah in Jesus to reverse this process. Historically, the church has preferred that Jewish believers become grafted into the church, adopting all of the church's customs and ways. Paul teaches clearly that these broken off natural branches can be grafted back into their *own* tree (Rom. 11:24). Gentiles are the ones who are grafted in contrary to nature.

Rabbi Elijah Benamozegh addresses the reconciliation needed between Christianity and its Hebrew roots. "The reconciliation dreamt of by the first Christians as a condition of the Parousia, or final advent of Jesus—the return of the Jews to the heart of the church, without which the various Christian denominations agree that the work of redemption must remain incomplete—this return, we say, will occur, not as it has been expected, but in the only serious, logical, and durable way, and above all in the only way which would be advantageous to the human race. This will be the reconciliation of Hebraism and the religions which were born of it. According to the last of the Prophets, as the sages called Malachi: 'He shall reconcile parents with children and children with their parents' (Mal. 3:24)."[5]

With a discerning eye, we can accept Rabbi Benamozegh's thoughts as worthy of our consideration with the notable exception of his view that Islam is an offshoot of Hebraism (it is not), as well as recognizing Christianity is not an offshoot of Judaism, but rather the fulfillment of Hebraic prophecy. Reconciling the fathers (Judaism) with their children (Gentile Christianity) is a lofty goal because many in the church have divorced their hearts and minds from considering any connection with their Hebraic roots.

We are urged to remember the new covenant was prophesied by the Hebrew prophets and understood to be *for the nation of Israel*. Thousands of Jews believed and entered into the new covenant by faith in the early days, including some Pharisees and a large number of Levitical priests (Acts 6:7; 15:5). Many Gentile believers have tried to negate the role of Israel by pointing out their rejection of the Messiah, forgetting the *partial* hardening of Israel that takes place until the Gentiles are reconciled to God (see Rom. 11).

Ignoring Paul's advice, some Gentile believers have become arrogant toward Israel, supposing God chose them *instead* of Israel and forgetting that God's calling and purposes for Israel are irrevocable (Rom. 11:25-32). Paul reminded us that our faith is rooted in the promises *given to Israel* and warned Gentiles about becoming proud, thereby losing their place (Rom. 11:20-21,25). The whole point of doing things this way is so Jew and Gentile alike come to the realization that it is through God's love and mercy that all believers are reconciled to Him, not: 1.) a special position as a chosen people, 2.) earned favor through deeds, or 3.) recognition for piety (Rom. 11:11-32).

If we could learn to view the Jewish practices mandated in the Word as the demonstrations or object lessons from which we learn the truth about God's ways and kingdom, we have made great progress. Think of all their ceremonial rituals and laws as a type of sign language. They are communicating messages from God to help us comprehend His plan, ways, kingdom, and will for us to be separate from the world. For example:

- the Sabbath points to the Jewish Messiah's Sabbatical reign;
- they separate themselves from what God deems as unclean, not allowing themselves a 'diet' of unclean things, for example, pornography, worldly philosophies, or religion polluted by a licentious culture;
- they are a small race, indicating that (proportionately) few will find the path to life and enter the kingdom (Isa. 41:14; Amos 7:2-5; Matt. 7:14).

The practices of Messianic Judaism are tied to the expression of traditional Judaic faith through the lens of the new covenant, much as was practiced by the early apostles. Is this a 'better' expression of faith for new covenant believers than what the Gentile believers practice? Only in the hearts of those predisposed to religious legalism. It would be similar to asking whether adherence to the practice of Cornelius or Paul would gain us more favor in God's sight. No religious practice earns favor in God's sight. Only belief in Jesus as God's Son, faith that He has reconciled us to God through *His* righteousness, and obedience to His will gives us right standing before God. Each of us now does our part: the Jews in the physical expression and demonstration of spiritual truth through the laws given them, and Gentiles in the spiritual understanding that this expression and demonstration imparts.

As Paul Liberman wrote, the pivotal issue has always been faith. "Messianic Judaism is living proof there is no essential difference between Christianity and the true Judaism of the Bible... In an honest search of the Old Testament Scriptures, a Jew must eventually concede it was faith in God's Word which distinguished his ancestral patriarchs... When we look at history, it is almost as if the organized church and synagogues have been eager to persuade the world that believers of the new covenant are something apart from their Jewish foundations. As a matter of fact, one cannot fully understand the Christian faith apart from its foundations. This alone should destroy the mistaken concept that true Judaism and true Christianity are opposed to one another. Christian faith depends upon the Jewish Bible. Even the New Covenant was written by Jews... The first Christian community was all Jewish, and the first great teacher of the Gentiles, Paul, was Jewish."[6]

We share many of the rich traditions of the Jewish culture. Many Gentile believers seek to participate in the worship style, *Torah* readings, emphasis on prayer and *tzedakah* (a word that means 'righteousness'; used for taking collections for the poor and needy), and Sabbath activities that promote faith and community as practiced in the Messianic congregations. There are many traditions in the church which are descended from Jewish practice. John D. Parsons wrote, "I think the ultimate point of the idea of "tradition" is to remind us that we are all linked together by faith. Our faith in the LORD God of Israel connects us to all the great heroes of the faith—and most especially to *Yeshua* Himself. Salvation is something "corporate," by which I mean it is something *shared.* We are part of the redeemed community or family of God."[7]

Abraham Is the Father of All Believers

> *For I have chosen him* **so that he will command his children** *and his house after him to keep the way of the LORD by doing what is right and just.* **This is how the LORD will fulfill to Abraham what He promised** *him.* -Gen. 18:19, HCSB

[Note: This passage is eye-opening. God states He will fulfill the promise made to Abraham because Abraham will instruct his children to keep the way of the Lord by doing what is right. God searches for those who pass this torch from their generation to the next, taking care that their progeny continue in the way of God. This is how we move in faith; it demonstrates that we believe God will redeem in the fullness of time all who believe. It also shows that we value God's promise of redemption as the only inheritance of true and lasting value for our children. Letting children 'find their own spiritual way' is contrary to biblical wisdom and negligence before God.]

In the beauty of His plan, God foreknew our tendency toward works to earn our way, and for this reason chose Abraham as the father of us all. As Noah and Enoch before him, Abraham was deemed righteous by faith. He was chosen centuries before the law was engraved on tablets and before the Sabbath was established as the sign that Israel had been chosen by God to bring forth the Messiah who would bring reconciliation, restoration, and rest. Abraham is the father of all who come to righteous faith in God.

Circumcision was given as the physical sign of the righteousness Abraham had by faith, which is a circumcised heart (Rom. 2:29). As an object lesson, uncircumcised Israelites would not be allowed to inherit the land, just as those without circumcised hearts will not be allowed to enter into the promises of God in the new covenant in Jesus. Just as no man is allowed to participate in Passover unless circumcised, we learn the uncircumcised in heart will not 'pass over' from physical death to eternal life. We also understand from the Word that mere outward circumcision as part of the Jewish tradition does not prove the lesson has been acquired inwardly (a circumcised heart).

Abraham is the prototype of saving faith for Jew and Gentile alike. The Jewish people have both an advantage and no advantage at all in the new covenant. The promised seed of Abraham requires all men to come *through faith* in order to be counted righteous. In this way, there is no advantage to being Jewish. All have fallen short and are reconciled to God by grace through faith, not race, gender, or works. Reconciliation to God by faith alone in the righteousness of Christ places the Jew and Gentile on equal footing. Both must look outside the law to receive forgiveness of sin, found only in the seed promised to Abraham *before* the establishment of the Mosaic law.

> **There is no advantage to being a Jew:** *What shall we conclude then? Do we have any advantage? Not at all! For we have already made the charge that Jews and Gentiles alike are all under the power of sin.* -Rom. 3:9, NIV

On the other hand, such a rich foundation of promises, covenants, and the very words of God has been entrusted to Israel. To Israel belong the patriarchs, adoption, the glory, the covenants, the law, the temple worship, and the promises, especially being chosen as the race of people to bring forth the Redeemer for all mankind as prophesied in Genesis 3:15 (see Rom. 9:4-5). In this way, there is a wonderful advantage to being Jewish.

> **There is an advantage to being a Jew:** *What advantage, then, is there in being a Jew, or what value is there in circumcision? Much in every way! First of all, the Jews have been entrusted with the very words of God.* -Rom. 3:1-2, NIV

The end of the matter is this: there is no place for boasting in nationality because through Christ all are justified by faith and reconciled to God, the Father of us all:

> **There is no place for boasting:** *Where, then, is boasting? It is excluded... For we maintain that a person is justified by faith apart from the works of the law. Or is God the God of Jews only? Is he not the God of Gentiles too? Yes, of Gentiles too, since there is only one God, who will justify the circumcised by faith and the uncircumcised through that same faith.* -Rom. 3:27a,28-30, NIV

Diversity of Roles, Unity of Purpose

> *There is neither Jew nor Greek, there is neither slave nor free man, there is neither male nor female; for you are all one in Christ Jesus.* -Gal. 3:28, NASB

This passage speaks of our oneness in Christ who is no respecter of persons. Yet in the apostolic letters we find specific directives for men, women, leaders, the mature, and the young. Distinctions are made in these writings, yet the concept of unity and the inclusion of all without respect to status, gender, age, or race is emphasized. Might we agree that there is also a role for the Jew, distinctive from the role for the Gentile? If not, the distinction made by the elders and apostles at the Jerusalem council makes no sense. The apostles nowhere imply we are all the same but rather stress each has a peculiar function in the body. Just as a physical body has many individual parts for specific purposes, yet is one body, so each believer has a specific function that supports the whole.

Through demonstration of the Mosaic laws, we are reminded of the prophetic nature of the *edot* and the *chukim*, much as we remember the Lord's death and resurrection by participating in the Lord's Supper. Not only this, but the fall observances of *Rosh Hasha-*

nah, *Yom Kippur*, and *Sukkot* (the Feast of Tabernacles) have yet to be fulfilled prophetically and teach us spiritual corollaries about the events to come. They point to the return of *Yeshua*, the atonement of Israel through recognition and acceptance of their Messiah, and the gathering of the nations under the headship of Jesus. The types and shadows of these festivals help us in our understanding of their prophetic fulfillment. While the Gentiles' portion is to understand these festivals in a spiritual way (although participation is encouraged as a 'hands-on' learning experience as well as to promote unity), the Jewish believers demonstrate these types and shadows to provoke our minds to search deeper into the applicable spiritual truths.

Are not wives the type and shadow of the church, the Bride of Christ, with husbands likewise functioning as the head as a type of Christ? Paul frankly stated that the relationship between a man and woman is a type and shadow of the relationship between Christ and the church. All recognize that this role only applies to married women and men as a prophetic shadowing. Can we not also conclude that following the *mitzvot* given at Mt. Sinai is part of the Jewish believers' portion in the body of Christ to foreshadow the prophetic plans and kingdom truths of God?

Think of this as being in a musical. Basically, there are five groups of people involved in the production: the actors, the choir, the orchestra, the stage hands, and the ancillary people who do everything else from providing costumes to babysitting children. All are under the direction of the conductor during the actual performance, though there are delegated subheads for each group. Each particular group typically hangs out with those who function in a similar role. Though there is no prohibition against fellowship between groups, the choir people usually hang out with the choir people, the stage hands spend more time with the other stage hands, etc. Yet all are like-minded in that they are working toward the same goal despite the widely divergent nature of their respective roles. Is this not how we should view the differing roles and giftings of the various 'groups' within the body of Christ? Perhaps we should confine our need for uniformity to the factories and brick makers.

Controversial Matters

> *Accept the one whose faith is weak, without quarreling over disputable matters...* **make every effort to do what leads to peace and to mutual edification**... *So whatever you believe about these things* **keep between yourself and God**. *Blessed is the one who does not condemn himself by what he approves.* -Rom. 14:1,19,22, NIV

When Romans 14 is read in context, Paul is speaking primarily regarding the festival days and dietary laws given to Israel. Because the leaders decided the Gentiles did not need to follow these laws, controversy was bound to develop. These matters became controversial only when rigid thinking made them so. By insisting our views are the only scripturally sound with regard to religious practice, we have once again erected a dividing wall of hostility. We will take a look at only a few controversial matters to point out how each mode of debate has potential flaws, rendering the conclusions unwarranted and divisive rather than what the debaters would hope to believe—that they are messengers of truth.

There are critical spirits in all camps which sit in judgment of others with opposing views, absolutely certain they have the mind of Christ on their side. Others, when they see Messianic Jews following the Mosaic law, are merely confused because they don't understand why they are following the law if they are in Christ. Likewise, *Torah* observant Messianic Jews can be put-off by the Christian's adherence to festivals that are not mandated in Scripture. We'll take a look at a few of the arguments aimed at certain religious practice issues to bring to the surface the faulty construct plaguing many of the debates.

Ancient Pagan Religious Customs

'Sunday observance has its origins in pagan worship.' Is it a valid argument that whatever predates a practice establishes the basis for later practice? Many of the practices legislated by God in Scripture through the Mosaic covenant had antecedents in pagan culture and were originally practiced by the Hebrews with this understanding on at least one occasion (see Ex. 32). For instance:

- **circumcision**: The earliest documented circumcisions took place in Egypt, c. 2400 B.C., before the Mosaic law[8] and before Abraham (c. 2000 B.C.)
- **law**: 'If..., then...' type codes of law [e.g., the Code of Hammurabi (1760 B.C.)] existed before the Mosaic law. "Earlier collections of laws include the Code of Ur-Nammu, king of Ur (ca. 2050 B.C.), the Laws of Eshnunna (ca. 1930 B.C.) and the codex of Lipit-Ishtar of Isin (ca. 1870 B.C.), while later ones include the Hittite laws, the Assyrian laws, and Mosaic Law. These codes come from similar cultures in a relatively small geographical area, and they have passages which resemble each other (e.g., 'an eye for an eye...')."[9]
- **covenants**: The similarity of the Mosaic covenant to earlier Hittite suzerain treaties of the 2nd millennium B.C. is noted by scholars.[10]
- **temple**: "Official (Egyptian) temples were important venues for private prayer and offering, even though their central activities were closed to laypeople. Egyptians frequently donated goods to be offered to the temple deity..."[11]
- **temple sacrifice with priests' portions**: Egyptian rituals are similar to and predate Jewish law: "There were numerous temple rituals... Some were performed daily, while others took place annually or on rarer occasions. The most common temple ritual was the morning offering ceremony, performed daily in temples across Egypt... when the god had consumed the spiritual essence of the offerings, the items themselves were taken to be distributed among the priests..."[12]
- **trumpet use**: The trumpet blown for decampment, at the gathering of the people, and on different cultic occasions, especially during sacrifices (cf. 2 Chron. 29:28; Num 10:1-10), was the signaling instrument of the Egyptian army.[13]
- **harvest festivals**: The ancient Egyptians celebrated a harvest festival in the spring as well as harvest celebrations held in honor of the god of fertility and vegetation.[14]

- **festivals, with prescribed measurements for offerings**: Egyptian practice predates Mosaic ceremonial law: "…festival calendars also contained explicit references to the offerings that were required by the deities associated with these events… such as the exact number of bread loaves, cakes, beer containers, meat, fowl, incense, cultic charcoal and such, which is listed beside each event. Even the amount of grain that went into making a certain type of loaf… "[15]
- **Passover and feast of unleavened bread**: Early nomadic herders celebrated a 'passover' festival each spring predating the Hebrew exodus story, requesting help from the gods for safe journey as they passed from the winter pastures to the cultivated lands each spring. This was followed by a feast of unleavened bread to welcome the firstfruits of the spring harvest.[16]

The Israelites were coming out of the paganism of Egypt, just as the Gentiles each came out of the paganism of their cultures. In both cases, God leads by the hand and shows us a better way if our heart seeks truth and we have faith in Him. Because many aspects of the Mosaic covenant and law have pagan antecedents, are we to jump to the conclusion that these God-given practices were extracted from their pagan forbearers, and therefore should be labeled pagan? Or did God give the Israelites commandments to define a new way to apply these customs to teach them about the coming Messiah through the prophetic types and shadows instilled in their practice?

The Sabbath

There are those who persist in the belief that **'the Christian practice of worship and rest on Sundays has origin in pagan worship of the Roman sun god.'** Using the same argument, some have also condemned Saturday worship as being rooted historically in the pagan worship of Saturn. They disapprove of both Saturday and Sunday worship for these very reasons despite the clear teaching of Scripture that God set the Sabbath apart for Israel to worship Him. If believers met on Thursdays, would they likewise be accused of worshipping Thor, the god of that day? There is no end to this type of muckraking. In light of the fact that Jesus rose on the first day of the week and that Gentiles are not bound to the laws of Israel, setting aside Sunday for worship cannot be construed as idolatrous. Indeed, any day of the week believers meet to fellowship in the Lord is appropriate.

The believers met to break bread and collect money for the poor on the first day of the week (Acts 20:7; 1 Cor. 16:2). This was done primarily because Jews generally frowned on handling money on the Sabbath. While the 'first day' can be understood to take place on the evening after the end of the Sabbath (which ends at sundown on Saturday), it is still the first day of the week. Historians show that Jews and Gentile God-fearers assembled in the synagogues for teaching on Sabbath days. For those who recognized Jesus as the promised Messiah, the synagogue welcome wore thin as the new believers were eventually labeled heretics. Subsequently, they were forced to meet after Sabbath in the evening or on Sunday to celebrate with their own fellowship meal in the Lord's Supper. From the time of Justin (A.D. 103-165), the historical record indicates the new covenant community met on the first day of the week, with the exception of strict Sabbatarians, and continued as "an unbroken historical sequence in the custom of Sunday observance."[18]

Robert Clanton gives us the reason behind Sunday observance in the heart of the Gentile believer. "In time, the celebration 'upon the first day of the week' was made a rest for the Gentile Christians as Sabbath was for the Jews. It had nothing to do with paganism but everything to do with being witnesses to the resurrection of Christ upon the Lord's own day of his resurrection... [and to] celebrate the Lord's Day in honor of the resurrection of Christ as commanded and prophesied in Ps. 118:19-24. The Lord's Day spoken of... is the day Christ was resurrected and was prophesied to be a day of rejoicing, for us to 'be glad in it' because the stone which the builders rejected became 'the chief corner stone.'"[17] Clanton also points out that Paul, by quoting Psalm 2 in reference to the day of Jesus' resurrection (see Ps. 2:7 and Acts 13:33), lends further weight to equating the new day of rejoicing with the day of resurrection. On the first day of creation week, God brought forth light, a befitting description of Jesus, the Light of the World that came to earth (John 1:4-5). God separated light from darkness on that first day, much as Jesus came as a light to shine in and dispel the darkness. As additional weight for the significance of the day, the Holy Spirit was given on *Shavuot* (Pentecost), which falls on a Sunday (Lev. 23:16).

In any case, Gentiles are not held to Sabbath observance but can participate with their Jewish brothers in *Yeshua* if they desire. Just as the Sabbath was instituted as a sign and reminder that God rested on the seventh day, Sunday observance is a reminder that Jesus rose from the grave on the first day, commemorating the day God separated light from darkness as well as the day the Holy Spirit was given. Even so, there is no scriptural mandate to gather for worship on Sunday, as some in the church believe, though there is scriptural evidence believers did so. This discussion is not to advocate switching from Sabbath to Sunday observance for new covenant believers, but rather to explain the origin of its practice, point out only Israel is bound to Sabbath observance as prescribed by Mosaic law, and show the argument against Sunday worship is unfounded. In the new covenant, the Jewish elders determined Gentile believers were not bound to Sabbath observance, though doing so encourages the oneness we have with our Jewish brothers in Christ.

Christmas

What about Christmas? '**Christmas is laced with pagan customs associated with the winter solstice and Saturnalia.**' In a way similar to the Mosaic covenant, which contains rites analogous to pagan customs predating the covenant, yes, Christmas has customs taken from pagan celebrations and adapted to point to truths of the birth of Christ and the gospel message. I can't think of one believing Christian who is worshipping his tree or Saturn at Christmas time. Opponents of Christmas have likened the Christmas tree to an Asherah pole, and use two primary 'proof texts' for condemning the practice.

> *You shall not plant any tree as an Asherah beside the altar of the LORD your God that you shall make.* -Deut. 16:21, ESV

Using this passage, *any* use of trees is condemned by those against the use of Christmas trees. But this passage is talking specifically about an Asherah grove or pole used in idolatrous worship next to worship at God's altar. The hypocrisy of serving other gods while feigning to serve God Almighty brought great judgment to Israel (see Ezk. 8). However, regarding the use of trees (not all trees are Asherah poles!), God actually sanctions their use to beautify His sanctuary, though not to introduce idolatrous worship:

> *The glory of Lebanon shall come to you, the cypress, the pine, and the box tree together, to beautify the place of My sanctuary.* -Isa. 60:13, NKJV

The second text used for the proscription on Christmas trees comes from Jeremiah:

> *For the customs of the peoples are futile; one cuts a tree from the forest, the work of the hands of the workman, with the ax.* **They decorate** ('overlaid,' CEB; 'adorn,' NIV) **it with silver and gold; they fasten it with nails and hammers so that it will not topple.** *They are upright, like a palm tree, and they cannot speak; they must be carried, because they cannot go by themselves. Do not be afraid of them, for they cannot do evil, nor can they do any good.* -Jer. 10:3-5, NKJV

In the eyes of those determined to discard Christmas as pagan, this passage is clearly referring to Christmas trees. But this interpretation wrenches the verse cleanly out of context, for throughout Scripture the type of 'decorating' described here is the overlaying of wood with gold and silver (see Isa. 40:19; 41:7; Hab. 2:19), much like the overlaying of the table of showbread in the tabernacle. Clearly, and the commentators agree, this passage refers to the lifeless idols constructed that cannot walk; whose eyes cannot see and ears cannot hear. I am not aware of any Christian who carved up a Christmas tree to look like a pagan deity and overlaid it with sheets of gold. I will sadly admit, however, like the Jewish customs for celebrating Passover or Hanukkah, the particular customs can take priority in the heart over the actual meaning of the day.

God does not have anything against trees—only the worship of trees or fashioning trees into objects of worship. He even describes Himself as a green fir tree:

> *I am like a green fir tree* ('pine tree,' HCSB). *From me is thy fruit found.* -Hos. 14:8, KJV

Christmas trees are not Asherah poles any more than the Jewish festival of Sukkot is an Egyptian celebration to the gods of harvest. Others have argued the custom of having Christmas trees was not widely practiced until the 18th century and therefore not part of the early church customs, thus invalidating the practice. Using this type of argument for Hanukkah would negate the use of potato latkes since potatoes were not brought to Europe from South America until the late 16th century. Many of the Jewish customs for celebrating the festivals were developed over time, such as the Passover Seder. The Passover *Haggadah* (the written framework for celebrating the Passover) was not developed until nearly two millennia after the Mosaic ordinance was given at Sinai. While the practices are in keeping with the spiritual significance and meaning of the celebration, the specific rituals were not mandated by Moses but rather handed down through Jewish tradition.

In the mind of the Gentile, the evergreen tree depicts the everlasting life provided for and love displayed by the miracle of Jesus' birth, the beginning of the fulfillment of the promised reconciliation to God. The birth of the Jewish Messiah reminds Gentiles they have not been forgotten. God loves and cares for them as well, including them in the way to life through Christ, grafting them into the tree of life. Like Purim and Hanukkah, Christmas celebration is not specifically mandated in Scripture, though the supernatural revelation to shepherds and wise men who worshiped at Jesus' birth attest to its importance.

Most scholars agree that Jesus' birth more likely happened in the fall at the time of the Feast of Tabernacles. Both Dr. David Stern (Messianic Jew) and Dr. David Pawson describe Christmas as the probable time of the overshadowing of Mary; the time of Jesus' conception by the Holy Spirit. Stern graciously views this time as a cause to celebrate, for what more appropriate time could there be for *Yeshua* to be conceived than at the time of Hanukkah, the festival of lights?

Easter

'Celebrating Easter makes Christians worshippers of Ishtar.' By this same reasoning, Jewish use of the Babylonian calendar makes them worshippers of Tammuz (a month on the Babylonian calendar the Israelites adopted as their own). The use of Easter eggs is criticized as being part of the spring fertility customs for the worship of Ishtar. Symbolic of new life, the egg is a token to the Christian of the new creation he is in Christ. By way of comparison, the Passover Seder plate, complete with its hard-boiled egg in salt water, is not part of the Mosaic code but has many emblems of significance that aid as object lessons when commemorating the Passover event, which points to the redemption we have in Christ.

The Lord's resurrection is typically celebrated on the first day of the week following Passover, commemorating the day the new covenant was ratified. Paul reminded us that Jesus is the Passover Lamb (1 Cor. 5:7) as well as the firstfruits (1 Cor. 15:20,23). The Jewish celebration of firstfruits occurs on the Sunday after Passover (Lev. 23:4-14), coinciding with day of Jesus' resurrection.

The incarnation of Jesus and His role as Shepherd and Judge can be seen in the types and shadows of Egyptian paganism in Osiris, who carries the crook (shepherd's rod) and flail (threshing instrument). Yet no believer would think to make this comparison to nullify the truth of Jesus' existence and mission, or to dismiss it as being rooted in paganism. Then why is it that we insist on the validity of our arguments on these other disputable matters? Just because the Egyptians worshipped cats, are we to give up our pets for fear of partaking in pagan worship? I hardly think so, do you? Chickens are used in occult rituals, so are we to stop eating chicken? The goat is a symbol of the unsaved or even Satan in some writings, so should we give up raising goats? Where do we cross the line into superstition and nonsense when we use types and shadows as literal harbingers of evil? These kinds of arguments and condescending remarks may be born of those who have the right heart in seeking after truth, but oftentimes come from a religious and self-righteous spirit. In either case, they do not point out indisputable truth but only cause division. Paul warned us to keep our opinions about special days and dietary beliefs between ourselves and God. By ignoring apostolic wisdom, we have upset the faith of some on issues we were not even to concern ourselves with in the first place. Let everything be done from a posture of faith. [Note: There are occult practices that obviously have no place in the practice of Christianity, e.g., divination, magic spells, worship of or praying to departed saints, etc.; I am not addressing those.]

Religious Celebrations

The Gentile should not be frowned on for observance of Jesus' birth and resurrection any more than the Jew who observes Hanukkah or Purim. Both honor the Lord when the observance is from the heart and draws the participant closer to the Lord, commemorating God's intervention and goodness demonstrated on their behalf. Paul made it clear we are not to judge each other in this regard. Our wrangling over these issues has reduced us to the same level as the Sadducees and Pharisees, who Jesus rebuked for their hypocrisy in traveling over land and sea to win converts.

> Therefore **no one is to act as your judge in regard to food or drink or in respect to a festival or a new moon or a Sabbath day**—*things which are a mere shadow of what is to come; but the substance belongs to Christ.* -Col. 2:16-17, NASB

The Gentile believer, not having been raised in the Jewish traditions, will be more focused on the events of Jesus' birth, death, and resurrection rather than the Jewish festivals. The latter were given to the nation of Israel as the types and shadows of Christ and the different aspects and timing of God's interaction with Israel in this age. These are foreign to the religious *practice* of most Gentile believers, though not to his spiritual *foundation*. Likewise, Gentile religious customs are foreign to Jewish practice and mindset, and some view these as hindering the Jews from recognizing Jesus as his Messiah.

The festivals, new moon celebrations, and Sabbath days are shadows of things to come. There are still events on the horizon, namely Jesus' second coming and the establishment of His kingdom. The festivals have utility because they are grand object lessons, rich in detail about the plans and purposes of God. Passover portrays Jesus as the sacrificial lamb, by whose power we are redeemed from bondage to sin. Jesus fulfilled the type and shadow in the feast of firstfruits, being the firstfruits of resurrection. Pentecost, the time at which the law was given on Mt. Sinai, becomes the time when the Holy Spirit arrives to write the law on our hearts. We move through the wilderness of life until we arrive at the 'promised land'—the Sabbath rest of the Lord as the type of Jesus' kingdom.

The types and shadows in the Jewish festivals are infused with imagery and spiritual truth that still speak to us today. Does this mean we should celebrate them? Those who want to, absolutely! But there is no stipulation that it is required. The festivals can be vibrantly alive with the depth of their meaning in Christ, tying together the law and the prophets, provided they are celebrated with the right heart posture (see warning at Isa. 1:12-14).

> [N]ow that you have come to know God... how is it that you turn back again to the weak and worthless elemental things, to which you desire to be enslaved all over again? -Gal. 4:9, NASB

This passage does not speak of the quality of the former principles to teach, but rather their powerlessness to save. None are required for righteousness, but we can learn a great deal from them through participation and/or study. A Messianic Jewish friend stated, "Christians celebrating the festivals is a great way to provoke Jews to jealousy, and to help them develop a love for Christians and the Messiah as they see them living a 'grafted in' life by celebrating the festivals established in the Tanakh." This is probably the strongest reason for participating in the festivals rather than merely studying the applicable spiritual truths, doing what we can to win some, as Paul exemplified (1 Cor. 9:19-23).

On a sad note, Jewish celebrations can be as secular as Christian ones. Nowhere is this seen more clearly than with Hanukkah and Christmas. Just as Christians can be inordinately attached to the tree, sweets, and gift-giving, Jews can also be likewise attached to the Hanukkah menorah, special foods, and gifts. Hanukkah menorahs come in all shapes and sizes, even with national sports team motifs. Believers must ask themselves: Would I be able to celebrate Jesus' birth if there were no tree, candy canes, lights, or presents? Would I be able to celebrate the meaning of Hanukkah without the menorah, latkes, dreidl, or gifts? If the answer is 'yes,' we have the holiday in proper perspective. If the answer is no, there may be a bit of unbalanced affection or even idolatry lurking in the shadows.

Temples and Churches

Temples had origins in pagan worship, as did the 'kirkes' (churches) of old, to which term many strongly object. While few seem to object to the use of the pagan word 'temple' to describe the temple in Jerusalem, they take great offense at the use of the word 'church' because of its pagan origins and its lack of presence in the original New Testament manuscripts. The historical record shows that 'church' was a later term and not originally used in the Bible. It surfaced in our modern English versions, replacing the Greek word *ekklesia* ('congregation or assembly,' used to distinguish new covenant believers in an assembly perhaps not exclusively Jewish from traditional synagogue meetings).

Whether this term offends someone or not is a matter of their own conscience. However, its widespread use today will not likely change because of the offense of a few. For those so disposed, it is best to view this as one of the many 'tares' in the present day *ekklesia* that will not be removed, for the sake of not uprooting the wheat, until the Lord returns.

Summary

In the chapter on covenants, we noted the Sabbath, holy days, and festivals are everlasting ordinances for the Jewish people. We can be certain the Feast of Tabernacles will be celebrated yearly in the age to come (Zech. 14:16-19). Whether our current celebrations and days for worship not *mandated* in the Word [Sunday worship, Christmas, Purim, and

Hanukkah will continue or not is a matter of speculation (Jesus' resurrection—Easter—is the one exception as it coincides with fulfillment of the Jewish day of firstfruits).

We may not agree on these issues, or even that each side has made unsound arguments, but perhaps we can agree each side has blind spots and filters which make us incapable of seeing the log in our own eye while we are trying to take the speck out of someone else's. Perhaps we could agree to fellowship without rancor or wrangling about the law, dietary practice, days, and customs, as Paul instructed, and instead focus on the common ground of all believers—the preeminence of Jesus *HaMashiach*, or *Yeshua* the Christ, and the work He did to save us all (juxtaposition intended). Celebrating special days are not to cause division. I have not brought up these issues to promote one side or the other. My heart is to see mutual respect in the believing community for those whose practice may differ from our own, rather than causing offense or hindrance on side issues. Those who have created division in this way must repent. The main thing must always remain the main thing—Jesus is the promised Messiah, and He's coming back.

The way in which the Gentile church remains connected to their Jewish roots is by staying connected to Jesus, the Jewish Messiah, who is the Word. If we make the Word our habitation (which includes the Old Testament), we gain clarity on the spiritual significance of Jewish practice, especially the rich understanding available in the festivals instituted by God in the Scriptures. Each gives deeper understanding of our Messiah and all He has accomplished and will complete on His return.

Paul emphasized each believer must be fully convinced in his own mind as to matters of religious practice (moral issues are nonnegotiable). We noted individual believers can have differences of opinion on observances of days or dietary regulations and still have right standing before God. It is the religious spirit in all of us that won't yield until all believers think, observe, and practice the way we do. Under the new covenant, we all come through grace by faith in Jesus. Paul maintained that we are to be totally convinced in our own minds without having to force those opinions on others. This assumes we are growing in our understanding of the Word. The main point is the practice of each believer must honor the Lord, come from faith, and line up with the Word and witness of the Spirit.

Jewish and Christian Conflict

Jews and Christians alike have been persecuted, murdered, and/or forced out of one country after another throughout history. Painfully, a good deal of Jewish persecution has come at the hands of supposed Christians. Jew and Christian alike have been at odds with one another, with respective anti-Gentile and anti-Semitic polemic in the writings of both camps. The persecution of early Jewish and Gentile believers by the Pharisees is well documented, though the Roman persecution of believers far outweighs any persecution received at the hands of traditional Jews. The Crusades were a hideous example in the history of the church of zeal without knowledge, ignorance of the Word, and racial prejudice, killing thousands of Jews under the banner of the cross.

SECTION 3 HARMONIZED VIEW OF LAW AND FREEDOM

There were seventeen million Jews in the world before the Holocaust in WWII Germany. Afterward, only eleven million remained. The loss of over one-third of this race of people as a result of the atrocities of Nazi Germany is overwhelming. Even more scandalous is the way in which a portion of the official German church rabidly supported Hitler's regime, alongside a large portion that remained silent.

Those who were neither supportive nor complacent formed the "Confessing Church." Though many criticize this church for watering down the ideals of those who spearheaded its formation, we have to ask ourselves whether there is any example in our own history that shows we championed the cause of the persecuted during a time of very real danger. Admittedly, many in this movement were focused primarily on protecting the church's right to govern themselves as a body (answerable only to God and not the state) more than protesting the injustice to Jews. But others were deeply afflicted in their conscience by what they saw taking place.

Dietrich Bonhoeffer, pastor and one of the founders of the Confessing Church, actively worked in opposition to the Nazi's but sadly was part of only a minority of church leaders who spoke out against the injustices against the Jews. Those who did were eventually arrested, sent to concentration camps, and executed. Bonhoeffer pondered the usefulness of religion that would not act on behalf of the persecuted: "We have been silent witnesses of evil deeds... we have learnt the arts of equivocation and pretence; experience has made us suspicious of others and kept us from being truthful and open; intolerable conflicts have worn us down and even made us cynical. Are we still of any use?"[19]

Bonhoeffer confronted himself with the insufficient results of good intentions. "Who stands firm? Only the one for whom the final standard is not his reason, his principles, his conscience, his freedom, his virtue, but who is ready to sacrifice all these, when in faith and sole allegiance to God he is called to obedient and responsible action: the responsible person, whose life will be nothing but an answer to God's question and call."[20] His reflection as stated here resulted from his work as a double agent in the German resistance movement under the guise of German military intelligence—work that required lying and culpability in assassination attempts on Hitler.

Marga Meusel, a Berlin church deaconess, is remembered as another voice with the courage, passion, and conviction to speak on behalf of the Jews, condemning the church for thinking more of its own religious civil liberties than the plight facing the Jews. The efforts of those who pleaded with the German church to intervene went largely unheeded, though some estimate over 2,000 Jews were rescued by members of the church who took these words to heart. In 1935, Meusel rebuked the Confessing Church for their cowardliness. "Why does the church do nothing? Why does it allow unspeakable injustice to occur?... What shall we one day answer to the question, where is thy brother Abel? The only answer that will be left to us, as well as to the Confessing Church, is the answer of Cain" ('am I my brother's keeper?' Gen. 4:9).[21] "She particularly condemned those who saw the Nazi persecution of the Jews as God's will: 'Since when has the evildoer the right to portray his evil deeds as the will of God?' It was imperative, she continued, that the church publicly oppose these measures and help everyone—Christian or not—affected by them."[22]

> To sin by silence when they should protest makes cowards of men. -Abe Lincoln

We must pray this gross negligence on the part of the church is never repeated. Though the Talmud requires Jews to help another whose life is in danger only if it does not jeopardize his own life,[23] Christians are to set a higher standard in that 'there is no greater demonstration of love than to lay one's life down for a friend' (John 15:13). [Note: The Talmud's loophole for helping only if it doesn't jeopardize one's own life comes short of biblical precedent. Esther risked her life to save the Jews in Medo-Persia (Esth. 4:16), and Obadiah risked his to save a hundred prophets from execution at the hand of Jezebel (1 Kings 18:3b-4).]

Pursuing peace and reconciliation with our Jewish brothers have become priorities for many in the church where intercession and targeted giving for helping the poor among Israel are routinely practiced. *The Jerusalem Prayer Team* and the *Hatikva Project* are just two charitable Messianic ministries that reach out in this way.

Worldwide, Christians have become the primary target for persecution if one is looking at sheer numbers. In the twentieth century alone, Italian journalist Antonio Socci estimates forty-five million Christians were martyred for their faith, stating, "Global persecution of Christianity is still in progress, but in most cases is ignored by the mass media and Christians in the West."[24] If this number sounds shocking to you, reconsider. If the rate of Christian execution equaled that of the Jewish mortality under Hitler, the number would be a staggering *seven hundred million*.

In no way do I want to minimize the persecution of Christians. Today, over two hundred million Christians are denied basic human rights in one way or another worldwide. "The persecution of Christians worldwide is growing and intensifying. The modes of persecution vary from discrimination to severe assault, imprisonment, arson, looting, torture, rape, and even death."[25] Archbishop Dominique Mamberti, Secretary for Relations with States for the Holy See, told the annual UN General Assembly general debate on Sept. 27, 2011, that "Christians currently suffer more persecution because of their faith than any other religious group."[26] This is sadly true even in the United States. Every other religion is allowed to parade their beliefs; only Christian beliefs are targeted for censure.

Much of the animosity some Jews and Christians feel toward one another is rooted in bitterness, unforgiveness, and unfounded prejudice. When we elevate our feelings, ambitions, or ill-considered beliefs over the standard of God's Word, we rapidly deteriorate in our understanding of what is right. This happened in the book of Judges. For many years I dreaded reading Judges 19-20 when it came up in my Bible study. I couldn't see how this story had anything to do with being 'profitable for reproof, instruction,' or anything else for that matter, as we were promised (2 Tim. 3:16). The cowardly Levite was infuriating, saving his skin at the expense of his concubine. The behavior of the

SECTION 3 *HARMONIZED VIEW OF LAW AND FREEDOM*

Benjamites was absolutely vile. The Levite's response to her death was unbelievably grizzly. I had no idea why such a story was included in the Word of God. Definitely PG-13 or R for disturbing images, thematic elements, and violence.

During one trip through these chapters, however, I noticed something I never saw before. In the first sixteen chapters of Judges, the lives of the individual judges of Israel are discussed. In the last five chapters, however, two seemingly unrelated stories are included with no connection to any judge being appointed by God. The first is about Micah and his Levite, and the convoluted events that ensued. The second is the disturbing story of the Levite and his concubine. So why were these stories included?

The answer seems to at least partly lie in the presence of two nearly identical verses that open and close this section of Scripture: 'In those days there was no appointed ruler in Israel. Everyone did what was right in his own eyes' (Jdg. 17:6; 21:25). It suddenly became clear to me that God was illustrating what happens when, 1.) there is no God appointed leadership, and 2.) people ignore God's Word. If the only standard we have is self and what we think should be done, we will default to the basest drives to preserve self and gain whatever profitable advantage we can. This also takes place when believers ignore the Word, settling for state religion and the comfort it has to offer the complacent, as in 1930's Germany.

As followers of Christ, we sit condemned for ignoring the Word that teaches us love keeps no record of wrongs. We have been keeping track of who did what to whom and on what day. We moved in zeal without knowledge, placing the church in the same place of hypocrisy as the Pharisees who persecuted the early believers. We viewed our own atrocities as a speck when we should have evaluated them as a beam. Out of suspicion, fear, greed, and/or misplaced understanding of making disciples of all nations, the countries of Europe expelled Jews or forced their 'conversions' at various times. This is a dreadful reminder of our pathetic lack of understanding of God's Word, an unthinkable deviation from the compassion followers of Christ are to demonstrate, and a shameful display of prejudice. Such action requires a heart made of stone. By this we were supposing to provoke the Jews to jealousy?

On the other side of the issue, there are wounds that refuse to heal. One Messianic Jewish writer gave a detailed account of all that the Jews suffered in Germany at the hands of 'Christians' who did nothing to stop Hitler. After reciting all of the faults of the silent majority, he wrote that it is 'no consolation' to then recount the actions of those Christians who risked and even gave their lives to help the Jews, not to mention those who suffered alongside them in the concentration camps. Even the Jewish Talmud would label these Christian benefactors as heroes. On the other hand, the aforementioned author painstakingly dismantled any charges of like atrocities committed by Jews, stating they were only 'Jews in name.'

It is only too easy to be offended by these types of comments. The author took pains in other portions of his book to make sure the reader could see the distinction between the actions of fringe Jews who did things not in keeping with the Judaic convictions of true faith in contrast with those who acted righteously. But when it came to offering the same generosity and grace to distinguish true Christian believers from mere pew sitters, the door was shut. However, after reading about the memorial in Israel to the righteous Gentiles who risked their own lives to save the lives of Jews in WWII, we gain a more balanced view that not all Jews feel the way this author did. At this point we must realize some pain is so deeply imbedded that personal hypocrisy is not even discerned.

The root problem with the silent 'Christians' during Hitler's rule was not primarily that they were silent, but that they were only socio-political Christians, whose convictions were less than skin deep, whose faith in Christ was fruitless and therefore worthless. Courage to stand for our convictions can only come if we have actually invested our lives in those convictions. These were not Christians by the biblical standard of what constitutes a Christian, but some anomaly that can only occur when people are deceived into believing national loyalty is the cornerstone of their faith.

Some in the church harbor feelings of condescension toward Jews because the Jewish people as a whole did not recognize or revere their Messiah. But can we honestly say that those in the Western church today truly revere the Lord they profess to follow? If Jesus is the Word and we profess Him as Lord, then why does Bible study have such low priority in the average Christian's daily routine in the West?

As another example, the Jewish oral traditions have been maligned by many in the church, but are they any different from all of the interpretive teaching the church has promulgated and to which many adhere? The oral traditions were merely the result of the best and most thoroughly trained and learned men in the *Torah* putting forth their interpretation or explanation of what was written, accompanied by regulations for what they thought to be the best way to live out *Torah* through the lens of that interpretation. Is the church's practice and scholarship any different?

Some judge the wrongful actions of their own forbearers by denouncing their actions as being out of the mainstream. But when they judge the actions of the other side's forbearers, they allow no such latitude and instead cling to bitterness and sharp criticism. Judging one's own party by rationale that diverts blame away from the group as a whole by offering plausible explanation becomes hypocrisy when that party does not afford the 'opposition' the same liberty. Whether born of a painful wound that won't heal, jealousy, prejudice, bitterness, or unforgiveness, the fruit is the same—a poisonous double standard that destroys unity and provides an excuse for continued prejudice or a bitter victim identity and mentality. Love and unity cannot flourish in such an environment.

In addition to these avenues for resentment and strife, worldwide prejudice and persecution of Jews and Christians is well documented, particularly in Muslim and Communist nations. The current Middle East conflict over the Jewish State, complete with unabashed talk of genocide, is continually in the news. As for Christians, ABC News ran an article last year on modern day Christian martyrs, calling the continual persecution and culling of the Christian population a 'creeping genocide.'

"Christians are 'the most frequently persecuted religious group globally'... The systematic persecution of Christians in the 20th century—by Communists in the Soviet Union and China, but also by Nazis—claimed far more lives than anything that has happened so far in the 21st century. Now, however, it is not only totalitarian regimes persecuting Christians, but also residents of Islamic states, fanatical fundamentalists, and religious sects... Experts speak of a 'creeping genocide.'"[27]

Jews and Christians must join together to defend, care for, and love one another in the distinctive role given to each. This is especially true of Gentile and Jewish believers in *Yeshua*. When Jesus separates the sheep from the goats, it will be determined by whether or not we helped our brothers in need (Matt. 25:31-46). Martin Niemoller's words are thought-provoking and worthy of remembrance. Initially a pro-Hitler anti-Semite, years of imprisonment alongside Jews dissolved his former prejudice, causing him to write the following: "First they came for the communists, and I didn't speak out because I wasn't a communist. Then they came for the trade unionists, and I didn't speak out because I wasn't a trade unionist. Then they came for the Jews, and I didn't speak out because I wasn't a Jew. Then they came for me, and there was no one left to speak out for me."[28]

Love Keeps No Record of Wrongs

We have great incentive to listen to Paul's words: love keeps no record of wrongs. Reconciliation is not a process in which I have much understanding according to the complex counseling processes of today. Those who understand the layers of complexity involved probably also understand the concept of a *niphal* conjugation in Hebrew. What I know about reconciliation has come through my own painful experiences:

- We put ourselves in a prison when we harbor anger and bitterness rooted in unforgiveness (Matt. 18:32-35); we are forgiven with the same measure we use to forgive others; unforgiveness is devastating to our relationship with God.
- We need to forgive from the heart, but sheer raw obedience to forgive void of any fuzzy feelings will at least open the door for the Spirit to work on the heart and let the poison of anger and bitterness out; this takes time.
- We are the biggest loser when we cling to bitterness and unforgiveness; the heart remains locked to others and to God, and we cannot experience the joy promised to believers—only blackness of soul.
- We cannot come to God's table to fellowship if we harbor something against a brother; there is only one loaf at the communion table.
- Healing can only take place when we let go of our 'right' to be angry, and choose life instead; clinging to anger will turn our hearts to stone.
- After we forgive the one who wronged us, renewing our mind by immersing ourselves in the Word will take us on the road to *shalom*.
- We must take every thought captive so we do not rehearse the wrong we have experienced, and by faith accept God's promise to make us whole.

Joseph, Our Example

The graciousness of Joseph can teach us all. He had a long time in slavery and unjust imprisonment to think about what his brothers had done to him, but he chose to forgive. Joseph saw God's greater plan in his suffering and was able to set aside any bitterness to which he may have been 'entitled.'

> *Joseph said to them, "Don't be afraid. Am I in the place of God?* **You intended to harm me, but God intended it for good** *to accomplish what is now being done, the saving of many lives. So then, don't be afraid. I will provide for you and your children." And* **he reassured them and spoke kindly to them.** -Gen. 50:19-21, NIV

Human nature naturally defaults to revenge when pain is caused from wrongdoing, wanting our persecutor to suffer as much as we were made to suffer. But this is not the way of Christ. We are commanded to put on the new nature so our old nature no longer controls us. Only by cooperating with the Holy Spirit and allowing His power to transform our mind and heart are we able to say as Jesus said, 'Father, forgive them…'

Many will say it is not that easy, groping for any excuse to hold onto bitterness and unforgiveness, the hallmarks of a victim identity rooted in self-pity, anger, and hatred. But the Word reminds us it is a matter of the will—nowhere is it ever implied this is an impossible task in 'special cases.' *Agape* love transcends emotion and is rooted in mental ascent, not feelings. What complicates the issue is the *strength* of our feelings, not inability to forgive. When the basis of our day-to-day behavior is the shifting sand of emotion, we have set a trap for ourselves like quicksand. Our feet must be firmly fixed on the foundation of rock solid truth—we can stand on no other foundation to remain in God's will. *Agape* love can only be expressed from this foundation, and from this foundation we experience true peace, freedom, and healing.

Those who have made their bitterness a harbor in which to dwell are quickly sinking into a mire of their own choosing. Unforgiveness will not harm the person who wronged us, but it will destroy those who cling to it. True believers who allow themselves to wallow in unforgiveness, bitterness, and resentment do so because they have chosen to do so, not because it is impossible to get out. The feelings associated with self-pity, depression, and bitterness are as addictive as alcohol or pornography, but God provides strength for us to be free. It is time to let go of the stones of offense and be made right with God and each other. Both Jesus and Joseph demonstrated eagerness to be reconciled with their persecutors. This is the goal of the overcomer in Christ.

Our African-American brothers and sisters in the Lord have suffered a good deal of abuse at the hands of Europeans, Americans, and their own brothers who betrayed them for mammon in Africa centuries ago. Many who have come to the Lord have demonstrated great dignity and strength through all their adversity, as Joseph did, rising above the cruel and unjust circumstances. The people who kidnapped and tortured their ancestors in order to bring slaves to Europe and the Americas meant it for harm, but God meant it for good. What good is that? Just think of the number of people of African descent who, by being forced out of Africa a few hundred years ago, have escaped the disease, poor living conditions, war, and genocide that plagues Africa in our day, and have turned from tribal worship practices to the worship of the one true God. Eternity with God is the beauty that God brought forth from the ashes of pain and abuse.

> We who lived in concentration camps can remember the men who walked through the huts comforting others, giving away their last piece of bread. They may have been few in number, but they offer sufficient proof that everything can be taken from a man but one thing: the last of the human freedoms—to choose one's attitude in any given set of circumstances, to choose one's own way. -Viktor Frankl

The strength of faith and character of those African-Americans who have chosen to forgive that part of the nation which refused to release their ancestors from bondage and the inhumane way in which many were treated is remarkable. By the grace of God, they have chosen to remember the others who fought for the slaves and gave their lives to see slavery quickly abolished in this nation, much like the Jews who remembered and honored those Christians who risked their lives to help them during WWII. For those still struggling, may the shackles of bitterness be removed and the heart unlocked to experience true freedom in Christ, and may we be one new man. Amen.

Closing Thoughts

You also, as living stones, are being built up a spiritual house, a holy priesthood, to offer up spiritual sacrifices acceptable to God through Jesus Christ. -1 Pet. 2:5, NKJV

This picture of living stones fitted together as only a master mason can do is an accurate picture of the spiritual house God is building. It is the direct antithesis of Nimrod's tower of Babel, built with bricks and bitumen. Bricks don't need to be fitted—any brick can go in any space that needs to be filled. Some churches treat their people this way, justifying their actions because of the 'grand vision' they are hoping to fulfill. Some would also like the practice of every believer to be uniform, that is, in the shape of a brick. But God calls us 'living stones' and takes the time to fit us in a place designed especially for us in His body. Jesus Himself holds the building together, unlike bitumen which turns to slime when tested by intense heat, causing the entire structure to fail.

There are many differences in the body of Christ. We often reject the unfamiliar, what we do not understand, and whatever doesn't make sense to us. The Lord is looking for those who will patiently wait for answers, not rejecting truth because it seems odd or doesn't make sense, but who do not grow weary in searching. Forming a rash opinion in order to quickly establish a foundation from which to work is not sound, nor will it last.

Envy and selfish ambition have no place in the church. Some who have been given an allotment or charge that is not in leadership or something they desire spend their days in futility trying to do or be something for which God has not equipped them. Few things are more painful than listening to a second alto trying to screech out a solo written for a first soprano, or a tenor trying to croak out the bass part. Each must stick to the part he is given if we are to perform the symphony God has written for the body of Christ.

It would be good for Jews and Gentiles to remember we are brothers in God's sight. The Jews, rich in the promises given to Abraham through Isaac and Jacob, would be provoked to jealousy by his Gentile brother who has found the secret of walking in God's favor and presence through the new covenant, partaking of the wealth of the kingdom to come (Rom. 10:19-20). Likewise, those who are grafted in need to give the respect due their Jewish brothers who walk out the richness of their heritage in daily life.

Jesus spoke the following words when the Pharisees harshly judged Him as having a demon when He healed a man on the Sabbath, violating their concept of keeping the day holy. Much of what has been called discernment or corrective teaching in the body of Christ has fallen into this trap of unrighteous Pharisaic judgment, criticizing the practice of others, chasing the children away, turning freedom in Christ into a yoke and chore. Teaching of this nature is called hay, wood, and stubble.

> *Stop judging according to outward appearances; rather judge according to righteous judgment.* -John 7:24, HCSB

The Jews criticized the apostles for eating common meats like the Gentiles as well as for entering their houses (Acts 11:3). Jesus was also criticized for eating with 'sinners.' In both cases, the criticism was determined as unfounded by the authority of the Word. Has not the body of Christ done the same thing when we criticize those who don't have our same view of proper days for worship, dietary guidelines, giving, or the role of the law? When we loudly proclaim our views on these matters as the only way to live righteously before God, we are engaging in empty and godless chatter that 'spreads like gangrene, upsetting the faith of some' (2 Tim. 2:16-18).

Think of all the families who have little traditions they do together, such as pizza night, movie night, prayer time, etc. All families have routines that define their particular family, and no two families are expected to look the same. In the movie, *Cheaper by the Dozen 2*, one daughter recalled, "[Dad] taught us there is no way to be a perfect parent, but there are a million ways to be a really good one." Perhaps we need to adopt this wisdom for our local congregations. Each local community of believers functions as a separate *mishpokha* (family)—delightfully unique, yet part of the whole extended family of the body of Christ. The blood that binds us together is truly thicker than water.

Albert Barnes rightly stated that 'young converts have often a special delicacy or sensitiveness about the lawfulness of many things.' This is exactly the case with younger children. They are offended by everything. 'Teacher, he's coloring outside the lines!' 'Mommy, he ate his tater tots with his fingers!' 'Daddy, she's wearing two different socks!' I'm afraid many of our arguments sound this way to our Father. We need to grow in grace and forbearance, mature in our own thinking through study of the Word, and choose our battles wisely. Only those practices or beliefs that clearly contradict the Word are to be addressed and vigorously refuted. Clamoring about the law, holidays, and eating habits are the mark of immaturity. We should be teachers by now, but instead we focused on our need to be right about matters Paul called disputable, or on finding fault with every other church to somehow elevate our own as superior. We are still infants.

We don't even know the Word or appreciate the gift we have in the Holy Spirit. How many believers can honestly say they have read the entire Bible? The translation of the Bible into English came at the price of the translators' lives, executed for disobeying the Roman church. Having the Bible has not provoked us to take advantage of the privilege of having the Word in our own language. We've procrastinated in our study of the Word, trying to get everything else done first. We are too focused on the baubles of worldly accomplishment and comfortable, entertaining lifestyles. We cannot expect to grow and mature if we ignore the very means we've been given for maturity. We are still children, arguing over matters that have no substance before God. We are where Paul feared we would be—complacent and immature, lacking fruit and possessing no larger picture than what our self-centered preferences and opinions dictate as a proper church.

> I don't like that man. I must get to know him better. -Abraham Lincoln

Sometimes we are offended by others for no apparent reason. Often, we only have greater appreciation for others and their views when we spend time getting to know and understand them. In a church I visited years ago, a Native American believer from the Inuit tribe brought out his *qilaut* (tribal hand-held drum) during worship. Some believers in the congregation immediately stiffened in anticipation of this 'pagan' instrument's effect. Rather than be offended, this steadfast warrior smiled and humbly explained how he only played his drum for the One who saved him. He began to play a very powerful and skillful accompaniment on his drum as he recited the 24th Psalm from memory. 'Who is this King of glory? He is the Lord, mighty in battle.' To this day, I can remember the confident smile of victory on his peaceful face. He played with remarkable dignity and strength. Graciously looking past the prejudice of the ignorant, he demonstrated that the peace which passes understanding had invaded his soul. He exuded the confidence one expects of a believer firmly established in the righteousness of Christ and living for the One he loves and serves. At 5'5", he stood as a giant of faith that day, rooted and grounded in love and the Word of God.

As bondservants, our focus must be on honoring Christ in thought, word, and deed. Moving in a spirit of humility and understanding that under the new covenant law and freedom may be expressed differently by individual believers, we can serve the needs of others without having to force them to be in agreement with the particulars of our religious practice. Guarding ourselves against divisiveness with regard to disputable matters is vital for our personal growth as well as body unity. Love is the better way and fulfills all the law and prophets. Only in loving unity can we partake of the Lord's Supper without bringing condemnation on ourselves. The Lord's body is one.

> *Always be humble and gentle. Be patient with each other, making allowance for each other's faults because of your love.* -Eph. 4:2, NLT

SECTION 4

WHOLEHEARTED LIFESTYLE OF OBEDIENCE

Chapter 12

Qualities of a Believer

> *For I desire steadfast love and not sacrifice, the knowledge of God rather than burnt offerings.* -Hos. 6:6, ESV

Our loyal love and growth in the knowledge of God are far more important to our heavenly Father than what we can give Him in offerings, sacrificial lifestyles, dedicated religious service, and achievements. A deepening relationship with God is the primary fruit of studying the Word with the Holy Spirit as Tutor. True love and mercy are a natural outcome of our relationship with God.

Jesus came to demonstrate God's priority that we walk in love and mercy with our fellow man by the many miracles He performed. He emphasized that understanding the law's foundational principles of mercy, justice, faithfulness, and love supersede its rules and regulations. The Jews acknowledged human endangerment warranted exception to carrying out the letter of the law, but Jesus went out of His way to demonstrate human need in general provided legitimate precedence. Legalistic observance of the law at the expense of another's welfare and need goes against the nature of our Father who values kindness and mercy more highly than ritual observance and sacrifice.

Lifestyle of Obedience

Our understanding of obedience is primarily enjoined with the idea of doing what is right. While this is a major component of obedience, the primary focus of God with respect to obedience is the heart. A circumcised heart will do the right thing even when no one is looking because of the desire to please God and remain in His light. An uncircumcised heart might obey when all are looking to gain the favor and approval of man, but will consider doing wrong if the desire to sin is present, opportunity knocks, and there is little chance of being caught. We must change our thinking to view obedience as primarily a *heart* issue and not a behavioral one. Once the heart is captured, the behavior will follow, though perhaps not perfectly in this age.

The purpose of the law was to confront man with his sinfulness and bring him to the realization he does not possess the moral constitution within himself to keep the letter *or* the spirit of the law. This realization kindles the longing for the promised Messiah who would fulfill the law and make a way for us to have God's laws written on our hearts through the presence and work of the Holy Spirit. God spoke through Ezekiel, giving His word He would accomplish this (Ezk. 11:19-20): 'I will give them an undivided heart and put a new spirit in them. Their heart of stone will be removed, and I will give them a tender, responsive heart; then they will be able to follow my decrees and carefully obey My laws. Our relationship will be restored.' This is not stated once but twice in Ezekiel. In the second passage, the Lord gives further detail, adding we will be cleansed from unrighteousness and declared clean (Ezk. 36:25-27). Stating this twice informs us the matter has been firmly established by God (cf. Gen. 41:32).

David came to the same realization that it was not sacrifice and ritualistic observance of the law that God was after but rather a heart that takes joy in doing the will of God.

> *I take joy in doing your will, my God, for your instructions are written on my heart.* -Ps. 40:8, NLT

The obedience God seeks is efficiently summed up by Jesus as love for God and love for our fellowman (Mark 12:29-31). Even though the scribe asked Him which was the most important commandment (singular), Jesus responds with these two commands. This teaches us that, in God's eyes, the two are inseparable. Love for others will be the natural outgrowth of true love for God.

Without the grace provided by the Holy Spirit, there is little chance of keeping the standards as outlined in the new covenant because these standards require *agape* love. Loving God and loving our neighbors requires the intervention of God Himself because it requires a heart change. Some people have a natural bent toward showing love to others, but often this is not done out of true *agape* love. Rather, the satisfaction one derives from doing something positive and admired by others drives the benevolent action. The failure of the law to enable men to obey through regeneration at the heart level is rectified by the gift of the Holy Spirit under the new covenant.

In essence, God has reversed the order of things through this new covenant by first blessing us with all spiritual blessings (Eph. 1:3), including the grace that enables us to be obedient. For this reason, having first received the blessing, we walk in a manner worthy of Christ (Eph. 4:1). Under the old covenant, the people were required to obey first, motivated by the promise of blessing. Under the new covenant, believers are motivated to obey because of the love poured out by God through Christ and the gift of the Holy Spirit. In other words, we obey because we have *already* been blessed, not in order to be blessed.

Obedience Kindled by Study of the Word

Obedience follows the washing of our hearts and minds with the Word. We must first be set apart *to* God, and then God helps us to be set apart *from* the world. To jump into obedience with religious zeal to do our best to follow the rules will only lead to despair and self-condemnation, or worse, self-righteousness and legalism. The process of changing our behavior starts with transforming our hearts. As we cooperate with the Holy Spirit, incrementally and over time, wrongful behaviors will cease to have power over us because of His grace. A dear friend once explained this at a church meeting, stating, "God doesn't show us every area that needs to be changed all at once because He knows we would freak out!"

> *Don't you see how wonderfully kind, tolerant, and patient God is with you? Does this mean nothing to you? Can't you see that his kindness is intended to turn you from your sin?* -Rom. 2:4, NLT

The moral code of God is part of the fabric of every human being prior to any searing of the conscience (see Rom. 2:14-16). The difference between the believer and unbeliever in this regard is that the believer has the Holy Spirit, who gives empowerment not to sin as well as conviction for unrepented sin. How then shall we live?

> *[Live] as children of obedience [to God]; do not conform yourselves to the evil desires [that governed you] in your former ignorance [when you did not know the requirements of the Gospel].* -1 Pet. 1:14, AMP

Love as the Basis for Obedience

There are many passages on obedience in the Word of God, but for now we will look to the New Testament writings to develop a theorem on obedience that incorporates the writers' general points. The basic premise is this: obedience must flow out of love and not robotic behavior.

> *And this is love: that we walk in obedience to his commands. As you have heard from the beginning, his command is that you walk in love.* -2 John 1:6, NIV

John gives us a loop: 'Love is walking in obedience to His command that we walk in love.' We will build on this verse by adding other relevant phrases regarding obedience. Each new phrase added will be expressed in italics in the theorem so we can better visualize the progression. The synthesized theorem that develops will give us a more comprehensive look at what walking in obedience born of love really looks like. [Note: There is obviously more than one way to do this.]

> *[W]e received grace and apostleship to call people from among all the Gentiles to the **obedience that comes from faith** for His name's sake.* -Rom. 1:5, NIV

This verse builds on the first and makes the loop look something like this: 'Love is walking in the *obedience that comes from faith* to obey His command that we walk in love.'

> *And we can be sure that **we know him if we obey** his commandments. If someone claims, "I know God," but doesn't obey God's commandments, that person is a liar and is not living in the truth. But **those who obey God's word truly show how completely they love him. That is how we know we are living in him**.*
> -1 John 2:3-5, NLT

SECTION 4 *WHOLEHEARTED LIFESTYLE OF OBEDIENCE*

'Love is walking in the obedience that comes from faith to obey His command we walk in love, *which is evidence we are truly His.*'

> *So everyone who hears these words of Mine and acts upon them [obeying them] will be like a sensible (prudent, practical, wise) man who* **built his house upon the rock**. -Matt. 7:24, AMP

'Love is walking in the obedience that comes from faith to obey His command we walk in love, which is evidence we are truly His, *having built our house upon His Word.*'

> *Therefore go and make disciples of all nations, baptizing them in the name of the Father and of the Son and of the Holy Spirit, and* **teaching them to obey** *everything I have commanded you.* -Matt. 28:19-20a, NIV

'Love is walking in the obedience that comes from faith to obey His command we walk in love, which is evidence we are truly His, having built our house upon His Word and *teaching others to do the same.*'

> **If you love me**, *you will obey what I command.* -John 14:15, NIV

'Love is walking in the obedience that comes from faith to obey His command we walk in love, which is evidence we are truly His *and love Him*, having built our house upon His Word and teaching others to do the same.'

> *Be doers of the Word [obey the message], and* **not merely listeners to it, betraying yourselves [into deception** *by reasoning contrary to the Truth].* -James 1:22, AMP

'Love is walking in the obedience that comes from faith to obey His command we walk in love, which is evidence we are truly His and love Him, having built our house upon His Word (*not deceiving ourselves into thinking we can be hearers only*) and teaching others to do the same.'

> *Whoever has my commands and obeys them, he is the one who loves me. He who loves me will be loved by my Father, and* **I too will love him and show myself to him**... *He who does not love me will not obey my teaching.* -John 14:21,24a, NIV

'Love is walking in the obedience that comes from faith to obey His command we walk in love, which is evidence we are truly His and love Him, having built our house upon His Word (not deceiving ourselves into thinking we can be hearers only) and teaching others to do the same, *resulting in the revelation of His presence in our lives.*'

> *[Y]ou have* **purified yourselves by obeying the truth** *so that you have* **sincere love for each other, love one another deeply, from the heart**. -1 Pet. 1:22, NIV

And finally, 'Love is walking in the obedience that comes from faith to obey His command we *walk in sincere love for our brothers, from the heart*, which is evidence we are truly His and love Him, having built our house upon His Word (not deceiving ourselves into thinking we can be hearers only), *having purified ourselves by obeying the truth*, and teaching others to do the same, resulting in the revelation of His presence in our lives.' This is the quality of love and obedience the Spirit desires to cultivate in the bondservants of God.

Supposed love for God that is not accompanied by obedience is not recognized by heaven as love at all. This feigned loyalty is viewed as lawlessness, a work of Satan. In the book of Revelation, there is no mistaking who true believers are—the people who are considered followers of Christ are those who obey Him (see also Rev. 14:12).

> *Then the dragon was enraged at the woman and went off to wage war against the rest of her offspring—***those who obey God's commands*** and hold fast their testimony about Jesus.* -Rev. 12:17, NIV

The Sermon on the Mount

The Sermon on the Mount records Jesus' description of what being a follower of God entails (see Matt. 5-7). For those who would be His disciples, Jesus first explained the blessings for those who embrace the character qualities pleasing to God (5:1-12). This transformation of our character can only come by washing our minds with the Word and the Holy Spirit's work of grace in our lives.

It should be evident to everyone we are believers, just as salt and light are known by virtue of their inherent qualities (5:13-16). We are not to parade our works before men to bring *ourselves* honor (6:1), but our works are to be seen by men to bring *God* honor (5:16). Salt and light are representative of the intrinsic qualities of Jesus' followers as revealed in the Beatitudes (5:1-12), affecting not only what we say and do, but what we think and desire. Without these qualities, the salt is not really salt, and the light we think we have is not light at all.

From there, Jesus unequivocally stated the commandments are still in effect (Matt. 5:17-20). He gave added dimension to the law, illuminating what it really means to actually follow God's commands in righteousness (Matt. 5:21ff.). God's commandments are to be understood within the context of grace, for the Lord does not turn the truly repentant away. This is not to be confused with cheapened grace, defined as willfully sinning and relying on a mistaken notion that God is obligated to forgive us if we say, 'sorry.' This is a false concept of grace, and we will lose our footing if we operate in this error. 'Anyone who sins with a high hand will be cut off...' (Num. 15:30; 2 Pet. 2:20-22; Heb. 10:26).

When discussing the commandments, we cling to the grace we have been afforded through Jesus so we run *to* Him instead of *from* Him when we stumble. Adam and Eve had not yet learned this when they hid from God. We have learned much since then, thanks to the revealed Word of God and the Holy Spirit. For the sincere, God longs to show compassion, and His mercies are new every morning.

Throughout the Gospels, Jesus qualified principles of the Levitical law as having some latitude with respect to the circumstances at hand. The Pharisees reduced everything to mere obedience without the flexibility necessitated by the qualities of compassion and discernment. If an ox falls into a well on the Sabbath, we need to get him out (Luke 14:5). If a male child is eight days old on the Sabbath, he will still be circumcised (John 7:23), and so on, as previously discussed.

Pharisaical Legalism

The Pharisees compounded their legalistic sin through their common practice of using rigid adherence to the law on minor points to preempt observance of weightier matters. Jesus defined the weightier matters of the law as being justice, mercy, and faithfulness (Matt. 23:23). For example, the Pharisees set aside gifts for God so as to excuse themselves from honoring parents with support since the funds they could have used to help them were already allocated to God (Mark 7:1-13). Even worse, the practice of tithing herbs took some attention to detail, yet they turned a blind eye to the many poor and needy around them (Matt. 23:23-24). To give a contemporary example, this would be the equivalent of being known at church as a good tither, but then not helping someone in need because there would be no tax credit for it. Jesus rebuked the Pharisees for allowing man-made traditions to nullify the Word of God (Mark 7:6-9,13).

In the Sermon on the Mount, we see the Word (Jesus) interpreting the Word for those listening to reveal the depth of what was written in the law. There is no fault in the law, but only in our understanding and practice of it (Rom. 8:3). The Lord never imparted the law so it would be a mere set of rules to be obeyed. The goal of the law is the transformation of the heart. Jesus directly challenged the oral traditions and ordinary interpretation of the law by the Pharisees, who had reduced the law to a set of behaviors and outward contrivances. Good outward behavior is not credited to us as righteousness if our thoughts and motives are selfish and evil. The deficiency of Pharisaism was that they defined sin as exclusively external in nature, devoid of any connection to the heart and will. Jesus called this hypocrisy.

> *They worship Me in vain, teaching as doctrines the commands of men.* -Mark 7:7, HCSB

In the woes pronounced to the Pharisees (Matt. 23), we get a picture of what obedience is not. It is not about being seen and honored by men or appearing righteous to all. It is about the heart posture of humility, compassion, justice, and faithfulness.

> *He has showed you, O man, what is good. And what does the Lord require of you but to do justly, and to love kindness and mercy, and to humble yourself and walk humbly with your God?* -Mic. 6:8, AMP

On several occasions the Pharisees castigated Jesus for not following their interpretation of keeping the Sabbath holy. Jesus' response came from the book of Hosea (6:6), answering the Pharisees the same way in which He answered Satan in the wilderness—with the Word:

> *And if you had only known what this saying means, I desire mercy [readiness to help, to spare, to forgive] rather than sacrifice and sacrificial victims, you would not have condemned the guiltless.* -Matt. 12:7, AMP

The Pharisees and scribes were consumed with the law and with demonstrating their perfect attention to the minutest details of even the oral law. Perhaps this was born of desire that searched for a solution to prevent another national exile. In their understanding, the exile came about from breaking the Mosaic law despite the fact those laws had *never* been kept perfectly, not even under Samuel or David. They ignored the prophetic voices that pinpointed the cause of their deportment: their hearts had strayed from God. Because they missed the heart of the matter, they developed a strict legalistic approach to the law. From the view of heaven, their practice was lawlessness. What natural man esteems highly (e.g., perfect performance, worldly accomplishment, monetary success, the praise of men, etc.) God disregards as contemptible.

> *Didn't Moses give you the law? Yet none of you keeps the law!* -John 7:19a, HCSB

A Higher Standard

In each of the issues raised beginning with the statement, 'You have heard it said...' (Matt. 5:21-48), Jesus revealed the higher level and deeper commitment He requires of His followers. His teaching explained the true essence of the law.

- Unchecked anger and insults incur the same judgment as murder.
- We don't have to commit sexual immorality to be guilty; merely allowing lustful thoughts to linger in our minds convicts us as guilty.
- Divorce is reserved for marital unfaithfulness, which can be understood to include the unfaithfulness that comes not only from immorality but also from fracturing the marriage bond through abuse (violates the marriage oath to 'love, honor, protect') or abandonment (violates 'til death do us part').
- Our words should come from a heart of integrity that needs no oath to validate the truthfulness of what we've said (see also Matt. 23:18-22).
- The correct response to situations which naturally provoke our desire to retaliate is meekness and mercy.
- As concerns our enemies, we need to imitate our Father who treats both the good and the evil with the blessings of the earth.

The Tongue

Our words can be a source of grief if we are not giving the Holy Spirit jurisdiction over our tongues. What we say issues forth from our heart and mind. Our only hope in this area is to follow the counsel of the Word: to purpose only to think on those things that are true, pure, noble, right, admirable, excellent, or praiseworthy (Php. 4:8). With the help of the Holy Spirit and the infusion of the Word, we have a chance to restrain our tongues.

> *Set a guard, O LORD, over my mouth; Keep watch over the door of my lips.* -Ps. 141:3, NKJV

The third commandment as given to Moses instructs us 'not to take the name of the Lord our God in vain, for the Lord will not hold him guiltless who takes His name in vain' (Ex. 20:7). Most of us have understood this to mean 'swearing' in the broadest sense of the word. But the type of swearing to which this passage refers is making an oath where we swear by God's name that we will do something. Swearing an oath in the name of God and then not following through on that oath profanes His name (Lev. 19:12). Jesus called this 'swearing falsely' (Matt. 5:33), and James warned us against taking any type of oath so we won't be condemned if we fail to follow through (James 5:12).

It can also be inferred that neither are we to use the name of God irreverently in casual conversation. To use profanity, which some call 'swearing,' is not a breach of the third commandment if God's name is not involved but rather falls in the category of unwholesome talk (Eph. 4:29). This manner of speech is unfitting for believers who are only to speak what is edifying. We will give an account for every careless (*argos*: idle, barren, useless) word we speak (Matt. 12:36-37).

> *If anyone considers himself religious and yet does not keep a tight rein on his tongue, he deceives himself and his religion is worthless.* -James 1:26, NIV

Examples of oaths that should not have been made are in both the Old and New Testaments. Jephthah's vow to sacrifice the first thing that came out of his house after his war victory cost him his daughter (Jdg. 11:29ff.). Saul's rash vow that would put to death anyone who broke the fast before sundown placed Jonathan under a curse and caused the other battle-weary men to transgress when they were too hungry to follow God's law regarding abstaining from meat with blood in it (1 Sam. 14:24ff.). And we never heard the outcome of the forty men who took oaths not to eat or drink anything until they killed Paul (Acts 23:12ff.), whose death did not take place until years later.

In fact, for many of us, it's best if we don't speak at all....

> *Even a fool is thought wise if he keeps silent, and discerning if he holds his tongue.* -Pr. 17:28, NIV

Give, Pray, Fast

In the next set of guidelines, we are called to a higher level in the way we execute good deeds and disciplines in our walk as believers. Jesus began His discussion on giving, praying, and fasting by saying *when* you give, *when* you pray, *when* you fast. These three are *givens* in a disciple's life, not variables. Jesus' presupposition is that His followers will naturally have it in their hearts to do all three, and for this reason each will be discussed in more depth in the following chapters.

Praying, fasting, and giving are *heart* issues, no matter what obstacles of rationalization and misunderstanding we may need to overcome to realize this. None are to be done to impress others but in secret so as to store up reward from God (*corporate* prayer, fasting, and giving are separate topics). Praying must be done in a manner that pleases God, not with an abundance of vain, repetitive words. The hypocrites do these things to be noticed and become our example of what *not* to do.

Satan corrupts our ability to follow through on Jesus' commands through our covetous nature. We covet wealth and things, which makes it problematic to give in a significant way. We covet our time and what *we* want to do with that time, making it virtually impossible to set aside time for prayer and meditation on the Word. We covet tasty and abundant food, evidenced by the fact we think about it so often, making it a tremendous challenge to fast. All three of these disciplines require relinquishing our wills and those commodities that protect our survival or further our personal interests.

In the parable of the Pharisee and publican (Luke 18:9-14), Jesus addressed the type of prayer, giving, and fasting that are a source of pride and therefore rejected by God. The practice of the Pharisee is an example of parading accomplishments before God as a garment of worth and achievement, one He views as a filthy rag, unfit for His presence because the emphasis is on self-righteousness. This is the way of Cain. Jesus told this parable to those who 'trusted in themselves for righteousness and viewed others with contempt' (v. 9). The publican, on the other hand, showed great humility before God, requesting only mercy. Jesus summed up the lesson by stating the publican went home justified because of his humility. If we exalt ourselves, we will be humbled by God when He rejects our life, just as He rejected Cain's offering.

We need to take this to heart because our obedience in the matters of giving, praying, and fasting must flow out of love and the realization that God has given us grace for obedience. When these actions flow out of relationship, gratitude, and humility, they are precious in God's sight and bear much fruit.

Behavior to Avoid

The Sermon then describes three behaviors to avoid: hoarding wealth, being anxious, and being critical of others. The remedy for hoarding wealth is to give generously to those in need. The solution for anxiety is to learn from the things around us that God is faithful and will take care of our needs. The prescription for the critical spirit is to understand our faults are to be viewed in our minds as *huge* in comparison with those things of which we are critical in others.

Both Jesus and Paul give caution to those in a position to confront someone who has gone astray. Jesus taught that even when our own faults have been dealt with and we can see clearly to move in the right spirit to help another (Matt. 7:1-5), we should not be hasty to reprove someone who does not have a teachable spirit, lest they turn on us with violence (Matt. 7:6; see also Pr. 1:7; 15:5; 23:9). Paul advised us to go about the process of confronting and restoring in a spirit of gentleness. The person steeped in sin must be approached with humility so we don't open an avenue for Satan to ensnare us through the sin of pride (Gal. 6:1).

From the command of both Jesus and Paul, only the mature who have dealt with their own sin issues and who walk in humility and compassion have the authority to confront another who is in sin. A person of this maturity would not think of going into a situation like this without prayer and leaning on his Beloved. This type of righteous judgment will not presume to judge by what is seen superficially, but will move forward with caution at the leading of the Spirit.

The vast majority of teaching in the Word regarding judging others warns us not to do so, especially in regard to matters of the law (James 4:11), religious practice (Rom. 14; Col. 2:16), and the worth of others based on distinctions not honored by God (James 2:4), though also including not judging others on sin issues because we are also guilty (Luke 6:37). Nowhere is this more clearly taught than in the story of the woman caught in adultery (John 8:1-11). Only those without sin would be allowed to cast a stone. After each one of her accusers dropped their stones and left, the only One qualified to throw a stone chose to forgive instead. *Selah*.

Most of us tend to minimize our own faults and magnify the faults of others. Judah found this out when he was ready to burn Tamar for her sexual impropriety (Gen. 38:24-26). Before acting out this hypocrisy, he came to the rightful conclusion that she was more righteous than he, for he was the father of her child (v. 26). It is the work of the Holy Spirit to convict of sin (John 16:8), which will lead to godly sorrow and repentance.

While most passages about judging others charge us not to do so, there are instances where we do make judgments in the church, as in the cases of: confronting someone living in unrepentant sin for which there are at least two witnesses (Matt. 18:16-17; 1 Cor. 5:11-13); exercising judgment regarding the meaning of teaching (Luke 7:43; cf. Acts 17:11); discerning the spiritual season (Luke 12:54-57); and mediating between two believers who are unwilling to reconcile their differences (1 Cor. 6:1-11). The end.

Keep Asking, Seeking, Knocking

> *But seek first the kingdom of God and His righteousness, and all these things will be provided for you.* -Matt. 6:33, HCSB

The next part of the sermon encourages us to keep asking for and seeking good things from the Lord, which by the witness of Scripture are the treasures of the knowledge of His Word, the Holy Spirit, righteousness, and wisdom. God praised Solomon for requesting discernment to govern wisely, forgoing the typical requests for money, possessions, honor, long life, or the destruction of enemies. As a result, God made Solomon wiser than any other king (1 Kings 3:9-12).

God has not changed—He still honors prayers for wisdom without finding fault in the one asking (James 1:5). Seeking counsel from the Lord is important, especially in major decisions. While the proverb 'there is safety in a multitude of counselors' (Pr. 11:14) is generally true, in some cases the majority consensus is incorrect (see 1 Kings 12:12-16; 26-28; 22:3-37; Hos. 8:4). The Holy Spirit and the Word provide us with the wisdom and discernment we need in any given situation. We are to seek these through prayer and sometimes fasting. King Rehoboam was judged as evil because he did not set his heart on seeking the Lord (2 Chron. 12:14). The Word records many occasions in which David inquired of the Lord for direction, an example for us to follow today (1 Sam. 23:2,4; 30:8; 2 Sam. 2:1; 5:19,23; 12:16; 21:1; 1 Chron. 14:10,14).

> *Look to the LORD and his strength; seek his face always.* -Ps. 105:4, NIV

God has promised that those who sincerely seek Him will find Him (Pr. 8:17; Jer. 29:13). By seeking the Lord, we demonstrate our reliance on His wisdom as well as accede our limitations. Seeking the wisdom and discernment from above demonstrates humility; the very act of requesting wisdom acknowledges our lack (Pr. 18:15). The Lord is good to those who place their hope in Him, not natural ability (Lam. 3:25; 1 Cor. 1:26-31). This requires faith that God keeps His Word and rewards those who diligently seek Him (Heb. 11:6).

Earnestly seeking God involves the passion of the heart as well as keeping His commands and following His ways (Ps. 119:2-3). The Word reminds us we have an active role in our quest for righteousness. We are to do righteous acts through demonstrating love for others by looking out for the poor and needy as God would. In addition, we are to 'break up' our unplowed ground so we can receive His Word. God's promise is that all who seek Him in this way will be showered with His righteousness, which is Christ (see Hos. 10:12).

For those who place their trust in the Lord, He is a refuge in times of trouble (Nah. 1:7). As we approach the close of the age, it is wise to remember Zephaniah's counsel:

> *Seek the LORD, all you humble of the land, you who do what he commands. Seek righteousness, seek humility; perhaps you will be sheltered on the day of the LORD's anger.* -Zeph. 2:3, NIV

Treatment of Others

> *So in everything, do to others what you would have them do to you, for this sums up the Law and the Prophets.* -Matt. 7:12, NIV

Paul advised us that what we do on disputable matters (issues unrelated to sin) boils down to a matter of loving our brother enough to restrain ourselves from doing something that would bother his conscience and doing everything from a posture of faith. This brings us back to our theorem on love and obedience: 'Love is walking in the obedience that comes *from faith* to obey His command that we walk in *sincere* love...'

An example of obedience that comes from faith is illustrated when Jesus tells Peter to let down his nets one more time (Luke 5:1-11). From a purely pragmatic analysis of the request, a carpenter is telling an experienced fisherman how to catch fish. If this carpenter had not also been the Messiah, mocking derision of the command would have been justifiable. But Peter knew Jesus after the Spirit and not the flesh. He had faith Jesus knew what He was doing. This act of obedience was rooted in submission to the Word. We need to walk in this revelation as Peter did.

Jesus told the Pharisees to learn the meaning of the prophet Hosea's statement, 'I desire mercy and not sacrifice.' Repeatedly, the Pharisees chose sacrifice by their rigid adherence to the law while matters of mercy were ignored. In the mind of the Pharisee, acts of mercy would interfere with their ability to have a perfect record of obedience. Why do it if it's not required by statute and we don't get credit for it? This type of hypocrisy is obvious to all except those with the pharisaical mindset.

To make matters worse, the Pharisees condemned those who prioritized mercy over their own traditional interpretation of the law (see Matt. 12:1-8). This is evident in the church today. For example, a believer who stops at the store on Sunday to pick up groceries for an elderly member of the congregation is condemned by those who view this as 'Sabbath breaking.' Likewise, a woman who wears jeans to help a disabled church member clean house and complete outdoor chores is condemned by church members who view this as 'dressing like a man,' prohibited in Levitical law. Which do you think the Lord would judge as acting in love, the merciful 'Sabbath breaker' or the critical legalist? The benevolent 'cross-dresser' or the judgmental 'expert in the law'?

Exhortations

Jesus then challenges us in four areas:

- **Enter by the narrow gate** (Matt. 7:13-14). The command in a parallel passage (Luke 13:24) is to strive, *agonizomai*, which means 'to exert great effort, to wrestle, to persevere in order to achieve the goal.' Passive Christianity is a contradiction in terms. We are to wrestle with our flesh until we bring it under subjection to the Spirit, and wrestle with the Word until we gain understanding.
- **Be wary of false prophets by discerning the fruit of their lives** (Matt. 7:15-20). Rather than the fruit of the Spirit, these will display strife, envy, fits of anger, rivalry, jealousy, selfish ambition, and all manner of sin, causing division, dissension, and enmity (Gal. 5:19-21).
- **Remember to cultivate intimacy and not be a mere performer** (Matt. 7:21-23). Those who only do things to garner the praise of men rather than quietly fol-

lowing the leading of the Spirit have two strikes against them: 1.) they are disobedient when they only do 'spiritual' activity to be seen by men, and 2.) they are not connected to or abiding in the Head.

- **Build your faith on the sure foundation of the Word of God** (Matt. 7:24-27). The Bereans were of noble character because they searched the Word daily to see if what they were being taught was true (Acts 17:10-11). It is the sum of God's Word that gives us a sure foundation, not little grains of truth taken out of context to construct a religion of our choosing. This is called sand and will cause us to stumble in the day of testing.

Everything Jesus did was based on what He heard from His Father. Relationship is the basis for obedience, not a to-do list that requires a strong will. We can only *sh'ma*, hear and obey, if we are in right relationship with God. Jesus is our perfect example, for He only did and said what the Father commanded (John 12:49-50).

In the same manner, we must learn to stay in step with the Holy Spirit as He guides us into doing all God has ordained for us to do (Eph. 2:10). This is the only way we will bear fruit for His kingdom and bring God glory. Abiding in Jesus, not adhering to biblical 'formulas' or law, keeps us connected to the Head so the Spirit can guide us on the race marked out specifically for us. Why don't formulas work? Because we are living stones with unique shapes, not standardized bricks.

Closing Thoughts

The hallmark of the bondslaves of Christ is their love for one another displayed in practical expressions of that love. For someone in the body of Christ to harbor hate is a sure sign that eternal life has escaped his grasp (1 John 3:11,14-18). Jesus demonstrated sacrificial love toward us, and as His body, He expects us to do the same.

> *My little children, let us not love in word or in tongue, but in deed and in truth.*
> -1 John 3:18, NKJV

Chapter 13

When You Give

> *But when you do a charitable deed, do not let your left hand know what your right hand is doing, that your charitable deed may be in secret; and your Father who sees in secret will Himself reward you openly.* -Matt. 6:3-4, NKJV

Jesus expected His followers to give generously out of love and compassion for the poor and needy as well as to those who have contributed to our spiritual growth (Gal. 6:6). This is a work of grace because few are inclined to do this in significant ways apart from the work of the Holy Spirit. The Spirit not only imparts grace for the desire to give, but transforms our character to the point where we are free from the covetousness that prevents us from giving the way God intended. Through this process, we slowly come to realize stewardship means we are merely entrusted with what belongs to God; no longer do we assume ownership of it.

This process is a psychological transfer of wealth. Realizing we are bondservants helps us understand everything we have belongs to our Master because slaves do not own property. All wealth placed in our hands is entrusted to us to carry out His will. As slaves, we in turn know our needs will be met without expectation our wants will also necessarily be supplied, though the generosity and kindness of God provide for this as well.

Steve Gregg points out that not only our wealth belongs to Him but also our time. "The Christian is a "steward," or "manager," of somebody else's (God's) possessions. He is not in a partnership with God in which God holds 10 shares and he holds 90. In coming to Christ, the repentant sinner surrenders everything to God, and claims ownership of nothing (Acts 4:32). From the moment of his conversion, the believer becomes responsible to manage every asset (monetary or otherwise) in the interests of his Master's profit. Those seeking to reserve a share of their lives for themselves need not apply (Luke 9:23)... All of the believer's time and all of his possessions belong to God; a fact foreshadowed in ceremonial law by the requirement of giving Him a representative token of each (one day of his week, and one tenth of his possessions)."[1]

Modeling Generosity

Giving reflects the nature and character of God. Jesus set aside His riches and became poor for our sakes so we could become (spiritually) rich. We must take His example to heart and strive to pattern our lives after His example. The riches that His poverty brought to man include reconciliation with God, the gifts and empowerment of the Spirit, hope for the future, and all the spiritual blessings of the believer's life. Because God has modeled generosity to His children and has given them the grace to willingly desire to be generous, He expects them to demonstrate generosity to others. Paul advised the Corinthians to encourage generosity in giving, not as a command but desiring that they excel in this gift as well as in the other spiritual gifts (see 2 Cor. 8:7-15). The genuineness of their faith would be tested in the area of giving, a sentiment James echoed in his letter (James 2:14-17).

According to Paul, only gifts given eagerly would be acceptable (2 Cor. 8:12, NLT). Giving was not to be done as a pledge (based on what they did not already have) but according to what they had. Paul was quick to add he in no way wanted their giving to put others in financial ease while leaving the giver in a state of financial hardship (v. 13). His point in the matter was that provision among believers should be equitable (v. 14). Financial wealth among believers must be viewed from God's perspective: as a gift and not the result of personal prowess, just as all the other gifts the Lord distributes for the edification of the body are to be viewed. In this way, the wealthier believers would share their wealth and possessions with those who have not been likewise gifted so that 'he who gathers much does not hoard, and he who gathered little has enough' (v. 15).

Only with this perspective can we understand the role of wealth in a believer's life. It is not a possession any more than the gifts of prophecy, preaching, or teaching are to be viewed as the possession of those so endowed. Do those with the gifts of teaching or preaching benefit personally from their gift in ways above and beyond what they share with others? Absolutely, just as those with monetary wealth will most likely have a higher standard of living when it comes to material things.

Those with spiritual wealth are expected, out of their abundance, to have a ready supply of insight and encouragement to share with whoever they meet, not selfishly hoarding that insight to themselves as if it were a commodity of value they earned, keeping the excess tied up in investments or for retirement. Did they spend themselves in laborious study over the Word? Definitely, just as the wealthy individual applied himself to his business or trade through his labor. But it is God's strength and grace working through both that increases the supply through the work given to each.

Where would we be if those with the gifts of teaching, preaching, and prophecy hoarded them as commodities to enrich only their own personal lives? Would we not view this as a selfish and foolish waste of the gift the Lord has given? Wouldn't we reason with them that they must share what the Lord has given them so others can benefit from their spiritual wealth in knowledge, revelation, and insight? Why is it, then, that we view the gift of giving so differently than the other spiritual gifts? Those who have been given the power to acquire wealth must use their gift of giving to edify the body, just as the teacher and preacher use theirs. We will be judged on how faithfully we administered the gift(s) we have been given. Having abundant material wealth must be viewed as a spiritual gift like any other.

On matters of giving, Paul explained it is not the amount that matters because each is to give from what he actually has. We are not to give to the point that we are now in need of assistance ourselves with regard to necessities. Many have given to affluent churches, where the staff are very well compensated as evidenced by their lifestyle and spending habits, while these needy givers cannot keep up with basic utilities and food. Paul clearly states giving is not to burden the giver in order for others to be in prosperous ease (2 Cor. 8:13).

At times, giving becomes burdensome as the result of a presumptuous pledge or 'faith promise.' Some people have gone into debt they cannot pay back, charging their gifts on credit cards—not wise, heroic, or biblical. If we are charging financial gifts without being able to pay them off, we have one of two problems: we have a cash flow problem that clashes with our unrealistic expectation of giving, or we have personal spending habits coupled with a generous heart that are at war with the checkbook, or a combination of the two. While there are occasions where the Lord prompts us to give in faith, apostolic wisdom tells us to base our regular giving on what we already have.

Equitable Giving

In the economy of God, things are purposefully inequitable in order to test us. The poor are tested in their faith that God will provide despite their circumstances, as well as in the arena of envy and covetousness. The wealthy are tested in their cooperation with the Spirit to be generous and in the areas of covetous spending, hoarding for self, and pride in self-sufficiency.

Both Nebuchadnezzar and Herod took prideful credit for their status. Sanity was taken from the first, and the other was struck dead on the spot and eaten by worms (Dan. 4:28-33; Acts 12:21-23). The sin of pride is not something trivial. We must acknowledge it is God who grants power to acquire wealth (Deut. 8:17-18) and that everything we have and give was first taken from His hand (1 Chron. 29:14).

> *There is a **grievous evil** which I have seen under the sun: **riches being hoarded by their owner to his hurt**.* -Ecc. 5:13, NASB

Paul wanted the church to exemplify the principle that 'he who gathered much did not have too much, and he who gathered little had no lack' (2 Cor. 8:15; cf. Ex. 16:18). For this to be true, those enriched with money and goods are to share with the needy so they are not found with 'too much' on Judgment Day. By this, the poor receive the necessities of life at the hand of the wealthy believers, despite having gathered little. The Lord desires equity in the fellowship of believers so there are no needy persons among us, evidence we actually believe all we have belongs to God. This was beautifully practiced in the early church (Acts 4:32-37).

It may take some doing to cleanse our minds of the notion that wealth denotes God's favor and approval or that it merely results from hard work and discipline. There are many poor who work just as hard if not harder but for a much smaller return. Is it wrong to be compensated for the added responsibility and accountability that come with running a business? Not at all. But it is what we do with the added compensation and our heart posture regarding the wealth with which we have been entrusted that will incur the approval or judgment of God in the end.

For those who study the Word, does not their knowledge also come with hard work and commitment? Do those with understanding of the Word take credit for that knowledge? Some do, but most would think it prideful to take credit for the obvious gift God has given them to comprehend the Word. Most who have received understanding are eager to share what they have acquired. If we have been given monetary wealth, we have to ask ourselves if we have this same eagerness to share what we have been given.

Many believers have taken the wealth with which the Lord has entrusted them and spent it on a higher standard of living for themselves without involving God in the decision. We must remind ourselves that Jesus gave up His wealth and became poor to meet our need to be reconciled to God. Do not read this to mean material goods and prosperity are wrong. The Lord intends that we enjoy the things He gives us, which we will only be able to do if we view all supply as His and if our hearts have truly adopted the nature of a bondservant. It is when we crave a higher standard of living and make this the goal for which we labor that it becomes unrighteous. Anything born of covetousness is not of God.

Giving Born out of Love

God does not honor giving as a sound business principle. Our giving is to be done eagerly from the heart and not reduced to an outward obedience tainted by inward greed for the hope of gain, or by fear of loss as a consequence for *not* giving. Many secular foundations have covert agendas, though on the surface they may appear compassionate and benevolent. All our behavior must be motivated by and result from love and faith.

> *And if I give all my possessions to feed the poor... but do not have love,* ***it profits me nothing.*** -1 Cor. 13:3, NASB

The centurion Cornelius is one of the best examples of a truly generous heart that caught the attention of God (see Acts 10). He and his entire household venerated and obeyed God. He prayed continually and gave much alms to the poor. An angel was sent to him with a personal message from God:

> *Cornelius, your prayer has been heard, and your acts of charity have been **remembered in God's sight**.* -Acts 10:31, HCSB

Cornelius' faith in God and love for God's ways naturally focused his attention on the poor and needy. The Word tells us God repays those who give to the poor. Cornelius was repaid through an angelic visitation, an appointment with Peter, and the salvation of his whole household. That is what is known as a 'high yield.'

> *Whoever is generous to the poor lends to the LORD, and he will repay him for his deed.* -Pr. 19:17, ESV

Generosity is not measured by the amount of the gift but rather defined by the love and faith of the giver, as exemplified in the story of the widow's mite (Mark 12:41-44). The box in which she placed her offering was not a place for tithes but for voluntary offerings for temple upkeep, wood for sacrifices, or perhaps even alms for the poor. Jesus judged her offering as greater than that of the heavy contributors because she gave all she had to live on. This proved she trusted God to provide her with those things she needed despite her lack of resources. This is faith. Here again, God takes notice of the sacrificial giving of a person with a trusting and generous heart. Trusting, for she did not concern herself with her lack of stores but relied on the Lord to take care of her (1 Tim. 5:5). Generous, because she gave all, not holding anything back for herself.

Our giving is estimated in His sight by the spirit in which it is given. Seizing this teachable moment at the offering chests in the temple, Jesus taught that all men, rich and poor, are in a state of equality before the Lord because it is the degree of heart engagement that is noted in giving, not the size of the gift.

[Note: We can also make a *drash* here on the desires of people to contribute to the Lord's work in areas they are not abundantly endowed. In the example of the widow, though bestowed with great faith, she also desired to give money despite her lack of monetary resources. Likewise, there are those who desire to edify the believing community by sharing the small morsel they have just learned in the Word. To despise what they have shared because it is not as profound or deep as that which was shared by one rich in insight by the gift of God is to show the same type of contempt as those who would view the widow's offering as trivial.]

Compassion Causes Us to Excel in Giving

> *Remember this: Whoever sows sparingly will also reap sparingly, and whoever sows generously will also reap generously.* -2 Cor. 9:6, NIV

Paul exhorted believers to excel in the ministry of giving, affirming that giving is important to God (see Rom. 12:8; 2 Cor. 8:7). We can be generous no matter what our income level. Determining whether we have sown sparingly or generously is determined by neither the actual *quantitative* amount we give nor the *percentage*, but by what we have given in comparison with the portion we hold back for ourselves (above and beyond our needs) and the heart posture with which we perform our giving before the Lord. Giving from right motives is critical, deciding in our hearts what to give rather than being motivated by an external standard or pressure.

> *Each one must give as he has decided in his heart, not reluctantly or under compulsion, for God loves a cheerful giver.* -2 Cor. 9:7, ESV

What we keep for ourselves above and beyond necessary food and clothes is a matter for discernment, as Steve Gregg explains: "We must also acknowledge that God would provide for the needs of His servants and their families. Therefore, a certain amount of our income must be devoted to the feeding, housing and clothing of our families (1 Tim. 5:8). Nor is there any forbidding of a few things for enjoyment alone (1 Tim. 6:17). How many such things? That is between the steward and his Master, and is not for another to judge (Rom. 14:4). However, we must be on our guard against our own pervasive tendency to judge our own actions (and expenditures) more favorably than the facts would suggest. In eternity, our rejoicing will be proportionate to our self-denial in this life and our generosity to the poor and to the work of God."[2]

Love and compassion will not allow us to buy ourselves a recreational boat when someone we know can't afford to fix the rundown vehicle they need for work. Love and compassion will not allow us to build a lighted basketball court on our property when a physically disabled church member is about to have his electricity turned off for not having the money to pay the bill. No, love and compassion will not allow this to happen—but covetousness and an entitlement spirit will. Sadly, these are real examples that took place in churches we've attended.

The only remedy for a covetous heart, which twists Scripture until it is convinced the accumulation of things is the entitlement and privilege of the child of God, is to give until it doesn't cause a tug-of-war in the heart anymore. This can take some time, but the Lord is patient with us as we cooperate in this area and will bring forth the character change needed for this to be accomplished.

Giving in the Early Church

All of the giving in the early church had to do with relief for those in need in their fellowships, teachers and followers alike. The requests made for collections were always done on behalf of others and not self. Jesus' instructions to His disciples before He sent them out to proclaim the gospel of the kingdom did not include instructions for collecting monetary wages, but for receiving wages in the commodities of food and shelter. This is one of the reasons why they were not to take a purse with them for the storing of money.

> *Do not take a purse or bag… Do not move around from house to house.* -Luke 10:4,7, NIV

Moving from house to house was viewed as searching for the person with the most favorable financial disposition. The disciples were not to engage themselves in finding the most lucrative situation but to seek out those who were hospitable. The gift of giving often included hospitality. The author of Hebrews instructed believers not to neglect or refuse to extend hospitality to strangers, for some have unknowingly 'entertained angels' because of this (Heb. 13:2). This is a hard directive in this age, for it is not wise to allow strangers into our dwellings without clear discernment from the Lord.

The early believers also concerned themselves with the plight of their fellow believers in other parts of the world (Rom. 15:26). There is no command to give to your local church first and then elsewhere, though it seems the proper principle is to take care of the poor in our families first (1 Tim. 5:4,8). Paul taught that those who did not care for their families were worse than unbelievers. Caring for the poor in our local fellowships and the poor among the believers worldwide came next, as the early church practiced. Providing relief for the unsaved poor of the earth, with no strings attached, witnesses to the love and generosity of God. *Voice of the Martyrs* is a reputable organization that earnestly looks out for and supplies the profoundly needy among the body of Christ worldwide with the necessities of life as well as encouragement that they are not alone, that others care for them, and that they are not forgotten. This is an outstanding organization to consider when we desire to help our brothers and sisters in need across the earth.

Heart Engagement Comes First

Jesus was delighted at Zacchaeus' change of heart when he declared he would give half of his possessions to the poor (Luke 19:1-9). In the early church, believers were known to sell property and donate all the proceeds for the needs of their brothers (Acts 2:44-45; 4:32-37). [Note: It cannot be stated with certainty what kind of property this was. In some cases, this may have included a personal residence, but in others it may have been more likely a field or perhaps a second residence.]

The delight God has over those who give generously stems not from the amount or the percentage, but because of the joy and compassion that prompts the giver to share in God's heart for the needy of the earth. In the early church, widespread persecution of believers resulted in their exclusion from trade membership, the outcome being a devastating loss of business revenue. As a result, pervasive poverty among believers became normative, and compassion and generosity became key virtues in the early church for its edification and survival. Believers alive in the time of great tribulation will again experience this as a direct result of exclusion from buying or selling (Rev. 13:16-17).

God honors and takes note of truly compassionate giving borne out of desire and not from compunction or for show. Jesus rebuked the Pharisees for their self-motivated, overtly law-oriented method of giving performed to appear righteous before men. In fact, these attentive tithers were inwardly filled with greed by God's evaluation. Only by giving what was 'inside' to the poor (giving up their greed and the money they clung to in their heart) would they be clean (Luke 11:39-41).

Give in Keeping with Income

> *Now about the collection for God's people: Do what I told the Galatian churches to do. On the first day of every week, each one of you should set aside a sum of money in keeping with his income.* -1 Cor. 16:1-2a, NIV

The act of giving is to be done on a regular basis in keeping with our incomes. This is not the same as tithing, which can best be understood with an illustration. Using simple figures, we will compare the giving habits of someone making $24,000/year ($2,000/mo.) to someone making $240,000/year ($20,000/mo.), each with a family of four.

In the first example, let's say the typical housing allowance at this income level is $500 for rent. Food for four, using the allowance allocated for food stamp users at $200/person/month, would equal $800/month. Take away FICA, Medicare, health insurance and misc. taxes from the gross pay (they will probably pay little, if any, Federal tax after deductions and exemptions, but not so with state and local taxes), and they will net about $1800/month. Subtract the food and housing allowance and we have $500 left. After subtracting for phone, gas for the house, gas for the car, electric, water, and trash collection at roughly $350/month, we now have $150 left each month for giving, clothes, incidental expenses like home and car maintenance or repairs, possibly a car payment, car insurance, dental visits, school supplies, medical deductibles, etc. It is easy to see that this family is near or below the poverty line.

Expecting such a family to give ten percent is unrealistic and would place them in further hardship. In fact, tithing would force this family to go into debt. While $200/month ($50/week) for giving may seem like nothing to some, it would deprive this family of food, necessities, or meeting their utility expenses. This is why the poor among the Israelites were not required to tithe but in fact received part of the tithe. Their endeavor to give at all puts them in the same class as the widow at the temple treasury or the poor but generous Macedonians. The Macedonian believers were filled with joy and a spirit of generosity despite the economic trials they were encountering themselves. Paul said they gave freely and far beyond their means for this special collection (this was not an ongoing commitment; see 2 Cor. 8:1-3).

The wealthier family, on the other hand, will have a greater tax issue, taking home a smaller percentage of the check but will still have much greater latitude. Let's say they keep $168,000 (70%), average for those who have charitable contribution deductions, business expense deductions, and so on, that reduce the amount of tax liability, leaving them with $14,000/month on which to live. They may or may not have a house payment, their financial status affording them the opportunity to pay cash for their house, but they will still have property taxes and insurance, perhaps totaling about $2000/month. They probably eat out more, spending the equivalent of $20-$30/person each day on food and drink (e.g., Starbucks), an average expense of about $3200/month. Utilities for a bigger house, additional wireless services, cable TV, etc. add $800 to the expenses. The grand total comes to $6000/month, more or less. If they tithe on their income, this adds another $2000. Higher insurance costs for the newer cars, expanded clothes budget, the family vacation, gym membership, salon appointments, entertainment, etc. will add another $3000 or more per month in expenses, bringing the total to $11,000/month. At the end of the day, they still have an additional $3000/month to allocate, more than the other family had to start with.

TITHING COMPARISON

EXPENSES	$2,000/mo	$20,000/mo
Tithe	200	2,000
Taxes, Medicare, FICA, etc.	200	6,000
Housing	500	2,000
Food	800	3,200
Utilities	350	800
TOTAL BASE EXPENSES	2050	14,000
Amount left for clothing, travel, house/car maintenance, car insurance, dental/medical, house/school supplies, etc.	-50	+6,000

In the one family, attempts to fulfill an unrealistic expectation regarding tithing may benefit the church a little, but it would cause this family financial affliction, contrary to apostolic wisdom regarding giving. The other family could reasonably give a double if not a triple 'tithe,' especially if they didn't spend quite as much on the less needful things. They could even be like Zacchaeus, giving half of their income to the poor each month if they scaled back their lifestyle for the aid of their fellow believers and the advancement of the kingdom of God.

Some have been unwise in their spending and investing, leaving them with debt obligations that preempt generosity. We cannot ignore our obligations to our debtors in order to give beyond what we have. It is a poor witness to the secular community if we contract services and don't pay for them just so we can 'make the tithe.' Wisdom is trampled when we take what we owe for goods and services and give it to the church instead, especially if the decision is based on fear of the supposed consequences of not tithing. Not paying our debts violates the Lord's command to keep our word, letting our 'yes' be 'yes' and our 'no' be 'no' (Matt. 5:37).

> *The wicked borrow and do not repay.* -Ps. 37:21, NIV

> *Fulfill your obligations as a citizen. Pay your taxes, pay your bills, respect your leaders.* -Rom. 13:7, THE MESSAGE

James exhorted us to help the poor and not just sympathize with their plight by offering mere words of comfort if we have the means to provide them with what they need (James 2:15-17). Faith that doesn't produce good deeds is not faith. We are to share what we have with those in need even if it isn't much—half a sandwich is better than none (see Luke 3:11). Those who have been truly hungry at some point in their lives (unrelated to voluntary fasting) understand this.

Neither are we to give of our resources in order to be paid back. It is very disconcerting to observe a common business practice where those who have wealth are given discounts or better deals unrelated to the volume of the transaction than the lower income people who truly need the break. The Word restrains us from showing this type of partiality, yet our business traditions are allowed to nullify the Word of God. Jesus told us to be generous to those who we know cannot pay us back (Luke 14:12-14; see also James 2:1-9).

There are times when the circumstances of life bring people to the place where they no longer have adequate resources, or when dramatic natural events and economic downturns devastate whole regions through no fault of those involved. To say, 'What a shame,' and do nothing when we have the power to help ignores the Lord's repeated command in both the Old and New Testaments to take care of the poor among us. To say, 'they must have deserved it' ignores Jesus' teaching that disaster does not come on the most deserving of judgment. Rather, He reminded us that *all* deserve judgment unless they repent. Any specific disaster is meant to remind the living of what awaits the unrepentant (Luke 13:1-5).

Warn and Teach Idle People

The discussion of taking care of the poor excludes helping the capable but crafty or lazy who will not work, for the Word also tells us that if a man *will not* work and idles about, he should not eat or partake in fellowship. These are not the true poor of the earth. They creep into the church to exploit the compassionate nature of believers. This is one of the reasons Jesus exhorted His followers to be shrewd in dealing with the worldly.

- Use wisdom in dealing with outsiders (Col. 4:5a).
- Do not fellowship with any brother who is idle and does not live according to apostolic teaching (2 Thes. 3:6).
- Warn those who are idle (1 Thes. 5:14).
- Believers must learn to apply themselves to good deeds, including honest labor, so they will be able to meet urgent needs, and not be idle, unproductive, or unfruitful (Titus 3:14).
- Only those who work are allowed to eat (2 Thes. 3:10).

Believers must also be wary of those holding cardboard signs, begging for cash. Several years ago, I stopped in response to a couple holding a sign, 'Will work for food.' I needed some help at a job site and offered them work. They hesitated but accepted. When we arrived at the site, I showed them the work I wanted them to do—neither complicated nor hazardous. They kept exchanging glances and after twenty minutes pulled me aside to tell me it wasn't worth their while to work if I was only going to pay them the going labor rate. 'Most people just give us money.' They made it clear their goal was neither work nor food—it was cash. The words on their sign were only meant to solicit empathy, not for the expectation of actually working to earn their food.

A police officer friend stated that many if not most of these have alcohol and drug addictions, which is where the money will go if we donate without prior knowledge of their true situation. Some fight over the more profitable corners for begging in bigger cities, even going so far as scheduling turns so each can get their 'fair share' of the take. Outsiders who try to get a piece of their action are treated harshly if not beaten outright. Some will bring out a cane, leg brace, or walker from the cart in which they keep their belongings, knowing this will solicit more sympathy and therefore more revenue. Because of the lucrative nature of this type of begging, one employed man was caught coming in from the suburbs, changing into worn old clothes, and begging after he finished his regular hours of work. Many of the beggars surpassed the police officer in what they 'earned' each day.

Humanistic compassion or a false sense that Scripture tells us to help *every* poor person cannot dictate believers' giving habits. The whole of Scripture encourages us to always be generous to the poor but cautions us against helping those who choose to be idle. Helping the poor may simply entail sharing the gospel with them.

There are many schemes to tug at our emotional heart strings in the area of giving. We are not to become callous toward the poor because of the craft of some, but we are to imitate Jesus, working only as the Father directs. This takes far more energy and watchfulness than making a blanket policy, for example, to *always* or to *never* give to someone with a cardboard sign. We cannot afford to be idle in our help to the poor, and neither can we be idle in dealing shrewdly with those who would deceive us.

Giving to the Church: Biblical Foundation

The rabbis expected to work at a trade to support themselves and their families, devoting as much time as possible after hours to the study and teaching of the law. "Every Jewish boy was expected to learn some trade. Rabbinic tradition declared that 'whoever does not teach his son a trade is as if he brought him up to be a robber.'"[3]

Paul was acutely aware of his right to expect a living from the gospel as an itinerant apostle, but he would not use this right for the sake of the gospel (see 1 Cor. 9:14-23). In *The Wycliffe Bible Commentary*, George E. Ladd explains this clearly: "It was customary for Jewish rabbis not to receive pay for their teaching, and therefore, Paul, who had been raised as a rabbi, had learned the trade of tent-making... Paul reminded the Ephesians of his custom of making tents not only to support himself but to provide for the needs of others with him… The main objective of giving in the early church was to provide for the needs of the poor brothers rather than to support the preaching of the gospel as is the case today."[4]

In his parting words to the elders of the Ephesian church, Paul shared wisdom the church should heed today. He exhorted the elders to be on guard over the flock, for even from among the elders would come those who distort the gospel message to draw disciples to themselves. With tears he spent three years warning, advising, and exhorting them to be alert and on their guard (Acts 20:28-31).

As he committed their welfare to the Lord, Paul seemed to suddenly switch gears by talking about money, stating that he coveted no man's money. He reminded the elders that he worked to meet his own needs and the needs of those with him. Paul cautioned the elders about coveting financial compensation. Rather, as his example testifies, he admonished the elders that working diligently to provide for the poor is preferable to having others provide for them (Acts 20:33-35; see also 2 Cor. 12:14).

By working to support himself, Paul distinguished himself from the typical itinerant preacher of his day. "This policy [working night and day] not only reflected a desire to be financially independent of those among whom they ministered, but it also marked them off from the ordinary religious traffickers of the day, and showed the converts a good example."[5] Working as a tent maker during the week in particular seasons of his ministry, Paul devoted Sabbath days to teaching in the synagogues. This gave him a rather full week, requiring that he labor with all the strength Christ gave him. Jesus' own comments about the Sabbath indicate God the Father and He likewise work on the Sabbath for the furtherance of the kingdom. The primary type and shadow of creation week with a seventh day of rest is a picture of the millennial reign of Christ that follows the 'week' of labor. In other words, the true 'Sabbath rest' will not arrive until Jesus returns. Until then, we work as He does.

The fact that Paul told these elders, who were not itinerant preachers, to follow his example is evidence his advice pertains to all who shepherd the flock. The specific conjugation of the verb 'assist' (Acts 20:35) indicates Paul was directing the elders to *personally* support the poor from their *own* means, not from the offerings collected from the believers under their charge. This is a far cry from our practice today, where rights, benefits, and privilege are the trademarks of the employment packages offered to church leadership in many of the more affluent congregations.

Receiving full-time support is neither condemned nor mandated as the will of God for the church or the furtherance of the gospel (1 Cor. 9:11-12). Church leaders did not receive a regular salary from God's people until the days of Constantine. Giving was focused on the relief of the poor up to that time. Today we have affluent churches with no want of resources and, at the same time and in the same city, food pantries, rescue missions, and shelters in dire need of goods. In these same churches, there are people struggling to keep their heads above water financially, laboring as Paul did for the basic necessities of life and trusting God to supply what they are unable to provide for themselves.

> *To the present hour we hunger and thirst, we are poorly dressed and buffeted and homeless, and we labor, working with our own hands.* -1 Cor. 4:11-12a, ESV

It is obvious that working in a service or trade keeps us walking in humility. When we cease to be involved in mundane labor, we often become out of touch with humility and humanity. Active service in common everyday chores can keep pride in check (or reveal its presence if we are incensed by doing something beneath our level of 'anointing'). When we are familiar with our trade (unlike high pressure jobs requiring all of our attention and mental focus), the need to fully concentrate on our tasks is no longer needed, affording us extra prayer time. Maybe Paul prayed in tongues more than anyone because he spent so much time making tents (1 Cor. 14:18-19).

The demands of today's ministry schedules most often limit any outside involvement in a trade of any sort. In my grandfather's day, he could both pastor a church and run a small farm. The pastor of the local church we attended in high school worked during the week as a butcher for a local grocer. Today, however, the demanding sheep who don't want to feed themselves, who crave the attention of the leaders, who spend a good deal of time airing opinions, who won't spend time in the Word which would release them from their needy behaviors, who demand programs to keep them interested and involved, and so forth, use up all the time and strength of the typical pastor. In these instances, the congregation will have to support the pastor they are wearing down because he can't get anything else done.

Supporting the pastor and the local church is important, but once again, to make a blanket policy for oneself about giving to the church does not allow for the input of the Holy Spirit. Under the new covenant, we are not to function robotically, one of the negative effects of the old covenant, but as bondservants who pay attention to their Master's voice. "The support of the Kingdom's ministers is similarly an expression of our duty to love God, to seek first the Kingdom of God (Matt. 6:33)... There is such a variety of ministry—some more and some less-needy, and some more, some less-worthy of support—that a conscientious steward will do a bit of prayerful research before committing the Master's funds to a given appeal for assistance. In the end, the discharge of one's stewardship requires a great deal of prayer and leading of the Holy Spirit. It is nothing like such a simple matter as writing a check to the local assembly (which might be looking to replace the carpeting for the third time this decade) for a tenth of one's paycheck."[6]

Watchman Nee also places the stewardship of money in the context of New Testament teaching, especially in the matter of supporting leadership. His view stresses we give not out of obligation to support the ministry, but out of love. Nee states that according to the new covenant, believers have no *obligation* to be responsible for ministers' needs.

Neither are those who minister the Word to demand such support but to trust God to move on the hearts of those being taught to generously give what is needed. This requires faith God will provide. No faith is required when we have a contract, the mainstay and security of the hireling[7] (see Jdg. 17-18), the covetous, and the weak in faith. "God has no use for an unbelieving worker, nor has He any use for a loveless church."[8]

Because our churches today more closely resemble corporations run like any other business than the early church, we have lost our ability to hear what the Spirit is saying to the church through the New Testament writers in this regard. Whether the solution is to return to the house churches as in the early days or not, I do not know, though many are doing this. But with our current manner of assembling and 'doing the Lord's business,' it is difficult, if not impossible, to steward giving in the manner the apostle Paul described. While we are to assist with the needs of our spiritual mentors, Paul moderated this principle by teaching we are to be satisfied with basic needs, defined as food and clothing. It can be assumed he was not envisioning silk suits or extravagant dining, let alone providing ministers with costly homes and vehicles, a 403b, private school tuition for their children, and expense accounts. One pastor I knew refused to be moved by all the benefits offered him. When the younger pastors rejoiced that the church gave them a regular salary and benefits, rather than just part of the 'take,' this faithful pastor testified, 'The Lord has always taken care of me, no matter what.'

Building Projects

In the matter of building projects and other efforts requiring special donations, we have a few stories in the Old Testament record where collections were taken for these purposes. When extraordinary projects were placed before the Israelites (constructing the tabernacle, building the temple, and repairing the temple), a free will offering was collected. The emphasis was on the willingness of the giver whose heart was stirred by the project (Ex. 35:5,21-22). The result was ample supply for the needs presented.

> ***The people bring much more than enough*** *for the service of the work which the LORD commanded us to do. So Moses gave a commandment... "Let neither man nor woman do any more work for the offering of the sanctuary." And **the people were restrained from bringing,** for the material they had was sufficient for all the work to be done—**indeed too much**.* -Ex. 36:5-7, NKJV

Because it was God's plan, the people gave generously—so generously, in fact, they had to stop the people from giving any more because they couldn't contain the gift. It would be hard to envision a ministry today turning away gifts because the need had been met.

If generous giving is absent for our church's building project, we have to ask ourselves, "Is God really in this?" If we are convinced that He is and the giving remains scanty, the next question is, "Why are these people so stingy?" Avarice and covetousness are rampant in the church, albeit insidious. Most church goers in the West work hard to get ahead to live a lifestyle they think they deserve, resulting in a seared conscience when it comes to differentiating needs from wants. With added appeals for money, many turn a deaf ear because their debt obligations for their 'needs' leave no room for extra giving.

So how does the leadership respond to this? In many churches, this leads to initiating proven tactics and methods to compel people to give. God calls these strategies *extortion*. Extortion in the body of Christ is a sad indication of where we are spiritually. By definition, extortion is 'to obtain money by manipulation, intimidation, threats, force, or abuse of authority.' The Lord warned the Israelites not to make their living by extortion, for the Lord repays people according to what they have done (Ps. 62:10-12). Many believers are afraid *not* to give because of the curses pronounced on the noncompliant. This is done by using passages intended to warn and rebuke Israel for breaking the stipulations of the old covenant. Those who use these passages teach that all who give are to expect reward, God's special favor, and blessing as well as avoid the curses of sickness and poverty stated in Deuteronomy and Malachi.

If our giving is motivated by guilt, fear, compulsion, greed, or pressure, we cannot hope it will be approved by God. When we give generously out of love, faith, compassion, and the leading and discernment of the Holy Spirit, there are great and precious promises for us, most of which are not monetary. The return we receive is evidenced by the grace we are given for the multiplication of good works, righteousness, and the treasures of His kingdom. The result is that many give thanks to God, and the giver is made rich 'in every way' so he can be generous 'on all occasions,' indicating wealth that includes but goes beyond mere monetary compensation, for money is not the remedy for every situation (2 Cor. 9:8-15).

It is no small matter that people will praise and give thanks to God for the generosity of His people. Giving to missions and evangelistic efforts allows each of us to participate in the preaching of the gospel to the poor. This the Lord will reward handsomely. Pure religion is to take care of those in need:

> *Religion that God our Father accepts as pure and faultless is this: to look after orphans and widows in their distress and to keep oneself from being polluted by the world.* -James 1:27, NIV

Tithing

[Note: Before beginning this section, I would like to give a special word of thanks to Dr. Russell Kelly, Robin A. Brace, and Dr. Kluane Spake. Their articles and resources on tithing have been very helpful. Throughout this section I have woven their ideas with my own. Each of us had many of the same thoughts and arguments on the subject, making it difficult to know who came up with which ideas first. Rather than riddle every thought with a footnote, I would invite you to explore their articles on your own as referenced in the endnotes.[9] Perhaps we can agree the Holy Spirit can impart like ideas in the same season to multiple believers who reach the same conclusions independent of one another. The bottom line is that I am grateful for their work and insight, giving me the much needed witness of the Spirit to write this portion of the chapter.]

"In the century following the apostolic age, the Christians understood that tithing had been replaced by full surrender to God."[10] There is no evidence the apostles taught new believers, who were mostly Jewish at that time, to pay the tithe to them instead of the Levitical priests. The early believers met in synagogues with no mention that the Jewish believers brought in tithes to the leadership there rather than the Levites in Jerusalem.

Tithing is a disputed matter in the body of Christ today. Some believe tithing expired with the fulfillment of the law in Jesus. Others base the continuation of this principle on the premise that tithing existed before the law was written. Still others argue tithing is for Israel alone and must come only from the land of Israel. *Let the games begin.*

Before we make up our minds on this issue, scriptural evidence must be weighed so each can be fully convinced in his own mind (Rom. 14:5). It has taken me a few decades to get to the point where I am fully convinced. Hopefully this discussion will help you accomplish this sooner. You may not agree with the conclusions offered here. But in the end, let each practice from a stance of faith, being fully convinced in his own mind.

Abraham's Tithe and Ancient Tithing Customs

The first mention of tithing in the Bible is the tithe Abraham gave to Melchizedek after going to war and rescuing Lot (Gen. 14). The Lord had endowed Abraham with great wealth. On meeting Melchizedek after the war, Abraham did not give a tithe to him of his personal possessions, but the Word records he gave a tenth of all the plunder from the war against the kings. Abraham gave the other ninety percent of the spoils away. Notice Abraham's payment of a tithe is only recorded once and followed the ancient pagan custom of tithing war spoils.

"The custom of tithing did not originate with the Mosaic law, nor was it peculiar to the Hebrews. It was practiced among other ancient peoples."[11] It was common practice to tithe the spoils of war not only in the Middle East among the pagan inhabitants, but in Athens, Rome, China, and Africa as well.[12] The practice of tithing and its widespread practice in the ancient world is well documented.

Not only was tithing practiced in pagan religion; tithes were also given to honor the local priest or ruler with a tenth of war spoils. "Giving a portion of one's profit or the spoils of war was known in the ancient world from Greece to China. Gifts were made as religious offerings, or given to a political authority as tribute or tax. Religious and political uses often combined since it was common to associate earthly and divine authority. Donation of a tenth portion, or tithe, was common apparently because most people counted in tens, based on ten fingers."[12]

Abraham's tithe had more to do with the customs of the day than following any divine or universal law of giving. Indeed, no such law for worshipping God had yet been written. In the book of Joshua, we learn Abraham's fathers served foreign gods on the other side of the Euphrates until God took Abraham from there and brought him to Canaan (Josh. 24:2-3). The pagan practices of the time were standard operating procedure honored by the majority of inhabitants with no record that it was a custom to be handed down for honoring the one true God.

If we are using Abraham as our prototype for tithing, keep in mind the practice was the custom of the culture of his time and the only recorded incident of Abraham tithing involved the spoils of war. We must also keep in mind that animal sacrifice and circumcision likewise predated the law as a common practice by God-fearing people and pagans alike, but no one has come forth to argue these practices should continue as a point of requirement for New Testament faith. How then do we keep a double standard to use this argument to justify the enforcement of tithing?

Another man of ancient time who had the favor of God was Job. God highly esteemed Job (Job 1:1,8; 2:3). He was the greatest man of the people of the east (Job 1:3) and endowed with great wealth. He gave generously to the poor, widows, and orphans, turning away no one in need (Job 29:12,16; 31:16-25). There is no mention he tithed, but he did offer sacrifices to God on a regular basis. Is anyone in the church today making an argument for offering sacrifices based on this righteous man's practice? Obviously not. It is important to note God considered Job blameless, not testifying to any practice of tithing but testifying to his generous giving to those in need. This is at the heart of New Testament giving.

Jacob's Vow

The second mention of tithing in the Bible comes from a vow Jacob made to God (Gen. 28:10-22). In a dream, Jacob saw a stairway extending from earth to heaven with angels ascending and descending on it. The Lord stood above the stairway and promised to multiply Jacob's descendants and give them the land on which he was lying. God also promised to bless the entire earth through Jacob and his offspring. The Lord further promised He would watch over Jacob wherever he traveled and bring him back to the land. When he woke up, Jacob realized the solemnity of the encounter and made an *if-then* vow to God that acknowledged and honored God as His source.

> Then Jacob made a vow, saying, "**If** God will **be with me** and will **watch over me on this journey** I am taking and will **give me food to eat** and **clothes to wear** so that I return safely to my father's household, **then** the **LORD will be my God** and ... of all that you give me **I will give you a tenth**." -Gen. 28:20-22, NIV

The next mention of tithing comes in the recording of the Levitical law with no further mention of Jacob's vow. Recall that in God's eyes, the name 'Jacob' also represented his promised descendants, the nation of Israel (a similar argument made in Heb. 7:9-10). Because Jacob's vow involved the promises God made to him and his descendants, we see a connection in the exodus story. God delivered Jacob's descendants from Egypt and brought them back to the land promised to their fathers, feeding them all the years they walked in the desert and keeping their clothes from wearing out (Neh. 9:21). This miraculous provision fulfilled God's promise to give Jacob food and clothing on his journey, accomplished vicariously through the whole company of his descendants. Jacob's vow would be fulfilled by the nation of Israel through adherence to the laws of tithing. God gave them manna and a land flowing with milk and honey. The tenth part belonged to God primarily because the land belonged to God, but the law can also be seen as enabling the fulfillment of Jacob's vow through his descendants, who many times are simply called 'Jacob,' especially in the prophetic writings.

Tithing Under Mosaic Law

Though the law for tithing was given at Mt. Sinai, there is no record of tithing until the Israelites entered the land forty years later. God makes clear that the land of Israel is His and though He has given it to the Israelites to steward, He expects His ownership to be acknowledged through the giving of tithes (see 2 Chron. 7:19-20; Ps. 85:1; Joel 2:18; 3:2).

> *The land, moreover, shall not be sold permanently, for* **the land is Mine**; *for you are but aliens and sojourners with Me.* -Lev. 25:23, NASB

> **Every tithe of the land**, *whether of the seed of the land or of the fruit of the trees, is the LORD's; it is holy to the LORD.* -Lev. 27:30, ESV

The Levites received no inheritance in the land. Their portion from the land would come in the form of the tithes set apart for God. The Lord would be the portion for the Levites (Num. 18:20-24; Deut. 18:1-2). The only tithe the Levites paid came from a tenth of the tithe received from the people, and this portion was given to the priests.

There is no evidence that the Levites actually tilled the ground to raise produce on the pasture lands set aside for them around the Levitical cities. These lands were solely for their herds and flocks.[14] The Hebrew word *sadheh* is used in Nehemiah 13:10 to denote the 'fields' the Levites were given around the cities. This word does not necessarily describe a crop field. The basic meaning is that the land is not mountainous, but level, like a meadow, for cultivating, pasturing, building, or other use.

The Levites were dependent on the tithes for produce as were those who typically had no inheritance of land in Israel: the orphans, widows, and foreigners who had no share in the land (Deut. 26:12). Whatever the case, these were all in need of sustenance, and the laws of tithing provided food for them. The basic principle of tithing is that those who have inherited part of God's land and benefit from it pay a tithe. Those who have no inheritance of land and are in need receive the tithe.

SECTION 4 *WHOLEHEARTED LIFESTYLE OF OBEDIENCE*

Three Different Tithes

According to Josephus, there were three tithes prescribed for the inhabitants of Israel. There is agreement among many historians this was the case, found in the Book of Jubilees and in the works of later church writers, Jerome and Chrysostom. Others believe the tithes prescribed in the third year replaced the solely Levitical tithe, which has been called the first tithe, or that the tithe was distributed differently depending on the year in the Sabbatical cycle. These views, however, are held by the minority.

"Let there be taken out of your fruits a tenth, besides that which you have allotted to give to the priest and Levites. This you may indeed sell in the country, but it is to be used in those feasts and sacrifices that are to be celebrated in the holy city: for ***it is fit that you should enjoy those fruits of the land which God gives you to possess***, so as may be to the honour of the donor... Besides those two tithes, which I have already said you are to pay every year, the one for the Levites, the other for the festivals, you are to bring every third year a third tithe to be distributed to those that want; to women also that are widows, and to children that are orphans."[15] (emphasis added)

All three tithes involved providing food for those in need: the Levites who had received no inheritance, the poor who had little or nothing with which to celebrate the festivals, and the poor in the towns where the farmers lived. While the first tithe was set aside for the Levites, a portion of the second and third tithes was shared with the poor. God made provisions in His law to ensure the poor were not excluded from temple activities just because they could not afford the offerings. These laws also prevented the abuse of the poor, which is rampant in our day (see Lev. 14:21-22; 25:6,25-28,35-38; 27:8; Deut. 14:28-29; 15:7-11; 24:10-22; 26:12; Mal. 3:5).

The command that the tithe consist of food is significant since money was clearly extensively used in the ancient world, the word and related words occurring over 230 times in the Bible (silver, shekels, coins, etc. included). Reference to these is found over thirty times in Genesis alone and more than sixty times in the Books of Moses, the majority of which pertain to laws for fines, dowries, taxes, and vows. Banking and usury laws were mentioned because these practices had already been established. Food was used for bartering purposes only after monetary resources had been depleted (see Gen. 47:15-17). Of the remaining passages related to money, over seventy are found in the New Testament, yet the Pharisees were still tithing food commodities.

Despite the presence of established banking and widespread use of money in the ancient world, the tithe consisted of food as prescribed by Levitical law. Even in the case of the Festival tithe, where the farmer from a great distance away could exchange his tithe for money before leaving to make the journey easier, the Levitical code instructed the farmer to use the money to buy whatever food and drink he liked when he arrived in Jerusalem (Deut. 14:24-27). He and his family would celebrate before the Lord with the things he had purchased. From this we can safely conclude one cannot legitimately make an argument for applying the law of tithing to giving *money* instead of *food* from an erroneous view that the law was originally defined in the context of an agrarian/barter economy. There is provision, however, for the individual who wanted to keep some of his tithe and bring money instead, but this required adding a stiff twenty percent monetary penalty to discourage the practice (Lev. 27:31).

In the case of a special project such as the repair of the temple, however, freewill *money* gifts were accepted:

> *All the money of the sacred things which is brought into the house of the LORD, in current money, both the money of each man's assessment* (i.e., the temple tax) *and all the money which any man's heart prompts him to bring into the house of the LORD...* (to) *repair the damages of the house wherever any damage may be found.* -2 Kings 12:4,5b, NASB (parentheticals added)

Different from Firstfruits

Many times the tithe is confused with the offering of firstfruits. The firstfruits, unlike the tithe, were meant only for the priests, not for the Levites. Firstfruits were a relatively small food offering given of what could be placed in a hand-held basket of the first produce that came from the ground (Deut. 26:1-10). The firstborn was also dedicated to the Lord and given to the priests, though the firstborn of man and unclean animals was to be redeemed with money (Num. 18:15-18). These offerings went directly to the temple for use by the priests on duty.

The following passage sums up the differences nicely. The passage has been split into sections, the first for the priests and the second for the Levites who serve in the temple (from Neh. 10:35-39, ESV).

Firstfruits for the priests at the temple (vv. 35-37a):

> **We obligate ourselves to bring the firstfruits** *of our ground and the firstfruits of all fruit of every tree, year by year, to the house of the LORD; also to bring to the house of our God,* **to the priests** *who minister in the house of our God, the firstborn of our sons and of our cattle, as it is written in the Law, and the firstborn of our herds and of our flocks; and to bring the first of our dough, and our contributions, the fruit of every tree, the wine and the oil, to the priests, to the chambers of the house of our God;*

Tithes for the Levites in the towns, including the tithe of the tithe that went to the priests (vv. 37b-39):

> *... and* **to bring to the Levites** *the* **tithes from our ground**, *for it is the Levites who collect the tithes in all our towns where we labor. And the priest, the son of Aaron, shall be with the Levites when the Levites receive the tithes. And* **the Le-**

vites shall bring up the tithe of the tithes *to the house of our God, to the chambers of the storehouse. For the people of Israel and the sons of Levi shall bring the contribution of grain, wine, and oil to the chambers, where the vessels of the sanctuary are, as well as the priests who minister, and the gatekeepers and the singers. We will not neglect the house of our God.*

From the Levitical tithes in the towns, the Levites brought portions to the temple in Jerusalem: the best tenth of what they received was given to the priests (Num. 18:25-32) with the remainder of the portion allocated for the Levites serving on rotation (see 1 Chron. 24-25). The Levites were not to eat of the firstfruits or the best tenth of the tithe allocated for the priests, but only of the remaining tithe.

As with the tithe, the firstfruits could only come from the produce or offspring of the land of Israel. The firstfruits and tithe were narrowly defined in the manner we have discussed. Part of their very definition is that these required donations: 1.) come from God's land, Israel, 2.) are food products of that land or taken from the flocks and herds in the land, and 3.) are only paid by the Israelites who had received an inheritance of land to farm and/or raise livestock (perhaps also includes those who had gardens).

Those who did not make their living off the land, for example, carpenters, weavers, fisherman, hired servants, perfumers, and so forth, were not required to pay the tithe. God's admonishment for the Israelite landowners to take care of the Levites was in effect for as long as they inhabited His land (Deut. 12:19). This suggests the converse—if they were removed from the land, this requirement would no longer be in effect.

It is interesting to note while the offering of the firstfruits came from the beginning of what was increased, the tithe came from the sum total at the end of what was brought forth (see Lev. 27:32). The distinction is more obvious in the case of tithing the increase of the herd or flock where the instruction required the tenth animal to be tithed. For example, if a man's flock increased by eighteen, only one animal was given for the tithe. If only increased by nine, no tithe was required. If by twenty-one, two were given.

Leviticus records that the tithed animal, 'the tenth that passes under the rod, whether good or bad,' was not required to be unblemished (Lev. 27:33). The requirement to be unblemished was only for offerings brought before the Lord, whether burnt, freewill, peace, or especially vow offerings (Lev. 22:17-25). The firstborn of the flock was brought to the temple to be sacrificed and eaten, unless it was blemished. The blemished are the only firstborn animals from the flock eaten in the towns (Deut. 15:19-23).

Israelite Landowners Alone Paid the Tithe

Those who received an inheritance of land in Israel were to view the privilege of tending the land as a means to serve the purposes of God through the gift of giving, albeit as a regulation through the giving of tithes. It is the precise equivalent of a ten percent property tax, though levied on what the land produced each year rather than being based on a fixed property valuation, as practiced in the U.S. The land, after all, belongs to God and they were the stewards of it. As such, it was God's desire that as the appointed stewards, they were to bring from their storehouses the portions prescribed. The first tithe provided the Levites their portion while on temple duty since they had no land inheritance. The second tithe supplied food for the landowner and for sharing with others at the festivals in Jerusalem. The third tithe provided sustenance for the Levites and the poor in the towns. This parallels the gift of giving assigned by the Spirit to believers in the new covenant.

The system of tithing reveals the generous nature of God as well as His compassion toward those who are not appointed to generate wealth, who are not of Israelite descent, and whose circumstances or station in life prevent them from providing themselves with necessities. God intended that those under the law would understand His purposes and remember they were stewards over what He had entrusted to them. To whom much is given, much is required in the service of God through serving others.

But what started out as a means to serve God and those in need ended up being a station of privilege. Subsequently, the landowners viewed their wealth as favor and entitlement for personal gain, resulting in contempt and condescension for the less privileged and hoarding the commodities with which God had entrusted them. The poor went unfed, the house of God fell apart, the needy were sent away empty-handed, and the Gentiles did not learn of God's goodness, concern, and compassion. The designated tithers did not understand what God was trying to teach them through the laws of tithing and how they related to stewardship, servanthood, and true community.

Tithing After the Exile: Nehemiah and Malachi

The following is a classic text used in defining the necessity of tithing. In our examination of this passage from Malachi, we will limit the discussion to the grammatical historical context. While this may take some time, looking at the original intent of the text is essential for arriving at a valid conclusion. Keep in mind that God reminded the Israelites they were under a curse for not following the Levitical tithing laws—the curse for those under the old covenant alone. There is no more curse if we are in Christ.

> *'How have we robbed you?' In your tithes and contributions. You are cursed with a curse, for you are robbing me, the whole nation of you. Bring the full tithe into the storehouse, that there may be food in my house. And thereby put me to the test, says the LORD of hosts, if I will not open the windows of heaven for you and pour down for you a blessing until there is no more need. I will rebuke the devourer for you, so that it will not destroy the fruits of your soil, and your vine in the field shall not fail to bear, says the LORD of hosts.* -Mal. 3:8b-11, ESV

The setting takes place in Israel after the second wave of Jewish captives in Babylon had returned to the land under the leadership of Ezra in 458 B.C. The people had received the Deuteronomic curses for breaking the covenant through the events prior to and including the exile from the land of Israel. Ezra, Nehemiah, and Malachi were contemporaries at a time when Israel was seeking to rebuild itself. Under Ezra's leadership, the men of Israel put away their foreign wives. Thirteen years later, Nehemiah arrived on the scene to rebuild the broken walls of Jerusalem.

In the midst of rebuilding, Nehemiah discovered the poor were being abused economically by the noblemen. He put an end to this practice, citing himself as an example to follow (see Neh. 5:15-19). Because he feared God, Nehemiah stated he did not 'lord over the people' by demanding his right as governor to exact a food allowance from the people. Moreover, rather than take tribute, he provided food from his own means for the many who sat daily at his table.

Note how closely Nehemiah's comments parallel Paul's on the subject of the rights and privileges of leadership. In the same vein of wisdom, both sacrificed their rights for the welfare of the people. "He disdains to take his legal right as governor to require a subsidy from the people for his official expenses. He did not domineer the people but rather paid for the expenses of his table from his own money. He did not consider common labor beneath his dignity as a governor, but diligently applied himself to the work on the wall."[16] The fear of the Lord kept Nehemiah from lording over the people by taking money from them, unlike the noblemen who thought nothing of charging usury and enslaving those indebted to them. Despite the challenges, the wall is finished in the month of Elul (Neh. 6:15), in time for the fall holy days the following month.

All Israel gathered for the Feast of Trumpets, and Ezra read from the 'Book of the Law.' Nehemiah recorded that the people were attentive to all he read and understood the teaching. Two days after celebrating the Feast of Tabernacles, the people gathered together to fast and mourn for the sins committed against God's covenant and the condition of their nation as a consequence (see Neh. 9). At the end of this time of confession and prayer, the leaders covenanted in writing and the people joined them in *entering into a curse* if they did not fulfill their oath to obey all God's commandments:

> Because of all this **we make a firm covenant in writing**... all who have knowledge and understanding, join with their brothers, their nobles, and **enter into a curse and an oath to walk in God's Law** that was given by Moses the servant of God, and **to observe and do all the commandments of the LORD** our Lord and his rules and his statutes. -Neh. 9:38; 10:28b-29, ESV

The remainder of Nehemiah 10 gives the main points of their vow before the Lord:

- They will not marry foreign wives;
- They will honor the Sabbath;
- They will honor the Sabbatical year and cancel debts;
- They will pay the temple tax for the temple work/upkeep;
- They will bring in the firstfruits/firstborn for the priests;
- They will bring the tithes for the Levites;
- They will not neglect the house of God.

We find under the firm yet righteous rule of Nehemiah, the people had rededicated themselves before God, 'entering into a curse and an oath' to serve Him as His commands required, particularly noting the oath to tithe (Neh. 12:47).

The historical record shows two separate periods in which Nehemiah governed Jerusalem. Nehemiah recorded the tithe was paid during his first governorship, from 445 B.C. (Artaxerxes' twentieth year, Neh. 2:1) to 433 B.C. (Artaxerxes' thirty-second year, Neh. 13:6). At that time, Nehemiah returned to the palace of King Artaxerxes, staying for a debated period of time.

Some years later, when Nehemiah heard reports of the corruption taking place in the temple, he returned with the king's permission to begin his second term as governor. The conditions he found when he arrived in Jerusalem, as described in Nehemiah 13, are in the list that follows. Notice Tobiah was given the room that normally held the food for the Levites, workers, and priests. We do not know if the people failed to give the tithes, or if the priests took them after giving Tobiah the room.

- Tobiah had been given the room in the temple used for storing the Levitical tithes and the priests' portions;
- The Levites had returned to their pastures because they did not have adequate provision, thereby leaving the temple unattended;
- Merchandising and regular labor were allowed on the Sabbath;
- The men of Judah had once again taken foreign wives.

It is during this time of backsliding, the interim between Nehemiah's two terms, when Malachi most likely entered the scene, though we have no definite dates to be certain. But the similarities between the conditions in Judah and the rebuke Malachi delivers are too well-matched to ignore. This is a very basic summary of the points made in the book of Malachi:

- the priests brought animals that were blind, sick, lame, or taken by violence as offerings to God (1:8,13);
- the priests no longer honored God's name with true instruction, nor by walking uprightly (2:5-8);
- Judah has married foreign women, divorcing the wives of their youth (2:11-16);
- they mocked God's Word and doubted His justice (2:17);
- they robbed God of the tithes and portions for the workers in the temple (possibly including a rebuke for giving the tithe storeroom to Tobiah; 3:8-10);
- they said it is vain to follow the Lord because nothing changes (3:14-15).

Those who feared God took Malachi's words to heart. Their conversations were recorded in God's book, and He called them His treasured possession—those He will spare in the day of judgment. The Lord's final word exhorted the people to remember the commands given through Moses, lest He strike the land with a curse (Mal. 3:16-4:6).

Remember, the returned exiles entered into a *curse* and an *oath* to follow God's statutes in Nehemiah's first term. By not following the statutes they pledged to honor, they brought the curse on themselves, which included drought, pestilence, poor crop yields, sickness, miscarriage, plunder—all of which would leave them confused, frustrated, and oppressed (see Deut. 28:15ff.). The whole nation was under a curse because they did not follow through on their oath (Mal. 3:9).

The book of Malachi is a rebuke, but it is the rebuke of a Father pleading with His people to open their ears to hear what He is saying, examine their hearts and behavior, and turn so these conditions could be reversed. Legally, they had agreed to the dire consequences if they failed to follow through on their oath. But thankfully, the Lord is slow to anger and abounding in kindness. He warned them of their untenable position and counseled them to return. The Lord wanted them to test Him at His Word that if they would only follow His commands and honor their oath, He would give them everything they needed to prosper.

The blessing resulting from 'opening the windows of heaven' refers to rain for their crops 'until there is no more need' (cf. Gen. 7:11; 1 Kings 8:35). In this way the whole nation would prosper as promised in Deuteronomy:

> *The LORD will* **open for you His good storehouse, the heavens, to give rain** *to your land in its season and to bless all the work of your hand.* -Deut. 28:12a, NASB

Judge for yourself. Is the Malachi passage exhorting new covenant believers to tithe money? Has anyone discovered apostolic teaching that even alludes to incurring a curse for not tithing? Does not the New Testament clearly state that because we are in Christ, the curse for violating the Mosaic law was nailed to the tree, and thus we are no longer under *any* curse? How can a curse from an expired covenant have any effect on believers under the new covenant, where no such curse is ever mentioned?

> *Christ has redeemed us from the curse of the law by becoming a curse for us, because it is written: Cursed is everyone who is hung on a tree.* -Gal. 3:13, HCSB

In *The New Treasury of Scripture Knowledge*, Jerome Smith had this to say about tithing: "The LORD commanded the Israelites to 'Bring the whole tithe into the storehouse, that there may be food in my house...' (Mal. 3:10). Christians are often urged to tithe based upon a mistaken appeal to this Old Testament text, which is wrested out of its rightful context, when applied to such a purpose... The storehouse is clearly the temple, not the church... Taken in context this passage lends no support to the mistaken doctrine of 'storehouse tithing,' whereby Christians have been directed to restrict all their financial giving to their own denomination or local church, or as a variation, church members have been directed to pay the tithe to the local church, and restrict giving to outside organizations to amounts over and above the church tithe... Tithing is not taught in the New Testament as an obligation for the Christian under grace... Because we are not under law, but under grace, Christian giving must not be made a matter of legalistic obligation, lest we fall into the error of Galatianism."[17]

Jesus' Teaching on Tithing

There are three passages in the Gospels where tithing is mentioned. The first two are parallel texts in which Jesus rebuked the tithing Pharisees for their lack of attention to the weightier matters of the law (see second text at Luke 11:42).

> *Woe to you, scribes and Pharisees, hypocrites! For you pay tithe of mint and anise and cummin, and have neglected the weightier matters of the law: justice and mercy and faith. These you ought to have done, without leaving the others undone.* -Matt. 23:23, NKJV

The historical context of this passage helps us understand Jesus' instruction to the Pharisees that they should do both: observe the weightier matters as well as follow the tithing laws. Notice that even though the economy in Jesus' day was based on money, the tithe was still being paid in agricultural products as required by the law given to Israel. Remember also Jesus was speaking to Jews, the only ones to whom the Mosaic law was given (cf. Matt. 10:5-8 where Jesus commands the disciples not to evangelize the Gentiles).

The third appearance of tithing in the Gospels is in a parable (Luke 18:9-14). As with the first two, this passage teaches that God does not honor arrogant holiness, an outward show of obedience without proper heart engagement, but rather a humble and contrite heart. The Pharisee in the parable trumpeted his attention to tithing, yet Jesus proclaimed this man did not receive approval from God.

Tithing does not automatically place us in position to receive blessing, as many have taught. Jesus chided the Pharisees for their legalistic attention to tithing without paying attention to the more important issues of justice, mercy, faithfulness, and the love of God. He also rebuked them for teaching the people if they devoted a gift to God, they were released from the charge to take care of their fathers and mothers. Neglecting the needs of our families and parents so we can pay the tithe and give offerings that 'count' is not approved by God (Mark 7:9-13).

There are only three examples of tithing in the Gospels, and each is the subject of rebuke. Jesus pronounced woes on each of the tithe payers in the examples given, the Pharisees, because they were filled with hypocrisy. Does this not contradict contemporary teaching, which asserts that those who pay tithes are *automatically* blessed and have the favor of God?

Apostolic Teaching on Giving

The teaching on giving from the book of Acts forward gives us clarity on the manner of giving practiced under the new covenant. Tithing is not even mentioned in the passages where the apostles teach on the subject of giving. In fact, Paul spends two chapters explaining proper giving under the new covenant and doesn't once mention tithing (2 Cor. 8-9). While we cannot make an argument from silence, does it not seem odd that the contemporary church has made its foundational principle for Christian giving on a topic the apostles do not even mention when discussing giving?

Because those who became believers under the new covenant had no regulations with which to govern the behavior of the new converts, the apostles set out under the guidance of the Holy Spirit to break ground for the emerging *ekklesia*. The basic precepts established by the apostles in the New Testament sought to provide for order in meetings, break down barriers in order to foster fellowship between Jew and Gentile, and put safeguards in place to prevent (as much as possible) division, heresy, and disorder.

The prevalent passages on giving under the new covenant reveal the following:

- Believers had all things in common to show compassion to the poor among them (Acts 2:42-47).
- They did not view their possessions as their own (Acts 4:32-37).
- Giving a gift is to be done generously; the ability to give is apportioned by the Spirit (Rom. 12:6-8).
- We are to excel in giving as the poor Macedonians did (2 Cor. 8:1-7).
- We give to prove our love is genuine (2 Cor. 8:8,24).
- We give according to what we have, not what we don't have (2 Cor. 8:12).
- The giver is not to be burdened/afflicted so another can be in ease (2 Cor. 8:13).
- Those with much should share with those with little (2 Cor. 8:14).
- We must handle gifts of money honestly, both to honor God and to be seen as having integrity by men (2 Cor. 8:20-21).
- We must always be ready and willing to give (2 Cor. 9:1-5).
- We need to sow generously (not a statement re: quantity, but rather in proportion to ability) to reap bountifully (2 Cor. 9:6).
- We give as we have decided in our heart (2 Cor. 9:7).
- We are not to give reluctantly or out of compulsion (a required amount or percentage), but from a cheerful heart (2 Cor. 9:7).
- We share in the fruit of the endeavor we help support (Php. 4:17).
- Givers will have their own needs met (Php. 4:19).
- The self-indulgent are dead while they live (1 Tim. 5:6).
- We show our faith by giving to those in need (James 2:14-20).

That's it. No command to give under compulsion or as a legal requirement, the precise definition of tithing under the law. No exhortation to bring all the money into the storehouse; no command to give of the 'firstfruits' (eisegetically interpreted to mean the first ten percent of our gross income); no hint of a curse for not giving; no statement that we will be blessed with luxurious living if we do—only that our needs will be met and we will always have a supply to give to others. We must learn to be content with what we have; otherwise we will fail miserably at these new covenant principles of giving.

Giving under the new covenant is based on freedom, similar to the freewill offerings in the law of Moses, and this freedom is to be exercised on behalf of those in need. Paul, a Pharisee who studied the law, would be quick to tell the new covenant believer that not only is money not a titheable commodity, he would also remind him that Gentiles have no obligation to the Mosaic law except for the four precepts laid down in Acts 15. Furthermore, Jews outside of Israel did not bring tithes in from other nations because the land outside Israel was not considered consecrated for the tithe.

Practicing apostolic teaching on giving results in having our own needs met. Those who give to the poor and needy store up treasure in heaven (Luke 12:33-34).

> *God is able to bless you abundantly, so that in all things at all times, having all that you need, you will abound in every good work.* -2 Cor. 9:8, NIV

Receiving Tithes

It is interesting to note the disciples, in their carnal minds, had not yet grasped the meaning of the new covenant at the Last Supper. Right after Jesus announced that the new covenant of His kingdom would be sealed in His blood, the disciples disputed about who among them would be greatest. Jesus replied:

> *The kings of the Gentiles lord it over them; and those who exercise authority over them call themselves Benefactors. But you are not to be like that. Instead, the greatest among you should be like the youngest, and the one who rules like the one who serves.* -Luke 22:25-26, NIV

Being a benefactor entitled the one so-called to loyalty and 'taxes,' the label the *Encyclopedia Judaica* gives the tithe. Nehemiah equated exacting his monetary rights as governor as the equivalent of 'lording it over the people' (Neh. 5:14-19). Like Paul, the needs of the people were his first concern, not his right to collect from them. He further knew that by *not* doing so the Lord would reward him, the reason for which Nehemiah asked the Lord to remember his actions done for the good of God's people. His heart was in the right place, and he considered the weightier matters of the law.

W.E. Vine addressed new covenant giving similarly. "Love and devotion to God! That imparts the real value to giving. And this perhaps serves to explain why no command as to the amount is laid down for believers. To obey a command stating the amount or proportion would be easy, but what exercise of heart would there be? Where would the motive lie? Loyalty would be superseded by mechanical religion. Love would be replaced by formalism. Both individuals and local churches would lose their sense of the high motive which should inspire in the offering a loving response to the love of the great Giver Himself."[18]

The only mention of tithing in the New Testament outside the Gospels is embedded in a section of Scripture dealing with the subject of the supremacy of Christ as the high priest of the new covenant (Heb. 5-9). The argument begins by quoting this Old Testament passage, which gives a foreshadowing of Jesus as high priest:

> *The* L*ORD* *has taken an oath and will not break his vow: "You are a priest forever in the order of Melchizedek."* -Ps. 110:4, NLT

The author of Hebrews made a series of statements in order to demonstrate the greatness of Melchizedek, a priest of high authority (Heb. 7:4-22). In order to establish Melchizedek as a higher authority than the Aaronic priests, the author pointed out that the Levites, resident genetically in Abraham as his future seed, gave a tithe vicariously to this priest when Abraham did. He further contended that the greater blesses the lesser, pointing out that Melchizedek blessed Abraham and, reading between the lines with his same argument, Levi was also blessed as the one of lesser authority.

From this precedent, the author then reasoned that if the goal was to be reached through the Levitical priesthood, then why was there a prophecy indicating God's chosen Davidic ruler (the Messiah) would come after the order of Melchizedek, rather than a descendant of Levi? He indicated Jesus became the high priest not on the authority of His genetic lineage, but because of the power of His indestructible life—sinless, and therefore immune to the curse of death. By His priesthood, we have better promises and can draw near to God. The summary statement proves this is the primary discussion:

> **[T]he point in what we are saying is this**: *we have such a high priest, one who is seated at the right hand of the throne of the Majesty in heaven, a minister in the holy places, in the true tent that the Lord set up, not man.* -Heb. 8:1-2, ESV

There is no focus in this section of Scripture on teaching tithing as the prototype for new covenant giving. It was merely to lend weight to his argument that since Levi paid Melchizedek a tithe through Abraham, Levi has a lesser authority than Melchizedek. Since Jesus is prophesied to be a priest after the order of Melchizedek, Jesus as high priest is, therefore, greater than the Aaronic priests. To use Abraham and his tithe to Melchizedek as our example for tithing would limit our practice to tithing the spoils of war, as previously mentioned. There is no evidence in this passage of Scripture to support the idea believers are being instructed to tithe.

Elliot Miller, writing for the *Christian Research Journal*, agrees. "When we examine this passage, we find neither an instruction to tithe nor an example of New Testament believers tithing. In fact, tithing is not even the theme of the passage, but rather the supremacy of the priesthood of Melchizedek over that of Aaron. An instance of tithing in the Old Testament is cited, but no suggestion is made that tithing has a New Testament application... If one does not assume beforehand that tithing is mandated for Christians this can only be seen as an illustration of the superiority of Christ's priesthood over the Levitical priesthood..."[19]

> ***No one takes this honor upon himself;*** *he must be called by God... So Christ also did not take upon himself the glory of becoming a high priest. But God said to him, "You are my Son; today I have become your Father." And he says in another place, "You are a priest forever, in the order of Melchizedek."* -Heb. 5:4-6, NIV

To make use of the example of Abraham with Melchizedek to justify the principle of tithing brings a couple of presuppositions to the table that conflict with clear New Testament teaching. Abraham gave the tithe to Melchizedek because Melchizedek was the one 'greater in honor.' The author of Hebrews expressly stated 'no one can take this honor for himself,' for not even Jesus, to whom the honor belonged, presumed to take it. For the leadership of a church to accept a tithe in this fashion is to take an honor not extended to them, as well as violate the Scriptures that say believers are to move in a posture of mutual submission and service to one another, not lording position over one another. We are to submit to one another out of reverence for Jesus (Eph. 5:21).

The main thrust in the argument in Hebrews is not the paying of tithes, but evidence and proof that Jesus, though not a descendant of Aaron, can and should be recognized as our high priest in the same way Melchizedek, also not descended from Aaron, was recognized as such. The last part of this section of Scripture summarizes this point unambiguously in straightforward words that leave no room for doubt as to the point of the argument.

The Melchizedek precedent will not hold up precisely because of these points, especially requiring that we have to appoint ourselves above our brothers in order to receive the tithe from the lesser. Rationalizing that the people are not providing tithes to the leaders of the church *per se*, but that the leaders are merely accepting tithes on Jesus' behalf, is less than honest in many cases. For the gainsayers, there will be a lot of explaining to do about the embezzling that has taken place. What else could explain the use of the Lord's funds for expensive homes, cars, extravagant lifestyles, investments, ad hoc... ad nauseum... *ad convictum*? And this while the poor go without care or consideration.

Is that not the very definition of embezzlement, to take the funds of the One you serve, exploiting them for personal use rather than in a manner in keeping with His wishes, which is to care for the poor and needy? Is this not, in actuality, the precise way in which He is robbed, rather than by the people who are not tithing? The reputation that 'the church is always after your money' is not undeserved because of the very vocal and questionable methods for soliciting money used by some very visible 'ministers' in the church. Truly, all who practice this, whether in the receiving or the legalistic giving, are under the curse for having placed themselves under the law. This is a blemish on the church and a poor witness to the unsaved. By this practice we are keeping people from entering the kingdom and from the truth that sets them free.

Consider also if we decide to arbitrarily observe the law in one area, we cannot dismiss the other aspects of the law. If we are tithing using Abraham as our example and not the rigors of the law, then this is a *voluntary* decision not to be imposed on others as a *rule* to follow. Paul warned us that on matters we have settled in our minds but are not settled in the minds of others, we are to respond in loving deference to the conscience and circumstances of our brother, so each one can carry out what he has purposed to do in his heart from a stance of faith (Rom. 14). Paul advised that whatever we believe regarding disputable matters we are to keep between ourselves and God.

In the *Wycliffe Dictionary of Theology* we read: "The silence of the NT writers, particularly Paul, regarding the present validity of the tithe can be explained only on the ground that the dispensation of grace has no more place for a law of tithing than it has for a law on circumcision."[20]

> *They have **freely scattered their gifts to the poor**; their righteousness endures forever.* -2 Cor. 9:9, NIV

Early Church Fathers on Giving

The early church fathers did not institute a system of tithing, as we have been lead to believe, but modeled the type of giving the apostles taught to the first believers. The weight of early church writings indicates that believers shared their possessions and gave freewill offerings as they were able, just as the apostles instructed. The following excerpts support this conclusion and speak for themselves (emphasis added).

- **Justin Martyr** (A.D. 103-165): *"And the wealthy among us help the needy*... and for all things wherewith we are supplied, we bless the Maker of all through His Son Jesus Christ, and through the Holy Ghost. And on the day called Sunday, all... gather together to one place... *And they who are well to do, and willing, give what each thinks fit;* and what is collected is deposited with the president, who succors the orphans and widows and those who, through sickness or any other cause, are in want, and those who are in bonds and the strangers sojourning among us, and in a word takes care of all who are in need."[21]
- **Irenaeus** (c. A.D. 200): "...for this reason they (the Jews) had indeed the tithes... but those who have received liberty *set aside all their possessions for the Lord's purposes,* bestowing joyfully and freely not the less valuable portions of their property, since they have the hope of better things [hereafter]; as that poor widow acted who cast all her living into the treasury of God."[22]
- **Tertullian** (A.D. 160-220): "Even the kind of treasury which we have is *not filled up with sums paid under a sense of obligation, as if they were the price of religion;* but each one places there a small contribution on a certain day of the month, or when he wishes, provided only he is both willing and able—for the *offerings are not compulsory* but voluntary... we are brethren in family possessions, which with you (Romans) generally dissolve brotherhood. In this way we, *who are united heart and soul, never hesitate to communicate our substance to one another.* All things are common amongst us..."[23]

Origin of Tithing in the Church

The majority of early church leaders took Jesus' instruction to the rich young ruler seriously and literally, taking vows of poverty. They supported themselves as Paul instructed in order to tend to the needs of the poor as the higher way of demonstrating love in the manner portrayed by the new covenant. Should we advocate vows of poverty today? I believe these early church leaders had their hearts in the right place. Commitment to living a simple lifestyle, working to supply our own needs, knowing the difference between needs and wants, and giving generously on every occasion is in keeping with apostolic teaching.

The Catholic Encyclopedia cites tithing as essentially unpracticed until A.D. 567, and then with only limited success as an edict from the church.[24] At the time of Charlemagne (A.D. 777), churches were legally allowed to collect the tithe. The concept of tithing eventually expanded to include sources not originally subject to the tithe, such as income of ordinary wage earners, and was exercised by the political rulers of the day. In the U.S., this practice parallels our federal income tax.

Though tithing was not practiced in the early church, by the sixth century both the church and ruling political authorities used the concept of tithing to tax the people. The great accumulation of land, goods, and money hoarded by those collecting the tithe stood in stark contrast to the abject poverty of the starving masses. The corruption that resulted from this abuse of Levitical law caused much dissension, especially in Europe. Many of the political tithing laws were eventually repealed. Perhaps the reason God regulated the tithe to exclude money was because He knew how it would affect those who received it.[25]

Dr. Kelly summarized the transition from the giving practiced by the early believers to the later practice of tithing: "New Testament doctrines concerning the church and giving experienced a drastic change from the end of the first apostolic century to the middle of the third century. The *first stage* of decline was the removal of spiritual gifts from the laity. The *second stage* was the distinction of the bishop as a level higher than the other (formerly equal) elders in the church. The *third stage* of decline occurred when the bishop was given a high priestly status with spiritual power over the laity. In the *fourth stage*, the bishops, elders, and (sometimes) the deacons were encouraged to stop performing secular work and devote themselves full-time to the church. Tithing became the *fifth stage* of this doctrinal decline.

"Instead of the priesthood of every believer replacing the Old Testament priesthood, the church had gradually reorganized itself to resemble the Old Testament hierarchy… Thus some type of tithing was introduced into the church only after a long period of at least 200-300 years of steady doctrinal decline and only to follow the pattern of Old Testament worship. Even then, tithing was not mandatory or compulsory for many more centuries."[26]

Appearance of Tithing in the U.S.

The practice of tithing in the U.S., no matter what we may believe about it, did not come in vogue until the late nineteenth century when churches found themselves in need of funds for building. James Hudnut-Beumler, Dean of Vanderbilt University, conducted a great deal of research on giving. In his book, *In Pursuit of the Almighty's Dollar: A History of Money and American Protestantism*, Professor Hudnut-Beumler tracks the history of giving in the church from the earliest days of the colonists in America.

This enlightening book clearly documents the inception of the tithe in the U.S. as taking place in 1873, hard to fathom for those of us who were led to believe the tithe was practiced from the church's beginning. "Tithing was attractive as a source of funding to the degree that clergy could convince themselves and others that it was a spiritual law, as unappealing as the laws of motion, force and gravity."[27] "The primary methods of church finance employed at the beginning of the century were now, in its last quarter, largely being pushed aside for the methods bearing more fruit... and sustained by a rhetoric of righteousness."[28] "By the 1890s, the offering was everywhere becoming a weekly ritual whereby parishioners would "present their tithes and offerings" to the Lord..."[29]

Malachi became the model for advocates of tithing: "...failure to give at least a tithe to the church was tantamount to 'robbing God'... the whole of the tithe needed to be given to the church, or storehouse... This contrasted with the emerging practice of systematic benevolence in which individuals gave to a variety of philanthropic causes directly. Finally the reward for trusting enough to tithe was the individual prosperity of 'an overflowing blessing.' Tithing businessmen who were asked how did they afford to tithe, could be expected to reply, 'How could I afford not to tithe?'"[30]

Those who state tithing was in existence *before* the law, thus justifying its application under the new covenant, use the passages *connected with* the law to solicit the tithe from the people, such as Malachi 3:8-12. Have we thrown out all of our precious hermeneutical principles—exegesis and literal historical-grammatical context—in order to promote a giving principle the apostles never taught as binding on the church?

The Unjust Steward

When faced with circumstances we don't like, most of us will try to figure out how we can change those circumstances to more favorable ones. This is exactly the situation in the parable of the unjust steward (Luke 16:1-14). According to John Wesley, the issue lamented here is that the worldly "are more consistent with themselves; they are truer to their principles; they more steadily pursue their end; they are wiser in their generation—that is, in their own way, than the children of light."[31]

The shrewd manager and those whose debts were lessened in this parable are all alike dishonest. It was not *Jesus* who commended his action, but the manager's likewise worldly master in the parable. In a modern example, think of a shady lawyer drafting legal papers to slash the tax liability of his clients to earn their favor before he is dismissed by his firm. Or think of heads of denominations with nearly empty treasuries who would like to secure more revenue for their ambitious projects. The passage could be updated to read: 'I don't know how to make tents, and I'm tired of begging for money from the congregants. I want to use my time to serve the Lord, not have a second job. If the people give more, I can start all those programs to bring in the lost, have a better building that will attract more people, and establish our church's reputation as successful for the kingdom.' This is what happened in 1873 in the U.S.

But as most pastors have discovered, the larger the building and the greater the number of programs, the less time the man of God will have to be in the Word and prayer. Soon his heart becomes colder with all his duty, but he justifies his lack of personal time with the Lord by thinking he sacrifices it for the good of the flock and all the fruit of his labor. This process is gradual and most often insidious until, like Samson, his eyes are no longer open to truth because 'he knew not that the Spirit of the Lord had left him.' At this point, most pastors experience the anger, despair, or frustration of leanness of soul, despite the fatness of the bank account for some, the 'success' of the programs and church for others, the popularity they experience with their people, or the esteem of their peers.

Sadly, the flock loves to have a busy church more than they love God or His Word so they can boast about accomplishment and the great things taking place, despite the fact their striving is void of true compassion or God's will. As in most business organizations, many think they are nobody unless they are known by the 'important' people in their congregation, fueling their ambitious goals to be noticed. Whatever happened to mutual submission and not lording over one another? Now we elevate being known by the platform or pulpit people over being known by God. If this mentality doesn't stagnate our hearts before God, we were never His to begin with. Things that are highly valued by man are detestable to God.

The way in which the children are not shrewd with worldly wealth is they assume God is blessing them so they can spend it on whatever worldly pleasure and whim suits their fancy. In order to be shrewd with the world's money acquired in this age, we must be generous in our support of the poor, those mentors who are in need, and worthy causes for furthering the gospel. Using worldly wealth in this manner gives us reward in the age to come. Using it for ourselves is *anti*-shrewd and will cause the loss of reward: the dividends of saved souls and the yield of poor fed in this life. Zacchaeus is a champion in this regard—an example of the shrewdness God is looking for in His people. James rebuked those who are not shrewd in this way. Their goods will testify against them in the final day, for God hears the cries of the poor (James 5:3; cf. Deut. 15:9; 24:15).

The Fruit of Tithing

People who are avid tithers cite giving a tenth as the starting place for Christian giving. In the mind of the tither, the acid test of faith and the avenue of blessing are anchored to giving ten percent. Ministers will often appeal to the people to give so they can receive blessing according to Malachi 3:8-12, as previously noted.

Dr. James Bollhagen, Professor of Exegetical Theology (Old Testament) at Concordia Theological Seminary, had this to say: "The Gospel is obscured when preachers, by way of a gross misinterpretation of God's call to faith in Malachi 3, entice people into greater giving by appealing to their fleshly, selfish desires: "If only you would give more money to church, you would have unparalleled business success and two new cars in your garage." Such talk turns Gospel giving into a business deal—"If you do this, God will do that"—and striking a deal with God is totally contrary to the Gospel. Even worse, business-deal language smacks of manipulation, the thought that God can be manipulated into doing this or that through one's own activity. This kind of divine manipulation characterized all the pagan Canaanite religions that surrounded the nation of Israel."[32]

Many Christians are fearful that if they *don't tithe*, God's hand of blessing will be removed from them and they will lose their shirts. This fear can border on superstition. Others are motivated by greed and desires for other things, believing God will bless them with more wealth if they *do tithe*. A third group tithes simply because they have been told it is the right thing to do and they really want to be obedient. The only group of tithers whose giving God honors is the third group, whose heart posture is right before God: that of a bondservant being obedient in faith.

As previously discussed, giving is the outflow of love and compassion without any expectation of return in this life. The first two postures in the previous paragraph are contrary to even the heart of the law, let alone Jesus' and apostolic teaching in the New Testament. Paul made it clear that Jesus redeemed believers from the curse of the law. The only people who receive the curses of the law are those who remain under the law to define their righteousness before God (Gal. 3:10).

Evidence that use of the Malachi 3 passage provokes fear of loss or greed for gain should raise red flags. Paul reminds us that the very failure of the law in the old covenant was due to its inability to draw forth the right heart response from our fallen nature. Its purpose was to help man understand that without the promised Messiah, the task was impossible to uphold. The Pharisees failed miserably because, even though they upheld the letter of the law, their hearts were filled with greed, not love or loyalty. Even David, who is highly esteemed by God for having the right heart posture, failed miserably in upholding the law in his actions.

The law could only be fulfilled by God in Jesus Christ as a Jewish man because *no other race was under the Mosaic law*. The law challenged us by revealing that we haven't the character or fortitude to walk perfectly in the statutes or to deal with sin as He prescribed. It revealed we do not have the goodness to keep ourselves from elevating or desiring to elevate ourselves over our brothers, whether by status, wealth, education, or power. It proved we are incapable of being free of covetousness without God's aid. It exposed our affinity for the safety of rules, which make us feel important if we have the strength of will to carry them out, resulting in self-righteousness and pride. On the other hand, if we are not so disposed or disciplined, self-condemnation, guilt, and self-abasement settle in if we fail. This is why the law will only bring fearful expectation of judgment if it is not carried out to the letter (Rom. 13:3; Heb. 10:26-28), or pride and self-righteousness if it is legalistically practiced.

Some believers have so consumed themselves with being faithful to this principle of tithing that they have gone into debt. The tithe was never meant to put anyone in the poor house, or to be a hindrance to taking care of our own family's needs. Here we must be careful how we define *need*. If we have squandered our resources or spent a great deal on the niceties of life, having nothing left at the end of the month for giving to those in need, we are without excuse before God for spending so much on ourselves.

Part of the tithe was meant to be given to the poor, not exacted from them. Because the firstborn son received the family inheritance of land, or at least the greatest share, the remaining sons often acquired a trade and worked as carpenters, fishermen, or some other business. The other members of the community provided services and labor for which they were compensated. Their skills were put to use for the benefit of others, much like a hireling is paid wages for his skill/work. We have no record of Jesus paying tithes as a carpenter, Peter paying tithes as a fisherman, or Paul paying tithes as a tent-maker. The tithe was exacted from those in possession of the farmed lands, not from the wages of laborers.

Skilled laborers supported the temple work through freewill offerings and the temple tax. The tithe, however, was paid on the increase of the crops, trees, flocks, and herds. Paying the tithe acknowledged the land belonged to God, and that He is the One who provided the increase by sending rain and favorable growing conditions, and by bringing life forth from the herds and flocks. Man cannot by his own will or strategy make the ground produce good crops, control the weather, or ensure the livestock birth healthy young.

Because Israel was a theocracy, these tithes were for the treasury of both the temple and the civil governance of the nation. The land belonged to God (2 Chron. 7:20; Isa. 14:25; Jer. 2:7; 16:18; Joel 3:2), and the tithe was His rightful due from the stewards who had received a portion of the land and cared for it, namely the Israelite people, or more specifically the Israelite farmers and herdsmen. Obligatory tithing was imposed by God on no other nation because God's covenant was with Israel, both the people and the specific land given by God (Lev. 27:34; Num. 18:24; Mal. 3:6-12). The tithe was only a part of the offerings given. They were for the Levites to use because they had no inheritance of land. Thus, the tithe was *given* by those who did inherit land and acquired increase from the use of it, and *received* by those who had no land. Today we would call it a property tax for the running of the services of the government, which in the case of a theocracy would include the running of the temple. Keep in mind that under the new covenant, believers have received no land from which to tithe.

The tithe was to be a celebration of the goodness and provision of God. The second tithe was to share a festive meal with the Levites and poor in honor of and evidence for the graciousness of God. *The tither ate the tithe* as part of a celebratory meal with the Levites who were serving on their rotation in Jerusalem (Deut. 14:22-27; 26:1-11,14). Every third year a tithe was to be given to the Levites, widows, orphans, and strangers in the local towns so their needs would be met and they could also rejoice in the Lord's benefits (Deut. 14:28-29; 26:12). The tithe was always associated with rejoicing, not duty. Dutiful observance is equated with the letter of the law that kills our spiritual life and relationship with God.

> *He has enabled us to be ministers of his new covenant. This is a covenant not of written laws, but of the Spirit. The old written covenant ends in death; but under the new covenant, the Spirit gives life.* -2 Cor. 3:6, NLT

If we want to get technical about tithing, the tithe was given to the Levites who took care of the menial tasks of temple upkeep, and the Levites gave a tenth of what they received as a heave offering to be set aside for the priest and his family (see Num. 18:25-28). The priest and the temple treasury received the *heave offerings*, the *freewill offerings*, and the *devoted things* (Num. 18:8-20), but the *tithe* was for the Levites—the servants of the priests and temple.

Those who run churches today cannot, for the most part, claim descent from the Levites. But if we would draw a parallel in today's language through eisegesis, the janitorial staff, secretaries, ushers, door greeters, Sunday school teachers, choir members, and musicians would receive the tithe from the congregation, and the pastors would receive their tithe from these members of the church staff. The Old Testament priests did not tithe at all. We cannot truthfully claim this is how we are doing it today, technically.

Whether we understand the finer points of tithing or not, this remains clear: *obligatory* tithing is part of the law to which Jews outside of Israel and Gentiles in general were never bound. *Voluntary* tithing, as exhibited by Abraham, is forever voluntary. Obligatory tithing can stagnate and lock the heart, eliciting a response toward giving that is antithetical to everything Jesus taught: 'I'm not required to give any more than that.' Voluntary giving, whether it is more or less than a tenth, provokes the giver to respond from the heart, 'I only wish I had more to give.'

Irenaeus acknowledged and taught this meaning to the early church. "And for this reason did the Lord, instead of that [commandment], 'You shall not commit adultery,' forbid even concupiscence; and instead of that which runs thus, 'You shall not kill,' He prohibited anger; and **instead of the law enjoining the giving of tithes**, to share all our possessions with the poor; and not to love our neighbors only, but even our enemies; and not merely to be liberal givers and bestowers, but even that we should present a gratuitous gift to those who take away our goods..."[33] (emphasis added)

The early Christians believed in the power of a changed life, and thus we have no evidence they either taught or practiced tithing. We cannot do the work of the Holy Spirit for others by imposing a rule about giving or even a highly encouraged principle for the 'real Christian.' Giving that flows from compassion, generosity, free will, godly wisdom, and the Holy Spirit is of great spiritual value.

> *Stand firm, then, and do not let yourselves be burdened again by the yoke of slavery.* -Gal. 5:1b, NIV

Sacrificial giving is a sign of servanthood and evidence that the carnal covetous nature of the heart has been circumcised. Jesus and the early church exemplified this principle. To deceive ourselves by happily accepting this freedom in giving because we can now keep more to spend on ourselves proves we have not matured enough spiritually to be free from the grasp of covetousness.

The desire of Ananias and Sapphira to receive praise for their giving is recorded in Acts 5:1-11. Is this not what is happening in churches where the tithers are paraded in front of the congregation as examples of people with the 'right faith'? Some who cannot responsibly tithe and meet their other financial obligations will lie about their giving and say they tithe in order to be included in this esteemed group. Is this any different from the lie told by Ananias and Sapphira?

If we heave a sigh of relief when we pay our tithe, we have to ask ourselves, 'Why?' For most, the answer would be that we feel 'covered' financially so our precious resources won't be attacked by the Malachi 3 curses. Jesus stated wisdom is shown to be valid by the children it bears (Luke 7:35). Herein lies the true acid test: If tithing provokes fear, greed, pride, lying, dutiful instead of joyful giving, closing eyes to the plight of relatives or neighbors because we already gave at the church, or worse, it has not been vindicated as the model for giving in the grace of Christ. Instead, it is proven inferior by being bound to that which is inferior—legalistic attention to the law, which brings condemnation and a fearful expectation of judgment on the one hand, or pride and self-righteousness on the other. The fruit of its practice is contrary to the fruit of the Spirit, and the weight of Scripture as well as the practice and teaching of the early church show it has no place in new covenant doctrine. Indeed, not even the Jews can practice tithing according to Mosaic law without a Levitical priesthood and temple in place.

Giving that comes from the heart brings peace, rejoicing, delight, and an ever-increasing measure of God's heart for the poor and needy as well as gratitude for those who serve us as overseers of our spiritual well-being. Paul stated that while all believers are to practice giving, it is also a grace or gift bestowed by the Holy Spirit. Because it is a gift that involves tangible goods, we often overlook giving as an operation of the Spirit.

Those who have been given this grace are not to neglect it, just as the other gifts are not to be buried in the ground. Where would the church be if no one taught, showed mercy to those in need, provided hospitality, or took care of the needed service and administrative needs of our churches? If the grace of giving has been given to us, we must fan it into flame by giving generously. The result will be that God will see to it we have a supply of funds with which to be generous on every occasion, resulting in the overflow of thanksgiving to God (2 Cor. 9:11-12).

Requirement for Membership

The following news report was aired in Columbus, Ohio, in 2006. It is a gross example of the extent to which tithing as a requirement for membership can go in preventing us from seeing how our actions in this realm negate God's Word, both in the Old and New Testaments, on caring for the poor. Notice the use of the phrase 'stopped making payments'—words you would only expect to see in financial circles.

Wheelchair-Bound Woman Kicked out of Church

> A 65-year-old wheelchair-bound woman with congestive heart failure was kicked out of her church because she was not paying her tithe, NBC 4 reported. Loretta Davis told NBC 4's Mike Bowersock she was shocked when she received a letter saying she was no longer considered a member of her church, The Living Word Tabernacle. Davis made an agreement with the church that she would give 10 percent of her income. Then she became ill and stopped making payments, so the church revoked her membership. "Since January 5th, I've been in the hospital 15 times," Davis said. "I've suffered with cellulites since I've had the open heart (surgery)." Davis is no longer paying the church $60 per month from her $592 per month Social Security check, Bowersock reported. "I have my tithes that I was supposed to pay, but I have not paid them since this has went on," Davis said. "In the time of (Davis') need, they should be caring, supporting, asking what she needs— help her if she needed help," said Teresa Meeks, who is Davis' daughter. "I was so hurt on what they did to her." The church moved out of its building in Waverly earlier this year and Davis' dismissal has become the talk of the town, Bowersock reported. In a letter to the editor of the local paper, the former pastor said it is true that Davis lost her membership for not paying her tithes. In the same letter, he said Davis was not kicked out of the church for not paying her tithes. The Rev. Paul McClurg, who started the church, said Davis is still welcome to attend church but is not allowed to be a member. The issue upset Davis' 83-year-old mother so much that she quit the church. The members have been holding services in a Lion's Club hall while waiting to build a new church. There are at least two former members who will not be attending with them.[34]

No compassion, shockingly calloused, just rules of operation, the letter which kills, ignoring the weightier matters of the law. Is this the fruit Jesus hoped for from people who claim to be His followers? Some would criticize a poverty stricken person such as Ms. Davis, self-righteously stating if she would only tithe and have faith, God would bless her. We do not have the poor in mind when we govern our churches in this way.

Provoking the Jews to Jealousy?

Additional fruit of the practice of tithing involves the way it has provoked the Jewish synagogues to jealousy when they see the financial stability of churches that compel their members to tithe. Most rabbis agree it is against Levitical law for the synagogue to collect the tithe. They have maintained a policy where dues and freewill offerings are collected to defray expenses and salaries, while *tzedakah* donations are collected for those in need. But with the economic downturn and its effect on giving, discussion among some rabbis has turned to imitating the tactics of Christian churches in order to acquire the needed revenues.

> ### With Synagogues in Jeopardy, It's Time to Talk About Tithing
>
> Why are so many [churches] so stable? Perhaps the tithe is the reason... Only one-tenth of 1% [of churches] sustains themselves through annual dues, as so many Jewish congregations do... Churches that talk the tithe do not necessarily enforce it, but when tithe is part of a conversation about stewardship, donation patterns appear higher and church leaders are likely to self-report financial stability... So what would happen if more synagogue leaders started talking about tithing? Giving to synagogues would likely double, with increased congregational financial stability and increased worship, study and program outcomes. What we need today in the synagogue world is a new approach to finances... Too many synagogues are finding out—or will soon find out—that the current annual dues system is insufficient for meeting budgetary needs. As Duane Rice of Evangelical Friends International recently told *The Wall Street Journal*, "If everyone gives 2% of their incomes because that's what they feel like giving, you aren't going to have enough money to pay the light bill and keep the doors open." In troubling times such as we now face—when cash flow may be in question and investment returns are lower than we have seen in many years—tithing would have a clear impact on congregations' financial resources... Synagogues need to start talking tithe—not as a threat or as a demand, but as a goal. Talking tithe increases the chances of a person giving accordingly; discussion of tithing alone can greatly increase membership support. It's time we moved talk about tithing from the Torah portion to the board meeting.[35]

Is this the type of fruit Paul hoped for when he stated that the Gentile believers would provoke the Jews to jealousy (Rom. 11:11)?

Closing Thoughts

Evidence that the laws of tithing have been misused and applied in a manner contrary to the Word is certainly prevalent in the church today. Tithing as a teaching of the church is an example of eisegesis and a direct result of perceived church need. It is amazing to note that the churches who say they are strict adherents of exegesis will promote tithing as near doctrine. Whether this is the result of misunderstanding, lack of careful scrutiny of Scripture, indoctrination, pressure from the boardroom, or from motives of greed or desperation (or a combination) is not for us to decide.

In the new covenant, tithing has been replaced with relinquishing ownership of *everything*. We give out of compassion and a grateful heart, desiring to share in the practice of true religion as God defines it: taking care of the poor, the needy, the stranger, the orphan, and the widow. Tithing in the church is on par with circumcision and has no apostolic support from the Word as new covenant doctrine. Paul warned the Galatians not to return to those elementary principles. They have the power to lock our thinking and hearts when we practice them 'religiously.' It is less than honest to teach tithing as anything other than an individual's decision to give in this manner of his own free will.

It is curious some churches will staunchly tell women they cannot even speak in church, adhering quite closely to Paul's literal teaching on this subject, and then ignore all literal instruction on the issue of giving and support of church leadership as previously discussed. In fact, some churches that profess to adhere to a literal grammatical-historical interpretation of the Word on the one hand, will on the other hand not only ignore apostolic teaching on giving and leadership support as irrelevant for the church today, but substitute an old covenant teaching—tithing—in its place, including the law's curse for disobedience. Let the hypocrisy and absurdity of this sink in for a minute.

Oddly enough, every study or statistic on giving demonstrates that the people who give the largest percentage of their income are the poor. According to the 'Malachi 3 principle,' these should have received the greatest out-pouring of wealth from the windows of heaven. But statistics also show that those in poverty usually remain so, their poverty increasing over time rather than improving. The blessings under the new covenant are not the same as the blessings under the old, and herein lies the failure of this passage to apply and bear fruit in the believer's life.

The preponderance of New Testament teaching on giving involves the care of widows and the poor, not sustenance of leadership. While Paul received gifts from the Philippians, he also stated he did not desire or ask for these. The Philippians took up the collection on their own initiative when they heard of his hardship because they loved him. There are several *warnings*, however, for leaders in the church not to use their position for monetary gain, and rebukes for those false leaders who do. Perhaps Paul knew what could happen to the hearts of leadership if they discovered preaching could be financially lucrative. Whatever the case, the emphasis in giving under the new covenant is on the poor among the believers.

Most churches weigh their options to determine how they will approach their stance on giving: make one indiscriminate eisegetical teaching on giving by combining tithing and firstfruits through the blessings and cursings in Malachi 3, or trust God to provide what is needed from voluntary freewill gifts. "Those who worry about how the church can survive without a tithing law may find that God had a better idea in mind all along."[36]

The pastorate in the West is largely adequately fed, housed, and clothed. Most of the excess goes for expensive church programs that could very well be rethought as the efficacy of the results from these outreaches has been overstated in most cases. In His Word, God repeatedly tells us to give to the poor, the needy (which include those who need to hear the good news, the specific function of organizations like Wycliffe), widows, orphans, and strangers as the hallmarks of true religion. All other giving may or may not be honored by God; this will be revealed when He returns to test our giving by fire. Cornelius was not noted for giving the temple a tithe of his wage or supporting the local synagogue leaders, but for giving alms to the poor. Such giving from the heart, motivated by love and compassion rather than duty, will always catch God's attention.

In his excellent article on tithing, Robin Brace of UK Apologetics wrote the following: "Tithing is... considered a particularly vital teaching in the prosperity gospel churches. Let us honestly admit that some of these groups only have the most superficial understanding of Christian theology. If a member encounters financial difficulties, it is too quickly thought by some that he or she could not have been tithing, or had been withholding part of the tithe. Apart from being a theologically perilous position to adopt in its own right, this appears to be the eager judgmentalism of the spiritually naive. I just wonder how many in those churches made prosperous through tithing realise the original purpose of tithing, that is, to assist the needy.

"Another—and very serious—problem can be noted in some congregations: The congregation becomes divided into two groups, the tithers and the non-tithers, but only the tithers can ever become 'members' of that congregation... ALL WHO HAVE REPENTED AND ACCEPTED CHRIST'S SACRIFICE IN THEIR OWN LIVES, BECOME MEMBERS OF THE CHURCH OF GOD IN ITS TRUE AND ETERNAL SENSE!! (Mr. Brace's emphasis)

"...the great majority of Bible scholars down through the ages have felt that Malachi 3:10 cannot be applied to the church... neither the apostle Paul nor the early church appeared to hold any concept of paying tithes, with the concept only emerging post-Constantine when a means was sought to finance huge 'church' and cathedral buildings. We have seen that the 'modern tithe' (which appears to have emerged in the late 19th century United States), bears little resemblance to the Levitical tithe. That tithe was concerned with meeting the needs of the poor of the land, whether the Levites who received no land inheritance, or others who wished to travel to the Levitical Feast days, or the poor in general. It was not the sort of tax which, as Samuel warned, kings would impose, thereby making themselves richer and financing their various projects... [T]he New Testament points out a financial approach which is best summed up by the word 'Koinonia' (sharing). We see this approach employed in the Book of Acts; it was a complete commitment by all Christians to each other, so that none should suffer lack or privation, and out of this, the preaching and advance of the Gospel was also funded. If this were practised today, it is fair to say that congregations would no longer have poorer members, though pastors might have to accept lower pay for their labours in some cases, especially in more affluent areas. It is also true to say that if this kind of total Christian sharing were practised today, third world missions would surely receive much greater financial support than is often the case at present."[37]

Am I against tithing? Absolutely not. I view it as any other spiritual discipline: a matter to be decided between the individual believer and God. The type and shadow provided by the Levitical tithing laws teach us responsibility in caring for others, an example for those given the gift of giving, as well as a way to acknowledge that all we receive is from God.

Will all believers spend the same amount of time studying the Word? Do all believers fast with the same regularity or frequency? The obvious answer is 'no.' Likewise, though we can use the laws of tithing to help us understand the spiritual principle of generosity to be practiced in the new covenant, making doctrine that *all* are to follow this principle as dictated under the law, complete with blessings for those who do and curses for those who don't, is contrary to apostolic teaching. We are already blessed with every spiritual blessing in Christ, and there is no more curse for those in Christ. Making tithing the standard for giving in the church places unwarranted guilt and condemnation on the poor. In our earlier example, I believe the Lord would be delighted if the poorer family gave ten dollars each week, only two percent of their income.

There is no exegetical evidence that the apostles imposed giving laws for believers under the new covenant. Just as disciplining ourselves to study the Word each day is beneficial, or setting time aside each week or month for a concentrated time of prayer and fasting is profitable, setting a personal standard for giving can also be a great way to discipline ourselves in giving until we become accustomed to hearing and following the inner leading of the Holy Spirit. Although spiritual disciplines are of great benefit to the believer, *enforcing* a specific standard for everyone promotes legalism and self-righteousness (or conversely, condemnation), not faith. If we choose to tithe, we have to ask ourselves which scriptural example of tithing provides the foundation for our conviction:

- adhering to the requirements of the law;
- following the ancient pagan custom to tithe spoils of war, as Abraham did;
- lifting Malachi 3:8-11 or Jesus' rebuke to the tithing Pharisees out of their grammatical-historical contexts to formulate a giving principle for new covenant believers; or
- deciding in our heart to give a tenth (2 Cor. 9:7), acknowledging God is our source.

I believe we can safely say the last reason alone is honored by God under the new covenant in Jesus because it is technically a freewill offering. On the other hand, perhaps the shrewd reinvention of the tithe in the 1870's by the leadership of several American churches will be viewed by God in the same way as the shrewd manager who saved his skin through some dishonest but clever maneuvering. But then again, this type of shrewd management is only to note that those whose eyes are on the things of this world are shrewd in gaining what the god of mammon requires.

Tithing as a matter of principle or spiritual discipline is in keeping with new covenant teaching if that is what we have purposed to do in our heart from a stance of love and faith. Giving financially to the family of God is thoroughly embedded in New Testament teaching, even if tithing is not. In our society where the average per capita income is more than adequate to provide for basic needs, tithing should be superseded with Zacchaeus' standard of giving—'I will give half away.'

We cannot be shaken by the magnitude of covetousness and greed in the present day church, but we must be provoked to intercede for the church concerning this matter. Before Jesus returns, we must pray the true church will be moving in sacrificial giving, with no one claiming what he has is his own, so there are no ~~greedy~~ needy persons among us. Then we will truly be, like Paul, content with food and clothes.

In the meantime, let each decide the matter between himself and God, not judging the giving of others, but moving in love, wisdom, compassion, generosity, and the leading of the Holy Spirit, not letting the left hand know what the right hand is doing, being fully convinced in his own mind so he can give from a posture of faith, giving thanks and glory to the God of all provision. Amen.

> ***If you spend yourselves in behalf of the hungry* and *satisfy the needs of the oppressed*, then *your light will rise in the darkness*,** *and your night will become like the noonday. The LORD will guide you always; he will satisfy your needs in a sun-scorched land and will strengthen your frame. You will be like a well-watered garden, like a spring whose waters never fail.* -Isa. 58:10-11, NIV

Sharing the burdens of others defines the way we fulfill the law of Christ (Gal. 6:2). James reminds us that pure and faultless religion looks after the poor and those in distress. This is what God is looking for and can only be accomplished if we are not polluted by the world's standard, which in the U.S. is the western lifestyle of excess (James 1:27).

Poor and wealthy alike can be extravagant in their giving, even if the poor man in the example earlier gives only two percent of his income—extravagant in the Lord's eyes because of how little he was given to work with. If the man in the second example, who probably tithes regularly and thinks everyone should, tried living on the same amount as the family in poverty, he could give away $18,750/month. If he were challenged to do so, the wealthier individual may think differently about tithing with respect to the plight of the poor man. Those who staunchly demand everyone must give ten percent are those who typically have enough to meet all their needs. They do not have the poor in mind when they say these things. Rather than attempt to extract the $200 dollar 'speck' from the poor man's eye, perhaps the 'beam' of legalism, covetousness, ulterior motives, ignorance, and/or the pride of self-satisfaction should be removed from our own.

God has chosen the poor to be rich in faith through greater experiential understanding of God's Word and possessing the love of God which casts out fear incited by dire circumstances. The rich, as James described, have been humbled by God in that what they do to acquire wealth will wither away. Those who are rich should be humbled in their view of themselves because God has chosen them to receive *worldly* monetary wealth (temporary riches that fade) to support the brethren. To others He has assigned the *spiritual* wealth of heaven (eternal riches that last) to enlighten those that have not. This is the way in which the rich are humbled and the poor are honored. Each is to use the gift of wealth he has been given, whether spiritual or monetary, for the edification and care of the believers and the poor among us (James 1:9-11). If we can change our paradigm of wealth to agree with the Word, understanding that the power to acquire wealth comes from God and that giving is a gift of the Holy Spirit (as are preaching and teaching), then we are on our way to having the right perspective.

The rich are both humbled and tested by the wealth they are given. They are humbled for the simple reason the wealth they toil for and generate will not last or credit their heavenly account unless they give it to the poor and needy (especially those who need to hear the gospel). They are tested because: 1.) the god of this age would have them believe they have acquired wealth on their own and deserve to spend it on themselves; 2.) the world elevates the wealthy as the important and successful people of earth; and 3.) wealth can bring worldly power, provoking the 'Nebuchadnezzar syndrome.'

Regarding new covenant freedom in giving, it would be no more conscionable for a wealthy believer to apply his freedom in giving as an excuse to keep more for self than it would be for a naive new believer to exercise his freedom in Christ to continue indulging in pornography. The Spirit of grace gives us the power to defeat both the lust of the eyes and the greed of the heart. The problem seen today is that many of the wealthy (not all; there are many wealthier believers who are always ready to help those in need) invest their monetary gain in higher standards of living (see Jer. 22:13-14). This is why it is so difficult for the wealthy to enter into the kingdom (Matt. 19:23-24).

Today we see the injustice of wages withheld from the poor even in our own nation (see James 5:4; cf. Rev. 6:6). This occurs when wages remain static in an economy burgeoning with inflation and skyrocketing corporate profits, hence the shrinking of the middle class. The poor neglect the study of the Word because they strive to acquire what the rich have. Now the needs of neither are met—the rich are wasting away spiritually, and the poor struggle to put food on the table.

If the one who has much in the bank or investments has gained the fear of the Lord in regard to giving, making a resolution to give more in the manner of Zacchaeus, and if the poor and destitute person has given up his guilt or fear of *not* tithing, then these words will have accomplished what they were sent to do. If not, I have failed. As the Jews zealous for the law found out when the new covenant was established, it is truly difficult, if not impossible, to sacrifice certain sacred cows...

> *Happy is one who cares for the poor; the LORD will save him in a day of adversity.*
> -Ps. 41:1, HCSB

Chapter 14

When You Pray

> *Let us therefore come boldly unto the throne of grace, that we may obtain mercy, and find grace to help in time of need.* -Heb. 4:16, KJV

Discussing prayer in a matter-of-fact fashion through the study of Scripture poses a challenge because it is founded on relationship, much like obedience. Prayer is communication with our Father who loves us as much as He loves His Son (John 17:23). This communication develops and matures over time. Like infants who have a hard time understanding what their parents are saying, but who nonetheless are loudly making their own needs known, we also at first reserve prayer for our needs and have difficulty understanding what and how our Heavenly Father communicates to us.

Though prayer may initially seem very one-sided, we come to realize the still small voice of God is heard primarily as we study the Word and gain understanding of Him and His ways. This does not ignore other modes of communication, such as visions or dreams as Peter and Paul received, but only points out the *typical* way in which we hear from God. Relationship, prayer, and the Word are inseparably woven together. Essentially, by His expectation we would spend time in prayer, Jesus is presupposing relationship.

Personal prayer is fellowship with God. It is conversation that includes listening, asking questions, and making requests as well as incorporating elements of quiet communion, worship, and admiration. It is the normal outgrowth of our relationship with God. The privilege that we are afforded access to God in prayer grips us more as the years go by and our relationship deepens. Hearing God most often takes place as we read the Word.

Corporate prayer takes on a different feel and is typically a bit more formal, but the element of relationship as the foundation for communication remains the same. This relationship is only established through the person of Jesus Christ and the Holy Spirit working and residing in us, teaching us how and what to pray. In contrast, the carefully crafted prayers of some politicians, who try to score points with Christians by feigning what they are not, do not fool believers who are walking in the discernment of God. Their words are like nails on a chalkboard, no matter how eloquent.

Requires Reliance on the Holy Spirit

> *Likewise the Spirit also helps in our weaknesses. For we do not know what we should pray for as we ought, but the Spirit Himself makes intercession... for the saints according to the will of God.* -Rom. 8:26a,27b, NKJV

Esther's reliance on Hegai to give her wisdom when it was her turn to encounter the king is an example of the believer's reliance on the Holy Spirit when we enter the presence of God (see Esth. 2:15-17). Unlike the other young women brought before the king, Esther did not ask for things she desired. She requested only those things which Hegai advised her to take. His counsel proved itself because Esther won the king's favor and grace, and he loved her more than any of the others.

Rather than presumptuously rushing into a one-sided conversation based on worldly needs, wants, or worse ('the sacrifice of fools'), wisdom charges us to first listen and seek the Lord's heart. Though making our requests known is also proper, prayer that puts God's agenda ahead of our own garners the attention and favor of the King.

> *Guard your steps when you go to the house of God.* **Go near to listen** *rather than to offer the sacrifice of fools, who do not know that they do wrong.* -Ecc. 5:1, NIV

The early believers took this privilege of prayer seriously. Everywhere we look, we find they were praying together for each other and the needs of the church. They were in 'full agreement' and devoted themselves to the apostles' teaching, the Lord's Supper, fellowship, and prayer (Acts 1:14; 2:42). If we examine the content of the apostolic prayers, we get a feel for their hearts and the occupation of their minds. The focus of their concern was the spiritual growth and maturation of the believers under their care (2 Cor. 13:7-9). Paul prayed 'night and day' and on all occasions, exhorting believers to do likewise (1 Thes. 3:10). He also asked them to pray for him so he would deliver the gospel message fearlessly (Eph. 6:18-20).

Paul encouraged the Thessalonians to pray without ceasing and be thankful in everything (1 Thes. 5:17-18). He urged believers to be faithful, devoted, and watchful in prayer, asking for the bold and clear proclamation of the gospel (Rom. 12:12; Col. 4:2-4). There are many examples of and teaching about prayer in the New Testament. We only have to open our eyes to see its utility and the importance the apostles and early believers placed on its practice.

> *Don't worry about anything; instead, pray about everything. Tell God what you need, and thank him for all he has done. Then you will experience God's peace, which exceeds anything we can understand.* -Php. 4:6-7a, NLT

Jesus as Our Example

Jesus' lifestyle and teaching give us the core elements of prayer. He gave examples of what prayer is and what it isn't. The very foundation of His perfect walk while on earth was based on His relationship with the Father and His submission to the Father's will. Jesus was one in spirit with His Father, doing only what He saw the Father doing, and speaking only the words the Father gave Him to speak (John 6:38; 8:28; 12:49; 14:10,24). The bar is very high.

So what do we know of Jesus' actual prayer habits? While Jesus was praying at His baptism, Luke recorded that heaven opened and the Holy Spirit descended as a dove on Him (Luke 3:21-22). Jesus also got up early, while it was still dark, to go to solitary places to pray (Mark 1:35). After He taught all day, He went alone to the mountainside to pray (Matt. 14:23; Mark 6:46) and often withdrew to lonely places to pray (Luke 5:16). Before He chose the twelve disciples, Jesus spent the night in prayer on the mountainside (Luke 6:12-13). He also had a favored place to pray that He often visited with His disciples in an olive grove away from the hustle and bustle of the city (John 18:1-2), much like the description of the dove in the chapter on cultivating intimacy. Unlike the disciples, Jesus took time to pray for those who had no status. He did not turn away the children but placed His hands on them, blessed them, and prayed for them (Matt. 19:13; Mark 10:13-16).

Jesus prayed with His disciples and on one occasion His appearance was transfigured before their eyes (Luke 9:28-29). Twice during prayer (at His baptism and on the mount of transfiguration), the Father bursts forth with loving affirmation of His Son: 'This is My beloved Son, in whom I am well pleased,' adding, 'Listen to Him' on the second occasion. On a third occasion, Jesus offered a direct plea to His Father in front of the crowd and the voice of the Father broke through:

> *"Father, glorify Your name." Then a voice came from heaven, saying, "I have both glorified it and will glorify it again." Therefore the people who stood by and heard it said that it had thundered. Others said, "An angel has spoken to Him." Jesus answered and said, "This voice did not come because of Me, but for your sake."* -John 12:28-30, NKJV

Some of us have held jobs that required the ability to discern the pitch, tone, and frequency of the various alarms of multiple pieces of electronic equipment, some requiring immediate action and others not. To the uninitiated ear, these alarms are difficult to distinguish from each other. But by repeated daily exposure to the alarms, those employed in such an environment eventually learn to differentiate the alarms by sound and not only by inspection. This allows prioritization by sound, saving time and adrenaline, for only certain alarms are truly 'alarming.'

It is the same with hearing the Lord's voice. Notice the three responses to God's voice in the above passage. Some heard the words and recognized the source. Others heard but thought an angel had spoken. A third group didn't recognize the source or the words, but interpreted it as a natural phenomenon. Those who said it thundered benefitted little. But the voice profited those with relationship and who were there to hear.

The Great Mercy of God

The prayers Jesus offered before His arrest, trial, and crucifixion are in every way models for us, just as the Lord's Prayer. The plea in Gethsemane may have been simple, but the strength of emotion that accompanied His prayer was intense (see also Mark 14:35-36).

> He knelt down and prayed, saying, "Father, if it is Your will, take this cup away from Me; nevertheless not My will, but Yours, be done." Then an angel appeared to Him from heaven, strengthening Him. And being in agony, He prayed more earnestly. Then His sweat became like great drops of blood falling down to the ground. -Luke 22:41b-44, NKJV

Jesus' plea was offered up three times 'with loud cries and tears to the One who could save him from death' (Heb. 5:7). David and Jesus both intimately knew the great mercy of God that will relent whenever possible from judgment or calamity if there is any other way. This 'great perhaps of God,' as it has been called by some, is provoked by the cries of His children as well as by the true repentance of the wicked (e.g., the sparing of Nineveh, Jonah 3; King Manasseh, 2 Chron. 33:10-13; etc.).

- The Lord instructed Jeremiah to preach a message, stating, '**Perhaps** the people will listen and turn **so I may relent** from sending the calamity decreed for them because of sin' (Jer. 26:2-3).
- Jonathan and his armor-bearer took courageous action, having faith that God did not need numbers to bring victory and seeking to know if '**perhaps the Lord will act on our behalf**' (1 Sam. 14:6).
- David fasted for his dying child, knowing the Lord is full of grace, saying, 'Who knows? **Perhaps the Lord will be gracious to me**' (2 Sam. 12:22-23).
- King Zedekiah asked Jeremiah to inquire of the Lord when Babylon attacked, hoping '**perhaps the Lord will help us** as He did in times past' (Jer. 21:1-2).
- Amos wrote that the people should hate evil, love good, and work justice in the courts, so '**perhaps God will have mercy** on Israel' (Amos 5:15).
- Zephaniah instructs the humble who obey God to seek righteousness, so '**perhaps they will be sheltered** in the day of God's wrath' (Zeph. 2:3).

Grace to Endure

God does not always answer our prayers the way we would like but instead gives us strength or grace to endure. The author of Hebrews wrote Jesus was heard 'because of His reverent submission' (5:7). This did not mean God the Father took the cup away as Jesus requested, but He sent His angel to strengthen Jesus to endure the trial set before Him to its completion. It was within Jesus' power to call off the ordeal He was about to undertake, but He submitted to it because it was the Father's will and necessary for Scripture to be fulfilled (Matt. 26:52-54). Laying aside His own will, Jesus demonstrated love that considers the interests of others first (in this case, man's eternal destination).

> My power is made perfect in weakness. -2 Cor. 12:9a, ESV

Recall Paul's request that the messenger from Satan be removed (2 Cor. 12:7-9). The Lord's response was to give Paul sufficient grace because God's power is 'perfected' in our weakness. Being given strength to endure the trial is every bit an answer to prayer from our loving Father as receiving precisely what we requested. Our natural human tendency is to remove ourselves from pain and suffering. But it is obedience through suffering that 'perfects' us. The Greek word *teleioo*, translated 'perfect' in this passage, means 'to complete, accomplish, or consummate' (in character). Obedience in the midst of weakness and suffering accomplishes the goal of our walk before the Lord in this age, that is, the completion of conforming our character to Jesus' example of obedience. This includes finishing the mandate specifically given to us by God. The bottom line is that God's power for accomplishing God's will and for being made one with Christ is made complete in us by grace, not our own strength.

The solution that seems the most favorable and even scriptural may not be the precise will of God in our situation at the time we make our request known to God. For example, under the old covenant, long life was one of the blessings promised the obedient (Deut. 32:46-47). Certainly Jesus was aware of this, and having lived in perfect obedience to the law, He had the right to this promise. But the higher good of God's plan was for Jesus to bear the sins of humanity as the perfect and blameless sacrifice. In Paul's situation, he could have claimed that in Jesus we have victory over the power of the enemy (Mark 16:18; Luke 10:19). But God had something more important in mind: He wanted to keep Paul from pride.

Timing Is Important

Many in the church would like to reduce prayer to a formula of reciting and claiming the promises in Scripture, upon which God must act according to His established Word. Jesus stated He only did what He saw the Father *doing*, and only said what He saw the Father *saying*. Both of these verb tenses indicate application of God's will *actively* at the *present* time. The Word of God has many promises that are irrevocable, but the timing for their fulfillment is determined by God as we cooperate with Him in prayer and in seeking His will. In other words, in every situation, Jesus yielded Himself to the Father's will *and timing*.

> *There is an appointed time for everything. And there is a time for every event* ('matter or purpose,' AMP) *under heaven... He has made everything appropriate in its time.* -Ecc. 3:1,11, NASB

Examples

David understood this concept of timing. Even though he had been anointed as successor to the throne, he had to continue to submit himself to King Saul. David waited patiently for the day God would fulfill His promise, not taking the throne by force through misapplication of the Word. Today, such a person might use Matthew 11:12 to support immediate action: 'From the days of John the Baptist until now the kingdom of heaven has suffered violence, and the violent take it by force.' Twice David countered the counsel of his men to take Saul's life and claim the throne (1 Sam. 24:1-10; 26:1-11). David knew he had been chosen by God to be king, yet he had to wait patiently for the appointed time, honoring the current king in the interim. Even Jesus has appointed times for the fulfillment of His prophesied commissions (cf. Luke 17:24; Heb. 10:13):

> *For **he must remain in heaven until the time** for the final restoration of all things, as God promised long ago through his holy prophets.* -Acts 3:21, NLT

Consider the lame man who begged at the gate Beautiful in Solomon's Colonnade when Peter and John walked by (Acts 3:1-4:22). In Herod's temple, the Colonnade, or portico, ran along the eastern wall in the court of the Gentiles. John recorded that Jesus walked through this colonnade and taught there (John 10:22-23). Because Luke noted that the lame beggar had been lame *since birth*, was carried *daily* to the Beautiful Gate in Solomon's Colonnade (Acts 3:2), and was *more than forty* years old (Acts 4:22), it is a very reasonable conclusion that Jesus saw this man when He was there. So why wasn't the man healed during Jesus' ministry?

To understand this, the most important result of this healing must be taken into consideration—the number of men grew to about five thousand (Acts 4:4). Jesus would have stopped to heal this man while He was there teaching if the timing had coincided with the purposes of God. Because it was not what the Father was doing *at that time*, Jesus restrained His compassion short of healing this man. As a result of this restraint, the man was healed at the *appointed* time, opening the door for the apostles to preach the gospel and resulting in the addition of a great number of believers. The timing of this healing also opened a door for Peter and John to testify in front of the rulers, elders, and chief priests (Acts 4:1-22).[1]

We cannot let humanistic compassion or what seems to be the most beneficial or edifying outcome, *by our own estimation*, dictate our prayers and expectation of God's intervention in any given situation. All the promises are 'yes and amen' in their proper season, which may or may not take place at the time we are hoping and praying. All the promises will be fulfilled when Jesus returns and we are given new and perfect bodies to match our 'perfected' souls. Our prayers cannot be reduced to incantations of Scripture or the 'power of positive thinking' that *must* yield the desired result. This is reserved for the faithless who have been deceived by the god of this age. Jesus did not model this, and neither did any of the apostles or early believers. We do, however, persevere in prayer for God to stretch forth His hand for healing, deliverance, and power to fearlessly preach His Word.

Notice both Jesus and Paul entreated the Father three times regarding their respective requests before receiving the strength needed to bear up under the strain of their trial. Their trials were not the result of any disobedience or sin. God's plan that they forbear through the trial rather than having the trial removed revealed a greater purpose exacted through their obedience and submission—in one case, the prevention of pride; in the other, the justification of all mankind.

This is in contrast with the example Jesus gave of the shamelessly impudent neighbor (see Luke 11:5-8). Hospitality for travelers was expected, and it was considered awkward if not disgraceful to be unprepared to take care of the basic needs of guests for food and shelter. For this reason, the host needed to find bread to properly care for his guest. The host's need was predicated on the need of another. This is an example of interceding on behalf of the needs of someone else, not necessarily our own.

We see a further illustration of tenacious and resolute prayer in the example of the persistent widow (see Luke 18:1-8). In this example, the judge was a godless man who initially refused to grant the widow justice. But because she relentlessly brought her plea before him, he gave in because he didn't want to be bothered any more. Jesus finishes His *kal v'homer* argument by saying:

> *So don't you think God will surely give justice to his chosen people who cry out to him day and night? Will he keep putting them off? I tell you, he will grant justice to them quickly! But when the Son of Man returns, how many will he find on the earth who have faith?* -Luke 18:7b-8, NLT

There is an appointed time to ask and a time to refrain (as in the examples of Jesus and Paul, mentioned previously). It is important to note two other things about this passage. This woman was seeking justice and not personal material wealth or possessions unrelated to an issue of justice. At the end, Jesus questions whether He will find this kind of persistent faith in prayer when He returns—prayer crying out for justice in a time when truth and justice are trampled in the streets. How shameful it will be in that day for those who, like the disciples in the garden, could not stay awake for their appointed hour to watch and pray. Much prayer will be offered in the closing hour of this age, rising as incense before the throne (see Rev. 5:8; 8:1-4).

Unauthorized fire (cf. Lev. 10:1-2) may be viewed as the fire that fuels passionate prayer outside of the heart of God—prayer with requests fueled by selfish motives, unwholesome desires, ambition, or desire for prosperous ease. The fire for this 'incense' does not come from sacrificing the lusts of the flesh but from fanning the flames of carnal desire. Having pure motives is difficult to attain in this age, underscoring the importance of the role of our great and merciful high priest who intercedes on our behalf.

Jesus' High Priestly Prayer

John recorded Jesus' final sermon, and if His first sermon preached moral and upright behavior by God's higher standards (Sermon on the Mount), His last sermon exuded tenderness, compassion, and hopeful expectation to calm the anxieties of those closest to Him (John 14-16). In this last discourse, Jesus told the disciples they had been declared 'clean' and were no longer only bondservants but friends privileged to know their Master's business. While the apostles continued to refer to themselves as the bondservants of Christ in the letters they later wrote, their dual identity as friends opened up a broader realm of revelation so they would learn the prophetic plans of God, as did the prophets of old.

After encouraging the disciples by giving them knowledge of the events in the immediate future, Jesus prays with the same tenderness with which He spoke to the disciples. The priestly prayer of Jesus, recorded in John 17, gives us a feel for the quality content of His prayers. Jesus prayed that God's glory would be seen through the authority the Father gave to the Son. There is a blend of request, proclamation of truth, and statement of reality in this prayer. Taking our lead from Jesus, we learn that although God knows everything in advance, it is proper to make our requests known with both a recounting of applicable truth and statement of current circumstances. In His prayer, Jesus defined eternal life as knowing the one true God and believing Jesus is Messiah.

- **Address/Request**: *"Father, the time has come. Glorify your Son, that your Son may glorify you. For you granted him authority over all people that he might give eternal life to all those you have given him.*
- **Proclamation of truth**: *Now this is eternal life: that they may know you, the only true God, and Jesus Christ, whom you have sent.*
- **Statement of what has taken place**: *I have brought you glory on earth by completing the work you gave me to do.*
- **Restated Request**: *And now, Father, glorify me in your presence with the glory I had with you before the world began."* (from John 17:1-5, NIV)

After His personal request, Jesus then prayed for His disciples (John 17:6-18). This blend of stating truth principles and the reality of how that truth applies in the situation is seen here as well. Jesus began by stating He made God's *name* known to them (John 17:6). "The word 'name' here includes the attributes or character of God. Jesus had made known his character, his law, his will, his plan of mercy—or, in other words, he had revealed God to them. The word 'name' is often used to designate the person and his authority."[2] This provides insight to help us understand why Jesus' *name* is above all names.

This prayer, because it is Jesus' last before the crucifixion, demonstrates those matters Jesus deemed most important for the disciples. He asks the Father to:

- keep them **in the knowledge of God** *so they may be one*;
- protect them from the evil one;
- sanctify them by the truth.

These three are the bondservant's primary needs. Finally, Jesus turns His attention to believers throughout the age before His return. In addition to restating these three, Jesus adds His request that the Father make future believers one *so that* (John 17:20-26):

- they will abide in God (rather than the doctrines or traditions of men);
- the world will know Jesus is Messiah;
- the world will witness the love of God.

Jesus then asks the Father to grant them to be with Him where He is: the place of sonship and eternal fellowship with God. Jesus closes by stating He will continue to reveal the knowledge of God so the love the Father has for Him would be in them, and that Jesus Himself would be in them. Albert Barnes stated, "It is worthy of remark here how entirely the union of his people occupied the mind of Jesus as he drew near to death. He saw the danger of strifes and contentions in the church. He knew the imperfections of even the best of men. He saw how prone they would be to passion and ambition; how ready to mistake love of sect or party for zeal for pure religion; how selfish and worldly men in the church might divide his followers, and produce unholy feeling and contention; and he saw, also, how much this would do to dishonor religion. Hence, he took occasion, when he was about to die, to impress the importance of union on his disciples..."[3]

Unity and love are to distinguish the *ekklesia* under the new covenant from all other groups, just as circumcision is the hallmark of the covenant with Abraham. Barnes commented: "This command he gave them as he was about to leave them, to be a badge of discipleship, by which they might be known as his friends and followers, and by which they might be distinguished from all others... is called new, not because there was no command before which required people to love their fellowman, for one great precept of the law was that they should love their neighbor as themselves... but it was new because it had never before been made that by which any class or body of people had been known and distinguished. The Jew was known by his external rites, by his uniqueness of dress, etc.; the philosopher by some other mark of distinction; the military man by another, etc. In none of these cases had love for each other been the distinguishing and special badge by which they were known. But in the case of Christians they were not to be known by distinctions of wealth, or learning, or fame; they were not to aspire to earthly honors; they were not to adopt any special style of dress or badge, but they were to be *distinguished by tender and constant attachment to each other*.

"This was to surmount all distinction of country, of color, of rank, of office, of sect. Here they were to feel that they were on a level, that they had common wants, were redeemed by the same sacred blood, and were going to the same heaven. They were to befriend each other in trials; be careful of each other's feelings and reputation; deny themselves to promote each other's welfare... 'As I have loved you, that ye also love one another.' His love for them was strong, continued, unremitting, and he was now about to show his love for them in death... This was a new expression of love; and it showed the strength of attachment which we ought to have for Christians, and how ready we should be to endure hardships, to encounter dangers, and to practice self-denial, to benefit those for whom the Son of God laid down his life."[4]

Does this mean we forget our differences and just get together to sing "Kumbaya"? This is hard to answer because the natural mind looks at the two millennia of factions and discord and says, 'no way.' But the prayer of Jesus and the power of God to answer His prayer forces us to admit it must be so. Paul prayed for love to abound among believers:

> *And it is my prayer that your love may abound more and more, with knowledge and all discernment.* -Php. 1:9, ESV

Jesus' prayer indicates we will be one as we are kept and continue in the ongoing revelation of the knowledge of God. Heresy must be battled in humility, truth, and love, not rancor, self-righteousness, or pride. Thus Paul also prayed we would know the love of Christ which *surpasses* knowledge (Eph. 3:19). One thing true believers can agree on as a point of commonality: salvation comes through Christ alone.

The Altar of Incense and the Mercy Seat

> *There is one God and one Mediator between God and mankind, the Man Christ Jesus.* -1 Tim. 2:5, NKJV

The apostles were committed to continual prayer and the ministry of the Word (Acts 6:4). We are to continually offer our sacrifice of praise as well (Heb. 13:15), foreshadowed by the incense which continually rose before God in the earthly temple. As we participate in this ministry of intercession, our prayers ascend before the throne as incense and are very pleasing to God (Rev. 5:8; 8:3-4).

> *Let my prayer be set before You as incense, the lifting up of my hands* (in submission) *as the evening sacrifice.* -Ps. 141:2, NKJV (parenthetical added)

Moses built the tent of meeting patterned after what he was shown on the mountain. It was a copy and shadow of the heavenly counterpart. The Lord instructed Moses that He would meet with him between the cherubim above the mercy seat (Ex. 25:22), appearing there in a cloud (Lev. 16:2). The incense itself sent forth a cloud to cover sin until blood could be applied to the mercy seat by the high priest, preserving the life of the one who entered the holiest place (Lev. 16:13-14). This is a picture of intercessory prayer covering the sinner until he receives the blood of Christ through repentance.

Inside the ark beneath the mercy seat are the tablets of testimony. These are the two witnesses that testify against sins committed against God and against man. The tablets represent the righteousness and justice that are the foundation of God's throne. Without the blood of atonement, the two witnesses within the ark condemn all who would presume to approach God on their own merit. Hence, the ark is a picture of God's throne where we come for either mercy or judgment (see also Ps. 97:2).

> *Righteousness and justice are the foundation of your throne; steadfast love and faithfulness go before you.* -Ps. 89:14, ESV

Steadfast love and faithfulness *go before Him* because His great love prefers to show mercy, and His faithfulness determines His response to the truly penitent. Judgment is God's 'strange act' (Isa. 28:21, KJV), and He is not pleased with the death of the wicked. Under the new covenant, we find this typology met in Christ. Jesus left the earth after the resurrection to assume His high priestly role in the heavenly sanctuary, ever interceding for those who are His. Jesus came with His own blood into the heavenly tabernacle, the only sacrifice ever needed to secure our place before the throne. Because of Jesus, we come to the throne with confidence, reconciled to the Father we yearn for.

As with the earthly copy before the mercy seat, the golden altar of incense in heaven is before the throne of God (Rev. 8:3). The earthly copy had to be atoned for each year by the blood of the sin offering, but the heavenly reality needed only one sacrifice: the innocent blood of the only sinless man, Jesus (Heb. 9:23-28). Jesus continues to serve in the true sanctuary in heaven to appear for us in God's presence (Heb. 8:1-2; 9:24). He intercedes for us before the throne night and day, for His blood 'speaks a better word than the blood of Abel' (Heb. 12:24). Because He endures throughout eternity, Jesus has a permanent priesthood and is therefore able to save completely those who come to God through Him by the intercession He continually offers (Heb. 7:24-25).

Jesus, Our Mercy Seat

Jesus' incense, as in the earthly copy, rises perpetually before the throne as He lives to intercede and pleads on our behalf before the mercy seat of God. *Hilasterion*, the Greek word used for 'mercy seat,' appears only twice in the New Testament. In its second occurrence, it is used in a description of the ark of the covenant (Heb. 9:5). The first occurrence, however, makes a direct reference to Jesus as *hilasterion*, translated 'sacrifice of atonement':

> *God presented Christ as a sacrifice of atonement* (**hilasterion**), *through the shedding of his blood—to be received by faith.* -Rom. 3:25a, NIV (parenthetical added)

Jesus *is* the mercy seat. When combined with the final events of the crucifixion, namely the rending of the veil that kept everyone from God's presence, we have a meaningful reminder of the work of redemption Jesus accomplished at the cross. Because His flesh was sacrificed for us, symbolized by the torn veil (Matt. 27:50-51a), we now have access to the holiest place where God dwells. The blood of the only righteous man provided us with the only means to gain entrance to the throne room of God without fear of judgment (Heb. 10:19-22). For all who are in Christ, the throne of God is a place of mercy.

By virtue of His indestructible life, Jesus' blood becomes an eternal sacrifice for all, satisfying the judgment of God. As long as we come by virtue of Jesus' righteous blood, we have access to the throne of God. Jesus is the *only* Mediator between God and man (1 Tim. 2:5). As in any court, when the King extends the scepter indicating His favor, it would be utter folly and an insult to the King to address some lesser person in the court to make our requests known. In parallel fashion, no one would dare think to address the bailiff or observers when the Judge is speaking directly to us in our earthly courts.

Likewise, the scepter of God has been extended to every believer who approaches through Christ. Our prayers must be addressed to God alone, not the observers in the court gallery, for example, the departed saints, venerated fathers, or a blessed mother. No Scripture supports this practice: there is *one* mediator between God and man—only one. Saints' medals won't help us ward off evil or illness anymore than a string of garlic around the neck. We cling to the only Savior of mankind, Jesus Christ our Mediator. This is wisdom founded on truth.

Any attempt to enter through good works or on our own merit leads to the fire of judgment issuing from the throne. Anyone who does so is under the curse of the law and will not receive mercy. By analogy, consider someone who commits a string of crimes but somehow believes his prior philanthropic deeds and volunteer work negate his sentence for the crimes committed. We would shake our heads at his ignorance for misunderstanding the difference between a legal judicial sentence for crime conviction, and the entirely separate matter of the performance of good deeds.

Under this false ideology, this man would be unpleasantly surprised when he enters a typical court of law. His charitable works do not change the sentence for his crimes. Furthermore, if he is even more unwise to ignore the exceptional legal counsel provided for him without cost, he is twice a fool and will likely be prosecuted to the full extent of the law, receiving the maximum sentence. So let us enter with humility and thanks, addressing our requests to God our Father through the righteousness of Christ.

> *Therefore, since we have a great high priest who has ascended into heaven, Jesus the Son of God, let us hold firmly to the faith we profess... Let us then approach God's throne of grace with confidence, so that we may receive mercy and find grace to help us in our time of need.* -Heb. 4:14,16, NIV

Jesus' Teaching on Prayer

> *One day Jesus was praying in a certain place. When he finished, one of his disciples said to him, "Lord, teach us to pray, just as John taught his disciples."*
> -Luke 11:1, NIV

The Lord's Prayer is the primary model Jesus gave the disciples after He told them how *not* to pray (Matt. 6:5-15; Luke 11:1-4). Those who loved to pray in order to be seen by men were counted as hypocrites, the praise of man being their only reward. These were not praying to the Father but to please or impress the crowd. Jesus instructed His followers to pray to the Father in secret without babbling repetitiveness like the pagans, who recite the same words over and over devoid of any heart engagement. These think they will be heard because of their 'many words,' *polulogia*. This Greek word is comparable to our English words *loquacity*: babbling or talking excessively; and *prolixity*: extending to great, unnecessary, or tedious length, or prolific talking in a rambling, wordy, or diffuse manner.[5] The bottom line—get to the point in a reverential way because your Father already knows what you need.

Jesus honors a heart posture of humility in prayer (Luke 18:9-14). If we come to prayer in self-righteousness, extolling our accomplishments or arrogantly demanding our rights as children of God, we have effectively closed our channel of communication with God. It takes much time spent in the Word in a posture of prayer to rid our hearts of these tendencies. Jesus instructed the disciples to pray like this:

> *Our Father in heaven, Hallowed be Your name. Your kingdom come. Your will be done on earth as it is in heaven. Give us this day our daily bread. And forgive us our debts, as we forgive our debtors. And do not lead us into temptation, but deliver us from the evil one. For Yours is the kingdom and the power and the glory forever. Amen.* -Matt. 6:9-13, NKJV

'Our Father in Heaven, Hallowed Be Your Name'

We begin by acknowledging God as Father. Jesus tenderly revealed that we are joined relationally to God as children are to a loving Father (Abba). At the same time, we must also approach in the fear of the Lord to honor His name.

> *The Lord is like a father to his children, tender and compassionate to those who fear him... "And I will sanctify My great name, which has been profaned among the nations, which you have profaned in their midst; and the nations shall know that I am the LORD," says the Lord GOD, "when I am hallowed in you before their eyes."* -Ps. 103:13, NLT; Ezk. 36:23, NKJV

'Your Kingdom Come; Your Will Be Done on Earth as It Is in Heaven'

The first petition requests God's kingdom be established and His will accomplished on earth as it already is in heaven. This request is based on the expectation of the restoration of the created order and removal of all injustice, unrighteousness, and deception. "The whole of the disciple's life is lived in reflection of what God will eventually do."[6]

> *[T]he God of heaven will set up a kingdom that will never be destroyed or conquered. It will crush all these kingdoms into nothingness, and it will stand forever... And I heard a loud voice from the throne saying, "Behold, the dwelling place of God is with man. He will dwell with them, and they will be his people, and God himself will be with them as their God"... And he who was seated on the throne said, "Behold, I am making all things new."* -Dan. 2:44, NLT; Rev. 21:3,5a, ESV

'Give Us This Day Our Daily Bread'

The request for bread is often viewed as making our physical needs known, but it is also and probably primarily a request for the spiritual food we need each day (Luke 12:22-

31). Just as yesterday's meals will not suffice for our physical body today, neither will yesterday's spiritual food be adequate for today.

> *Do not labor for the food that perishes, but for the food that endures to eternal life, which the Son of Man will give to you. For on him God the Father has set his seal.* -John 6:27, ESV

'And Forgive Us Our Debts, as We Forgive Our Debtors'

Our request for forgiveness will be as complete as the forgiveness we have given to those who have wronged us (see Matt. 18:23-35). Forgiveness for our sins comes by God's grace and should not be viewed as an entitlement. The New Testament clearly teaches here and elsewhere (Matt. 6:14-15; Mark 11:25-26; Luke 6:36-38) that it is contingent based on the degree of forgiveness we have shown to those who have (or who we perceive have) wronged us.

> *When you stand praying, if you hold anything against anyone, forgive him,* **so that your Father in heaven may forgive you** *your sins.* -Mark 11:25, NIV

Jesus prefaced the parable of the unmerciful servant by teaching about sin and church discipline (see Matt. 18:15-22). He instructed His followers to take aside a believer caught in sin and discuss his error privately. If he listens, there is reconciliation. If he doesn't, we are to take one or two witnesses and again address the wrong committed. If he still refuses to listen, the matter is to be brought before the assembly.

If there is still no repentance, fellowship must be discontinued. Jesus then explained that what we decide on earth regarding the retained sin of an unrepentant believer will have already been bound to that person in heaven—a sin retained because of a heart that will not turn. Peter asked how often we are to forgive someone who sins: 'up to seven times?' Jesus responded by saying 'seventy times seven' (Matt. 18:21-22). The mathematical mind will calculate this out. But Jesus meant *every time* and *completely*.

The two or three witnesses in Jesus' teaching are those who, out of love and concern, confront the wayward brother (Matt. 18:16). If he doesn't repent, his sin is retained because of the testimony of the witnesses (vv. 17-18). John also recorded that after Jesus breathed on the disciples to receive the Holy Spirit, He gave them authority to forgive or retain the sins of others (John 20:22-24). Jesus reiterated this in Matthew 18:19. The witnesses who are in agreement regarding a brother in habitual sin have the power to keep his sin bound to him: not forgiven and not covered until he repents. The flow of thought in this entire section (Matt. 18:5-35) deals with sin and forgiveness.

> *Truly I say to you, whatever you bind on earth* **shall have been bound** *in heaven; and whatever you loose on earth* **shall have been loosed** *in heaven. Again I say to you, that if two of you agree on earth about anything that they may ask, it shall*

> *be done for them by My Father who is in heaven. For where two or three have gathered together in My name, I am there in their midst.* -Matt. 18:18-20, NASB

To take this passage out of its context to come up with a principle for prayer that was not intended by the text depicts the way in which we practice eisegesis (reading into a passage something that is not actually there). While I believe in the power of agreement in prayer, especially as practiced by the early church that operated in one mind and heart, to interpret this particular passage in that way should be viewed as homiletical.

Jesus then moved right into the parable of the unmerciful servant, helping us understand the immeasurable quality of the forgiveness He bestows on us in comparison with the petty nature of our unforgiveness and the harsh vindictiveness with which we act toward those who have wronged us. Jesus brought this up to warn us to place top priority on reconciliation of our wayward members through repentance, rather than on 'cleaning house' in a legalistic fashion to rid our gatherings of all those who are not compliant with our list of do's and don'ts. Those who are the 'two or three witnesses' must love the sinner and be in pain over his pending removal from the fellowship, possessing enough agony of heart that they will fast and pray for his repentance and restoration to fellowship (contrast with the witnesses of Deut. 17:6-7).

> *Pay attention to yourselves! If your brother sins, rebuke him, and if he repents, forgive him, and if he sins against you seven times in the day, and turns to you seven times, saying, 'I repent,' you must forgive him.* -Luke 17:3-4, ESV

Jesus gave the church the authority of heaven to bind unrepented sins and loose repented sins with the presupposition that the witnesses have the mind of Christ, the heart of the Father, and the witness of the Holy Spirit. The decision has already been rendered in heaven, noted by the verb tenses in Matthew 18:18. As previously quoted, the NASB translates these in keeping with the Greek ('shall have been'). The congregation is merely following through on what has already been decided in heaven.

Discipline and mercy must be held in proper tension in the church. The community of believers must divorce itself of professing Christians who continually and habitually sin with a 'high hand' so neither the sinner nor those outside the church will delude themselves into thinking a believer can still be in bondage to the world and inherit eternal life. In so doing, we keep ourselves from the sin of silence when God has instructed us to warn those who choose the way of sin, which leads to death.

> *Now if a righteous person turns from his righteousness and practices iniquity, and I put a stumbling block in front of him, he will die.* **If you did not warn him, he will die because of his sin** *and the righteous acts he did will not be remembered. Yet **I will hold you responsible for his blood**. But if you warn the righteous person that he should not sin, and he does not sin, he will indeed live because he listened to your warning, and you will have saved your life.* -Ezk. 3:20-21, HCSB

The goal of church discipline is true repentance, covering the sin, and reconciliation. Peter encouraged the believers to have 'intense and unfailing love for each other' so they could disregard the offenses of others (1 Pet. 4:8). Paul instructed the believers in this same vein, advising them to walk in compassion, kindness, humility, gentleness, and patience so they will be able to forbear and forgive one another as the Lord had forgiven them. Only love will bind us together in perfect unity (Col. 3:12-14).

Binding and loosing are issues of judicial authority in the case of a sinner brought before the congregation. Paul reminded us we will one day judge the world and angels (1 Cor. 6:2-3). Our faithfulness to this duty in this age prepares us for the judicial authority we will be given to exercise in the age to come. This will most likely go to those who have been faithful to discharge this duty *in spirit and truth* in this age.

'And Do Not Lead Us into Temptation'

The next petition in the Lord's Prayer will only make sense to us in light of other passages of Scripture. The thought is better understood by this paraphrase: 'Father, do not allow the enemy to tempt us without alerting us and showing us how to escape his scheme to cause us to fall. Help us focus on You and not the lure of sin.'

Charles Finney points to our weakness as the basis for this request. "You will observe, moreover, that this petition does not by any means imply that God leads men into temptation in order to make them sin, so that we must needs implore of Him not to lead us thus, lest He should do it. No, that is not implied at all; but the spirit of the petition is this; O Lord, Thou knowest how weak I am, and how prone to sin; therefore let thy providence guard and keep me that I may not indulge in anything whatever that may prove to me a temptation to sin. Deliver us from all iniquity—from all the stratagems of the devil. Throw around us all thy precious guardianship, that we may be kept from sinning against Thee. How needful this protection, and how fit that we should pray for it without ceasing!"[7]

We see three principles at work in regards to temptation. *First*, Satan has to ask permission to tempt us. As in the examples of Job and the disciples, Satan must bring his case before God regarding the trial and temptation through which he wants to put the believer. From the record in Job, it would seem Satan makes the initial accusation and states his premise before the Court of Heaven—that the individual will sin in response to the trial. When God gives His consent to the trial, it is important we realize God does not tempt us to sin. James makes this clear by stating God tempts no man to sin (James 1:13). God's purposes in a trial are redemptive: to give us strength to overcome or to expose what is lurking in our hearts. God may even warn us ahead of time about the trial to come, as when Jesus warned Peter that Satan had asked to sift them as wheat:

> **Satan has asked to sift all of you** (plural) **as wheat. But I have prayed for you, Simon, that your faith may not fail.** -Luke 22:31-32a, NIV (parenthetical added)

[Note: Satan did not ask to sift only Peter; the 'you' in v. 31 is plural. This is in keeping with Jesus' statement as recorded in Matthew 26:31 that they would *all* fall away.]

Second, no trial is more than we can bear for two reasons: 1.) there is nothing new under the sun—all temptation is common to man, and 2.) God promised to give us the strength we need to overcome. The temptation Satan meant for our harm, God intends to use for our good. We have foreknowledge that God has given us grace to pass the test if we don't let our carnal nature take over.

> *But God is faithful [to His Word and to His compassionate nature], and He [can be trusted]* **not to let you be tempted and tried and assayed beyond your ability and strength** *of resistance and power to endure, but with the temptation He will [always]* **also provide the way out** *(the means of escape to a landing place), that you may be capable and strong and powerful to bear up under it patiently.*
> -1 Cor. 10:13b, AMP

And *third,* anyone who falls in a time of testing does so because he allowed himself to be enticed by the temptation, giving birth to the evil desire conceived in his heart. But the one who perseveres under trial and overcomes temptation receives a crown of life (see James 1:12-15). (This will be discussed in greater depth in Section 5.)

Trials test our faith, producing steadfastness that leads to maturity and a heart that is perfect toward God (James 1:2-4). Suffering produces perseverance, the tool by which the Lord fashions our character. By the transformation of our character, we have hope of being blameless when Jesus returns (Rom. 5:3-4)

> *God disciplines us for our good, that we may share in his holiness. No discipline seems pleasant at the time, but painful. Later on, however, it produces a harvest of righteousness and peace for those who have been trained by it. Therefore, strengthen your feeble arms and weak knees.* -Heb. 12:10b-12, NIV

'But Deliver Us from the Evil One'

In the second half of this petition regarding temptation, Jesus taught His disciples to ask for deliverance from evil. He has promised to show us the way of escape, and we must pray to find that way. At Gethsemane, Jesus admonished the disciples to pray *so that* they would not fall into temptation. Without prayer, we will be taken by temptation unawares, and our chances of succumbing to temptation are much greater. Even when Jesus warned Peter that Satan asked to sift him, it was Jesus who prayed. Peter fell asleep instead of praying, as did all the rest, and all stumbled headlong into the trap of the enemy a few hours later. This type of prayer is preventative medicine for the soul against the danger of falling into sin.

Jesus also instructed us to love and pray for our enemies and those who persecute us (Matt. 5:44; Luke 6:27-28), for God is not willing that any should perish but that all would come to repentance (2 Pet. 3:9). This is one of the most difficult things to accomplish during a trial, but the Holy Spirit will enable us if we are willing.

Both Jesus and Stephen modeled this with their dying breaths (Luke 23:34; Acts 7:59-60). When we have ungodly leadership, governmental or otherwise, no matter how our feelings want us to think and act toward them, we can always pray they would learn to shun evil and embrace righteousness and truth so we, as believers, can live in peace, free to worship God. God wants all men to be saved and know truth (1 Tim. 2:1-4).

Prayer in the Church

The church is to be a house of prayer, not a mere social network, or worse, a market place (Matt. 21:13). We are to pray for workers to be sent out into His harvest (Luke 10:2). We are to keep watch and constantly be on our guard because we don't know how or when trials will come (Matt. 26:41; Mark 14:33-34,38; Col. 4:2; 1 Pet. 5:8). By maintaining a watchful posture in prayer, we can avoid being taken unawares by a time of testing ('falling into temptation,' Luke 22:40).

> *But keep on the alert at all times, praying that you may have strength to escape all these things that are about to take place, and to stand before the Son of Man.* -Luke 21:36, NASB

Peter reminded the believers we are in the last days and therefore must be clear-minded and self-controlled so we can pray (1 Pet. 4:7). Believers have been afforded an incredible privilege in that we have access to the throne room of God and can enter boldly with our requests. Jesus taught the disciples that if they had faith and believed, they would receive whatever they asked for in prayer (see also Matt. 21:21-22; Mark 11:22-25; John 14:12-14; 16:23-28).

> *Ask and it will be given to you; seek and you will find; knock and the door will be opened to you. For everyone who asks receives; he who seeks finds; and to him who knocks, the door will be opened... If you then, though you are evil, know how to give good gifts to your children, how much more will your Father in heaven **give the Holy Spirit to those who ask** him!* -Luke 11:9-10,13, NIV

The idea that we can ask for anything in prayer and receive it creates tension with other passages that can only be resolved by qualifying Jesus' statement with the underlying truths explained in the whole counsel of God. The qualifying passages include Jesus' own statements about only doing and saying what He saw the Father doing and saying. If Jesus is our example, we must always first seek God's will and timing in each situation. Otherwise, how can we have bold confidence and faith that we have what we ask unless the request first originated in God's will? The apostle John agrees:

> *Now this is the confidence that we have in Him, that if we ask anything **according to His will**, He hears us. And if we know that He hears us, whatever we ask, we know that we have the petitions that we have asked of Him.* -1 John 5:14-15, NKJV

Furthermore, what may seem like an overtly sound scriptural request to us at present may not be in keeping with God's decision in the matter. We do not have all the details that are available to God. Our confidence must be grounded in obedience and submission to His will.

> *Dear friends, if our hearts do not condemn us, we have confidence before God and receive from him anything we ask, because we obey his commands and do what pleases him.* -1 John 3:21-22, NIV

Prayer in its full New Testament meaning is addressed to God as Father, in Jesus' name as Mediator, and through the Holy Spirit as enabler by His grace. There is no evidence prayer was ever reduced to a continual barrage of requests for material goods. This mentality has truly defiled the church.

No one in their right mind would think to barge into the White House and demand a new car as our right as Americans. Yet One greater than the president is here and has availed His heavenly throne room to us for our requests. Yes, we go as children, but which children do you look forward to spending time with: those who want to be with you because they enjoy your company and share your interests, or those who constantly demand another toy, gadget, or even their inheritance ahead of time because of impatience, selfishness, and/or an improper sense of entitlement?

Judicial Format of Prayers for Justice

The more we study prayer and the trials Christians will undergo, the more apparent it becomes we are involved in judicial and legal proceedings taking place in the High Court of Heaven. We may not presently relate to this point, failing to see its importance in our personal relationship with God. But at the close of the age, with escalated persecution of Christians and Jews, prayers for justice will increase, and these are the prayers Jesus said will be answered quickly. At this point, we will only take a brief look at this principle, finishing the discussion in the next chapter.

Peter and John

After Peter and John were released from prison, they prayed in a manner similar to what Jesus demonstrated (see Acts 4). This pattern of prayer follows a logical judicial progression. Prior to the prayer, the injustice currently taking place is recorded. The apostles were arrested and put in prison for healing the lame beggar (v. 3). The next day they were released after being threatened and commanded not to speak in Jesus' name (vv. 17-21).

The apostles open their prayer by addressing the Heavenly Court properly, giving honor to the One addressed, the Benefactor and Judge who renders decisions on the requests brought forth. This opening statement acknowledges God's authority, establishing His 'jurisdiction' over the matter they are presenting (akin to addressing the Court, 'Your

Honor'). Peter and John first proclaim acknowledgment of the Lord as the Creator and Sovereign over the entire earth (Acts 4:24).

Next, the case is stated briefly so as not to waste the court's time, laying a foundation from relevant established parameters and examples in the Word (using 'case law' to establish precedent). The 'precedent' is then applied to the current plight as support for their position (statement of the injustice taking place). In this example, Peter and John proceed to remind God of His Word in Psalm 2 regarding the plotting of the nations against the Lord's anointed (vv. 25-26). They apply this to their current situation by then stating the details of what was taking place around them: they were being threatened by the governing authorities in Jerusalem for proclaiming Jesus as Messiah (vv. 27-29a).

Finally, the request is made (legally termed a 'motion') for which the Judge will render a decision. In this example, the apostles asked for boldness to speak despite the threats, and for signs and wonders to confirm their message (vv. 29-30). As the accuser, Satan will also make his motion. Just as in a court of law, whichever motion the Judge accepts is entered into the official record as the verdict and is favorably acted upon. In this case, the Heavenly Judge decided in the apostles' favor.

> *After this prayer, the meeting place shook, and they were all filled with the Holy Spirit. Then they preached the word of God with boldness.* -Acts 4:31, NLT

This type of language is also used in the book of Revelation when Babylon receives her judgment, evidence that the believers are crying out for justice during this time:

> *Rejoice over her, O heaven, and you saints and apostles and prophets, because* **God has pronounced judgment for you** *against her.* -Rev. 18:20, NASB

Jehoshaphat

A look at this Old Testament passage shows the same judicial progression (2 Chron. 20:1-17). The events leading up to this prayer placed the nation of Judah in a very precarious position (vv. 1-4). The Moabites, Ammonites, and Mt. Seir made war on Jehoshaphat by sending a vast army. The King resolutely inquires of the Lord and proclaims a fast. All of Judah came together to seek God's help.

- **Addressing the court and establishing jurisdiction** (vv. 5-6): Jehoshaphat begins his prayer: 'O LORD, God of our fathers, are You not the God who is in heaven? You rule over all the kingdoms of the nations. Power and might are in Your hand, and no one can withstand You.'
- **Citing case law/setting precedent** (vv. 7-9): The king reminds God of how He had driven out the inhabitants of the land to give the land to Israel because of the covenant God made with His friend Abraham. He builds his case by reminding God that Israel built the temple for God's name, and of the foundational prayer made by Solomon: 'If calamity comes upon us, whether the sword of judgment,

plague or famine, we will stand in Your presence before this temple that bears Your Name and cry out to You in our distress, and You will hear and save us.'
- **Stating the current injustice** (vv. 10-11): Ammon, Moab, and Mt. Seir, whose land God prohibited the Israelites from invading, were now repaying the kindness by trying to drive out Israel from the land God gave them.
- **Motion** (v. 12): 'O our God, will You not judge them? For we have no power to face this vast army that is attacking us. We do not know what to do, but our eyes are upon You.'
- **Verdict on the motion** (vv. 13-17): Everyone stood there waiting for the Lord. The Spirit of the Lord spoke through Jahaziel: 'Do not be afraid or discouraged because of this vast army. For the battle is not yours, but God's... You will not have to fight this battle. Take up your positions; stand firm and see the deliverance the LORD will give you. Do not be afraid; do not be discouraged. Go out to face them tomorrow, and the LORD will be with you.'

(Exciting conclusion at 2 Chron. 20:18-30.)

Hezekiah

With the threat of attack from Assyria, Hezekiah offers a prayer in similar format (2 Kings 19:15-19). The preexisting conditions are explained in 2 Kings 18:9-19:14, and the verdict recorded as given by Isaiah (2 Kings 19:20-34).

- **Addressing the court and establishing jurisdiction** (v. 15): Hezekiah prayed, 'O LORD, God of Israel, enthroned between the cherubim. *You alone are God over all the kingdoms of the earth*. You have made heaven and earth.'
- **Citing case law/setting precedent**: (included in the opening address; establishing jurisdiction also states the precedent that *God alone* has authority over the earth, not the king of Assyria who boasted of his might and showed contempt for God)
- **Stating the current injustice** (vv. 16-18): Hezekiah asks the Lord to see and listen to the taunts of Assyria that insult the name of the living God, adding that Assyria has laid waste the other nations and destroyed their gods.
- **Motion** (v. 19): The king then asks for deliverance so that all kingdoms will know that the Lord alone is God.
- **Verdict on the motion** (vv. 20-34): Isaiah reported the Lord's decision that Assyria will neither attack nor enter the city, but return the way he came. 'I will defend this city and save it, for My sake and for the sake of David My servant.'

As a result, 185,000 Assyrians were killed that night by the angel of the Lord, and Sennacherib, king of Assyria, broke camp and withdrew (vv. 35-36).

In plain everyday terms, these prayers are initiated by acknowledging God as Sovereign, having authority over all the earth. Next, passages of Scripture or concepts from the Word that pertain to the situation to validate the request are verbalized in the prayer.

These may not be direct quotations from specific passages, but they will certainly embody one or more of the many truths or concepts in God's Word. A brief recounting of the current circumstances follows in order to bring to God's attention the injustice of the present situation. The petition is completed with the applicable request for justice in the situation (the motion).

Not all prayer will be in this format, for not all prayer offered is about injustice and dire circumstances. Sometimes we just need to go to *HaShem* as our Father and pour our hearts out before Him, whether in spontaneous exuberant praise or out of despair or longing from an afflicted heart and soul. We don't have to search far and wide to find these types of relational prayers in the Psalms. But the prayers for justice have their place. Both Old and New Testament writers record their use and the favorable results for God's people. These prayers will have particular significance at the close of this age.

Apostolic Prayers

When we examine the prayer requests of the apostles, we get a broader idea of what should take priority in our own prayers. Many prayer gatherings across the earth have turned their focus to the apostolic prayers because of the wisdom and priority these requests have in the heart of God. In addition to the apostolic prayers are the themes of God's heart for the believers in the new covenant. These prayers include requests for:

- the power of the Holy Spirit to be witnesses (Acts 1:8)
- visions, dreams, and the ability to prophesy (Acts 2:17-21)
- boldness in preaching followed by healing, signs, and wonders (Acts 4:29-31)
- all Israel to be saved (Rom. 10:1; 11:26-27)
- like-mindedness (unity) among believers (Rom. 15:5-13; Eph. 4:3)
- understanding and readiness of speech (1 Cor. 1:5-6)
- no lack in spiritual gifts (1 Cor. 1:7-8)
- wisdom and revelation in the knowledge of God (Eph. 1:17-19)
- inner strength, Christ's presence, and grounding in Christ's love (Eph. 3:16-19)
- love to abound as we grow in knowledge and discernment (Php. 1:9; Col. 3:14)
- discernment to approve what is worthy (Php. 1:10)
- sincerity without compromise or offense (Php. 1:10)
- evidence of righteous fruit (Php. 1:11)
- knowledge of His will with wisdom and understanding of His purposes (Col. 1:9)
- walking worthy of the Lord, fully pleasing to Him (Col. 1:10)
- fruitfulness in every good work (Col. 1:10)
- increase in the knowledge of God (Col. 1:10)
- strength for patience during trials (Col. 1:11)
- gratitude for our share in the inheritance of the saints (Col. 1:12)
- open doors of opportunity to share the gospel (Col. 4:3)
- more of His Spirit to complete what is lacking in our faith (1 Thes. 3:10)

- power and resolve for every good work of faith (2 Thes. 1:11-12)
- the message of the Lord to spread quickly and be received (2 Thes. 3:1)
- deliverance from wicked and evil men (2 Thes. 3:2)
- believers to be active in sharing their faith (Phile. 1:4-7)
- leadership to have a clear conscience and live honorably (Heb. 13:18)
- equipping the saints (Heb. 13:21)
- being pleasing to the Lord (Heb. 13:21)
- health (3 John 1:2)

Isaiah cried out to God to 'rend the heavens and come down to make His name known to His enemies and cause the nations to tremble at His presence' (Isa. 64:1-3). This will be the cry of the remnant of believers at the close of the age, and the book of Revelation testifies this prayer will be answered. This is also true of all the yet-to-be-answered prayers of Jesus and the apostles. Making these requests a priority in especially our corporate gatherings shows wisdom and a mind 'set on things above.'

Silent Prayer and Faith

Though praying biblical promises out loud in a corporate setting benefit all that are present, we cannot make a formula that only the prayers proclaimed audibly will be honored. Prayer does not have to be spoken out loud for it to be effectual, as some claim. Nehemiah prayed to God silently while he prepared to speak to the king (Neh. 2:4-5). Certainly it is obvious this prayer was not spoken out loud, given the strict protocol of that day for behavior in the presence of the king. His prayer was answered and his petition granted—a petition that benefitted the entire nation of Israel.

The woman with the issue of blood was undoubtedly silent in her prayer for healing as she reached out to touch the hem of Jesus' garment (or more precisely, the *tzitzit* of His prayer shawl), particularly as recorded in Matthew (Matt. 9:20-22; see also Mark 5:25-34). While her actions were in violation of the letter of the law (Lev. 15:25), out of desperation she did what Jesus taught was the spirit of the law. She perceived the grace present in Jesus and quietly but boldly laid hold of it for her healing because of her great need. Jesus praised her for her faith in Him and did not 'condemn the innocent' for violation of the ceremonial law.

The prayer of faith is foremost faith that Jesus is who says He is: the Son of God whose power is limitless. He alone received the Spirit without measure. The woman with the issue of blood did not possess a mere entity of faith or belief in healing. Her faith rested squarely in the One she specifically sought out for healing—Jesus. If her faith was the object and not Jesus, there would be no point in specifically seeking Him for healing. It is evident from the story that the object of her faith was Jesus Himself, who she believed had the power to cure her.

The faith with which we boldly enter the throne room of grace is not resident in ourselves as a commodity that in and of itself has properties to bring the desired results. The faith we have has been imparted to us by God ('God has allotted to each a measure of faith,' Rom. 12:3b). It is based on the way made for us by Jesus to be reconciled to God. Hence, we can enter with confidence to make our requests known.

Jacob had faith in God's promises, which prompted him to be bold in his prophetic blessings for each of his sons for the future, translated *'for the last days'* in some versions (see Gen. 49:1-27, KJV, NKJV, AMP, YLT, ASV, DARBY). The author of Hebrews also implied this when giving a list of men and women of faith (Heb. 11:21). He defined faith as believing what we have not seen, and having assurance of those things we hope for. This described all the people listed in the 'faith chapter.'

In the opening example of faith in Hebrews 11, the text reads, 'by faith, we understand God created the universe by His Word even though we were not there to witness it' (paraphrased). This is far different from stating, 'God created the universe by faith,' which is how this passage has been understood by some, somehow elevating faith (as an entity with its own power) to a level not intended. With close scrutiny of each of the examples, we notice the pattern is the same, 'by faith, so-and-so...' The first 'so-and-so' mentioned is 'we': 'By faith, *we* understand the universe was created by the Word of God...' (Heb. 11:3), not 'By faith God created the universe...' *We* are the ones who by faith believe God created the universe because we did not witness the event.

> *These were all commended for their faith, yet none of them received what had been promised.* -Heb. 11:39, NIV

It is also important to note that those listed in this chapter of Hebrews did not receive what they had faith and hoped for but were commended nonetheless for their faith. This is the exact opposite of what is preached in some circles, where we are taught we did not get what we hoped and prayed for because our faith was too small.

Jesus taught 'little faith' is in operation when we worry about provision (Matt. 6:30), when we are gripped with fear in dire circumstances (Matt. 8:26; 14:31), when we cannot grasp Jesus' teaching (Matt. 16:8), or when we are unable to cast out a demon (Matt. 17:20). In other cases, the problem is not lack of faith but misunderstanding the timing of God. There are other occasions where we don't get what we ask for because we are just plain asking for wrong things or with selfish motives (James 4:3). *Selah*.

Hindrances to Prayer

Knowing that Satan stands as our opposition when we bring requests forward in the court of God, we come to realize our requests can be contravened by his accusations. These accusations consist of pointing out sinful behaviors and thought patterns to which we still cling, heart motives that are impure, character flaws not yet dealt with, and/or immaturity of faith that has not yet been tested (whether simply being a new convert, or due to lack of attention to the Word, thereby stunting spiritual growth).

Satan also uses the tactic of calumny, 'a false and malicious statement designed to injure the reputation; slander with intent to defame'[8] (see Job 1:9-11; 2:3-4). This form of accusation, however, will have little chance of holding up in court. Unfortunately, with the exception of the new believer where immaturity is inherent and not an occasion to find fault, most of us have given Satan enough legitimate ammunition to keep our requests from being answered in our favor. The Word tells us prayer is hindered when:

- husbands do not treat their wives considerately and with respect (1 Pet. 3:7);
- when we ask with wrong purposes and evil, selfish motives to spend it on lavish living (James 4:2b-4); and
- when we are living in sin or entertain sin in our hearts (Ps. 66:17-19; 1 Pet. 3:12; cf. 2 Chron. 7:14; 1 Kings 8:35-36).

In light of the Sermon on the Mount, we become more and more aware that what is going on in our hearts affects the outcome of our requests as we stand before God. Knowing this provokes us to rely on the Word and the Spirit to bring about the heart change we have no hope of accomplishing on our own.

As we cooperate with the Holy Spirit and grow in our understanding, our hearts are transformed. Perfect performance is not required in order for our prayers to be heard, but we do need to be committed to obey the Lord. The opposite of this is sinning with a 'high hand,' a sure indication we have no intention of being loyal to God.

> *[C]onfess your sins to each other and pray for each other so that you may be healed.* ***The prayer of a righteous man is powerful and effective.*** -James 5:16, NIV

James reminds us that Elijah was a man with a human nature just like ours, not a super saint. His earnest prayers were heard and rain was withheld. When he prayed again, the rain returned (James 5:17-18). Prayers offered in faith that are in agreement with the Word as well as with the timing and purpose of God accomplish more than we know. By the examples of those who have gone before us, we must persevere in prayer and not give up hope, even if the results may not be seen in our lifetimes.

Praying for Others

Praying for the welfare of others was frequently recorded in the Word and modeled in the early church. We learn from Samuel that *not* praying for others is a sin against the Lord:

> *Moreover, as for me, far be it from me that I should sin against the LORD in ceasing to pray for you.* -1 Sam. 12:23a, NKJV

The New Testament gives examples of praying for the sick among us, those in danger, the downtrodden, those who mourn, the weak, and leadership who need courage and open doors. By praying for others, we open our hearts to their burdens and tenderize our conscience to someone other than ourselves. In this way, we learn and acquire compassion, which in turn helps promote and develop a sense of community and moral responsibility for the family of God and all those who are in need.

We also offer prayer on behalf of the ungodly, those who persecute us, government leaders, and nations. It is easy to pray for those we love or with whom we agree, but the true test of *agape* is whether we will pray for those who have offended or wronged us, for government leaders whose policies cause us to shudder, or for nations who persecute Christians, Jews, or other minorities, including those still in the womb. In these cases, we have to ask ourselves if we have enough faith to believe God can change people, governments, and whole nations. All it takes is a grain of faith the size of a mustard seed for God to work.

> *I urge you, first of all, to pray for all people. Ask God to help them; intercede on their behalf, and give thanks for them. Pray this way for kings and all who are in authority* **so that we can live peaceful and quiet lives marked by godliness and dignity**. *This is good and pleases God our Savior, who wants everyone to be saved and to understand the truth.* -1 Tim. 2:1-4, NLT

A group of people who pray together by the leading of the Spirit can accomplish much in the spiritual and physical realms. The unity that such prayer fosters cannot be obtained through potlucks, gym days, choir, or even Bible classes. Perhaps the lack of unity in the church that we see today is due in great measure to the low priority given to prayer. There is no lack of teaching in the body of Christ, yet this has not brought unity. Nor have special programs or outreaches accomplished unity or maturity of the saints.

> *Whereas* **the object and purpose of our instruction and charge is love**, *which springs from a pure heart and a good (clear) conscience and sincere (unfeigned) faith.* -1 Tim. 1:5, AMP

Closing Thoughts

Because the results of prayer are mostly not seen immediately, we grow impatient with its practice and opt for the activities that are 'fun' or give us a sense of accomplishment. Prayer is born out of obedience and *agape* love, the mark of a bondslave on the way to maturity, provided it is practiced in humility and by the guidance of the Word and Spirit. Without unity, the effectiveness of corporate prayer is questionable. But thankfully, the wisdom of God provided for our shortcomings by giving us the Holy Spirit as our guide and Jesus as our mediator.

- **Holy Spirit**: intercedes for us in keeping with God's will (Rom. 8:26-27)

- **Jesus**: 1.) keeps us from condemnation before God by declaring us righteous, giving us right standing before God and the privilege of making our requests known (Rom. 8:33-34; see also Heb. 7:25; cf. Isa. 53:11-12); and 2.) intercedes on our behalf because He is able to identify with our shortcomings during trials and testing (Heb. 2:16-18; 4:14-16; 1 John 2:1; see also Luke 22:31-32)

The ministry of both Jesus and the Holy Spirit functions on our behalf in a comprehensive way and places us in a position of grace before the throne of God. This makes prayer our most powerful weapon in combating darkness and adversity as well as for receiving the power and grace of God to accomplish all He has ordained for us to do. What could be more advantageous than having the Judge of the entire universe as our Father, and having expert legal counsel on our side?

In the temple ceremonies, coals from the altar of sacrifice were taken to heat the incense placed before the curtain veiling the holy of holies. Under the new covenant, we are the sacrifice, dying daily to our wants and the desires of the carnal nature, taking on the form of a bondservant to do the will of another. It is through this sacrifice, kindled by God's sanctifying fire through the work of the Holy Spirit, that our prayers can send forth the sweet aroma of incense and be pleasing in His sight.

While we are praying, it is vital we remember Jesus' passion for the unity of His body in His final recorded prayer before the cross. Paul shared this passion, and we must make it a priority in our own prayers.

> *[If] you have any encouragement from being united with Christ, if any comfort from his love, if any common sharing in the Spirit, if any tenderness and compassion, then* **make my joy complete by being like-minded, having the same love, being one in spirit and of one mind.** *Do nothing out of selfish ambition or vain conceit. Rather, in humility value others above yourselves, not looking to your own interests but each of you to the interests of the others.* -Php. 2:1-4, NIV

Chapter 15

When You Fast

> *But the days will come when the bridegroom will be taken away from them; then they will fast in those days.* -Luke 5:35, NKJV

Fasting can be done for many reasons, physical or spiritual, and is practiced by nearly all religions across the world. Some Christians claim this is why they do not fast, because it is no different from what the pagan religions do. Singing is also done for many reasons and practiced by nearly all religions across the world, yet is not shunned by the same individuals who shun fasting for this reason. What sets Christianity apart is the heart posture of the believer who is compelled to worship God through obedience in spirit and in truth. This includes fasting, singing, praying, giving, speaking truth, and so on.

The emphasis of this discussion will primarily focus on the circumstances that provoke us to fast. There are a number of works dealing with the mechanics of fasting readily available in books and on the web. Some have made the argument that everyone in times past knew how to conduct and break a fast because of its widespread practice. While this is probably true, we cannot jump to the conclusion the majority of people undertook *lengthy* fasts, which do require a bit of restraint and common sense when eating is resumed.

To have the type of detailed teaching we possess on the subject today would have been unnecessary because earlier cultures were not saturated with unhealthy 'food.' Meat was not eaten very often except by the well-to-do. Grains, vegetables, and fruit supplemented with a bit of dairy or fish were the daily fare of the majority of people. With only these choices and common sense, there was little need for volumes to be written on breaking a fast, especially considering most of their fasting was likely of shorter duration.

The Acceptable Fast

Before we get into the reasons for fasting, however, we will take a look at what acceptable fasting entails. Jesus expected His followers to fast, giving them instruction on what an acceptable fast requires in contrast to a fast done just for appearances. Once again, we observe that heart posture is the deciding factor:

> *And when you fast, do not look gloomy like the hypocrites, for they disfigure their faces that their fasting may be seen by others. Truly, I say to you, they have received their reward. But when you fast, anoint your head and wash your face,*

that your fasting may not be seen by others but by your Father who is in secret. And your Father who sees in secret will reward you. -Matt. 6:16-18, ESV

The Lord rebuked Israel for fasting religiously without heart involvement or a change in behavior or attitude (Isa. 58). It may seem odd that the Lord reproved them for fasting to please themselves (v. 3), but like the practice of tithing or public prayer, those who fast without the necessary heart involvement can derive pleasure from their ability to look and feel spiritually superior.

They ask me to take action on their behalf, **pretending they want to be near me.** *'***We have fasted before you!*'** *they say. '***Why aren't you impressed?*** We have been very hard on ourselves, and you don't even notice it!' I will tell you why... It's because* **you are fasting to please yourselves.** *Even while you fast, you keep oppressing your workers.* **What good is fasting when you keep on fighting and quarreling?** *This kind of fasting will never get you anywhere with me. You humble yourselves by* **going through the motions of penance**... *Is this what you call fasting?* **Do you really think this will please the LORD?** -Isa. 58:2b-5, NLT

Fasting and heart issues are intimately connected. The Lord wants our fasting to be birthed in our hearts because we have the same yearning for relationship and justice as He does—justice born out of compassion and mercy.

In Zechariah, the Lord asked the people and priests to honestly answer whether or not they were really fasting unto the Lord for the seventy years prior. In the same vein, He asked them if they could honestly say their feasts were in honor of Him and not just times of feasting for themselves with a day off from work (Zech. 7:4-6). In response to these questions, the Lord reminded Israel of the right way to conduct their fasting:

Render true judgments, show kindness and mercy to one another, do not oppress the widow, the fatherless, the sojourner, or the poor, and let none of you devise evil against another in your heart. -Zech. 7:9-10, ESV

Because the people hardened their hearts and would not listen to the Lord's words through the prophet, the Lord rebuked the people of Israel and told them He would not listen to them either (Zech. 7:11-14). It matters how we conduct ourselves at the heart level when we fast. Our prayers are actually *hindered* if we do not listen to the Lord's advice to pay attention to these weightier matters through all of our religious practice.

Fasting, like tithing, does not earn God's favor. In fact, those who feel confident before God because of their successful fasting and tithing (or who lack confidence if they have 'failed') are in a dangerous place. Though one has pride and the other misplaced self-condemnation, both seek to justify themselves through works and good behavior. God is looking for those with a broken heart and contrite spirit who recognize their inadequacy to obtain grace by their own merit. It was the Pharisee who was rebuked by Jesus for boasting about and taking confidence in his regular fasting ('I fast twice a week,'

Luke 18:11-14). His fasting, praying, giving, and good behavior did not earn justification or right standing before God but rather rejection because of his pride.

The Word exhorts us to fast in secret and for the right reasons. There are general guidelines in Isaiah 58 governing fasting honored by God:

- free those who are wrongfully imprisoned
- lighten the burden of others, especially those who work for you
- let the oppressed go free
- remove the chains that bind people
- share your food with the hungry
- give shelter to the homeless
- give clothes to those who need them
- do not hide from relatives who need your help
- satisfy the needs of the afflicted
- stop criticizing and spreading vicious rumors
- help those in trouble

If we fast in this way, God promises deliverance will come and our wounds will quickly heal (v. 8). Righteousness will guide us and the Lord Himself will protect us. Those who fast in this manner demonstrate their loyalty to God's heart for the needy and oppressed. To these God promises His presence, light, guidance, and strength. 'Light' in this passage can mean different things, including knowledge and understanding.

> **Then when you call, the Lord will answer.** *'Yes, I am here,' he will quickly reply...* **Then your light will shine out from the darkness,** *and the darkness around you will be as bright as noon. The Lord will guide you continually, giving you water when you are dry and restoring your strength.* -Isa. 58:9-11a, NLT

Fasting for the wrong reasons, in the wrong way, or not fasting at all are each contrary to Jesus' teaching. While religious fasting as prescribed by the law does not apply to the Gentile believer (e.g., on the Day of Atonement), forgoing our necessary food to embrace voluntary weakness for the purposes of God is a fundamental part of our walk as bondservants of God. It requires humility that acknowledges God's strength, not ours, bears fruit for His kingdom.

Disregarding Jesus' direction to fast can only be attributed to lack of biblical teaching on fasting, misunderstanding the purposes or reasons for fasting, fear of fasting, or the lack of motivation to give up a meal. The Word exhorts us not to let our appetites control us but rather to subdue them for the sake of the advancement of God's kingdom so we are not disqualified from receiving the imperishable crown that awaits us (1 Cor. 9:25-27). While this is not talking about fasting specifically, it is telling us to discipline ourselves by not allowing our appetites to control us. Paul warned those who do, stating they are headed for destruction because their god is their appetite (Php. 3:19-21).

Most of the examples of fasting in the Bible have similar basic elements: yearning for restoration, desperate need for justice, preparation for intercession or a new season of ministry, and/or the need for revelation of the Lord's will and plans. Technically, it could be shown that each fast has the same essential feature of seeking justice in one way or another, but for the sake of showing relationship they have been divided into four categories: restoration, justice, preparation, and discernment fasts.

The Restoration Fasts

Fasting for restoration can be applied to the repentant sinner seeking to be reconciled with God. In addition, the burdened intercessor who longs for the community of believers to walk in God's light or who seeks national restoration to righteousness in God will fast as part of his dedication to serve God's purposes. As we near the close of the age, we will see more bondservants fasting due to longing for Jesus' return.

The Fast of the Penitent

The fast of the truly penitent person who turns to God with sorrow is always honored by God. The consequences for their sin may or may not be removed, but God is always faithful to forgive the sincerely repentant (1 John 1:9). God, in fact, passionately pursues reconciliation as evidenced by sending His Son to provide restoration. This ministry of reconciliation has been passed on to us as we witness to others the power of Christ to bring the lost back to God and make them whole (2 Cor. 5:18-20).

Godly sorrow produces a broken heart over personal iniquity that longs to be in right standing and fellowship with God. Though David had originally been content to hide his sins of murder and adultery, he later expressed this kind of sorrow and was restored to a right relationship with God (2 Sam. 12:1-14). Worldly sorrow brings death because the pain experienced is not over the sin or the severed relationship with God, but over the consequences and humiliation of being caught. Had no consequences come or if the sin had not been found out, the person with worldly sorrow would quite happily continue in his life of sin.

> *For the kind of sorrow God wants us to experience leads us away from sin and results in salvation. There's no regret for that kind of sorrow. But worldly sorrow, which lacks repentance, results in spiritual death.* -2 Cor. 7:10, NLT

The story of Jonah illustrates the great lengths to which God is willing to go in order to bring us to repentance and reconciliation. Jonah, perhaps having been prophetically shown the future attack and plunder of the northern kingdom by the Assyrians, did not have the same desire for these people to be reconciled as God did. While the story does not state this, there is a very real possibility Jonah did not want to be recorded in Israelite history as the prophet who was instrumental in saving the Assyrians so God could later raise them up to dismantle the northern kingdom of Israel (Isa. 10:5).

SECTION 4 *WHOLEHEARTED LIFESTYLE OF OBEDIENCE*

Whatever the case may be, the Ninevites actually listened to the message and repented. They called a fast, and everyone put on the clothes of humility, saying, 'Who knows? Perhaps God may turn and relent from His anger so we will not perish.' Note the Ninevites were eager for the mercy God *may* show them. This is another example of 'the great perhaps of God.' When God saw they turned from their evil and humbled themselves before Him, He relented from the disaster He had planned (Jon. 3:5,9-10).

The Lord gave instruction in His Word detailing the specific action to take when a nation is under judgment because of sin. While this is spoken to Israel, it can be applied to other nations as well, using the example of Nineveh to support such a view:

> *If I shut up the heavens so that there is no rain, or if I command the locust to devour the land, or if I send pestilence among My people, and **My people who are called by My name humble themselves and pray and seek My face and turn from their wicked ways, then I will hear from heaven, will forgive their sin and will heal their land.** Now My eyes will be open and My ears attentive to the prayer offered...* -2 Chron. 7:13-15, NASB

We observe this precise scenario in Joel (see Joel 1-2). At God's charge, the prophet Joel called the nation to sound the alarm, declare a fast, and repent. This is all evidence of the love and mercy of God, who warns us when we have pursued a course that is legally indefensible in His court. If we heed His warning, repent, and turn our face to God, His mercy provides for the legal loophole we need to avert disaster.

The Court of Heaven, however, is not fooled by feigned repentance. Turning toward God in sincere repentance 'with all of our heart' provides the only way to approach God. In so doing, we find He is gracious, merciful, and abounding in steadfast love. The Word states God is 'slow to anger.' In order to understand the anger of God, we must realize His anger is always linked to injustice—the transgression of His standards. He is 'slow to anger' means He gives us latitude because of our fallen nature and allows us time to repent (Rom. 2:4; 2 Pet. 3:9; cf. Rev. 2:21). He is slow in executing the just sentence we deserve for breaking His law, always warning us ahead of time to turn from our indefensible position. In the book of Joel, people turned to the Lord in repentance, and 'He became jealous for His land and had pity on His people' (Joel 2:18).

During the reign of Rehoboam, the Lord warned the leadership of Judah that He was going to hand them over to Shishak (king of Egypt). In response, the king and princes of Judah humbled themselves, which most agree denoted fasting (cf. Ps. 35:13). Because of this, God lessened the consequences of their sin (2 Chron. 12:5-8). Even when King Ahab of Israel and King Manasseh of Judah, recorded as the two most evil kings, humbled themselves before the Lord in true repentance, the compassion of the Lord was kindled and He forgave them (see 1 Kings 21:25-29; 2 Chron. 33:10-13). The Lord was so moved by their penitent hearts that the consequences of their evil were delayed.

CHAPTER 15 *WHEN YOU FAST*

The Fast to Serve God's Purposes

The purposes of God to restore the nation of Israel, all humanity, and the earth to a righteous and just rule through the promised Messiah becomes the focus of all who serve the Lord night and day through prayer and fasting. As quoted before, 'Will not God bring justice for His people, who cry out to Him day and night? Will He continue to put them off? No, He will see to it they get justice quickly' (Luke 18:7-8).

Anna, the prophetess found daily at the temple serving through prayer and fasting, was present when Jesus was dedicated. Her devotion and discipline to serve God in the manner she was able put her in the right place at the right time to see the promised Messiah. Immediately upon the revelation that Jesus was the promised Messiah, she began spreading the good news (Luke 2:36-38).

Daniel was also attentive to God's plans as revealed in His Word, serving Him through prayer and fasting. After discovering the length of time determined for Israel's exile, Daniel reminded God of His Word and petitioned Him to accomplish that Word. This may seem odd at first, but God has advised us by His Spirit that spiritual matters are spiritually discerned, not reasoned by the mind of man. God's declared will in the Word and His will by the witness of the Holy Spirit are both to be taken before the throne in prayer to petition that His will be done on earth as it is in heaven.

> *I, Daniel, understood from the Scriptures… So I turned to the Lord God and pleaded with him in prayer and petition, in fasting, and in sackcloth and ashes.*
> -Dan. 9:2a,3, NIV

The Fast of the Bride for Jesus

The longing in the believer's heart for Jesus' return to restore His presence on the earth awakens a desire not satisfied by the legitimate pleasures of life. This yearning produces a mourning or ache typified by the expression, 'pining away.' When asked why His disciples did not fast as John the Baptist's disciples or the Pharisees did, Jesus responded that while the Bridegroom was present, there was no reason to mourn (fast) in this way.

> *But the days will come when the bridegroom will be taken away from them, and then they will fast.* -Matt. 9:15, NKJV

Here again Jesus stated His disciples *will* fast but only after He leaves. There are no regulations governing this fast of mourning for Jesus' return. The Pharisees and devout Jews practiced fasting on a regular basis as an act of piety and worship motivated by tradition. By the examples Jesus gave to illustrate His point (old wineskins cannot hold the new wine, etc.; see Matt. 9:16-17), He explained that the new plan God is initiating through Him cannot be synchronized with the old ways and practices. Fasting during Jesus' absence will be from a heart longing for His return, not disciplined days set aside regularly in the manner of religion.

The additional thought in the Luke account, stating those who have had the old wine will not immediately desire the new (Luke 5:39), reflects Jesus' unerring knowledge of the way our mind works. For many of us, it is far easier to have a schedule and know ahead of time when we will fast, for example, fast on Monday and Thursday every week like clockwork; no food, only water. To call a regularly scheduled fast a 'fast of longing' seems paradoxical; who can schedule longing? Picture a bride whose betrothed is overseas. Would she fast in this manner? Or would she burst into tears on certain days, ignoring her daily meals because of the intense and overwhelming longing in her heart?

Whether this is the kind of syncretism Jesus reproved in this passage (taking the old methods of regular fasting in Judaism and trying to fit them with the fast of longing for the Bridegroom) is not entirely clear. Like other spiritual practices (studying the Word, praying, giving), sometimes disciplining oneself on a schedule to develop a good habit precedes the heartfelt desire to do those things without the guardianship of the 'to do' list. The test comes when we honestly evaluate our response to disciplined practice. Do we feel we've accomplished something worthy of God's favor, or do we feel our love and tenderness for our Lord deepening? For most of us, the response would be 'yes' on both accounts, revealing the bit of religious pride lurking about in the process of growing in Christ. But the day *will* come when love is awakened, and then we will fast with true longing. In the meantime, there are plenty of other fasts to choose from...

The Justice Fasts

Prayers offered to seek God's intervention in an unjust situation are often accompanied by fasting. It is when we embrace voluntary weakness that we open a spiritual window for God to display strength. Injustice comes in many forms: a sickness unrelated to any sin issue; a national crisis due to an aggressive regime; persecution of the innocent or due to religious affiliation; and so on. Fasting in this way can be done individually or corporately. [Note: There is some overlap with the other fasts.]

The Fast to Avert Crisis Unrelated to Sin

Ezra proclaimed a fast among the returning exiles before he approached the Lord for protection. The route over which they had to travel back to Jerusalem was dangerous for both the people and their possessions (Ezra 8:21-23). This type of fasting was typically 'water only' and of short duration because of the imminent nature of the need. Ezra ended the account by stating God listened to their request.

Esther requested that all Jews fast for her so that would have she had every spiritual advantage possible for succeeding in her quest to avert the Jews from annihilation. This fast was extremely pressing and urgent because of the Jewish genocide Haman planned. No one ate or drank for three days. This passage makes evident Esther understood God was not required to honor her request for favor and protection just because they fasted ('if I perish, I perish,' 4:16). The story concludes by relating God's intervention that not only protected the Jews but also exacted retribution on those who acted unjustly.

Jehoshaphat called the people to fast when they were about to be attacked by Ammon, Moab, and Mount Seir unrelated to any revealed sin issues (2 Chron. 20:1-30; see v. 3). The address to God (v. 6), establishment of precedent (vv. 7-9), statement of current situation (vv. 10-11), and motion (v. 12) are all present in this judicial prayer, as previously discussed in the chapter on prayer. The motion put forth demonstrated their utter dependence on God for deliverance: 'O our God, will You not judge them? For we have no power to face this vast army attacking us. We do not know what to do, but our eyes are on You.' God acted favorably on their behalf in a most unusual way (vv. 13-30), which provoked fear in all the surrounding nations and accomplished more than Jehoshaphat could ask or even think.

The Fast for Healing and Deliverance

Since the fall of Adam and Eve in the Garden, sickness and infirmity have plagued man, not always as a result of sin (cf. John 9:2-3). Jesus came to destroy the works of Satan, and He continually confronted this injustice while He was here on earth.

David fasted for his opponents who were ill, mourning for them as for a close friend if they were not healed. This is a typical example of how David's heart was like the Lord's—blessing enemies and praying for those who persecuted him.

> *They reward me evil for good, to the sorrow of my soul. But as for me, when they were sick, my clothing was sackcloth;* ***I humbled myself with fasting…*** *I paced about as though he were my friend or brother; I bowed down heavily, as one who mourns for his mother.* -Ps. 35:12-14, NKJV

When the disciples could not cast the demon out of a boy, Jesus chided them for their lack of faith (Mark 9:19-29). After Jesus delivered the boy of the evil spirit, the disciples privately asked Him why they could not accomplish the deliverance. Jesus replied, 'this kind cannot come out except by prayer and fasting' (Mark 9:29, NKJV). This is an example of God's strength being made manifest when we are weak physically. It takes the love of God and the mind of Christ to fast and pray for others, especially when it is done privately and not for an outward show. Only when Jesus returns will we have any idea of the strength and humility possessed by those who have fasted and prayed in secret when the results attributed to their requests are made known.

The Preparation Fasts

The wisdom of fasting in preparation for a new season of ministry or for a time of testing focuses our spirit on the discernment we need to remain in God's timing and move forward in a way that honors God. Likewise, fasting as a means of humbling ourselves before God in preparation for intercession is also demonstrated in the Word.

The Fast to Prepare for Testing

After His baptism, the Holy Spirit led Jesus into the wilderness to be tested before His public ministry began. Because the specific purpose for being driven into the wilderness was to be tempted by Satan, Jesus chose to fast during this time to strengthen Himself spiritually. Satan came to tempt Jesus at His weakest point physically, the most logical and reasonable time to exploit one's opponent. But God's strength is made perfect or complete in our weakness, and Jesus did not succumb to any of Satan's devices. Though fasting makes the body weak, it makes the spirit strong with the strength God provides. This type of fasting prepares the believer for the heightened level of attack that often accompanies an increase in responsibility from the Lord.

> *Then Jesus was led up by the Spirit into the wilderness to be tempted by the devil. And after fasting forty days and forty nights, he was hungry. And the tempter came and said to him, "If you are the Son of God..."* -Matt. 4:1-3a, ESV

Note the text states Jesus became hungry, evidence He abstained from food but not from water. Anyone who has undertaken a three day absolute fast (no water or food, as in Esther's fast) will tell you the only thing on their mind is water, not food. Most experts agree man can survive only 8-14 days without water.[1] The Word testified that Jesus was tested on every point as a man, just as we are. If He had been given supernatural grace to fast from food *and water* as Moses had received (see Ex. 34:28), the test would have been invalidated and this Scripture nullified on that point:

> *For we do not have a high priest who cannot sympathize with our weaknesses, but was **in all points tempted as we are**, yet without sin.* -Heb. 4:15, NKJV

The Fast in Preparation for Judicial Intercession

In this example, the use of fasting to humble ourselves before judicial intercession adds weight to the case brought before the Court of God. As the judicial prayers explained earlier, these prayers follow the same pattern with one or two additional steps. Before offering the judicial prayer, a period of fasting is declared, which may include mourning over sin if the calamity is the result of sin. When sin is involved, confession and repentance are typically offered after the opening address to the Judge and before the establishment of precedent in the Word. This can be viewed as 'agreeing with our accuser quickly,' as Jesus advised us to do.

Examples of fasting before judicial intercession where sin is an issue are recorded in Nehemiah and Daniel. Nehemiah received news of the returned exiles' plight and the depressing conditions of Jerusalem, provoking him to weep, mourn, fast, and pray for many days (Neh. 1:1-4). In similar fashion, Daniel realized the time of Israel's exile for breaking the covenant would soon be completed. This led him to prepare his heart for intercession through fasting and denying himself comforts (Dan. 9:1-3).

The period of fasting that preceded their intercession involved mourning over the sin that caused the consequences, which are part of the conditions addressed and the request presented in the prayer. The judicial prayer format is seen in both examples with the additional step of confession after the opening honorable acknowledgment. God is honorably addressed (Neh. 1:5-6a; Dan. 9:4), confession of sin is offered (Neh. 1:6b-7; Dan. 9:5-8), precedent is established (Neh. 1:8-9; Dan. 9:9-12a), the situation is stated (Neh. 1:10; Dan. 9:12b-15), and the motion is submitted (Neh. 1:11; Dan. 9:16-19). In both cases, the Court of Heaven responded favorably to their requests.

The Discernment Fasts

This occasion for fasting originates with the desire to obtain God's direction, wisdom, and divine will for a given situation, or to receive understanding and discernment of the truth in God's Word, visions, or dreams. When we are not sure which direction to take, or experience frustration because we are having difficulty grasping a concept or prophetic imagery in the Word or in prophetic experiences (visions, dreams), fasting can place us in a position before God to hear, see, and receive more clearly what the Spirit is trying to impart. This is an example of the strength of God given to us when we embrace voluntary physical weakness: 'then your light will come forth…' (Isa. 58:8-12).

The Fast for Direction

The apostles and early believers included fasting with worship and prayer. They sought direction and discernment from the Holy Spirit when they needed to make decisions regarding leadership. This is the way in which elders were appointed and committed to the work of the Lord in each church (Acts 14:23).

> *While they were worshiping the Lord and fasting, the Holy Spirit said, "Set apart for me Barnabas and Saul for the work to which I have called them." Then after fasting and praying they laid their hands on them and sent them off.*   -Acts 13:2-3, ESV

The Fast for Understanding

Daniel fasted for wisdom and discernment to understand the disturbing visions he received. The text reveals Daniel *set his heart and mind* to gain understanding, foregoing his customary comforts and routine (Dan. 10:2-3,12, AMP). His lifestyle of prayer, humility before God, and willingness to relinquish his right to comfort and abundant food by virtue of being one of the highest ranking officials in the Babylonian and Medo-Persian kingdoms was remarkable. Daniel remained humble before God and devout in his lifestyle of prayer because he purposed in his heart *ahead of time* to walk in a manner worthy of God's name. This was accomplished in part by not defiling himself with the food and drink of the king (Dan. 1:8). His heart posture was set early in his life, decades before he received the visions from God.

> *Then he continued, "Do not be afraid, Daniel. Since the first day that **you set your mind to gain understanding and to humble yourself** before your God, your words were heard, and I have come in response to them... Now I have come to explain to you what will happen to your people in the future, for the vision concerns a time yet to come."* -Dan. 10:12,14, NIV

We see another example at the time Paul encountered the risen Messiah. Because of his experience on the Damascus road and resultant blindness, Paul was stunned into the reality he had been acting contrary to God's will. This so impacted him that he then sought and waited upon the Lord in fasting to give him understanding about what was taking place (Acts 9:8-9).

Practical Issues

On a practical note, fasting as a lifestyle requires that we fast with wisdom. While there are lengthy fasts recorded in the Word, there is no evidence any individual did this repeatedly throughout his lifetime. Having been involved in fasting for over thirty years in various ways and with various motives, I can now say in hindsight this bit of information would have been very useful on the front end.

Pride can come with Pharisaical-type scheduled fasting as well as through lengthy feats of 'water only fasting.' Some people just have more strength of will than others in this area. Because of the havoc repeated and unwise *lengthy* fasting will have on our endocrine system, which controls everything from ability to sleep, energy to meet the demands of the day, metabolism, growth, repair, mood, and a host of other functions, this type of fasting should only be undertaken at the true leading of the Holy Spirit. Women are even more susceptible in this area due to a more involved hormonal system.

We can undertake the shorter fasts judiciously for their intended purposes, as stated in the previous examples. Like giving, fasting that comes from the heart and not only as the result of self-induced behavior modification is of great worth before God. When we fast in this way, we share in what moves God's heart. What father is not drawn to those who truly, at the heart level, share his vision and willingly forego their legitimate needs for physical sustenance in the hope of entering more fully into the concerns of his heart? This type of fasting bears lasting fruit.

For many, however, food has become an idol in the heart, some barely finishing one meal before craving the next. Many are controlled by the desire to eat continually. We have become infirm by the food of our culture, which can be addicting and teratogenic. Abundant food has defiled the church in the West, evidenced by the fact that a bagel or sandwich accompanies every gathering in the name of fellowship. Fellowship here is translated 'so people will show up.' One couple even confessed they arrived early so they could be in the front of the line for the church potluck in order to get the best and most of what was offered. We are the Corinthians.

It is a cruel irony that the very thing that will deliver us from this idolatry is the very thing we have the most difficulty doing—abstaining from food. The covetous person is tested in releasing his money in order to give, the ambitious person is tested in giving up his time to pray and study the Word instead, and the lover of food is tested in giving up food to fast. All three are learning to give God their whole heart. Only the genius of God would come up with such a simple plan to remove the things that capture our affections in an unholy way and at the same time advance the purposes of His kingdom.

Fasting Does Not Guarantee 'Results'

As briefly mentioned in the example of Esther, fasting does not guarantee results,. David fasted for the life of his first son with Bathsheba, but the son still died (2 Sam. 12:16-23). There are also examples where God does not honor the fast of those who have not had true godly sorrow for their actions but merely want to avert the consequences or judgment (see Jer. 14:12).

The Lord chided the Israelites for fasting without heart involvement or intent to honor what God honors (Isa. 58). This type of religious fasting accomplishes nothing. True fasting reflects the heart posture of longing for justice, yearning for understanding and discernment, pain over the Lord's absence, and mourning over sin that aches for reconciliation with God (godly sorrow). The Lord favorably responds to fasting in this manner.

Those who are satisfied with what the world has to offer will never fast for the superior pleasures found only in God. They will not long for Jesus to return because their longing is anchored to the trappings of worldly success and pleasure. If we continually satisfy and comfort ourselves with the pleasures of this life, especially legitimate pleasures like food, the longing for His kingdom to be established will likely stay below our conscious radar. How then will we ever hunger for the banquet He has prepared for us, which includes God's presence and understanding His Word (Luke 14:24)?

Here is another loop: the longing we need to have for His kingdom and presence is ignited through fasting, but the desire to fast originates in the longings of the heart. We must conclude that this can only be accomplished through the work of the Holy Spirit. Only the Spirit of God can transform our desires. Fasting can be difficult, but if we desire to have His heart and be moved with what moves God, the Holy Spirit will work in us so that we are willing to fast. This produces desire to follow through with what we have purposed in our heart to do, and in that day we will fast.

Closing Thoughts

Obedience comes from the heart of someone who loves the Lord and is being filled with God's nature of mercy and compassion with longing to see His kingdom established. By submitting ourselves to the will of God, we offer ourselves as living sacrifices to God as

SECTION 4 *WHOLEHEARTED LIFESTYLE OF OBEDIENCE*

our spiritual act of worship, acceptable in His sight. Worship in spirit and in truth mandates a lifestyle of obedience.

> *I appeal to you therefore, brothers, by the mercies of God, to present your bodies as a living sacrifice, holy and acceptable to God, which is your spiritual worship.* -Rom. 12:1, ESV

God prepared a body for Jesus so He could model obedience to the will of God based on love. Love is superior to legalistic or mere outward compliance to the law. The lifestyle of obedience has now become the spiritual equivalent of the daily burnt offerings. We are now the sacrifices, which is the reason we die daily to our own wills and thus participate at the heart level in the morning and evening sacrifices. Like Christ, as part of His body we willingly say, 'Here I am; I have come to do Your will.'

Numerous passages in the New Testament establish the expectation that our life is to be sacrificed daily through the killing of our own wills to serve the purposes of God (Matt. 10:38-39; 16:24; Mark 8:34; 10:21; Luke 9:23; Rom. 6:5; 8:36; 1 Cor. 15:31; 2 Cor. 4:10; 6:9). This obedience involves resisting our own flesh as well as the temptations of the adversary. Gratefully, we have the intercessory ministries of Jesus and the Holy Spirit who will show us the right path (if we are willing to see it) and give us the strength to embrace this lifestyle. God will even impart the desire to do this if we are still struggling to get to the starting block in any of these areas.

We must always bear in mind that the Holy Spirit transforms our hearts as we cooperate with Him. Just as natural parents do not expect a six month old to run, change the oil in the car, clean house, or do calculus, our heavenly Father does not place burdens on us for which His grace has not provided the empowerment. The reason Jesus could say with confidence that His followers will fast, give, and pray is based on His foreknowledge of the Holy Spirit's grace and empowerment. These disciplines and the underlying heart posture that prompt their practice are brought forth in a believer's life over time and as we mature in the Lord. [Note: This is not to be confused with those whose walk is stagnant. No one would accept a twelve year old who is still in diapers and demanding a bottle as normal.]

Each of the three primary disciplines of prayer, giving, and fasting are a test of stewardship. Our first test is to steward our time so we do not overcommit our schedules, even with good activity, in order to have time with the Lord in prayer and study of the Word. We are tested in the area of our resources to teach us to be satisfied with basics and share the rest with the needy. Where eating is concerned, the Lord wants us to be satisfied with what we need and not what we crave. By this, even our restraint in forgoing the delicacies our stomachs desire is seen as fasting by our Father when our hearts are postured before Him in love and the desire to do His will rather than our own.

Just as giving is a heart issue and not a matter of percentage, fasting and prayer are also birthed in the heart and not a matter of regulation. Some will give up their web surfing, soccer games, TV viewing, or shopping excursions to better steward their time before the Lord in prayer and Bible reading. Others will cut back on their dining out or eating 'choice' foods in order to afflict their flesh before the Lord, saying, 'My desire to know You and for the establishment of Your kingdom is stronger than my desire for my customary food,' or in some cases, '...my necessary food,' if the fasting is more stringent than what the prophet Daniel practiced. Our individual fasting is not meant to be a list of do's and don'ts any more than the way we conduct our giving or devotional time (though corporate fasting for a crisis can be governed a bit differently).

Spiritual disciplines are profitable as long as they don't give us confidence before the Lord for our faithful commitment and execution of them, puffing us up with pride, or rob us of confidence if we fail, filling us with self-condemnation and shame. Placing ourselves before the Lord to study and pray through the Word is our priority. By the transforming power of the Holy Spirit and the Word, all the other disciplines and the heart posture God desires to accompany them will follow. We have only to trust that He will do as He promised and cooperate with Him in the process. Amen.

> *I have esteemed and treasured the words of His mouth more than my necessary food.* -Job 23:12b, AMP

SECTION 5

TACTICAL KNOWLEDGE OF THE ADVERSARY

Chapter 16

Role as Adversary

> *The god of this age has blinded the minds of unbelievers, so that they cannot see the light of the gospel that displays the glory of Christ, who is the image of God.*
> -2 Cor. 4:4, NIV

'The whole world lies in the power of the evil one' (1 John 5:19). The New Testament writers attest that Satan is still the god of this age and active in the lives of men—believers and unbelievers alike. We are warned he continues to operate, roaming the earth to seek whom he may devour, for how could the *god* of this age also be *bound* in this age? But we know he has no hold on the believer because:

- he cannot do as he wills in the believer's life without the permission of God;
- we have been given the Holy Spirit and have the power to resist temptation to sin;
- we have the mind of Christ, with understanding and discernment available to us so Satan cannot outwit us.

Jesus has authority above all principality, might, power, dominion, and name in this age and the age to come (Eph. 1:20-22). All who are in Christ partake of His authority because He is the Head of the body of believers. Through Christ, we have been delivered from the dominion of Satan into the kingdom of light. But as we shall see, the activity of Satan continues but without the power to enslave the believer.

Jesus prayed we would be protected from the evil one (John 17:15). For this reason, it behooves the believer to have tactical knowledge of their adversary, Satan. Armed with this knowledge, we can be on our guard and withstand falling prey to his strategy. This includes discerning between the voice of truth and the voice of error.

> *After he has gathered his own flock, he walks ahead of them, and they follow him because they know his voice. They won't follow a stranger; they will run from him because they don't know his voice.* -John 10:4-5, NLT

Who Is Satan?

Some have convinced themselves Satan is not real and that our 'evil inclination' is the adversary. If that were so, how could Jesus have been tempted in the wilderness? We know that Jesus had no such 'evil inclination' yet was tested by Satan. The Word tells us that because Jesus was without sin (2 Cor. 5:21), Satan had no hold on Him (John 14:30) even though he tempted Jesus in every way (Heb. 4:15).

SECTION 5 TACTICAL KNOWLEDGE OF THE ADVERSARY

In the Old Testament, we see three specific incidents where Satan is referenced directly by name. The first is in the book of Job, where Satan asked God for permission to test Job by causing destruction and attacking Job's health (Job 1:6-12; 2:1-7). The second is when he incited David to sin (1 Chron. 21:1). The third is when he accused Joshua, the high priest, after the exiles returned to Israel (Zech. 3:1-2).

By cross-referencing Revelation 12:3,9, where Satan is called the devil, the ancient serpent, and described as a dragon with seven heads, we can also determine that the serpent who tempted Eve (Gen. 3:1-5), and the sea dragon/coiled serpent that God will one day punish (Isa. 27:1) are also references to Satan. This forms the base of objective information we have received to understand our adversary from the Old Testament.

Some of the descriptive names for Satan in the New Testament are:

- the Devil (Matt. 4:1)
- Beelzebub (Matt. 12:24)
- wicked one (Matt. 13:38)
- the enemy (Matt. 13:39)
- thief; steals the Word (Mark 4:15)
- liar/father of lies (John 8:44)
- murderer from the beginning (John 8:44)
- prince of this world (John 12:31)
- god of this world (2 Cor. 4:4)
- serpent (2 Cor. 11:3)
- masquerades as an angel of light (2 Cor. 11:14)
- prince of the powers of the air (Eph. 2:2)
- ruler of darkness (Eph. 6:12)
- the tempter (1 Thes. 3:5)
- roaring lion (1 Pet. 5:8)
- a sinner from the beginning (1 John 3:8)
- ancient serpent (Rev. 12:9)
- great dragon (Rev. 12:9)
- deceiver of the whole world (Rev. 12:9)
- accuser of the brethren (Rev. 12:10)

[Note: Conspicuously absent from this list is 'angel' except for the warning that he *masquerades* as one. I searched in vain to find a passage that actually called Satan a 'fallen angel,' or an angel of any sort, for that matter. We will return to this point later.]

Activity of Satan

In the Old Testament, we are introduced to Satan's craft at the time of the fall of Adam and Eve into sin. By perverting the Word, causing doubt, and inciting covetousness, he was able to trap Eve in his deceit (Gen. 3:1-7). We also find Satan making accusations against righteous Job and bringing disaster and devastation to Job's property, family, and health (see Job 1-2:7). Satan later incited David to number Israel contrary to the law (1 Chron. 21:1). When the exiles returned to Israel, he stood in God's presence to make accusations against Joshua, the high priest (Zech. 3:1-2). Perverting the Word, causing doubt, inciting to sin, accusing before God, wreaking havoc with circumstances, bringing disease on the righteous—these are the venues through which Satan works to bring death to men and halt the progress of God's kingdom.

These tactics are also found in the New Testament. Paul warned us not to give him any occasion or cause to slander or accuse us before God (1 Tim. 5:14; see Rev. 12:9-10). Satan hinders the advancement of God's kingdom by:

- sowing 'tares' among believers (Matt. 13:37-40);
- tempting believers to avoid the difficult things God has ordained for them to do (Matt. 16:21-23; Mark 8:31-33);
- immediately stealing the Word from those who hear the gospel so they do not believe (Mark 4:15; Luke 8:12);
- binding people in infirmity (Luke 13:16);
- entering the heart of the offended, whose loyalty is to their own feelings, opinions, or money (Luke 22:3; 13:27; see Matt. 26:6-16; Mark 14:3-11; John 12:4-6; 13:2; Acts 5:1-4);
- requesting permission to test believers' professed love and loyalty (Luke 22:31);
- tempting believers to act deceitfully in order to make themselves appear more spiritual (Acts 5:3);
- tempting a spouse who lacks self-control over his physical passions during a time of fasting (1 Cor. 7:5);
- outwitting believers who walk in unforgiveness (2 Cor. 2:10-11);
- masquerading as an angel of light, or figuratively, as a 'messenger of knowledge' (2 Cor. 11:14);
- inflicting some type of physical limitation or weakness (2 Cor. 12:7);
- getting a foothold through a believer's anger (Eph. 4:26-27);
- hindering believers from fellowship (1 Thes. 2:17-18);
- trapping believers who operate in pride or conceit (1 Tim. 3:6);
- instigating false doctrine (1 Tim. 4:1-3; see 2 Tim. 4:3-4);
- ensnaring opponents of truth who love to quarrel over controversial matters (2 Tim. 2:24-26);
- convincing believers it is alright to sin or hate another (1 John 3:8-10);
- persecuting or imprisoning believers via the agency of government (Rev. 2:10).

In the New Testament, Jesus and the apostles addressed the activity of Satan in order to forewarn and therefore forearm the followers of Christ. After Jesus endured testing in the wilderness at the hand of Satan (Matt. 4:1-11; Mark 1:12-13; Luke 4:1-13), Satan left Him until an opportune time. An opportunist, in the negative sense, is the kind of criminal who checks car doors in a parking lot to see which doors have been left open as an invitation for theft. Peter reminded us of Satan's opportunistic nature (1 Pet. 5:8), and we are warned on several occasions not to give the devil an opportunity to trip us up.

Satan's activity in the lives of the unsaved is evident because of the rampant practice of sin. A girl with a demon followed Paul (Acts 16:16-18), demonstrating that demon possession still takes place in this age (see also Acts 19:11-16). Proof that he still operates after Jesus' victory at the cross is also readily seen in the lives of Ananias and Sapphira ('how is it Satan has so filled your heart,' Acts 5:3). In His revelation to Paul on the Damascus road after His ascension, Jesus Himself attested that Satan still has power:

> *I am sending you to open their eyes, so that they may turn from darkness to light and **from the power of Satan to God**, that they may receive forgiveness of sins and a place among those who are sanctified by faith in me.* -Acts 26:17b-18, ESV

Through Jesus' death and resurrection, the process of reversing the power of Satan over individual lives began. When someone comes to repentance, sin as the agency of death no longer has power over him. As each individual takes a stand against sin and the trappings of the world, the kingdom of God advances and the power of Satan is restricted.

Satan *will be* but *is not yet* crushed under our feet by God Himself (Rom. 16:20). Paul called the age we are living in 'this present *evil* age' (Gal. 1:4). Believers stubbornly sinning were handed over to the dominion of Satan for the destruction of their sinful nature (1 Cor. 5:5; 1 Tim. 1:20). Satan prevented Paul from reaching his destination (1 Thes. 2:18), and sent Paul a messenger to torment him (2 Cor. 12:7). He can still outwit us if we are not sober and watchful (2 Cor. 2:11). He operates as an angel of light to introduce error into the church (2 Cor. 11:14), and some have already fallen away to follow him (1 Tim. 5:15). Are these the activities of someone who is bound? His activity may be restricted in the believer's life, but he is a cunning strategist and opportunist, ever watchful and ready to seize any misstep we may make.

The author of Hebrews stated we do not yet see everything in subjection to Jesus, though He has been granted authority over all (Heb. 2:8). The judicial decision granting Him power and authority will not be fully actualized until the millennial reign is inaugurated, the time His *diadem* (crown of kingship) is conferred (Rev. 19:12; similar to David's anointing as king; he did not come into his full authority as king until many years later). Prior to this time, Jesus functions as our high priest crowned with the victor's (*stephanos*) crown. Paul explained the order in which this takes place. Christ was the first to be resurrected, then those who are Christ's at His return are resurrected or transformed directly. He returns wearing the *diadem* and puts an end to all rule, authority, and power. Jesus then delivers the kingdom to the Father. He concludes by saying death is the last enemy destroyed (1

Cor. 15:23-26), attested to in Revelation where John recorded that Death and Hades are thrown into the lake of fire after the thousand year reign of Christ (20:14).

How do we reconcile this with the passage that tells us Jesus 'nullified' death (2 Tim. 1:10)? Again, we remember all of God's promises are 'yes and amen' from the view of eternity. In this case, we also notice the remainder of the verse qualifies this statement by applying it to the gospel message. Those who are in Christ learn through the light of the gospel that death no longer has a hold on them because they have been given *power not to sin*. Therefore death has no hold on them—its power has been nullified. Though believers still die physically in this age, they will be resurrected at Jesus' return, and those who are alive and remain will be instantly transformed to have incorruptible flesh that will never die (1 Thes. 4:13-17).

According to the Word, it is the devil who presently has the power of death because of the presence of sin (Heb. 2:14). By inciting people to sin, Satan brings death to all because all have sinned, and the penalty for sin is death (Rom. 6:16). The believer, however, is not under Satan's sway in this regard because he has been set free from the power of sin and has been made righteous in Christ. In this way, the activity of Satan is curtailed in the believer's life as long as the believer clings to this power to be free from sin. We are free from sin and therefore death because of the resurrection to come for all who are in Christ, even if our body dies in the meantime (Rom. 8:2).

Is Satan bound in this age? The Word is clear: though the activity of Satan in the believer's life is 'bound' (or more accurately, 'curtailed') in the ways mentioned, Satan will not be officially and completely bound until Jesus returns (Rev. 20:1-3).

The Subtlety of Satan

The final deception is going to be the greatest deception ever. It will look and sound advantageous to the undiscerning ear. It will not look blatantly evil to the unspiritual mind, which is unable to accurately discern. If it were, no one would be in danger of being deceived. This is the same tactic our adversary used in the garden and has used repeatedly throughout history. The first description of Satan in the Word exposes his primary trait as *subtlety*, lending cover to his cunningly devised schemes. A little acronym will help us remember that from the beginning, his chief, foremost, fundamental, principal tactic of operation—his *modus operandi*—has been subtlety: S̲atan's s̲ubtle s̲trategies. 'Sss'… the sound of a serpent.

> Now **the serpent was more subtle and crafty than any living creature** of the field which the Lord God had made. -Gen. 3:1a, AMP

Part of the preparation of believers, especially as we near the close of the age, includes taking the revealed things in the Word regarding our adversary, Satan, and learning from them. Sports teams and military forces who know the tactics of their opponents are much better equipped to outmaneuver them. Paul warned us we should not let our adversary outwit us by being unaware of His schemes (2 Cor. 2:10-11). So what are his schemes? While this discussion is not exhaustive, it will give the reader an idea of who we are up against. Our focus and faith are to be squarely placed on the Lord, not the swirling waters around us or the enemy that would seek to entrap us. Be anxious for nothing. The Bible frequently charges us to have courage and fear not, for greater is He who is in us than he that is in the world (1 John 4:4). The Bible also charges us to be sober and watchful. Accurate knowledge of how our enemy operates will help us keep that charge.

The Beginning

How does the Word define who Satan is and how he became our adversary? Many believe Satan to be a fallen angel named Lucifer based on the language of Ezekiel 28 and Isaiah 14. Others define Satan simply as the adversary of man. We will take a brief look at the available passages from Scripture and offer a conclusion for your consideration that may differ from your own. May we be granted discernment to know truth, and perhaps recognize our limitations as well.

Ezekiel 28

Jesus stated Satan was a murderer *from the beginning* and the father of lies (John 8:44). Many reputable scholars view Ezekiel 28 as an allegorical representation of Satan's fall from glory, defining Satan as a fallen angel (read Ezk. 28:1-19 if you are unfamiliar with this passage). This is derived from the passage where the King of Tyre is metaphorically called the 'anointed cherub that covers' (v. 14).

I am uncomfortable adopting the view of Satan as a fallen angel as there is no unallegorized support for this elsewhere in Scripture. If he was blameless from the day he was created (Ezk. 28:15), how then can Jesus say he was a murderer from the beginning? Is not the Ezekiel passage talking about the wanton pride of the King of Tyre, so much so that he fancied himself a god, as Ezekiel 28:1-10 charges? Consider these points:

- The word 'cherub' is used poetically in this description, whereas in the rest of Scripture the word is used in conjunction with factual descriptions of cherubim (with possible exceptions in 2 Sam. 22:11 and Ps. 18:10). Poetic language is not to be assumed literal without further investigation, nor is it an invitation to allegorize.
- God is elsewhere described as enthroned above the cherubim (Ps. 80:1; Isa. 37:16), and in combination with Ezekiel's description that the cherubim go in the direction God ordains (Ezk. 10), the symbolic description of the King of Tyre as a cherub in Ezekiel 28 is not out of line with what we know of God's sovereign placement of governmental leaders. God sets the boundaries for their authority and the seasons for their rise to power for His specific purpose. They are God's arm to execute His judgments in the earth (Rom. 13:1-4; cf. Isa. 10:5-6).

- Recall that cherubim cover the ark of the covenant, symbolically guarding the laws entrusted to mankind by God. This is in keeping with the mandate given to Noah that man is to justly govern his fellowman. Hence, cherubim symbolically 'cover' the activities of men by ensuring justice is preserved under the direction of God. The cherubim posted at the Garden of Eden prevented men from usurping their just sentence of death by keeping them from partaking of the tree of life (Gen. 3:22-24). Cherubim safeguard the just decrees of God.
- Between the cherubim are coals of fire, which speak of the purifying judgments of God (Ezk. 10:2; cf. Isa. 6:6-7).

The human authorities God appoints on the earth are placed in those positions to accomplish His purposes for justice, similar to the function of cherubim as guardians of God's judgments and righteous decrees. By describing the King of Tyre as a cherub that covers, this passage is painting a picture of someone who was given authority to protect those under his care by upholding justice and walking in wisdom. Instead, he chose to traffic in greed to fuel his covetous heart and pride.

As further support this passage is only talking about the King of Tyre, consider that many of the ancient kings in Egypt, Canaan, Babylon, Rome, and others were given god-like status and seen as governing from on high or with the help of a deity.[1] Scripture likewise makes reference to rulers as gods (Psalm 82). Pharaoh was identified as a reincarnation of the god Horus, the 'morning star.' Rulers and their governments are frequently expressed in poetic terms in the Bible, being depicted as:

- mountains (Job 9:4-5; Ps. 30:7; 36:6; Isa. 41:15; 45:2; 64:1-4; Jer. 50:6; 51:25; Ezk. 6:1-3; Dan. 2:35-45; Mic. 4:1; 6:1);
- trees (Isa. 10:33; 37:24; Jer. 11:15-17; 46:22; Ezk. 17; 20:28; 31:1-18; Dan. 4:10-22; Hos. 14:6);
- ascending to heaven (Gen. 11:4; Ps. 139:8; Jer. 51:53; Amos 9:2; Obad. 1:4; Isa. 26:5);
- objects of beauty (Ps. 48:2; 50:2; Isa. 4:2; 13:19; 23:9; 33:17; Jer. 48:17; Lam. 2:15; Ezk. 16:14; 27:3; 28:17; 31:7; Dan. 4:20-22).

These expressions are poetic and not typically treated as literal descriptions. Angels (Job 38:7; Rev. 1:20; 9:1; 12:4) and men (Gen. 37:9; Num. 24:17; Dan. 8:10; Jude 1:13) are both depicted as stars. When Deborah was judge in Israel, she sang a song of victory after the battle against Sisera. In it she spoke of either the actual troops who fought or the divine help they received as 'the stars who fought from heaven to defeat Sisera' (Jdg. 5:20). We find another example in Obadiah's message to Edom that God will bring him down from his place 'among the stars' (Obad. 1:4). The ten spies described the cities of Canaan as being 'fortified to heaven' (Deut. 1:28; see also 9:1). The king of Babylon is depicted as 'mounting up to heaven' and fortifying his 'strong height' (Jer. 51:53).

Knowing these examples should give us adequate reason to question the assumption Ezekiel 28 is referring to the fall of Satan rather than the literal King of Tyre who, like the King of Assyria (Isa. 10:5-19), reached beyond the authority given him to grasp at more.

Three times Ezekiel recorded what God said about this king's heart: he believed himself to be a god 'sitting in the seat of the gods' (Ezk. 28:2,6,9; cf. Ps. 82).[2] Notice the similar theme in this passage from Job regarding the wicked and godless:

> *Though his height mount up to the heavens, and his head reach to the clouds, he will perish forever.* -Job 20:6-7a, ESV

The Lord's speech as recorded in Ezekiel 28 starts with, 'A lament for the King of Tyre.' A lament for this man's demise is in keeping with God's nature that He is not pleased with the death of the wicked but wants all men to come to repentance, here expressed in poetic language. This man was chosen by God to execute justice on the earth through government ('I placed you on the mountain of God,' v. 14b). He had been given divine wisdom as a foundation for governance ('you were in Eden, the garden of God,' v. 13; cf. Pr. 3:18), and built on it with precious wisdom and truth ('every precious stone was your covering,' v. 13; cf. 1 Cor. 3:12). But instead of continuing in this beauty, he succumbed to unrighteous trade, taking pride in the wealth he created, thereby filling his kingdom with violence and corruption (vv. 15-18).

Consider also the similar language used poetically to describe Pharaoh as a tree in the garden of God (Ezk. 31:8-9,18). No tree in the garden of God could compare with his beauty (v. 8). He was so beautiful that all the trees in Eden envied him (v. 9). Perhaps this is an allegorical picture of Satan as the tree of knowledge, using the same process of reasoning exercised in concluding the anointed cherub that covers is Satan before his demise. But is there a second witness in the Word to either of these theoretical extrapolations?

A man governing on earth who looks at all he has accomplished and in pride sees himself as divinely endowed above other men with authority to rule because of his own majesty and strength, is grasping beyond his station. Repeatedly, we see rulers who were given authority to govern vast kingdoms succumbing to pride. They reached beyond what they had been given authority to govern, treating their captives with cruelty (Isa. 14:5-6; Amos 1:13), glorying in the wealth they had plundered (Isa. 10:12-14; cf. Pr. 16:19), and refusing to recognize God as the Sovereign who gave them their power and kingdom (Isa. 10:13; Dan. 4:30; Acts 12:21-23).

The lament for the King of Tyre in the Ezekiel passage deals with this type of wanton pride. In similar fashion, God dealt with the arrogance of Nebuchadnezzar, who was given a sentence of insanity as a result. In the end, Nebuchadnezzar knew it was God who ruled over all and that man has no power of his own.

Manslayer from the Beginning

When Jesus stated Satan was a manslayer from the beginning, He used the word *arche*, which speaks not of 'a' beginning, but of an extremity of time, or origin. In other words, if Satan was a murderer from his *origin*, we would be hard pressed to reconcile Jesus' statement with an allegorical text presumed to be depicting Satan as a cherub who fell from glory through pride. Jesus taught Satan was our adversary from the point of origin: from the beginning. John also described Satan as sinning from the *arche*: the beginning or commencement. How can this be harmonized with the poetic description of the King of Tyre, presumed to be a veiled reference to Satan, which states he was the signet of perfection, perfect in wisdom, blameless in his ways from the day he was created?

> *...the devil has been sinning from the beginning.* -1 John 3:8b, ESV

There is a passage in Timothy that seems to support the view of Satan as a fallen angel, but on closer inspection of the original Greek text, it becomes evident the translators' own bias may have affected some versions. Taking a look at a couple of different translations in comparison with the Greek will show us how bias can affect how we arrange words and interpret a text based on presuppositions:

> **Greek**: Not/ newly planted/ so that/ not/ having been puffed up/ unto/ condemnation/ he may fall/ of the/ devil (1 Tim. 3:6).

Several of the English translations insert the word 'same' or 'like' (or some equivalent) into the verse, which are not in the original text (NIV; GWT; CEV; GNT; NCV; CJB; NKJV: the word inserted is italicized; AMP: the word inserted is in brackets; NASB: 'incurred by the devil,' qualified by putting the original translation in the footnote), rendering the passage similar to these translations:

- **NIV**: He must not be a recent convert, or he may become conceited and fall under the *same* judgment as the devil.
- **GW**: He must not be a new Christian, or he might become arrogant *like* the devil and be condemned.

The word translated 'judgment' in this passage (*krima*) means a judicial decision, sentence of condemnation, or a legal suit brought before court. 'He may fall,' translated from the Greek word *empipto*, means literally 'to be entrapped by.' Notice the difference in the following versions, represented by both literal and paraphrased translations:

- **YLT** (literal): not a new convert, lest having been puffed up he may fall (*empipto*, be entrapped by) to a judgment (*krima*, judgment, legal accusation) of the devil
- **NLT** (paraphrased): not be a new believer, because he might become proud, and the devil would cause him to fall
- **KJV** (literal): not a novice, lest being lifted up with pride he fall into the condemnation of the devil.
- **THE MESSAGE** (paraphrased): not be a new believer, lest the position go to his head and the Devil trip him up.
- **ISV** (literal-idiomatic): not be a recent convert, so that he won't become arrogant and fall into the devil's condemnation

In keeping with what is known of Satan from other passages of Scripture, which we will soon explore more fully, perhaps we can consider this verse is meant to say that 'an overseer must not be a new believer, lest he fall into the trap of the devil because of pride, leading to a legal accusation/judgment of condemnation in the Court of Heaven.' This is in keeping with Paul's further instruction to Timothy regarding younger widows, and supports the concept that Satan searches for those who can be devoured because of pride or other sin (1 Pet. 5:8):

> So I would have younger widows marry, bear children, manage their households, and **give the adversary no occasion for slander.** -1 Tim. 5:14, ESV

Isaiah 14

Other scholarship finds a reference to Satan in Isaiah 14 where the judgment of the King of Babylon is described (see Isa. 14:3-23). This passage is labeled as a 'taunt.' The people of Israel are instructed to pronounce it against Babylon when they are freed from their captivity. The word 'taunt' is translated from *mashal*, a Hebrew word defined as 'a condescending epithet, usually of a metaphorical nature.'

The portion believed to reference Satan begins in verse 12 (KJV): "How art thou fallen from heaven, O Lucifer, son of the morning! How art thou cut down to the ground, which didst weaken the nations!" Keep in mind this passage has already been defined by the Spirit of God as being metaphorical in nature. The word translated 'Lucifer' in this passage originated in the Latin translation called the Vulgate, written by Jerome and completed in A.D. 405. Jerome translated from the Hebrew and Greek texts available at the time. *Heylel*, the Hebrew word from which 'Lucifer' was derived, means 'shining one, light bearer, or morning star.' The Greek Septuagint, completed c. 132 B.C., used the word *eosophorus*, also translated 'morning star.' The *Jewish Publication Society Tanach* (Old Testament) translates *heylel* 'day-star,' while the *Complete Jewish Bible* (Messianic) renders *heylel* as 'morning star.'

Many early English translators merely took Jerome's Latin translation 'lucifer' and left it untranslated. Martin Luther, however, translated this word 'Morgenstern' in his German translation (1534). "Many Latin words were taken from the Vulgate into English nearly unchanged in meaning or spelling."[3] This also occurred with the words 'Calvary' and 'Golgotha.' Some assume these are the proper names of two different places near Jerusalem, adding fuel to their premise that the Bible contradicts itself. But both are descriptions of the 'place of the skull,' not proper nouns—one translated from Latin and the other from Aramaic.

"**Lucifer** is a Latin word derived from two words, *lux* (light; genitive of *lucis*) and *ferre* (to bear, to bring), meaning *light-bearer*. Lucifer does not appear in Greek or Roman mythology; it is used by poets to represent the Morning Star at moments when 'Venus' would intrude distracting imagery of the goddess. 'Lucifer' is Jerome's direct translation in his *Vulgate* (4th century) of the Septuagint's Greek translation, as *heosphoros*, 'morning star,' literally 'bringer of the Dawn,' of a phrase in *Isaiah* that originally intended no reference to Satan."[4]

Though the word 'lucifer' was not the translation of a Hebrew, Greek, or Aramaic proper noun, it evolved into that status over time. The translators of the 1611 King James Version showed tremendous restraint and humility in expressing the uncertainty of translating certain words by including alternate renderings in the margins (see discussion in Chapter 7). While later versions of the KJV removed these margin notes, they remain intact in the 1611 version. It should come as no surprise that in the margin next to Isaiah 14:12, the translators included an alternate translation for 'Lucifer': 'day-starre.'

Most commentators agree this description is plainly a reference to the King of Babylon. John Gill stated, "[T]he king of Babylon is intended, whose royal glory and majesty, as outshining all the rest of the kings of the earth, is expressed by those names; and which perhaps were such as he took himself, or were given him by his courtiers. The Targum is, "how art thou fallen from on high, who was shining among the sons of men, as the star Venus among the stars.""[5] [Note: The Targum is the Aramaic translation of the Hebrew Bible.]

Recall also that men are depicted as 'stars' in several other passages of Scripture, as previously mentioned. So does this Isaiah passage posit a veiled reference to Satan, who may have gone by the name Lucifer when he was the 'anointed cherub that covers' from Ezekiel 28? I don't think there is enough evidence to come to this conclusion with any sense of certainty. One thing we do learn is that God uses the proud thoughts of our hearts to reveal the folly and futility of our vain imaginations.

These passages are taunts against those kings who got too big for their britches and fancied themselves as deity, or at least as the power behind their vast empires. Both Ezekiel 28 and Isaiah 14 show the presence of the antichrist spirit, which seeks to exalt itself above the authority God has given, or in pride believes that authority to be the result of one's own merit or effort. Extrapolating metaphorical language to conclude Satan is a fallen angel without any direct literal description elsewhere in the Word that he is such can be slippery footing for a doctrinal stance. The weight of Scripture merely defines him as the adversary inciting men to sin, accusing men in the Court of Heaven, requesting permission from God to test them on the matters for which he accuses them, and thwarting them from staying on the path marked out for them to subvert God's purposes in their lives.

Even the early church fathers "tended to see the devil as different from the angels..."[6] While I think it is an untenable position to staunchly hold onto the idea of Satan as a fallen angel, I would also say it is not an impossible position. Because of the lack of reliable or clear-witness from either the Word or the Holy Spirit, I would be hard pressed to either promote or staunchly refute. In this case, I would say we just don't have enough information to make such a statement. What we do know is this: he exists to accuse and slander, to lead astray, and to destroy.

If we are looking for a veiled reference to Satan, I would like to rather suggest Job 40:15-41:34. Here we have descriptions of two beasts, one an immensely strong land animal and the other a coiled or twisted serpent of the sea with multiple heads (cf. Ps. 74:14). In God's description of these beasts, He proclaims their invincibility with respect to the efforts of man to tame or destroy them (40:24; 41:1-8,26-29; 'the hope of man is false,' 41:9). Leviathan is described as having a heart of stone (41:24), *created* to have no fear, and the king over all the proud:

> On earth there is nothing like him, which is made without fear. He beholds every high thing; **He is king over all the children of pride.** -Job 41:33-34, NKJV

Satan is elsewhere also described as a dragon with multiple heads (Rev. 12:3) with no fear of man. He functions with cunning to disinherit those who are recipients of God's promises. Because of this, we wisely cling to Christ and remain humble before God, for it is the proud who belong to Satan. At the end of the millennial reign, he will receive his sentence at the hand of God, no more to trouble mankind. Isaiah prophesied his demise, calling him Leviathan—the twisted serpent who lives in the sea just as described in Job:

> In that day the LORD will punish Leviathan the fleeing serpent, with His fierce and great and mighty sword, even Leviathan the twisted serpent; and He will kill the dragon who lives in the sea. -Isa. 27:1, NASB

Fearless in nature with a heart of stone, the view of Satan as a beast is attested to elsewhere in Scripture (Rev. 12:3; 13:1). From the Genesis account, he is described as a serpent (Gen. 3:1; cf. 2 Cor. 11:3), and in Revelation he is described as the *ancient* serpent (Rev. 12:9; 20:2). The word 'ancient' used here is *archaios*, which does not mean merely old, as in the case of *palaios*, but from the point of his origin. From a plainly analytical standpoint of the weight of Scripture, it is easier to demonstrate Satan's origins as a beast than as a fallen angel.

God Defines Good

So if Satan is a created beast, murderer, and sinner from his origin, how do we reconcile this with God's proclamation that everything He created was good? In order to interpret God's statement with greater accuracy, we will take a look at the meaning of the Hebrew word 'good' as well as at further revelation regarding what God has created.

All God planted on the earth was labeled 'good' (Hebrew *tov*). Yet we find God planted the tree of knowledge of good *and* evil in the garden. How do we reconcile the seeming contradictory nature of creation judged 'good' by the Creator with the presence of a tree with the knowledge of evil? I believe the answer is found in two principle ideas: 1.) God's definition of good may not be the same as our own; and 2.) we, like Job, do not possess the grid to understand how the earth's foundation was laid in wisdom (Job 38-41).

Of further interest is God's evaluation of the trees of the garden as 'pleasant' to look at (Gen. 2:9), from the Hebrew *chamad*, 'to delight in; to desire; to be desirable; to covet.' The next time this word is used occurs during Eve's conversation with the serpent. Eve longingly looked at the forbidden fruit of the tree of knowledge, noting it was desirable (*chamad*) for making one wise (Gen. 3:6). The third time *chamad* is used surfaces in the Ten Commandments: 'You shall not covet...' (Ex. 20:17). What do we learn? Desire is not necessarily evil, unless we are provoked to desire something we do not have or are not allowed to have. At this point, desire becomes covetousness. The object of our desire is not necessarily evil, but our unchecked desire for what has been forbidden is.

The Hebrew word *tov* is defined as that which is good in the *broadest* sense of the term. It includes goodness in the sense of being beneficial, fruitful, or wise, as well as other applications.[7] Since we know 'wisdom' was present at creation (Pr. 8:22-31), perhaps we can note that in God's wisdom He created a tree with the knowledge of evil in the midst of the Garden (Gen. 2:9). This aids in understanding the following passages:

> *I form the light, and* **create darkness***: I make peace, and* **create evil***: I the LORD do all these things... I have* **also created the ravager to destroy***.* -Isa. 45:7, KJV; 54:16b, ESV

The word 'create' in these passages is the same word used in Genesis for the creation of the world, *bara*. The subject of the creation of evil is difficult for the mind to fathom. Perhaps this stems from the dichotomy that exists between God's definition of good and ours. In the book of Job, we find that Job understood God could send both good and evil: 'Shall we receive good at the hand of God, and not receive evil?' (Job 2:10b). In Zephaniah, the Lord rebuked those who said He would do neither good *nor* evil (Zeph. 1:12).

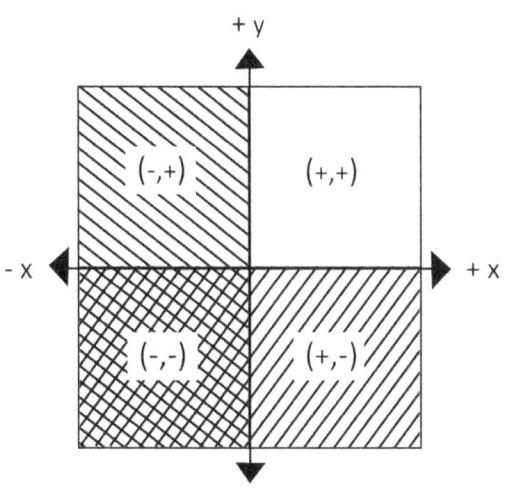

The graph at left gives a visual way to understand this concept by using the typical x-y graph of the Cartesian coordinate system, where coordinates are expressed as (x,y). As a straightforward look at the difference between what man defines as good in contrast with God's definition, consider for our example that the 'x' axis represents circumstances, and the 'y' axis represents both the morality of our actions and the effect the circumstances have on our character development.[8]

Worldly people would view anything that leads to positive circumstances as good, whether they are the result of morally good behavior or unrighteousness (e.g., cheating on taxes to keep more money), or whether those nice circumstances produce morally righteous character or the opposite (e.g., pride, greed, immorality, etc.). They see everything to the right of the 'y' axis as good (represents positive circumstances).

Many believers tend to narrowly view 'good' as beneficial circumstances resulting from morally righteous behavior, denying good circumstances might conversely corrupt their character, as the Word attests (e.g., 'those who desire to be rich fall into a trap'). Similar to the worldly, they would tend to see anything to the right of the 'y' axis as good, naively believing they will not fall into any trap as a result of prosperity, power, or a comfortable lifestyle. Any negative circumstances are viewed as the result of Satan's activity, and therefore rejected as worthless or having no place in the life of a believer.

God loves to bless His children with good things, but He is more interested in their character and eternal destiny. Through the witness of the Word, we know trials and testing are the tools God uses to produce righteous character in us. The Word testifies God sends both good and adverse ('evil') circumstances. God views everything above the 'x' axis as good, as this represents both upright moral action and righteous character development.

Satan, on the other hand, will try to ensnare us through either bad circumstances (causing us to fall into sin or to distrust God), or through good circumstances (to corrupt our character or cause us to forget God). He sees everything *below* the 'x' axis as to his advantage. All the fruit in this area is negative.

Far Side of the Moon

As far as the creation of Satan the manslayer, the subject may just be the 'far side of the moon.' I say this because from the earth's point of view, we never see one side of the moon. Some also call this the *dark* side of the moon. The moon's 'day' requires one full revolution around the earth to complete, and therefore we always see the same side of the moon. There are some mysteries about this heavenly body created to rule the night, and likewise there are mysteries the Bible does not expressly address concerning the how and why of Satan's existence.

For this reason, I believe exercising restraint in formulating conclusions about Satan's creation is important, whether we believe he is a fallen angel, created evil beast, or otherwise. We can only go so far before we cross over into speculation or allegorization of phrases more likely meant only to be poetic metaphors to describe the stated subject matter. We breach the safe boundary of Scripture into matters too lofty for us to obtain when we formulate *doctrine* on issues requiring more than we are given to understand. As Job found out, we cannot even fully understand God's created order. How then can we suppose we fully understand the wisdom of God?

> *No one is ferocious [enough] to rouse Leviathan; who then can stand against Me?* -Job 41:10, HCSB

There is only one person we can trust who will always do what is in our best interest. Remember Jesus' words, 'There is only *One* who is good...' (Matt. 19:17). Even if we don't understand the wisdom that took place behind closed doors when the earth was founded, we must trust the decisions rendered without leaning on the reasoning or wisdom of man, lest we become angered without remedy in our pain, foolish in our shortsighted conclusions, or filled with mocking derision in our pride. There is only One we can safely trust whose end purpose justifies His means. It is not wrong to search out God's purposes or struggle to find understanding from God's perspective. But it is about not accusing Him with wrongdoing or neglect. We need the fear of the Lord to keep us from being wise in our own eyes, for 'God does not regard any who are wise in their own conceit' (Job 37:24).

We must remember who we are: created beings made in the image of the Almighty Eternal God who founded the universe in wisdom, righteousness, and justice. Though made in His image, we do not possess the wisdom, knowledge, or understanding that designed the interwoven intricacies of the entire universe. In our shortsightedness, we cannot shake our fists at God when we do not understand, or in our anger and limited understanding claim to have a more righteous plan for governance, lest we hear this:

> *Who is this that darkens counsel by words without knowledge?... **Shall a fault-finder contend with the Almighty**? He who argues with God, let him answer it... Will you even put me in the wrong? **Will you condemn me that you may be in the right**?* -Job 38:2; 40:2,8, ESV

Since each will be judged on every idle word spoken, I'd like to suggest having the following verses memorized in anticipation of the rebuke we will surely receive:

> *I have uttered what I did not understand, things too wonderful for me, which I did not know... therefore I despise myself, and repent in dust and ashes.* -Job 42:3b,6, ESV

This would be a very good answer.

Perhaps...

In His wisdom, God did not reveal all the details of His plans when He established the world in righteousness and justice. Some things have been kept secret from the foundation of the universe (Matt. 13:35). Those things which were kept secret most likely include the wisdom that went into the creation of Satan and evil. With pride in his cunning and seeming invincibility (see Job 41, particularly vv. 8-9,34) except in regard to his Creator (vv. 10-11), Satan's objectives are to keep humanity trapped in sin (ensuring their death) and to keep his 'authority by default' over the kingdoms of earth.

Causing man to fall proved only too easy for the lying manslayer. As a result of the fall, authority over the earth was delivered to Satan until a man could demonstrate by his life that he could walk in full obedience to God. Keeping men in bondage to sin through the generations demonstrated the inevitable corruptibility of men once the knowledge of evil had been revealed (a theme Paul emphasized in Romans). Since only a righteous man could reverse this curse, Satan's victory seemed absolutely certain in the pride of his own wisdom and his arrogant reliance on his cunning and near invincibility.

SECTION 5 TACTICAL KNOWLEDGE OF THE ADVERSARY

Only a righteous man could receive back the legal right to govern the earth. With the information Satan possessed regarding the nature of man, defeat of his plan to keep his legal right to the earth seemed impossible because the character of man was so easily corrupted. The piece of information he may have been missing was that God would get the job done Himself because of His love for man, the crown of His creation. This teaches us that finitude, no matter how close to infinitude, will never be without blind spots.

Through the incremental unveiling of God's plan in the prophetic word, Satan understood the timing, circumstances, place, and lineage of the promised redeemer man. This allowed him to formulate tactical countermeasures either to prevent the prophetic word from taking place or to destroy its effects if it did. Perhaps what he did not take into account was the power of a life totally committed to the will of God—the incarnate God, otherwise known as Jesus the Messiah. The resurrection of Christ established that death had no hold over Him because He was judged sinless before God. Now Satan's strategy would have to include damage control.

In any case, we know that the king of pride will spend eternity in the lake of fire. Those who patiently endure the trials and testing of this life by abiding in Jesus and staying in step with the Holy Spirit will inherit eternal life. The following verse captures succinctly the end of both Satan and the patient overcomer:

> **Better is the end of a thing than its beginning**, *and the patient in spirit is better than the proud in spirit.* -Ecc. 7:8, ESV

Satan's Role as Adversary

Satan, which means 'adversary,' primarily operates as *the* adversary, his function being the prosecutor of all men in the Court of Heaven. His kingdom is one of darkness because he blinds people to the truth through subtle alterations, especially those alterations that appeal to our finite reason and skewed sense of fair play. Keep in mind this darkness affects body, soul, and spirit. Many of the battles we fight with this enemy will be in our minds as carnal thinking and error battle with God's truth. Half-truths are not truths but lies, of which he is the father (John 8:44).

A murderer from the beginning, he tricked Eve into choosing death (the tree of knowledge) instead of life (the tree of life). Perhaps Eve thought she could have both. Satan will always highlight the seeming advantages of sin and disobedience, or elevate teaching that appeals to the shallow reasoning and vanity of men, and either lie about, downplay, or remain silent regarding the consequences. The bottom line, as Eve found out, is that we cannot have both life and our own, selfishly-motivated way.

Satan assured Eve she would be wise like God, but he lied about the cost to her life. He didn't tell her that knowledge of sin would arouse desire to sin. Without the Holy Spirit giving us power over sin, we become enslaved to what has gripped our affections, causing us to sin (Rom. 7:5-25). The weight of the sentence of death, the loss of innocence before God, and the forfeiture of man's position of authority over the earth came to all mankind. Let's get something very clear: we *never* became wise like God, the promised result of this disobedience. Instead, we became slaves to sin and adulterated in our natural minds. We bear the weight of condemnation on our conscience for all our acts of disobedience, and the entire planet has been corrupted as a consequence.

Satan introduces a mixture of truth and error in *subtle* ways simply because few of us would be baited by anything blatantly evil or false (Gen. 3:1-7). Without being connected relationally with God, knowing the Word, and listening for the discernment of the Holy Spirit, we will be deceived. Of this there is no doubt, for if sinless, intelligent human beings who walked with God were deceived, what chance do we think we have? Satan deftly wove a few phrases into his conversation with Eve to instill a little doubt in Eve's mind about the truth of God's Word. 'Did He really mean what He said about the tree, about death? Surely He must not because this fruit will open your eyes to know good… and evil of course, but that is so you will be wise like God. Come, let us reason together. Does it make sense that God would hold these things back from you?'

His words no doubt provoked Eve to wonder why God would hold back this 'gift' that was, from surface evaluation, beneficial to the body ('good for food'), gratifying to the soul ('delight to the eyes'), and profitable to the spirit ('to be desired to make one wise') (Gen. 3:6). After Adam and Eve took part in his deception by eating the fruit, Satan claimed his prize: the authority originally given to man to have dominion over the earth and the souls of men. Satan stated that authority over and the glory of kingdoms had been given to him, and he gives it to whom he wills (Luke 4:5-6; John 14:30; 2 Cor. 4:4).

[Note: If we understand that authority and power to rule test the heart of a man, as in the case of Nebuchadnezzar, *et al*, it is not difficult to find the congruency of Satan's statement with the assertion all authority and sovereignty belong to God. Satan confers the authority in the permission of God to cause a ruler and/or nation to fall into his plan to bring corruption. God sets up authority to test the ruler and/or nation for its good, as well as use them as His 'rod' to bring justice for the wickedness of wayward nations.]

Both Old and New Testaments teach that Satan roams the earth seeking whom he may devour, tempt, or test (Job 1:7; 1 Pet. 5:8). He also has access to the heavenly throne room to accuse us before God (Job 1:6; Zech. 3:1; Luke 22:31; cf. Rev. 12:10). His role as adversary and accuser of believers is well documented in the Word. Even so, Satan is limited in what he can do by God's allowance or denial of his requests, at least in the lives of the righteous (Job 1:6-12; 2:1-7; Luke 22:31; 1 Cor. 10:13).

Only God wields authority over Satan (cf. Job 40:19, 'only its Creator can threaten it'; see also 41:9-10). Granting Satan's request to test us may or may not have to do with a weakness in our character. Even Jesus was tested (Matt. 4:1; see also Job 2:3). We are told, rather, that trials and temptations are for the testing of our faith to promote the spiritual growth we need—training for those destined to rule with Christ.

SECTION 5 *TACTICAL KNOWLEDGE OF THE ADVERSARY*

Slander and Accusation

Though it is debatable whether Satan was 'the cherub that covers,' we know for sure he is *the accuser who exposes*. The Hebrew word for 'Satan' is pronounced *saw-tawn,* and simply means 'to accuse, to attack, to be an adversary/opponent, to resist, an enemy in war or in a court of justice.' Satan's name is not only who he is but also describes his function. Zechariah 3:1 shows the wordplay of the proper name of Satan, *ha Saw-tawn,* and the verb to accuse, *saw-tan*. Zodhiates defines Satan's activities: "He seduces men and then accuses them like a prosecuting attorney in the courtroom of God."[9]

> THEN [the guiding angel] showed me Joshua the high priest standing before the Angel of the Lord, and Satan standing at Joshua's right hand to be his adversary and to accuse him. -Zech. 3:1, AMP

I experienced this tactic first hand while giving a deposition before a trial where I was retained as an expert witness for the prosecutor. During a break, the defense attorney became congenial, engaging me in what seemed to be casual conversation about my professional experiences. This had the effect of lowering my guard by making me feel at ease in the presence of the opposition. When the break was over and the deposition resumed, this attorney tried to use some of my own statements against me, twisting my words to suit his agenda. My naiveté evaporated as I learned what it means to be innocent as a dove but shrewd as a serpent.

In the next passage, the Amplified Bible points out the judicial nature of Satan's accusations. It is quite obvious he plays the role of prosecutor in the heavenly court, particularly against those who are moving in God's purposes. Knowing this is critical for understanding what is taking place in Revelation 12. The Lord alone can rebuke Satan, just as only the Judge can issue a citation of contempt in our earthly courts. This is in keeping with the Greek word translated 'rebuke' in the following passage, *epitimao*, which means 'to censure or forbid, but without the weight of conviction or any effectual consequence on the one being rebuked,' as would be the case with the use of the word *elegcho,* 'to reprove so that the offender is convicted of (acknowledges) his wrong' (e.g., Rev. 3:19). In other words, *epitimao* is the equivalent of being found in contempt of court.

> But when [even] the archangel Michael, contending with the devil, **judicially argued** (disputed) about the body of Moses, he dared not [presume to] bring an abusive condemnation against him, but [simply] said, The Lord rebuke (**epitimao**) you! -Jude 1:9, AMP (bold parenthetical added)

'Slander' is another way the word *sawtan* can be interpreted. Accusations leveled against believers are as to be expected: a mixture of truth and calumny. We see this being carried out against Joshua in the Zechariah passage. His clothes were filthy, and likewise the priest's turban on his head, symbolizing that his actions and mind were defiled. Satan stood to accuse him on these points, and the Lord defended Joshua by saying, 'Is not this man a burning stick snatched from the fire?' (v. 2). This is a statement permeated with the language of mercy and compassion.

How did this statement silence Satan? The answer lies in the prophetic words of Isaiah: 'A bruised reed he will not break, and a faintly burning wick he will not quench; he will faithfully bring forth justice' (Isa. 42:3, ESV). After reading this, we come to the realization our God *loves us so much* and *so zealously guards* His purposes in our lives that He has sown phrases into the Word He can use to defend us against Satan's accusations.

This is profound foresight and shrewd strategy, the benchmarks of divine wisdom. For example, this verse could be used to defend Peter: 'Whoever speaks a word against the Son of Man will be forgiven' (Matt. 12:32). Amazing—it boggles the mind. It is our turn to be overwhelmed by both the love and genius of God. We could not ask or even think of a better defense attorney than Jesus, *the Word*. The entire Bible is a book of case law to be used in our defense, a sword for offense as well as defense against the wiles of the adversary, and a witness against the unrepentant. *Selah*.

Satan's role as accuser is a powerful one, and he is not to be trivialized, as some of us have heard and read. He is powerful and far superior to our created design in every way. He is still considered one of the heavenly dignitaries, to be rebuked by the Lord alone (Zech. 3:1-2; 2 Pet. 2:10-12; Jude 1:8-10; cf. Job 41:8-10). Michael the archangel will not accuse him, implying Satan's authority is even higher than his. Only one Name has been given authority over all rule, power, principality, authority, title, and dominion, in this age and the age to come—Jesus, *the Word* (Col. 2:9-10; Eph. 1:19-23).

By His obedience in becoming the perfect sacrifice, Jesus nailed the curse against us to the cross, 'disarming the powers and authorities' by depriving them of the legal right to accuse us according to the law (Col. 2:14-15). These are maliciously evil forces, both on earth and in heaven, against which we struggle through our trials in this age. But greater is He who is in us, and no longer can these powers bring legitimate charges against those who are *in Christ*.

Satan is the author of all mischief in the world.[10] Jesus instructed us to pray for deliverance from evil (Matt. 6:13). Paul exhorted us to take up the shield of faith to combat the evil one's trap (Eph. 6:16). Both passages use *poneros*, a Greek word meaning malicious evil, 'aptness to do shrewd turns; delight in mischief, evil, and tragedy; perverseness.'[11] This defines Satan's work, demonstrating his commitment to harm man (a murderer from the beginning) through subtle and shrewd devices (lies and misuse of the Word) as well as turn men from God through tragedy (circumstances) and entrapment to sin.

It is not within the realm of our authority to bind Satan as his function in this age has been given to him by God. Nor can we inflict any harm upon him by accusation (cf. Job 41:28, 'the arrow cannot make him flee'). While we have been given authority over his works or activities through appropriate use of God's Word, as previously discussed, we cannot bind him with our words, cast him into the abyss, or bring accusation against him before God in the Court of Heaven. Revelation 20:1-2 tell us that an angel from heaven, as the agent of God's Court, will bind him when Jesus returns.

The sentence for the slanderer is predicated on the sentence he intended to see imposed on the ones he falsely accuses. Levitical law states if a malicious witness perjures himself to falsely accuse a man of a crime and his perjury is discovered, the witness who has been proved a liar will receive the sentence he intended for the man he falsely accused (Deut. 19:16-19). Satan's accusations and slander are made with the precise goal of making us fall, bringing God's judgment of death to the disobedient. Because he brings false testimony, Satan is destined for the punishment he sought for others: the lake of fire made for him and his angels.

> *The wicked lie in wait for the righteous, intent on putting them to death; but the* ***LORD will not leave them in the power of the wicked or let them be condemned when brought to trial.*** -Ps. 37:32-33, NIV

The Role of Trials and Testing

> *Remember how the LORD your God led you all the way in the wilderness these forty years,* ***to humble and test you in order to know what was in your heart,*** *whether or not you would keep his commands.* -Deut. 8:2, NIV

This concisely sums up our lives in this age: to be humbled and tested. Paul forewarned the Thessalonians that trials are inevitable so they would not be unsettled when testing arrived. We are destined for trials and persecution (1 Thes. 3:3-4). Learning to humble ourselves under the hand of God through the tests and trials of life is critical because it requires the transformation of our hearts from prideful self-centeredness to humble bondservanthood. Those who pass advance to rule and reign with Messiah in the age to come.

So what are the differences between the testing of God and the temptations of Satan? As far as can be determined from the various words used, the difference seems to boil down to objective. Satan tempts us with the goal to see us fall, but God tests us with the goal of exposing what lurks inside our hearts as well as to test and bring forth the good He has instilled in us through His Word and the sanctifying work of His Holy Spirit.

- God tests the heart and is pleased with integrity (1 Chron. 29:17).
- The Lord judges righteously, testing the mind and heart (Jer. 11:20).
- The Lord knows us and examines our heart's attitude toward Him (Jer. 12:3).
- The Lord searches the heart and tests the mind to reward each man according to his ways and the fruit of his deeds (Jer. 17:10).
- The Lord tests the righteous and sees the heart and mind (Jer. 20:12).

Both God and Satan are described as testing us by use of the Greek words *peirasmos* (to put to trial, temptation, testing), and *peirazo* (to test, scrutinize, discipline, entice). "Peirazo involves entangling a person in sin, or discovering what good or evil, weakness or strength, was in a person..."[12] This also describes the testing of Jesus by the Pharisees (Matt. 16:1; 19:3; 22:18,35; Mark 8:11; etc). When God brings *peirasmos*, His goal is that we gain experience in leaning on His strength and not our own understanding (see John

6:6; Heb. 11:17), *not* to cause us to sin. Through the testing God allows in our lives, we learn how weak and vulnerable we are to sin, and whether or not His Word has taken root in us. Jesus illustrated this principle when He described the rocky ground. The Word did not take root in these, which becomes evident during a time of testing because they quickly fall away (Luke 8:13).

God's purpose is not to make us fall ('God tempts no one to sin,' James 1:13), but to either prove our faith genuine or expose those hindering issues of which we may not even be aware (2 Cor. 12:7-10).[13] On this later issue, God's purpose in exposing sin is redemptive in nature and not for the purpose of making us fall. This is evident by the use of the Greek words *dokimion* and *dokimazo*:

> *Wherein ye greatly rejoice, though now for a season, if need be, ye are in heaviness through manifold temptations (**peirasmos**): That the trial (**dokimion**) of your faith, being much more precious than of gold that perisheth, though it be tried (**dokimazo**) with fire, might be found unto praise and honour and glory at the appearing of Jesus Christ.* -1 Pet. 1:6-7, KJV (parentheticals added)

Dokimazo (translated 'test, try, trial, or prove') is the Greek word used where the goal is to prove or bring forth good from a trial, and thus is never used of Satan's activity. It also means 'to approve what is good or worthy to be received.'[14] This word is often used for the testing or proving we do to examine teaching, our hearts, and our work (2 Tim. 2:15; 2 Cor. 13:5; Rom. 2:18; 12:2; Gal. 6:4; Php. 1:10; 1 Thes. 5:21; 1 John 4:1).

When Satan tempts us, on the other hand, he does so with the intent to make us fall or enter into the temptation by causing us to entertain the pleasures or benefits of the sin while minimizing or not even mentioning the temporary nature of illegitimate pleasure or the consequences (Pr. 28:14,18; Amos 3:5; Matt. 26:41; Mark 14:38; Luke 22:40; 1 Tim. 3:7; 6:9; James 5:12). Satan cannot make us sin, for if we 'walk in the Spirit we will not gratify the desires of the flesh' (Gal. 5:16), but he leads us to the brink of it, hoping to ensnare our mind, heart, and will where sin is conceived (James 1:14-15). We, however, are 'not ignorant of his devices' (2 Cor. 2:11) and counter his attack by 'rightly dividing the word of truth' (2 Tim. 2:15).

God's Objective for Testing

> *It was good for me to be afflicted so that I might learn your decrees... in faithfulness you have afflicted me.* -Psalm 119:71,75b, NIV

Victor Frankl reflected, "What is to give light must endure burning." God's objective for testing is to approve, *dokimos,* when He allows us to be tested, *peirasmos, peirazo.* The goal of our faith is perfection (*teleion*). "God's perfection is absolute; man's is relative, reaching the goal set for him by God with each individual differing according to his God-given ability... the goal for which he was intended, namely, to be a man obedient to Christ."[15] As we mature, testing is no longer a set of circumstances to grimly or gratingly endure, but is instead accompanied by the hopeful expectation of victory and good fruit that prepares us for what lies ahead so that we are complete, lacking nothing. With this mind, we can count it all joy when we are tested (see also 1 Pet. 4:12-13).

> *My brethren, count it all joy when you fall into various trials (**peirasmos**), knowing that the testing (**dokimion**) of your faith produces patience. But let patience have its perfect work, that you may be perfect (**teleion**) and complete, lacking nothing.* -James 1:2-4, NKJV (parentheticals added)

God always provides a way of escape when He allows us to be tempted. The Spirit led Jesus into the wilderness in order to be tempted by Satan. Jesus knew the purpose of the wilderness time, and the first strategic measure He employed in His warfare was fasting. We witness the wisdom of fasting during trials and temptations by observing Jesus' triumph over Satan's tactics during the wilderness test. Denying our flesh by humbling ourselves through fasting allows God to display His strength.

In pride we would like to believe we are able to resist temptation because of our own convictions and love for God. But, as Peter found out, at the end of the day this type of strength will leave us in a state of sorrow because sin will overtake us. Pride in our own moral rectitude is still pride; only the humble receive grace from God. Fasting is one way in which we humble ourselves before God, essentially agreeing we have no strength of our own and are in need of His. If our all-powerful God be for us, nothing can prevail against us (Ps. 62:11; Rom. 8:31).

> *I have said these things to you, that in me you may have peace. In the world you will have tribulation. But take heart; I have overcome the world.* -John 16:33, ESV

If humbling Himself through fasting is the way in which Jesus prepared to overcome temptation, should we not also use the weapon of humility given to us in order to receive grace from God during trials and temptations? James and Peter both quote Proverbs 3:34 (from the Septuagint): 'God *resists* the proud, but gives grace to the humble' (James 4:6; 1 Pet. 5:5). In hindsight, many of us will honestly admit that the testings we failed occurred due to foolishly trying to deal with the temptation in our own strength, *sans humilité* before God.

> *Do not lift up your horn* (strength) *on high, do not speak with insolent pride.* -Ps. 75:5, NASB (parenthetical added)

Jesus went through many *peirasmos* (Luke 22:28). All of His trials, testings, tribulations, and temptations served to make Him the sympathetic high priest who intercedes for us when we are tested, just as He did for Peter. Even the Pharisees and teachers of the law tested Jesus on many occasions. He went through these in order to be 'perfected,' fit for the office of high priest and intercessor as our Advocate before the Father. He is the tested, costly, firmly placed cornerstone for the foundation of our faith (Isa. 28:16). The incense of His intercession for us continually rises before the throne of God in this age.

> *Because he himself suffered* (in that He had to submit His will to the Father) *when he was tempted, he is able to help those who are being tempted... For we do not have a high priest who is unable to empathize with our weaknesses, but we have one who has been tempted in every way, just as we are—yet he did not sin.* -Heb. 2:18; 4:15, NIV (parenthetical added)

We likewise must go through trials of many kinds: temptation to sin, test of handling the Word, test of following the Spirit, trial of persecution for our beliefs, test of rejection, test with stewardship of resources, test of our response to the praise of men, trial of tragic or undeserved circumstances, test of faith when we are in need, etc. We experience sorrow, loss, pain, fear, disappointment, separation, and detours. Jesus intercedes on our behalf through all of these. We cannot allow our finite perspective on trials to dictate our response to God, especially during the more difficult times of testing.

The mark of a mature believer is not that they have fewer trials, but that they endure trials with joy. Through many trials we will enter the kingdom of God (Acts 14:22). We are able to view trials positively when we remember they produce perseverance, character, and hope (Rom. 5:3-5). C.S. Lewis reminds us we must not be surprised that believers are in for a rough time. "God is forcing him on, or up, to a higher level: putting him into situations where he will have to be very much braver, or more patient, or more loving, than he ever dreamed of being before. It seems to us all unnecessary: but that is because we have not yet had the slightest notion of the tremendous thing He means to make of us."[16]

Cooperating with the Holy Spirit will keep us from entering into temptation, just as we are taught to pray, 'lead us not into temptation.' Taking every thought captive so it is in line with the Word of God keeps us from letting our mind entertain sin, the place where sin is conceived. We have been told ahead of time that a way of escape has been made for us in every temptation with which we are confronted. 'The Lord knows how to rescue the godly from trials' (2 Pet. 2:9). The only reason we might miss the way of escape is if our gaze lingers too long in the other direction.

> **No temptation has overtaken you that is not common to man.** *God is faithful, and he will not let you be tempted beyond your ability, but with the temptation he will also provide the way of escape, that you may be able to endure it.* -1 Cor. 10:13, ESV

God also tests our loyalty and love for Him in the realm of prophecy. Oftentimes it is only by the witness of the Spirit that we are able to discern whether something is truly of God (Deut. 13:1-4). The Lord instructed the Israelites to test the prophets who appeared among them performing signs and wonders to validate their claims, especially if that claim promoted a false god. If our hearts are captured by supernatural signs more than by God Himself, we will have a very difficult time in this area of testing.

Exploitation of Desires

Temptation will exploit our desires, and this is why it is so crucial that our desires be transformed. If we truly love God with our whole being and love our neighbor as ourselves, desire will be secondary to fulfilling those two commands. Falling or entering into temptation occurs at the point where carnal desire becomes king, for 'each person is tempted when he is drawn away and enticed by his own evil desires' (James 1:14).

We are to be watchful and learn from our failures in testing. 'A prudent man foresees evil and hides himself, but the foolish keep going and are punished' (Pr. 22:3). Like Jesus, we are not here to please ourselves (Rom. 15:3), but in all patience we are to endure trials and testing of various kinds to bring us to maturity, the goal of our faith. This is how God tests our hearts (1 Thes. 2:4). By giving us the Holy Spirit, the carnal 'lines of code' in our hearts are being rewritten. Cooperating with the Holy Spirit is essential for guarding our heart in times of testing. God's Spirit residing within causes believers to walk in His righteous ways, as prophesied by Ezekiel (Ezk. 36:27).

Knowing the Word is imperative in this war waged against powers and principalities. This is the weapon we use in combating the subtle lies of the enemy. Our mind and desires are transformed degree by degree as we place ourselves before the Word in a teachable way (Rom. 12:2). Moreover, we also add to our arsenal the only ammunition effective against the attacks of our adversary: the sword of the Spirit, which is the Word of God (Eph. 6:17b).

'Discretion will preserve you, and understanding will keep you' (Pr. 2:11). By repeatedly washing our minds with the Word and growing in our relationship with God, our desires begin to change. This is critical in our warfare against temptation simply because sin starts in the realm of desire. When our desires are transformed, it is far more difficult for sin to be birthed. By cooperating with the Spirit and abiding in the Word, the avenues for temptation to sin become narrower and fewer, making us less vulnerable to attack in the arena of sin issues, 'for it is God who works in you, both *to desire* and *to do* His good pleasure' (Php. 2:13).

> *With my whole heart have I sought Thee... Order my steps in Thy Word: and let not any iniquity have dominion over me.* -Ps. 119:10a,133, KJV

Prayer is vital in overcoming temptation. Our struggle against temptation is won in the place of prayer, just as Jesus demonstrated at Gethsemane. Weak flesh keeps us from praying as we ought, but as with any discipline, regular exercise of the discipline curtails the howling of the flesh to be king. Soldiers are adept at keeping watch because they understand the dangerous nature of the situation. The enemy will exploit any perceived weakness. Likewise, believers must keep watch in prayer so they are not taken unawares by entering into temptation (Matt. 26:41; Luke 22:40).

We are driven to prayer in order to wage a successful campaign against temptation. Through testing, we are being trained for the ministry of intercession as Jesus was so we can empathize with others. The Lord puts people in our path that will have in common some of our same trials. Having gone through those trials ahead of time, we can provide comfort and share their burden, building the body up in love.

Blessed be the God... of all comfort, who comforts us in all our tribulation, that we may be able to comfort those who are in any trouble, with the comfort with which we ourselves are comforted by God. -2 Cor. 1:3a,4, NKJV

Confidence in Christ

If we place our confidence in Christ and not secure circumstances, we can respond as David did, or as the Shulamite, in anticipation of or in response to testing. Both asked for testing, knowing that testing would bring them closer to their Beloved (Ps. 139:23-24; Songs 4:16a). Both placed their confidence in the Lord and desired to be pure in His sight, understanding that perfection comes through trials and testing. Death to our carnal nature brings forth the fragrance of myrrh before God, a pleasing aroma.

God tests us in various ways to determine the nature of our faith in His promises, our loyalty to His purposes, the depth of our convictions, or even our reliance on His direction so we can properly respond during the test.

- **Joseph**: tested by God's prophetic word to him (the dreams he received, Gen. 37:5-11), whether he had faith God's promises would come to pass (Ps. 105:19).
- **Hezekiah**: tested by the Babylonian envoys: 'God left him to himself, in order to test him and to know all that was in his heart' (2 Chron. 32:31).
- **Ahab**: tested by lying spirits in the mouths of 'political' prophets (1 Kings 22:22).
- **David**: incited by Satan to take an unlawful census (1 Chron. 21:1).
- **Believers**: tested to see if the Word we have received has taken root and to expose the problem if it has not (Matt. 13:18-23).

Learning from the object lesson of our physical bodies, we better understand the role of trials. The food we eat greatly affects the health of our bodies. We stay healthier if we choose healthy foods to eat. Though good nutrition is important, regular exercise is also vital to maintaining physical health. Many of us excuse ourselves from this part, saying we don't have enough time to exercise. But if the truth be known, many of us just simply don't want to put forth the discipline and effort required because we feel worn out from working.

The parallel for our spirit man is obvious. We 'eat' the Word as the healthy 'food' for our spiritual well-being rather than the junk food from TV, web surfing, magazines, and so on. Trials and testing, like physical exercise for the body, are for strengthening our spirits. God places trials in our lives to bring about the needed spiritual maturity. By co-operating with God's methods born of His infinite wisdom, we submit under this pressure and allow Him to bring forth the treasure He has placed in each one of us, the character of Christ. Trials and testing give us spiritual 'muscle.'

Satan can test us in various ways: by destroying our possessions (Job 1:12); harming our bodies and keeping them bound in infirmity (Job 2:7; Luke 13:16); offering us fame, power, and wealth if we will put these first instead of God, His plan, and His timing (Matt. 4:8-

11); inciting us to sin (1 Chron. 21:1); introducing error into our thinking (2 Pet. 2:1); or preventing us from reaching our destination(s) (1 Thes. 2:18). In Paul's case, a messenger of Satan was sent to keep Paul from pride (2 Cor. 12:7-9). Satan will even use the Word to test us as he did when he tempted Jesus (see Matt. 4:1-11; Luke 4:1-13).

Responses to Testing

These are examples of positive responses to testing:

- not faltering, but turning everything over to the wisdom of God;
- becoming confused initially, but leaning on the Word to keep our focus on God and not circumstances;
- fearing the circumstances, but coming to the realization the Lord is bringing to the surface everything that hinders love in order to dismantle lies against the true knowledge of God ('perfect love casts out fear');
- falling into sin's trap, but then running to God for mercy that is new every morning.

Test me, LORD, and try me, examine my heart and my mind; for I have always been mindful of your unfailing love and have lived in reliance on your faithfulness.
-Ps. 26:2-3, NIV

Negative responses include:

- anger that turns into bitterness toward man and/or God;
- wallowing in self-pity because of circumstances, establishing a victim identity;
- self-condemnation for failing;
- a continued state of vacillating between two opinions because of slothfulness in putting forth effort to seek out truth;
- rejection of the testing as solely a device of Satan, clinging to inaccurate paradigms of the nature of testing;
- ongoing fear due to lack of trust in God's goodness;
- becoming ensnared by the sin we fell into, allowing it to become habitual.

Do not harden your hearts... as in the day of trial in the wilderness. -Ps. 95:8, NKJV

It is what comes out of a person that defiles, including our response to testing. Notice positive outcomes are the result of mental ascent, which elevates the rock solid foundation of truth above ever-changing feelings, desires, or circumstances. The negative outcomes are all based on feelings, carnal desire, and ignorance of truth. One particular lie that plagues many believers is that our circumstances indicate whether or not God loves us.

David's Census

In the following story, the Israelites had incited the anger of God, presumably by the idolatry or immorality that started this chain of events. Though the situation may seem unjust from our view (the 'innocent' people died because of what David did), it was the unrighteousness of the people that provoked God's just anger in the first place. Once again, by taking a look at the cross reference of this story, we see the involvement of the accuser, Satan.

> *Now again the anger of the LORD burned against Israel, and it incited David against them to say, "Go, number Israel and Judah."* -2 Sam. 24:1, NASB

> *Satan stood up against Israel, and provoked David to number Israel.* -1 Chr. 21:1, KJV

There may initially seem to be a contradiction in these two accounts. Some foundational truths help us understand what is taking place. *First,* we remember the Lord is sovereign and reigns in the affairs of men. We must also understand He sends testing because of His perfect wisdom and understanding as well as to reveal our faults (see also Rom. 5:3-4). This includes exposing the motives of our heart (1 Cor. 4:4-5). Those who are patient under trial, standing firmly against temptation, receive the crown of life (James 1:12).

Second, though God is not the author of sin or evil actions, He did create darkness as well as disaster in order to test the character and motives of man (Amos 3:6; Isa. 45:7). An example of the Lord bringing disaster through the agency of Satan can be found in the entire book of Job. Job was considered blameless by God, and this trial was a matter of testing/reproving.

We find a similar situation in the life of evil King Ahab, though in Ahab's case the testing was done to bring forth justice. This evil king had joined himself to a priestess of Baal, and the entire northern kingdom had been corrupted by his rule. God had shown him mercy, but Ahab did not repent fully. God, armed with foreknowledge of our nature, particularly our weaknesses, knows how we will respond to testing as shown in this passage:

> *And the LORD said, 'Who will persuade Ahab to go up, that he may fall* (be killed) *at Ramoth Gilead?' So one spoke in this manner, and another spoke in that manner. Then a spirit came forward and stood before the LORD, and said, 'I will persuade him.' The LORD said to him, 'In what way?' So he said, 'I will go out and be a lying spirit in the mouth of all his prophets.' And the LORD said, '**You shall persuade him, and also prevail. Go out and do so**.' Therefore look! The LORD has put a lying spirit in the mouth of all these **prophets of yours**, and the LORD has declared disaster against you.* -1 Kings 22:20-23, NKJV (parenthetical added)

Knowing this, we must be grateful for the revelation that believers are not tested beyond what they can endure and are always provided with a way of escape. Jesus intercedes on our behalf when we go through this kind of testing. Without the Lord's help, which of us could hope to stand?

In the example of David being incited to take a census, we note God's anger was kindled against the *people* of Israel. Having brought his accusations against the Israelite people before God, Satan is given permission to incite David to take a census, which will result in the outbreak of plague by God's own decree in the laws given through Moses (see Ex. 30:12-13). Taking a census fuels pride by feeling the strength of numbers and bolsters one's confidence at the military advantage strong numbers suggest. By appealing to his pride, authority, and position, David was incited to count the people out of the timing and regulations of God, for the census was only to be done for collecting the temple tax or when going to war. This was established when Moses received the law. If the people were numbered, they had to be ransomed by giving a half shekel to the Lord for each person counted lest a plague (death) break out.

This test had two broad objectives: reveal the pride in David's heart and bring judgment on the people who were sinning against God. God's purposes here are redemptive. This action would dissuade further apostasy among the people, which would have warranted harsher measures from God because of the curses for dishonoring the covenant, including being expelled from the land at the hand of an invader. In essence, even though the people broke their part of the covenant, God brought this lesser punishment both as justice *and as mercy* because of the deterrent it imposed to further apostasy. A modern day example would be similar to having a speeding ticket for twenty M.P.H. over the speed limit reduced in court to the much lesser charge of defective speedometer.

Though he initially fell into Satan's trap, David properly responded to this test. When given the choice of punishments for his sin, David chose to rely on the 'great perhaps of God.' He clung to the merciful nature of his all-powerful God rather than taking a chance on the vindictive cruelty of much weaker men. In humility, David expressed his sincere repentance, listened to the words God spoke through the prophet, and offered a sacrifice at the designated location—the future sight of the altar for burnt offerings in the temple (1 Chron. 21:7-22:1).

Superior Knowledge of Scripture

Many of us have seen the play, "Heaven's Gates and Hell's Flames." There is a quote in this play that has stuck in my mind for over a decade: Satan sneers, "I know Scripture better than any one of you." Chilling. Satan will use the Word of God in many ways to tempt us, typically by combining truth with error. Other ways in which he accomplishes this is through misapplication, invalid or inaccurate interpretation, faulty conclusions, or presumption, thereby provoking us to sin and disobedience by moving out of God's timing and/or will. His attempts to incite us to sin are defeated by correctly handling the Word of God and through the discernment of the Holy Spirit, though this will not prevent him from further efforts to seduce us (Luke 4:13).

The prophets provide an example of suffering and patience for the purposes of God. Those who endure are counted as blessed because the result of testing is to experience the compassion and mercy of God (James 5:10-11). By responding positively to the testing of God, we build victory upon victory in our faith, even when we actually fail the test but still learn something from it. This produces constancy and an unswerving faith in the face of adversity.

By standing firmly on the bedrock of truth and following in the footsteps of the Holy Spirit, we can set our faces like flint to complete all that has been set before us, rather than: 1.) turning back in fear to find we haven't the heart to complete anything; or 2.) turning away from God in anger because we didn't understand the nature and purpose of testing. We conquer by patient endurance and keeping our gaze fixed on Jesus rather than on the raging water of circumstances around us. Knowing beforehand the purpose and role of testing helps us to persevere and to 'count it all joy.'

> *Who shall separate us from the love of Christ? Shall tribulation, or distress, or persecution, or famine, or nakedness, or peril, or sword?... in all these things we are more than conquerors through Him who loved us. For I am persuaded that neither death nor life, nor angels nor principalities nor powers, nor things present nor things to come, nor height nor depth, nor any other created thing, shall be able to separate us from the love of God which is in Christ Jesus our Lord.* -Rom. 8:35,37-39, NKJV

Victory Comes Through the Word and the Spirit

When Jesus was tempted in the wilderness, He used the Word each time to fight Satan's temptations. After Satan's third attempt, enticing Jesus to move into His place of authority before God's timing and in a way contrary to God's plan, he left *until an opportune time* (Luke 4:13). Notice Satan offered Jesus what would one day be rightfully His (all the kingdoms of the world). But it was offered here with strings attached—compromises—and out of God's timing (Matt. 4:1-11).

In the first two temptations, Satan baits the hook with a taunt or challenge about Jesus' relationship with God. 'If God really is your Father…' In our lives it would surface as, 'If you really are a child of God…' This immediately puts us on the defensive because our relationship with God has been questioned.

Typically, a scriptural issue that has two (often paradoxical) sides is used to incite us to focus on one side without taking into consideration the whole counsel of God. In the example of Jesus' testing, Satan quoted Psalm 91 to goad Jesus into doing something presumptuous—throw Himself down because God said He would send His angels to our rescue. After all, hadn't God promised He would make sure we wouldn't be hurt?

Satan crafts the taunt that accompanies this challenge in such a way as to question the validity of our relationship with God. If you *really* are God's child, then He has promised to protect you, to heal you, to give you the miracle you need this hour, to make you a lender and not a borrower, the head and not the tail, to make you walk in abundant provision, to impart greater works than these, and so on. Does any of this sound familiar?

Jesus wisely countered Satan's taunts by quoting Deuteronomy 8:3 and 6:16 (the third temptation was countered with Deut. 6:13). We cannot allow the deceptive provocation of the enemy to goad us into presumptive acts or thinking. Some have been completely blown off course by this type of testing, walking in a presumptive world of their making, claiming all of the promises day after day in a whimsical world where only blessings and healing await every believer who has enough faith to believe the promises because the curse has been reversed.

While the hand of God does break through for miraculous healings and interventions, He is not bound to do so simply because we quote biblical promises. All of the promises are 'yes and amen' from the perspective of eternity. It is by His grace and mercy, as well as in accordance with His plans and purposes, that He breaks through in the present age for healings and miracles. This 'perhaps of God' prompts us to pray in all circumstances.

> *Therefore submit to God. Resist the devil and he will flee from you. Draw near to God and He will draw near to you. Cleanse your hands, you sinners; and purify your hearts, you double-minded.* -James 4:7-8, NKJV

The defense against the devil is to know the Word, shun evil so we do not give the devil a 'foot in the door' (Eph. 4:17-32), keep our focus on God rather than the trappings of life in this age, and put on the whole armor of God (Eph. 6:10-18). God's truth will be our shield and buckler, something that surrounds us (Ps. 91:4), all the more reason to make study of the Word our priority. Jesus' name is called 'the Word of God' (Rev. 19:13), and on this relationship our whole well-being in this life and the next rests.

The Armor of God

The different aspects of our spiritual armor are likened to physical armor (Eph. 6:10-18). Like those who helped rebuild the wall under Nehemiah's direction, taking tools for rebuilding in one hand and a sword in the other, we are called not only to works of faith but to always be ready to do battle with our spiritual enemies. Paul begins and finishes his description of the armor by encouraging believers to be alert with all perseverance, ever mindful that we wrestle against spiritual powers by the strength of God's might. Only in this way are we able to withstand evil and stand firmly in the truth. The armor is based on:

- **Truth**: revealed in the whole counsel of God upon which our defense rests. Jesus stated that He is the Truth.
- **Righteousness:** found only in the righteousness of Christ so our hearts are protected from both self-righteousness and self-condemnation. The enemy cannot entice us to pride or shame when we are in Christ's righteousness.
- **Readiness:** based on firmly standing on the solid foundational knowledge of the gospel. Jesus is the cornerstone—the Rock—on which our whole foundation rests. We speak and move in the Holy Spirit's leading.

- **Faith:** established in the person and work of Jesus, the Word, and founded on Him alone. It is a gift given by the Holy Spirit and enables us to trust His Word.
- **Salvation:** given through Jesus alone by the sanctifying work of the Holy Spirit to transform our minds and hearts from worldly to godly.
- **The Word**: provides our only actual weapon for both offense and defense. Jesus is the Word, and the Holy Spirit gives us the words to say as we lean on His counsel.
- **Prayer**: places us in the throne room of God. It is to be done at all times in the Spirit, with Jesus as our high priest to plead our cause.

Everything in our armor depends on Christ and the Holy Spirit. Those who are *in Christ* can expect victory over any scheme of the enemy because God always causes us to triumph in Christ (2 Cor. 2:14). This does not always mean our circumstances will change, but our *response* to those circumstances will be in line with the character of Christ. This brings honor to God if we follow the way of victory He has prescribed. Be strong in the Lord and the power of *His* might (Eph. 6:10).

Fiery Darts

Our 'shield of faith' enables us to extinguish the fiery darts the enemy shoots our way to defeat us, interfere with our mandate from God, or cause us to give up hope. Barnes noted, "By the 'fiery darts of the wicked,' Paul most likely refers to the temptations of the great adversary, which are like fiery darts... They are—blasphemous thoughts, unbelief, sudden temptation to do wrong, or thoughts that wound and torment the soul.

"In regard to them, we may observe: 1.) that they come suddenly, like arrows sped from a bow; 2.) they come from unexpected quarters, like arrows shot suddenly from an enemy in ambush; 3.) they pierce, and penetrate, and torment the soul, as arrows would that are on fire; 4.) they set the soul on fire, and enkindle the worst passions, as fiery darts do a ship or camp against which they are sent. The only way to meet them is by the shield of faith, by confidence in God, and by relying on his gracious promises and aid. It is not by our own strength; and, if we have not faith in God, we are wholly defenseless. We should have a shield that we can turn in any direction, on which we may receive the arrow, and by which it may be put out."[17]

The Word defines the 'arrows' of the enemy primarily as accusations and slanderous statements. The enemy's work is often depicted as coming from the shadows. The following reveal some of the tactics Satan uses against us, likened to arrows:

- The wicked bend their bow and shoot their arrows secretly from the shadows at the upright in heart (Ps. 11:2).
- Tongues are sharpened like swords; bitter speech aimed like arrows (Ps. 64:3).
- We are not to fear arrows (accusations) that fly by day (Ps. 91:5).
- A false accuser or slanderer is likened to a sharp arrow (Pr. 25:18).

- The tongue of the slanderer and liar is called a 'murderous arrow' (all are descriptions of Satan); the one who speaks deceitfully has a heart that lays snares and waits in ambush for his neighbor (Jer. 9:8).

Understanding this aids our grasp of the need for the shield of faith, which is wielded to put out the enemy's fiery arrows. How can those who don't expose themselves to the Word hope to be prepared to withstand the enemy's strategy? Those who have squandered the time the Lord has given them by pursuing selfish desires or what the world values or expects can reverse the course of their life as Zacchaeus did. *Carpe diem*!

> Be sober, be vigilant; because your adversary the devil walks about like a roaring lion, seeking whom he may devour. Resist him, steadfast in the faith, knowing that the same sufferings are experienced by your brotherhood in the world. -1 Pet. 5:8-9, NKJV

The Old Trick Still Works

These tactics of Satan have been used repeatedly throughout history because they work on our finite minds, fears, and self-centered desires. We naturally default to formulas that 'have to work' when it comes to spiritual realities, preferring predictable 'objective' methods to discerning the voice of God for every specific situation. Satan knows us well. We are dealing with a supernatural being with superior wisdom and tactics *by design*, operating under the authority of God. Formulas can displace our faith in Christ to faith in methodology.

We must remember that the Holy Spirit is credited with driving Jesus to the place of testing. We also recall that Jesus stated He did not say anything unless it came from the Father. If Jesus relied upon the very words the Father spoke in His time of testing, we must assume this also provides the pattern for us to follow. Jesus taught the disciples that the Holy Spirit would give them the words to say in the hour they were needed, and that they did not need to prepare speeches beforehand.

For this reason, we cannot hope to be victorious without reliance on the leading of the Holy Spirit and the Word. Satan attacks our will, affections, and intellect by using mixtures of truth and error to deceive and corrupt three general categories in our lives: our *perspective* on life and eternity, our *understanding* of truth, and our *actions* that flow out of the first two paradigms (discussed in the next two chapters). Only by reliance on the Holy Spirit to illuminate the error will we have the right response in the day of testing, regardless of which of these areas are tested.

Closing Thoughts

Satan has a special role in heaven as one of the 'heavenly dignitaries,' as Peter called him (2 Pet. 2:9-12; see also Jude 1:8-10). While his role as prosecutor, accuser, and tempter of all mankind is adversarial to our well-being, we cannot act like brute beasts by walking in authority that has not been granted to us, speaking scurrilous judicial accusations or judgments against him, scoffing at things we do not fully understand. Destruction awaits those who do (2 Pet. 2:10-12; Jude 1:8-13).

Peter differentiated the angels from these supernatural beings, and stated even angels will not bring blasphemous judgments against those beings. Peter also noted these angels who won't bring accusations are greater in power, authority, and strength than we are. The Greek words used imply *dominion authority* in addition to the *supernatural power* of angels. As Peter stated, we clearly do not understand these matters, and to scoff at what we do not understand will be done to our own hurt. His point in this passage is that we turn our eyes to the Lord who will rescue the godly from trials (v. 9), just as He did Noah and Lot.

Our role is to seek justice from God through intercession. In other words, when we address the High Court of Heaven, we direct our comments to God Himself, not the prosecuting attorney. Could we even imagine someone in one of our courtrooms today having the audacity to breach courtroom etiquette and begin a tirade of accusation against the prosecuting attorney? Not only would we be silenced before we could finish, we would be held in contempt of court and possibly thrown out of the courtroom altogether.

Our demeanor before the High Court of Heaven must be one of humility coupled with the confidence we have because of the finished work of the cross. Add to this the knowledge that we have standing with us in our defense the most wonderful and compassionate defense attorney we could possibly have—Jesus the Messiah Himself, the Word made flesh. Moreover, the Holy Spirit will intercede for us with groanings too deep for words as well as bring to our remembrance the Word He has planted in our hearts to remind us of His promises. He will give us the exact words to speak in every situation to counter the lies of the enemy; words that also provide the proper legal precedent to counter the accusations made against us. Add to this the knowledge that the One seated on the throne is our Father who *desires* to show us mercy and longs to display compassion for the children He loves. Now that is a defense team we can count on.

> *By steadfast love and faithfulness iniquity is atoned for, and by the fear of the LORD one turns away from evil.* -Pr. 16:6, ESV

Chapter 17

The Process of Corruption

> *The thief comes only to steal and kill and destroy; I have come that they may have life, and have it to the full.* -John 10:10, NIV

An ambitious person who desires to accomplish a malicious agenda would be hard pressed to goad his intended victims to cooperate of their own free will through divulging his purpose outright. In contrast, a subtle plot implemented step by step, sown while the victims are unaware and developed only incrementally over a course of time will have a much greater chance of succeeding. This is especially true if the thinking of the victims insidiously changes during the process to conform to or even embrace the intended outcome.

One danger in this process is that victims view too highly their own ability to reason *and* underestimate their malevolent manipulator. A strategy of Karate advises us to enter every confrontation with the assumption our opponent is faster and stronger, requiring we move with wisdom and not strength or pride in skill. For believers, it is vitally important we stay connected to the Head and wait for the discernment of the Spirit. If we have the mind of Christ and the timing of the Spirit, we will not fall prey to the adversary's schemes. With the mind of Christ, we will win every time over the strategy of Satan.

> *Keep me free from the trap that is set for me, for you are my refuge.* -Ps. 31:4, NIV

This is an excellent verse to pray, for oftentimes Satan sets a trap for us we cannot perceive. As any good hunter will explain, the key for a successful trap is to hide the trap by luring the prey with desirable bait. Typically, the prey will only see and focus on the delight of their eyes and not the trap set for them. We are forewarned.

Devaluing Our Perspective

> There is no need to be worried by facetious people who try to make the Christian hope of "Heaven" ridiculous by saying they do not want "to spend eternity playing harps." The answer to such people is that if they cannot understand books written for grown-ups, they should not talk about them. -C.S. Lewis[1]

Our perspective is based on our knowledge, beliefs, and desires. If we focus on our life in this age, we will make decisions and choices geared toward getting the most out of this life. Our decisions will be motivated by pleasure, accomplishment, recognition, status, power, wealth, self-actualization, or even goodwill—whatever the culture views as worthwhile and successful. If our perspective is rooted in eternity, we will focus our energies on those values that are relevant to the age to come.

When we are deceived into believing this age possesses the best life has to offer—even if we are believers bound for heaven—we focus our thoughts, energy, and time on accomplishing and experiencing all we possibly can in our eighty-year lifetime. 'After all,' the mind reasons, 'we only get one life to have fun and make our mark. After that, we'll be singing in a choir for eternity...' Our mind views everything and everyone as either helping or hindering our plans and goals, and we feel the pressure of time bear down on us as we age. This self-centered and short-sighted mindset is directly reflected in our prayers, which remain focused on personal desires and ambitions with little thought for the plans, purposes, and timing of God or the establishment of His kingdom.

Worse yet, we interpret the Word from this short-sighted perspective. Through repeated exposure to superficial yet cunning manipulation of the Word, we see all God's promises as being fulfilled in this life if we only have enough faith. Trials and testing are to be rebuked, negative circumstances are not to be acknowledged, and any failure is the result of sin or a lack of faith. We spend our energy pursuing those blessings to which we feel entitled in this life. After even a few weeks of listening to this kind of mixture, our mind and heart grow warmer to the comforts and successes the world has to offer, and colder to the true riches Jesus said are available to those who put Him and His kingdom first. We begin to accept that the only proof we have enough faith is the evidence of abundant provision, health, protection, and recognition in our lives.

> *For he who sows to his flesh will of the flesh reap corruption, but he who sows to the Spirit will of the Spirit reap everlasting life.* -Gal. 6:8, NKJV

The God of This Age

> *The god of this age has blinded the minds of unbelievers, so that they cannot see the light of the gospel that displays the glory of Christ, who is the image of God.*
> -2 Cor. 4:4, NIV

It goes against our nature to lay down our worldly aptitude and potential in order to serve Christ. Receiving the praise of others, accomplishing something noteworthy and esteemed in the eyes of men, or even merely living our lives as we please, naturally competes with the teaching of Christ who instructs us to lay down our lives for the sake of the kingdom as He did. Laying our lives down does not necessarily mean physical martyrdom, but that we give up our right to determine our course. Our culture, very much adopting the philosophy of the god of this age, blindly accepts pleasure, success, wealth, health, and self-fulfillment as the only way to keep from wasting our lives.

Paul explained to the Corinthians that the wisdom and reasoning of the world is foolishness to God precisely because it is finite and does not address the true purpose of our life in this age. Following the wisdom of the world toward a fulfilling life is a contradiction in terms, for only the One who *gave* us life knows the way in which we are truly fulfilled. True living is only realized in Him. If God intended that we pursue all the natural ability and potential we have, then why did He ordain that Jesus would be a carpenter rather than a statesman, or a quantum physicist, for that matter?

Solomon reflected on the worldly paradigm of life and came to some depressing conclusions. 'All labor and achievement spring from man's envy of his neighbor… what I have toiled to achieve is meaningless. It is all chasing after the wind. Nothing has been made better' (Ecc. 2:11; 4:4). This is, of course, in reference to the life lived for one's own glory and desires. This perspective is truly a veil that keeps us from comprehending what God has planted in our hearts and minds—a view based on eternity and the realization that we have a significant role in the age to come.

> *He also has **planted eternity in men's hearts and minds** [a divinely implanted sense of a purpose working through the ages which nothing under the sun but **God alone can satisfy**].* -Ecc. 3:11a, AMP

Need for an Eternal Perspective

When we let go of the ill-considered perspective that life in this age deserves all our affection and instead embrace the eternal, our eyes are opened to what truly makes a difference: the Word and kingdom of God. To think and do otherwise jeopardizes our eternal destiny. Furthermore, much to the dismay of all who chase after the things they thought would make them happy, in the end they find they are lonely, disillusioned, and in a state of even greater unhappiness.

> *I have seen that **everything [human] has its limits** and end [no matter how extensive, noble, and excellent]; **but Your commandment is exceedingly broad and extends without limits [into eternity].*** -Ps. 119:96, AMP

Jesus warned that if we cling to our lives in this present age, we will lose them and miss out on the far superior pleasures of a life lived in the eternal presence of God. The only way we can keep our lives for all eternity is to empty our heart of the love we have for the world's ways (John 12:25). This change in perspective comes only by the work of the Holy Spirit and the persistent washing of the Word.

As believers, we are given trials in this age to perfect our faith and draw forth the character of Christ planted in us at our new birth. We nurture the little seed placed in us when we received the free gift of salvation in Jesus by studying the Word. It grows as we cooperate with the Holy Spirit when He convicts us of sin and helps us pass the trials and testing sent our way to conform us to the nature of Christ—obedient in all things.

An eternal focus requires we have at least a little knowledge of what is to come. We know from the Word that we receive new, transformed, indestructible, ageless bodies with the hairs of our head numbered, and that we will live on the earth with authentic, meaningful work. We will rule and reign over the earth with Jesus as the Head over all. This will not be a virtual reality experience. After Jesus subdues all enemies under His feet with the Bride of Christ as His suitable and effectual partner in this governance, heaven descends to earth as we are reunited with the Father. The tree of life is once again made available for man to partake of forever. The perspective of eternity primarily centers on reconciliation: man with God, the earth with man (dominion authority), and heaven with earth. This will be anything but monotonous as we live as God originally intended for us to live—forever in His presence on earth.

> *You make known to me the path of life; in your presence there is fullness of joy; at your right hand are pleasures forevermore.* -Ps. 16:11, ESV

The wisdom of man changes with each successive generation because it is founded on man's finite mind and duplicitous heart. God's Word, in contrast, changes not. Satan has blinded the minds of unbelievers (2 Cor. 4:3-4). They have a misplaced confidence in the value of corrupted intellect (1 Cor. 2:6), rather than the true wisdom that comes from above and can withstand the fire of testing. Jesus gave Himself for us to rescue us from the god of this age (Gal. 1:4) as well as from the sin and wrong thinking in which those who follow Satan indulge, profaning body, soul, and spirit in the process (Eph. 2:1-2).

Adulterating Our Understanding of Truth

> *If anyone teaches a different doctrine and does not agree with the sound words of our Lord Jesus Christ and the teaching that accords with godliness, he is puffed up with conceit and understands nothing. He has an **unhealthy craving for controversy and for quarrels about words**, which produce envy, dissension, slander, evil suspicions, and **constant friction among people who are depraved in mind and deprived of the truth**.* -1 Tim. 6:3-5a, ESV

When we believe the god of this age—that all 'truth' is God's truth, that all roads lead to heaven, that truth and morality are relative—we are well on our way to a depraved mind, *adokimos nous*. These Greek words mean an 'unapproved, rejected, and worthless intellect or mind.' In other words, we have traded down for a mind whose thinking has become futile, lacking anything of value, believing anything and everything, slithering into rationalized acts of sin with the approval of a veiled conscience. In the Court of Heaven, man's wisdom is legally defined as *katargeo*—entirely useless (see 1 Cor. 1:18ff.).

From this position, we can be convinced God holds back good things from us. We begin to doubt the goodness and truth of God's love, ways, words, and leadership. When any little thing doesn't go our way or we are hindered from reaching a goal, we blame God and convince ourselves He is somehow 'out to get us' or that He doesn't care. Every catastrophe in the world becomes proof God doesn't love us or that He isn't truly good, or even that He doesn't exist at all.

We are deceived into scoffing at the Lord's ways and plans because we are not able to reason or perceive the purpose behind them. Since we now doubt the truthfulness and trustworthiness of God's Word, we do not waste our time reading or listening to it. The rift between us and God grows until it is a chasm, far and wide in our minds, affections, and desires. Yet there is an unsettled quality in our soul and spirit that cannot be shaken off—a restless agitation that expresses itself as depression, despair, unpredictable bursts of anger, anxiety, darkness, frustration, annoyance, emptiness, impatience, fear, or confusion. These are present in those estranged from God, whether acknowledged or quietly lurking in the shadows of the mind and heart.

When we are exposed to the subtle lies of Satan, confusion often results. The most insidious danger here and the primary cause of that confusion is that we begin to substitute intellect for trust in God and the Holy Spirit's illumination. This is not to say we throw our brains out the window when we become Christians. Quite the contrary, our minds will be stretched beyond their natural limits because of the work of the Holy Spirit. The mind of Christ far exceeds the limits of even the most brilliant genius ever born, and we are promised we have the mind of Christ as believers through the transforming work of the Holy Spirit (1 Cor. 2:16).

Satan does not want this to happen. Before we even begin to enter into the fellowship of the Holy Spirit, Satan will move to cause doubt in our minds through questions appealing to our sense of finite reason. We find ourselves saying, 'Hath God really said…?' Or we question the inerrancy of the Word, the motives of God, or the interpretation of the Word as a literal historical document laced with the trustworthy prophetic revelation of God. When we stray from trusting the Word (as it was given in the original languages; differentiated from *minor* disagreements regarding translated word choices or word order), we place ourselves in jeopardy because we have removed our foundation. Without our plumb line—the confident assurance that the Word of God is true—we quickly stray from the narrow path.

When confronted with subtle mixing of fragments of Scripture with error or lies, the struggle that follows in our mind will be far more difficult to resolve if we do not know what the Word actually says. Our mind can be easily convinced by fine sounding arguments. When given a few key statements, our minds will search to bridge any gaps in those statements in order to draw conclusions, usually erroneous ones. We must remember, 'our faith cannot rest on man's wisdom' (1 Cor. 2:5).

It is an odd phenomenon that the greater a person *perceives* his ability to reason and analyze, the more precarious his position with regard to truth. Those so inclined have a greater chance of accepting error disguised as a logical argument when presented in a way that appeals to his pride and god—intellect. Do not read this to be referring to all those endowed with above average intelligence. I am saying that it is problematic for those who *consider* themselves this way and in pride always want to appear so, even before God. In His wisdom, God saw to it that the world would never know Him through human wisdom (1 Cor. 1:21).

> *As the Scriptures say, "I will destroy the wisdom of the wise and discard the intelligence of the intelligent."* -1 Cor. 1:19, NLT

Though the mind may accept man-reasoned 'truths' as sound and reasonable, the conscience of a man will not because man is made in God's image. While consciously he assents to these plausible but fallacious arguments with his finite mind, subconsciously he is vexed by the dichotomy between what his mind has accepted as truth and what his God-given conscience recognizes as authentic. It is the difference between high-fructose corn syrup and real maple syrup.[2]

Depending on the strength of the person's will, this confusion can be displayed in different ways but often as cold-hearted ambition, a merciless drive for success, teeth-grinding pursuit of power, heartless view of other people as commodities, seething anger, acerbic condescension or patronizing contempt toward those of differing views, or darkness and disquiet of soul when left alone to deal with the unrelenting conflict waging war within. Deep within, the cry for an authentic revelation of truth begs to be satisfied.

Paul wrote that what is known about God is evident and made plain in our inner conscience. God's eternal power and divine nature are obvious from the created things. Even though the inner man recognizes God, many refuse to acknowledge God in their pride and blind acceptance of man's wisdom. Their thinking becomes futile and godless, devolving to 'vain imaginings, foolish reasoning, and stupid speculations.' Paul defines these as fools, despite their view of themselves as wise (Rom. 1:19-22). This was true in Paul's own life. Absolutely convinced he was in the right, Paul persecuted believers with vengeance. His finite grasp of truth persuaded Paul's mind that his acts were justifiable, despite the murderous anger (the fruit) that accompanied those acts (Acts 9:1-2).

When Paul recounted his Damascus road experience to King Agrippa, a few more details were released that give insight into the nature and extent of his anger-motivated persecution and Jesus' intervention (see Acts 26:9-14). Paul starts out by saying he was convinced it was his duty to do everything possible to oppose the followers of Jesus. Having obtained authority from the chief priests, Paul hounded the new believers, put them in prison, and gave approval to their executions. As he went from synagogue to synagogue, Paul admitted he tried to force them to blaspheme. In his obsession ('bitter fury,' AMP), Paul pursued believers into foreign cities to persecute them there. It was on one of those journeys that Jesus blinded Paul with His light, asking him, 'Why are you persecuting *Me*? It is hard for you to kick against the goads.'

Goads were sharp sticks used to prod oxen to keep them moving and prevent them from straying from the furrow. Goads were and are used in many cultures as imagery for sharp urging of the reluctant, wayward, or slothful. Using the *remez* interpretation of Deuteronomy 25:4, Paul elsewhere comments that 'ox' is a metaphor for God's workers (1 Cor. 9:7-11). Jesus is describing Saul (Paul) as an 'ox' who is defiantly resisting the wisdom of God, defined as Jesus Himself (1 Cor. 1:24), by moving in his own understanding and vehemently opposing Christ (*"Why do you persecute Me?"*).

> **The words of the wise are like goads,** their collected sayings like firmly embedded nails—*given by one Shepherd.* -Ecc. 12:11, NIV

SECTION 5 *TACTICAL KNOWLEDGE OF THE ADVERSARY*

Described by many as a brilliant theologian, Paul did not recognize the truth because it takes the Spirit of truth to reveal this to us, not fine sounding arguments and personal acumen. The man without the Spirit cannot understand spiritual truth because he has no discernment from God (1 Cor. 2:14-16), no matter how high his IQ or how extensive his training and education.

Jesus' response to Paul boggles the mind: no condemnation for the persecution of Jesus' followers; no mention of the unjust imprisonments or the murders; no guilt-provoking stare or rebuke for his self-righteousness and pride; no biting, sarcastic, or critical remarks for a person with his knowledge of Scripture to be so blind as to be unable to recognize the truth that Jesus is the prophesied Messiah. Jesus graciously gives only a clear description of His will for Paul's life as well as the promise of protection (Acts 26:15-18; with God on your side, you'll be surprised what you can live through, as Paul would soon find out). Paul's own assessment of his life prior to this encounter was much less gracious, admitting he was a blasphemer, persecutor, and insolent opponent (1 Tim. 1:13).

This makes it clear to us that God patiently bears with us and that none of us receive a calling from God because we deserve it or have earned it. We run our race only by His grace and to suit His purposes. We wisely take note of how Jesus treated Paul, following our Master's example in the way we should treat others who are moving in zeal without knowledge. *Selah*.

With his mandate to evangelize the Gentiles, Saul began using his Roman name, 'Paul,' which means 'little.' Switching to his Roman name spoke of his mission to the Gentiles and provides a picture of who he really was: not a prominent intellectual Pharisee, self-appointed to rid the world of those in error who were polluting Judaism, but a 'little' child in need of the wisdom of God. This realization defines where all need to be before God if we are to have the mind of Christ and the truth that sets us free.

Clandestine Operations in the Church

> Satan knows right well that one devil in the church can do far more than a thousand devils outside her bounds. -Charles Spurgeon[3]

Satan meddles covertly in the affairs of the church. He masquerades as an angel of light and his servants masquerade as servants of righteousness (2 Cor. 11:13-15). We are told his servants creep into the church unnoticed (Gal. 2:4; Jude 1:4), and through them he introduces destructive heresies and causes division (2 Pet. 2:1). C.S. Lewis stated that Satan often introduces error as *pairs of opposites*, encouraging us to choose one side or the other based on which side we strongly disagree with. But we cannot be fooled, because *both* are error.[4] Once again, we see Satan's subtlety at work because these workers look like sheep, not the wolves they really are, sent to devour (Matt. 7:15; Acts 20:29). Several popular *secular* speakers also fit this description. They have put forth a doctrine of mixture many in the church have accepted because it is palatable for our culture, and because those who accept this teaching do not know what the Word really says.

The unsaved are already his slaves, and it is not expressly stated whether Satan needs permission from God to operate in their lives. It would seem, however, that since they are his, Satan does not need to meet the same requirement to operate in their lives as he does for those who are believers. We are slaves to the one we obey (Rom. 6:16) or whatever defeats us (2 Pet. 2:19).

> *Formerly, when you did not know God, you were enslaved to those that by nature are not gods.* -Gal. 4:8, ESV

When the lives of unbelievers are exposed to the Word of God, Satan moves quickly to steal the Word so they cannot understand or believe and be saved (Luke 8:4-5). The hardened path where this seed falls became so through constant traffic due to painful circumstances and the trials of life, the constant barrage of the vain philosophies of men that brainwash and sear the conscience, bitterness or hatred, love for sin, obsession with self and the success the world has to offer, pride in intellect that will not humble itself before its Creator, love for a fast-paced life filled with amusements and distractions, or any other preoccupation placing men on the broad path. Without the Holy Spirit's intervention nudging those hardened to the gospel to plow their fallow ground to seek truth and a higher purpose in life, the Word will not take root. This is why prayer and gracious, compassionate, godly living are two of the best evangelistic tools we have.

Prayer is one of the weapons of our warfare and can prepare the ground of the unbeliever's heart by the working of the Holy Spirit. Godly living (not to be confused with acrimonious holiness) can cause people to pause and take notice, awaken longing in those who are searching, and draw them to seek genuine purpose and a plumb line of truth. Longing can take root in the heart of an unbeliever when they notice something different about a true believer. They may not recognize that longing at first, but through the work of the Holy Spirit and the Word aptly spoken at the right time, the ray of light will crack the shell around the heart so the seed can be sown on good ground.

Satan can enter those who have given themselves over to ungodly desires (Luke 22:3). He also operates in the lives of those who lead 'good' lives by their own (man's) standards. When we judge our behavior by the standard of our culture, we prove our lack of wisdom (2 Cor. 10:12). Recall good and evil are from the same tree (Gen. 2:9,17), and that no good works apart from being in Christ are of any value to our eternal destiny. We are not made right with God *by* works, but *for* works (Rom. 3:28; Eph. 2:8-10).

Thwarting the Advancement of the Gospel

When Jesus sent out the disciples two-by-two into the towns of Israel to proclaim the gospel ahead of Him, He gave specific instructions as to how they were to accomplish this (see Luke 10:1-11,16). Upon their return, the disciples exclaimed even demons were subject to them in Jesus' name (Luke 10:17). Jesus responds by saying something that has typically been used to substantiate the belief Satan was cast down from heaven at this time. The Amplified most closely preserves the meaning of the original word:

SECTION 5 *TACTICAL KNOWLEDGE OF THE ADVERSARY*

I saw Satan falling like a lightning [flash] from heaven. -Luke 10:18, AMP

When we look at the entire passage, a different conclusion may be drawn than that of Satan being 'thrown down' at this time. Consider that when Satan witnesses the sending out of the disciples to proclaim the gospel, he moves 'swift as lightning' to come down from heaven in order to thwart the gospel from going forth. Jesus deployed counter measures to Satan's strategy by giving the disciples authority over all Satan's power, assuring them nothing would harm them (Luke 10:19).

This interpretation is not only in keeping with the Greek word meanings used in this passage, but it also lends a greater and more cohesive understanding of the context of this comment within the text. Jesus sends out the disciples to preach, Satan retaliates by coming swiftly from heaven to interfere, and Jesus counters by giving the disciples His own authority over the activities of the adversary.

When the Lord sends us out to proclaim the gospel, we can count on Satan's interference. If it is the Lord who has sent us out, we can be sure He will also give us authority to trample the works of darkness sent to impede the progress of the kingdom of God. Even when tragedy strikes, as in the life of Jim Elliot when he reached out to the primitive Auca tribe in Ecuador, God's purposes brought forth fruit when the tribe who killed him witnessed the love and forgiveness of Jim's wife, Elizabeth Elliot.[5]

Guard Yourselves

There is no room for complacency in the life of a believer. We are to be sober and watchful, knowing Satan prowls around looking for the unsuspecting, the unwary, those preoccupied with this life, those who place confidence in their own intellect, and those who have drifted off the narrow path—even if only for a moment. We are exhorted to be ready in season and out (2 Tim. 4:2), to keep from entangling ourselves in the affairs of 'civilian' life (2 Tim. 2:3-4), to be strong in the Lord with His power (Eph. 6:10), and to pray in the Spirit on all occasions with all kinds of prayers and requests (Eph. 6:18).

Jesus told us Satan 'comes only to steal, kill, and destroy' (John 10:10). We must take to heart Paul's advice to Timothy, especially regarding the philosophies of this age (authored by the god of this age), and the error they introduce into our minds and hearts:

> *O Timothy, **guard and keep the deposit** entrusted [to you]! **Turn away** from the irreverent babble and godless chatter, with the vain and empty and worldly phrases, and **the subtleties and the contradictions in what is falsely called knowledge and spiritual illumination**.* -1 Tim. 6:20, AMP

In our culture and age, sin has been redefined to discredit the Bible's teaching and relevancy for our day. Others teach we can continue to sin in the grace of God because God knows how weak we are and will always forgive us. These also teach it is impossible for a believer to fall from grace, no matter how much they willfully sin. While this may be what many want to believe, it is far from God's truth and will bring destruction.

CHAPTER 17 *THE PROCESS OF CORRUPTION*

The apostles gave us the right perspective on sin. Their words are also the most convicting for believers (1 Cor. 10:13; 1 Pet. 5:8-9; James 1:14). They discredit the notion that the struggle and failure we have with sin is uniquely unbearable or impossible to overcome in our lives. Our struggle is *common* to man, not unique to our situation as we would like to believe in order to provide ourselves with an excuse for failure. Even Solomon taught there is 'nothing new under the sun' (Ecc. 1:9). Worse yet, God provides the way of escape *if we are looking*. By the grace of the Holy Spirit, we need to open our eyes to the way of escape and let go of everything that hinders, never looking back again.

With Jesus as our example and the writings of the apostles, we learn the unconventional nature of our warfare. Arguing with and reviling our opponent in a battle may feel right and reasonable, fulfilling our natural inclination to get the upper hand and advance through our own strength and tactics, but we won't win this way. Victory comes through appealing to the righteousness of Christ and wielding the Word on the counsel of the Holy Spirit. The Word of God is our weapon against attack and temptation, and the shield of faith our defense against the accusations of the enemy. This benefit comes through our faith in Jesus as our righteousness and as our great high priest and intermediary before God.

> *For **the weapons of our warfare are not carnal but mighty in God** for pulling down strongholds, casting down arguments and every high thing that exalts itself against the knowledge of God, bringing every thought into captivity to the obedience of Christ.* -2 Cor. 10:4-5, NKJV

The Final Outcome

The gospel message establishes that Satan, sin, and the flesh are overcome by Jesus' sacrifice and the provision of the Holy Spirit, who enables us to be victorious over Satan's schemes. The kingdom of God has been advancing since the days of John the Baptist. Jesus began destroying the works of Satan's kingdom 2000 years ago through overcoming temptation, delivering the demon-possessed, healing the sick, and proclaiming truth. The full establishment of kingdom authority will not be realized until His return, bringing Satan's reign of pride and seduction to an end. The last enemy to be destroyed is death at the end of the millennial reign (1 Cor. 15:26).

Jesus testified that when He returns, Satan will be bound in chains for a thousand years (Rev. 20:1-3). Matthew and Mark record Jesus as saying a strong man's house cannot be plundered unless the strong man is first bound (Matt. 12:29; Mark 3:27). In Luke we find further explanation of this strong man:

> *When a strong man, fully armed, guards his own palace, his goods are in peace. But when a stronger than he comes upon him and overcomes him, he takes from him all his armor in which he trusted, and divides his spoils.* -Luke 11:21-22, NKJV

Now we can better understand Paul's teaching to the Corinthians, which stated Jesus must reign until He subdues all of His enemies, the last of which will be death itself. In the Luke passage, Jesus established that a strong man in full armor can only be overcome by one stronger who takes away the armor in which he trusted. This armor is metaphorically described in Job 41 as impenetrable: 'Who can penetrate his double layer of armor?' (Septuagint, v. 13). We also learn from this chapter of Job that God alone, who created this beast, is more powerful. Therefore, we see that at Jesus' return this strong man is completely bound so Jesus can plunder the kingdom previously delivered unto Satan (the kingdoms of the world). This is why Jesus reigns *until* He subdues all His enemies. The plundering of Satan's kingdom takes place over the course of Jesus' reign (cf. Dan. 2:34-35).

The Word, which cannot lie, promises that Satan loses and we win (Rom. 16:20). He is cast out of heaven just before the Great Tribulation (Rev. 12:7-12), thus ending his days of *accusation* in the Court of Heaven (Rev. 12:10-11). This event triggers his days of intense *fury* on the earth (Rev. 12:12), evidenced by escalated persecution of believers (Rev. 13:5-7). But after this, he is *bound* for a thousand years (Rev. 20:1-2), *deceives* the nations on earth one more time at the end of this sentence (Rev. 20:3,7-9), and is subsequently *thrown into the lake of fire* for eternity (Rev. 20:10).

While Satan can still cause great damage as our enemy, his cause is ultimately lost. Jesus went before us, overcoming Satan's power and providing the Holy Spirit to those who believe, enabling them to overcome Satan as well. 'He who is in you is greater than he who is in the world' (1 John 4:4b). Overcoming Satan is a matter of clinging to Jesus, the Word, no matter what happens, and not letting go of Jesus no matter what we are offered or experience. The ways of the world, including the wisdom and intelligence of man, are hopelessly corrupted and will destroy us if we cling to them.

Closing Thoughts

Paul's description of believers as soldiers of Christ must be thoughtfully considered. No one serving as a soldier entangles himself in civilian affairs, but is committed to serving his commanding officer (2 Tim. 2:3-4). Being a soldier requires shrewdness in discerning the enemy's objectives and knowing his tactics, and vigilance in being alert and prepared for any avenue of attack. The bondservant remains sober, guarding himself against becoming an open target by divorcing himself from attachment to this world and remaining pure in regard to sin. In addition, the bondservant understands the nature of this warfare and relies on the strength of his beloved Redeemer and the unconventional means he has been given to overcome his adversary.

> *Behold, I send you out as sheep in the midst of wolves; so be shrewd as serpents and innocent as doves.* -Matt. 10:16, NASB

Chapter 18

The Goal: Corrupting Our Actions

> *Then, when desire has conceived, it gives birth to sin; and sin, when it is full-grown, brings forth death.* -James 1:15, NKJV

Corrupt and debased actions flow out of a defiled perspective and a desecrated mind. Our adversary desires this result, for Satan knows actions speak louder than words in the High Court of Heaven. We may profess with our mouths we are Christians, but if our actions do not validate this claim, or worse are *contradictory*, our profession is perjurous.

> *For the wages of sin is death, but the free gift of God is eternal life in Christ Jesus our Lord.* -Rom. 6:23, ESV

We Are Accountable

Some may object this is not fair because we are fallen and vulnerable to being despoiled by an enemy more powerful and intelligent than we are. This will not be a valid argument because the Word will testify against us. God avails His strength to all who are in Christ, trumping the power of Satan. The Word was there all along to correct, rebuke, train, and warn in order that we would have all the tools necessary to overcome our opponent's strategy.

> *Every Scripture is God-breathed (given by His inspiration) and profitable for instruction, for reproof and conviction of sin, for correction of error and discipline in obedience, [and] for training in righteousness (in holy living, in conformity to God's will in thought, purpose, and action).* -2 Tim. 3:16, AMP

Moreover, we have been given the Holy Spirit. 'Greater is He that is in you than he that is in the world.' 'Do not fear little flock, I have given you the keys.' 'Behold, I have overcome the world.' 'He disarmed principalities and powers and is Head over all.' With this power available to us, our excuses are invalidated. If we continue to sin with a 'high hand' as believers, we have no defense before the throne of God.

To the contrary, sin results when we are carried away by the lusts of our mind, flesh, and will. Though Satan tempts us, sin itself is birthed in our own mind and heart. The proverb, 'You can lead a horse to water, but you can't make him drink,' applies here. In a time of trial and testing, Satan can lead us to the place of sin or put us in a position to sin, but the desire to sin is birthed *in us.* In the garden, Eve was never *told* to eat the fruit. Satan merely awakened her desire with his lies, resulting in disobedience to the command of God. 'Such a fulfilling and wise goal must be worth taking the risk of defying the Lord's command. Surely God would want us to carry out the desires of our hearts. Hadn't He put those desires there to be fulfilled by the 'opportunities' placed before us?'

The answer to this last question is both 'yes' and 'no.' The Lord has given each of us noble desires and longings instilled into the very fabric of our nature. They include the desires for beauty, greatness, and the hope of making a lasting impact or contribution, alongside the yearning to be fascinated, enjoyed, and wholehearted in intimate relationship with God.[1] These are God-given desires, and their existence is known to Satan. Satan, however, will test and tempt us by offering us illegitimate ways to have these longings and desires fulfilled out of God's timing, God's will, and/or God's ways.

At Satan's provocation with sketchy but carefully calculated information, Eve's mind focused on the attainment of what she desired. The sentence of death did not come until she acted on her desire. The point is this: we are accountable for our actions in response to the testings and temptations in our lives.

God's Word warns that we need to be prepared for the devices and traps with which Satan will try to ensnare believers in his goal to keep them from entering God's kingdom. Many Christians have deluded themselves, rationalizing sinful behavior by comparing it to the norms of our culture rather than the light of God's Word. We cannot allow ourselves to be deceived by cultural norms, the accepted practices of this age, or the arguments of learned men with what is falsely called knowledge. Only the Word of God is eternal and worthy of our trust (see also Isa. 40:8).

> *Your word, O LORD, is eternal; it stands firm in the heavens.* -Ps. 119:89, NIV

Making Sin Acceptable

Paul wrote of some of the major sins that our enemy will entice us to embrace in order to cause us to lose our position of grace. As we come closer to the end of the age, each one of these sins is becoming more and more acceptable to society as a whole in the name of tolerance and relativism. Incrementally and subtly, Satan has made evil seem okay, and those who stand up for good are labeled intolerant, with intolerance considered *the* evil by contemporary society. Once again, we have been forewarned of the snares that await us.

In the Sermon on the Mount, Jesus conveyed the truth that sin is merely the expression of what is taking place in the heart. A heart filled with lust has already committed sexual immorality of whatever category through imagining the act (Matt. 5:28). A heart filled with anger and rage is equated with murder (Matt. 5:21-22).

> **From within, out of men's hearts,** *come evil thoughts, sexual immorality, theft, murder, adultery, greed, malice, deceit, lewdness, envy, slander, arrogance and folly. All these evils come from inside and make a man 'unclean.'* -Mark 7:21-23, NIV

Only by taking every thought captive and submitting them to Jesus (the Word) can we hope to be presentable before God (2 Cor. 10:5). Paul exhorted the Philippians to focus their minds on those things that are true, noble, just, pure, lovely, admirable, virtuous, and praiseworthy (Php. 4:8).

Leprosy: The Picture of Sinning with a 'High Hand'

But the person who does anything with a high hand, whether he is native or a sojourner, reviles the LORD, and that person shall be cut off from among his people. -Num. 15:30, ESV

What exactly does it mean to sin with a 'high hand'? The NASB describes sinning with a 'high hand' as sinning defiantly, whereas the NKJV translates this as sinning presumptuously. Under the new covenant, presumptuous or defiant sin would entail a rationalization for sin something like this: 'Well, God has to forgive me because I believe in Jesus and I'm under grace. It doesn't matter how much I sin because I am already forgiven for every sin I commit. Besides, the area of sin that I commit isn't hurting anyone, and I actually derive pleasure or benefit from this sin. Wouldn't God want me to be happy and prosperous? Besides, aren't God's standards relative, dependent on the times we live in?' Here is what the Bible tells us about sin:

- The wages for sin is death (Rom. 6:23).
- Full-grown sin brings death (James 1:15).
- Those who sin harm their own soul and choose death (Pr. 8:36).
- Death entered the world because of sin and spread to all mankind (Rom. 5:12).
- Sin reigned in death (Rom. 5:21).
- Sin kills us (Rom. 7:11).
- The sinner who turns from sin saves his soul from death (James 5:20).

The common denominator for nearly all biblical teaching on sin is that it leads to death. John talked of a sin that does not lead to death, and we can only conclude this sin is committed by the believer who has godly sorrow for having committed it (1 John 5:16-17). God is faithful to forgive those in Christ who fall into sin and sincerely repent.

As mentioned before in the section on covenants, sinning with a 'high hand' under the new covenant brings the same result as leprosy under the old covenant: it effectively annuls the covenant. Leprosy has to be judged as greater than skin-deep in order to be labeled as such, a picture of the degree to which sin has hold of us. It must also be differentiated from a wound in the process of healing. Evidence that leprosy has spread over the course of a specified time confirms the diagnosis when involvement of raw flesh is seen (see Lev. 13:1-14:32). Leprous individuals were to live outside the camp (Lev. 13:46), an object lesson about those with sin that parallels Jesus' teaching on church discipline as explained in Matthew 18. Paul also taught that those who sin habitually are to be 'handed over to Satan for the destruction of their fleshly ways' (1 Cor. 5:5).

If healing takes place, the Mosaic law required that the individual repeat the blood of sprinkling to renew the covenant through bringing guilt, sin, and burnt offerings to complete the reinstatement to the covenant community (see Lev. 13:1-14:32). The guilt and sin offerings represent the substitutionary blood atonement every man needs to be made acceptable before God. This requires acknowledgment not only of sins committed, but of the inherent inclination to sin as well. It must be accompanied by faith in the promised Redeemer who would restore the repentant to life through forgiveness.

Isaiah prophesied the coming Messiah would be the guilt offering (Isa. 53:10), and the author of Hebrews stated Jesus became the sin offering to do away with sin (Heb. 9:26). The Levitical priests ate the guilt and sin offerings because these offerings sanctified the one who partook of them. This is why these holy offerings were only to be eaten by the priests in a holy place. Under the new covenant, believers become a kingdom of priests (Rev. 1:6; cf. Isa. 61:6), partaking of the Lord's body as the sacred offerings (guilt and sin offering) to make them consecrated for God's work.

The blood of guilt and sin offerings was used to purify the priests and the tabernacle as well as the sinner who sought reinstatement. The guilt and sin offerings were to be followed by the burnt offering. The burnt offering represented the repentant worshipper's pledge of obedience, an expression of total devotion as all the purifiable parts of the sacrifice are arranged on the altar and burned completely as an aroma pleasing to God—nothing was held back to be eaten (though the hide was removed prior to the sacrifice). This parallels the bondservant who delights to walk in full surrender to God.

Under the new covenant, there is only one sacrifice that provided the blood of sprinkling to seal the covenant—the blood of Jesus. Accepting this holy blood must be followed by a pledge of bond servitude, the equivalent of the burnt offering. The reason willful sin displays contempt for Jesus' name is that the habitual practice of sin denies Jesus' power to deliver from sin's bondage. To scorn the power available to the believer to overcome sin treats Jesus' sacrifice as common rather than holy (able to consecrate that which it touches), and is evidence the sinner has rejected the Spirit's empowerment (grace) to overcome sin:

> *Of how much worse punishment, do you suppose, will he be thought worthy who has trampled the Son of God underfoot, counted the blood of the covenant by which he was sanctified a common thing, and insulted the Spirit of grace?* -Heb. 10:29, NKJV

Paul contends that Jesus released us from sin by becoming the sin offering so that the righteous requirements of the law would be met *in us* (Rom. 8:3-4). The picture of reinstating the leprous under the old covenant demonstrates the mercy of God toward those under the old covenant who had not received the abiding presence of the Holy Spirit. Under the new covenant, we have been given the Spirit's enabling power, dispelling the need for a provision of reinstatement through additional sacrifice.

> *[He] is **able to keep you from stumbling**, and to make you stand in the presence of His glory blameless with great joy.* -Jude 1:24, NASB

To continue in habitual sin without remorse after we have been restored from our spiritually leprous state through repentance and rebirth by the power of the Holy Spirit is to reject the new covenant blood of sprinkling and the power to overcome sin. Sinning with a 'high hand' is the equivalent of leprosy more than skin-deep; evidence of a seared conscience that will not repent. It invades the entire body by eating away the flesh. This is a picture of the affect of sin. It 'consumes' us and brings death.

Under the old covenant, the one with leprosy was isolated outside the camp and reexamined after seven days. If the leprosy had not changed or progressed, the individual was to remain isolated an additional seven days. If the questionable lesion had faded and did not involve underlying tissue, the person was declared clean and reinstated to the community. If, however, raw flesh became visible, the person was pronounced unclean. Only when the skin turned white and there was no evidence that raw flesh was involved could the person be declared clean.

Under the new covenant, there is no provision for reinstatement of one who returns to his leprous state *with no evidence of repentance*. The provision to prevent this from happening is included in this covenant—the gift of the Holy Spirit. By neglecting so great a gift, we have ignored the only provision we have for inoculation against this type of 'leprosy.' The author of Hebrews warned that deliberately sinning after we have received the truth brings only the terrible expectation of God's judgment. There is no more sacrifice to reconcile us to God because Jesus' death cannot be repeated (Heb. 10:26-31).

The apostles continually addressed sin because sinning under the new covenant must be the exception in our daily walk and not the rule. Sin, because of its association with death, is the opposite of the life of freedom we have in Christ, including freedom from the power of sin. There is no life in sin. Those who continue as slaves of sin, no matter what their theology may be, will find they have lost the eternal security they thought was theirs. If we remain in a state of sinning with a 'high hand,' callously indifferent to the Spirit's leading and defiant before God in this age, we will find there is no more sacrifice for sin to make us right before God, resulting in rejection when Jesus returns.

Satan knows this well, and he will do everything in his power to place obstacles in our path in his attempt to draw us into a life of sin. He knows very well if we give ourselves over to sin, we have forfeited our inheritance. We will be the slave of whatever we obey (Rom. 6:16). Death is the result of sinning with a 'high hand.' After warning those who continued sinning after accepting the blood of the new covenant, the author of Hebrews reminds us:

> *It is a terrifying thing to fall into the hands of the living God.* -Heb. 10:31, NASB

Avenues for Treachery

There are many avenues through which the enemy tries to derail our walk with God. This discussion is not exhaustive and will highlight only a few. Our focus will be limited to prosperity, ambitious zeal without knowledge, covetousness, anger, persecution, and seeking after miraculous signs in an inordinate way.

SECTION 5 *TACTICAL KNOWLEDGE OF THE ADVERSARY*

Prosperity Tests Our Loyalty to God

> You may say to yourself, "My power and the strength of my hands have produced this wealth for me." But **remember the LORD your God, for it is he who gives you the ability to produce wealth.** -Deut. 8:17-18a, NIV

Times of prosperity test us as much as times of want. If we have worked hard to be prosperous, pride and feelings of self-sufficiency are the temptations we must battle. This was the sin of Nebuchadnezzar. Jeshurun, a symbolic name for Israel that means 'upright,' also became self-satisfied by the abundance of prosperity God had given (Deut. 32:15-16). They rebelled against God who had established the Israelite nation in the first place. Worse, they pursued other gods and forgot the one true God (Hos. 13:6).

The termination of Sodom and Gomorrah was not only about sexual immorality. These cities were very prosperous, having an abundance of material wealth which promoted pride, idleness, and selfish indulgence. The poor went hungry despite the abundance of food, and God judged them for it (Ezk. 16:49-50).

Remembering it is God's grace and His power working through us that accomplishes anything of worth will help us retain the proper heart posture during prosperous times. Isaiah spoke of this, saying, 'All that we have accomplished You have done for us' (Isa. 26:12, NIV). David also knew where his prosperity and blessing originated, acknowledging that the gifts brought before the Lord were first taken from His hand (1 Chron. 29:14). When we are blessed, we must remember it is the Lord who gives us power to prosper.

> Nearly all men can stand adversity, but if you want to test a man's character, give him power. -Abraham Lincoln

Knowing that the Lord provides us with the circumstances to create wealth should keep us humble. If we do not keep this perspective, we will fall into a trap of the devil to boast in our accomplishment. This promotes an entitlement spirit that seeks to satisfy the cravings of the flesh for a better lifestyle. Others will fuel their ambition for the power to control others that often accompanies monetary wealth. Those fixated on the power of wealth live by a different golden rule, asserting instead that 'he who has the gold makes the rules.'

> *The LORD makes some poor and others rich; he brings some down and lifts others up... No one will succeed by strength alone.* -1 Sam. 2:7,9b, NLT

Zeal Without Knowledge

> *For I bear them witness that they have a zeal for God, but not according to knowledge.* -Rom. 10:2, NKJV

Satan can also incite believers to oppose the plans of God through pride, unsanctified mercy, or misunderstanding God's will. This type of temptation results from 'zeal without knowledge,' seen in Paul before his Damascus road experience as well as in the Jews who wanted the Mosaic law to be enforced for Gentile converts. New converts have a great deal of zeal but are especially prone to pride if they are promoted too soon. Oftentimes, our heart can be in the right place but our zeal misplaced, which is what got Peter into trouble:

> *Jesus turned to Peter and said, "Get away from me, Satan! You are a dangerous trap to me.* ***You are seeing things merely from a human point of view, not from God's.****"* -Matt. 16:23, NLT

Prophetic paradigms out of line with God's Word can be a real problem for those more loyal to their viewpoint than God's. Others will struggle with unsanctified zeal due to their magnanimous, compassionate hearts not harnessed by the control of God's Spirit. This type of humanistic mercy comes from viewing things from our perspective and not God's, placing greater importance on the comfort and needs of men than on God's purposes, the sanctifying work of the Holy Spirit, and the furtherance of God's kingdom. This is where the discernment of the Holy Spirit prevents us from overstepping the authority God has given us for specific good works.

> *It is not good to have* ***zeal without knowledge****, nor to be hasty and miss the way.* -Pr. 19:2, NIV

Paul used the concept of this proverb specifically when addressing the Jews who were zealous for the law, but it can apply to all who handle God's Word in a divisive way, promoting knowledge that leads to arrogance rather than the way of humility through love. There are many who campaign for their viewpoints in the church, some solely interested in truth and others with agendas to fulfill. Whatever the case, we should put our zeal to the test, always searching for the witness of the Word and the timing of the Spirit, doing all things from faith and for the hope of unity in love and truth.

Covetousness

Covetousness is far more pervasive in the lives of especially Western believers than we are willing to admit. Notice that the people who were said to be filled with Satan in the New Testament were people of covetousness (Judas, Ananias, and Sapphira).

> *Those who desire to be rich fall into temptation, into a snare, into many senseless and harmful desires that plunge people into ruin and destruction.* -1 Tim. 6:9, ESV

In the story of Ananias and Sapphira (Acts 5:1-11), Satan was credited as being the one to have taken over their *affections*, causing them to lose their fear of the Lord and to lie to the Holy Spirit. Satan will use the natural inclination of the heart to covetousness to incrementally steal the devotion and loyalty of our hearts from the Lord. We cannot underestimate the insidious nature and power of covetousness. Most of us will not even acknowledge it is lurking in the shadows.

> *You have spent your years on earth in luxury, satisfying your every desire. You have fattened yourselves for the day of slaughter.* -James 5:5, NLT

Many times we will disguise it subconsciously, calling it good stewardship or wisdom, so that our minds do not recognize it for what it really is. It could be labeled the 'spirit of Achan.' Achan saw nice clothing, gold, and silver, and hid the articles in his tent despite the command to destroy everything when Israel attacked Jericho (Josh. 7). How many of us today would be able to destroy silver and gold, knowing its value and usefulness, or give away the clothes in our closet, especially the ones we still wear and really like?

When we save more than our houses can hold, reasoning it would be a waste to get rid of things that still have use in them, we need to suspect the presence of avarice. Avarice is defined as 'insatiable greed for riches and *abnormal hatred in parting with money or possessions.*' This strong aversion to letting go of money and things is evidenced in the lives of those who worry about a bank account that has gone under a thousand dollars, or who have houses filled with possessions they haven't used in years. The sad thing is that many with garages and shops filled with useful things cannot find what they need when they need it. They usually end up buying another one of whatever it is they cannot find. Or even worse, they do find it and discover it is so antiquated it is no longer of use to anyone.

King Saul was tempted in this way when he and his men saved the best of the livestock and 'all that was good,' despite being told to destroy everything (1 Sam. 15). The Word states they were *unwilling* to destroy the best of the plunder (v. 9). Saul had deceived himself into thinking he had done the will of God, and that the plunder he took would be pleasing in God's sight. He rationalized his disobedience, reasoning it would be sacrificed before the Lord (which, of course, they would partake of the sacrifice by eating it). Hadn't he been a good steward? But the kingdom was taken from him because he disobeyed and in arrogance tried to substitute his own reasoning and wisdom for God's will.

> *Does the LORD delight in burnt offerings and sacrifices as much as in obeying the voice of the LORD?* **To obey is better than sacrifice**, *and to heed is better than the fat of rams. For rebellion is like the sin of divination, and* **arrogance like the evil of idolatry**. *Because you have rejected the word of the LORD, he has rejected you as king.* -1 Sam. 15:22-23, NIV

The sins of King Saul were counted as *rebellion* by rejecting God's way of doing things, and as *arrogance* by substituting his own plan through human intellect and reason (rationalization). Noteworthy is that this arrogance disguised as reason and wisdom—all rooted in the finite intellect of man—was seen as *idolatry* in God's eyes.

When Jesus was anointed at Bethany, an outcry of indignation went up as those present were offended by the waste of the expensive perfume, justifying their offense by reasoning it could have been put to better use by helping the poor (Mark 14:3-9). The Word tells us their thoughts of helping the poor were *very* secondary to their thoughts about the value of the perfume. In the John 12 recounting of this event, we learn this is exactly so. Judas objected to the waste, asking why the perfume hadn't been sold and the money given to the poor (vv. 4-5). John records that Judas did not ask this because he cared about the poor, but because he was the treasurer and a thief, helping himself to the money in the purse (v. 6). It was right after this event that Judas sought to betray Jesus to the priests (Mark 14:10-11).

Covetousness is rooted in greed and presents itself with subtlety, attempting to disguise itself as stewardship, wisdom, and prudence. We must take this seriously, for covetousness, like the arrogance of rationalization, is seen by God as idolatry.

> *You can be sure that no immoral, impure, or greedy person will inherit the Kingdom of Christ and of God.* **For a greedy person is an idolater,** *worshiping the things of this world.* **Don't be fooled by those who try to excuse these sins***.* -Eph. 5:5-6a, NLT

Inordinate desire for and pursuit of things above and beyond basic needs is covetousness. To have these things and appreciate the use of them as blessings from the Lord, however, is not covetousness unless we are driven to have them and cannot conceive of a contented life without them. The love of money includes greed for more, avarice, hoarding accumulation, and craving earthly possessions (Heb. 13:5a, AMP). Without the Holy Spirit's conviction, it is very difficult to be honest with ourselves on this point.

> *Guard yourselves and* **keep free from all covetousness** *(the immoderate desire for wealth, the greedy longing to have more); for a man's life does not consist in and is not derived from possessing overflowing abundance or that which is* **over and above his needs***.* -Luke 12:15, AMP

Selfish Hoarding

Storing up for *ourselves* on earth is a no-no. The Lord wants us to have a different view of stewardship than merely getting the most bang for your buck. Jesus taught that we are not to store earthly wealth for ourselves because this would divide our affections. We cannot serve both God and money (Matt. 6:19-21,24). John the Baptist promoted something called sharing:

> *The man who has two tunics is to share with him who has none; and he who has food is to do likewise.* -Luke 3:11b, NASB

Stored or hoarded wealth will be a witness against us in the last days when food and supplies will be especially scarce for those who will not be allowed to buy or sell. Whether the next verse is to be applied to those days or merely the last days of a person's life is up for debate. Either way, sharing what we have is shrewd in God's eyes. The alternative is to have these witnesses testify against us as we stand before the Lord:

> *Now listen, you rich people, weep and wail because of the misery that is coming upon you. Your wealth has rotted, and moths have eaten your clothes.* **Your gold and silver are corroded. Their corrosion will testify against you** *and eat your flesh like fire.* **You have hoarded wealth in the last days***.* -James 5:1-3, NIV

The New Living Translation puts it this way: "The very wealth you were counting on will eat away your flesh like fire. This treasure you have accumulated will stand as evidence against you on the day of judgment."

Jesus used the illustration of the rich fool to show the absolute futility of hoarding wealth for ourselves (Luke 12:16-21). This is not the same as the God-given wisdom Joseph received to store food, which would save *many people* during the seven years of famine. The rich fool, to the contrary, was not concerned for the welfare of others but for *himself*. Many Christians have labeled investing as wise and prudent, but from a biblical standpoint, it is only wise and prudent if it is done from a posture of faith, not hoarding for fear of lack or without concern for the welfare of others.

The wisdom from above is first of all pure (James 3:17), which can be read as 'wisdom that won't allow us to deceive ourselves.' Retirement investing is wise if we are saving in faith and not fear. Here is the question we need to ask ourselves: If our retirement investment(s) went belly up and nothing was left, a very real possibility in this economy, would this invoke fear and/or anger in our hearts? Or would our response be one of faith that God would provide for us another way? This is one way to examine ourselves to see whether we have acted in faith or have operated in fear disguised as wisdom.

Another lesson to be learned from the story of the rich fool and the story of the rich man and Lazarus (Luke 16:19-31) is that these men did not concern themselves with the plight of others. There are those who have well-cushioned retirement funds and in condescension view those who are not likewise prepared as lacking the discipline and wisdom they exercised in working and saving. They have no intention of sharing what they have put away because they view their investment as reward for diligence, and view those who have nothing as getting the consequences due the foolish.

> *Whoever closes his ear to the cry of the poor will himself call out and not be answered.* -Pr. 21:13, ESV

Fear-Based Hoarding

Others who invest do so out of fear. They are afraid there won't be enough for themselves, and it is this fear that prevents them from sharing with those who have nothing. The boy with the five loaves and two fish had only enough for himself, yet he was willing to share and the results were dramatic for the greater than five thousand who were fed (John 6:1-13). If we have retirement funds or other investments, they must be handled with open hands and faith, not grasping tightly for fear of loss or of not having enough, nor holding back from those we have judged harshly for not being likewise prepared.

Jesus' desire is that we trust Him to provide all our needs. 'Keep your life free from love of money ('covetousness,' NKJV), and be content with what you have, for He has said, I will never leave you nor forsake you' (Heb. 13:5). This reminds us God is with us and will take care of us in all circumstances. He never changes and is worthy of our trust.

As previously discussed with regard to giving, the Lord gives power to obtain wealth, and if He has favored us with that power, we are to share with those He has not similarly blessed. In the same manner, those poor in finances He has made rich in the things of God, who also share what they have received. It is a divine exchange program, and we all benefit by having both our spiritual and physical needs met (James 2:5; 2 Cor. 8:15).

> *Blessed… are you poor and lowly… (destitute of wealth, influence, position, and honor), for the kingdom of God is yours!* -Luke 6:20, AMP

Investing

Investing can be a touchy subject in the body of Christ. Those who are avidly in favor of investing cite the Wisdom literature to validate their arguments (Ps. 17:14; 112:5; Pr. 6:8; 13:22; 21:20, etc.). Those who lean against this use of resources typically cite New Testament teaching (Matt. 6:19-21; Luke 12:21,33-34; 14:33; 19:8; Acts 4:32-37; James 5:3). Much that justifies or condemns the use of money for investment boils down to the investor's heart motive and the integrity and dealings of that in which he invests.

When the soldiers asked John the Baptist what they should do, John replied they should be content with their pay (Luke 3:14). Jesus exhorted his followers not to store up treasures on earth (Matt. 6:19). Paul told us to be satisfied if we have clothing and food (1 Tim. 6:8), and to be content in all circumstances (Php. 4:11-13). He also told Timothy that godliness accompanied by contentment is of great value (1 Tim. 6:6-7). If we are storing up treasure because we are not content with what we have, which is different from not knowing what to do with what we have, we are on unstable ground.

Motives aside for a moment, there are issues of method regarding investing that need to be addressed. The Lord wants us to be aware of what we are doing because ignorance of what we are involved in does not exonerate us before the Lord, though the sentence is lessened for that ignorance:

> *That servant ('slave,' NASB) who knows his master's will and does not get ready or does not do what his master wants will be beaten with many blows. But the one who does not know and does things deserving punishment will be beaten with few blows.* -Luke 12:47-48a, NIV (parenthetical added)

Admittedly, this is not all that comforting.

Usury and unjust gain are unequivocally condemned in the Bible, especially when exacted from the poor (Ex. 22:25; Deut. 23:19). The sins of greed and usury were apparent even when the Israelites returned to Jerusalem from captivity and were pursuing a fresh start. This sad story shows those who took shrewd business advantage of the situation were clearly in the wrong (Neh. 5:2-13). Nehemiah held a great assembly against them, shaming them into doing what was right in *God's* sight, rather than taking advantage of (i.e., exploiting) the situation through the skillful maneuvering and ingenuity of the craft of business.

After berating the noblemen for selling their brothers back into slavery, Nehemiah castigates them for their lack of mercy and fear of the Lord. The wealthy men had nothing to say in their defense.

> ***Should you not walk in the fear of our God*** *in order to avoid being mocked by enemy nations?... let us stop this business of charging interest.* ***You must restore*** *their fields, vineyards, olive groves, and homes to them this very day.* ***And repay the interest you charged*** *when you lent them money, grain, new wine, and olive oil.* -Neh. 5:9b,10b-11, NLT

There are many institutions making money hand-over-fist today by defrauding the poor through interest. Covetousness, like pride, is vastly pervasive, whether we recognize it or not. Speaking through Jeremiah, the Lord stated 'from the least to the greatest, everyone was given to covetousness' ('greed for unjust gain,' Jer. 6:13, AMP). Ezekiel records similarly, 'they express devotion with their words, but their hearts are greedy for unjust gain' ('idolatrous greed for gain,' Ezk. 33:31, AMP).

Because man leans heavily toward covetousness and lust for wealth in spite of the cost to others' lives—even brothers—the Lord instituted the year of Jubilee every fifty years. In this way, all land would return to the original owners. In addition, all debts were released every seventh year. This would prevent the rich from getting richer, concentrating all the land and wealth in the hands of just a few. Likewise, these measures would prevent the poor from losing everything, becoming perpetual slaves in order to eat and survive (Lev. 25).

We see this in evidence today as those with money are acquiring vast amounts of land, and the poor are forced to charge even their food on credit. They have a very slim chance of ever getting out from under the weight of this kind of debt. The Lord has His eye on the poor to see they get justice. This includes poorer nations who have been defrauded by skillful market manipulation and currency devaluation. It is from the lack of the fear of the Lord that we exploit the poor in this way (Lev. 25:35-37).

> ***He will bring justice to the poor of the people****; He will save the children of the needy, and **will break in pieces the oppressor**.* -Ps. 72:4, NKJV

In Deuteronomy 15, we learn the Israelites were instructed to cancel all debts to their brothers every seven years so there would be no poor among them and they would be blessed among the nations. The Lord, knowing the covetousness of the heart, warned the wealthy not to be tight-fisted toward the poor needing to borrow when the seventh year drew near. They were to give ungrudgingly, even while knowing they would not be fully repaid. They were to remember Who had given them the power to acquire wealth in the first place. Was not wealth given to them to test them on this very point?

> *For there will never cease to be poor in the land. Therefore I command you, 'You shall open wide your hand to your brother, to the needy and to the poor, in your land.'* -Deut. 15:11, ESV

The Lord's urges His children to share in ministry to the poor:

- Those who increase their wealth through usury and unjust gain end up gathering it for those who will pity the poor (Pr. 28:8).
- Whoever gives to the poor will also have his own needs met; those who close their eyes to poverty will be cursed (Pr. 28:27).
- The righteous concern themselves with the plight of the poor (Pr. 29:7).

If we get involved in investing, we must take care the increase we receive is not from unjust gain. Sanitizing our financial activities by using sterile, industry specific jargon, from basic yields to the controversial and more difficult to understand hedge funds and derivatives, does not cloud the issue in God's eyes. Even if we don't look into these matters out of fear of what we may find out or because they are too difficult for us to comprehend, we are not excused from accountability. Keep in mind the craft of banking makes money by creating debt through loans and credit card accounts.[2] Using the expression 'yields' for mutual funds hides the fact that a portion of the payouts may have come from usury and not only actual growth in business through products and services. Oppressing the poor through usury to increase our own wealth will bring poverty to the one seeking increase (Pr. 22:176). God will not be mocked in this regard.

> Behold, therefore, **I beat My fists at the dishonest profit which you have made**. -Ezk. 22:13a, NKJV

> What sorrow awaits you who build big houses with **money gained dishonestly! You believe your wealth will buy security**, putting your family's nest beyond the reach of danger. -Hab. 2:9, NLT

The true test of whether we have acted in wisdom is the fruit it bears—'wisdom is vindicated by her children' (Luke 7:35). If fear of loss or anxiety over how the markets are doing continually grips our heart and attention, a red flag should go up in our spirit. If our mind is persistently at war over what we should do with our money and investments, consider the very real possibility the Lord may be prodding us to give to the poor what we have saved. *Compassion International* is another organization to consider for such giving.

We don't want to be found holding the money bag when Jesus returns, sheepishly remarking, 'Here is what you gave me. I wasn't sure what to do with it. I gave away some, but this was just too much to give away. I invested it just in case I lost my job...' Does not this reasoning stand in contrast with the Word, which expressly states we are to spend ourselves on behalf of the poor, needy, orphans, widows, and oppressed? If we have been given resources to spare, we must aggressively seek discernment on how the Lord would have us handle those resources.

Perhaps we are to invest so down the road the money will underwrite an orphanage. Maybe we are to send the money to fellow believers who have neither adequate food nor clean water to drink, or who are in prison. Funding Bible translation into a remote language may be the right course. The author of Hebrews challenges us not to neglect helping the needy, especially among believers (Heb. 13:16). It is *after* we spend ourselves on behalf of the poor that we receive light—the wisdom and revelation of God (Isa. 58:10).

For doubts to remain after we've heard the plain truth of Scripture, requiring further proof, or saying, 'Yes, but…' to the Word of God should also raise a red flag in our spirits. Hoarded wealth does not help but rather harms the owner and is called a 'grievous evil' (Ecc. 5:13). Even the Wisdom literature advises us to stop giving attention to acquiring wealth, wearing ourselves out to get rich (Pr. 23:4). 'Cease from your consideration of it' (NASB). 'Do not toil to acquire wealth; be discerning enough to desist' (ESV). 'Do not wear yourself out to get rich; have the wisdom to show restraint' (NIV). This is the opposite of the aspirations of our culture and generation. Some have been given power to acquire wealth by God. If submitted to God's will, these will be at peace with what they do and have gained. Like Job, they joyfully and regularly extend their wealth to those in need.

I have stayed as neutral as I can on the subject of investing, for in my mind it is a disputable matter. Recall that Jesus told the unprofitable servant that collecting interest on money was the *least* he could have done with what had been entrusted to him (Luke 19:22-23, NLT). So to the man who invests, let him do it from faith, not because of doubt, fear, or lack of contentment, being fully convinced in his own mind, not judging those who think and act differently, giving thanks and honor to God who grants power to create wealth *for the edification of the body and the care of the poor*. Amen.

Cannot Serve Two Masters

The story of the rich young ruler helps us understand the true nature and cost of discipleship (Matt. 19:16-26). It is not enough to robotically obey the commandments without concern for others. Obsessively striving for a track record of perfect outward obedience to God's law shows concern for the welfare of only one person. We must also have love and compassion for the plight of others, even if that means putting a dent in our perfect performance of religious traditions. A truly obedient heart will have no attachment to worldly things and aspirations, for this would divide the heart's loyalty. The more tightly we cling to the things of this life, including those things we would like to accomplish apart from God's will, the more loss we will suffer.

> *Remember what happened to Lot's wife!* **If you grasp and cling to life on your terms, you'll lose it,** *but if you let that life go, you'll get life on God's terms.*
> -Luke 17:32-33, THE MESSAGE

Jesus warned His followers not to store up treasure on earth because He knows how quickly our hearts can be turned by this powerful master. He desired that we demonstrate generosity to benefit the poor and needy who are always among us. With so many in the world suffering from true physical hunger and in need of other basic necessities, it will be difficult to explain to the Lord when He returns why there are Christians with large sums of money sitting in the bank or tied up in investments.

The *Complete Jewish Bible*, a translation by Dr. David Stern, captures the meaning of the Jewish idiom 'a good eye' in the parenthetical he placed in the following text. The primary context speaks of generosity vs. covetousness, confirmed by the verses before and after that discuss issues of money (see Matt. 6:19-21,24):

> *'The eye is the lamp of the body.' So if you have a **'good eye'** [that is, if you are generous] your whole body will be full of light; but if you have an 'evil eye' [if you are stingy] your whole body will be full of darkness. If, then, the light in you is darkness, how great is that darkness!* -Matt. 6:22-23, CJB

> *He who has a **generous eye will be blessed**, for he gives of his bread to the poor.* -Pr. 22:9, NKJV

While there are other very appropriate applications, the main thrust in this teaching deals with matters of wealth and our heart posture toward it as evidenced by the particular idioms used. As another consideration, the 'single eye' (KJV) speaks not only of generosity, but also of a mind and heart that are not divided between two opinions, or in this case, two masters.

Though the New Testament writers frequently record we are to give all we have to be followers of Christ, the message is not well received by a society that praises and pursues accumulation. The Bible emphasizes placing everything we have at God's disposal. Forsaking what we have may not necessarily mean giving every little thing away, but primarily divorcing ourselves from our attachment to it at the heart level. Jesus repeatedly stressed relinquishing the hold worldly goods have on us:

- Sell your possessions and give to the poor. For where your treasure is, there your heart will be also (Luke 12:32-34).
- Whoever does not forsake all he has cannot be My disciple (Luke 14:33).
- Sell everything you own and give it away to the poor; *then* come and follow Me (Luke 18:22; Matt. 19:21).

Desperately hoping these teachings can be labeled hyperbole, we look for teachers who preach we can keep everything and still be disciples (2 Tim. 4:3). We are not to cling to any monetary wealth in our hearts. If the thought of parting with investments really bothers us, we must pray that the grip they have on our hearts be dissolved. Does God always require us to give up everything? Probably not literally (e.g., Zacchaeus), but certainly He wants us free of its grip on our affections. There are Christians who have financial interests that keep them from seeing the truth of these words. Our eyes are not single, and because of a fear- or lust-driven desire to cling to wealth, we are gripped with confusion and double-mindedness on the matter of wealth.

Jesus makes it clear, however, that we are to lay aside our wealth for the benefit of others and allow the Lord to direct its use. He did this not only by His words but by His example as well. Though rich, Jesus became poor so we might become rich (2 Cor. 8:9). We have not truly comprehended the riches Jesus laid aside for our sake. Letting go of our baubles in this life is really a baby step compared to what He laid aside for us.

Entitlement

There are other destructive teachings in the church today that view the use of Scripture 'spoken in faith' as the means to procure entitled wealth in this life. These teachings, like the voice of Satan during Jesus' temptation in the wilderness, start out with the clause, 'If you are a child of God, then...' This theology focuses on material wealth as evidence we have the right faith and favor of God, just as the Pharisees believed.

Jesus stated as we seek His kingdom *first*, all we need will be added to us because our Father knows what we need (Matt. 6:31-33). This is difficult at first; we naturally desire to build *our* kingdoms first in order to look successful in our own eyes and the eyes of the world. But as our minds are washed with the Word and we spend time in His presence, those desires are transformed.

For those who are already poor, the risk of covetousness is no less. It is unmistakable in this next passage that what God desires to give the poor to bring relief into their situation is *the good news*, not wealth.

> *The blind see and the lame walk; the lepers are cleansed and the deaf hear; the dead are raised up and the poor have the gospel preached to them.* -Matt. 11:5, NKJV

The first five show the results we expect as the remedies for the specific circumstances mentioned, for example, the blind receive sight. But for the poor, though it seems obvious to us money would be the answer for their specific plight, the Lord promises the good news. If this disappoints those who are poor, who may have been hoping God would make them wealthy (or simply break even), we need only to redefine 'wealthy.'

Does this mean we should not pursue betterment of our circumstances? Not at all, for the Lord would want each of us to be in a position not only to provide for ourselves but to help others in their time of need as well (Eph. 4:28; 1 Thes. 4:11; 1 Tim. 6:18). We are instructed to do honest labor so we are dependent on no one and always have something to share with those in need.

When Zacchaeus repented, he had a sudden change of heart toward money. He exclaimed he would give half of his wealth to the poor and repay those he had swindled. [Note: If every politician, CEO, Wall Street broker, and banker in our nation would come to repentance as Zacchaeus did, I suspect we would have the money needed to pay off the entire U.S. deficit.] Jesus, delighted by his affirmation, responds to Zacchaeus by stating he has received the light of salvation and is a true son of Abraham (Luke 19:8-9). Notice the pattern again: he gave, and then Jesus declared he had received light. The action was proof that faith had taken hold of Zacchaeus' heart. 'The real children of Abraham, then, are those who put their faith in God' (Gal. 3:7).

Deal with It Now

Covetousness is a fantastically big issue today, even if we don't recognize it in our lives. It will be an even bigger issue in the days to come. If we deal with it now, we will be less likely to compromise when an economic plan is introduced to enslave men through fear of not being able to acquire the things they 'need' for life through economic access. Of course, it will not be packaged as *enslavement* but as *privilege*. We must be sober, not deceiving ourselves, and pray with the psalmist:

> *Incline my heart to Your testimonies, and not to covetousness.* -Ps. 119:36, NKJV

Anger

The issue of anger, like covetousness, can be artfully hidden. We have all tried to justify our anger by blaming the other guy for provoking us. Christians will shrewdly dismiss the conviction of their consciences by relabeling their anger as righteous indignation, which more often than not is disingenuous.

> *[B]e quick to hear, slow to speak and slow to anger; for* **the anger of man does not achieve the righteousness of God.** -James 1:19b-20, NASB

The Word rescues us from the dangers of anger if we not only hear the Word but also do what it says (James 1:21-22). It is precisely this tendency to vindicate, justify, and otherwise excuse our anger that Jesus adds an illustration to show what is really happening when we harbor unrepentant anger in our hearts.

> *Agree with your adversary quickly, while you are on the way with him, lest your adversary deliver you to the judge, the judge hand you over to the officer, and you be thrown into prison.* -Matt. 5:25, NKJV

The adversary in this example is most likely Satan, who accuses us before God. Hanging onto anger gives Satan a foothold (Eph. 4:27; see NLT). To 'agree with our adversary quickly' requires restraining ourselves from justifying our behavior before God, our Judge, and appealing instead to the righteousness of Christ. This requires humility because it is our nature to bandy words when we are accused. If we validate our anger, refusing to let it go or to acknowledge our complicity in the charge brought forth, prison awaits—the prison of a locked heart, or worse. If this involves seething, smoldering hatred and unforgiveness, we are in danger of much worse (Matt. 5:22). Jesus gives us the remedy for anger. He tells us to love our enemies (Matt. 5:44), for 'love is not easily angered' (1 Cor. 13:4-5). Remember, this is *agape* love, which is based on mental ascent, not feelings.

One of our enemy's schemes is to keep us bound, soul and spirit, through unforgiveness, bitterness, anger, hatred, and perceived wrongs (2 Cor. 2:10-11). The way in which we are bound is that our own sins are retained because we have not forgiven another and therefore do not receive forgiveness for ourselves. Those in Christ are always free to be loosed from sin by seeking God's forgiveness. But if we do not show the same forgiveness to others, Jesus taught we are prisoners by choosing not to forgive.

There are believers with locked hearts due to the pain of wrongs suffered (real or perceived). Some have little desire to be free of their self-imposed prisons—self-imposed because the key to their prison cell has been given to them. This key is the Word of God:

> *If you abide in My word, you are My disciples indeed. And you shall know the truth, and **the truth shall make you free**... Therefore if the Son makes you free, you shall be free indeed.* -John 8:31b-32,36, NKJV

The Word tells us that the *truth*, God's Word, sets us free. Jesus is the Word. Rather than spend time in the Word, many hurting and wronged believers have become slaves to their pain, anger, bitterness, and unforgiveness. It consumes their thoughts and emotions, severely stunting spiritual growth. While biblical counseling has its place, especially when the issues cause confusion and we are desperately trying to get our bearings, it is no substitute for personal time in the Word. Many cannot even read the Word because of the wall these types of feelings can create between the believer and the Lord. Words aptly spoken by other believers in the timing of God can be the key that helps propel the wounded on the road to healing. True and lasting healing comes as we continually and persistently wash our minds and hearts with the Word. This is the only way to be truly set free and experience *shalom*.

> We should be too big to take offense and too noble to give it. -Abraham Lincoln

Persecution

Sin issues and error aside, Satan also makes use of injustice, slander, and persecution to provoke or defeat believers. The Lord's purpose in allowing the trial is, of course, the testing and maturing of our faith. After speaking boldly in the temple, the apostles were brought before the Sanhedrin. They testified to Jesus and told the council they had to obey God rather than men. Due to their maturity and conviction, they were able to rejoice in the beating they received for defying the council. They were delighted that God counted them worthy to suffer disgrace for the name of Jesus (Acts 5:40-41).

Circumstances and the actions and words of others (believers and unbelievers alike) can be used in the testing sent to refine us. Satan will use whatever means are available to make our hearts grow cold toward God. Trials are one of the avenues through which he tries to diminish, steal, or destroy our faith in and relationship with God. Remaining steadfast through trials can only be accomplished by a heart gripped by the love of God. A cold heart will not stay the course because it neither loves nor trusts God. Those who persevere under trial are those who love *and* trust God. These will receive the crown of life (James 1:12).

Jesus and the New Testament writers warn us to expect testing and encourage us to recognize it is this very testing that will strengthen our faith and render us worthy for the kingdom of God. The church at Smyrna, who received no rebuke for wrongdoing, was told they must be tested first (Rev. 2:10). By suffering persecution, we share in the sufferings of Christ because we relinquish our will and submit ourselves to the hand of God (1 Pet. 4:12-13; cf. Php. 3:10). Endurance is the fruit of testing, and when it is fully developed, we will be perfect, lacking nothing (James 1:2-4). Keep in mind the consequences that follow sin are not technically trials. Those consequences may sorely vex us, but we did bring those on ourselves (1 Pet. 2:19-20; 3:17).

The heart of a believer under trial pursues an even closer relationship to the Lord through prayer and meditation on the Word, trusting God to bring forth the intended fruit that is pleasing to Him and fulfills His purposes. Trials forge the character of Christ in us. Pursuing God and trusting Him are the keys to remaining steadfast. While we are to take authority over these trials by the Word of God, we must remember that authority flows out of relationship. It is not simply a matter of reciting verses from the Word as if they were incantations that had to be obeyed. The seven sons of Sceva, sons of a priest, found this out in a painful way (see Acts 19:11-20).

> *Who is there who speaks and it comes to pass, unless the Lord has commanded it?* -Lam. 3:37, NASB

Pleasant circumstances in this life can become an idol set up in the heart. Some who rebuke the testing sent by the Lord are maligning the very circumstances meant to bring them closer to God. This is usually the result of not knowing or understanding the Word and the methods God uses to refine us.

Rebuking the Enemy

Does this mean we never rebuke the enemy? In the New Testament, we are shown our authority to rebuke is in the realm of taking authority over the *demons* (to be differentiated from principalities, powers, and the princes of the air) and the *devices* of Satan, but not Satan himself. We find examples of rebuking *demons* (Matt. 17:18; Mark 1:25; 9:25; Luke 4:35; 9:42), *illness* (Luke 4:39), *those in error* (Mark 8:33; Luke 9:54-55; 2 Tim. 4:2; Titus 1:9,13), *those in sin* (Luke 17:3; 1 Tim. 5:20), and *the elements* that try to harm us (Mark 4:39; Luke 8:24). In another example, God's authority is sought over Satan's tactics, but no authority is granted ('the thorn in the flesh,' 2 Cor. 12:7-9). Even when riots broke out in Ephesus due to allegiance to Artemis, no believers spoke against the goddess (Acts 19:37).

Both Peter and Jude remind us not even God's mighty angels rebuked Satan. When Satan presented himself to meddle in the affairs and purposes of God in Israel, his interference came in the form of legal arguments and accusations. The two examples recorded in Scripture supporting this involve the (legal) dispute over the body of Moses as recorded in Jude (1:9), and the accusation made against Joshua, the high priest after the Israelites returned from exile (Zech. 3:1-2). In both examples, the one opposing Satan said, 'The Lord rebuke you.' This can be understood when we remember John told us the Lord Jesus is the Word of God. This is none other than the Word being used to rebuke Satan, as previously pointed out. In other words, this statement could read, 'The *Word* rebuke you.' Or put another way, we use the Word to rebuke our adversary, just as Jesus did in His wilderness testing.

On one occasion, Jesus cast out a demon and then came under attack by the Pharisees, who said Jesus cast out demons by Beelzebub (see Matt. 12:22-29). Jesus countered by exposing the absurdity of their statement (why would Satan drive out Satan?), and their hypocrisy in judging Him but not the others who expelled demons. By stating no one can plunder the strongman's house without first tying him up, Jesus indicated He has overcome the power of Satan and has authority to plunder his house—both Satan's rule and his works. He came to destroy the works of Satan, and the process of plundering Satan's 'house' will be completed in the millennial reign, as previously discussed.

Jesus personally overcame Satan's power while being tested in the wilderness, essentially binding Satan's ability to have any power over Him in those circumstances. Satan had to wait until an opportune time presented itself to tempt Jesus again. By this, Jesus was not giving a precedent for binding Satan with a command, but demonstrating His authority by the power of an indestructible life (sinless life) over which Satan has no dominion. The demons obeyed Jesus by virtue of His authority, not because of a proven formula of specific words to say. The demons recognized the authority of Jesus and Paul, who walked with integrity and obedience before God as overcomers, but not of those loud proclaimers who had reduced Jesus' name to a magical word (Acts 19:13-16).

Miraculous Signs

An unhealthy preoccupation with signs, healings, and miracles can set us up for deception. The Word tells us there will be counterfeit miracles and signs in the last days. Those who have focused their energy and affections on these things instead of pursuing relationship with God and knowledge of His Word will find themselves short on discernment when these days arrive. Satan is counting on it.

Jesus called the Pharisees wicked and adulterous for seeking a sign that would validate Jesus' ministry (Matt. 12:38-42). They were looking for something more spectacular than healings and deliverances, which they had seen in abundance and had attributed to Beelzebub. Referencing Jonah's three day fish entombment, Jesus informed the Pharisees that the only sign they will receive is His own three day burial and resurrection.

Jesus' rebuttal increases in intensity by stating the heathen Ninevites repented and turned to God just by hearing Jonah preach; the pagan Queen was convinced merely by the wisdom spoken by Solomon. Both examples took place in the absence of signs and were accomplished through men of less authority than Jesus. These Gentiles are depicted as more righteous than the Pharisees. In other words, Jesus points out that this generation (when He walked the earth) does not need a sign to validate He was sent by God other than the message He has proclaimed and the miracles they have already witnessed.

Their rejection of His message and request for a sign will testify against them by the two witnesses, Nineveh and the Queen, who turned *without* signs. The Pharisees' hardened hearts have insulted the Spirit of grace, the only sin which will not be forgiven because it comes from a heart that will not recognize God or repent. How can there be forgiveness without repentance? The reason this sin cannot be forgiven is because there is no remorse for having committed it.

Jesus laments in the next section that this generation will be worse off than it was before He arrived (Matt. 12:43-45). They refused the Holy Spirit who would have taken up residence in the 'house' Jesus spent His life cleaning. This was not merely a simple task of deliverance but also of correcting the mindsets of traditional interpretations of Scripture. The Pharisees had kept the hearts of the people enslaved to obey the letter of the law rather than free them to love God and walk in the spirit of the law.

Enter by the Narrow Gate

Jesus wants us to have every opportunity to flee from those things that may hinder entrance into His kingdom. The free gift of righteousness opens the door that had been previously locked and barred to everyone. Entering the kingdom comes with perseverance and striving by cooperating with the Holy Spirit. Jesus warned that not all who seek to enter will be allowed to do so (Luke 13:24).

> *Let us therefore **be zealous and exert ourselves and strive diligently to enter** that rest... that no one may fall or perish by the same kind of unbelief and disobedience.* -Heb. 4:11, AMP

The open door (the free gift of righteousness) is accompanied by the infilling of the Holy Spirit who enables us to be conformed to Christ and overcome the world. Striving to cooperate with the Spirit defines how we work out our salvation and qualifies us to enter the kingdom. If we pause at the door and longingly look back at the sin or lifestyle we left behind, we endanger our entrance into the kingdom. Lot's wife found this out too late as did the Israelites who longed to be back in Egypt instead of taking the Promised Land.

Being found worthy to enter the kingdom comes from our continual struggle to reach for righteousness in thought, word, and deed. This process is designed to lead the repentant to forsake sin, even if not perfectly in this age. It is about a heart posture gripped with affection for God despite the war that continues in our soul over those affections. This is not the same as sinless perfection, but it means the transformation of our desires and will to conform to the righteous pattern of Jesus.

> *Work out your own salvation with fear and trembling.* -Php. 2:12b, NKJV

The Amplified defines fear and trembling as "self-distrust, with serious caution, tenderness of conscience, watchfulness against temptation, timidly shrinking from whatever might offend God and discredit the name of Christ." Repeatedly, the Word teaches only those who have clean hands (righteous actions) and a pure heart (righteous desires) can approach God. In Jesus we have both, provided we abide in Him and stay in step with the Holy Spirit.

> *O LORD, who may abide in Your tent? Who may dwell on Your holy hill? He who walks with integrity, and works righteousness, and speaks truth in his heart... He who does these things will never be shaken.* -Ps. 15:1-2,5b, NASB

Closing Thoughts

Remember this—no matter how good Satan makes evil appear or how hopeless the situation may feel because evil seems to have the upper hand, we must never forget he loses. We don't want to give in to temptation *or despair,* and find ourselves on the wrong side when Jesus returns and sets the dividing line between the sheep and the goats. Satan's goal is to prevent men from believing in God, from believing in the true way of salvation in Christ, from walking in the Holy Spirit, and from striving to die to sin. Satan knows if we believe in God and His Son, accept the blood of sprinkling of the new covenant, and receive the Holy Spirit, his only hope of keeping us from eternal life is to entice us into a life of sin—sin that is more than skin-deep.

Everything Satan does is geared toward the temptations thrown at Eve, Job, Saul, David, Jesus, Peter, and all the other examples in the Word. He will do anything he is given latitude to do in order to cause the people of God to lose their inheritance. This is especially true when it comes to getting something before its time, whether the knowledge of good and evil, marital pleasures, rulership, or any other thing our heart might desire. It is also true when it comes to trying to use worldly means to gratify desires only God can satisfy.

C.S. Lewis stated, "Creatures are not born with desires unless satisfaction for those desires exists... If I find in myself a desire which no experience in this world can satisfy, the most probable explanation is that I was made for another world. If none of my earthly pleasures satisfy it, that does not prove that the universe is a fraud. Probably earthly pleasures were never meant to satisfy it, but only to arouse it, to suggest the real thing. If that is so, I must take care, on the one hand, never to despise, or be unthankful for, these earthly blessings, and on the other, never to mistake them for the something else of which they are only a kind of copy, or echo, or mirage. I must keep alive in myself the desire for my true country, which I shall not find till after death; I must never let it get snowed under or turned aside; I must make it the main object of life to press on to that other country and to help others to do the same."[3]

Our life in this age boils down to giving loyalty to one side or the other. If our loyalty is to self, the good of mankind, money, worldly pleasure or accomplishment, or any of the vices known to humanity, we are on Satan's side and have become his slaves, whether we acknowledge his existence or not. Those whose loyalty is bound to God and His kingdom are the bondservants of God. These have repented, accepted the blood of sprinkling, and received the Holy Spirit. They exert strength and attention, striving to stay on the narrow path in order to be able to enter by the narrow gate. These will be raised to immortality to rule and reign with Christ on the earth.

> *Despite all these things, overwhelming victory is ours through Christ, who loved us.* -Rom. 8:37, NLT

SECTION 6

RESPONSIVE DEPENDENCE ON THE HOLY SPIRIT

Chapter 19

Ministry and Work of the Holy Spirit

> *I will give you a new heart, and I will put a new spirit in you. I will take out your stony, stubborn heart and give you a tender, responsive heart.* -Ezk. 36:26, NLT

The Holy Spirit plays a vital role in the life of the believer. After we are made clean by the blood of Jesus, we enter into the new covenant with our old, stony, stubborn hearts replaced with new, tender, responsive hearts. Responsive hearts do not merely listen to the Word but respond to what has been heard by taking appropriate action. God gave the Holy Spirit to guide us to walk in careful obedience.

The foundation for understanding and walking in obedience to the Word and growing in revelation and discernment of the times is unquestionably identified with the presence and work of the Holy Spirit. Jesus placed a high priority on the work of the Holy Spirit. So high, in fact, that He told the disciples to wait in Jerusalem until the Spirit was given (Luke 24:49). The presence of the Holy Spirit is our guarantee God will deliver His promise to resurrect our bodies and give us a place in His kingdom (2 Cor. 5:5).

Repentance, Holy Spirit, and Fire

The Holy Spirit came upon Jesus after He attended to the initiating rite of the new covenant—the baptism of repentance. John's baptism was a baptism of repentance, or in Jesus' case, a public declaration of obedience to God through the ordinance God prescribed. Just as circumcision was given as the symbolic introduction to the Mosaic covenant, whereby the act symbolized the circumcision of the heart, the baptism of repentance is the symbolic act representing a cleansed conscience that has turned to God. Jesus subjected Himself to both in fulfillment of all righteousness, which is obedience to God.

The next baptism comes with the impartation of the Holy Spirit, followed by testing in the wilderness. After Jesus was baptized by John, the Holy Spirit rested on Him in the form of a dove and then led Him into a period of testing (Mark 1:10). Matthew and John stated the Spirit rested or remained on Him (Matt. 3:16; John 1:32). Luke recorded that Jesus went into the wilderness testing full of the Spirit (Luke 4:1). John also stated Jesus was given the Spirit without measure (John 3:34). Testing and fiery trials are the baptism of fire promised to all who are in Christ (Mark 9:49; 1 Pet. 1:6-7; 4:12).

This sequence of baptisms—repentance, Holy Spirit, and fire (the fire of testing, fire of zeal for God, fire of the Word—cf. Deut. 9:10; Ps. 105:17-19; Jer. 23:29)—are noted by John (Matt. 3:11; Luke 3:16), manifested in Jesus' life (Matt. 3:11,15,16b; 4:1; Luke 12:49-

50), and possibly referred to as 'baptisms' by the author of Hebrews (Heb. 6:2). All three are necessary in the life of the believer and typically proceed in that order. [Note: Fire is also equated with judgment; see Isa. 66:16; Amos 7:4; 2 Pet. 3:7; cf. Heb. 12:29.]

Without true repentance, the gift of the Holy Spirit is not given (John 14:17). Without the Holy Spirit, we cannot go through the fiery trials sent to sanctify and perfect us. It is the empowerment of the Holy Spirit that enables us to endure and pass testing. In addition, without the Spirit we will not have the zeal to finish the work ordained for us to accomplish, known as our charge in this age.

Repentance has two components—sorrow over past sin, and turning or changing the worldly mind to embrace divine truth. Once repentance has taken place and belief in Christ is ignited, all the other ameliorations of the Holy Spirit become available. The Holy Spirit's premier work is to bring conviction and testify to Christ, the Word. The Holy Spirit brings conviction of sin followed by granting repentance (Acts 5:31; 11:18; 2 Tim. 2:25). He then helps us understand truth and apply it to our walk as believers.

Sent to Convict of Sin, Righteousness, and Judgment

> *He* (the Holy Spirit) ***will convict the world of sin,*** *and of **righteousness,** and of **judgment**: of sin, because they do not believe in Me; of righteousness, because I go to My Father and you see Me no more; of judgment, because the ruler of this world is judged.* -John 16:8b-11, NKJV (parenthetical added)

The Holy Spirit came to instruct and convict at the heart level the truth about sin, righteousness, and judgment. Ignorance on these issues keeps us from acknowledging the work of Christ as authentic and necessary for salvation. Without understanding these issues with the wisdom from above, we drift hopelessly with manmade speculation based on what makes sense to our finite minds and distorted sense of justice. In our fallen condition, we tend to prefer to determine what is right in our own eyes, setting our own standards of behavior based on our limited wisdom. This results in a self-righteousness of our own choosing, which puts us in an indefensible position in the Court of Heaven. This was the mistake of the Pharisees and all who followed them.

Sin

> *[T]hese things I write to you, so that you may not sin. And if anyone sins, we have an Advocate with the Father, Jesus Christ the righteous.* -1 John 2:1, NKJV

The truth about sin is that all have sinned and fallen short of eternal life. This negates the teaching that Mary the mother of Jesus was sinless. Even Mary called the Lord, 'My Savior' (Luke 1:47), the sentiments of one who knew her sinful state before God and her need for the Messiah.[1] John plainly states if we think we have not sinned, we are deceived and do not know the truth (1 John 1:8). Any deeds we attempt to do in our own righteousness are declared profane in the sight of God because He sees what lurks in our hearts. No law can make us morally right before God, even though we may carry the law out to the letter. It is only by the privilege of repentance that we view the subject of sin as God does.

Repentance is not an end in itself. It is the means by which we begin the process of sanctification. With the Holy Spirit as our teacher and guide, we learn to forsake sin not because the law tells us to, but because we also now hate sin (Heb. 1:9). The presence of sin in our lives tests our conscience. If we feel struck to the core and have remorse, hating what we have done, we are demonstrating godly sorrow and are on our way to life. If we secretly plan to commit the sin again, hoping no one sees what we are doing, then we must examine ourselves to see if we really are in the faith, for this type of thinking paves the broad road to condemnation.

Paul emphasized that we are saved so we no longer sin but abide by the law of God through life in the Spirit (Rom. 8:3-17). By gaining self-control over our sinful nature through the working of the Holy Spirit, we gain life (Rom. 8:13). This dying to sin daily leads us to be 'done with sin' (1 Pet. 4:1). Jesus gave Himself for this very purpose: 'to redeem us from all lawlessness' (Titus 2:14). Continuing in sin without true repentance carries the same penalty as it has from the beginning, whether we profess to know Christ or not—the wages of sin is still death. True repentance is evidenced by the fruit of repentance, expressed as gratitude for Jesus and desire to live morally upright.

In his counsel to Titus, Paul encouraged him to remind believers to be careful to restrain their carnal nature and instead devote themselves to doing what is good (Titus 3:3-8). Believers are reminded they were once 'foolish, disobedient, and enslaved to sin,' but now have received the mercy and love of God through Jesus for salvation without any merit on their part. Paul stated God saved us (vv. 5-7):

- **through the washing of rebirth**: made right before God through repentance
- **by the renewal of the Holy Spirit**: sanctification of our desires and actions
- **so that we may become heirs of eternal life**: the transformation of our physical bodies to become incorruptible and eternal

In his letter to the Galatians, Paul underscored that if we walk by the Spirit, we will not fulfill the desires of the flesh, which are by nature contrary to the Spirit of God (Gal. 5:16). Only in this way can we fulfill the entire law by keeping one command, 'love your neighbor as yourself.' If we are out of step with the Holy Spirit, we will surely devour each other through divisiveness born of ambition, conceit, envy, need to be right, demand to be first, and our unmerciful critical natures that put self-interest before the well-being of others (Gal. 5:15,25-26). We have been delivered from the power and condemnation of sin, though not the presence of it. Our natural bent to self-centeredness is continually confronted by God's Spirit in the process of sanctification.

> *Those who live only to satisfy their own sinful nature will harvest decay and death from that sinful nature. But those who live to please the Spirit will harvest everlasting life from the Spirit.* -Gal. 6:8, NLT

Righteousness

> *As the Scriptures say, "No one is righteous—not even one."* -Rom. 3:10, NLT

The truth about righteousness is there is no one righteous except Christ, and only in Him are we declared righteous before God. Adherence to God's law will not make us righteous before God because self-righteousness is no righteousness at all in His sight (Rom. 9:31; 10:2-4; Gal. 2:21). Our righteousness comes through faith alone in the Messiah—the righteousness provided for us by God Himself.

> *Therefore, as one trespass led to condemnation for all men, so one act of righteousness (**dikaioma**) leads to justification (**dikaiosis**) and life for all men.*
> -Rom. 5:18, ESV (parenthetical added)

The 'one righteous act' in this verse refers to Jesus' obedience to die on the cross. By using *dikaioma* in this instance, we are better able to grasp the legal implication of the death of an innocent life as the substitute for those who deserve to die. It is often translated 'judgment' or 'decision' in a legal sense, as the root word *dikaioo* suggests. The word justification (*dikaiosis*) in this verse has the same root, but a slightly different nuance in the meaning. It denotes an act which establishes someone as justified *legally* but not in personal essence. *Inherent* righteousness can only describe God and His righteous decrees.[2]

> *We are made right with God by placing our faith in Jesus Christ. And this is true for everyone who believes, no matter who we are.* -Rom. 3:22, NLT

Jesus, who did not sin and therefore was not under any legal sentence of death, willingly laid His life down in our stead. We are declared legally righteous in God's Court by believing in Jesus and by accepting His blood in our place by faith. Once we accept that we are made righteous in His sight through belief and faith in the righteous sacrifice of Jesus alone, we are in a position to do righteous acts before God. This helps us understand James' statement that we are 'justified by works and not only faith' (James 2:24).

The word James used for 'justified' in this verse is translated from *dikaioo*, describing righteousness brought out of a person, or action taken to make a person righteous in a legal sense.[3] This is in keeping with Paul's thoughts that the *doers* of the law are justified, not those who merely hear (Rom. 2:13). The apostles remind us we are either slaves of sin (our own desires and moral deficiencies) or slaves of righteousness. Only by the power of the Holy Spirit in the heart of the truly repentant can there be hope to follow the way of righteousness. This is the desire of every bondservant of God.

Paul was anxious for believers in Jesus Christ to follow the way of righteousness, citing the following reasons (Rom. 6:16-19):

- We are the slave of what we obey, either God or sin.
- Obeying God leads to righteousness; sin leads to deeper sin and death.
- Jesus freed us from bondage to sin.

> *Now you must give yourselves to be slaves to righteous living so that you will become holy.* -Rom. 6:19b, NLT

'Thou didst love righteousness, and didst hate lawlessness' (Heb. 1:9a, YLT). No truly repentant believer can cling to sin. In order to be conformed to the character of Christ, we, too, must love righteousness and hate sin. This must take place first in our own lives. The writer of Hebrews pointed out that the teaching about righteousness is for the mature who have trained themselves to distinguish evil from good (Heb. 5:11-14). This righteousness is also the fruit of testing (Heb. 12:11). Walking in righteousness is at the very core of the process of sanctification, the primary purpose for which we were given the Holy Spirit.

> *For the eyes of the LORD are on the righteous, and His ears are open to their prayers; but the face of the LORD is against those who do evil.* -1 Pet. 3:12, NKJV

Judgment

> *The wrath of God is being revealed from heaven against all the godlessness and wickedness of people, **who suppress the truth by their wickedness**.* -Rom. 1:18, NIV

The sentence for sin and unrighteousness has never changed, for 'the wages of sin is death' (Rom. 6:23). There were those in the early church who believed they could continue in sin without losing their place in God's kingdom. The apostles refuted this ideology repeatedly, making it very clear that those who persist stubbornly in sin will incur God's wrath. We cannot fool ourselves on this point. God knows whether we are truly repentant and struggling to overcome the sin that so easily besets us, or whether we have given ourselves over to carnal desires. This latter depiction is sin that has gone beyond 'skin-deep,' resulting in death.

What separates man from the animals is that he was given a conscience straight from God Himself. This means God's sense of right and wrong is part of the makeup of every human being. Since the fall, this God-given conscience exists alongside man's carnal nature, which demands the throne of his will until he comes to repentance. Paul testified that God's eternal power and divine nature are clearly understood from creation. It is sin and wickedness in our lives that suppress this truth, rendering our ability to reason futile because the darkness of unrighteousness prevents the heart and mind from true wisdom and understanding (Rom. 1:21-22).

What better way to deny the witness of creation than to discredit it through a scientific theory of evolutionary chance. By definition, science gains systematic knowledge through observation and experimentation. It is impossible to define the origin of life through 'science' because it is outside the scope of its own inherent limitations. Serious evolutionists admit the theory's probability is beyond reason, but have no other suitable theory for their worldview. Science itself was originally defined as a philosophy because one's paradigm directly affects any hypothesis put forth.[4] While many in the church

SECTION 6 RESPONSIVE DEPENDENCE ON THE HOLY SPIRIT

have different ideas about the timing and length of the creation process, as believers we must accept the Bible's clear teaching and the witness of an orderly creation: God alone is due credit for the creation of the universe. To believe otherwise is to grasp at man's inconstant base of knowledge, finite perspective, faulty premises, and ulterior motives.

When we no longer acknowledge God, we easily make the transition into moral relativism because our mind is no longer able to discern truth from error or even right from wrong (Rom. 1:28-31). This bears the fruit of 'unrighteousness, wickedness, greed, and evil.' Paul stated these people think nothing of gossiping, backstabbing, slandering, hating God, disobeying parents, or inventing evil. They are disrespectful, arrogant, boastful, without understanding, untrustworthy, heartless, and ruthless.

> *Although they know the ordinance* ('righteous judgment,' NKJV) *of God, that those who practice such things are worthy of death, they not only do the same, but also give hearty approval to those who practice them.* -Rom. 1:32, NASB (parenthetical added)

When we scrutinize the lists of the practices of darkness, it strikes us at the heart because all of these are seen in the church (see Gal. 5:19-21; Eph. 5:3-18; Col. 3:5-9). If our members are struggling with any of these issues, we forgive and bear each others' burdens in prayer. But for the unrepentant, discipline is required in the hope they will turn from their sin. Judgment is certain, and this will either strike fear in the unrepentant who believe God exists, or mocking disdain in those who are so hardened they have denied the obvious. For those who are in Christ, however, all fear is gone because of the perfect love of God which brings life to those who believe.

Belief is not only mental ascent, but as with *sh'ma*, requires obedience as proof this belief exists. In this way, we can be convinced of the judgment to come, where those who are abiding in Christ receive resurrected life by inheriting incorruptible bodies of glory. The demons believe and shudder, knowing the judgment to come (James 2:19). James reminded the church that belief without obedience to God is worth no more than the belief of demons who know their fate for disobeying God.

When Paul preached before Felix about righteousness, self-control, and judgment, the procurator became afraid. Felix was steeped in covetousness and felt the sentence of God on his life as the Holy Spirit convicted him through the words Paul spoke (Acts 24:25-26). Felix was not seeking to be reconciled to God by hearing Paul, but was hoping to receive a bribe. The fear of judgment, however, came upon him just the same.

> *But because you are stubborn and refuse to turn from your sin, you are storing up terrible punishment for yourself. For a day of anger is coming, when God's righteous judgment will be revealed. He will judge everyone according to what they have done.* **He will give eternal life to those who keep on doing good,** *seeking after the glory and honor and immortality that God offers. But* **he will pour out his anger and wrath on those who live for themselves,** *who refuse to obey the truth and instead live lives of wickedness.* -Rom. 2:5-8, NLT

All judgment has been entrusted to the Son so that all will honor the Son as they do the Father (John 5:22). Without the righteousness of Christ there is no justification, no matter how our interfaith culture may object. This is not intolerance—it is truth. If you told me the surface of the sun is hot, but I hold the view it is cold, would you be labeled intolerant of my view for insisting that it is hot? Or is it a matter of what is true?

Those who shrink back from the truth for political correctness, love of sin, or any other reason will face the same judgment as the ungodly. 'Those who shrink back are destroyed' (Heb. 10:39). The resurrection will occur either to enter into eternal life or for the condemnation of the unrighteous (John 5:28-29).

When Jesus stated the Holy Spirit will convict of judgment (John 16:8), the word used is *krisis*. This word emphasizes not the result of judgment, but rather the legal verdict of a judge's decision, whether positive or negative.[5] The primary thrust appears to be the idea of separation.[6] All of our actions become witnesses for or against us in the Court of God. If we are *in Christ*, all of our sins are removed—even if we still struggle with sin—and it is only our deeds that will be judged. Those who are steeped in habitual sin are not abiding in Christ; their sin still clings to them and brings death. If we only have in our account deeds done to please or promote self, we will be found wanting at the judgment seat of Christ. This should not surprise us, for Jesus also told John to tell each of the seven churches that He takes note of and judges their *works*, encouraging those with deficiencies to overcome them by listening to His Spirit (see Rev. 2-3).

The word translated 'evil' in the next passage literally means 'worthless' (*kakos*). The person who does such things is usually not malicious, trying to pull others down with him, but has sufficiently corrupted his own actions as to make himself worthless. The root of this word means 'to turn back' or 'retreat.'[7]

> *For we must all appear before the judgment seat of Christ, so that each one may receive what is due for what he has done in the body, whether good or evil* (**kakos**). -2 Cor. 5:10, ESV

The teachings about resurrection and eternal punishment were considered elementary (Heb. 6:1-2). Truth teaches us that each man is appointed to die *once*, and afterwards face the judgment his deeds deserve (Heb. 9:27). Reincarnation is an invention, not truth, and will lull its adherents into thinking they will be given another chance. Likewise, those who deliberately keep on sinning after receiving knowledge of the truth will find that what they hoped for will not be given them. They chose to believe a lie because of their craving and stubborn desire to continue in unrighteousness (Heb. 10:26-27). The only way we can have confidence in the day of judgment is to live as Jesus did (1 John 4:17). Peter warned believers to be on their guard so the error of 'lawless and wicked people' would not carry them away, causing them to fall from their current firm position in Christ (2 Pet. 3:17).

The Gift of the Holy Spirit

> *[Y]ou have received the Holy Spirit, and he lives within you, so you don't need anyone to teach you what is true. For the Spirit teaches you everything you need to know, and what he teaches is true—it is not a lie. So just as he has taught you, remain in fellowship with Christ.* -1 John 2:27, NLT

Jesus considered the Holy Spirit to be the best gift that could be given to His followers. The Holy Spirit is critical for our survival and witness, and a blessing for our comfort, encouragement, and understanding. The term *parakletos*, which primarily means 'to help,' is a Greek word often used to signify a proxy, pleader, or legal counsel or advocacy.[8] This describes His work in this age as the proxy for Christ and as our legal counsel that pleads on our behalf. When we realize this judicial connection, we have greater understanding and appreciation for the words He gives us to speak in any situation warranting the right 'precedents' to accomplish a legal decision in our favor.

With the Holy Spirit resident in believers, they can be transformed to understand the Word and equipped for every good work. The Holy Spirit guides them into all truth and reveals the things to come (John 16:13-15). All the things Jesus was restrained from saying, the Holy Spirit would be able to give Jesus' followers when they were ready (John 16:12). Believers would not have to worry about what to say during their trials because the Spirit would give them the most effective words to say (Mark 13:11; Luke 12:12).

The gifts of the Holy Spirit would be given to believers just as they were needed: bold preaching, prophetic encouragement and warnings, timely giving and hospitality, administration of aid to the needy, healing for the sick, signs to confirm the message tailored to the crowd being addressed, and so on. From God's perspective, the combination of the Holy Spirit and the Word would accomplish everything needed for the perfection of the believer, the maturation of the body of Christ, and drawing in the lost.

Comprehending all the Holy Spirit does in a believer's life makes obvious Jesus' consideration of Him as the best possible gift we could ever need or want. As parents, we require our children to be responsible. We don't give them everything they want but teach them what they need to know for life. We do this not just because it is good for their character but also because they need it for their survival. Should we expect anything less from our Heavenly Father in His dealings with us? The Holy Spirit is the only gift we truly need for our survival and perfection as believers. Our part is to cooperate and yield to His leading to have a life that brings honor to God by bearing much fruit.

Feast of Tabernacles

At the Feast of Tabernacles, the custom of pouring water out of a gold pitcher into a basin at the base of the altar symbolized prayer for rain as well as prayer for the fulfillment of the prophesied outpouring of the Holy Spirit on the people of Israel. This took place on the seventh day of the celebration and was accompanied by blowing trumpets, waving branches, and singing. In the midst of this celebration, the closing verses of the *Hallel* (Ps. 113-118) surely struck Jesus:

> *Blessed is he who comes in the name of the Lord... The Lord is God, Who has shown and given us light.* -Ps. 118:26a,27a, AMP

Jesus bursts forth with the following invitation in the presence of all the priestly divisions partaking in the festival. His heart overflowed with longing that the people would recognize Him as the answer to the prayer they just offered. With the inauguration of the new covenant in Jesus' blood, the Holy Spirit would be poured out as the covenant's provision for every partaker.[9]

> *On the last day of the feast, the great day, Jesus stood up and cried out,* **"If anyone thirsts, let him come to me and drink.** *Whoever believes in me, as the Scripture has said, 'Out of his heart will flow rivers of living water.'"* **Now this he said about the Spirit,** *whom those who believed in him were to receive, for as yet the Spirit had not been given, because Jesus was not yet glorified.* -John 7:37-39, ESV

The Holy Spirit was promised as a gift to those who repent with godly sorrow over past sin, are baptized for forgiveness of sins (Acts 2:38), and who live in obedience and submission to God (Acts 5:32). He is given to:

- enable us to be witnesses (Acts 1:8);
- give us clear and specific direction (Acts 8:29; 10:19ff; 11:12; 13:4; 16:6);
- give us power for healings, miracles, and deliverances (Acts 9:17; 10:38);
- enable us to pray in and by the Spirit (Acts 2:4; Rom. 8:26; Jude 1:20);
- empower us to speak boldly (Acts 4:31);
- give us wisdom in handling congregational affairs (Acts 6:3; 15:28);
- enable us to forgive those who persecute us (Acts 7:60);
- bring encouragement to the church (Acts 9:31);
- give us warning regarding the future (Acts 20:23; 21:4,11);
- raise the dead (Rom. 1:4);
- pour God's love into our hearts (Rom. 5:5; Col. 1:8);
- help us in our weakness and intercede for us (Rom. 8:26);
- bear witness with our conscience (Rom. 9:1);
- fill us with hope (Rom. 15:13);
- make us acceptable to God through sanctification (Rom. 15:16);
- enable us to say 'Jesus is Lord' in spirit and truth (1 Cor. 12:3);
- give life, transforming us to the image of Christ (2 Cor. 3:18);
- allow us to come to the Father (Eph. 2:18); and
- bring unity (1 Cor. 12:13).

SECTION 6 *RESPONSIVE DEPENDENCE ON THE HOLY SPIRIT*

The Holy Spirit ensures we have all the good things we need to accomplish the race marked out for us—all the tasks ordained for us. He can even transport us to the destination He so desires if it suits His purposes (Acts 8:39-40).

The Holy Spirit is imparted through preaching (Acts 10:44; 11:15), by believing the message (Gal. 3:2), while gathered together in unity (Acts 1:14 with 2:1-2), and through the laying on of hands (Acts 8:17; 9:17; 19:2-6). The gift of the Holy Spirit cannot be bought (Acts 8:18) or earned through the law (Gal. 3:2). We are not to hold the work and gifts of the Holy Spirit with contempt (1 Thes. 5:19). The gifts are imparted as He wills (Heb. 2:4), though we can seek the gifts that would be most helpful (1 Cor. 14:12).

> *For the Spirit searches all things, yes, the deep things of God.* -1 Cor. 2:10b, NKJV

The work of the Holy Spirit stays in perfect synch with the timing and purposes of God. Through His work and the Word we stay connected to the Head and bear fruit for God's glory. We cannot presume to know, analyze, or logically deduce His activity. It is spiritually discerned and moves in a way that is felt and heard by men, but not necessarily seen or in a pattern that can be predicted. Jesus described the Holy Spirit as wind. Though we hear and feel the wind's activity, we don't know where it came from or where it is going. 'This is how it is with those born of the Spirit' (John 3:8).

The Holy Spirit Bears Witness to Christ

> *When the Advocate comes, whom I will send to you from the Father—the Spirit of truth who goes out from the Father—he will testify about me.* -John 15:26, NIV

In addition to convicting the world of sin, righteousness, and judgment, the Holy Spirit bears witness to Jesus as the Savior of mankind. The signs, wonders, miracles, and gifts of the Holy Spirit testify to the salvation of the new covenant in Jesus' blood, just as the exodus signs and wonders testified to God's redemption of Israel from Egypt.

For this reason, we are to pay close attention to the salvation we have been given so we do not drift away and incur God's punishment rather than His favor and eternal life (see Heb. 2:1-4), as did those who died in the wilderness for disobeying God in the exodus story. In the new covenant, His laws are written on our hearts and guide us to live righteously. An incredible benefit of this is that 'our sins and lawless acts He no longer remembers' (Heb. 10:15-18). By the Holy Spirit, we no longer fear punishment as slaves do when owned by sin and death, but rather we receive the assurance that accompanies our adoption as sons (Rom. 8:15-16). There is no conflict in the dual identity of bondslaves of Christ and sons of God. The assurance of our adoption by the witness of the Holy Spirit gives us confidence to go before God as our Father, not as our task master.

The identity as bondservants defines our willingness to do all God requires of us. In fact, Christ had this same dual identity as both the Son of God and the bondservant of God.

Perhaps for some it will be easier to grasp this dual identity if we view our adoption as sons as the legal description defining our relationship to the Father, and understand our role as bondservants as primarily the posture of our heart. It is out of this heart posture of love, gratitude, and humility that our actions flow.

> ***Have this attitude in yourselves which was also in Christ Jesus****, who, although He existed in the form of God, did not regard equality with God a thing to be grasped, but emptied Himself,* ***taking the form of a bond-servant****, and being made in the likeness of men.* -Php. 2:5-7, NASB

After His resurrection, Jesus breathed on the disciples saying, 'Receive the Holy Spirit (*pneuma*)' (John 20:22). The word *pneuma* primarily denotes 'wind,' a fitting description of something unseen yet capable of great power. When used of the spirit of man, it speaks of man's ability to relate to God, while the word for soul (*psuche*) speaks of man's ability to relate to his environment.[10] In his commentary, Adam Clarke describes this wind/breath: "Every word of Christ which is received in the heart by faith comes accompanied by this Divine breathing; and, without this, there is neither light nor life."[11]

> *The one who keeps God's commands lives in him, and he in them. And this is how we know that he lives in us: we know it by the Spirit he gave us.* -1 John 3:24, NIV

Ask, Seek, and Knock

In the well-known passages about asking, seeking, and knocking (see Matt. 7:7-11; Luke 11:9-13), both accounts convey the same message, namely that by continuing to ask, seek, and knock, the Holy Spirit will be given to us. While Matthew does not record that the 'good gifts' to which Jesus is referring are the gifts and person of the Holy Spirit, Luke states this outright (compare Matt. 7:11 to Luke 11:13).

The picture that comes to mind when we see the words 'good gifts' may or may not line up with God's definition. The good gift He has given believers is the Holy Spirit. Paul exhorted us to be filled with the Holy Spirit, even as Jesus was filled with the Spirit without measure for all good works and the proclamation of the kingdom. Every gift we need for our perfection comes from God who does not change (James 1:17). God intends to give us all the good gifts we need for life—for serving and doing the works He has planned for us to do. The gift of the Holy Spirit accomplishes all of this. If He did not even spare His own Son for us, won't He give us everything we need (Rom. 8:32)?

> *For the LORD God is a sun and shield; the LORD gives grace and glory; no good thing does He withhold from those who walk uprightly.* -Ps. 84:11, NASB

Does this mean persistent asking is not for other requests, our own healing, for example? Not at all. Prayers in keeping with the priorities God has revealed in His Word (e.g., destroying the works of darkness, which includes physical infirmity) or in harmony with other examples of requests or statements of God's will in Scripture can corroborate the validity of any request brought before the throne. Our own *priority*, however, must be in keeping with God's plan, purpose, and timing for the advancement of His kingdom and not what suits our own objectives. Even Jesus qualified His personal request in Gethsemane with, 'not My will, but Yours be done.'

What sets prayer to our God apart from the magic arts is that God is not compelled to give us what we ask for. Some believe if we will only say the right combination of Bible verses, or if we loudly and persistently insist a certain verse be manifested in our lives, the creative power of God's living Word must yield the desired result. The words in the Bible are treated as entities with power in and of themselves apart from the will of God. This reduces the Word of God to a book of spells and incantations. The element that raises prayer above incantation is the sovereign will of God, who works everything out for our good. Only when *God* sends forth His Word will it accomplish that for which it is sent (Isa. 55:11). When *we* send forth His Word, there is no inherent creative power unless it is energized by the Spirit of the living God (Lam. 3:37; cf.). The sons of Sceva discovered this, as previously mentioned.

If we set aside the pain and intense anxiety we all experience when going through any crisis in order to say with trust in our heart, 'not my will and what makes the most sense to me in this situation and what I would *really like* to see accomplished, but Your will be done,' God will intervene with the best possible solution. Only He can see the impact and results of granting or denying our request. He takes into consideration not only the immediate benefit and relief we are seeking, but the ramification to those around us, the transformation of our mind and character, and the long term significance of the outcome. The posture of the bondservant's heart must be loyal to whatever outcome brings God the highest glory.

Whether He gives us our request or gives us grace to endure, we have established in this kind of prayer that we trust His judgment to do what is right and brings the most glory to His kingdom (and hopefully the least pain for us). If we walk away angry at a request denied, we miss out on the fragrance of myrrh the Lord purposed to bring forth in our lives—the fragrance of someone who is willing to die to their own desires for the will of God, as Christ did.

This is truly an aroma pleasing to God. Prayers offered in this manner rise as pleasant incense before His throne. When we purpose to do everything our way, which leads to death, the stench of rotting flesh comes before the Lord. When we let go of our plans and determine to agree with His no matter what, even as Abraham did, the Lord transforms the stench of self-will into the fragrance of self-sacrifice—myrrh—for 'He makes all things beautiful in their time' (Ecc. 3:11).

Paul exhorted us to *be* filled with the Spirit (Eph. 5:18). This is why we need to keep on asking, seeking, and knocking. The Holy Spirit will guide us into truth and reveal what we need to know for what lies ahead. He even shares wonderful news as He did with Simeon, telling him he would see the Messiah before he died (Luke 2:25-26). The Holy Spirit is our guarantee we are God's own and that He will give us the inheritance He promised (Eph. 1:13-14; 4:30). To have the Holy Spirit is proof of God's acceptance (Acts 15:8).

We have been bought with a price and have been given the Holy Spirit as a deposit. By this we become the temple of the Holy Spirit and must strive to honor Him by what we do and say (1 Cor. 6:18-20). Paul counseled believers to be careful to devote themselves to doing what is good because of the Holy Spirit (Titus 3:4-10). The spiritual gifts we receive are to be used to serve one another, not make a name for ourselves or secure a following for our ministry (1 Pet. 4:10; Acts 20:30). Peter explained that the prophets were not serving themselves by the things they wrote, but us. Even angels long to look into the things we have been given in the new covenant by the Holy Spirit (1 Pet. 1:10-12).

Repentance Is the Key

Unless you repent (change your mind for the better and heartily amend your ways, with abhorrence of your past sins), you will all likewise perish and be lost eternally. -Luke 13:5, AMP

There is no salvation without repentance. John the Baptist, in fulfilling the prophetic announcement of his ministry as forerunner, fearlessly preached the requirement of repentance because of the Messiah's imminent approach. This prepared the way of the Lord by causing those who listened to have fertile ground for the message Jesus would bring. Jesus came to teach about the kingdom of God—the new covenant—with demonstrations of power and great authority. Those with repentant hearts were prepared to receive His message and recognized Jesus as the Messiah.

John's diet of locusts and honey heralded the two basic outcomes connected with repentance—judgment and mercy. Refusing to repent leads to judgment. Wholehearted repentance leads to the mercy of God in Jesus Christ. Just as Ezekiel had to eat the scroll of prophetic pronouncements for Israel (Ezk. 3:1-11), sweet as honey in his mouth but filled with the judgments of God, John ate the honey of mercy and the locusts of judgment to portray the kindness and severity of God. Repentance is the place where all who would trust in Christ for salvation must begin their journey.

The goal of repentance is two-fold—a change of heart and a change of mind. When the foolishness of preaching is accompanied by a spirit of conviction, those who listen either turn aside to discern the message or harden their hearts against it. Those who turn aside, as Moses did when he saw the burning bush, experience conviction and godly sorrow for sins committed. These actively repent, reflected by the active voice of the verb in the Greek text. The fundamental tenets of the gospel are repentance and forgiveness in Jesus' name. This is what the disciples were instructed to preach to all nations (Luke 24:47). John the Baptist (Matt. 3:2), Jesus (Matt. 4:17; Luke 13:3), and the disciples (Mark

SECTION 6 RESPONSIVE DEPENDENCE ON THE HOLY SPIRIT

6:12) each preached repentance (*metanoeo*) with the goal of reaching those who would hear and turn. In these passages, the verb 'repent' is in the active voice, indicating the sinner is the one who takes action. In Peter's first sermon on the day of Pentecost, he called the people to repent (active voice) and be baptized into the new covenant. The Holy Spirit would be given to all who would come in this way (Acts 2:38).

Repentance (*metanoia*) means primarily to "change ones' mind from evil to good," the mind here depicted as the "agent of moral reflection,"[12] that is, the place where altering one's views occurs. *Metanoeo* is related to *metanoia* and means to change one's mind *accompanied by regret of heart*, a true change of heart toward God. "It signifies a change of mind consequent to retrospection, indicating regret for the course pursued and resulting in a wiser view of the past and future. Most importantly, it is distinguished from *metamellomai*, to regret because of the consequences of one's actions." To clarify on this last point, Dr. Zodhiates is talking about regret over consequences without being struck in the conscience. Being struck in our conscience would cause regret over the action itself that caused the consequences.[13] Paul differentiated the two by calling one 'godly sorrow' that leads to life, and the other 'worldly sorrow' that leads to death (2 Cor. 7:10).

Albert Barnes explains the nature of changing our view on sin as the result of repentance: "Repentance implies sorrow for sin as committed against God, along with a purpose to forsake it. It is not merely a fear of the consequences of sin or of the wrath of God in hell. It is such a view of sin, as evil in itself, as to lead the mind to hate it and forsake it. Laying aside all view of the punishment of sin, the true penitent hates it. Even if sin were the means of procuring him happiness; if it would promote his gratification and be unattended with any future punishment, he would hate it and turn from it. The mere fact that it is evil, and that God hates it, is a sufficient reason why those who are truly penitent hate it and forsake it.

"False repentance dreads the consequences of sin; true repentance dreads sin itself. These persons whom Peter addressed had been merely alarmed; they were afraid of wrath, and especially of the wrath of the Messiah. They had no true sense of sin as an evil, but were simply afraid of punishment. This alarm Peter did not regard as by any means genuine repentance. Such conviction for sin would soon wear off, unless their repentance became thorough and complete. Hence, he told them to repent, to turn from sin, to exercise sorrow for it as an evil and bitter thing, and to express their sorrow in the proper manner."[14]

From this place of godly sorrow, the repentant not only turns from sin, but his mind is now open to God's truth. This opening of the mind to truth—the lifting of the veil—is the work of the Holy Spirit. When Peter explained his visit with Cornelius to his Jewish brothers, he told them how the Holy Spirit had been given to Gentile believers, just as they had received the Holy Spirit. When the Jews heard this, they no longer complained about Peter fraternizing with Gentiles. They realized 'God has also given the Gentiles the *privilege of repenting* to receive eternal life' (Acts 11:18). The gift of the Holy Spirit is equated with the *privilege* of repentance leading to eternal life. In this use, God is the one actively involved, *granting* repentance to open the mind to divine truth.

Being *granted* repentance (removing the veil) is considered an act of God and His desire for every man (2 Pet. 3:9). Paul instructed Timothy to gently teach opponents in the hope God would *grant* them repentance leading to knowledge of truth, causing them to turn from wrong thinking to escape the devil's trap. Paul bluntly stated that those who do not know truth have been taken captive by the devil to do his will (2 Tim. 2:25-26). The goal of preaching is transformation of the mind and heart: *metanoeo*. When the sinner perceives and accepts conviction for sin, *actively* repenting of that sin, he is given the Holy Spirit who then *grants* repentance: lifts the veil that prevented his mind from understanding divine truth. This two-step process is the cooperation of the free will of man and God's intervention. Pausing to turn our attention to God causes God to turn to us (James 4:8). Again we are reminded, 'today, if you hear His voice,' take the time to turn aside, hear, and obey. Those who do will be rewarded with truth that sets them free.

Baptism of Repentance

Following repentance, public profession and subsequent baptism declare to all that *metanoeo* has taken place and that Jesus has been embraced as Savior. Unwillingness to profess one's belief and faith publicly is evidence no such belief or faith exists. Barnes stated, "Baptism is the application of water, as expressive of the need of purification, and as emblematic of the influences from God that can alone cleanse the soul. It is also a form of dedication to the service of God… There is nothing in baptism itself that can wash away sin. That can be done only by the pardoning mercy of God through the atonement of Christ. But baptism is expressive of a willingness to be pardoned in that way, and is a solemn declaration of our conviction that there is no other way of remission. He who comes to be baptized, comes with a professed conviction that he is a sinner; that there is no other way of mercy but in the gospel, and with a professed willingness to comply with the terms of salvation, and to receive it as it is offered through Jesus Christ."[15]

Baptism is symbolic of the washing of the heart and mind from the old way of carnal thinking and desire that led to sin and death. It also symbolizes washing away sins of the past because of the *metanoeo* that has taken place. Peter calls this baptism 'the pledge of a clear conscience toward God' (1 Pet. 3:20-22). Jesus commanded the disciples to baptize those who believe and come to repentance. Anyone who has repented of his former way of life and thinking by believing in Jesus must be baptized if at all possible. When the Ethiopian eunuch heard the gospel message, he was eager to be baptized so he could be included in the new covenant in Christ (Acts 8:36). Cowardice, age, physical limitations, and/or embarrassment are not legitimate excuses for forgoing baptism.

Prior to the new covenant, Israelites circumcised in heart and God-fearing Gentiles were included in the redemptive grace of God. Since the days of John the Baptist, however, the baptism of repentance became the outward expression of the inward condition in the new covenant. Obedience is required. But Jesus left a possible example of one who experienced true repentance without following his repentance with the rite of baptism, yet was certainly allowed entrance into 'paradise' (the same term also used by Paul to describe his supernatural experience, 2 Cor. 12:4) by Jesus' own promise: the thief on the cross. Under these circumstances, the thief's change of heart and public profession were sufficient because of the dire circumstances and great mercies of God (Luke 23:40-43). [Note: An argument could be made here that since the thief repented *before* the new covenant was inaugurated by Jesus' death, resurrection, and the giving of the Holy Spirit, the requirement for baptism did not apply. Yet we also note that many people were baptized by John the Baptist and the disciples prior to Jesus' death and resurrection. Jesus' disciples were baptized *before* the cross (Mk. 1:4-5; Lk. 3:3ff.; Matt. 3:5-15), though the new covenant baptism of the Holy Spirit was not given until Pentecost.]

Nowhere in Scripture do we find support for the view that baptism is a supernatural act in itself that saves a person. It is a symbolic token demonstrating what has already taken place in the heart of the believer. Similarly, circumcision held no supernatural power to transform the heart but was an outward symbol of inclusion in Israel's promises. Paul specifically stated that circumcision is useless unless accompanied by a circumcised heart. It is the same with baptism. If we have been baptized as infants, the Lord will be looking for a heart that is tender with 'the pledge of a clear conscience toward God.' Sprinkling or dunking people in water in the name of the Father, Son, and Holy Spirit without their consent or without repentance has no supernatural power to save that person or make them believe unto salvation. This was the faulty premise seen in the practice of forced 'conversions' in the Middle Ages.

Is supernatural grace present at baptism? Certainly, because it is the Holy Spirit who grants us the privilege of repentance that opens our mind to the truth. Baptism is an act which honors the Lord through obedience to His command and must be done with reverence for His name. Baptism places the repentant in the community of believers, initiating accountability before God and man for the way he conducts himself. But to ascribe magical saving power to a symbolic act falls in the same category as using the Word as a magic spell, and is similar to the mistaken belief that external circumcision can save. The Word states specifically that he who *believes* and is baptized will be saved, but he who *does not believe* will be condemned (Mark 16:16). The pivotal factor is *belief*.

This is probably the strongest argument for the questionable efficacy of baptizing infants. Some use the examples of the 'whole households' that were baptized to legitimize the practice of infant baptism. But if we take a closer look at each of these passages, the prerequisite of belief in Jesus is met in each example, precluding any assumption that infants were involved (with the possible exception of Lydia's household).

- **The Philippian jailer**: He and his whole household were baptized because, 'he and his whole household *believed*' (Acts 16:33-34).
- **Crispus**: He and his entire household '*believed* and were baptized' (Acts 18:8).

- **Lydia**: Already a worshipper of God, the Lord opened her heart to respond to Paul's message; she and her whole household were baptized (though no mention is made specifically that her household believed; Acts 16:14-15).

In the example of Cornelius, we note he *and his whole household* were God-fearing and devout in the first place (Acts 10:2,33). Cornelius immediately sent for Peter after his visitation with the angel and stated he and his household were gathered to hear, Greek *akouo*. This word has the same implication as *sh'ma*: to hear with the intent of obeying. These people were committed to obey everything God would say through Peter. They were already bondservants of the Lord. As Peter began speaking to them about Jesus, the Holy Spirit 'fell on them' and they began speaking in tongues and praising God. The gift of the Holy Spirit came through believing what was preached, proving to the Jewish disciples who witnessed the event that this gift was indeed meant for the Gentiles as well. Again, we see that belief and devotion to God were present beforehand. As a result, Cornelius' whole household was baptized right away (Acts 10:47-48).

Jesus gives two conditions for entering the kingdom of God: being born of water and the Spirit (John 3:5). Being born of water most likely refers to the baptism of repentance initiated when John the Baptist heralded the arrival of the new covenant. Those that have remorse over past sin and whose minds have been opened to embrace truth must then seek to make public profession of their *metanoeo* through literal baptism. This act, like circumcision, sets the believer apart from the rest of the world and validates that the mind of the new believer has turned from following the world's ways to following God's will. While there are other interpretations possible, this interpretation is in keeping with other passages that teach repentance is required before the Spirit is given.

Baptizing infants should be regarded in the same way as Jewish circumcision (cf. Col. 2:11-12). Physical circumcision is an act emblematic of the circumcised heart hoped for in the child's life, and a commitment on the part of the parents and relatives to make sure the child receives proper instruction and an environment conducive to the realization of this hope. Likewise, baptism of infants has similar merit because it is a public pronouncement by the parents and godparents that they intend to see to the spiritual instruction of the child for the hope of his salvation. Certainly, as an act of commitment on the part of parents and godparents and as an act of dedication of the newborn to the Lord, infant baptism has merit. Whether it fits New Testament criteria or not is a matter for the grace of God to determine, keeping in mind that baptism without heart change is as useless as circumcision without the same, no matter how holy we think the baptismal water is.

The baptism of the new covenant requires repentance on the part of the one being baptized, which demands adequate cognitive function and the development of the conscience, neither of which infants possess. If the child is brought up in the faith, this heart change will be seen as evidence of the Holy Spirit's grace and work in answer to prayer for the baptized child. However, it is unsupported scripturally to conclude that every infant who is baptized and later enters adulthood in unrepentant sin, overtaken by love for the ways of the world, is saved. Furthermore, this false confidence will be exposed at Christ's return when the unrepentant hear, 'Depart from Me, I never knew you.' The ways of religion can have eternally devastating results if they are not scripturally sound and give someone false confidence before God.

The apostles taught that baptism saves us from death because of the resurrection of Christ. In baptism, we are buried with Christ into His death with the confidence we will be resurrected as He was (Rom. 6:3-4). We go into the water spiritually dead and are raised out of the water in newness of life. I remember a pastor telling of an African man who came to Christ and asked to be baptized. The pastor baptized the man by immersion. When the pastor attempted to bring the man out of the water, a struggle ensued. The man did not want to come up from the water! When he was finally brought out of the water, the African said he hadn't died yet and would have to go at it again. His faith was so huge that he actually thought baptism meant he was to be drowned in the water, and then Christ would resurrect him on the way out of the water. There was no doubt in this man's mind as to the power of God. He understood that through baptism, we exchange our sentence of death for eternal life in God.

Paul described baptism as 'circumcision without hands' because it entails removing (crucifying) the flesh (old nature; Col. 2:11-12). Peter recorded that Noah and his family are an example of baptism, having been 'saved through water' as we are now saved through the water of baptism (1 Pet. 3:20-21). Paul likewise compared baptism to the Red Sea crossing, bringing us to a place of separation (consecration to God) from that which formerly held us in bondage (sin and death; 1 Cor. 10:2).

This idea of exchanging our sentence of death for eternal life by being obedient in baptism is noted in a passage of Scripture difficult to grasp. On first glance, it seems as though Paul is talking about being baptized for people who have died and didn't get a chance to be baptized. The flow of the entire chapter (1 Cor. 15:1-58), however, seems to be making an argument for Christ's victory over death, the resurrection to come, and the final destruction of death itself when Jesus returns. Otherwise, Paul argues, if these things are not true, what reason would there be for baptism in order to escape eternal death, or for putting our lives in jeopardy for the sake of being obedient to God? If there is no resurrection of the dead or the final annihilation of death, why would we bother to comply with baptism or endure trials? The literal translation makes this difficult to see (taken from the NASB): "Otherwise, what will those do who are baptized for the dead? If the dead are not raised at all, why then are they baptized for them?"

The intended meaning seems to more closely parallel the following paraphrased translation, particularly noting that the Greek word *huper* (typically translated 'for, in exchange, instead of, on behalf of') includes both exchange and equivalence.[16] In other words, we are baptized *in exchange for* death; we suffer persecution and lay our lives on the line now because we know we will be resurrected later.

> *[P]eople are baptized because the dead [will come back to life]. What will they do? If the dead can't come back to life, why do people get baptized as if they can [come back to life]? Why are we constantly putting ourselves in danger?* -1 Cor. 15:29-30, GW

To be baptized in the name of Jesus alone can be misunderstood as somehow different than Jesus' own command to baptize in the name of the Father, Son, and Holy Spirit (Matt. 28:19; Acts 2:38; 10:48; 19:5). Being baptized in Jesus' name merely signifies the baptism of repentance and forgiveness afforded by the grace of God through the new covenant inaugurated in Jesus' blood. This can be compared with those who went through the Red Sea and were baptized 'into Moses,' which refers specifically to the Mosaic (old) covenant (1 Cor. 10:2). The baptism of repentance in the new covenant reconciles us with the Father through the blood of Jesus, granting us the gift of the Holy Spirit. It is at this point we are enabled to bear fruit in keeping with repentance (Luke 3:8). Hence, we are baptized 'into Jesus'—into the new covenant—in the name of the Father, Son, and Holy Spirit.

> *I preached that they should repent and turn to God and demonstrate their repentance by their deeds.* -Acts 26:20, NIV

The supernatural result of repentance and baptism patterned after Scripture is that we are moved to live holy because we are now 'clothed with Christ' (Gal. 3:27). Producing fruit in keeping with repentance means to shun evil and do good works; to live a life separated unto God according to His will. The gift of the Holy Spirit makes this possible. For the believer baptized into Christ, this will include striving for unity because we are 'baptized by one Spirit into one body' (1 Cor. 12:13). The bondservant will carry this out because of love and not the fear of punishment.

> *Repent therefore and be converted, that your sins may be blotted out, so that times of refreshing may come from the presence of the Lord.* -Acts 3:19, NKJV

The Seal

> *And you also were included in Christ when you heard the message of truth, the gospel of your salvation. When you believed, you were marked in him with a seal, the promised Holy Spirit.* -Eph. 1:13, NIV

The presence of the Holy Spirit is critical in the life of the believer. True repentance is followed by the granting of the Holy Spirit, who is the seal of a true believer. 'Seal' is translated from *sphragizo* and means 'to stamp for security, or to attest.' It is taken from *sphragis*, which means 'a signet—fencing in, protecting from misappropriation, a mark of genuineness.'[17] This seal guards the deposit entrusted to each believer (2 Tim. 1:12-14), including the treasures of Christ as well as the specific calling and works ordained. Barnes reminds us, "One of the best methods of preserving the knowledge and the love of truth is to cherish the influences of the Holy Spirit."[18] Blasphemy against the Holy Spirit is unforgiveable because it essentially removes this seal (Matt. 12:31).

SECTION 6 *RESPONSIVE DEPENDENCE ON THE HOLY SPIRIT*

Not only is the Holy Spirit the seal of security that we are God's, He is also the earnest deposit given to assure us that God's Word is true and all His promises will be fulfilled (2 Cor. 1:22; Eph. 1:14). This gives the believer great confidence regarding the things to come, particularly resurrection from the dead and an immortal body. Paul referred to our bodies as a house or tent, teaching that our 'earthly tent' will be replaced by a 'house in heaven,' defined as an 'eternal body made for us by God Himself' (2 Cor. 5:1-5). He also talks of our longing for this eternal body so our inner man will not be found naked at Jesus' return. Paul stated God created us for this precise purpose, and gave His Spirit to us as guarantee of this promise.

In the Garden of Eden, Adam and Eve discovered they were naked only after sin entered their lives. Prior to this, they had been clothed in righteous immortality. Likewise, the church at Laodicea is counseled to 'buy white raiment' to cover their nakedness. This white raiment would cost them their indolence and self-centeredness. In other words, they would have to die to themselves in order to show their faith by their works through obedience to the Holy Spirit. Then they could hope to be clothed with righteous immortality at the Lord's return, rather than suffering shame.

The Holy Spirit is our guarantee that God will give us new heavenly bodies as He promised so we will be 'clothed' at His return. Clarke stated, "The Holy Spirit in the soul of a believer is God's seal, set on his heart to testify that he is God's property, and that he should be wholly employed in God's service."[19] One of the ways in which we stay in step with the Holy Spirit is to discipline ourselves to study the Word and stay connected to the Head. The only sure foundation is Jesus (the Word), our Rock and Redeemer.

> *Listen to me, you who pursue righteousness, you who seek the LORD: look to the rock from which you were hewn.* -Isa. 51:1a, ESV

Transformation of Desires

With the help of the Holy Spirit, we can count on having our desires transformed, even if we are not really sure we want this at first. Most of us have at some point reordered the following verses in our minds to say, 'He will give me everything I want if I seek His kingdom first; He will give me all my desires if I delight in Him.' The focus of each of these revisions becomes *our* wants and desires, rather than delighting in Him, His kingdom, and righteousness.

> *Seek the Kingdom of God above all else, and live righteously, and he will give you everything you need.* -Matt. 6:33, NLT

> *Delight yourself in the LORD; and He will give you the desires of your heart.* -Ps. 37:4, NASB

Our delight always starts out with the hope *our* desires will be fulfilled. Whatever captivates our heart and preoccupies our thoughts—work, entertainment, wealth, success, reputation, education, politics, houses, vacations, food, alcohol, drugs, sex, even ministry accomplishment—is our *de facto* delight. From these verses, we see the order is reversed from what typically occupies our minds. New or immature believers naturally preoccupy themselves with worldly desires because their minds are not yet captivated by the superior pleasures of knowing God and His incredible plans to reconcile and restore.

> *For those who live according to the flesh set their minds on the things of the flesh, but those who live according to the Spirit set their minds on the things of the Spirit.* -Rom. 8:5, ESV

Paul reminded the Ephesians to put off the old self corrupted by deceitful desires (Eph. 4:22). He also advised Timothy to flee youthful desires and passions and instead pursue righteousness, faith, love, and peace as one who calls on the Lord from a pure heart (2 Tim. 2:22). Peter likewise told us to think clearly and exercise self-control:

> *[L]ive as God's obedient children. Don't slip back into your old ways of living to satisfy your own desires.* -1 Pet. 1:14a, NLT

Personal desires and motivations change through the power and work of the Holy Spirit as we continually wash our minds with the Word. Our part in this process is to discipline ourselves to read the Word with a willingness to commit the posture of our heart and will in obedience. Reading the Word and committing to comply is a simple concept, but like pulling the roots of a tree stump out of the ground, we really have to put our backs into it to get the job done.

- Loving God means keeping His commands by the Spirit of truth (John 14:15-17,26).
- The Spirit gives us desires opposite of what the sinful nature desires (Gal. 5:17).
- God's promises enable us to share His divine nature and escape the world's corruption caused by human desires (2 Pet. 1:4).
- God gives us the desire *and* power to do what pleases Him (Php. 2:13).
- By clothing ourselves with Christ, we do not think about how to gratify the desires of the sinful nature (Rom. 13:14).
- We arm ourselves with Jesus' attitude to suffer as He did; then we are finished with sin, no longer chasing our desires but anxious to do God's will (1 Pet. 4:1-2).

It is painful at times to let go of desires, expectations, and dreams that do not line up with the Word or God's specific plans for us as individuals. At this point, some believers will look in the Word to find some way to keep their worldly desires and still remain in the favor of God. When we remold Scripture to justify and exonerate our wrongful desires, we essentially recreate the Word to fit the image we want. This is exactly what the Israelites did when they molded the golden calf to worship God in the image they desired and with which they were familiar (Ex. 32:4-6).

Old desires, goals, and ways have no place in our lives as believers. We all go through stages in our growth as believers where we are more focused on our circumstances than God's kingdom. This is not problematic if we don't camp here but eventually move on to maturity. Regrettably, some halt here, trying to find ways to legitimize their pre-

SECTION 6 RESPONSIVE DEPENDENCE ON THE HOLY SPIRIT

occupation with the material things this world has to offer through twisting, isolating, or forcing certain Scriptures to justify their paradigm.

If we try to cling to these, searching for ways to make Scripture comply with our ambition in order to have the best of both worlds, we end up with a hybrid religion that is no more honored by God than the mixture detailed in the incident with the golden calf. Everyone involved in this crossbred worship was killed in the desert, and their names were blotted out of God's book (Ex. 32:33). This is serious error that jeopardizes our salvation. We must let it go and move forward to maturity.

We have been warned beforehand that people would seek doctrine that suits their own desires, no longer wanting to hear truth (2 Tim. 4:3). Others will mock the truth in order to justify their determination to follow their carnal desires (2 Pet. 3:3). Discrediting what we don't want to believe so we can legitimize what our sinful nature wants to do is not a new tactic. Only by allowing the Holy Spirit to guide our lives will we be able to forgo what our sinful nature craves (Gal. 5:16). Those dominated by their fallen nature only think about those things which satisfy their carnal desires. On the other hand, those controlled by the Spirit have their minds focused on what pleases God (Rom. 8:5).

Even quibbling over peripheral issues can be a way to satisfy the carnal nature for those who love to get the upper hand in a debate, something we are warned to avoid (1 Tim. 6:4). These arguments invariably lead to division and trammeled understanding rather than edification. Jude described others as grumblers and complainers who live only to satisfy their desires (Jude 1:16). The bottom line for believers is to turn from love of the world's ways because it squelches love for God:

> **Do not love this world nor the things it offers you,** for when you love the world, you do not have the love of the Father in you. For **the world offers only a craving for physical pleasure, a craving for everything we see, and pride in our achievements and possessions. These are not from the Father,** but are from this world. And this world is fading away, along with everything that people crave. But anyone who does what pleases God will live forever. -1 John 2:15-17, NLT

We cannot be deceived into thinking *God* placed materialistic desires in our hearts. John directly refutes this idea (v. 16, above). Any material blessing that comes from God, above and beyond our necessary food and clothing, is a blessing only secondary to the superior blessings found through the presence and work of the Holy Spirit. Material blessings and riches are not to be sought after but merely shared and enjoyed in the grace of God as we walk in obedience to Him.

In the story of the prodigal son, Jesus illustrated the mentality of those who want their inheritance prematurely. They demand to have all that is promised ahead of time to spend on their own desires and pleasures, just as the prodigal did. The Lord will take such children back if they return to Him in humility, as illustrated in the parable. The last phrase of the following passage teaches us that our full rights and new bodies will come at the same time, specifically at Jesus' return (see Isa. 40:10; 62:11; Rev. 22:12):

*We, too, **wait with eager hope for the day** when God will give us our full rights as his adopted children, including the new bodies he has promised us.* -Rom. 8:23b, NLT

Our desires must line up with the examples we have in the Word. Jesus stated the righteous saints of old *desired* to see the promises fulfilled (Matt. 13:17; Luke 10:24). The Corinthian believers *desired* to help other believers through giving (2 Cor. 8:11). Paul *desired* to depart to be with Christ (Php. 1:23). The believers included in the list of the faithful focused their *desire* on the promises yet to be manifested (Heb. 11:13-16). The apostles' prayers give us a good idea of their desires for the community of believers. Paul exhorted believers to eagerly *desire* the most helpful spiritual gifts for the edification of the *ekklesia*, and to follow the way of love (1 Cor. 12:31; 14:1).

By these examples, we learn what our desire should be set upon according to the will of God and the apostles' exhortations. We can discern the maturity of our walk by what we delight in and desire. The content of our prayers testifies for or against us regarding the transformation of desires; whether His words actually abide in us rather than merely being stored in our brains for recitation. 'To abide' in or by something means 'to act in accordance with; to keep; to concede or agree to; to remain steadfast and faithful in that to which we have submitted.' By abiding in Christ, our desires are transformed. Then we will receive what we desire and ask for in prayer:

***If you abide in Me**, and My words abide in you, **you will ask what you desire**, and **it shall be done for you**. By this My Father is glorified, that you bear much fruit; so you will be My disciples.* -John 15:7-8, NKJV

God is glorified when we abide in His Word and experience transformed desires so that our prayers can be answered. This yields fruit that lasts for His kingdom. If we only pray according to what our carnal nature craves, our unsanctified prayers remain barren because they lack the necessary evidence that we are abiding in His Word. The Holy Spirit has been given to transform our desires so we have hope of gaining the prize for which we run our race. Our walk is not about faultless performance or accomplishment, but about the transformation of our heart (affections/desires), mind (paradigms/mindsets), and will (ambition/goals). God synchronizes all of them if we set ourselves before His Word in humility, allowing Him to sanctify us in the process.

Blessed are those who hunger and thirst for righteousness, for they shall be filled. -Matt. 5:6, NKJV

Sanctification

*Pursue peace with all men, and the **sanctification** (hagiasmos) **without which no one will see the Lord**.* -Heb. 12:14, NASB (parenthetical added)

In this verse, *hagiasmos* (translated 'sanctification') describes the *state* of being sanctified rather than the *process* of sanctification. It is the result of justification by Christ through recognizing God's legal right to the sinner's life. Acknowledging God's ownership establishes the proper paradigm for the bondservant identity. This realization compels him to pursue what pleases God through love, gratitude, and obedience. Zodhiates explains, "Hagiasmos means not only the activity of the Holy Spirit to set men apart unto salvation, but also enabling him to be holy even as God is holy."[20]

The process of transforming our desires and behavior results in sanctification, which renders us separated unto God for His purposes. This involves separation from worldly desires by being granted fellowship with God. The result of Jesus' imputed (freely given) righteousness and the transformation of our minds is sanctification (purification) of our actions. This gives us confidence that we will be fully redeemed at Jesus' return. Through Jesus' sacrifice, we have been made holy or sanctified (*hagiazo*) unto God with no further blood sacrifice required (Heb. 10:10). We now legally have an indestructible life as Jesus does because His righteousness has been legally ascribed to us.

Recall that Jesus said only those who are born of water *and the Spirit* will enter the kingdom (John 3:5). We have already noted that the baptism of repentance defines the way in which we are born of water. This parallels the redemption of the Israelites from Egypt as they crossed the Red Sea and entered the wilderness for testing, just as Jesus was driven to the wilderness for testing after His baptism, and as all believers are also thus led. But how are we born of the Spirit? The exodus story portrays the process of being born of the Spirit in the following instruction:

> *See, I am sending an angel before you to protect you on your journey and lead you safely to the place I have prepared for you.* ***Pay close attention to him, and obey his instructions. Do not rebel against him****, for he is my representative, and he **will not forgive your rebellion**. But **if you are careful to obey him**, following all my instructions, then I will be an enemy to your enemies, and I will oppose those who oppose you.* -Ex. 23:20-22, NLT

This precisely parallels New Testament teaching that exhorts us to honor the Holy Spirit. Continuing with our example of the Israelites, the Spirit of God led them all the way to Kadesh, at which time the twelve spies were sent to explore the land. After forty days, all but two returned with a report based primarily on human reasoning to give weight to their fear. This fear caused the Israelites to shrink back from the command of the Lord to take the land, and it cost them their place in the land of promise. They were sentenced to die in the wilderness (Num. 14:26-38). Those twenty years old and older were sentenced to this fate because they rebelled against God through unbelief on ten separate occasions (Num. 14:22)—sinning with a 'high hand.' Only those under twenty, the age of accountability as determined by God in this story, would be allowed to enter the Promised Land.

What do we learn from this? The parallel is that we will only be allowed into the 'promised land' (the kingdom of God) through obedience to the Spirit of God, something that can only be accomplished by someone who trusts God as a child. Those who died in the wilderness as judgment for their sin of rebellion were certainly redeemed from slavery in Egypt. Each experienced baptism when they crossed through the Red Sea. The baptism of repentance must be followed by the baptism of the Spirit in order for us to gain entrance into the Promised Land—the kingdom of God. The first baptism of repentance, typified by the Red Sea crossing, reconciles or restores our relationship to God but does not give us automatic entrance into His kingdom. This is what the exodus story seeks to teach us through the types and shadows written for our benefit. Paul made several points in his spiritual analysis of the story (1 Cor. 10:1-6):

- Each person was brought safely out of slavery, just as new covenant believers are granted repentance and are no longer slaves to sin.
- Each was baptized into the Mosaic covenant, just as the repentant are baptized into the new covenant ratified in Jesus' blood with the law now on the heart.
- Each ate the supernaturally provided food and drink, just as the new covenant believer receives spiritual food by the ministry of the Holy Spirit and the Word.
- Those who were willfully and repeatedly disobedient, allowing their behavior to be dictated by the confines of their own reasoning, fears, and carnal desires rather than the leading of the Spirit, are not allowed entrance into the Promised Land, just as those under the new covenant who walk in carnality and willful disobedience to the Holy Spirit are not allowed into the kingdom of God.

> *Every sin and blasphemy will be forgiven people, but the blasphemy against the Spirit will not be forgiven.* -Matt. 12:31, ESV

Resisting the Holy Spirit is an eternal sin that cannot be forgiven (Mark 3:29). John acknowledged there is a sin that won't be forgiven and leads to death (1 John 5:16). So what manner of men should we be? There is only one road for us: the road to sanctification by transformation through the activity of the Holy Spirit. To continue in sin, callously ignoring the prompting of the Holy Spirit, is to bring ourselves back under the penalty of death. The goal of the transforming work of the Holy Spirit is sanctification, and the goal of sanctification is eternal life.

> *[Y]ou have been **set free from sin** and have become slaves of God, the fruit… **leads to sanctification** and **its end, eternal life**. For the wages of sin is death, but the free gift of God is eternal life in Christ Jesus our Lord.* -Rom. 6:22-23, ESV

This freely given 'salvation package' includes: 1.) conviction of sin, leading to godly sorrow; 2.) being granted repentance, whereby the veil is removed so we can discern truth; 3.) being declared righteous before God because of Jesus' atoning sacrifice; 4.) receiving the Spirit as a seal to protect, instruct, guide, and preserve; and 5.) guidance in the process of transformation of desires and actions in this age. The fruit of this package is sanctification, which brings the promised eternal life. To reject any part of this package is to reject the process of salvation *through sanctification* (2 Thes. 2:13), without which no one will see God. Though freely given, it will cost us everything the world values in

SECTION 6 *RESPONSIVE DEPENDENCE ON THE HOLY SPIRIT*

this life. But the exchange rate for what we receive compared with what we relinquish is off the scale. How can we escape God's judgment if we ignore so great a salvation?

The author of Hebrews reminded us that the message of the old covenant which God delivered by angels stood firm and every violation was punished. If this was so under the old covenant, he argued, how much more is this so under the new covenant delivered by the Lord Himself? He advised us to listen carefully to the truth we have received so we do not drift from it. God confirmed this new covenant with signs, wonders, miracles, and the gift of the Holy Spirit, just as He did with the old (Heb. 2:1-4). [Note: Just as the old covenant was established with profound signs and wonders, so has the new covenant been established with signs and wonders. We should remind ourselves the supernatural work of God continued in Israel after their deliverance from Egypt and after the establishment of the covenant, just as it continues today at the discretion of the Holy Spirit.]

In Jesus we live and move and have our being, for He is our wisdom, righteousness, sanctification, and redemption (1 Cor. 1:30). Only by the Spirit of God living in us can we hope to be sanctified. Our cooperation is required, but He provides the power and desire to those who pursue truth and love for God. In this way, no one can boast because He has provided everything we need for salvation. Does this mean it is easy? Certainly not, for the roots of the world are deeply rooted in each of us as well as the cares and anxieties of life. For this reason, Paul repeatedly warned the new believers to flee from sin, especially sexual immorality. If we reject this teaching, we have rejected God (1 Thes. 4:3-8; see also 1 Cor. 6:18-20).

We have an active role in the process leading to sanctification. Every test we are given builds on the previous test, similar to beginning a weight-lifting program. At the beginning of a weight-lifting program, lighter weights are emphasized to promote good form and prevent muscle soreness or damage. Over time, the amount of weight lifted and the number of repetitions and exercises performed change to reflect the strength and endurance gained. Likewise, in matters of faith and the transformation of our hearts and minds, the Holy Spirit typically guides us at a workable pace with the faith we have been given. If we have truly repented and received the Holy Spirit, our love for God compels us to cooperate in this phase of salvation. God calls us out of uncleanness so He will welcome and relate to us as Father rather than Judge. We cleanse ourselves from everything that defiles flesh and spirit in order to make our sanctification complete (2 Cor. 6:17-17:1).

Paul spoke of our salvation as coming through sanctification and through belief in the truth. We must cease thinking of salvation as if it were an RSVP for a wedding, something we either accept or reject and then continue on with life as usual until the day of the wedding. To be granted repentance requires we turn our back on the ways of the world to pursue truth and transformation by the Holy Spirit. By this we are sanctified and made acceptable to God (Rom. 15:16).

True repentance brings with it a love for the truth. Some will not accept love for the truth because of the change it will require in their comfortable, pleasurable lives. 'For this reason God sends them strong delusion so they believe what is false' (2 Thes. 2:10-12). This is how God gives someone over to what they stubbornly cling to, insisting on having their own way.

We can no longer live life as we did in the futile thinking and practices of an unrenewed mind. Our focus must be on truth and staying in step with the Holy Spirit so our hope of eternal life is not founded on the self-deception that we can do as we please once we have prayed the sinner's prayer. This thinking serves only to placate the seared conscience of the unrepentant. Those who have trusted God for salvation must be careful to devote themselves to doing what is good (Titus 3:8). Paul stressed the importance of upright behavior so new believers would be blameless at the Lord's return:

> *Now may the God of peace Himself sanctify you completely. And may your spirit, soul, and body be kept sound and blameless for the coming of our Lord Jesus Christ.* -1 Thes. 5:23, HCSB

In His final words to His followers, Jesus clearly revealed He knows our *works*, and it is on works that He will base His judgment. To those who *hear* what the Spirit says to the churches, great and precious promises are given (Rev. 2-3). Just as Jesus overcame the world (John 16:33), we overcome worldly lusts by our love for the truth and faith in Jesus (1 John 5:4-5) and overcome evil with good (Rom. 12:21).

> *If anyone cleanses himself from these things, he will be a vessel for honor, sanctified, useful to the Master, prepared for every good work.* -2 Tim. 2:21, NASB

Unity in the Spirit

> *Since you are so eager to have the special abilities the Spirit gives, seek those that will strengthen the whole church.* -1 Cor. 14:12, NLT

The gifts of the Spirit are primarily for the purpose of confirming the gospel message and building up the church. Edifying the body of believers cannot come when individuals demand stage time to parade their gifts, but only as those gifts are exercised in the spirit of love for the promotion of unity and building up others in their faith. The body of Christ naturally promotes teaching gifts, but this practice has come with a high price tag. If teaching is not done in spirit and truth with the goal of unity in the faith and in the knowledge of God, we will reap the fruit of works of the flesh (Gal. 5:19-21). Unhealthy promotion of talents or natural ability in platform ministry void of heart involvement is not born of the Spirit but of the natural inclination of our culture to judge by the outward skill rather than the inward condition.

In other instances, those who desire to be recognized for superior spirituality may seek to validate their claims through false visions, encounters, and dreams. These claims are rooted in pride and the need for man's approval. Many insist on an ascetic lifestyle as the primary means to greater experiential revelation (dreams, visions, etc.) rather than steadfast attention to studying the Word (Col. 2:18). Jude stated those who 'rely on their dreams' have a secret life of immorality and defy authority (1:8, ESV). The only remedy for those so disposed is to cling to the Word and deny the flesh, which clamors to be seen before men.

Because human nature is predictably fascinated with the supernatural and at the same time predictably slips into self-aggrandizement, Paul gave exhortations to counter these natural inclinations with respect to the operation of the gifts of the Spirit. We are not to think of ourselves more highly than we ought (Rom. 12:3), and love is the more excellent way (1 Cor. 12:31-14:1). The goal of Paul's instruction when speaking of the spiritual gifts was not to emphasize the gifts themselves, but the oneness of the body in which the diversity of gifts is given. The whole point of the operation of gifts in the believing community is for building up the body, not to cause division through pride or envy. Jesus taught that if we love one another, the world will know we are His disciples. It is the Spirit of God who gives us love (2 Tim. 1:7), and love is first on the list of the fruit of the Spirit (Gal. 5:22). We are to strive for unity of the faith by demonstrating love.

> *Whatever happens, conduct yourselves in a manner worthy of the gospel of Christ... stand firm in the one Spirit, striving together as one for the faith of the gospel.* -Php. 1:27, NIV

While we are to earnestly desire the gifts which have greater strength in building up the *ekklesia*, the preeminent quality that builds the body is love. The gifts are secondary in importance. The goal of both is to build up the church in unity, 'for we were all baptized by one Spirit so as to form one body' (1 Cor. 12:13). Only by the work of the Holy Spirit will there be 'one new man' established in love. Paul earnestly prayed the Ephesians would be rooted and established *in love*, not the gifts, so they would be able to grasp the immeasurable nature of Christ's love for us—a love that *surpasses* knowledge (Eph. 3:16-19). Effort must be exerted on the part of believers to maintain unity in the Spirit because much of our carnal nature is still in the process of being sanctified (Eph. 4:3). Paul wanted believers to be like-minded and move in one spirit. This would require denying selfish ambition and vain conceit that desires and strives for supremacy. We are to humbly value others above ourselves, watching out for their interests before our own (Php. 2:1-4), always clinging to truth.

Impartation of Wisdom and Understanding

> *The Advocate, the Holy Spirit, whom the Father will send in my name, will teach you all things and will remind you of everything I have said to you.* -John 14:26, NIV

Of all the wonderful benefits of having the Holy Spirit, this is one of the most amazing. Many of us have experienced the forbearance of God as we place our dull minds and hearts before the Word. While all benefit greatly from the teaching of the many gifted minds in the body of Christ, nothing can compare with the exhilaration of being taught by the Spirit of God—discovery is its own reward. This gift is available to all who persistently place themselves before the Word. Jesus reminded us that understanding God's Word is not reserved for lettered professionals. It was God's good pleasure to reveal the treasures of His Word to the common laborers in the land (Luke 10:21; cf. 1 Cor. 1:26-29).

Paul focused on asking for impartation of wisdom and understanding in his prayers. God is no respecter of persons and delights in giving good things to His children. Paul asked and kept on asking for wisdom and revelation to be poured out on the community of believers so we would know God and His ways better (Eph. 1:17), which enables us to live lives worthy of the Lord. Breaking down Paul's prayer to the Colossians, we learn the themes of his heart that prompted what he wrote (see Col. 1:9-10). In his prayers, Paul continually asked God to fill believers with the knowledge of God's will, which would be accomplished through the wisdom and understanding the Holy Spirit imparts. His purpose in praying this was so they would live a life worthy of the Lord by:

- pleasing Him in every way;
- bearing fruit through good works;
- growing in the knowledge of God; and
- being strengthened with His power.

We need God's power for endurance and patience to stick with the process of sanctification, which includes trials and testing. Gratitude is forged as we begin to comprehend the incredible grace we have been given to share in the inheritance of God's people. In a very pragmatic way, the Holy Spirit gives us pertinent passages of Scripture and revelation when we are faced with situations warranting a higher degree of His intervention, additionally giving expert legal advice on the way in which to express that counsel. A perfect example of this took place when Stephen was challenged by synagogue leaders. 'They could not argue against the wisdom given him by the Spirit' (Acts 6:10).

The teaching of the Holy Spirit includes helping us understand the many types and shadows given in the old covenant (Heb. 9:7-9). Only the Spirit of God can search the deep things of God, another indication that not everything in the Word is to be taken at a mere historical or factual level. If it were, we would not need the intervention of the Holy Spirit to understand. God gave us the Holy Spirit so we might know the things freely given to us. This also reveals the simple fact that what we have been given *freely* does not also mean it is understood *automatically*. We must seek and keep on seeking the treasures in the Word—answers freely given to those who persevere in their search.

Paul reminded the Corinthians that God has revealed His Word to us by His Spirit. Only the Holy Spirit searches and knows the hidden or deep knowledge in the heart of God. Therefore no one knows the thoughts of God except His Holy Spirit, the same Holy Spirit we have received so we might understand these very things. Because the things freely given to us are spiritually discerned, only those who have been given the Holy Spirit will also be granted the mind of Christ to understand spiritual matters (1 Cor. 2:10-16).

Grieving the Holy Spirit

And do not grieve the Holy Spirit of God, by whom you were sealed for the day of redemption. -Eph. 4:30, NKJV

The context of this command centers on instruction pertaining to unity in the Spirit through the bond of love (Eph. 4:1-16). This stands in contrast to the darkened understanding and corrupt actions of the worldly who are apathetic toward righteousness (Eph. 4:17-20). In order to demonstrate that the teaching of Christ existed in their lives, Paul counseled the Ephesians to:

- put off the old man with its corrupt ways and lustful desires;
- be renewed in the spirit of the mind;
- put on the new man created after God's character;
- keep from falsehood;
- keep anger in check;
- work rather than steal;
- keep from corrupt conversation;
- speak those things that edify;
- guard against bitterness, rage, harsh words, malice, and slander;
- be kind and tenderhearted to one another; and
- forgive one another.

By doing these things, believers will avoid grieving the Holy Spirit. Especially on the point of our conversations, there is nothing that breaks unity more than words harshly spoken, divisive opinions loudly ventilated, words of encouragement or thanks neglected, and critical judgments or gossip freely given. To an even greater degree, our refusal to forgive others surely affects the Holy Spirit's operation in our lives.

Albert Barnes explains how we grieve the Spirit: "There is a course of conduct which will drive that Spirit from the mind as if he were grieved and pained—as a course of ingratitude and sin would pain the heart of an earthly friend, and cause him to leave you... Often he prompts us to pray; he disposes the mind to seriousness, to the perusal of the Bible, to tenderness and penitence. We neglect those favored moments of our piety, and lose those happy seasons for becoming like God... Christians often resist the Holy Spirit. He would lead them to be dead to the world; yet they drive on their plans of gain... All that is needful for a Christian to do in order to be eminent in piety, is to yield to the gentle influences which would draw him to prayer and to heaven."[21]

Grieving the Spirit also occurs when we have no use for His wisdom, evidenced by minimal time spent in prayer in contrast with hours spent in the board room planning. Disregarding His guidance and promptings invariably lead to a sense of darkness of soul. Gill stated, "There are many reasons why he should not be grieved; as because he is God, and... because he is the saints' comforter, their advocate, helper, and strengthener; and their constant companion, who dwells in them, and will remain in them, until death."[22]

Through the Spirit's grace, we pursue love and the transformation of our minds, character, and actions, learning to serve one another and growing in faith. By choosing other priorities, we are in danger of quenching the work the Holy Spirit planned for us. Clarke stated, "Grieve not the Holy Spirit of God by giving way to any wrong temper, unholy word, or unrighteous action... [to] so grieve this Holy Spirit that it shall withdraw both its light and presence; and, in proportion as it withdraws, then hardness and darkness take place; and, what is still worse, a state of insensibility is the consequence; for the darkness prevents the fallen state from being seen, and the hardness prevents it from being felt."[23]

Discerning the leading of the Holy Spirit is developed over time. Our primary responsibility is to keep ourselves grounded in the Word and pray for the work of the Holy Spirit to continue in our lives. This leads to transformation of character and usefulness for God's kingdom. Both Old and New Testaments warn us: 'today, if you hear His voice, do not harden your hearts' (Ps. 95:7-8; Heb. 3:7-8).

Revelation of Things to Come

> *I have much more to say to you, more than you can now bear. But when he, the Spirit of truth, comes, **he will guide you into all the truth**. He will not speak on his own; he will speak only what he hears, and **he will tell you what is yet to come**.* -John 16:12-13, NIV

Jesus told His disciples that these are the things for which they would ask after He returned to the Father (John 16:23-28). Wisdom and understanding of the things to come would be revealed in the Father's timing through the agency of the Holy Spirit.

Peter was inspired to quote an Old Testament prophecy on the day of Pentecost to describe the outpouring of the Holy Spirit they experienced. Joel prophesied that the Holy Spirit would be poured out in the last days to impart dreams and visions as well as the gift of prophecy to the bondservants of God (Acts 2:17-18). Prophecy, dreams, and visions are part of the Holy Spirit's work, and there is ample evidence this activity continued in New Testament times:

- Joseph received direction through dreams (Matt. 1:20; 2:12-13,19,22).
- Ananias received specific instructions in a vision (Acts 9:10-16).
- Cornelius had a vision of an angel speaking with him (Acts 10:1-6).
- Agabus prophesied a famine (Acts 11:28).
- Peter had the vision of the clean and unclean animals (Acts 10:10-16).
- Paul was warned of prison and hardships (Acts 20:22-23).
- Paul had a vision of the Macedonian man (Acts 16:9-10).
- Paul supernaturally perceived the shipwreck (Acts 27:10).
- An angel visited Paul (Acts 27:23-24).
- Paul was caught up to the third heaven (2 Cor. 12:1-7).

- The coming of the lawless one was revealed (2 Thes. 2:1-12).
- The latter days' apostasy was prophesied (1 Tim. 4:1).
- The apostles prophesied of scoffers in the latter days (Jude 1:18).

The revelatory work of the Holy Spirit is seen throughout the Old Testament writings. Peter testified 'prophecy never had its origin in the human will, but prophets, though human, spoke from God as they were inspired by the Holy Spirit' (2 Pet. 1:21).

Closing Thoughts

As this age comes to a close, the Holy Spirit will reveal in the timing of God clearer understanding of the events on the horizon before the Lord's return. The sealed things of the book of Daniel (Dan. 12:4,9-10) and the words of the seven thunders (Rev. 10:4) have not yet been fully understood or disclosed. But we have assurance that in the latter days, those with the wisdom from above will understand perfectly and instruct many by the working of the Holy Spirit.

The presence and work of the Holy Spirit is indispensible in the believer's walk and necessary for his survival. He is the Spirit of God brooding over the waters at creation, bringing forth life and order out of darkness. This took place when the will of God went forth through His Word by the dynamic power or breath of the Spirit. This Holy Spirit overshadowed Mary and by the will of God brought forth the Word in her womb in the form of a man. This same Holy Spirit has been given to us with the power to preserve us and bring forth life from our broken existence. How can we ignore so great a salvation?

> *May the grace of the Lord Jesus Christ, the love of God, and the fellowship of the Holy Spirit be with you all.* -2 Cor. 13:14, NLT

Chapter 20

Discernment

> *And this I pray, that your love may abound still more and more in real knowledge and all discernment, so that you may approve the things that are excellent, in order to be sincere and blameless until the day of Christ.* -Php. 1:9-10, NASB

Paul's prayer is critically important for our day. Cultivating unity and discernment come only as believers abound in love grounded in knowledge of God by the illumination of the Holy Spirit. Paul did not exaggerate when he wrote spiritual matters can only be discerned spiritually. The wisdom of this world, humanistic logic, analytical reasoning, and intellectual acumen will not enable us to fully comprehend the treasure hidden in God's Word, especially in regards to prophecy. Only the Holy Spirit knows God's thoughts and intentions; only He can impart true understanding to believers.

> *For this world's wisdom is foolishness (absurdity and stupidity) with God... The Lord knows the thoughts and reasonings of the [humanly] wise and recognizes how futile they are.* -1 Cor. 3:19-20, AMP

Understanding the real implication of news worthy events in our day requires discernment. There is no true discernment apart from the Holy Spirit, only reasonable deductions, speculation, and suspicion. There is no direction or knowing God's will aside from the Holy Spirit, only pragmatic solutions from limited perspective. There is no sanctification without the Spirit's work, only valiant attempts to quiet the war within through self-regulated behavior control. There is no wisdom independent of the Spirit's guidance, only judgments made from superficial inspection and limited knowledge of principles. We can't even correctly divide the Word aside from the Spirit's enlightenment, but rather only draw conclusions that are a hopeless combination of truth and short-sighted opinion or presupposition, causing much strife, controversy, and quibbling. There is no hope we will get along and have unity without the Spirit's intervention, only vying for position, just as the disciples did before they received the Spirit.

Missing Link in the Church Today

> *No wisdom, no understanding, no counsel can avail against the LORD.* -Pr. 21:30, ESV

We desperately need the Holy Spirit to come in our midst to fill us and operate as He did among the early believers. By attending to the Holy Spirit's promptings, the restoration of His wisdom, understanding, revelation, and unity in the bond of peace will be seen in

SECTION 6 *RESPONSIVE DEPENDENCE ON THE HOLY SPIRIT*

the *ekklesia*. We must continually keep asking for more of His presence, power, and gifts so the church can be built up in love, understand the will of God, discern between truth and error, have true knowledge and understanding of the things to come, and move in one accord with one mind and heart. As a whole, the church today is lacking each of these in adequate measure.

Asking for more of the Spirit because of our fascination with supernatural workings or a desire to have 'powers' to impress other people is contrary to the very nature and purpose of the Holy Spirit's ministry. When the Pharisees asked for a sign, Jesus pronounced them evil and adulterous because everything about Jesus' life already pointed to Him as the promised Messiah. No further sign was needed to validate His ministry (Matt. 16:1-4). When the disciples displayed a lack of discernment in an instance when Jesus spoke metaphorically about bread, the misunderstanding was not attributed to immaturity or lack of knowledge. It was attributed to hardness of heart (Mark 8:17). Being undiscerning is a spiritual issue requiring we ask, seek, and knock for understanding and wisdom before we jump to conclusions or move ahead in untempered zeal.

Not everything that happens in the church today that is *called* the Holy Spirit *is* the Holy Spirit. But the way in which many in the community of believers determine whether an activity is of the Spirit takes place not through divine discernment but often through opinion or suspicion. We must look at everything through the lens of the Word *and* the discernment of the Spirit to judge correctly. Many of the false prophets in the Old Testament claimed to have dreams, visions, or the 'word of the Lord.' They led the people astray because their messages were what the people wanted and expected to hear, not what God wanted to say. Laying down our expectations of what we would like to see happen, or what makes sense to us, opens our hearts to receive discernment. The Word and the Spirit are the only reliable witnesses to verify prophecies, dreams, or visions.

Even those who have established ministry in this area will not always be accurate because the Lord wants us to rely on Him for discernment, not the reputation of the speaker. Admittedly, it is much easier to say, 'This guy is okay. We can believe what he is saying.' By so doing, however, we have turned off discernment and have judged by the flesh, not the Spirit. On the other hand, when an unknown individual comes forth to offer prophetic insight, we are on red alert, straining to shift our idle discernment into high gear, typically ending up with only a severe case of counterproductive suspicion.

> *Beloved, do not believe every spirit, but test the spirits to see whether they are from God, for many false prophets have gone out into the world.* -1 John 4:1, ESV

Hold Fast to What Is Good

Paul exhorted the Thessalonians to examine everything carefully. The Bereans were praised for their noble character because they searched the Scriptures daily to see if what they had been taught was based on truth. The Word is the standard by which we weigh and examine the teaching of others and especially our own beliefs. Many beliefs I held for years had to be adjusted or significantly overhauled once I delved into the Word of God and no longer relied on the reputation of teachers or denominational systems of belief. The only way we can hope to embrace God's truth is if our loyalty to God surpasses our loyalty to our denomination, traditions, or personal opinions.

> Sir, my concern is not whether God is on our side; my greatest concern is to be on God's side, for God is always right. -Abraham Lincoln

A word of caution: reading through the Bible once, twice, or even a dozen times will not be adequate to instruct our minds sufficiently to know all there is to know. 'In the multitude of counselors there is safety,' and wisdom advises us to have a circle of Bible-believing friends with whom we can discuss teaching as well as receive constructive feedback based on the Word.

We are to examine all teaching carefully and hold onto the parts that are good (1 Thes. 5:21). By holding fast to what is good, we find common ground with those who may come short in other areas. In this way, we can both encourage the good doctrine others hold while gently refuting the error. Finger pointing or attacking another's beliefs typically causes offense rather than turning their minds to the truth in God's Word.

With basic knowledge of the Word, we can still run amuck if we do not listen for the witness of the Holy Spirit. One person may have a true prophetic word but speaks out of the timing of God. Another may also have a true word, but mixes his own opinions in with it. Still another may be scripturally accurate, but the word is delivered void of the purposes or heart of God—in the wrong spirit. Without the witness and discernment of the Holy Spirit, we will miss the way.

> *So let two or three prophets speak [those inspired to preach or teach], while the rest pay attention and weigh and discern what is said.* -1 Cor. 14:29, AMP

Exercise Discernment

Exercising discernment mandates an active rather than passive role on our part. We are equipped to recognize truth by exercising discernment and paying attention to both the Word and the Spirit. The ability to discern sharpens with use and study of the Word. Only by this combination will we have the necessary tools to discern prophetic words given to the church.

> *But solid food is for the mature, for those who have their **powers of discernment trained by constant practice** to distinguish good from evil.* -Heb. 5:14, ESV

Passively listening to a sermon once a week with no personal knowledge of the Word may be where we start, but it is not the place to stay. Even an infant has to exercise its jaws and facial muscles to drink the milk it needs for survival. Our public school model has trained us to be passive rather than active learners, brainwashing us into believing that without the spoon-feeding of the 'trained experts,' we will not learn anything, or at best learn only inadequately. This has carried over into the church. We must shake ourselves free from this mode of spoon-fed learning and become actively involved in our spiritual growth by reading the Word and exercising discernment.

Ignoring the Holy Spirit

Many have ignored, rejected, or scorned the work of the Holy Spirit because of misunderstanding His role or having aversion to the excesses witnessed in the church. There is as much error in shunning the Holy Spirit as there is in feigning His presence. We are instructed not to grieve the Spirit (Eph. 4:30), insult or disdain the Spirit (Heb. 10:29), or quench the Holy Spirit's work (1 Thes. 5:19-20). Casting aside the Holy Spirit to safeguard the community from 'imbalance' is hazardous to our eternal destiny. Ignoring the discernment available to us will not keep us safe, as the application of the old adage 'ignorance is bliss' would have us believe. Ignorance when it comes to the Word of God and the Spirit's discernment does not bring bliss but rather confusion and death. Allowing this verse to sink into our spirits will help us remember this:

> *For **this is a people without discernment**; therefore he who made them **will not have compassion on them**; he who formed them will show them no favor.*
> -Isa. 27:11b, ESV

If we make a lifestyle of neglecting or refusing discernment from the Holy Spirit because of complacency, fear of feigned activity, or hardness of heart, we will be unable to understand or discern when we need it most. It was not without cause we are admonished, 'today if you hear His voice, do not harden your heart.' The author of Hebrews instructed us to warn each other every day so we will not be deceived by sin and hardened against God. Only by being faithful to the end will we share in Christ's inheritance (Heb. 3:13-15).

Greater love for the ways of the world will harden our hearts toward the things of God through indifference, laziness, and inattentiveness to the Word. The consequences of hardness toward God are costly. Our hearts and eyes will be closed to truth, knowledge of God, and discernment of the times. Like Samson, the gradual drift away from God goes unnoticed, and we don't even perceive when the Spirit of the Lord has departed from us (Jdg. 16:20). Subtle changes in the wrong direction are often felt as a vague sense of uneasiness in our minds or sluggishness toward the things of God. The following passage is aimed at those who have already decided to embrace the world instead of God.

> *They know not, nor do they discern, for he has shut their eyes, so that they cannot see, and their hearts, so that they cannot understand. No one considers, nor is there knowledge or discernment.* -Isa. 44:18-19a, ESV

Effort and Time Are Required

We must keep our guard up, which takes far more work and labor in discernment than either rejecting or accepting everything. The nature of man with regard to religion is to become lackadaisical and passive, preferring an inert list of expected behaviors and honored traditions to the dynamic relationship offered by God through the Holy Spirit. The latter would require time and effort, which in the Western lifestyle is consumed by jobs, techno-gadgets, extracurricular sports, various hobbies, and taking care of big houses and yards. We continually run to and fro with little attention to what is truly important. Philanthropic volunteer work can also become a hindrance if we place little priority on knowing God because of the pressing needs of the people. Even Jesus got away from the demanding crowds to spend time with His Father.

Accumulation, accomplishment, and a well-rounded resume have become our top priorities in the West. The time required to get to know God is already apportioned out elsewhere for the activities we deceive ourselves into thinking have to be done. We suppress the small whisper in our spirit beckoning us to come away for awhile and be refreshed at the feet of Jesus (the Word) and through the fellowship of His Holy Spirit.

We must wake up, repent, and embrace the discernment the Holy Spirit desires to give us. This discernment comes if we will only keep asking, seeking, and knocking until it is imparted to us. We have been so focused on baubles (comfort, material wealth, fun activities, and success in life—ministry or otherwise) that we have neglected the precious jewels promised to those who ask. The concept of asking, seeking, and knocking for understanding, wisdom, and discernment is not something new. It can be found in the Old Testament wisdom literature.

> *Yes, if you cry out for discernment, and lift up your voice for understanding, if you seek her as silver, and search for her as for hidden treasures; then you will understand the fear of the LORD, and find the knowledge of God.* -Pr. 2:3-5, NKJV

It is difficult and surely tries the patience to wait for discernment, but the alternative is to move forward without the Spirit in presumption, error, or worse. Jumping to hasty conclusions is in opposition to discernment (see Isa. 32:4). We must wait for the Lord and keep asking, seeking, and knocking. Letting these passages sink into our hearts to speak patience and longing to our spirits helps us prioritize and stay focused on God:

> *In the morning, O LORD, you hear my voice; in the morning I lay my requests before you and wait in expectation.* -Ps. 5:3, NIV

> *Wait for the LORD; be strong, and let your heart take courage; wait for the LORD!* -Ps. 27:14, ESV

> *Our soul waits for the LORD; he is our help and our shield.* -Ps. 33:20, ESV

> *For you, O LORD, do I wait; it is you, O Lord my God, who will answer.* -Ps. 38:15, ESV
>
> *I wait for the LORD, my soul waits, and in His word I do hope.* -Ps. 130:5, NKJV
>
> *The LORD favors those who fear Him, those who wait for His lovingkindness.*
> -Ps. 147:11, NASB
>
> *I will wait for the LORD, who is hiding his face... I will put my trust in him.*
> -Isa. 8:17, NIV
>
> *But as for me, I will watch expectantly for the LORD; I will wait for the God of my salvation. My God will hear me.* -Mic. 7:7, NASB
>
> *I say to myself, The LORD is my portion; therefore I will wait for him.* -Lam. 3:24, NIV
>
> *Yet those who wait for the LORD will gain new strength; they will mount up with wings like eagles, they will run and not get tired, they will walk and not become weary.* -Isa. 40:31, NASB
>
> *I will climb up to my watchtower and stand at my guardpost. There I will wait to see what the Lord says...* -Hab. 2:1, NLT

The words translated 'wait' in these verses include several nuances of meaning—watchfulness, hopeful expectation, patient and enduring trust, tarrying in confidence. This confidence and trust is based on the Lord's own Word that He will be found by those who diligently seek Him. Waiting on the Lord involves prayer and continual study of the Word. The frustration we feel will incrementally begin to lift until the day star rises in our hearts and we gain understanding.

> *But when I thought how to understand this, it seemed to me a wearisome task, **until I went into the sanctuary of God**; then I discerned...* -Ps. 73:16-17, ESV

The Fruit of Discernment

God's discernment brings forth fruit, ranging from personal to national and beyond. Consider Joseph and Daniel, both praised for their unusual God-given discernment. In Joseph's situation, the wisdom and discernment he received from God saved the lives of many people during a regional famine (Gen. 41:38-40). Likewise, Daniel had discernment that saved the wise men of Babylon (Dan. 2). Nebuchadnezzar sought for someone who could tell him both his dream and the meaning, declaring he would kill all the wise men if no one could satisfy his demand. Daniel enlisted the help Hananiah, Mishael, and Azariah to seek God's mercy. That night God revealed the mystery to Daniel in a vision, who related the dream and interpretation to the king. This not only saved the lives of the wise men but also brought promotions for all four of these intercessors.

Abigail was praised for her discernment because it kept David from avenging himself (1 Sam. 25:32-33). Solomon was blessed because he asked for wisdom and discernment instead of wealth, honor, and long life (1 Kings 3:5-15,28). David guided the people with discernment, skill, and an upright heart (Ps. 78:72), and God declared he was a man after His own heart. Part of Paul's mission was to impart God's heart so that all may come to recognize and acknowledge truth (Titus 1:1). This would equip believers to discern truth from error.

God desires that we come to know, discern, and correctly understand eternal truth (1 Tim. 2:4). Anyone who diligently seeks truth will be rewarded with the only truth anchored to a sure and everlasting foundation: the Word of God. Wisdom and discernment begin with the Word (Heb. 4:12), and are an operation of the Holy Spirit (see 1 Cor. 12:4-11 on the gifts of the Spirit). The Word furnishes the primary vehicle the Holy Spirit uses to give discernment and wisdom for any given situation. Ignoring the Word is to forego *the means* by which we gain understanding, wisdom, and discernment. Disregarding the Holy Spirit is to relinquish *proper application* of the Word for understanding, wisdom, and discernment. They are interconnected and inseparable.

The fruit of discernment, on a personal level, brings forth knowledge of God's will for our lives. When we have knowledge of the Lord's Word—His plans and His heart—and the presence of the Holy Spirit, we are better able to discern His will correctly. Every living person searches for his specific meaning or purpose in life. Only by the Spirit of God can we know this in truth. Paul prayed we would have deep and clear knowledge of God's will, accompanied by spiritual understanding, wisdom, and discernment (Col. 1:9).

Guardian Against Deception

The final days before Jesus returns will be the greatest days of deception in the history of the world. Without discernment, many are destined to fall for this subterfuge. Those who have no love for truth will be easily deceived by the strong delusion sent into the world to deceive those who have chosen the ways of the world over the ways of God. The Word states they simply cannot understand these spiritual matters (1 Cor. 2:14).

Though spiritual discernment is reserved for believers, it is not automatically imparted to new believers but rather comes by: 1.) constant use through studying the Word, 2.) being transformed by the work of the Spirit, and 3.) testing. Believers content with a distorted view of salvation as merely the means to escape judgment, or who have been erroneously led to believe they can continue their worldly and self-focused way of life because of an adulterated view of the grace of God, have stunted the spiritual growth that could have been theirs.

Worse, their eternal destiny is in jeopardy. Our priority must be to know the Word under the guidance of the Holy Spirit, the means by which we grow in discernment (Rom. 12:2). This keeps us from being conformed to the world and enables us to approve what is acceptable to God.

SECTION 6 RESPONSIVE DEPENDENCE ON THE HOLY SPIRIT

> *And I pray this: that your love will keep on growing in knowledge and every kind of discernment, so that you can approve the things that are superior and can be pure and blameless in the day of Christ.* -Php. 1:9-10, HCSB

Paul prayed that the Philippians would grow in discernment so they would be rendered pure and blameless at Jesus' return. This comes only through progressing to maturity in the Word (Heb. 5:13-14). Discernment is critical for our spiritual growth in knowledge and understanding, the catalysts for transformation into the new man we were saved to become. Those who surrender to the training required for such transformation will be the peculiar possession for which Jesus returns, fit to rule and reign with Him.

Unlike the many false prophetic voices in the world today from various religious and secular groups or individuals, there is only one voice that has the required testimony of two or three witnesses to establish its authenticity and supremacy for all time. This is none other than the testimony of Jesus. He received the witness of His Father when God spoke from heaven to testify that Jesus is His Son, and the witness of the prophets who foretold His coming with such precision and detail.

Peter stated the apostles did not follow cleverly devised stories but were eye witnesses of Jesus as both God and man. He called attention to the fact that prophecy did not originate in the will of men, but prophets spoke as God guided them by the Holy Spirit. These prophets foretold of the Messiah's coming in detail—prophecies Jesus fulfilled. Furthermore, the disciples heard God Himself pronounce from heaven that Jesus is His Son in whom He is well pleased.

Knowing that the prophecies about the Messiah came true gives us faith that the other events foretold will also take place. Peter exhorted us to pay attention to the Word of prophecy until understanding dawns and the light of truth is planted in our hearts (see 2 Pet. 1:16-21). The essence of prophecy provides a clear witness to Jesus (Rev. 19:10b). Not only the voice from heaven and the prophets testify about Jesus. John wrote that the Holy Spirit, the water, and the blood are in agreement that Jesus is the Son of God and Savior of mankind (1 John 5:7-8).

- **The Holy Spirit**: attested to Jesus' birth, baptism, miracles, and resurrection; the promise of the outpouring of the Holy Spirit on Pentecost also testified that Jesus is the promised Messiah and the author of the prophesied new covenant.
- **The water of His baptism**: testified that Jesus' ministry inaugurated the prophesied new covenant based on repentance from a heart that has been washed; the voice which spoke from heaven at His baptism testified to Jesus' deity.
  [Note: Abraham was accepted by God as one circumcised in heart, yet later he still partook of the covenant right of physical circumcision that symbolized his tender heart. Similarly, though Jesus' heart, mind, and actions were already in line with the will and knowledge of God, He also partook of the covenant rite of baptism which symbolized what He already possessed.]

- **Jesus' shed blood**: verified Jesus was truly man, He had certainly died, and the prophesied new covenant was sealed by His atoning sacrifice and resurrection.

The Subtlety of the Final Deception

Jesus revealed that the days of trouble will be cut short for the sake of the elect. Very convincing false christs and false prophets will arise, even performing counterfeit signs and wonders with the hope to mislead the elect. He warned us not to be deceived by those who claim Christ has returned, inviting us to come and see him. Everyone will see Jesus all at once when He returns—there will be no need for anyone to tell us He has arrived. 'Just as lightning comes from the east and is seen even to the west, so all will see the coming of the Son of Man' (Matt. 24:27; see also Rev. 1:7).

This cannot be emphasized enough. Our culture craves the supernatural and many spend much time and money to go see the latest revival. In contrast, we exert little energy to enter into the Lord's presence through personal study of the Word. This will prove to be our undoing in the latter days if we don't correct our course now. Jesus stated it would be difficult for even the elect to discern this last deception if it were not for the fact they had been warned ahead of time. Peter echoed this warning, emphasizing the subtlety because all things will look just as they have from the beginning. In other words, there would be nothing new under the sun to get our attention.

> [S]coffers will come in the last days with scoffing, following their own sinful desires. They will say, Where is the promise of his coming? For ever since the fathers fell asleep, **all things are continuing as they were from the beginning of creation...** The Lord is not slow to fulfill his promise as some count slowness, but is patient toward you, not wishing that any should perish, but that all should reach repentance. But **the day of the Lord will come like a thief...** therefore, beloved, knowing this beforehand, **take care that you are not carried away with the error of lawless people and lose your own stability.** -2 Pet. 3:3-4,9-10a,17, ESV

The Normalcy Bias

When the status quo changes only by increments, very few recognize the change because it is viewed as the natural progression of life. When the changes are positive, little notice is taken of their presence. When the cumulative effect of those changes is negative, it is usually noticed by the majority of the people only after it is too late. Even in the case of alarming change, a phenomenon known as the 'normalcy bias' can prevent us from taking action—even in the face of imminent danger.

"The normalcy bias refers to a mental state people enter when facing a disaster. It causes people to underestimate both the possibility of a disaster occurring and its possible effects. This often results in situations where people fail to adequately prepare for a disaster, and on a larger scale, the failure of the government to include the populace in its disaster preparations. The assumption that is made in the case of the normalcy bias is that since a disaster never has occurred then it never will occur. It also results in the inability of people to cope with a disaster once it occurs. People with a normalcy bias have difficulties reacting to something they have not experienced before. People also tend to interpret warnings in the most optimistic way possible, seizing on any ambiguities to infer a less serious situation."[1]

During times of turbulence, those accustomed to making decisions by analysis alone—weighing options, checking historical patterns, and so forth—are the most likely to default to the normalcy bias. This has occurred in times of war, persecution, economic upheaval, and natural disasters, where people convince themselves things won't be as bad as predicted, and they therefore take no precautions to prepare. This is particularly true of those who have the most to lose, or those who are affected the most emotionally by the thought of losing the comforts to which they are accustomed and have worked so hard to secure.

"The normalcy bias actually refers to our natural reactions when facing a crisis. The normalcy bias causes smart people to underestimate the possibility of a disaster and its effects. Basically… people have a really hard time preparing for and dealing with something they have never experienced. The normalcy bias often results in unnecessary deaths in disaster situations. For example, think about the Jewish populations of World War II… As Barton Biggs reports in his book, *Wealth, War, and Wisdom*:

> "By the end of 1935, 100,000 Jews had left Germany, but 450,000 still [remained]. Wealthy Jewish families… kept thinking and hoping that the worst was over… Many of the German Jews, brilliant, cultured, and cosmopolitan as they were, were too complacent. They had been in Germany so long and were so well established, they simply couldn't believe there was going to be a crisis that would endanger them. They were too comfortable. They believed the Nazi's anti-Semitism was an episodic event and that Hitler's bark was worse than his bite. [They] reacted sluggishly to the rise of Hitler for completely understandable but tragically erroneous reasons. Events moved much faster than they could imagine. This is one of the most tragic examples of the devastating effects of the 'normalcy bias' the world has ever seen."

"Just think about what was going on at the time. Jews were arrested, beaten, taxed, robbed, and jailed for no reason other than the fact that they practiced a particular religion… Their houses and businesses were seized. Yet most Jews still didn't leave Nazi Germany, because they simply couldn't believe that things would get as bad as they did. That's the normalcy bias… with devastating results."[2]

The Crucial Nature of Discernment

Can we begin to comprehend how valuable this gift of discernment is to us? It is our very lives, spiritual and physical, particularly as we approach the close of the age. Without discernment, we are fated to the confused floundering of the unbelieving around us when in the midst of alarming reports and tumult. Ferocious anxiety leading to paralysis, worldly wisdom leading to futile decisions, or naive complacency leading to disaster—these are the fate of the unspiritual who are unable to grasp the wisdom and discernment of God. But we have the mind of Christ available to us by the working of the Holy Spirit.

> *For the god of this world has blinded the unbelievers' minds [that they should not discern the truth].* -2 Cor. 4:4a, AMP

Jesus stated there would not be an atmosphere of apprehension and alarm in the last days, but of just the natural events of life. People were eating; hence, no famine, at least not everywhere. People were drinking; hence, no shortage of water, at least not everywhere. People were getting on with life. If there were periodic cataclysmic events, the normalcy bias prevented people from seeing them as anything other than natural occurrences. In the following passage, does Jesus' description of the day of His return sound like a panic-stricken world in utter chaos to you?

> *Just as it was in the days of Noah, so also will it be in the days of the Son of Man. People were **eating, drinking, marrying** and being given in marriage **up to the day** Noah entered the ark. Then the flood came and destroyed them all. It was the same in the days of Lot. People were **eating and drinking, buying and selling, planting and building. But the day Lot left** Sodom, fire and sulfur rained down from heaven and destroyed them all. **It will be just like this on the day the Son of Man is revealed.*** -Luke 17:26-30, NIV

Yet we also know Jesus stated there will be devastating judgments prior to His return (Rev. 16). The period of travail that occurs prior to Jesus' return 'shakes' the earth with wars, famines, earthquakes, and tumults among nations (Matt. 24:6-8; Mark 13:7-8). Though the day of His return is prophesied as a time of *relative* peace and safety globally, similar to the 'peace' in the days of the *Pax Romana*, believers and all those who don't conform will be persecuted (Dan. 7:21-22; Rev. 12:17; 13:15-17).

> *For you yourselves know perfectly well that the day of the [return of the] Lord will come [as unexpectedly and suddenly] as a thief in the night. **When people are saying, All is well and secure, and, There is peace and safety**, then in a moment **unforeseen destruction (ruin and death) will come upon them as suddenly** as labor pains come upon a woman with child; and they shall by no means escape, for there will be no escape.* -1 Thes. 5:2-3, AMP

SECTION 6 *RESPONSIVE DEPENDENCE ON THE HOLY SPIRIT*

Jesus, Peter, and Paul are in agreement that the day of Jesus' return will be a time of relative peace and safety with most people carrying on with life. Paul encouraged the Thessalonians, *who thought the day had arrived and passed*, reminding them they are not in the dark about these things and therefore the day will not take them by surprise. He advised them to remain sober and watchful, reminding them they are not appointed to condemnation but salvation through Jesus (1 Thes. 5:4-9; 2 Thes. 2:2). This is held in tension with the arrival of the bowl judgments as described in Revelation 16.

The threat of persecution cannot sway the believer's steadfast trust that God will preserve them through tough times. Jesus told His disciples they would not be harmed by the tribulation and trials they would undergo (John 16:33, AMP; 1 John 5:18). From God's perspective, the harm that can be done to our eternal soul is of far more importance to Him than what happens to our mortal bodies, which He will replace at Jesus' second coming. Most of us have this backwards. We have a great deal more concern for our physical bodies than our souls, which is like worrying about the candy wrapper and disregarding the chocolate. *Selah*.

History records that some believers were tortured, burned, crucified, beaten with rods, sawn in two, and stoned. Because of this, we must conclude the harm to which Jesus referred indicates harm to our spiritual well-being. Our spirit man, the real and eternal part of who we are, would be kept safe from harm. A new, glorified, perfect body will be given to us for all eternity to replace the one we have today. How else can we explain passages where Jesus stated we will be persecuted and put to death, but He will keep even the littlest physical detail about us intact (using hair as the example; Luke 21:12-19)? This can only come with a focus on eternity.

> *[D]o not be afraid of those who kill the body and after that can do no more. But I will show you whom you should fear: Fear him who, after the killing of the body, has power to throw you into hell... Indeed,* **the very hairs of your head are all numbered. Don't be afraid;** *you are worth more than many sparrows.* -Luke 12:4b-5,7, NIV

It is our inner man (soul and spirit) that is in danger in this age. Our soul and spirit are not replaced when Jesus returns. If we have accepted Jesus' righteousness and the sanctification that comes through faith, we will be rewarded with immortal bodies to replace the old, worn out ones. This new body will 'house' our sanctified soul and spirit. If we have ignored our inner man, giving attention only to the outer man or appearing successful to the world, we are already dying on the inside with no promise of life in the age to come. This is shortsightedness at its worst, with eternal, devastating results.

The whole point of our existence in this age is to be trained, equipped, tested, and matured through trials and the circumstances of life so we will be found worthy to stand alongside Jesus in ruling and reigning on the earth. What makes us worthy? Completing the race designed specifically for us, making us fit and prepared in spirit and character.

Who is wise? He will realize these things. Who is discerning? He will understand them. The ways of the LORD are right; the righteous walk in them, but the rebellious stumble in them. -Hos. 14:9, NIV

Love and Discernment Bound Together

In the opening passage of this chapter (Php. 1:9-10), Paul expressed his longing that our love would abound more and more in our continued growth in knowledge and discernment. This love is founded not on blind affection, but rather on an enlarged view of God. Only in this way will we be able to promote the priorities of God's heart and know His will through discernment in any given situation. The goal is to be a believer whose love increases alongside knowledge and discernment, forging neither indiscriminate love nor coldhearted knowledge.

This love grows as we are taken into the King's chambers and learn in His presence by the Spirit who guides us into all truth (Songs 1:4; John 16:13). Through ever deepening knowledge of God, we are changed to become as He is: able to love freely with grace and mercy. No longer are we *self*-centered, but *God*-centered by all that defines Him. The discernment that accompanies this gradual transformation enables us to determine those matters truly worthy of our attention.

It is the difference between a three year old with constant complaints of 'he took my cookie,' 'she took my bear,' 'I don't like peas,' and a mature adult who chooses his battles carefully based on their importance and worth when held against the standards of truth, mercy, love, and justice. This perspective enables us to cease from quarreling over disputable matters, no longer driven to force others to practice precisely as we do. With an enlarged perspective, we can begin to discern and appreciate the diversity God has instilled in the human race, and His desire to include all in His plan of redemption.

Barnes commented, "It is remarkable here how anxious the apostle was not only that they should be Christians, but that they should be intelligent Christians, and should understand the real worth and value of objects... The word 'sincere' means literally without wax... that is, honey which is pure and transparent. Applied to Christian character, it means that which is not deceitful, ambiguous, hypocritical; that which is not mingled with error, worldliness, and sin; that which does not proceed from selfish and interested motives, and where there is nothing disguised. There is... nothing more lovely in the character of a Christian than sincerity. It implies... that he is truly converted—that he has not assumed Christianity as a mask... The wish of the apostle is, that they might show abundantly by their lives that they were truly righteous... If we wish, therefore, to honor God, it should not be merely with the lips... it should be by a life devoted to him. It is easy to render the service of the lips; it is far more difficult to render that service which consists in a life of patient and consistent piety; and in proportion to the difficulty of it, is its value in his sight."[3]

Closing Thoughts

Discernment is imperative in our day. As one of the benefits of close relationship with the Holy Spirit and training in the Word, it is bewildering that the church today is sorely lacking this trait that is fundamental for its survival. With much uncertainty on the horizon, whether natural disasters, political unrest, economic upheaval, or even the deceptive teaching that has rooted itself in the church, we must be resolute and vigilant in our pursuit of walking in the discernment available to us through the ministry of the Holy Spirit. It is through discernment that we grow in the true knowledge of God, understand His will, and become the obedient bondservants for which He is searching.

To be blameless in the sight of God means having our lives held up to the scrutiny of His light with the confidence that the Spirit of God has transformed our hearts to such a degree that He "shall not be able to discover a fault that the love of God has not purged away... as strong as the word perfection itself."[4] C.S. Lewis reminds us that the level of perfection or maturity ordained for each believer is individualized, taking into consideration the lot each was dealt in life (environment, parental involvement, socioeconomic status, tragic circumstances, etc.): "[God] meant what He said. Those who put themselves in His hands will become perfect, as He is perfect—perfect in love, wisdom, joy, beauty, and immortality. The change will not be completed in this life, for death is an important part of the treatment. How far the change will have gone before death in any particular Christian is uncertain." Lewis also reminds us that the Christian "does not think God will love us because we are good, but that God will make us good because He loves us."[5]

Obedience defines the foundation for 'perfection,' for the truly obedient heart overcomes the carnal nature in order to put God's will first. The pursuit of the believer is to abide in the Spirit and the Word, preoccupied with both for the hope of complete sanctification before God. Discernment is critical throughout the process of sanctification as well as a benefit of fellowship with the Holy Spirit.

> *Do not be conformed to this world, but be transformed by the renewal of your mind, that by testing you may discern what is the will of God, what is good and acceptable and perfect.* -Rom. 12:2, ESV

SECTION 7

DESTINATION OF BONDSERVANTS

Chapter 21

Eternal Salvation

> *Having been perfected, He became the author of eternal salvation to all who obey Him.* -Heb. 5:9, NKJV

Bondservants eagerly anticipate their promised destination: to be in the presence of God, in this life and the next. Just as a bride longs to be with her bridegroom, the bondservant yearns for oneness with God. He is consumed with getting to know God and living his life in wholehearted obedience before his Master and Savior. The opening passage reminds us that obedience defines the bondservant. Eternal salvation awaits all who *sh'ma*—who hear and obey God.

In this age, a bondservant occupies himself with whatever activity brings him closer to the object of his desire, whether engrossing himself in study of the Word or performing obedient acts that connect his heart to the Father's. The father heart of God breathes compassion for the poor, needy, and lonely, and the bondservant will be likewise disposed. Bondslaves are not anxious about food or clothes because it is a 'given' that their Master provides these for them. Their primary concern is to do the Master's bidding and delight in His presence.

The heart of the bondservant grows in gratitude, longing, and love as his relationship with God deepens. One by one, the tethers the world placed on him are severed until they have no more hold on him. He is free indeed, by the truth and the power of the Holy Spirit. His life becomes simplified because he is no longer a person of diversity, but of one desire.

> **One thing I have desired of the LORD**, *that will I seek: That I may dwell in the house of the LORD all the days of my life, to behold the beauty of the LORD, and to inquire in His temple.* -Ps. 27:4, NKJV

In our busy culture with distractions to suit every preference, it is truly miraculous and a testimony to the power of the Holy Spirit when an individual shuns what the world has to offer and chooses God instead. 'Few there are that find this' (Matt. 7:14). We must actively shun the traps our enemy has set to ensnare our hearts with that which does not last. To do so is to choose *life*.

Attached to the Door

> *Then Jesus said to them again, "Most assuredly, I say to you, I am the door of the sheep... If anyone enters by Me, he will be saved."* -John 10:7,9a, NKJV

SECTION 7 *DESTINATION OF BONDSERVANTS*

Jesus described Himself as 'the door.' Recall that the bondservant is symbolically attached to the door. By this attachment, we demonstrate and pledge our loyalty to Jesus. Because Jesus is the door and also the Word, we can accurately say our affection and attention would be rightly placed on study of His Word. The understanding we receive through deliberating over Scripture brings the bondservant to the same conclusion as the man healed of his blindness: 'One thing I know—I was blind but now I see' (John 9:25).

In contrast, the Pharisees who claimed to be experts in knowledge of *Torah* were actually *preventing* people from entering the door by their rejection of Jesus and by teaching the Word with hypocrisy and error (Matt. 23:13). Entering into life, described as knowing God, comes through Jesus alone, not the reasonable doctrines or traditions of men.

Jesus admonished His disciples to keep asking, seeking, and knocking so the door would be opened to them. This can be applied to the concept of wrestling with the Word for understanding. Jesus also called Himself the 'bread of heaven' (John 6:32-35), the spiritual truth behind the object lesson given by the manna provided on the wilderness journey (Ps. 78:23-24). This is the bread we labor for and acquire as we sit before the Word under the Holy Spirit's tutelage.

Three other applications of door imagery are pertinent to the life of the bondservant. The first uses the door to describe the posture of our heart as either open or closed before God. Jesus described the bondservants as poised and ever waiting and available for the Master to return to the door (Luke 12:36). This not only portrays Jesus' return, but also those seasons of visitation where He imparts His understanding, encouragement, will, and heart. The Laodiceans were told likewise if any would hear His voice and open the door, He would share a meal with them (Rev. 3:20), a banquet found in the illumination of His Word. This is the bread for which Jesus exhorted us to labor (John 6:27).

The second application refers to opening a door for 'effective work' (1 Cor. 16:9; see also 2 Cor. 2:12; Col. 4:3). Cyrus, as the Lord's agent, also received an open door so the Lord's purposes for Israel would be accomplished (Isa. 45:1).

Third, an open door will be set before the church of Philadelphia which, if taken in context with the open door set before John the apostle fourteen verses later, has to do with divine revelation of the things to come (see Rev. 3:8; 4:1). This is the portion of the bondservants who have kept God's Word with patient endurance. In the latter days, they will understand perfectly.

Salvation: A Dynamic Process

For this reason we must pay much closer attention to what we have heard, so that we do not drift away from it... [H]ow will we escape if we neglect so great a salvation? -Heb. 2:1,3a, NASB

Our salvation requires our attention and is not a static entity as some suppose. The apostles wrote of the dynamic nature of salvation because of the need for our thoughts, desires, and actions to be sanctified following our cleansed conscience, now free from guilt and the power of sin. The author of Hebrews exhorted believers to *pay attention* to the Word. Peter spoke of the need to *grow* in our salvation by craving the Word (1 Pet. 2:2). *To ensure* our salvation, we must persevere in paying attention to our conduct and teaching (1 Tim. 4:16). Salvation comes *through sanctification* by the Spirit and faith in the truth (2 Thes. 2:13). Jesus *brings* eternal salvation to all who wait for Him (Heb. 9:28).

The word 'salvation' as used in various passages in the Word carries seemingly paradoxical thoughts. Some describe salvation as a free gift, others advise us to study the Word and exert effort to ensure our salvation, and still others tell us that Jesus brings salvation with Him at His return. How can these thoughts be woven together to form one cohesive portrayal of the salvation we have been given?

Scripture supplies three recurring but different thoughts on salvation in addition to the foundational truth that salvation is found only in Jesus (Acts 4:12; Heb. 5:9; cf. Luke 2:25-30). Confusion creeps into our thinking when we fail to discern the differences between these various aspects and uses of the word salvation as taught by Jesus and the apostles. This has led to forming opinions that are at one side of the spectrum or the other. But perhaps we should consider these truths on salvation as an integrated whole with definite components in a process in order to see how all of these passages fit together, rather than explaining away or ignoring passages that don't fit our views.

Our salvation has elements involving: 1.) reconciliation with God, 2.) transformation of our desires, will, thought processes, actions, and discernment in this age (Titus 2:12), and 3.) redemption of our bodies at Jesus' return. This is why we must pay attention. It is not as simple as repeating a sinner's prayer without an actual change in heart posture and the way in which we live. We must check to see if we really are 'in the faith' as evidenced by these changes. Sincere desire to change and godly sorrow over sin are definite signs the Holy Spirit is at work, even in the absence of 'perfect' behavior.

The three basic thoughts on salvation can be viewed as three distinctives: justification, sanctification, and redemption. Though we freely receive salvation when we experience true repentance, there is more to it. The *first* part of salvation resets our conscience to the truth and restores our relationship to God through repentance and forgiveness. This part of salvation provides reconciliation, which is the first step Jesus spoke of when He said we had to be born of water—the baptism of repentance with the result that we now stand **justified** (made righteous in Christ) before God with a cleansed spirit.

The *second* part of the process in our salvation involves the baptism of the Holy Spirit, the means by which we become sanctified in thought, word, and deed. Through sanctification, our mind, will, and affections are transformed so that the desire of our soul is to know God and obey His will. On this evidence we will either be granted entrance to the kingdom at Jesus' return or denied. Sanctification is an integral part of salvation and cannot be ignored. Peter exhorted us to *make every effort* to live a blameless life (2 Pet. 3:14). By submitting to the Holy Spirit for **sanctification**, we go on to receive the prize of our faith and perseverance, the *third* part of this process—**redemption** of our bodies at Jesus' return (1 Cor. 9:24-27; 2 Tim. 4:8; Rom. 8:23; 1 Pet. 1:3-5).

Jesus: Our Righteousness, Sanctification, and Redemption

> *It is because of God that you are in union with the Messiah Jesus, who for us has become wisdom from God, as well as our **righteousness, sanctification, and redemption**.* -1 Cor. 1:30, ISV

In the wisdom of God, we are provided with complete salvation by Jesus' atoning sacrifice (justification/righteousness before God), the washing of our minds with the Word under the guidance and guardianship of the Holy Spirit (sanctification of our souls), and the power of God to transform our decaying bodies into glorious, incorruptible, eternal homes for our soul and spirit (redemption of our bodies). Jesus' death provided payment for the penalty of our sin, and His resurrection established our legal justification before God (Rom. 4:25). All the repentant receive justification (righteousness) before God, which renders the conscience (spirit) clean. The gift of the Holy Spirit guides us in sanctifying our desires (soul) and therefore our actions. When Jesus returns, we are transformed from perishable flesh (mortal bodies) to a glorified state like Jesus. Each is the result of grace; our part is cooperation in faith. Paul tidily summed up the tripartite nature of salvation in the verse quoted above: Jesus is our righteousness or **justification** (*dikaiosune*), **sanctification** (*hagiasmos*), and **redemption** (*apolutrosis*).

Dikaiosune: Justification Through the Righteousness of Christ

> *Through one Man's righteous act the **free gift** came to all men, **resulting in justification** of life.* -Rom. 5:18b, NKJV

Dikaiosune, typically translated 'righteousness' or 'justification,' is defined as "the state commanded by God." Only this state can withstand the fire of His presence. "God's righteousness is imputed and imparted as a gift to man but cannot be earned. It results in God's act of justification of man by his faith through Christ." It is a legal verdict that restores our relationship with God and gives us right standing before Him by faith in Christ alone. It is also recognition of God's rightful claim on man, whom He has created for His purpose. This realization can only come through repentance.[1] Absolutely free, justification in Christ gives us reconciliation, peace, and right standing with God (Rom. 3:24; 5:1). All the charges brought against us for transgressing His laws are dropped, and we hear the Judge's ruling in our favor: 'Case dismissed.'

Paul reminded the Ephesians that even our faith to receive the righteousness of Christ has been given to us as a gift from God (Eph. 2:8). We can boast about nothing except that God is merciful. Justification before God rests solely on the righteousness of Christ and the finished work of the cross. It is the first step in our salvation and can be remembered as the gift to the heart because it takes place at the heart level (Rom. 10:10). Justification reestablishes communication with God.

- We are justified by faith through the atoning work of Jesus (Rom. 1:17; 3:25,30; 9:30; Gal. 3:24; Php. 3:9).
- We are justified freely by God's grace apart from works of the law (Rom. 3:20,24,28; Gal. 2:16; 3:11; see also Rom. 5:16).
- Having been justified in Christ, we are delivered from the penalty of God's wrath poured out on the ungodly (Rom. 5:9).

The goal of our justification is that we become heirs of eternal life (Titus 3:7). Those who turn from sin through repentance are justified in Christ (made righteous) and receive the Holy Spirit as Mentor and Guide. Every believer is granted this deposit at repentance.

Hagiasmos: Sanctification by the Holy Spirit and Truth

Most often translated 'sanctification' or 'holiness,' *hagiasmos* corresponds to the work of the Holy Spirit in our salvation. It signifies the Spirit's activity consecrating us for salvation, resulting in the state of being sanctified. This is in contrast with *hagiazo*, which means 'to be hallowed or separate from the world' because our relationship with God has been restored. Using the word sanctified in this way correlates with justification, and is the way in which Paul described the Corinthians as sanctified in Christ, even though their behavior was still carnal (1 Cor. 1:2; 6:11; see also 1 Tim. 4:5; Heb. 10:10). *Hagiazo* sets us apart as useful for God's work (2 Tim. 2:21).

Sanctification (*hagiasmos*) follows justification and includes the cleansing of our paradigms, thoughts, desires, and actions by the power of the Word and the Spirit. The Holy Spirit enables us to actually 'be holy even as God is holy' (1 Pet. 1:15).[2] This part of salvation furnishes the evidence verifying that our relationship to God has been reconciled through faith in Jesus. While it is also a gift of grace as God's power works through us, it requires our cooperation and effort, granting us entrance into His kingdom.

> **Make every effort** *to... be holy* (**hagiasmos**); *without holiness no one will see the Lord.* -Heb. 12:14, NIV

We are sanctified through the work of the Holy Spirit (Rom. 15:16), primarily by:

- the truth found in God's Word (John 17:17,19);
- separating ourselves from the ways, cares, and distractions of the world (Luke 12:29-31; John 12:25; Rom. 12:2; Gal. 6:14; 2 Tim. 2:4);
- being obedient to the righteous standards of God (Rom. 6:19; 2 Tim. 2:19); and
- trials and testing (John 16:33; Acts 14:22; James 1:12; 1 Pet. 1:5-7).

The goal of sanctification, like justification, is that we receive our inheritance in Christ (Acts 20:32; 26:18), which is eternal life (Rom. 6:22). Our salvation comes *'through* sanctification by the Holy Spirit and belief in truth' (2 Thes. 2:13). Paul pictured Jesus as cleansing His Bride with the water of the Word, which is truth (Eph. 5:26). On this same theme, Paul prayed we would be thoroughly sanctified so our spirit, soul, and body would be preserved completely without blame at Jesus' return (1 Thes. 5:23).

Fornication

Paul defined sanctification as abstinence from sexual fornication (1 Thes. 4:3-8). Fornication portrays the type or symbol of disloyalty to God because it is grounded in the belief we can have relationships or find fulfillment with the things the world offers and still think we are faithful to Jesus, our Betrothed. We are warned about sexual immorality over thirty times in the New Testament alone, if for no other reason than it pollutes our bodies, which are the temples of the Holy Spirit.

It is no coincidence that with the rise of personal spiritual apostasy in the church, primarily fueled by our love for what the world has to offer, there has been a rise in physical fornication as well. Pure and undefiled religion as defined by God takes care of the needy and remains undefiled by the world (James 1:27). Whoever lives by the world's pattern of success has made himself an enemy of God and is defined as 'adulterous' (James 4:4). Apostle John warned that we cannot love the Father and the ways of the world at the same time. 'The cravings of the flesh, the desires of the eyes, and pride in possessions' do not come from God but the world. The world and its desires will pass away, but whoever does God's will abides forever (1 John 2:15-17).

Hypocrisy in the church on this issue is subtle. Many of the older members of the church are embarrassed by and harshly critical of the young people caught in fornication and unwed parenthood. Yet we do not hold ourselves to the same judgment for having given our lives over to love for the world, as evidenced by our drive to succeed and acquire wealth as the world does. God describes pursuit of wealth and worldly ways as spiritual fornication. Our spiritual fornication has led to rampant physical fornication in the generation that followed us. How can we judge the young people when we have a beam of adulterous worldly affection in our own eyes? We have become the Pharisees. We cannot be betrothed to our Bridegroom and also emotionally attached to the world's ways.

Sanctification Is Incremental

When all is said and done, the incremental process of sanctification is actually very gentle for those who cooperate with the Holy Spirit. For those who don't respond to His gentle drawing and 'bands of love' (the restrictions He places on our lives for righteousness' sake), He will capture our attention and discipline us with 'the rod of men' (Hos. 11:3-5; cf. 2 Sam. 7:14). Insisting on our own way is futile. We must remember we have been bought at a price (1 Cor. 6:20), and our lives are not for us to decide:

I know, Lord, that our lives are not our own. We are not able to plan our own course. So correct me, Lord, but please be gentle. Do not correct me in anger, for I would die. -Jer. 10:23-24, NLT

Jesus advises us to take His yoke and learn from Him because He is gentle and humble in heart. In so doing, we will find rest for our souls (Matt. 11:39). Striving will get us nowhere. David also knew this quiet place of rest where he learned from the Lord, and he acknowledged this is what made him great.

Your gentleness has made me great. -Ps. 18:35b, NKJV

Apolutrosis: Redemption from the Curse of Death

Because Jesus reversed the curse of death (Gal. 3:13), we who are in Christ may die physically in this age but are promised eternal bodies in the age to come, nevermore to die. This part of our salvation is known as redemption, 'a release on payment of ransom.' Zodhiates identifies this ransom as that which releases captives (sinners) from captivity (sin).[3] Being released from the curse of sin (death) carries with it the understanding that the former slave of sin will not want to return to his former slavery. Jesus paid our ransom for sin at the cross, and all who are found in Him by the seal of the Holy Spirit will be transformed at His return. At that time, the final part of His redemptive plan will be manifested by the transformation of our physical bodies.

We ourselves, who have the firstfruits of the Spirit, groan inwardly as we wait eagerly for adoption as sons, the redemption of our bodies. -Rom. 8:23, ESV

Jesus told His disciples their redemption would take place at His return (Luke 21:28). In his letter to the Ephesians, Paul explained the progression of salvation as starting with faith that came by hearing the Word of truth (the gospel), followed by the seal of the Holy Spirit guaranteeing our inheritance until the 'day of redemption' (Eph. 1:13-14; 4:30). Because the blood of Jesus paid the ransom price for our redemption, Peter exhorted us to conduct ourselves in this age with the fear of the Lord (1 Pet. 1:17-19). The bondservant understands he has been purchased from death and therefore owes his life to his Benefactor, prompting him to say, 'Take me to the door, I will not go out free.'

The redemption of our bodies makes it possible for our adoption as sons. The goal, then, is eternal life with God as heirs with Jesus, ruling and reigning on the earth without threat of death.

*[H]e will appear a second time, not to bear sin, but **to bring salvation** to those who are waiting for him.* -Heb. 9:28b, NIV

Saved for Works

The apostles are in agreement that we are saved for works, which are the *evidence* we have received the righteousness of Christ and have been released from the power of sin. This *tangible evidence* will be presented before the Court of Heaven as sufficient cause to validate the plea that the person has indeed received the free justification found only in Christ.

- **Paul**: We are saved by grace through faith for the works God has ordained for us to do (Eph. 2:8-10).
- **James**: We are justified by works (the evidence) and not faith alone (James 2:24).
- **Peter**: We are to conduct ourselves in the fear of the Lord, knowing we will be judged (given a legal verdict) on the basis of our works (evidence) (1 Pet. 1:17).
- **John**: Whoever practices righteousness is righteous; whoever makes a habit of sin is of the devil (1 John 3:7-10).

Jesus also testified to the necessity of works as proof the gift of salvation has been received. In the book of Revelation, Jesus rebuked the Laodiceans for being lukewarm, advising them to buy white garments to cover their nakedness (Rev. 3:14-18). These white garments are elsewhere defined as the 'righteous deeds of the saints' (Rev. 19:8). Without these white garments, or righteous deeds, we will be found naked at His return and experience shame.

> *Truly, truly, I say to you,* **he who hears My word, and believes** *Him who sent Me,* **has eternal life,** *and does not come into judgment, but has passed out of death into life.* -John 5:24, NASB

Jesus' words here do not support a doctrine of salvation without the evidence of works, but rather support the Jewish understanding of *sh'ma*. To hear God is to obey what we've heard. Hearing and obeying are inseparable if we have received the free gift of justification (righteousness) in spirit and in truth. Before we get confused on the issue of works, we must keep in mind several things:

- God has ordained specific works for each individual.
- His yoke is easy and His burden light.
- He will not ask us to do anything He has not also given us the power to accomplish.
- This is not a contest where we strive to get to the front by doing 'great' or 'important' works by man's standard.
- God's works flow out of relationship—His Spirit working through us.
- The nature of the works can change as we mature.
- The works tailored for us will enlarge our hearts to receive more of God.
- For most of us, the struggle against sin and selfish desires will demand our greatest effort. This requires the patience of the overcomer.

Doing and saying what the Father gave Him to do and say defined Jesus' walk on the earth. From this we learn that our words are every bit as important as our deeds. In fact, Jesus taught this very principle by first defining that what we speak originates in our heart. If our hearts are good, our speech will likewise be good. In addition, He taught that we will give an account for every idle word we have spoken, for by our words we will either be justified or condemned on the day of judgment (Matt. 12:34-37). Just as works are the evidence of our faith, our words are the evidence of a heart that has been changed by His grace. On this evidence—works and words—we will be judged at Jesus' return. When words are multiplied, sin is not absent (Pr. 10:19). Therefore, our conversations are to be sprinkled with salt (the eternal Word of God) and of good confession (Col. 4:6; Rom. 10:9-10).

Overcomers/Perfection

> *In the world you will have tribulation; but be of good cheer, I have overcome the world.* -John 16:33b, NKJV

Through active faith in Jesus and attention to the Holy Spirit, the bondservant overcomes the world, just as his Master did. With the emergence of repentance in our lives, we are no longer overcome by evil but now overcome evil by the power of the Holy Spirit (Rom. 12:21). When we fix our hope on Jesus and abide in His Word, we purify ourselves from everything that hinders our relationship with Him.

The person who continues sinning is not abiding in Christ. John warned us not to be deceived into thinking we could keep sinning or hating others and still be declared righteous (see 1 John 3:8; the passage uses the present participle, indicating that he is referring to habitual, ongoing sin). Jesus came to give us a fresh start; a clean slate by the free gift of grace so we would learn righteousness and shun lawlessness (1 John 3:3-10). The bondservant works diligently to this end by the Holy Spirit's power working in him.

> *For **everyone** who has been **born of God overcomes the world**. And this is the victory that has overcome the world—our faith.* -1 John 5:4, ESV

Jesus and the apostles spoke often of the perfection of our faith. The words typically used mean 'to complete' with the connotation of establishing something (*katartizo*), or 'to accomplish or fulfill a goal,' such as maturity or a specific purpose (*teleios*). Previously, we shared Zodhiates' definition of *teleios*—'perfection'—as being uniquely determined for each individual by God Himself. The goal for every believer is to be obedient to God according to the ability given him by God. This is God's definition of 'perfection' and the moral goal for all who abide in Christ.[4]

This is important, and the author of Hebrews verified that those made righteous by the free gift in Jesus are given entrance to heaven through their 'perfection.' There is no 'maturity inventory,' a checklist for assessing whether the *teleios* has made the mark. Each is assessed individually, taking into consideration the measure of faith imparted, the time given, degree of ability, personal obstacles to overcome, and the obedience demonstrated, particularly when personal desire conflicted with God's will.

SECTION 7 DESTINATION OF BONDSERVANTS

> *But you have come to Mount Zion... to the general assembly and church of the firstborn who are registered in heaven, to God the Judge of all,* **to the spirits of just men made perfect** (**teleioo**). -Heb. 12:22-23, NKJV (parenthetical added)

The 'spirits of just men' are those who have accepted the free gift of being made right with God through Jesus (justification). They are then made 'perfect' by learning to obey the Holy Spirit and thus have been sanctified to the degree that God has ordained for each specifically. Jesus' sacrifice perfected forever those who are sanctified (Heb. 10:14). Those who are sanctified are those who, having gained fellowship with God through Christ, have withdrawn themselves from fellowship with the world.[5]

Here is our eternal security: 1.) if we repent and accept Jesus' free gift of reconciliation with God (justification), and 2.) divorce ourselves from the world, striving to cooperate with the Holy Spirit as He conforms us to the character of Christ, fulfilling the degree of maturity God has determined for us (sanctification), then 3.) we are judged 'perfected forever' at Christ's return. From this place we can never be snatched from His hand.

[Note: These three steps were seen before in the mission of the Holy Spirit to convict the world of sin (leading to repentance), righteousness (leading to sanctification), and judgment (leading to a legal verdict with the emphasis on separation, i.e., if separated from the world, we are 'perfected forever' and receive imperishable bodies; conversely, if separated from God, we are assigned a place with the hypocrites).]

Requires Effort

Paul spoke of laboring to see this maturity (the obedient character of Christ) brought forth in the new believers (Gal. 4:19), hoping he had not labored in vain. Epaphras was also noted to pray that believers would stand mature and complete in all the will of God (Col. 4:12). The entire context of the new covenant supports an active faith that *struggles* and *labors* to be free from the world and sin so we will be deemed blameless at Jesus' coming. This evidence witnesses that true salvation has taken place. Notice in the next passage that Paul considered his labor fruitful if the believers stand before the Lord untainted by the world, firmly established in the Word.

> *Do everything without complaining and arguing, so that no one can criticize you.* **Live clean, innocent lives as children of God,** *shining like bright lights in a world full of crooked and perverse people.* **Hold firmly to the word of life; then, on the day of Christ's return, I will be proud that I did not run the race in vain** *and that my work was not useless.* -Php. 2:14-16, NLT

Anxious that believers would mature enough to go beyond elementary teachings of repentance, faith, baptisms (repentance, Spirit, fire), the laying on of hands, resurrection, and eternal judgment, the author of Hebrews exhorted them to be diligent to the end and not sluggish *so they will inherit* the promises (Heb. 6:1-2,11-12). Does this sound like an effortless, automatic process to you? We should not fool ourselves into thinking that by diligence and struggle he meant only church attendance. Personal pursuit of the knowledge of God and staying in step with the Holy Spirit as He transforms our thoughts and desires are what require our diligence and attention. The author of Hebrews admonished us to *strive* to enter so we will not fall due to disobedience (Heb. 4:11).

> *We proclaim Him, warning and teaching everyone with all wisdom, so that we may present everyone mature in Christ. I labor for this, striving with His strength that works powerfully in me.* -Col. 1:28-29, HCSB

In his rebuke to the Corinthians for arguing about which human leader they followed, Paul discussed the nature of teaching (see 1 Cor. 3). He stated specifically that those who build on the foundation with costly materials (gold, silver, and precious stones) will receive a reward. Those who teach error, not doing their homework but relying on worldly wisdom, must lay hold of God's wisdom instead. To build on the foundation of Christ with this 'hay, wood, and stubble' would render their work worthy of fire rather than reward. It is important we handle the Word of God with care.

To be saved as though by fire means having all labor destroyed. These are the sincere but immature or careless, who in their 'zeal without knowledge' run ahead of God's plan. They are anxious to teach, not having the patience to wait for the Holy Spirit to instruct them in the Word or for the timing of God. Each must build with care (1 Cor. 3:10). This ensures the salvation of both the teacher and those who listen to him:

> **Pay close attention to yourself and to your teaching**; *persevere in these things, for as you do this* **you will ensure salvation both for yourself and for those who hear you.** -1 Tim. 4:16, NASB

In his second letter to Timothy, Paul stated the Word of God is able to make us wise *for salvation* through faith in Jesus (2 Tim. 3:15). Our knowledge and understanding of God's Word comes through diligent, careful, and prayerful study. Paul exhorted us to be mature in our understanding, not children (1 Cor. 14:20). It is a difficult process on purpose. Disciplined study of the Word tests our resolve and perseverance as well as our faith that God will deliver what He promised—His Spirit who will guide us into all truth.

John went further, stating *those who treasure and keep the Word of God* are the ones whose love for God has been perfected—made complete and mature (1 John 2:5-6). Abiding in Him means to conduct ourselves as Jesus did, doing and saying only what the Father gave Him to do and say. If we live for self and worldly desires, we will lose everything (Matt. 16:25). Paul warned us ahead of time that persecutions would come. This warning came to prevent us from falling away during a time of testing due to misunderstanding its purpose. Satan, on the other hand, tempts us with the intent to invalidate our faith so that we have run in vain (1 Thes. 3:4-5).

> *Let nothing move you. Always give yourselves fully to the work of the Lord, because... your labor in the Lord is not in vain.* -1 Cor. 15:58b, NIV

SECTION 7 DESTINATION OF BONDSERVANTS

Paul counted everything he thought he had accomplished prior to knowing Jesus—all those things by which the world would define him as successful—as loss because of the incomparable worth to be found in knowing Jesus as Lord. His wholehearted desire was found in Christ and His righteousness. Paul was willing to undergo the sufferings Jesus went through in order to *attain* the resurrection of the dead (Php. 3:8-11). Paul advised all the mature to have this same view, *pressing on* to maturity for the promise of resurrection and eternal life with God (Php. 3:14-15).

In recounting his Damascus road experience, Paul witnessed to Jesus' words, stating he was commissioned to bring understanding of the gospel to turn people from the domain of Satan. They could then receive forgiveness and an inheritance along with all who have been sanctified (Acts 26:18). This sanctification was discussed previously, *hagiazo*, accomplished only through separation from that which defiled us in the first place. All the bondservants of Christ have this mind: to turn from the world, embrace God, and be obedient no matter the cost. Legal sanctification happens instantly at rebirth, but the step-by-step process occurs as the Spirit guides the believer throughout life. The Word bears witness that it is these sanctified who receive the promised inheritance.

> *No, dear brothers and sisters,* **I have not achieved it,** *but I focus on this one thing: Forgetting the past and looking forward to what lies ahead,* **I press on to reach the end of the race and receive the heavenly prize** *for which God, through Christ Jesus, is calling us.* -Php. 3:13-14, NLT

When he wrote this, Paul did not judge himself to have yet attained perfection, required for taking part in the resurrection from the dead (Php. 3:10-14). Perfection deals primarily with the sanctification of our character to the extent God has ordained as well as the accomplishment of His will for our lives through self-sacrificing obedience. It is an individualized process that does not look the same in any two believers' lives but has the same foundation in obedience. Maturity will look different for each person. For the rich young man, this entailed selling his possessions and giving the money to the poor. This is what was ordained for him so he would be 'complete' (*teleios*; Matt. 19:21).

Jesus had a goal to be accomplished in His earthly ministry as well, and He felt the pressing nature of the burden His Father had given Him until it was completed (Luke 12:50). The apostles emphasized striving for the maturity (also called 'perfection' or 'completion') specifically ordained for us by:

- **separation from sin and the world**: cleansing ourselves from every defilement of body and spirit so that holiness (separation) is made complete (2 Cor. 7:1);
- **sanctification of our desires and actions**: persevering through trials so we can be mature and complete, lacking nothing (James 1:4); and
- **obedience to our specific charge**: accomplishing the works ordained for us so our faith is made complete (James 2:22; see also Heb. 13:21).

The works ordained for us will mostly entail caring for the poor and those in need around us, which includes sharing the gospel and raising godly offspring. If we are focused on our careers more than on the righteousness of our children, we have stepped away from wisdom. God does not value the worth of our 'works' in the same way we do.

The subject of apostolic prayers offered on behalf of the believers frequently included requests that they be brought to completion or maturity. The apostles were entrusted with proclaiming Jesus, admonishing and teaching the new believers so each person would be presented to Christ complete (obedient, *teleios*) in their faith (Col. 1:28). They also exhorted the believers to be made complete (2 Cor. 13:11), indicating they expected them to participate in the process by cooperating with the Holy Spirit in the way they stewarded their time, resources, and affections. As we abide in Christ (the Word), we are made complete (Col. 2:10, NASB, AMP) because our souls are purified through obedience to the truth (1 Pet. 1:22). By the presence of the Holy Spirit, we have assurance that He who began this work in us will bring it to completion at the day of Jesus Christ (Php. 1:6).

> *Now may the God of peace himself **sanctify you completely**, and may your whole spirit and soul and body be kept blameless at the coming of our Lord Jesus Christ.* -1 Thes. 5:23, ESV

We actually desire the process of salvation through sanctification if true repentance has taken place. To have an emotional experience that does not lead to a lasting change in values, desires, or behavior that lines up with the Word of God is not repentance and therefore not salvation. People also have strong emotional responses to secular music and movies, or in response to eloquent speeches crafted to elicit such a response. Emotional responses by themselves cannot be our barometer of whether true repentance has taken place. We must examine ourselves to see if we are in the faith by the criteria established in the Word of God.

The believer who has experienced true *metanoia* will have a desire to increase in his knowledge of the truth. Godly sorrow will accompany any participation in sin. We become concerned with the true meaning of the Word. Our heart becomes warm to the idea of obedience to the Word, and we grow in faith as we lay hold of truth. Compassion for the less fortunate grips our heart in a heightened way, and injustice fuels our passion to see the 'King in His beauty'—Jesus' righteous rule when He returns. This is how we know if we are in the faith. These changes take place gradually as we are transformed by the power of God's Word through the ministry of the Holy Spirit.

At repentance, it is as if we have been granted a place in a prestigious race, the entrance fee being so astronomically high that *no one* could possibly pay its price. But through Jesus, our entrance fee has been paid and we have been given a place on the starting line. This race is unique because each entrant is given an individualized course. Though similar in basic quality, each race is different from all others with regard to length, duration, number of obstacles, weather conditions, and terrain. As an added bonus, a Personal Trainer/Advisor has been provided so each entrant will have all the help he needs to finish his particular race, including refreshment along the way.

To be placed in this race as a free gift comes with the understanding the entrant will not just sit at the starting gate *because the prize is waiting for him at the finish line* (cf. Php. 3:13-14). To linger at the starting line is to forgo the reason for being in the race in the first place. Whatever the reason that prevents the runner from taking the first step, whether ignorance, slothfulness, fear, feelings of unworthiness, or looking back at what must be left behind in order to run this race, those who do not move forward will not receive the prize that awaits them.

For some, the race will be as short as a sincere public profession of faith in Jesus to redeem, as in the life of the thief on the cross. The 'works' ordained for this man were designated as one solitary act of obedience. For others, it will be years of hardship, labor and persecution ending in martyrdom, as in the life of Paul. In the life of John the Baptist, a six-month preaching engagement ending in execution preceded by thirty years of wilderness training fulfilled his race. For most of us, it will be somewhere between these extremes. Whatever the case may be, frantically trying to figure out what has been ordained for us to do will get us nowhere. Growing in wisdom and revelation through study of the Word and following the Holy Spirit will get us where we need to be. If we focus on our relationship with God, 'all these things will be added.'

> *[Y]ou have been set free from sin and have become slaves of God, the fruit you get leads to sanctification and its end, eternal life.* -Rom. 6:22, ESV

Importance of the Word

> *Who is this coming up from the wilderness, leaning upon her beloved?*
> -Songs 8:5a, NKJV

The more we study the Word, the more we come to realize our trust is wisely placed in God and the Word He has given for our edification. In the story of the Shulamite, we see the progress of the Shulamite from 'dark but lovely' (Songs 1:5) to this place of maturity where she leans on her Beloved, who is none other than Jesus, the Word. Leaning on the Word is the mark of maturity, something seen as weakness by the world but which is the very definition of the bondservant. Reliance on the Word and the guidance of the Spirit rather than our own understanding demonstrates our loyalty and trust.

Jesus and the apostles emphasized abiding in the Word by directing us to abide in Christ. Reading and studying Scripture with the Holy Spirit's tutoring establishes our faith firmly in the Word and enables us to remain steadfast in the face of trial. The Word of God is likened to both bread and water, the two commodities typically designated as the basic necessities for life. Our spiritual sustenance comes from the Word and is the primary means by which we grow in our relationship with God.

Throughout the Bible, we find frequent reminders meant to impress us with the invaluable nature of the Word. The vitality of our walk depends on knowing and understanding God and His ways. Scripture goes to great lengths to remind us the Word is our very life:

- 'It is not an idle word for you; it is your life' (Deut. 32:47).
- 'Turn my eyes from worthless things; sustain me through Your word' (Ps. 119:37).
- 'Your word has given me life and is my comfort in affliction' (Ps. 119:50).
- 'Whoever hears My word and believes has eternal life' (John 5:24).
- 'Only the Spirit gives life; the words I speak are spirit and life-giving' (John 6:63).
- Peter said, 'You have the words of eternal life' (John 6:68).
- Jesus is the word of life—the eternal life (1 John 1:1-3).

Paul exhorted believers to hold firmly to the Word of Life (Php. 2:16a), which stands in sharp contrast to our own words—the source of much folly, futility, and chasing after wind (Ecc. 5:3; 6:11). Solomon wrote, 'when words are many, sin is not lacking and therefore the prudent restrain themselves' (Pr. 10:19). Only the foolish multiply words (Ecc. 10:14a), one of the reasons why Jesus recommended we get to the point when we pray. The remedy for speaking too much is to fear God who will judge every idle or worthless word we have spoken (Matt. 12:36-37). Fearing God is the beginning of wisdom, and wisdom is rooted in Christ, the Word (1 Cor. 1:30).

Prayer itself is rooted in the Word. Communication with God is not merely a matter of assuming a posture of prayer and making our requests known to God, although this is part of it. The conventional concept of prayer leaves out a large part of the definition of communication because this practice is often very one-sided. When we place ourselves before the Word, we allow God to communicate His heart to us, and often this is where we receive the answers to our questions and requests. We have all met people who monopolize the conversation with no intention of letting others speak. This can be frustrating for those listening, especially if they have something important to contribute to the topic. By narrowly defining prayer as requests made to God without including the fellowship we experience while studying the Word, we miss out on one side of the conversation. Prayer and Bible study are inseparable facets of communication with God. In fact, routinely using passages and the language of Scripture in our prayers is not only wise, it is modeled in the Word by the servants of God (e.g., David, Mary, etc.).

Closing Thoughts

Be sure you put your feet in the right place, then stand firm. -Abraham Lincoln

Bondservants are attached to the door, the metaphor Jesus used to describe Himself. He is the door to everything the bondservant desires. Keeping ourselves in fellowship with God through the Word and guidance of the Holy Spirit will take us to the place of perfection God has ordained for us. Though not complicated, it can be unsettling at times when the trials and tests sent our way prove whether the Word of God has taken root or not. This crucial process requires our cooperation and determination to see it through for the promise of eternal salvation in God's presence. Eternal life cannot be undervalued by trivializing and reducing the scope of God's redemptive plan to a nebulous musical experience in the clouds forever. Eternal salvation means we are immortal with bodies that do not age or get sick. It means we will be appointed to work in the government of God as He reunites heaven with earth and man once again lives in paradise. Is there anything in this age that is worth the risk of missing out on this promise?

> "No eye has seen, no ear has heard, and **no mind has imagined what God has prepared** for those who love him." -1 Cor. 2:9, NLT

C.S. Lewis provided much needed insight into the necessity of regular attention to spiritual growth and faith: "Now Faith... is the art of holding on to things your reason has once accepted, in spite of your changing moods. For moods will change, whatever view your reason takes. I know that by experience. Now that I am a Christian I do have moods in which the whole thing looks very improbable: but when I was an atheist I had moods in which Christianity looked terribly probable. This rebellion of your moods against your real self is going to come anyway. That is why Faith is such a necessary virtue: unless you teach your moods "where they get off," you can never be either a sound Christian or even a sound atheist, but just a creature dithering to and fro, with its beliefs really dependent on the weather and the state of its digestion. Consequently one must train the habit of Faith. The first step is to recognise the fact that your moods change. The next is to make sure that, if you have once accepted Christianity, then some of its main doctrines shall be deliberately held before your mind for some time every day. That is why daily prayers and religious reading and church going are necessary parts of the Christian life. We have to be continually reminded of what we believe. Neither this belief nor any other will automatically remain alive in the mind. It must be fed. And as a matter of fact, if you examined a hundred people who had lost their faith in Christianity, I wonder how many of them would turn out to have been reasoned out of it by honest argument? Do not most people simply drift away?"[6]

> *You have been believers so long now that you ought to be teaching others.*
> -Heb. 5:12a, NLT

This verse is another indication that Bible school or a seminary education is not required in the economy of God. Spending time in the Word, praying for understanding, and receiving instruction from other believers and the Holy Spirit eventually bring the believer to the place where he can instruct others. If this is not true in our lives after being a believer for more than a few years, we need to examine ourselves to see if we are spending enough time in the Word, prayer, and fellowship with other believers. We should also take an honest look at our hearts to determine whether our hunger for God has been replaced by hunger for the world.

> *Abide in Him, that when He appears, we may have confidence and not be ashamed before Him at His coming.* -1 John 2:28, NKJV

Chapter 22

Adoption as Sons

> *[Y]ou did not receive the spirit of slavery to fall back into fear, but you have received the Spirit of adoption as sons, by whom we cry, "Abba! Father."* -Rom. 8:15, ESV

The way of the bondservant leads to adoption as sons. By attaching ourselves to the door of God's house, we have made the statement we belong to Him and have given up the right to rule our own lives. There are no rights or privileges of sons for those who do not also walk in the dual identity of the bondservant, as Jesus did. Jesus is the door, and it is by His sacrifice and example that we come to God's house and commit ourselves to the way of humility (meekness) before God. Our ears must be circumcised at the entrance in order to walk in the way of obedience.

The covenant relationship we have with God is unique. We were purchased with the blood of Jesus and freely given His righteousness, no more to stand condemned before the Court of Heaven. As part of this new covenant, we are given the Holy Spirit to guide and train us, giving us power to overcome evil as well as power to be obedient to the will of God. As God's bondservants, our part is to cooperate in our sanctification and training in knowledge of the truth.

In addition to the gift of the Holy Spirit, God has promised to provide our basic needs in this life and transform our bodies at Jesus' return. Paul stated we were given this hope of the resurrection and eternal life with God when we were saved, and therefore we wait patiently and confidently (Rom. 8:24-25). Transformation of our bodies seals our sonship forever.

> *A slave does not remain in the household forever, but a son does remain forever. Therefore if the Son sets you free, you really will be free.* -John 8:35-36, HCSB

The transition from bondservant to sonship does not negate our desire to be obedient to all of God's will, but rather deepens our love, respect, and thanksgiving for the intense love God has for us and the great lengths to which He will go to include us in His family forever. In a culture of entitlement, grateful hearts are hard to come by. But thankfully, by the power of the Holy Spirit we can be transformed in this area of our lives as well. The incredible privilege of becoming part of God's family is available to all who receive and abide in Christ.

> *[A]s many as received Him, to them He gave the right to become children of God, to those who believe in His name.* -John 1:12, NKJV

SECTION 7 *DESTINATION OF BONDSERVANTS*

The 'place' our Father has prepared for us is an imperishable dwelling for our spirit and soul. Our 'tent' in this life is only a temporary dwelling place for our inner man. This explains why Jesus taught believers not to be afraid of those who can hurt the body. From the perspective of eternity, our present bodies last only a day. Whatever we have to go through in the 'one day' of our existence in this age in order to have entrance into life as the sons of God for eternity is worth every sacrifice we have to make.

> *In My Father's house are many dwelling places; if it were not so, I would have told you; for I go to prepare a place for you.* -John 14:2, NASB

Bondservants: The Friends of God

> *But know that the LORD has set apart the godly man for Himself; the LORD hears when I call to Him.* -Ps. 4:3, NASB

The godly are those who obey out of a heart connected to God in love. The disciples grew to love their Savior and gave their last breath to demonstrate their loyalty and obedience. Before He went to the cross, Jesus told the disciples He no longer called them servants, but friends. The difference between being a servant of God and a friend of God is not the issue of obedience, but rather the issue of knowing what the Master is doing. Obedience to God as a servant leads to friendship with God, where the obedient heart receives understanding and revelation of the Master's business.

Abraham and Moses are good examples of this (Gen. 18:2,17-20; Ex. 33:11) as are the apostles. Even after Jesus called the disciples His friends, they continued to identify themselves as bondservants of Christ in their epistles. From this we see that not only does the bondservant identity form the basis for sonship but for friendship as well. This same transition occurs when our children grow up and become adults. The parents now also view the child as a friend, though he will never cease to be their child.

> ***You are My friends if you do what I command*** *you. I do not call you slaves anymore, because **a slave doesn't know what his master is doing. I have called you friends, because I have made known to you everything** I have heard from My Father.* -John 15:14-15, HCSB

Revealing the Father's business fulfills part of the new covenant promise. The Holy Spirit, who we received at repentance, will give us revelation of the things to come in the timing of God.

> *ON MY BONDSLAVES, BOTH MEN AND WOMEN, I WILL IN THOSE DAYS POUR FORTH OF MY SPIRIT, and they shall prophesy.* -Acts 2:18, NASB

Jesus, the Word, reveals Himself to those who love and obey Him. This revelation not only includes comprehending the truth in God's Word and the deeper meanings of biblical teaching, but also understanding the prophetic events as recorded in the Word. How

CHAPTER 22 *ADOPTION AS SONS*

do we know this? 'The testimony of Jesus is the spirit of prophecy' (Rev. 19:10), and Jesus has promised to reveal *Himself* to His friends the bondservants.

> ***The one who has My commands and keeps them is the one who loves Me.*** *And the one who loves Me will be loved by My Father. I also will love him and* ***will reveal Myself to him.*** -John 14:21, HCSB

Our love for God expressed through obedience has great reward not only in the life to come but in this life as well. Understanding God's heart and plans for the hour in which we live is invaluable, both for our spiritual and physical well-being.

Sons of Issachar: Prophetic Foreshadowing

> *Of the sons of **Issachar**, **men who understood the times, with knowledge of what Israel should do**, their chiefs were two hundred; and all their kinsmen were at their command.* -1 Chron. 12:32, NASB

The Aramaic (Peshitta) translation reads, "And of the children of Issachar, men who had understanding in their times, who did good and upright deeds before the LORD," similar to bondservants who have become God's friends. Some ministers have used this homiletically to describe the prophetic voice in the present day community of believers. They designate this special gifting as the 'Issachar anointing,' an insightful application. The prophetic blessings spoken over Issachar by both Jacob and Moses support this use.

> **Jacob:** *Then Jacob summoned his sons and said, "Assemble yourselves that I may tell you **what will befall you in the days to come**... Issachar is a strong donkey, lying down (**rabats**; by implication, 'to brood') between (**beyn**; literally 'a distinction,' but only used as a preposition) the sheepfolds (**mishpath**; also translated 'burden'). When he saw that a resting place (**menuchah**; rest) was good and that the land was pleasant, he bowed (**natah**; by implication, submitted) his shoulder to bear burdens, and became a slave (**abad**; related to ebed, bondservant) at forced labor (**mas**; a burden causing one to faint)."* -Gen. 49:1,14-15, NASB (parentheticals added)[1]

Issachar is likened to a strong donkey, a humble beast of burden highly valued in Middle Eastern culture (Gen. 24:35; Ex. 13:13; 20:17; 23:4-5,12; Luke 13:15). From the Hebrew words used, we get a picture of one given strength to bear burdens as a donkey, lying down under or brooding over the burden in the sense of 'mentally separating or distinguishing' in order to understand or discern the burden. Recall that Jesus entered Jerusalem 'humble and riding on a donkey' (Matt. 21:1-8) in fulfillment of prophecy (Zech. 9:9). This is a picture of a donkey bearing Jesus, the Word, on his shoulders.

Though a different form of the word is used (*massa*), there are examples of the prophetic words of the Lord being called 'the burden of the Lord' (e.g., Ezk. 12:10; Zech. 9:1; 12:1; Mal. 1:1). We also note Issachar found that rest was good, speaking of the rest one finds when at peace with the Lord (Ps. 62; 131; Jer. 6:16; Matt. 11:29). The land of Israel is a

SECTION 7 *DESTINATION OF BONDSERVANTS*

type and shadow of the 'better country' to which the author of Hebrews refers (Heb. 11:10,13-16). Knowing this, we can apply these types to Jacob's blessing to Issachar. When Issachar saw that resting in the Lord was good, and the promise of a better country pleasant, he willingly submitted himself to the Lord's will (bond servitude), shouldering the burden given. Like Paul, this burden would cause him to pour himself out as a drink offering (Php. 2:17; 2 Tim. 4:6), the implied meaning of the Hebrew word *mas* (Gen. 49:15).

> **Moses:** *"Rejoice, Zebulun, in your going forth, and, Issachar, in your tents. They will call peoples* ('am; "a group which has certain unified, sustained relationships within itself"[2]) *to the mountain; There they will offer righteous sacrifices; For they will draw out the abundance of the seas, and the hidden treasures of the sand."* -Deut. 33:18-19, NASB (parenthetical added)

In Jewish tradition, these blessings reveal the special bond between Zebulun and Issachar. "Rashi interprets the Blessing in the context of Yissachar being a hard laborer in the field of Torah. He will "bend his shoulder" to bear the yoke of Torah, and will have great success in that field… In his blessing to the Tribe of Yissachar, Moshe Rabbeinu joins Yissachar with his brother Zevulun in his final words to the Tribes, foreseeing a partnership relationship where Zevulun devotes itself mainly to traveling the seas in pursuit of commerce, while supporting the Tribe of his brother, Yissachar, which devotes itself to the study of Torah; and the heavenly reward for the study of Torah is split between them. Moshe says, "…Rejoice, O Zevulun in your seafaring excursions, and Yissachar in your tents." (Devarim 33:18)… The great merchandising ability of the Tribe of Zevulun will draw traders from many nations to do business with its members. Once they got to the territory of Zevulun, they would say to each other, 'Let us go and observe how this nation worships its G-d.' They would proceed to Yerushalayim to observe the practices of the Jewish People (as taught by the great Torah scholars of the Tribe of Yissachar)… The Torah scholarship of the Tribe of Yissachar was so great that the Sages said, "No scholar could be found who would provide guidance in Torah Law besides a descendant of the Tribe of Levi or the Tribe of Yissachar."[3] [Note: 'Moshe Rabbeinu' refers to Moses; cf. Gen. 49:13 re: Zebulun being a merchant of the sea.]

Here again we note the historical understanding of the blessing to Issachar involving 'bearing' the Word as a way of life. According to this interpretation, Zebulun fully shares in the reward given to the *Torah* scholars of Issachar because he funded them in an equal partnership, an example of equitable giving as previously discussed (Chapter 13; see Matt. 10:41; Php. 4:14-19). The sons of Issachar do not have to divide their attention between working for the necessities of life and study of the Word due to the generosity of their brother Zebulun. This is detailed in the business *halakha* of the Jewish people.[4]

Calling the people to the mountain can be understood symbolically as being called to enter into God's presence (Ex. 19:1-20:21; Heb. 12:22) for instruction and revelation (see Ps. 3:4). Offering righteous sacrifices can only come from those with circumcised hearts—who live in obedience to what they hear from their Master. The 'abundance of the seas' in Moses' blessing most likely refers to the portion ordained for Zebulun—wealth through business. The concealed treasures are Issachar's portion, likely referring to the treasures of God's Word (Ps. 119:162; Pr. 15:6; Pr. 21:20; Isa. 33:5-6; Matt. 13:44). The reference to sand, which is preceded by 'in the' or 'of the' in most English translations but lacking in the Hebrew, might reasonably be referring to the innumerable quantity of treasure. This is in keeping with the frequent use of 'sand' in the Old Testament to describe something that cannot be counted (Gen. 22:17; 41:49; Josh. 11:4; Jdg. 7:12; 1 Sam. 13:5, etc.). God gave Solomon wisdom and great insight, as measureless as the sand (1 Kings 4:29). Paul described God's wisdom as unsearchable because of its depth and magnitude (Rom. 11:33; see also Eph. 3:10). In summary, Moses' blessing to Issachar symbolically depicts the treasure he will be given for devoting himself to study of God's Word—the vast and concealed treasure reserved for the bondservants of God (see also Matt. 13:52; Col. 2:2b-3; 2 Tim. 1:14).

> *Do not plow with an ox and a donkey yoked together. Do not wear clothes of wool and linen woven together.* -Deut. 22:10-11, NIV

The Mosaic instruction that oxen and donkeys are not to plow together is intriguing. Paul likens oxen to the workers the Lord sends forth to bring the gospel to the lost (1 Cor. 9:9-14; 1 Tim. 5:17-18). In Job, we find that 'the oxen plow and the donkeys graze' (Job 1:14). Isaiah stated that 'the ox knows his master though Israel does not; the donkey knows his owner's manger, but Israel does not understand' (Isa. 1:3). These hints reveal the two different functions of 'oxen' and 'donkeys' in the community of believers. The oxen know their Master and are driven to plow—to bring God's light to the lost (reconciliation) and plow the fallow ground. The donkeys know their Master's manger and are compelled to graze—to continually forage for understanding in the Word.

The parallel language of the types of clothes (v. 11) may also hint about the type of work in which each engages. The oxen and wool primarily suggest ministering to people. The donkey and linen may point to the emphasis on ministering to the Lord through study of the Word. Recall that a donkey 'restrained the prophet Balaam's madness,' alluding to the donkey's role of discerning prophetic messages by virtue of his understanding of Scripture (Num. 22:21-33; 2 Pet. 2:16). The admonishment that the two are not to be yoked together may simply be due to the different focus of each. For an 'oxen' to insist everyone plow and minister as he does is to ignore the unique calling of the 'donkeys'—to graze continually on the Word of God to bring forth understanding of the concealed treasure. There are not enough hours in the day for oxen to also be donkeys, or donkeys to take on the allotment given to the oxen. Though their duties are not mutually exclusive, they must concentrate their efforts on the portion ordained specifically for them.

Adoption

> *[C]reation waits with eager longing for the revealing of the sons of God... not only the creation, but we ourselves, who have the firstfruits of the Spirit, groan inwardly as we wait eagerly for adoption as sons, the redemption of our bodies.*
> -Rom. 8:19,23, ESV

SECTION 7 *DESTINATION OF BONDSERVANTS*

The goal of Jesus' ministry is to reconcile us to God and sanctify our inner man so that we might receive the adoption as sons (Gal. 4:5), which is the redemption of our bodies. James Strong's Greek Lexicon defines the word used for adoption in this passage (*huiothesia*) as 'the placing of a son.' In this age, while we reside in corruptible flesh, we are justified in Jesus and sanctified by the Holy Spirit so our character can be transformed to the character of Christ, the firstborn son. As bondservants, we lay aside our agendas to submit to this process of acquiring the *character* of obedient sons. Through this work of grace, we are brought through to the day when we experience our full adoption (the redemption of our bodies) at Jesus' return and are given the *placement* of sons in God's kingdom. In other words, sanctification transforms our character (*inner man*) in this age; adoption transforms our body (*outward* man) when Jesus returns.

Paul used this expression to define all those who believe and abide in Christ. While adoption has been specifically determined for the faithful in Israel (Rom. 9:4), Paul reminded us that racial background does not determine who the children of the promise are but rather faith (Rom. 9:8). Paul saw the salvation of Gentiles as a fulfillment of Hosea 2:23: 'I will call them My people, who were not My people' (see Rom. 9:25). Jesus will gather into one not only the loyal and faithful remnant in the nation of Israel, but also the Gentile children of God scattered abroad (John 11:52).

> *This mystery is that through the gospel the Gentiles are heirs together with Israel, members together of one body, and sharers together in the promise in Christ Jesus.* -Eph. 3:6, NIV

Believers are the sons of God through faith and therefore heirs according to the promise made to Abraham (Gal. 3:26,29). Paul made this clear when he stated not only the circumcised would inherit the promise, but all who share the faith of Abraham. In this way, Abraham is the father of many nations (Rom. 4:16-17). God's plan to bring many sons and daughters to glory is realized only through Jesus (see Heb. 2:10-13 and John 1:12-13 for this discussion) by the grace of God (Eph. 1:5-11). All who turn aside, repent, and come to faith in Christ are foreordained to be conformed to His likeness (Rom. 8:29).

> *He chose us in Him before the foundation of the world, that we should be holy and without blame before Him in love, having predestined us to adoption as sons by Jesus Christ to Himself, according to the good pleasure of His will.* -Eph. 1:4-5, NKJV

The author of Hebrews called Jesus the founder of our salvation, made complete by what He suffered. Those who are sanctified by Jesus are one with Him, and He is therefore not ashamed to call them His brothers. As the Head over all who believe in Him, Jesus is described as revealing God to the heirs of redemption and is also called the firstborn among many brethren (Rom. 8:29b).

> *And if children, then heirs—heirs of God and fellow heirs with Christ, **provided we suffer with him** in order that we may also be glorified with him.* -Rom. 8:17, ESV

The word 'suffer' in this passage is *pascho*, the implication being to experience feeling, usually negative. Zodhiates defines this as being the opposite of free action.[5] Applied to Jesus' conduct, who did not initiate anything of His own will but only did and said what the Father gave Him to do and say, suffering in this manner entails giving up our right to decide our way. In this manner, we also *pascho*, suffer, by giving up our will for God's.

The role of the Holy Spirit in our adoption starts with being granted repentance. Those who then follow the Spirit's leading through the process of sanctification are delivered from fear and given instead the spirit of adoption by which we come to God as our Father. Finally, we have the witness of the Holy Spirit in our heart that we are the children of God (Rom. 8:14-16; Gal. 4:6). This gives us confidence before the Lord in this age as well as confidence that He will deliver what He has promised when Jesus returns: the redemption of our bodies and eternity in His presence.

> *In the fear of the LORD there is strong confidence, and His children will have a place of refuge.* -Pr. 14:26, NKJV

As we mature, we begin to eagerly long for our adoption to be made manifest. Though it has not yet been revealed what we will be like, we know we will be like Jesus when He is revealed the second time from heaven. John declared those who hold this hope will purify themselves to be like Jesus (1 John 3:2-3; see also Heb. 9:28; cf. Acts 1:11). The Holy Spirit accomplishes this work through sanctification. Because He loves us and calls us sons, God also disciplines us 'with the rod of men' and other means when we stray from the path of righteousness (2 Sam. 7:14; Deut. 8:5; Pr. 3:11-12).

Enduring hardship as discipline from our Father demonstrates we are truly and legitimately His children. The objective of His discipline is that we might share in His holiness (*hagiotes*), which is the *essence* of His character, not the result or process of sanctification. This describes the harvest of righteousness—the transformation of our character—that God has in mind when we are tested and persevere through the hardships sent to refine us. Sharing in the essence of *God's* holiness is profound, for we do not possess holiness by nature. God is 'totally other than' in His holiness. As a result of the work of righteousness in our lives through God's discipline, we can experience the peace of God no matter what our circumstances (Heb. 12:5-11).

> *Come out from among them and be separate… Do not touch what is unclean, and I will receive you. I will be a Father to you, and you shall be My sons and daughters, says the LORD Almighty.* -2 Cor. 6:17-18, NKJV

Notice this is new covenant teaching, even though it mirrors the old. In one way or another, the theme of being separated from the world is repeated throughout the Bible. The way in which we become blameless and pure, 'sons of God without fault in a warped and crooked generation,' results from paying attention to our salvation, working it out in the fear of the Lord. Doing so allows us to 'shine like stars' among the ungodly. Peacemakers will be called the sons of God (Matt. 5:9). They have disciplined themselves to imitate God

(Eph. 5:1), who 'makes the sun rise on the evil and the good, and gives rain to the just and unjust.' By their Father's example, His children learn to bless and love those who persecute, malign, and curse them (Matt. 5:44-45). We stumble in this process when we respond by complaining and arguing (see Php. 2:12-15). We are to let our light shine before men so they will glorify God for the good we do in His name (Matt. 5:16).

At Jesus' return, the sons of God will be revealed, an event all creation longs to witness (Rom. 8:19). The world does not presently recognize the children of God because it does not know God (1 John 3:1). On the appointed day, the sons of God will 'shine forth as the sun' in their Father's kingdom (Matt. 13:43). We will no longer be considered slaves (cf. Luke 17:10) but fully adopted sons (Gal. 4:7).

Kingdom Parables

"Lord, are only a few people going to be saved?" -Luke 13:23, NIV

The very fact this question was asked leads one to believe Jesus' teaching implied its truth. Keep in mind 'many' and 'few' are relative terms. Some have estimated the total number of human beings to have ever lived at somewhere between 100 and 115 billion.[6] While we are unable to make any predictions, we do know the number of people from all languages, races, and nations throughout history, saved and standing before God's throne, is a vast multitude that could not be counted in John's vision (Rev. 7:9).

Jesus' response to the above question established that many who try to enter God's kingdom won't be allowed because they are not known by God. Once the door is shut, no amount of pleading will reopen the door. This is precisely what happened at the time of the flood. Once God shut Noah and his family in the ark, all others were lost (Gen. 7). The chance for entrance was past, causing remorse in all those who ignored the command, 'today, if you hear His voice, do not harden your heart…'

> **Work hard to enter** the narrow door to God's Kingdom, for many will try to enter but will fail. **When the master of the house has locked the door, it will be too late.** You will stand outside knocking and pleading, 'Lord, open the door for us!' But he will reply… 'I tell you, **I don't know you** or where you come from. Get away from me, all you who do evil.' -Luke 13:24-25,27, NLT

Those who are not allowed entrance are told God does not know them and they are evildoers. They have no relationship with God from His perspective because those who love Him also obey His commands. Entrance into God's kingdom depends upon relationship and obedience. When Jesus commands us to 'work hard' or 'make every effort,' to which all the New Testament writers agree, how can we possibly ignore or dismiss this instruction as not pertaining to entrance to the kingdom?

Yes, we freely receive righteousness through Christ, which requires nothing on our part so that no man may boast. Through the spirit of conviction when the gospel is preached, we repent, are reconciled to and given right standing before God, and are blessed with the gift of the Holy Spirit. But why all this talk of effort, striving, and contending against sin and the god of this age *so we can enter the narrow door* if entrance comes automatically with professed belief in Jesus as Savior? The answer is that the High Court of Heaven is looking for bona fide proof—evidence—that repentance has indeed taken place.

Many have been deceived into thinking that once they receive the free gift of salvation through repentance, they are 'in' and are now free to do as they please because of the mistaken notion God will forgive every sin they willfully commit. Those who believe this will be in for a rude awakening. To say we have faith in God, yet not keep His commands or live righteously *by the power of the Holy Spirit,* is to be rewarded by being assigned a place with the hypocrites, complete with weeping and gnashing of teeth.

Parable of the Ten Virgins

When Jesus taught the disciples about the signs at the close of the age just prior to His return, He finished His discussion with two parables. In the parable of the ten virgins (Matt. 25:1-13), each virgin took her lamp to go out to meet the Bridegroom. The wise took flasks of oil with their lamps, but the foolish did not. The Bridegroom was delayed and all fell asleep.

At midnight, the cry went out that the Bridegroom had arrived. The foolish found they had no oil left in their lamps, but the wise refilled their lamps and advised the foolish to go to the dealers to get oil. In the meantime, the Bridegroom opened the door for the marriage feast, the wise were let in, and the door was shut. When the foolish returned, they were not allowed in because the Bridegroom *did not know them*. At the end of the parable, Jesus admonished the disciples to be watchful because they do not know the day or hour of His return.

If all were virgins, all had lamps, and all fell asleep, then our only variable is oil. Being a virgin is a description of a believer, betrothed to one Husband (2 Cor. 11:2). But what do the lamps represent? While there are other interpretations possible, we know from the Word that David referred to the Lord as his lamp (2 Sam. 22:29; cf. Rev. 21:23) and declared that the Lord keeps his lamp burning by turning his 'darkness into light' (Ps. 18:28). In addition, the spirit of man is described as the lamp of the Lord (Pr. 20:27). When we receive the deposit of truth in our spirit man, our darkened understanding gives way to the light of truth: 'Thy Word is a lamp unto my feet' (Ps. 119:105). This is the lamp of the Lord we freely receive at repentance that guides us onto the path of life. Metaphorically described as a lamp, God's Word—Jesus—comes to us at repentance.

The oil can represent many things. It was used for consecration and purification (Ex. 29:21; 40:9-15; Lev. 8:1-2); to accompany offerings (Lev. 2:1-7; 7:10); as a symbol of unity (Ps. 133) as well as righteous rebuke (Ps. 141:5); to oil battle shields (Isa. 21:5); for healing (Mark 6:13; James 5:14); and for anointing priests and kings (Ex. 30:25; 40:9-15; Lev. 21:10; 1 Sam. 10:1; 16:1,13; 1 Kings 1:39). The wise stored 'precious treasure and oil' in their dwellings (Pr. 21:20). All of these uses of oil describe the activities of the Holy Spirit in a believer's life on the road to sanctification, including the oiling of our shields for battle. Obtaining oil from olives required beating, pressing, and waiting for the separation of the oil from the olives' other components, very similar to the role of trials in our walk as believers.

Because we are given the Holy Spirit at repentance and also exhorted to *be filled* with the Holy Spirit as believers, we may conclude that the measure of oil in the lamp we received came with repentance, but that the oil in the flask is acquired as we attend to the deposit given to us. This multiplies our supply. By using this analogy of the consumable commodity of oil, we see another parallel. The flame causing our lamp to burn brightly when we repent and come to the Lord will not keep burning once the initial measure of oil runs out. Thus we understand the imperative nature of the command to continually *be filled* with the Spirit. Only one Man was given the Spirit without measure—Jesus of Nazareth (John 3:34).

The Greek word *chrisma* is used in particular of oil for anointing. It appears three times in the New Testament, and only in one chapter of John's writings. Each use is associated with the concept of teaching. The oil of anointing is equated with the Holy Spirit guiding us into all truth, as Jesus promised. In fact, the NLT translates *chrisma* as 'Holy Spirit' in this passage, though here translated as 'anointing' in the HCSB.

> *You have an anointing from the Holy One, and you all* **have knowledge**... *The anointing you received from Him remains in you, and you don't need anyone to* **teach you**. *Instead,* **His anointing teaches you** *about all things, and is true and is not a lie; just as it has* **taught you**, *remain in Him.* -1 John 2:20,27, HCSB

Jesus, as the Head of the *ekklesia*, is the anointed one, *Christos*. The depiction of Jesus as high priest makes the description of Aaron in Psalm 133 very appropriate in light of New Testament teaching on unity:

> *Behold, how good and how pleasant it is for brethren to* **dwell together in unity!** **It is like the precious oil upon the head running down** *on the beard, the beard of Aaron, running down on the edge of his garments. It is like the dew of Hermon, descending upon the mountains of Zion; for there the LORD commanded the blessing—***Life forevermore***.* -Ps. 133, NKJV

The five foolish virgins failed to get this oil, which comes by fellowship with the Holy Spirit primarily through study of the Word. The use of oil for consecration (a common translation of *teleios*, which is often rendered 'perfect') illustrates the believer's consecration as he is perfected through sanctification. The foolish virgins ignored the greatness of their salvation through erroneous understanding of their charge. They neglected to acquire more oil because either they thought the original allotment was all they needed, or they were too busy to get more. Along this theme, Paul told the believers at Ephesus to 'be filled with the Spirit' (Eph. 5:18). The verb 'be filled' in this passage is written in the present passive imperative, meaning that the action it describes is a command for an ongoing or habitual action. "The Present Imperative is often a call to a long-term commitment and calls for the attitude or action to be one's continual way of life (lifestyle)."[7]

Because it is written in the *passive* voice, it indicates action done *to* us rather than *by* us. The only way in which a command like this can be carried out, then, is to pray that God would keep on filling us with His Spirit. This is in agreement with Jesus' teaching that we are to keep on asking (present *active* participle) for the Holy Spirit (Luke 11:9-13). We are commanded to keep our lamps burning so we are ready when He returns, in season and out. Without the oil of the Holy Spirit providing fuel for our lamps, we have no hope of accomplishing this.

> *Be dressed for service and **keep your lamps burning**, as though you were waiting for your master to return from the wedding feast. Then you will be ready to open the door and let him in the moment he arrives and knocks.* -Luke 12:35-36, NLT

John the Baptist, the greatest man ever born of a woman, is described as a 'burning and shining lamp' (John 5:35), the desire of every bondservant. This is the description of one who abides in the Word. Peter described the prophetic word as a 'shining lamp in the darkness' (2 Pet. 1:19). God's Word is the lamp that delivers knowledge and understanding of God and His kingdom, but only the oil of the Holy Spirit provides fuel for comprehension. A lamp without oil cannot shed light. This reminds us that the Bible cannot be understood the way God intended without the Holy Spirit—the oil—to guide and teach us. We have no light for knowing truth without the Holy Spirit.

The parable of the ten virgins highlights the effort (continual prayer and meditation on the Word, and asking for more of the Holy Spirit) we must put forth to obtain oil to keep our lamps burning, which in turn helps us grow in our relationship with God as we are sanctified by truth. To neglect this part of the salvation process is to neglect building our relationship with God. This is why the foolish virgins were told, 'Truly, I do not *know* you.'

Parable of the Talents

In the second parable in this series, Jesus illustrates a similar point (see Matt. 25:14-30). The master in this story entrusted varying amounts of his property to his *bondservants* before departing on a journey. By definition, a bondservant is one who has voluntarily committed himself to obedience out of love for his master. The first was entrusted with five talents and through his labor acquired five more. The second bondservant received two talents, earning two more through his labor. The third bondservant, however, willfully contrary to his master's wishes, dug a hole and hid the one talent with which he had been entrusted; out of sight, out of mind. [Note: The NIV footnote explains a talent was worth about twenty years' wages for a day laborer.]

When the master returned, the first two were rewarded for their work, praised by the master for their faithful attention to the portion they were given, and invited to enter into the master's joy. The third, however, demonstrated he neither knew his master nor used sound reasoning to justify his disobedience to the master's command. He kept his portion hidden for whatever reason—slothfulness, greater desire to fulfill his own agenda, etc. As a result, this bondservant received a scathing rebuke from his master who called him 'wicked and worthless,' had his talent taken away and given to the first bondservant, and was *not allowed to enter in*—he was cast to the place of weeping and gnashing of teeth.

Notice all three bondservants received their initial deposit freely; not because they earned it, but because the master had his own purposes in mind. This parable differs from the parable of the minas in that here each was given a different amount (though the principle is similar). Underscoring the unique nature of the charge God has ordained for each person, this parable reminds us we are not uniform bricks but living stones with different shapes. Because God apportions to each as He desires, we must be careful in making any judgments as to what constitutes a faithful or fruitful walk with the Lord when we evaluate our own or someone else's labor. Despising the day of small things will cause us to be unfaithful with what we've been given. If we judge our portion by comparing it with someone else's, we have cast wisdom aside (2 Cor. 10:12b).

> *Pay careful attention to your own work, for then you will get the satisfaction of a job well done, and you won't need to compare yourself to anyone else.* -Gal. 6:4, NLT

After receiving their initial portion, the first two bondservants labored in loving obedience to multiply the deposit they received, just as Jesus and the apostles likewise instructed believers to walk in obedient labor in the process of sanctification through the strength given by the Spirit. Afterward, the master praised their industrious work and welcomed them into his joy. The third, however, did nothing with his deposit. Because of this, what he had been freely given was taken away from him—he proved unfaithful. Even though he was a bondservant, he *did not hear* (sh'ma) his master's instruction, evidenced by his failure to follow through on his commitment to obey (2 Cor. 5:10).

Eternal Security

Remember our discussion of *sh'ma*, to hear with the resolve to obey? Circumcision of the heart through repentance is the spiritual equivalent of piercing the ear with an awl. Those so marked have pledged themselves to *sh'ma*. In light of the spiritual definition of what true hearing entails, we can look at the next passage with greater understanding.

> *My sheep **hear** (akouo) **My voice**, and **I know** (ginosko) **them**, and **they follow** (akoloutheo) **Me**. And I give them eternal life, and they shall never perish; **neither shall anyone snatch them out of My hand**.* -John 10:27-28, NKJV (parentheticals added)

In the opening phrase, Jesus stated His sheep **hear His voice**. We know this means to hear for the purpose of obeying, *unlike the third bondservant* in the second parable who was *willfully* disobedient. In new covenant language, this is the equivalent of resisting the Holy Spirit's guidance and refusing the strength He provides to accomplish God's will. By definition, a bondservant is one whose ear has been pierced in his voluntary pledge of obedience. *Akouo* means primarily 'to hear,' or 'to hearken,' implying intent to obey. It also means 'to hear with the mind,' indicating understanding of what has been heard.[8] Even with the Greek word, the primary thrust is to hear with the intent to obey, just as with the Hebrew equivalent, *sh'ma*. The main idea conveys the heart posture of one committed to obey the Master's voice. Though the third bondservant experienced repentance, he resisted his master's will and did not follow through on his commitment to obey.

Jesus then stated He **knows them**, unlike the five foolish virgins who were told the opposite. The use of the word *ginosko* signifies knowing through experience rather than only cognitively.[9] It is the same verb used when describing the intimacy of a husband and wife (Matt. 1:25; Luke 1:34). Paul described his zeal for the Corinthians to be presented as a pure virgin betrothed to Christ, their one Husband (2 Cor. 11:2). A virgin, by definition, is one who has pledged himself to Christ and shunned the world. Being one with Jesus is the goal of every believer pressing forward to possess the mind and character of Christ. The primary intent focuses on growth in the knowledge of God by abiding in the Word through the illumination of the Holy Spirit. Works for God without a heart engaged in ongoing and deepening intimacy with Him through study of the Word and fellowship in the Holy Spirit are not honored by God. The five foolish virgins failed to attend to their initial deposit of oil, perhaps focusing on works as the Ephesians did (Rev. 2:2-5). Jesus declared that even though the Ephesians had worked hard, they were in danger of losing their place because they had left their first love. The foundation and driving force behind our obedient works must be love for God. Jesus warned that those who focus only on works will hear this: 'Depart from Me, I never knew (*ginosko*) you' (Matt. 7:21-23).

Jesus' sheep are thirdly identified by the fact that they **follow Him** (*akoloutheo*: 'to be in the same way with'). The components that make up this word crudely mean 'to move quickly and straight, together on a path.' Zodhiates pinpoints the intended meaning: "The individual calling to follow Jesus involved abiding fellowship with Him, not only for the sake of learning as a scholar from his teacher, but also for the sake of salvation known or looked for, which presented itself in this fellowship. The first thing involved in following Jesus is a cleaving to Him in believing trust and obedience, those cleaving to Him also following His leading, acting according to His example. Hence the constant stress laid by the Lord Jesus upon the need for self-denial and fellowship with Him in the cross."[10] The concept of denying our wills so we can be obedient to God's will and purpose is again linked with our eternal destiny. The primary emphasis is on the believer's willingness to give up his personal goals, agenda, and rights to fulfill God's will.

These three components must be present in order to be called His sheep, who alone receive the gift of eternal life. To summarize, those who *hear* Jesus' voice as evidenced by obedience (*akouo*), are *known* by Jesus intimately through growing in knowledge of the Word by the Spirit (*ginosko*), and *follow* Jesus by giving up their own will to do His (*akoloutheo*), are His sheep and will be redeemed at Jesus' return. No one is able to snatch these out of His hand, ever.

SECTION 7 *DESTINATION OF BONDSERVANTS*

Shipwrecking Our Faith

> *Cling to your faith in Christ, and keep your conscience clear. For* **some people have deliberately violated their consciences**; *as a result, their faith has been shipwrecked.* -1 Tim. 1:19, NLT

Accepting the free gift of righteousness is the unearned deposit entrusted to us by God. The response of the bondservant to this gracious gift is to strive with all the power given him through the Holy Spirit so that the deposit bears fruit. This defines the will of God for everyone who has repented, accepted the righteousness of Christ, and received the Holy Spirit as a guarantee of their adoption as sons.

In the above passage, we learn it is possible to shipwreck our faith by not clinging to the faith we were given and by doing those things which lead to a sullied conscience. Repeatedly, we are warned that those who habitually walk in unrighteousness will not inherit the kingdom. If we do not strive to keep God's commands to love and obey, we will hear what all the disobedient dread to hear in that day: 'Depart from Me, I never knew you.'

While some teach belief alone keeps us in the hand of God for all eternity, the Scriptures teach otherwise. We do not earn righteousness in order to be reconciled with God, but our works are the evidence true faith exists. Jesus used the parable of the sower for a reason. The only evidence that the seed germinated and took root is the emergence of the plant. The initial deposit is hidden. We find the same object lesson in pregnancy. If a woman told you she was pregnant, you would expect to see a protruding abdomen by the second trimester. If abdominal growth is absent, you would assume she either had a miscarriage, an abortion, or perhaps was never pregnant in the first place. In the case of those who mistakenly thought they were pregnant with the purposes of God, they found they only gave birth to wind (cf. Isa. 26:18).

> *Jesus answered and said to them, "This is the work of God, that you believe in Him whom He sent."* -John 6:29, NKJV

In order to believe in the One sent by God, it is crucial we understand that the type of belief this passage describes includes all that Jesus taught *and did*. It is not merely believing He is the Son of God—the demons believe this and shudder, knowing their fate (James 2:19). In light of all Scripture, this means we embrace Jesus' teaching about the kingdom as well as the labor required on our part after we freely receive His righteousness. The Holy Spirit has assigned each believer a measure of faith, and out of this faith flow the works ordained for each to do—the believer's charge. Those led by the Spirit are the sons of God, dying daily to the desires of the flesh (Rom. 8:13-14).

Contending

> *Beloved, although I was very eager to write to you about our common salvation, I found it necessary to write* **appealing to you to contend for the faith** *that was once for all delivered to the saints.* -Jude 1:3, ESV

Jesus and the New Testament writers agree—through much toil and hardship we enter the kingdom. One can sense the urgency and alarm in the apostles' words when it became apparent some believers used the grace of God as an excuse to sin, while others did nothing with the deposit given to them. Many focused on self-accomplishment and adherence to religious ceremony to justify the righteousness of their walk. Still others used the gospel for their own profit or to cause division by focusing on debatable matters and issues of the law, hoping to attain a following of their own. Others, like the man who showed up to the wedding banquet improperly dressed, believed entering the kingdom of God is a 'come as you are' event, neglecting to don the robe provided. Like the Laodiceans, who fancied themselves wealthy and beyond reproach, these will be ashamed at His coming because they did not clothe themselves with the righteous acts God ordained for them to do, nor will they be clothed with righteous immortality.

The parables Jesus taught frequently developed themes of receiving punishment, suffering loss, or being disqualified because of:

- allowing the lure of the world to choke out the Word planted in our hearts (Matt. 13:22);
- using the duties of life as an excuse for neglecting our invitation (Matt. 22:1-14; Luke 14:16-24);
- shrinking back in anger, pain, or cowardice when trials beset us (Matt. 13:20-21);
- having knowledge of His will, but neglecting to do the works ordained for us (Matt. 25:14-30; Luke 12:47-48);
- not keeping our lamps burning by neglecting to get oil (Matt. 25:1-13);
- not forgiving others (Matt. 18:21-35);
- neglecting to abide in Christ, the Word (John 15:1-17);
- pride and self-righteousness; treating others with contempt (Luke 18:9-14);
- abusing the sheep entrusted to us (Luke 12:42-46);
- hoarding wealth for ourselves (Luke 12:16-21; 16:19-31);
- hearing the Word but not obeying it (Matt. 21:28-32; Luke 6:49);
- being barren in the faith we were given (Luke 13:6-9);
- neglecting the poor and needy (Matt. 25:31-46); and
- coming to repentance, but ignoring the process of sanctification (Luke 19:11-27).

Paul not only taught others to exercise self-control but also disciplined his own body to keep its desires under control so he would 'not be disqualified' (1 Cor. 9:27). Peter warned the believers not to 'lose their stability' by being carried away by the error of lawless people, whether in sin, legalism, or doctrinal error (2 Pet. 3:17). John admonished believers to be watchful so they would not lose what had been achieved, and to be diligent so they 'receive their full reward' (2 John 1:8). The author of Hebrews advised us to pursue holiness, being careful we do not 'fall short' of the grace given to us by God (Heb. 12:14-16).

Furthermore, Jesus and the apostles addressed the issue of being ashamed when Jesus returns. Jesus warned the Laodiceans, as previously mentioned, of the impending shame they would experience when their 'nakedness' would be brought to light at Jesus' return. When Jesus assessed this church in the area of their works, He stated they were neither hot nor cold but lukewarm. Jesus, the Word, stood at the door of their hearts, knocking to come in and have fellowship with them. It seems these believers were either unprovoked or ignorant of the necessity of developing their relationship with God through feasting on His Word. In addition, they were indifferent toward doing the works God ordained for them to do, preoccupied with their wealth and perhaps ignorant of the role works played in the process of salvation. They are counseled to buy eye salve so they can see their true condition—precarious because of a false confidence in ideology that ignores the reason for which they were saved, namely works.

Likewise, the apostles were concerned that we not suffer shame at Jesus' return. None who believe in Jesus will be put to shame (Rom. 10:11), but this word 'believe' does not merely mean mental ascent. *Pisteuo*, often translated 'belief' or 'faith,' comes from the word *pistis*, 'to be persuaded.' The one who is persuaded does not merely acknowledge teaching, but puts it into practice. John instructed us to abide in Jesus, which requires relationship. This means following His leading and adhering to the truth so we will not be ashamed at His coming (1 John 2:28). We are to be sober-minded and keep ourselves free from sin and therefore free from shame, unlike those who have no knowledge of God (1 Cor. 15:34).

Suffering Loss

Those who teach are held to a stricter standard (James 3:1). A bondservant who has been made a steward over other bondservants (see Luke 12:42-44) must be diligent to show himself approved by God through accurately handling God's Word (2 Tim. 2:15). Paul likened teaching to building, emphasizing that Jesus is the foundation (see 1 Cor. 3:10-15). Each person who teaches builds on this foundation with either gold, silver, and precious stones, or with hay, wood, and straw. At Jesus' return, fire will test what has been built. If the work survives the fire of God's scrutiny when held up to His eternal Word, that builder will receive a reward for having correctly handled the Word in what he taught. If a teacher's work is found unfaithful to the Word of God, all he has 'built' will be burned away and he will suffer loss. Though he himself will be saved, the one who built poorly and without care will come through this testing with only the smell of smoke to fill God's nostrils.

Surely the fear of the Lord is required when we build upon the gospel's foundation. Jude appealed to the believers to contend for the faith because ungodly people had wormed their way into the church, teaching that God's grace allows us to live immoral lives in direct contradiction to the Word (Jude 1:4). Jude described these people:

> [T]hey are **like dangerous reefs that can shipwreck you**. They are like **shameless shepherds who care only for themselves**. They are like clouds blowing over the

*land without giving any rain. They are like trees in autumn that are **doubly dead**, for they **bear no fruit** and have been **pulled up by the roots**. They are like wild waves of the sea, churning up the foam of their shameful deeds. **They are like wandering stars, doomed forever to blackest darkness.*** -Jude 1:12-13, NLT

We cannot drift along with every wind of teaching that comes our way, lest we be taken in the error of others and shipwreck our own faith. Whether we accept teaching is not a matter of checking the reputation of those who would be our leaders. Neither is acceptance of doctrine determined by simplistically granting someone the right to dictate our beliefs by virtue of impressive credentials, such as a doctorate of theology, a prestigious position on a denominational board, an honorable appointment on a faculty, or a seat of authority in Rome. We are instructed to be diligent and watchful, checking everything against the sum of God's Word.

Losing Our Position

As far as the believer who returns to a life of sin, Peter and the author of Hebrews warn us that those who turn from righteousness to embrace a life of sin will not be saved. Ezekiel also recorded God's words on this matter, and the passage can be broken down into two thoughts. First, the righteous behavior of righteous people will not save them if they turn to sin. And second, the wicked behavior of wicked people will not destroy them if they repent and turn from their sins (Ezk. 33:12).

Regarding the righteous who turn to sin, the Lord further states:

> *When I tell righteous people that they will live, but then they sin, expecting their past righteousness to save them, then none of their righteous acts will be remembered. I will destroy them for their sins.* -Ezk. 33:13, NLT

The Lord then expounds on the wicked who turn from their sin, as Nineveh did:

> *And suppose I tell some wicked people that they will surely die, but then they turn from their sins and do what is just and right. For instance, they might give back a debtor's security, return what they have stolen, and obey my life-giving laws, no longer doing what is evil. If they do this, then they will surely live and not die. None of their past sins will be brought up again, for they have done what is just and right, and they will surely live.* -Ezk. 33:14-16, NLT

When the people of Israel heard this, they protested that it wasn't fair (Ezk. 33:17). The Lord then repeated what He had already said (Ezk. 33:18-19), indicating the matter had been decided (cf. Gen. 41:32). At the close of this section of Scripture, God reminds us that He judges each person according to their works (v. 20), a concept carried over into the New Testament (Matt. 16:27; 1 Cor. 3:13-15; 1 Pet. 1:17; Titus 1:16; James 2:2,9,13,19-20; Rev. 2-3). The deeds that have been ordained for us to do (confessing faith in Jesus, knowing truth, helping the needy, overcoming our sin nature, having compassion on the poor, etc.)

are not to be confused with religious or ceremonial works (lighting candles, celebrating holy days or Sabbaths, dietary restrictions, etc.). Being *judged* by works is not the same thing as being *justified* by Christ. We are *justified* freely when we come to repentance and believe in Christ, accepting His righteousness by faith. This allows us to be *judged* at His return when our works either vindicate or condemn us by providing evidence of what we have done with the deposit we have freely received. Put differently, those in Christ are judged on their works when He returns, having had all sin removed; those steeped in sin will be judged for their works with their sin still clinging to them—requiring the sentence of death—at the end of Jesus' millennial reign (Rev. 20:11-15; Dan. 12:2).

> *O people of Israel, you are saying, 'The Lord isn't doing what's right.' But I judge each of you according to your deeds.* -Ezk. 33:20, NLT

On the issue of a believer falling from grace, the book of Hebrews makes certain we have no question about this. By first spelling out precisely the targeted subject, the author leaves little room for doubt that he is referring to believers who had experienced true repentance but later turn back to be slaves of sin (parentheticals/bullets added):

> *For it is impossible, in the case of those who have:*
>
> ♦ once been enlightened (*photizo*; made to see/understand; cf. Eph. 1:18; Heb. 10:32)
> ♦ tasted (*geuo*; experienced) the heavenly gift
> ♦ shared (*metochos*; partaker) in the Holy Spirit (given *only* to the truly repentant)
> ♦ tasted (*geuo*; experienced) the goodness of the Word of God
> ♦ and [have experienced] the powers of the age to come,
>
> *and then have fallen away, to restore them again to repentance.* -Heb. 6:4-6a, ESV

Why is this? Unlike the old covenant, which provided for the reinstatement of physical lepers to right standing in the covenant through a repetition of the ceremony of sprinkling, there is no more sacrifice for sin under the new covenant. There is only one sacrifice that provided the blood of sprinkling for the new covenant, the death of Jesus on the cross. Everyone who repents has received the blood of sprinkling, placing them under the new covenant in Jesus' blood and providing them with power over sin. For those who later return to sin, giving themselves over to it by hardening their hearts to the cleansed conscience they received, there is no more sacrifice for sin (Heb. 6:6b-8).

Peter testified to this same theme, making certain to clearly spell out that true believers are the subject of his warning (note the use of *epignosis*: clear, exact knowledge; and *epiginosko*: fully acquainted):

> **For if, after they have escaped the defilements of the world through the knowledge (epignosis) of our Lord and Savior Jesus Christ**, they are **again entangled** in them **and overcome**, the last state has become worse for them than the first. For it would have been **better for them never to have known (epiginosko) the way of righteousness than after knowing it to turn back** *from the holy commandment delivered to them.* -2 Pet. 2:20-21, ESV (parenthetical added)

The reason they are worse off in the second state is that in their first condition, hope of reconciliation exists through coming to repentance. This condition must be differentiated from the believer in a backslidden state. A backslidden Christian knows what they are doing is wrong. Even though they are deriving some benefit or pleasure from their sin, they still have guilt over it. Another example of a backslidden believer is the one who has drifted from the Lord by pursuing worldly goals, consuming all his time and energy in the process. Yet even while pursuing fame, fortune, or 'the American dream,' he senses a constant nagging in the back of his mind that gnaws at his conscience to turn back to God. These backslidden are not lost, but they are in danger of crossing the line into a seared conscience and hardened heart. We must pay attention to the internal promptings of the Holy Spirit, lest like Samson we don't even notice when the Spirit of God has left us to our own desires.

> *Therefore, since the promise of entering his rest still stands,* **let us be careful** *that none of you be* **found to have fallen short** *of it.* -Heb. 4:1, NIV

After reading all the apostles have to say on the matter of warning believers of the danger of being ensnared again by sin, we must pause to ask, 'Why?' If the believer has eternal security by his decision to accept Christ's righteousness, with no possibility of losing that security through defiant, habitual sin, then why did the apostles use up so much ink to warn believers they could fall short of entering into this salvation through entrapment to sin? The Word gives us the answer: the wages of sin is still death.

Inheritance in God

> *Blessed are the meek, for they shall inherit the earth.* -Matt. 5:5, NKJV

The meek are those who do not demand their rights but move in humility for the greater good. They forbear and yield rather than assert themselves in situations which warrant this response. Quiet confidence in the ways and will of their Master, these will not judge by what they see with their eyes or hear with their ears, but wait for the Lord to provide the just solution each situation merits (cf. Isa. 11:3-4). These are the ones to whom God will entrust governance of the earth under the headship of Jesus.

Our inheritance in God has two major components: eternal life and adoption as sons. It is 'imperishable, undefiled, and unfading, kept for us who are being guarded through faith for a salvation *to be revealed* in the last time' (1 Pet. 1:4-5). When Jesus returns, our mortal bodies are transformed to immortal bodies, finalizing our adoption into the family of God.

> *Just as we have borne the image of the man of dust,* **we shall also bear the image of the man of heaven***... When the perishable puts on the imperishable, and the mortal puts on immortality, then shall come to pass the saying that is written: "Death is swallowed up in victory."* -1 Cor. 15:49,54, ESV

SECTION 7 *DESTINATION OF BONDSERVANTS*

Those who are dead in Christ will be transformed first, rising from their graves at the sound of His voice, just as Lazarus was raised. Those who are alive at His coming will be caught up together with these departed saints to be in the presence of the Lord forever (1 Thes. 4:14-18). Because Jesus' resurrection took place as prophesied, we have confidence that our inheritance will also take place just as God promised. David prophesied of this hope (as quoted by Peter; Acts 2:25-28), that we who are the Lord's:

- will not be shaken because the Lord is at our right hand to help;
- are given knowledge of the path or way to life;
- dwell in hope of resurrection, knowing our souls will not be abandoned in death; and
- will be full of joy in His presence forever.

> *Christ died for us so that, whether we are dead or alive when he returns, we can live with him forever.* -1 Thes. 5:10, NLT

We experience eternal life in a limited way in this life by walking in the Spirit and growing in our understanding of truth. Increasing our knowledge of God gives us a foretaste of eternity by placing us in His presence by the power of the Holy Spirit. The Word reveals God's nature and desires. This also prepares the ground of our hearts to walk in agreement with God's prophetic plan for the close of the age and the millennial reign of Christ.

> *And **this is eternal life, that they may know** (ginosko) **You**, the only true God, and Jesus Christ whom You have sent.* -John 17:3, NKJV (parenthetical added)

This spark of eternal life is present in us in this age as we come to know God through study of the Word and the power of the Spirit. This spark is what Jesus will be looking for when He returns to reign. The kingdom of God will fill the earth (Dan. 2:34-35,44-45), and the bondservants of Christ will inherit that kingdom. They will reign with Him, exercising judicial powers in the millennial kingdom in the capacity to which they are appointed (Rev. 20:6; cf. Luke 19:17). Just as Jesus became a bondservant with respect to the Father's will without jeopardizing His position as Son, we also have a dual role, progressing from bondservants and friends to full adoption as sons. Sons with the character of Christ delight in doing the Father's will, not out of duty but born of love. Adoption as sons makes us heirs with Christ.

> *When Christ who is our life appears, then you also will appear with Him in glory.* -Col.3:4, NKJV

Paul instructed that although we have been grafted in, we can be cut off if we don't continue to abide in Christ. Likewise, those who turn from unbelief can be grafted back in (Rom. 11:20-23). As stated earlier, this is nothing new and is proof that God not only delights in showing mercy but is also serious about dealing with sin (Ezk. 33:10-20). By looking at the entire counsel of both Old and New Testament writers, it becomes apparent that only with continued attention to our sanctification and the will of God will we be found faithful at Jesus' return.

Ask yourself this question: When the rich young ruler asked what he must do to inherit eternal life, how did Jesus respond? Did He say, 'Just believe that I have taken away your sins?' No, he told the young man to do something—to give away his wealth and take care of the poor. From Jesus' own teaching we are to understand that entrance into the kingdom is granted to those who have been declared righteous by the blood of Christ, *and* who then strive to complete the work given to them (cf. Matt. 5:13).

Part of the work ordained specifically for each believer is designed to take him to the place of overcoming those things which have gripped the heart's affection in an inordinate way. For the wealthy, greedy, and covetous, their work will entail giving away those things they have accumulated that are not necessary. For the lustful, their challenge will be to remain faithful to their spouse. For the cowardly, their 'work' will be to make public confession of their faith. For the intellectual, the Lord may just give them divine insight, which is foolishness to the natural man who takes pride in his intellect. For those proud and conceited because of their status and reputation, the Lord may require humble service doing menial tasks among the believers. The works we have been given to do may not be 'works' in the sense of our own preconceived definition, but those things which help us to be overcomers of our character flaws and deficiencies when measured against the character of Christ.

Being set free from sin entails more than being forgiven for our sins. It also encompasses empowerment *not* to sin. By this freedom we are no longer slaves to sin but to God. There isn't a third choice—we are slaves of one or the other. Being a slave to self is slavery to sin. The fruit of repentance leads to sanctification, and the goal of sanctification is eternal life. Only in Jesus will we find this life (1 John 5:11-12), and it is intrinsically linked to piety and knowing truth through the process of sanctification by the power of the Spirit (Titus 1:1-2). Paul warned us not to be deceived in thinking those who participate in habitual wrong-doing *as God defines it* will inherit life (1 Cor. 6:9-10).

To truly know God involves understanding the importance of the finished work of the cross. We are no longer bound to sin and have received an avenue back to God. With repentance comes the desire to obey. The gift of the Holy Spirit enables us to accomplish this. Those who receive eternal life abide in God's presence, increasing in their knowledge and affection toward Him. Eternal life is yet another identity of our Savior:

> *The life appeared; we have seen it and testify to it,* **and we proclaim to you the eternal life***, which was with the Father and has appeared to us.* -1 John 1:2, NIV

We have eternal life if we:

- have been declared righteous by grace through faith in Christ, leading to devotion to good works (Titus 3:7-8);
- hear His Word and believe God sent Jesus (John 5:24);
- forsake our lives for His sake (Matt. 19:29);

SECTION 7 *DESTINATION OF BONDSERVANTS*

- feed on the Word and take part in the new covenant (John 6:54);
- sow to please the Spirit (Gal. 6:8);
- fight the good fight of faith, actively taking hold of eternal life (1 Tim. 6:12);
- trust in God and not our wealth, evidenced by freely sharing what we have (1 Tim. 6:17-19);
- know the truth about how to live a godly life and pursue that end (Titus 1:1-2);
- abide in Christ and walk in obedience as He demonstrated (1 John 2:5-6);
- keep away from anything that would take God's place in our hearts, for He is eternal life (1 John 5:20-21); and
- have the seal of the Holy Spirit, guaranteeing our inheritance (Eph. 1:13-14).

We do not have eternal life abiding in us if we hate our brother, which is murder (1 John 3:15), or sow to please the flesh (Gal. 6:8). Sowing to please the flesh includes greed, division, discord, selfish ambition, envy, anger, and hatred, as well as doing things our own way. Although these sins of the heart and mouth cannot be legislated against, they are abominable just the same. The New Testament writers provided lists of negative behaviors that disqualify those who will be denied entrance to God's kingdom (1 Cor. 6:9-10; Gal. 5:19-21; Eph. 5:5; Rev. 21:8). 'Do not be deceived,' and 'do not fool yourselves'—those who habitually and with a seared conscience practice these sins will not inherit the kingdom (1 Cor. 6:9), which will be on earth (Rev. 19:11-15; 20:4-21:7).

> *The righteous will never be removed, but the wicked will not inhabit the earth.*
> -Pr. 10:30, NKJV

Paul wrote we can be sure 'anyone living this sort of life will not inherit the kingdom' (Eph. 5:5; Gal. 5:21). None who practice these things will inherit the kingdom because the evidence of ongoing sin denies the presence of repentance or the Holy Spirit. The author of Hebrews unequivocally warned that those who give up their inheritance for the fleeting pleasures and self-indulgences of this life will not be able to regain it after the 'door is shut,' no matter the weeping and gnashing of teeth through which they might seek to regain that inheritance (Heb. 12:16-17).

Notice in the next passage that the unbelieving are listed separately. Put differently, unbelievers and those who think they are saved but are cowards (those who shrink back from the will of God or are gripped with the fear of man), liars, fornicators, and so on, will not receive what they had hoped for because they were deceived into believing the doctrine of cheap grace. [Note: This is not referring to the person who struggles with these issues from time to time, or even on a regular basis, but to those who have a seared conscience and *habitually sin without remorse*.]

> *But the cowards, unbelievers, vile, murderers, sexually immoral, sorcerers, idolaters, and all liars—their share will be in the lake that burns with fire and sulfur, which is the second death.* -Rev. 21:8, HCSB

Eternal life is linked to the idea of feeding on God's Word and accomplishing His will in His strength. Evidence we are on the way to life requires obeying God's command to love others through acts of compassion and mercy, and crucifying our carnal or worldly desires. We are warned by the example of Esau not to give up our inheritance for a fleeting indulgence of our flesh (Heb. 12:16).

> *Do not labor for the food that perishes, but for the food that endures to eternal life, which the Son of Man will give to you. For on him God the Father has set his seal.* -John 6:27, ESV

The presence of the Holy Spirit in our lives guarantees what is to come. If we have been like the five foolish virgins, who ignored this part of their salvation, we will be shocked by what happens at Jesus' return. Like Samson and King Saul who did not know that the Spirit of God had left them (Jdg. 16:20; 1 Sam. 16:14), those who continually and habitually do things their own way will be utterly stupefied and possibly outraged to find the door to the kingdom has been closed to them. We must exert effort now to enter into the promise of eternal life because our inheritance is not automatic. It comes through self-denial and heeding the voice of the Holy Spirit.

> *[D]o not become sluggish, but imitate those who **through faith and patience inherit the promises**.* -Heb. 6:12, NKJV

The Overcomer's Crown

An imperishable crown of glory awaits those who faithfully persevere (1 Cor. 9:25). Peter described a crown of glory, never fading, given to those who have been faithful in their leadership as an example to the flock, not for monetary gain or using their position to domineer (1 Pet. 5:1-4). Whether the crown of righteousness awarded to all those who long for His appearing (2 Tim. 4:8) is the same or different from the crown of life given to those who love the Lord and persevere under trial (James 1:12; Rev. 2:10) remains unclear to me. It is obvious only those who are obedient to Him would long for His return. The rest anxiously put this thought out of their minds, hoping they can do as they please and turn to God in time to be saved.

The New Testament speaks of two types of crowns. The *stephanos* crown is given as a symbol of honor for accomplishment. The *diadem* crown is conferred upon one given authority to rule. The *stephanos* crown was typically made of leaves or flowers, and was given to the victor of a race, those who displayed valor in battle, or those who made noteworthy contributions to benefit the community—any praiseworthy action. It is a crown given for deeds judged as genuine, venerable, and in compliance with established criteria (cf. 2 Tim. 2:5). *Stephanos* crowns were also worn by bride and groom and at other joyful celebrations. All of these describe activities of believers. *Stephanos* is used each time we see a reference to a crown believers receive at the Lord's return.

SECTION 7 *DESTINATION OF BONDSERVANTS*

The *diadem* is only mentioned three times in the New Testament: once in reference to the seven diadems of the dragon, Satan (Rev. 12:3); once in reference to the ten diadems of the beast from the sea, the 'antichrist' (Rev. 13:1); and once in reference to the many diadems Jesus wears when He returns to rule the kingdoms of the earth (Rev. 19:12). Prior to Jesus' return, the author of Hebrews reminds us that we do not yet see everything in subjection to Jesus, but He has been crowned (*stephanos*) because He was obedient through His suffering and death (Heb. 2:8-9). Before Jesus' *de facto diadem* is conferred and His royal reign inaugurated, Satan has been given authority over the earth. In the last days, Satan will give that authority to a man who will do what Jesus would not—worship (obey) him in order to have authority and power over the kingdoms of the earth.

Receiving the crown of life is reserved for the faithful overcomers. In the discussion of the seven churches, crowns are only mentioned in the discussions of Smyrna and Philadelphia, the two churches found without fault when Jesus judged their works. Our patience and perseverance in the process of sanctification is vitally important, worth all the attention we can give to its completion.

> *I am coming soon. Hold fast what you have, so that no one may seize your crown.* -Rev 3:11, ESV

Closing Thoughts

> *Eye has not seen, nor ear heard, nor have entered into the heart of man the things which God has prepared for those who love Him.* -1 Cor. 2:9, NKJV

The genuineness of our faith is of greater worth than gold precisely because of God's promise to adopt His bondservants as sons. For this reason, Paul could say without hesitation that he considered all he had achieved and possessed as loss in comparison with the surpassing worth of knowing Jesus as Lord (Php. 3:8). Embracing Jesus not only as the author of our faith (justification), but also as the finisher of it (sanctification of our inner man and redemption of our bodies), places us in a position of eternal security. It is to the thirsty and the overcomers that Jesus made these promises:

> *I will give of the fountain of the water of life freely to him who thirsts.* **He who overcomes shall inherit all things**, *and I will be his God and he shall be My son.* -Rev. 21:6-7, NKJV

The importance of leaning on the Word and the Spirit in this age cannot be stressed enough. Doing so will fuel our passion for more of God's presence in our lives as well as equip us to separate ourselves from sin and those things the world values. Those who voluntarily embrace the role of bondservant through obedience to the charge given to them by God will also become the friends of God as they abide in the Word. These friends of God receive discernment of the times and have wisdom for the hour in which

CHAPTER 22 ADOPTION AS SONS

they live, described by some as the Issachar anointing. They understand the plans and purposes of God as He makes them known in His timing.

Those who: 1.) treasure their relationship with the Lord, evidenced by growing love for God and His ways, 2.) keep the charge entrusted to them by the power of the Holy Spirit, 3.) follow Jesus' example of self-denial no matter the cost, and 4.) are not ashamed of His Word, will find themselves in good standing at Jesus' return (Matt. 7:21-23; Mark 8:38; John 10:27-28; 1 John 2:28). While this may not be lived out perfectly, just as in David's imperfect life, the heart can be postured 'perfectly' before God.

The author of Hebrews recorded that the Lord is not ashamed to call 'brothers' those who are *being sanctified* (Heb. 2:11). Later in Hebrews, he also wrote that God is not ashamed to be the God of those who *long for the heavenly city* He has prepared for them (Heb. 11:16). Our hearts must be focused on completing the course of sanctification uniquely created for us and postured to long for His kingdom.

Cooperating with the Holy Spirit and allowing the Word to reset our thinking to be synchronized with God's defines our responsibility in the salvation we have been given. The power we receive when we come to Christ gives us everything we need for a godly life through ever increasing knowledge of God. The promises we have been given are great and precious, enabling us to actually participate in the divine nature of God. For this reason, we make every effort to cooperate with the Holy Spirit's work in our lives to bring forth fruit that is pleasing to God, adding to the faith we have received the traits of goodness, knowledge, self-control, perseverance, godliness, harmony, and love (2 Pet. 1:5-7).

> **[W]ork hard to prove** *that you really are among those God has called and chosen.* **Do these things, and you will never fall away.** *Then God will give you a grand entrance into the eternal Kingdom of our Lord and Savior Jesus Christ.*
> -2 Pet. 1:10-11, NLT

In closing this discussion on the bondservant's eternal destiny, I would like to take the words from Paul's prayer to the Thessalonians and pray them for every single reader who persevered through this entire book:

> *We keep on praying for you, asking our God to enable you to live a life worthy of his call. May he give you the power to accomplish all the good things your faith prompts you to do.* -2 Thes. 1:11, NLT

Amen.

Epilogue

> *I love my master... I will not go out free.* -Ex. 21:5, ESV

Voluntarily reading a book this size is an accomplishment. Those who have made it this far have demonstrated they have both hunger and perseverance. Throughout this book, I have attempted to emphasize the need for the believer to view his relationship with God as a bondservant who walks in the dual identity as a son. The various disciplines and doctrines discussed were chosen to give a broad foundation and provide the basic understanding needed for walking in this identity. The bondservant identity lived authentically before the Lord in spirit and truth leads to friendship with God, the place where God reveals His prophetic plans. Our desire to study prophecy will be frustrated if we have not taken time to know our God and walk in the fundamental commands to love God with all our heart, soul, mind, and strength, and our neighbor as ourselves.

By understanding the foundational concepts presented, the believer can be freed from self-condemnation and a religious spirit that insists on uniformity in religious practice. This will, in turn, foster unity in the body of Christ. Realizing that correctly dividing the Word of God requires the Spirit's intervention helps us grow in our dependence on Him. Spiritual disciplines incite us to grow in our relationship with God and share in His heart. Understanding the role of our Adversary and his goal to prevent us from entering into life keeps us sober and vigilant, aiding our grasp for the need to forbear with others who are also struggling in their effort to overcome sin and temptation. Knowing the glorious and eternal outcome of believers helps us focus on what truly matters. Each section of this book was written with the goal of laying a solid foundation from which the bondservant could walk out his faith in love toward God and his fellowman unencumbered by doubt, misgivings, or the need to control and criticize others who think or practice differently on side issues.

Challenging mindsets that impose unnecessary barriers to fellowship provokes us to take a step back from our own traditions to seek the mind of Christ. Believers who remain indifferent to the need for unity in the body of Christ forego sharing God's heart in this regard. A study of John 17 bears this out. With great earnestness, Jesus prayed that His followers would be one. This requires we love one another and that the main thing must always remain the main thing: Jesus has saved us from death, we must strive to enter into the kingdom, and He is coming back to redeem our physical bodies and appoint us to reign with Him in His kingdom.

The journey we undertake to gain understanding of the Word requires perseverance. I want to encourage you to pursue your own study of the Word and to be anxious for nothing. I began my study of the Bible without even knowing the role of the Holy Spirit to teach and illuminate the Scriptures. I started as one steeped in the ways of the world with many religious traditions I took for granted were scriptural. Though I had a professional degree, I had no training in biblical studies to speak of.

Perhaps you have training in an unrelated field as well. Let me assure you—God has leveled the playing field when it comes to understanding His Word. He will not turn away those who hunger and thirst and place themselves humbly before the Word and Spirit to gain understanding of and intimacy with their heavenly Father.

> *The Lord is like a father to his children, tender and compassionate to those who fear him.*
> -Ps. 103:13, NLT

But remember, understanding does not come without effort. Thomas Edison persevered through one failure after another to find the right material for his incandescent bulb. He was determined to accomplish his goal to bring the world inexpensive light through electricity and undaunted by thousands of failures. How much more should followers of Christ be determined to lay hold of the eternal light of truth!

> *The entrance and unfolding of Your words give light; their unfolding gives understanding (discernment and comprehension) to the simple.* -Ps. 119:130, AMP

Amos was a farmer, David a shepherd, and the disciples were common laborers. God is no respecter of persons. Before you think you are disqualified from being a bondservant of God or don't have the ability to understand God's Word, read this list that has been circulated on the web. If it doesn't make you smile, you are taking yourself too seriously. The next time you feel like God can't use you, remember...

- Noah got drunk
- Abraham was too old
- Sarah laughed at God's promise
- Isaac was a daydreamer
- Jacob was a liar
- Leah was average looking, not a beauty queen
- Joseph was abused, a slave, and a prisoner
- Moses was slow of speech
- Gideon was afraid
- Samson had long hair and was a womanizer
- Rahab was a prostitute
- Jeremiah and Timothy were too young
- David had an affair and was a murderer
- Elijah was suicidal
- Jonah didn't show up for work
- Naomi was a widow
- Job went bankrupt
- Esther was fearful
- John the Baptist ate bugs
- The Centurion and Syrophoenecian woman had racial issues
- Peter succumbed to man-pleasing
- The disciples fell asleep while praying
- Martha worried about everything
- The Samaritan woman was divorced, more than once
- Zacchaeus was too small and a swindler
- Paul was a religious fanatic and a parolee
- Timothy had an ulcer...
- And Lazarus was *dead*!

This demonstrates that the Lord will always work with what we've got if we turn to Him. He takes our five loaves and two fishes and multiplies them to create a banquet.

Remember the Levites, who came to the Lord's side during the golden calf fiasco? Originally, the Lord had set aside the firstborn of each Israelite family to serve Him in the sanctuary. But the Levites demonstrated their loyalty to God with zeal for the honor of His name when all Israel went astray at Sinai. Therefore God took the Levites instead (Ex. 32:29; Num. 3:41,45). This is a picture of who He is looking for today—those whose hearts are loyal to Him and have zeal for His purposes. For those in Christ, there is no distinction as to race, status, gender, age, education, or physical ability to disqualify anyone. Heart posture and the righteousness of Christ are the only considerations for inclusion in the service of God.

> *I will not leave you as orphans.* -John 14:18, ESV

We are never alone, for Jesus promised to never leave us or forsake us. In addition, the Lord sets the lonely in families (Ps. 68:6). For the repentant, God's presence is *real*. God has given us His Word and His Spirit to supply all we need. Oftentimes, it is while we are in the Word that we sense His presence. He is waiting and watching over those who are His. When we are overwhelmed, we can run to Him and find the refuge we need. He takes us to a place that is above self and the cares of this world. With a broader perspective—*God's* perspective—we can overcome all things.

> *From the end of the earth I will cry to You, when my heart is overwhelmed; lead me to the rock that is higher than I.* -Ps. 61:2, NKJV

Studying the Word of God does not have to break the bank. Having your own library of reference and other materials may be convenient, but all that is really needed to start is a Bible. I personally love the *Daily Bible* with comments by F. LaGard Smith for those starting out. It uses the NIV, which is written in today's English, and places the text of the Bible in chronological order. It is divided into 365 readings, and the comments give background information on the passage introduced. This Bible is ideal for those who have had trouble getting started or sticking with reading the Bible all the way through.

Even buying a Bible is not actually needed if you have computer access because of the many versions available online. There are dozens of other resources available as well, including thousands of articles on every subject (though these must be read with discernment). If you don't have a computer at home, you can use the computers at your local library. The only real requirement for Bible study is time, though I highly recommend getting copies of Spiros Zodhiates' *Complete Word Study* for both Old and New Testaments (neither are available online that I am aware of).

Some excellent resources can be found on these web sites, including various translations, commentaries, concordances, lexicons, interlinear texts, parallel texts, bible encyclopedias and dictionaries, Hebrew and Greek grammar decoding, and historical information:

biblegateway.com	biblestudytools.com	mechon-mamre.org
biblos.com	bible-history.com	preceptaustin.org
studylight.org	Scripture4all.org	sacred-texts.com

The thought that God pursues a relationship with us may be new to some. This idea is expressed in a striking way by Francis Thompson (1859-1907), former opium addict, in his poem, "The Hound of Heaven," chronicling a hound chasing a hare. "As the hound follows the hare, never ceasing in its running, ever drawing nearer in the chase, with unhurrying and imperturbed pace, so does God follow the fleeing soul by His Divine grace. And though in sin or in human love, away from God it seeks to hide itself, Divine grace follows after, unwearyingly follows ever after, till the soul feels its pressure forcing it to turn to Him alone in that never ending pursuit."[1]

After reading this poem, David Scott wrote, "God is 'our Father in heaven,' as Jesus taught us to pray to him. He is the origin and goal of our lives, and the loving sustainer of all points in between. He put us here. He knows where we came from, where we have been, and where we are now. And he knows where we should be heading—always on the road back to him. In his poem, Thompson calls God 'this tremendous Lover.' He is out to get us. He hounds our days and hounds our nights. He knows what we need even before we ask, and he knows that he alone is what each of us is searching for... This is the God revealed in the pages of the Scriptures. The drama begins with God making the first man and woman in his own image to share his life. Quickly his children spurn his love. He pursues them, calls to them with words that will resound through the pages of biblical history, and in every human heart today—'Where are you?' God, the Hound of Heaven."[2]

God reveals Himself in His creation and His Word, and we must turn aside to pursue understanding and discipline ourselves to diligently seek truth. It will cost us everything this life has to offer, yet we will gain the peace that passes all understanding.

Most leaders in the church today are desirous of going deeper in the Word to know truth. Some, however, are interested in acquiring truth only if they do not have to change their long-held and cherished beliefs, even if those beliefs do not line up with the Word of God. All of the builders (teachers of the Word) will give an account before God and are held to a stricter judgment. To stick with faulty doctrine to save face now will cause great shame when we stand before Christ. We must choose today who we will serve: our denomination, or the King of kings; our comfortable religious views, or the Way, the Truth, and the Life; the teaching complacent congregants crave, or the truth that will set them free.

> There is no greater adventure than the true Christian life, and there is nothing more boring than religion. -Rick Joyner

If you are frustrated in your walk as a believer, let me encourage you to persevere in nurturing your relationship with the Lord through reading the Word. An unknown author wrote, "Make time for the quiet moments, as God whispers and the world is loud." We can't hear His voice if our mind is overloaded with worldly traffic. Declutter your schedule to make room for the One who loves and desires you. It may mean something as simple as giving up watching the news in the morning. Involve yourself in a group of believers who love the Lord and cherish His Word. This may be a group of friends and family, a house church, or even a much larger traditional church. Whatever the case may be, the Spirit of God is in the midst of those who fear Him and take His Word to heart. Their conversations are recorded in God's book of remembrance (Mal. 3:16-18).

> *Finally, all of you, have unity of mind, sympathy, brotherly love, a tender heart, and a humble mind.* -1 Pet. 3:8, ESV

Michael W. Smith and Christine Dente sang a song entitled, "Prepare a Place." Though this is a Christmas song, the words are appropriate as a call for every believer at all times, especially as we approach the close of this age.

Prepare a Place

Prepare a place, while you're waiting.
Prepare a place for the coming One.
Prepare a place and be patient,
While you wait for the coming One.

> Prepare your heart, while you're waiting.
> Prepare your heart for the coming One.
> Set time aside and be quiet,
> While you wait for the coming One.

Abraham was God's friend, and he kept God's *mishmereth* in his generation. *Mishmereth* can be interpreted as the 'watch' or 'charge' of God given to each person in his generation. Many have shunned the small part they were given to do, proving themselves unfaithful to God's charge. From geometry and physics, we know if a spacecraft's trajectory is off by only a fraction of a degree, it will completely miss its target. Likewise, because so many in the church have ignored the watch given to them by God, deeming it as insignificant or unworthy of their time or attention, the church has missed the mark as well. But through resolve, courage, and obedience, this can change.

Most of us are unsure of the charge we have been given by God. Viktor Frankl, an Austrian neurologist/psychiatrist and Holocaust survivor, shared words of wisdom that can be applied to the believer searching for the charge God has specifically given to him:

> Don't aim at success—the more you aim at it and make it a target, the more you are going to miss it. For success, like happiness, cannot be pursued; it must ensue... **as the unintended side effect of one's personal dedication to a course greater than oneself.** -Viktor Frankl

We find our charge as we spend our energy getting to know our God through the Word and extending His love in practical ways to those we meet. This must be our focus if we are to be found faithful. For the bondservant, guarding the purposes of God entrusted to him in his generation, no matter how small, is a mark of friendship with God and the mandate by which he prioritizes his life. Each believer must keep the charge God has given him. Faithfulness in doing our part will make an eternal difference, no matter how small the duty or how little time we have left. This is the mark of the bondservant's loyalty and pledge.

> *I will stand my watch at my guard post, and station myself at the lookout tower, to watch what He will say to me.* -Hab. 2:1

Abraham Lincoln said, "In the end, it's not the years in your life that count. It's the life in your years." Putting 'life' into our years comes through relationship with Jesus, 'the Way, the Truth, and *the Life*.' We may not have started strong, but by the grace of God and the power of His might, we can finish strong. That is what God is looking for, and that is what He remembers. For the repentant, the judgment seat of Christ is not so much about ministry accomplishment as it is how well we loved both God and our fellow man in thought, word, and deed. Without this love, everything we've done is judged as 'nothing'—burned away leaving only a cloud of smoke. Therefore, forgetting what lies behind, we press on for the prize that awaits—the redemption of our bodies and eternity in the presence of God.

> *We have come to know and have believed the love which God has for us. God is love, and the one who abides in love abides in God, and God abides in him. By this, love is perfected with us, so that we may have confidence in the day of judgment; because as He is, so also are we in this world.* -1 John 4:16-17, NKJV

END NOTES

PREFACE
1. Mike Bickle taught this Jan. 30, 1999, as a guest speaker at a church I was visiting in Colorado.
2. Whipkey, Randall L. & Calvin J. Hamilton. Copyright 2000-2007. http://www.crpuzzles.com/logic/logic0133.html
3. Logic Problem Solution: Sally Salada bought a different number of lbs., from 1-5, of each of the five items she purchased at the Meyersdale Farmers Market. By clue 1, three of the items that Sally bought are red lettuce, the fruit or vegetable she bought at the Raindrop Acres stand, and the one of which she purchased 1 lb. By clue 4, Sally bought more white potatoes than of what she picked at Freshly Fruit & Vegetables, so the white potatoes aren't the 1 lb. purchase in clue 1; and by clue 7, she didn't get the white potatoes at the Raindrop Acres stand. Therefore, the white potatoes are the fourth item purchased to the three in clue 1. Sally didn't buy the white potatoes (4), red lettuce, or fruit/vegetable of which she got 1 lb. (8) at the Freshly Fruits & Vegetables stand. Therefore, the purchase at the Freshly Fruits & Vegetables stand is the fifth to the four already named. By clue 3, Sally Salada made a 2 lb. purchase at Grow Bros. Produce. Since her purchase at Freshly Fruits & Vegetables was for more than 1 lb. (8), by clue 4, she bought at least 3 lbs. of white potatoes. So, Sally bought 2 lbs. of red lettuce at the Grow Bros. Produce stand. Her purchase of 5 lbs. of Granny Smith apples (5) wasn't at Freshly Fruits & Produce (4) and was at the Raindrop Acres stand. By clue 4, then, Sally bought 4 lbs. of white potatoes and 3 lbs. of food at Freshly Fruits & Produce's stand. The purchases of 1 and 3 lbs. were of blueberries and peaches or vice versa. By clue 2, therefore, Sally Salada got the white potatoes at the Tiller Gardens stand. By elimination, the 1 lb. purchase was at the Sunset Farm stand--of blueberries (6), with the peaches then the item bought at the Freshly Fruits & Produce stand. In sum, Sally Salada's Meyersdale Farmers Market purchases were: 1.) 5 lbs. of Granny Smith apples at Raindrop Acres; 2.) 4 lbs. of white potatoes at Tiller Gardens; 3.) 3 lbs. of peaches at Freshly Fruits & Vegetables; 4.) 2 lbs. of red lettuce at Grow Bros. Produce; 5.) 1 lb. of blueberries at Sunset Farm.

CHAPTER 1
1. I have elected to write 'new covenant' in lowercase letters throughout the book in keeping with the practice of the majority of English Bible translations.
2. "Book of Revelation." Subhead "Dating." *Wikipedia, The Free Encyclopedia*. Wikimedia Foundation, Inc. Web. 17 Feb. 2011. http://www.wikipedia.org

CHAPTER 2
1. Definition at thebondservant.org
2. Fischer, Mike. "The Bondservant." http://www.cke1st.com/sr_2pet11.htm
3. Fischer, Mike. Ibid.
4. Wiggs, Evan. "The Bondservants of the Most High." http://www.evanwiggs.com/articles/bondserv.html

CHAPTER 4
1. Zodhiates, Spiros, Th.D. *The Complete Word Study New Testament*. Chattanooga: AMG Publishers, 1991. p. 947 (hereafter *WSNT*).
2. Spurgeon, Charles H. *The Treasury of David*. 1869-85, public domain. Commentary on Ps. 131:1, at http://www.sacred-texts.com/bib/cmt/index.htm
3. Keil, Carl Friedrich and Franz Delitzsh. *Biblical Commentary on the Old Testament*. 1857-78, public domain. Notes on Psalm 131, at http://www.sacred-texts.com/bib/cmt/index.htm
4. Zodhiates, Spiros, Th.D. *The Complete Word Study Old Testament*, Chattanooga: AMG Publishers, 1994. p. 2379 (hereafter *WSOT*).

CHAPTER 5
1. Bickle, Mike. *The Song of Songs*. Available at the Forerunner Bookstore at http://www.ihop.org
2. Gill, John. *Exposition of the Entire Bible*. 1746-63, public domain. Notes on Songs 6:5, at http://www.sacred-texts.com/bib/cmt/index.htm
3. Josephus, Flavius. *Antiquities of the Jews*, book III, ch. 7, sec. 4, at Perseus Digital Library, http://www.perseus.tufts.edu/hopper/

4. Lewis, C.S. *Mere Christianity*. New York: Scribner, 1943, 1945, 1952. pp. 102-103.

CHAPTER 6
1. *Star Trek: The Next Generation*. Episode TNG 202: "Darmok." Season 5 Episode 2. Air date 9-30-1991.
2. *Monty Python and the Holy Grail*. Scene 5. Transcript at http://www.sacred-texts.com/neu/phg/mphg.htm
3. "Postulate." At http://www.definitions.net/definition/postulate
4. "The Best Lines of Yogi Berra." At http://www.jokesaboutbaseball.com/the-best-lines-of-yogi-berra.html
5. "Dale Berra Quotes." At http://www.quotes.net/quote/10722
6. Stern, David H., Ph.D. *Jewish New Testament Commentary* (hereafter *JNTC*). Clarksville: Jewish New Testament Publications, Inc., 1992. pp. 11-12.
7. Stern, Ibid. pp. 11-12.
8. Adapted from Dr. Stern's *JNTC* on the cited passages.

CHAPTER 7
1. "Fruit Tree Pollination." Subhead "Apple." *Wikipedia*. Ibid. 22 Mar. 2011
2. "What Is a Wolf Tree?" At http://www.wisegeek.com/what-is-a-wolf-tree.htm
3. Mack, Norman, ed. *Back to Basics: How to Learn and Enjoy Traditional American Skills*. Pleasantville, Montreal: Reader's Digest Association, 1981. p. 82.
4. Material on chapter and verse history adapted from: Schaff, Philip and Johann Jakob Herzog. *The New Schaff-Herzog Encyclopedia of Religious Knowledge*. Vol. 2. New York: Funk & Wagnalls, 1908-1912, public domain. Article: "Bible Text." At http://www.ccel.org/ccel/schaff/encyc02.html?term=Bible%20Text
5. "Vision 2025." At http://www.wycliffe.org/Explore/WhenWillWeFinishtheTask.aspx
6. "Exegesis." *Wikipedia*. Ibid. 3 Apr. 2011
7. "Eisegesis." *Wikipedia*. Ibid. 3 Apr. 2011

CHAPTER 8
1. Abegg, Martin. "Paul, 'Works of the Law' and MMT." *Biblical Archaeological Review*. 20:06, Nov-Dec 1994. pp.53-55. At http://www.hebroots.org/hebrootsarchive/0404/0404b.html
2. Baruch ben Daniel. *The Dead Sea Scrolls and Apostle Paul*. 2001. At http://www.mashiyach.com/scrolls.htm
3. http://www.dumblaws.com/laws/united-states
4. Went, Jonathan. *Hebrew Word Studies*. "*Towrah*—Instruction, Teaching, Guidance, Law." At http://www.Biblicalhebrew.com/wordstudies/torah.htm
5. Went. Ibid.
6. Zodhiates. *WSOT*. Ibid. p. 2380.
7. Rosensweig, Rabbi Michael. "*Zot Chukat haTorah*: The Role of *Chukim* in Torah Study and Commitment." At http://www.Torahweb.org/torah/2007/parsha/rros_chukas.html
8. Spurgeon, Charles H. *The Treasury of David*. 1869-85, public domain. Notes on Psalm 119, at http://www.biblestudytools.com/commentaries/treasury-of-david/
9. Blizzard, Roy. Foreword. *The Spirit of the Law* by Ron Moseley. Sherwood: Mozark Research Foundation, 1993. At http://www.haydid.org/spiritta.htm
10. "Talmud." http://www.new worldencyclopedia.org/entry/Talmud
11. Rich, Tracey R. *Judaism 101*. "Love and Brotherhood." At http://www.jewfaq.org/brother.htm
12. American-Israeli Cooperative Enterprise. "Mitzvot." 2011. At http://www.jewishvirtuallibrary.org/jsource/Judaism/mitzvot.html
13. Luther, Martin. "How Christians Should Regard Moses." Sermon delivered on August 27, 1525. Trans. and ed. by Theodore E. Bachmann. *Luther's Works* (first ed.; now public domain). *Word and Sacrament I, Vol. 35*. Philadelphia: Muhlenberg Press, 1960. pp.161-174. At http://www.wordofhisgrace.org/LutherMoses.htm

CHAPTER 9
1. Jablonowski, Paul. *Sons to Glory*. Chapter 7, "The Millennial Temple." Harvest: (Self-published), 2006 and 2011. Online book at http://sonstoglory.com/book.htm
2. Koniuchowsky, Rabbi Moshe Yoseph. *Children of Salt*. At http://www.hebroots.org/hebrootsarchive/0209/0209b.html

3. Zodhiates. *WSNT*. Ibid. p. 954.
4. Zodhiates. *WSOT*. Ibid. pp. 2371-2372.
5. Zodhiates. *WSNT*. Ibid. p. 936.
6. Zodhiates. *WSNT*. Ibid. p. 934.
7. Adapted from a line in the movie, *Facing the Giants*. Written by Alex and Stephen Kendrick. Directed by Alex Kendrick. Albany: Sherwood Pictures. 2006.

CHAPTER 10
1. Zodhiates. *WSNT*. Ibid. p. 953.
2. Zodhiates. *WSNT*. Ibid. p. 894.
3. Adapted from *The Agora Bible Commentary* on Titus 2:11-14. At http://www.christadelphianbooks.org/agora/index.html
4. Ryrie, Charles C. *The Grace of God*. Chicago: Moody Press, 1963. pp. 51-52.
5. Zodhiates. *WSNT*. Ibid. p. 943.
6. Ritenbaugh, John W. *The Forerunner Commentary*. "Five Teachings of Grace." Notes on Titus 2:12, at http://www.bibletools.org
7. Zodhiates. *WSNT*. Ibid. p. 944.
8. Kierkegaard, Soren. *Assorted Remarks and Observations*. Chapter 1, "Worldliness." 1813-1855, public domain. At http://members.optushome.com.au/davidquinn000/Kierkegaard/Kierkegaard01.html
9. Barnes, Albert. *Barnes' Notes on the Bible*. 1834, public domain. Notes on Rom. 14:1, at http://www.sacred-texts.com/bib/cmt/index.htm
10. Clarke, Adam. *Commentary on the Bible*. 1831, public domain. Notes on Rom. 14:1, at http://www.sacred-texts.com/bib/cmt/index.htm
11. Scofield, C.I. *Scofield Reference Notes*. 1917, public domain. Notes on Rom. 14:1, at http://www.sacred-texts.com/bib/cmt/index.htm

CHAPTER 11
1. Vincent, Marvin R. *Vincent's Word Studies*. 1886, public domain. Notes on Php. 1:9-10, at http://www.godrules.net/library/vincent/vincent.htm
2. Zodhiates. *WSNT*. Ibid. p. 910.
3. Barnes. Ibid. Notes on Eph. 4:3.
4. Russell, Rusty. *The Tabernacle of Ancient Israel*. 2003. "Table of Shewbread." At http://www.bible-history.com/tabernacle/TAB4The_Table_of_Shewbread.htm
5. Benamozegh, Elijah. *Israel and Humanity*. Trans./ed. by Maxwell Luria. Mahwah: Paulist Press, 1995. p. 59.
6. Liberman, Paul. *The Fig Tree Blossoms*. Indianola: Fountain Press, 1976. pp. 5-8.
7. Parsons, John D. *Interpretation and Tradition*. 2010. At http://www.hebrew4christians.com/Articles/Interpretation_and_Tradition
8. "History of Male Circumcision." *Wikipedia*. Ibid. 12 May 2011.
9. "Code of Hammurabi." *Wikipedia*. Ibid. 12 May 2011.
10. Kline, Meredith G. *The Treaty of the Great King: The Covenant Structure of Deuteronomy*. Grand Rapids: Wm. B. Eerdmans, 1963.
11. "Ancient Egyptian Religion." *Wikipedia*. Ibid. 12 May 2011.
12. "Ancient Egyptian Religion." *Wikipedia*. Ibid. 12 May 2011.
13. Quasten, Johannes. *Music and Worship in Pagan and Christian Antiquity*. Portland: Pastoral Press, 1983. p. 65.
14. Falsetto, Sharon. "History of the Harvest Festival." 2009. http://www.suite101.com/content/the-history-of-the-harvest-festival-a144496
15. Springer, Ilene and Jimmy Dunn. "Grand Festivals in Ancient Egypt." http://www.touregypt.net/featurestories/festival.htm
16. Elimelech David Ha-Levi Web. "Passover Seder Meal History –Origin of the Passover Celebration." 1999-2011. http://www.angelfire.com/pa2/passover/passover-seder-meal.html
17. Clanton, Robert. "The Lord's Day Worship (Sunday) Origins." http://www.auburn.edu/~allenkc/lordsday.html
18. Hanson, Thomas D., Sr. "The Origins of Sunday Worship in the Church." Subhead 'Justin.' At http://www.gci.org/law/sabbath/hanson.

19. Bonhoeffer, Dietrich. Eberhard Bethge, ed. *Letters and Papers from Prison.* "After Ten Years." New York: The Macmillan Company, 1971. pp. 16-17.
20. Bonhoeffer. Ibid. p. 5
21. "Confessing Church." Subhead "Aftermath." *Wikipedia.* Ibid. 23 May 2011.
22. Barnett, Victoria. *Dietrich Bonhoeffer.* United States Holocaust Memorial Museum, essay at http://www.ushmm.org
23. Rich, Tracey R. Ibid.
24. Socci, Antonio. *The New Persecuted: Inquiries into Anti-Christian Intolerance in the New Century of Martyrs.* Cited in Chuck Colson's article "A New Century of Martyrs: Anti-Christian Intolerance." June 17, 2002.
25. Yogarajah, Godfrey, "Disinformation, Discrimination, Destruction and Growth: A case study on persecution of Christians in Sri Lanka." *International Journal for Religious Freedom.* Vol. 1:1, 2008. p. 86.
26. The Sofia Echo staff. "Christians Now 'Most Persecuted Religious Group in the World,' Vatican Tells UN." 9.28.11. www.sofiaecho.com
27. Von Mittelstaedt, Juliane, and Christoph Schult, Daniel Steinvorth, Thilo Thielke, Volkhard Windfuhr. ABC News/International. "Christanity's Modern-Day Martyrs: Victims of Radical Islam." March 1, 2010. At http://abcnews.go.com/International
28. "First They Came..." *Wikipedia.* Ibid. 23 May 2011.

CHAPTER 13

1. Gregg, Steve. "Is Tithing for Christians?" March 9, 2005. At http://www.thenarrowpath.com/ta_tithing.html
2. Gregg. Ibid.
3. Dana, H. E. *The New Testament World*, 3rd. ed. Nashville: Broadman, 1937. p. 149.
4. Pfeiffer, Charles F. and Everett F. Harrison, eds. *The Wycliffe Bible Commentary.* Chicago: Moody, 1990. Notes by George E. Ladd on Acts 18:1-4 and 20:34.
5. Wenham, Motyer, Carson and France, eds. *New Bible Commentary.* Downers Grove: IVP Academic, 1994. Notes on 1 Thes. 2:9-10.
6. Gregg. Ibid.
7. Recommended reading: Reidhead, Paris. "Ten Shekels and a Shirt." At http://www.sermonindex.net/modules/mydownloads/
8. Nee, Watchman. *The Normal Christian Church Life.* Anaheim: Living Stream Ministry, 1980. pp. 152-153.
9. **Brace, Robin A.** "Tithes and Tithing: Can We Honestly Face Up to the Truth?" At http://www.ukapologetics.net; **Kelly, Dr. Russell E.** "Should the Church Teach Tithing?" At http://www.tithing-russkelly.com; **Spake, Dr. Kluane.** "On Reconsidering Tithe." At http://www.etpv.org/2001/ontith.html
10. Gregg. Ibid.
11. Douglas, Hillyer, Bruce, eds. *The Illustrated Bible Dictionary.* Downers Grove: IVP, 1998. p. 1572.
12. Parker, David M. "Tithing." Alphacrucis College, 2010. PDF file p. 1, footnote 4. At http://www.agnz.org/media/Tithing.pdf
13. Elwell, Walter A. ed. *Baker Theological Dictionary of the Bible.* Grand Rapids: Baker Book House, 1996. Article: "Tithe, Tithing," by Brian K. Morley.
14. Wigoder, Geoffrey, ed. *The New Encyclopedia of Judaism.* New York: NYU Press. 2002. Entry on "Levites." http://www.answers.com/topic/levite
15. Josephus. *Antiquities of the Jews.* Book 4, chapter 8, sections 8 and 22. http://earlyjewishwritings.com
16. Elwell, Ibid. Article: "Nehemiah," by Paul Ferguson.
17. Smith, Jerome. *The New Treasury of Scripture Knowledge.* Nashville: Thomas Nelson, 1992. pp. 1026, 1152.
18. Vine, W. E., M.A. *The Church and the Churches.* Fincastle: Scripture Truth Book Company, n.d. Part 2: "The Churches," Ch. 17, "Giving." At http://awildernessvoice.com/Church&Churches-Chapt17.html
19. Miller, Elliot. "Tithing: Is It New Testament?" *Christian Research Journal.* Vol. 26, No. 3, 2003.
20. Harrison, Everett F., Geoffrey W. Bromiley, and Carl F. Henry, eds. *Wycliffe Dictionary of Theology.* Peabody: Hendrickson Publishers, 1999. p. 525.

END NOTES

21. Martyr, Justin. *First Apology*. Chapter LXVII, "Weekly worship of the Christians." http://www.earlychristianwritings.com/text/justinmartyr-firstapology.html
22. Irenaeus. *Against Heresies*. Book IV, Chapter XVIII, "Concerning Sacrifices and Oblations, and Those Who Truly Offer Them." http://www.ccel.org/ccel/schaff/anf01.ix.vi.xix.html
23. Tertullian. *The Apology of Tertullian*. Chapter XXXIX. Trans. by T. Herbert Bindley, M.A. Oxford: Merton College, 1890. http://www.tertullian.org/articles/bindley_apol/bindley_apol.htm
24. Herberman, Pace, Pallen, Shahan, Wynne, Eds. "Tithes." *Catholic Encyclopedia*. New York: The Encyclopedia Press, 1913. http://en.wikisource.org/wiki/Catholic_Encyclopedia_%281913%29/Tithes
25. Brace, Robin A. "Tithes and Tithing: Can We Honestly Face Up to the Truth?" 2002. At http://www.uk apologetics.net/tithe.htm
26. Kelly, Russell Earl, Ph.D. *Should the Church Teach Tithing?*" New York, Lincoln, Shanghai: Writers Club Press, 2000, 2007. p. 247.
27. Hudnut-Beumler, James. *In Pursuit of the Almighty's Dollar: A History of Money and American Protestantism*. Chapel Hill: The University of North Carolina Press, 2007. p. 51.
28. Hudnut-Beumler. Ibid. p. 52.
29. Hudnut-Beumler. Ibid. p. 55.
30. Hudnut-Beumler. Ibid. p. 57.
31. Wesley, John. *Explanatory Notes on the Whole Bible*. 1754-1765, public domain. Notes on Luke 16:1-14, at http://www.sacred-texts.com/bib/cmt/index.htm
32. Bollhagen, James, Th.D. "Tithing: The 10% Rule and the Church." Broadcast July, 2001. Transcript at http://stjohnyorkpa.com/TithingThe10PercentRuleandtheChurch.htm
33. Irenaeus. *Against Heresies*. c. A.D. 150-200. Book 4, chap. 13, paragraph 3. At http://www.sacred-texts.com/chr/ecf/index.htm
34. Bowersock, Mike. NBC 4, Columbus, OH, 2006. Transcript at http://www.hydesvilletithing.com
35. Ross, Dennis and Robert Evans. "With Synagogues in Jeopardy, It's Time to Talk about Tithing." Op-ed. *The Jewish Daily Forward*. Published April 24, 2008, issue of May 02, 2008.
36. Miller, Elliot. "Tithing: Is It New Testament?" *Christian Research Journal*. Vol. 26, No. 3, 2003.
37. Brace. Ibid.

CHAPTER 14
1. I heard this teaching from John Bevere in 2001.
2. Barnes. Ibid. Notes on John 17:6.
3. Barnes. Ibid. Notes on John 17:23.
4. Barnes. Ibid. Notes on John 13:34.
5. Entries at http://www.definitions.net
6. Osborne, Grant R., ed. *IVP New Testament Commentary*. Downers Grove: IVP Academic, n.d. Commentary on Luke 10, at http://classic.biblegateway.com/resources/commentaries/IVP-NT/Luke/Discipleship-Looking-Our-Jesus
7. Finney, Charles. "Conditions of Prevailing Prayer." Sermon 1847, public domain. Points 80-81 as transcribed at http://www.charlesfinney.com/finney/finney.php?op=327
8. Entry at http://www.definitions.net

CHAPTER 15
1. Fontaine, Ron. "Importance of Adequate Water." April 20, 2011. http://www.survivaltopics.com

CHAPTER 16
1. "The kings of ancient Egypt were an integral part of religion. They formed a bridge over the chasm dividing the people and the gods. In pre-dynastic times the kings were considered to be gods. In later times, around the third dynasty, the kings became "transformed into" gods." At http://www.touregypt.net/gods1.htm
2. Regarding 'the gods,' there is evidence regarding the heavenly powers in both the Old (Jer. 2:11; Dan. 10:13,20; Mic. 4:5) and New Testaments (Rom. 8:38; Eph. 1:21; 2:2; 3:10; 6:12; Col. 1:16; 2:10,15). The hierarchy of power involves at least the governance of man on the earth; the powers or princes of the air which govern regions (e.g., the princes of Persia and Greece that Gabrielle had to withstand; see

Dan. 10:13, 20); Satan as the ruler over the powers of the air (Eph. 2:2); and God who sits enthroned *above* the heavens (Ps. 8:1; 57:5; 113:4-6; 148:4; also Jesus, Heb. 7:26). We as believers are seated in the heavenly places with Christ (Eph. 2:6). God has sovereign rule over all (Deut. 10:14).
3. "Vulgate." *Wikipedia*. Ibid. 5 Jun. 2011.
4. "Lucifer." http://www.wordiq.com/definition/Lucifer
5. Gill. Ibid. Notes on Isa. 14:12.
6. Russell, Jeffrey Burton, Ph.D. *Satan: The Early Christian Tradition*. Ithaca, London: Cornell University Press, 1981. p. 97.
7. Zodhiates. *WSOT*. Ibid. p. 2320.
8. This idea came to my very mathematical daughter while we were discussing this topic on a long road trip. Children truly are a blessing from the Lord.
9. Zodhiates. *WSOT*. Ibid. pp. 2372-2373.
10. Zodhiates. *WSNT*. Ibid. p. 949.
11. Zodhiates. *WSNT*. Ibid. p. 949.
12. Zodhiates. *WSNT*. Ibid. p. 946.
13. It is important that we understand James' statement that God tempts no man (James 1:13). The Greek translation is 'God/ without temptation (*apeirastos*)/ is/ of evils (*kakon*)/ he tempts (*peirazei*)/ neither/ Himself/ anyone.' From this we understand what we previously established:
    - God is 'without temptation' to cause *kakos* evil. This evil is not malicious in the sense of *poneros* evil (a description of Satan that indicates willful and malicious harm of others), but has everything to do with the wickedness and corruption of sin.
    - Neither does God test anyone *to cause them to sin* (this clarifies the dual nature of the Greek word *peirazo*; as previously discussed can mean to test to draw out good, or tempt to do evil).

    In his discussion on the purpose of testing, James finished by stating that 'every good and perfect (*teleion*) gift comes from God' (James 1:17). This confirms that God has established testing as something 'good' which brings about our 'perfection' (teleios) through obedience.
14. Zodhiates. *WSNT*. Ibid. pp. 906-907.
15. Zodhiates. *WSNT*. Ibid. p. 960.
16. Lewis, C.S. *Mere Christianity*. New York: Scribner, 1943, 1945, 1952. p. 159.
17. Barnes. Ibid. Notes on Eph. 6:16.

CHAPTER 17
1. Lewis, C.S. *Mere Christianity*. New York: Scribner, 1943, 1945, 1952. p. 106.
2. From a sermon given by Pastor Gaylord Lemke at Brookfield Assembly of God, Brookfield, WI.
3. Spurgeon, Charles H. as quoted by David Guzik in *1-2-3 John and Jude Commentary*. Santa Barbara: Enduring Word Media, 2005. Point 5.a.i., at http://www.studylight.org/com/guz/
4. Lewis, C.S. *Mere Christianity*. New York: Scribner, 1943, 1945, 1952. p. 145.
5. The movie, *End of the Spear*, is an excellent dramatization of this story.

CHAPTER 18
1. Bickle, Mike and Deborah Hiebert. *The Seven Longings of the Human Heart*. Kansas City: Forerunner Media, 2006.
2. Brown, Ellen Hodgson. *The Web of Debt*. Baton Rouge: Third Millennium Press, 2010. Highly recommended reading on basic economics and the history of banking and money.
3. Lewis, C.S. *Mere Christianity*. New York: Scribner, 1943, 1945, 1952. p. 106.

CHAPTER 19
1. From a sermon on Luke 1 delivered by Pastor Greg Blanc at Calvary Chapel, Rapid City, SD.
2. Zodhiates. *WSNT*. Ibid. p. 905-906.
3. Zodhiates. *WSNT*. Ibid. p. 905-906.
4. "Science." Subheads, "History and Philosophy," and "Critique." *Wikipedia*. Ibid. 28 Jan. 2012.
5. Hill, Dr. Gary and Dr. Gleason Archer, co-eds. *Helps Word Studies*. Helps Ministries, Inc. "Krisis." Pegged to Strong's #2920, available at biblos.com as part of their interlinear Greek resources.
6. Zodhiates. *WSNT*. Ibid. p. 930.

END NOTES

7. Zodhiates. *WSNT*. Ibid. p. 924.
8. Zodhiates. *WSNT*. Ibid. p. 944.
9. Stern, David. *JNTC*. Ibid. pp. 178-179.
10. Zodhiates. *WSNT*. Ibid. p. 948.
11. Clarke. Ibid. Notes on John 20:22.
12. Zodhiates. *WSNT*. Ibid. p. 936.
13. Zodhiates. *WSNT*. Ibid. p. 936.
14. Barnes. Ibid. Notes on Acts 2:38.
15. Barnes. Ibid. Notes on Acts 2:38.
16. Zodhiates. *WSNT*. Ibid. p. 963.
17. Strong, James. *New Strong's Exhaustive Concordance*. 1890, public domain. Greek entries 4972, 4973.
18. Barnes. Ibid. Notes on 2 Tim. 1:14.
19. Clarke. Ibid. Notes on Eph. 4:30.
20. Zodhiates. *WSNT*. Ibid. p. 879.
21. Barnes. Ibid. Notes on Eph. 4:30.
22. Gill. Ibid. Notes on Eph. 4:30.
23. Clarke. Ibid. Notes on Eph. 4:30.

CHAPTER 20
1. "Normalcy Bias." *Wikipedia*. Ibid. 14 Aug. 2011.
2. Stansberry and Associates Investment Research. Baltimore. Video presentation. At http://www.stansberryresearch.com/pro/1103PSIEOAVD/PPSIM369/PR
3. Barnes. Ibid. Notes on Php. 1:10-11.
4. Clarke. Ibid. Notes on Php. 1:10.
5. Lewis, C.S. *Mere Christianity*. New York: Scribner, 1943, 1945, 1952. pp. 161, 49.

CHAPTER 21
1. Zodhiates. *WSNT*. Ibid. pp. 904-905.
2. Zodhiates. *WSNT*. Ibid. p. 879.
3. Zodhiates. *WSNT*. Ibid. p. 891.
4. Zodhiates. *WSNT*. Ibid. p. 960.
5. Zodhiates. *WSNT*. Ibid. p. 878.
6. Lewis, C.S. *Mere Christianity*. New York: Scribner, 1943, 1945, 1952. p. 109.

CHAPTER 22
1. Strong, James. Ibid. Hebrew entries 7257, 996, 4942, 4496, 5186, 5647, 4522.
2. Zodhiates. *WSOT*. Ibid. p. 2350.
3. "Yissachar." Orthodox Union. *Judaism 101: A Glossary of Basic Jewish Terms and Concepts."* At http://www.ou.org/about/judaism/yissachar.htm
4. **Citron, Aryeh**. "The Torah Business Partnership." At http://www.chabad.org/library/article_cdo/aid/999756/jewish/The-Torah-Business-Partnership.htm; **Shpitz, Rabbi Tzvi**. *Business Halacha*, translated by Rabbi Aaron Tendler. *Hilchos Choshen Mishpat*. Vol. 3, No. 15. "'Yissachar-Zevulun' Arrangements." At http://www.torah.org/advanced/business-halacha/5757/vol3no15.html#
5. Zodhiates. *WSNT*. Ibid. p. 946.
6. "World Population." *Wikipedia*. Ibid. 14 Aug. 2011.
7. Greek Quick Reference Guide. At http://www.preceptaustin.org/
8. Zodhiates. *WSNT*. Ibid. p. 883.
9. Zodhiates. *WSNT*. Ibid. p. 898.
10. Zodhiates. *WSNT*. Ibid. p. 883.

EPILOGUE
1. The Neumann Press Book of Verse, review. 1988.
2. Scott, David. "God's Unhurrying Chase." http://www.catholiceducation.org

www.ingramcontent.com/pod-product-compliance
Lightning Source LLC
Chambersburg PA
CBHW080721230426
43665CB00020B/2574